THE
COLLEGE
PRESS
NIV
COMMENTARY

DEUTERONOMY

THE
COLLEGE
PRESS
NIV
COMMENTARY

DEUTERONOMY

GARY H. HALL, PH.D.

Old Testament Series Co-Editors:

Terry Briley, Ph.D.
Lipscomb University

Paul Kissling, Ph.D.
Great Lakes Christian College

COLLEGE PRESS
PUBLISHING COMPANY
Joplin, Missouri

Library of Congress Cataloging-in-Publication Data

Hall, Gary Harlan.
    Deuteronomy/Gary H. Hall.
        p.   cm. — (The College Press NIV commentary. Old
    Testament series)
    Includes bibliographical references.
    ISBN 0-89900-879-8
    1. Bible. O.T. Deuteronomy—Commentaries.   I. Title.
II. Series.
BS1275.3.H35 2000
222'.1507—dc21

                                            00-050897

A WORD
FROM THE PUBLISHER

Years ago a movement was begun with the dream of uniting all Christians on the basis of a common purpose (world evangelism) under a common authority (the Word of God). The College Press NIV Commentary Series is a serious effort to join the scholarship of two branches of this unity movement so as to speak with one voice concerning the Word of God. Our desire is to provide a resource for your study of the Old Testament that will benefit you whether you are preparing a Bible School lesson, a sermon, a college course, or your own personal devotions. Today as we survey the wreckage of a broken world, we must turn again to the Lord and his Word, unite under his banner and communicate the life-giving message to those who are in desperate need. This is our purpose.

ABBREVIATIONS

ABD . . . . . . *Anchor Bible Dictionary*

ANEP . . . . *Ancient Near Eastern Pictures Relating to the Old Testament*

ANET . . . . *Ancient Near Eastern Texts Relating to the Old Testament*

Ant. . . . . . . *Josephus's Antiquities of the Jews*

AUSS . . . . . *Andrews University Seminary Studies*

BA . . . . *Biblical Archaeologist*

BAR . . . . . . *Biblical Archaeology Review*

BASOR . . . *Bulletin of the American Schools of Oriental Research*

BHS . . . . . . *Biblia Hebraica Stuttgartensia, the most recent authoritative Hebrew text of the Old Testament*

Bib . . . . *Biblica*

BibSac . . . . *Bibliotheca Sacra*

BRev . . . . . *Bible Review*

CBQ . . . . . . *Catholic Biblical Quarterly*

CT . . . . *Christianity Today*

EncyJud . . . *Encyclopaedeia Judaica*

ET . . . . *The Expository Times*

EvQ . . . . . . *The Evangelical Quarterly*

GTJ . . . . . . *Grace Theological Journal*

HTR . . . . . *Harvard Theological Review*

IDB . . . . . . *The Interpreter's Dictionary of the Bible*

IDBS . . . . . *The Interpreter's Dictionary of the Bible Supplement*

Int . . . . *Interpretation*

ISBE . . . . . *International Standard Bible Encyclopedia, rev.ed.*

JBL . . . . . . *Journal of Biblical Literature*

JETS . . . . . *Journal of the Evangelical Theological Society*

JJS . . . . *Journal of Jewish Studies*

JNES . . . . . *Journal of Near Eastern Studies*

JQR . . . . . . *Jewish Quarterly Review*

JSNT . . . . . *Journal for the Study of the New Testament*

JSOT . . . . . *Journal for the Study of the Old Testament*

KJV . . . . . . *King James Version*

LXX . . . . . . *The Septuagint*
MT . . . . *The Masoretic Text of the Hebrew Old Testament*
NASB . . . . . *The New American Standard Bible*
NBD . . . . . . *New Bible Dictionary, 2nd ed.*
NIDNTT . . *The New International Dictionary of New Testament
            Theology*
NIDOTTE . *The New International Dictionary of Old Testament
            Theology and Exegesis*
NIV . . . . . . *New International Version*
NRSV . . . . . *The New Revised Standard Version*
NT . . . . *The New Testament*
NTS . . . . . . *New Testament Studies*
OT . . . . *Old Testament*
RestQ . . . . . *Restoration Quarterly*
RSV . . . . . . *Revised Standard Version*
TB . . . . *Tyndale Bulletin*
TDNT . . . . *Theological Dictionary of the New Testament*
TDOT . . . . *Theological Dictionary of the Old Testament*
VT . . . . *Vetus Testamentum*

( ) [ ] . . . . . *A number in parentheses or brackets following a verse
            number indicates a different versification in the Hebrew text.*

Simplified Guide to Hebrew Writing

Heb. letter	Translit.	Pronunciation guide
א	ʾ	Has no sound of its own; like smooth breathing mark in Greek
ב	b	Pronounced like English B *or* V
ג	g	Pronounced like English G
ד	d	Pronounced like English D
ה	h	Pronounced like English H
ו	w	As a consonant, pronounced like English V or German W
וּ	û	Represents a vowel sound, pronounced like English long OO
וֹ	ô	Represents a vowel sound, pronounced like English long O
ז	z	Pronounced like English Z
ח	ḥ	Pronounced like German and Scottish CH and Greek c (chi)
ט	ṭ	Pronounced like English T
י	y	Pronounced like English Y
כ/ך	k	Pronounced like English K
ל	l	Pronounced like English L
מ/ם	m	Pronounced like English M
נ/ן	n	Pronounced like English N
ס	s	Pronounced like English S
ע	ʿ	Stop in breath deep in throat before pronouncing the vowel
פ/ף	p/ph	Pronounced like English P *or* F
צ/ץ	ṣ	Pronounced like English TS/TZ
ק	q	Pronounced very much like כ (k)
ר	r	Pronounced like English R
שׂ	ś	Pronounced like English S, much the same as ס
שׁ	š	Pronounced like English SH
ת	t/th	Pronounced like English T *or* TH

Note that different forms of some letters appear at the end of the word (written right to left), as in כָּפַף (*kāphaph*, "bend") and מֶלֶךְ (*melek*, "king").

Vowels in Hebrew (except where the ו is used to represent a vowel sound), are represented by "vowel points" added to the consonant. For example: הַ (*ha*, "the"). The letter *yod* (י, *y*) also becomes a *part of* certain vowel sounds, as in the conjunction כִּי (*kî*, "that"). Originally, Hebrew was written as "unpointed" text, with just the consonants. For convenience, the different vowel points are shown below on the letter Aleph (א).

אָ	ā	Pronounced not like long A in English, but like the broad A or AH sound
אַ	a	The Hebrew short A sound, but more closely resembles the broad A (pronounced for a shorter period of time) than the English short A
אֶ	e	Pronounced like English short E
אֵ	ē	Pronounced like English long A, or Greek h (eta)

אִ	i	Pronounced like English short I
אִ	î	The same vowel point is sometimes pronounced like אִ (see below)
אָ	o	This vowel point sometimes represents the short O sound
אֹ	ō	Pronounced like English long O
אֻ	u	The vowel point ֻ sometimes represents a shorter U sound and
אוּ	ū	is sometimes pronounced like the וּ (û, see above)
אֵ	ê	Pronounced much the same as אֵ
אֵ	ê	Pronounced much the same as אֵ
אִי	î	Pronounced like long I in many languages, or English long E
אְ	ə	An unstressed vowel sound, like the first E in the word "severe"
אֳ, אֲ, אֱ	ŏ, ă, ĕ	Shortened, unstressed forms of the vowels אָ, אַ, and אֶ, pronounced very similarly to אְ

PREFACE

Attempting to write a commentary provides a lesson in humility. First of all, it is presumptuous to try to clarify God's Word. It is able to stand on its own. "For the word of God is living and active. Sharper than any double-edged sword . . ." (Heb 4:12). Secondly, a commentary cannot be written without the assistance of numerous people. An enormous amount of valuable in-depth study of Deuteronomy has occurred over the years. Dependence on others will be apparent on almost every page of this work.

Nevertheless, it was with great anticipation that I undertook the task of writing this commentary. Only the Psalms surpass Deuteronomy in importance for understanding the rest of the Old Testament. Deuteronomy's covenant-based theology and deep understanding of God's will for Israel had profound impact on Israel's historians and prophets. It has been a rich experience to mine the depths of this book.

Despite Deuteronomy's theological depth, its message is simple: love and obey God. The call to love God is central to Deuteronomy (6:5) and the Old Testament. Jesus' teaching was not original to him (John 14:15-21) but was based on a profound understanding of Deuteronomy. This fact illustrates just one reason why, in my opinion, Christians should allot a significant amount of time to studying Deuteronomy. They would then understand the New Testament much better.

Deuteronomy was written in sermonic style and involves a great deal of repetition. Moses was an outstanding preacher, and he constructed his sermons so they could be remembered. Consequently, there is considerable intratextual referencing in Deuteronomy. Moses comes back to the main points over and over. The commentary utilizes numerous cross-references so that the reader who might study only one passage can get a sense of this internal unity and emphasis.

The student of Deuteronomy will discover afresh the greatness of God's grace and love for his people. Jesus and Paul did not invent these ideas; they are core attributes of God's character. These essentials of life with God are at the heart of the book. Deuteronomy exhibits their impact in Israel's life again and again.

It is only by God's grace and because of God's people that I have come this far. I am deeply indebted to God for his blessings. It is impossible to thank all the people who have influenced my life. But it is necessary to acknowledge my deep appreciation to several. Lincoln Christian Seminary has been a wonderful place to do teaching and research over the years. Dean Wayne Shaw's leadership and pastoral concern have encouraged me. A sabbatical in the fall of 1998 enabled me to accomplish a significant amount of writing. The "Son-Seekers" Sunday School class at Lincoln Christian Church encouraged me through prayer and responded warmly to a lengthy series of lessons on Deuteronomy. Colleagues and students who continually asked how my work was going kept me on my toes.

However, important as friends are, none of this work would have been accomplished without God's special gift, my family. My wife, Cheryl, will never know how much her faithful support has encouraged me. Loving companionship is one of God's greatest blessings. Stephanie and Nathan, our two children, have brought untold joy. In addition, Stephanie undertook the arduous task of proofreading the rough draft of this book. It is with deep love and gratitude that I dedicate this book to them.

INTRODUCTION

A study of Deuteronomy quickly dispels some false impressions held by many Christians about the Old Testament and the Old Testament law. Deuteronomy is anything but an outdated, irrelevant, dry, legal text. It brims with profound theological insight. Its laws are set in a specific context that brings them to life. Its language is the lively exhortation of a master preacher and teacher whose admonitions transcend time and culture.

Deuteronomy had a profound influence on the New Testament. It is one of the four most quoted and alluded to Old Testament books.[1] Furthermore, it was Jesus' favorite book in the Pentateuch.[2] He often quoted from it in his teaching and preaching. He resisted Satan by quoting from Deuteronomy (Matt 4:4,7,10). For him, the greatest commandment was Deuteronomy 6:5 (Matt 22:36-38). Consequently, Christians will reap great dividends from a careful study of Deuteronomy.

---

[1] The four are Isaiah, Psalms, Deuteronomy, and Genesis. Exact numbers of quotations are difficult to uncover because of differing definitions of what is a quote and what is an allusion. The United Bible Society's Greek Text lists 195 quotes and allusions in the New Testament from Deuteronomy. Elizabeth Achtemeier believes there are 83 quotes from Deuteronomy in the New Testament (*Deuteronomy, Jeremiah* [Philadelphia: Fortress, 1978], p. 9). Other authorities give different figures. J. Gordon McConville's assessment of the influence of Deuteronomy on the New Testament is exemplary, but his assertion that Deuteronomy is cited more frequently in the NT than any other OT book is inaccurate (*Grace in the End* [Grand Rapids: Zondervan, 1993], p. 145).

[2] When Jesus quotes or alludes to the Pentateuchal books in his teaching, Deuteronomy is referenced two times as often as any other of the five books.

TITLE OF THE BOOK

Deuteronomy is the fifth book of the Old Testament and the last book in the Pentateuch.[3] The title of Deuteronomy in the Hebrew Bible, אלה דברים (*'ēlleh debārîm*, "these are the words") follows the custom of naming a book after the first few words in the text. The English title, Deuteronomy, comes from the Latin Vulgate translation *Deuteronomium* that was dependent on the Greek Septuagint title, *Deuteronomion*. The Greek title was based on its translation of Deuteronomy 17:18, "this second or repetition of the law." The translators apparently understood the Hebrew to refer to a second law in addition to the law of Exodus. However, the Hebrew text means "a copy of this law," not a second law.[4]

The Hebrew title accurately reflects the fact that Deuteronomy is both the words of Moses (1:1) and the words of God that he told Moses to speak. It is not merely a copy of the law of Exodus but a restatement and expansion of the original covenant and covenant law. The new time and setting, forty years after the original reception of the law at Sinai (Exod 20–24), required both updating of the law and a renewal of the covenant.

AUTHORSHIP AND DATE

The traditional view of Christian and Jewish scholars until the eighteenth and nineteenth centuries was that Moses was the author of Deuteronomy. This view did not deny that there might be post-Mosaic material in the book (chapter 34 on Moses' death, for example), but it affirmed that the majority of the book came from Moses. This traditional view was based on the many references to Moses' speaking (1:1,5,9; 5:1; 27:1,9; 29:2; 31:1,3; 33:1) or writing (31:9,24). Other Old Testament books attributed the book to Moses also (Josh 1:7-8; Judg 1:20; 3:4; 1 Kgs 2:3; 2 Kgs 14:6; Ezra 3:2). Christian schol-

---

[3]Pentateuch is the name given to the first five books of the Bible, reflecting that they are seen as a discrete unit of books. Jewish tradition refers to them as the Torah.

[4]Deuteronomy is also known among Jews as *Mishneh Torah* from the Hebrew of 17:18.

ars gave great weight to the numerous New Testament references that suggested that Moses wrote the Pentateuch and, by implication, Deuteronomy (Matt 19:8; Mark 12:26; Luke 24:27,44; John 7:19,23; Acts 13:39; 15:5; 28:23; 1 Cor 9:9; 2 Cor 3:15; Heb 9:19; 10:28).[5]

Mosaic authorship implies the setting and date of the book. The place was the plains of Moab just east of the Jordan River.[6] The date was nearly forty years after receiving the law at Sinai, at the end of the wilderness period, just prior to Moses' death. Israel was poised to enter into the Promised Land in fulfillment of God's promise to Abraham. The generation that had exited Egypt with Moses was dead. The new generation needed to renew their covenant relationship with God and hear the law once again. This generation also needed to be prepared for the transition to a new leader, Joshua. Furthermore, they needed instruction on how to live in the land and deal with the many social and religious pressures they would experience there. Moses, through sermonic exhortation and teaching, prepared them for what was ahead. The key for Israel's future was faithfulness to the covenant through obedience to the covenant law.

The exact time of Moses' preaching Deuteronomy is a matter of debate. Two dates have been proposed: around 1400 B.C. and somewhere in the thirteenth century B.C. The details are too involved to be included in this brief introduction.[7] Whichever date is accurate, the cultural and historical situation in Canaan was similar. The Promised Land was inhabited by Canaanites who were distinguished by their religious fertility cults. These posed an extreme threat to Israel and were to be destroyed (chapter 12). There was also a power vacuum in the land. Neither Egypt nor a Mesopotamian country was in control of Palestine. This presented Israel with an opportune time to move in and take the land.

---

[5]There were a few scholars through the centuries who expressed doubts about Mosaic authorship, but they were in a minority. See the survey by R.K. Harrison, *Introduction to the Old Testament* (Grand Rapids: Eerdmans, 1969), pp. 3-11.

[6]See comments on chapter 1:1-5.

[7]For convenient and detailed discussion see any of the following: Eugene H. Merrill, *Kingdom of Priests: A History of Old Testament Israel* (Grand Rapids: Baker, 1987), pp. 66-75; W.H. Shea, "Exodus, Date of the," *ISBE*, 2:230-238; K.A. Kitchen, "Exodus, The," *ABD*, 3:700-708. Merrill and Shea support a late fifteenth century date, Kitchen supports a mid-thirteenth century date.

DEUTERONOMY IN MODERN OLD TESTAMENT STUDIES

Beginning in the early nineteenth century the traditional view on the date and authorship of Deuteronomy was called into question and eventually abandoned. In 1806, W.M.L. de Wette, a German scholar, published a work that revolutionized Old Testament study.[8] De Wette identified the law book discovered by the high priest Hilkiah in 2 Kings 22:8 as the book of Deuteronomy. He also suggested that the book had been written at that time (622 B.C.). Based on a purely history-of-religion approach and his views on Deuteronomy, de Wette asserted that the biblical view of Israelite religion was false. There was no central sanctuary in Jerusalem until the time of Josiah, and the books of Chronicles read later developments back into the past. Further, the complex priestly laws of Leviticus were late, not early. Therefore, the history of early Israel presented to us in the Pentateuch is myth.

De Wette's ideas had little impact at the time because of conservative opposition from scholars such as Hengstenberg and Keil. However, in 1878 Julius Wellhausen published a brilliant synthesis based on de Wette's position and made it the "cornerstone" of Pentateuchal studies.[9] Wellhausen showed that Israel's history had three periods: 1) the early monarchy with its many sanctuaries, simple religion, absence of priests, and much spontaneity, as seen in the books of Samuel and Kings; 2) the seventh century,which was marked by Josiah's reform and the centralization of worship at Jerusalem based on the newly discovered book of Deuteronomy or some form of it; 3) the postexilic period when the priesthood gained control and instituted elaborate sacrificial rituals. In this scheme the late seventh-century date of the book of Deuteronomy and its contents

---

[8]His doctoral thesis (*Dissertatio critica, qua Deuteronomium . . .*) in which he argued for his view was written in 1805. More detailed arguments were published in his *Beitrage zur Einleitung in das Alte Testament*, vol. 1 in 1806. For a convenient discussion see the essay on de Wette in Donald McKim, ed., *Historical Handbook of Major Biblical Interpreters* (Downers Grove, IL: InterVarsity, 1998), pp. 298-302.

[9]E.W. Nicholson, *Deuteronomy and Tradition* (Philadelphia: Fortress, 1967), p. 1. Wellhausen's book has been published in English as *Prolegoma to the History of Ancient Israel* (Edinburgh, 1885).

became the "linchpin" in Old Testament studies.[10] Language in the Pentateuch could now be styled as "pre" or "post" Deuteronomic. The details of the history of Israel's worship and theology could also be identified as being earlier or later than Deuteronomy.[11]

A further feature has come to dominate Old Testament studies. Scholars have recognized that the history of Israel contained in the books of Joshua through Kings was written from the perspective of the book of Deuteronomy. These books are now called "The Deuteronomistic History."[12] Thus the importance of the book of Deuteronomy for current Old Testament studies is enormous.

Chapter 12 is crucial to modern scholars' understanding of Deuteronomy. It calls for Israel to destroy all Canaanite sanctuaries (12:2-3) and to worship at "the place the LORD your God will choose" (12:5,11,14,18,21,26). For Wellhausen and others this place was Jerusalem, and Josiah's reform, which included the destruction of all sanctuaries outside of Jerusalem (2 Kgs 23:8-9,15), was based on Deuteronomy 12.[13] For scholars chapter 12 has become a major text and its contents a major theme of the book.[14]

The language of Deuteronomy has become another key point in modern discussions of its date.[15] The language of the book is clearly distinct from the rest of the Pentateuch. It is sermonic, verbose, repetitive, and sprinkled with words and phrases that do not occur elsewhere in the first four books of the Old Testament. Its language does, however, resemble that of several written compositions that undeniably come from the seventh and sixth centuries B.C. such as the book of Jeremiah and the books of Kings.

---

[10]Gordon Wenham, "The Date of Deuteronomy: Linch-pin of Old Testament Criticism," *Themelios* 10,3 and 11,1 (1985): 15-20 and 15-18.

[11]R.E. Clements, *Deuteronomy* (Sheffield: Sheffield Academic Press, 1989), p. 9.

[12]Martin Noth first proposed this idea. See *The Deuteronomistic History* (Sheffield: JSOT Press, 1981) which is a translation of his *Uberlieferungs-geschichtliche Studien*, 2nd ed. (Tubingen, 1957), pp. 1-100. We cannot go into any details here on this issue. Those interested can consult Walter Rast, *Joshua, Judges, Samuel, Kings* (Philadelphia: Fortress, 1978).

[13]See the commentary on chapter 12 for more observations on this issue.

[14]"The law of the central sanctuary in Deut. 12:2-14 must certainly be regarded as one of the most distinctive features of the Deuteronomic legislation." R.E. Clements, *Deuteronomy*, p. 27.

[15]Wenham, "Linch-pin," p. 17.

Other arguments have been advanced for denying Mosaic authorship.[16] 1) The perspective in Deuteronomy seems to be from the west side of the Jordan, not the east side. 2) The laws in Deuteronomy presuppose conditions after Israel had been settled in the land for some time and city life had developed. 3) Chapter 17 assumes kingship had been instituted. 4) The priestly functions described in chapter 20 come from a later time since the priesthood was not developed in Moses' day. 5) The person of address in Deuteronomy changes from singular "you" to plural "you" and back again which points to different sources. 6) The form of the book resembles ancient Near Eastern treaties from the seventh century B.C. not the fifteenth century as once thought.[17]

Although the Wellhausen scheme for the development of Israelite religion has been maintained, de Wette's position that Deuteronomy was a fiction from Josiah's time has been abandoned.[18] Many scholars recognize that major portions of the book had to be earlier and could not have been a late, pious fraud. They have advanced conflicting theories about where and how the material in Deuteronomy originated. We can present only a few of the ideas here.

Several scholars have seen evidence of strong influence from the Northern Kingdom on the book. G. von Rad suggested that much of Deuteronomy originated in priestly and Levitical circles in the north. The Holy War traditions and the fight against Canaanite religion fits well the situation in the north. Much of the material was connected with the cult, and therefore the old worship site of Shechem or Bethel may have been the original setting (ch. 27). The date would have been mid-eighth century. These traditions were brought to the south and revived by Levitical priests in Josiah's day.[19]

---

[16]Ian Cairns, *Word and Presence: A Commentary on the Book of Deuteronomy* (Grand Rapids: Eerdmans, 1992), pp. 1-2; Achtemeier, *Deuteronomy, Jeremiah*, p. 10. The texts in Deuteronomy used to support these arguments are open to other interpretations that support Mosaic authorship. The case for Mosaic authorship is made below. Comments throughout the commentary address these issues as well.

[17]For more discussion on the treaty form see below on structure of the book.

[18]S.R. Driver led the way over a century ago (*A Critical and Exegetical Commentary on Deuteronomy* [Edinburgh: T. & T. Clark, 1895], pp. lvi-lxii).

[19]Gerhard von Rad, *Deuteronomy* (London: SCM Press, 1966), pp. 23-26.

E.W. Nicholson believes prophetic, not priestly, circles in the Northern Kingdom were responsible for much of the book. Disciples of these circles took the sermons and reflections south after 722 B.C. and wrote them down during the dark days of Manasseh in Judah. They hoped the material would be used for reform in the south. Nicholson thinks chapter 27 was a later addition.[20]

N. Lohfink thinks the language of Deuteronomy is more probably that of the court rather than country priests. Many texts in the book were originally legal and liturgical texts to be read to large assemblies. Its origin is most likely Jerusalem. Therefore, it should be connected with the court of Hezekiah in the late eighth century when the king instituted the first reform movement. In Josiah's time the court secretary Shaphan and the priest Hilkiah played important roles in the discovery of the law.[21]

Moshe Weinfeld believes that the time from Hezekiah to Josiah was a time of religious revival all over the ancient Near East. Under this influence, a group who was familiar with the treaty forms of the day revived the traditions of the old covenant and brought in wisdom traditions. Some northern influence came in, especially from the prophet Hosea. Some of the material may go back to Joshua's day, and some even back to Moses' time. According to Weinfeld, the book itself was created by a school of scribes during the time of Hezekiah who intended it as a handbook for the king (ch. 17).[22]

From the time of de Wette, many scholars challenged the perspective on Deuteronomy presented above.[23] These challenges can only be considered briefly. The reader should consult the sources listed for fuller discussion.

---

[20]E.W. Nicholson, *Deuteronomy and Tradition*, (Philadephia: Fortress, 1967), chapter IV.

[21]N. Lohfink, "Deuteronomy," *IDBS*, pp. 229-232.

[22]Moshe Weinfeld, *Deuteronomy 1-11* (New York: Doubleday, 1991), pp. 44-53.

[23]Not all were conservatives. For a detailed review see Harrison, *Introduction*, pp. 33-82, although he covers the larger area of source criticism also. James Orr, *The Problem of the Old Testament* (New York: Scribners, 1906), pp. 245-284, provided an early, detailed critique. R.N. Whybray, *The Making of the Pentateuch: A Methodological Study* (Sheffield: JSOT Press, 1987), provides a recent critique from within the critical school. Many of the criticisms he proposed were those put forth by conservative scholars over the last century and a half.

1) Deuteronomy claims to be from Moses and consists of three sermons (ch. 1–4, 5–28, 29–30) and two poems from him (32, 33). This claim should be taken seriously unless there is overwhelming evidence to the contrary. There is no clear evidence of pseudo-authorship in the Old Testament with a possible exception of Ecclesiastes.[24] Often arguments against Mosaic authorship proceed on assumptions about development of laws and concepts from simple to complex, with complex automatically being later.[25] Suggestions that Deuteronomy was not written by Moses but expresses "authentic Mosaic tradition"[26] seem like attempts to circumvent the persistent claim of the book. However, it is necessary to recognize that there are non-Mosaic additions to the book. Chapter 34 is a clear example. What other portions might be additions is unclear.[27]

2) The concept of inspiration suggests the integrity of what the Bible claims and goes closely with point one. Not all scholars who claim a non-Mosaic authorship and a late date deny inspiration. Their understanding of inspiration would include pseudo-authorship, anachronistic language, and complex source theories. However, it is certainly proper to raise the question whether a biblical view of inspiration and these theories are compatible.

3) The argument from language usage is difficult to nail down. Style is dictated by genre. Wenham has pointed out how both religious language and literary language are basically conservative. There are examples in both ancient Babylon and Egypt of this conservatism. Old Babylonian remained as a literary language for a millennium after the spoken language was changed. In Egypt, Middle

---

[24]Pseudo-authorship refers to a text's claim that someone other than the real author wrote it. Ecclesiastes claims that a "son of David" wrote it. Tradition and many scholars believe this to be Solomon. However, since Solomon is not actually named in the book, Ecclesiastes would not seem to fit the category of "pseudo-authorship." "Son of David" could refer to any Davidic king. For the case both for and against Solomonic authorship see Duane A. Garrett, *Proverbs, Ecclesiastes, Song of Songs* (Nashville: Broadman Press, 1993), pp. 254-267.

[25]Clements, *Deuteronomy*, pp. 24-27, is a good example of this kind of thinking.

[26]Ibid., p. 69.

[27]J.A. Thompson, *Deuteronomy: An Introduction and Commentary* (Downers Grove, IL: InterVarsity, 1974), pp. 67-68.

Egyptian was the universal written language for one thousand years.[28] In the modern era the influence of the King James Version of the Bible for three hundred and fifty years is an example of the same conservatism. Therefore, in ancient Israel so-called Deuteronomistic language could have been invented long before the seventh century. That would explain "Deuteronomistic" language elsewhere in the Pentateuch, in the eighth century prophets, and in seventh and sixth century compositions.

4) The relationship between Deuteronomy and the eighth century prophets is open to different interpretations. There is a close relationship between Deuteronomy and Hosea. Both are grounded in the Sinai covenant and find God's saving act in the Exodus. Hosea faults Israel for disobedience and wages war on syncretism and apostasy, which were concerns of Deuteronomy. Both view Israel's election as based solely on God's love.[29] There are similarities in other prophets as well. Which way did the influence go? Were prophetic Deuteronomistic editors following Hosea? Or is it more sensible to suppose that Deuteronomy was an authoritative work that influenced Hosea, Amos, other prophets, and the compilers of Kings?[30]

5) It is true that Deuteronomy 12 is concerned about worship at one place, but there is no evidence in the book that the place was Jerusalem. Could not Moses, as the greatest of the prophets (34:10-12), point to Jerusalem as the place if that was his intention? The one site that Deuteronomy does specify as the place to worship is Mt. Ebal near Shechem (chapter 27:4-8; cf. Josh 8:30-35; 24; 1 Kgs 12).[31] Worship in the Pentateuch and Samuel–Kings centered on the Ark of the Covenant, not a place. The Ark was housed at several

---

[28]Wenham, "Linch-pin," 10,3:18-19.

[29]Nicholson, *Deuteronomy*, p. 70. These ideas, which are scattered throughout Deuteronomy, are found in Hosea in the following texts: 11:1ff; 4:1-2; 5:3-4; 6:7-8; 6:5; 12:11; 4:12; 8:5-6; 2:14-23.

[30]Wenham suggests that if every trace of Deuteronomy influence were excised from Hosea and Amos, as some scholars try to do, there would be little left. This suggests Deuteronomy was already an authority for the prophets. ("Linch-pin," 10,3:18).

[31]It is hardly logical to suggest that chapter 27 is a later addition (Nicholson, *Deuteronomy*, p. 34). The chapter is an integral part of the covenant renewal nature of the whole book. Furthermore, under what circumstances would a later editor think it appropriate to add such a reference to a book whose major function was to centralize worship in Jerusalem?

different places including Gilgal, Shechem, Bethel, and Shiloh.[32] Eventually David moved the Ark to Jerusalem and made it the place of worship. The important issue was theological, not geographical.

6) Josiah's reform in the late seventh century began several years before the law book was discovered in the temple (see 2 Chr 24). Furthermore, Josiah's response to the law which he read was to vigorously eliminate idolatry from the land, not demand worship in Jerusalem (2 Kings 23). Idolatry even existed in the temple.[33]

7) Many of the laws make sense if from an early period, but not from later. Most of the laws that are unique to Deuteronomy are aimed at protecting Israel from Canaanite influence, which fits an early date well but not a later period.[34] Many of the laws stand closer to the situation pictured in the book of Judges than to the seventh century. They reflect reinterpretation of older laws in the light of God's new act, the gift of the Promised Land.[35]

8) Major theological themes of Deuteronomy can already be found in the Song of Moses in Exodus 15, a hymn that is recognized by everyone as ancient. These themes include commitment to one God, God as a Warrior and King, and the centrality of the Exodus event.[36] These key features support an early date for the material in Deuteronomy.

9) The structure of Deuteronomy is similar to ancient Near Eastern treaties. The book more nearly parallels the Hittite treaties from the mid-second millennium than Assyrian treaties from the seventh century (see the discussion below).

Further observations on these issues will be made throughout the commentary. The position taken here is that Deuteronomy is Mosaic. The sermonic and teaching style of the book is more likely to come

---

[32]Jeremiah 7:12 asserts that Shiloh was a place where God had placed his name. This was in a sermon preached after Josiah's death. Jeremiah apparently did not understand Deuteronomy 12 to refer to Jerusalem as many modern scholars do.

[33]Of course elimination of idolatry throughout the country would result in concentrating worship at the temple in Jerusalem. But that was a consequence, not the central focus.

[34]G.T. Manley, *The Book of the Law* (London: Tyndale, 1957).

[35]J.G. McConville, *Law and Theology in Deuteronomy* (Sheffield: JSOT Press, 1984), pp. 66, 87, 122-123, 155.

[36]Peter Craigie, *The Book of Deuteronomy* (Grand Rapids: Eerdmans, 1976), pp. 61-66.

from one brilliant leader and thinker than a committee. One can easily visualize Moses during the nearly forty years in the wilderness era constantly teaching and exhorting the people to obedience to the law. Forty years is a lifetime career for most people.[37] Moses could have taught and preached the same themes many times (see 4:5). Deuteronomy would then represent the best of his sermons and teaching, presenting one final call to faithfulness and obedience.

STRUCTURE

The structure of Deuteronomy can be analyzed in several ways. The book itself suggests the contents focus around three speeches by Moses: chapters 1-4, 5-28, 29-30. References to Moses words (1:1) or his speaking (5:1; 29:2) introduce these sections. In addition the poems in chapters 32 and 33 are ascribed to Moses. Recognizing smaller discrete units in the book often further refines this macrostructure. Chapters 5-11 share a common exhortation to obey the law. Chapters 12-26 form the core of the Deuteronomic law itself. Chapters 27-28 sum up the presentation with a focus on blessings and curses.

A close analysis of the poetic features of Deuteronomy has yielded a concentric literary pattern in the book.[38] This pattern is sometimes called chiasmus. It consists of balancing the sections in a composition. The initial units lead up to a central focus or theme. The following units repeat the themes of the first units in reverse order away from the center until the composition ends where it began. This technique is common in Hebrew poetry but is also found in Hebrew narrative. It appears often in Deuteronomy. Christensen has suggested a macrostructure for the book.

   A. The Outer Frame: A Look Backward (Deut 1-3)
      B. The Inner Frame: The Great Peroration (Deut 4-11)
         C. The Central Core: Covenant Stipulations (Deut 12-26)
      B'. The Inner Frame: The Covenant Ceremony (Deut 27-30)
   A'. The Outer Frame: A Look Forward (Deut 31-34)[39]

---

[37]A well-known evangelical preacher and scholar who died in his early 60s in August of 2000 wrote and contributed to over 60 books.

[38]Duane Christensen, *Deuteronomy 1-11* (Dallas: Word Books, 1991).

[39]Christensen, *Deuteronomy*, p. xli.

Christensen suggests the outer frame could be read continuously since it is connected by the figure of Joshua. The inner frame could also be read continuously, for chapter 11 ends with references to a covenant ceremony at Mounts Ebal and Gerizim and chapter 27 continues with the details.

Concentric structures are found throughout the book of Deuteronomy. Chiasm is a poetic device and lends itself to the sermonic and teaching style of Deuteronomy. The macrostructure has implications for the unity of the book and for how it should be read.

Deuteronomy is also structured around the Decalogue. Chapters 6–26 are organized according to the arrangement of the Ten Commandments.[40] Although some details are not precise, this organizing principal seems well established. Details can be found in the outline below. Recognition of this order helps explain the logic of laws in chapters 12–26.

Several decades ago scholars discovered that ancient Near Eastern vassal treaties all exhibited similar structure. They also realized that Deuteronomy followed this structure. The treaties had several main features that are paralleled in the book.[41]

A. Preamble, that identified speaker and recipient (Deut 1:1-5)
B. Historical prologue, that reviewed the history of relations between the two parties (Deut 1:6–4:49)
C. General stipulations, that outlined the treaty in general terms (Deut 5–11)
D. Specific stipulations, that listed the specific requirements the overlord or state made on the vassal (Deut 12–26)
E. Blessings and curses, promulgated as sanctions and motivations for observing the treaty (Deut 27–28)
F. Witnesses, called upon as enforcers of the treaty

---

[40]Dennis Olson, *Deuteronomy and the Death of Moses* (Minneapolis: Augsburg Fortress, 1994); John Walton, "Deuteronomy: An Exposition of the Spirit of the Law," *GTJ* 8 (1987): 213-225.

[41]Meredith Kline, *Treaty of the Great King: The Covenant Structure of Deuteronomy* (Grand Rapids: Eerdmans, 1963); G.E. Mendenhall, "Covenant Forms in Israelite Tradition," *BA* 17,3 (1954): 50-76; idem., *Law and Covenant in Israel and the Ancient Near East* (Pittsburgh: Biblical Colloquium, 1955); Craigie, *Deuteronomy*, pp. 20-29.

G. Disposition of the treaty, which was usually to be stored and brought out on special occasions for public reading (Deut 31:9-13,24-26)

The vassal treaties were employed in the ancient Near East by a great power, usually a conquering nation, to impose conditions on a smaller state, the vassal. The treaty rehearsed the relations between the two countries and explained the duties of the smaller state in maintaining the relationship.[42] Ancient Israel could have adapted the treaty form, for God was conceptualized as the Great King and Israel as the vassal. But Deuteronomy was not merely a treaty between God and Israel, as this structure would suggest. It contains much more than requirements for the vassal. Moses adapted the form of the treaty to make a powerful statement about loyalty and covenant obedience.

The treaty pattern observable in Deuteronomy bears directly on the debate about the date of the book. The first ancient Near Eastern vassal treaties found were Hittite treaties from the fourteenth and thirteenth centuries B.C. They provided the basis for comparison with Deuteronomy.[43] This comparison seemed to provide strong grounds for an early date for the book.[44]

Deuteronomy has also been compared to ancient Mesopotamian law codes that have a structure similar to the treaty form. The Code of Hammurabi, for example, consists of a preamble, historical prologue, laws, and blessings and curses. The law section especially seems to fit Deuteronomy better than the stipulation section of the treaties.[45] This would seem to add further evidence for an early date for Deuteronomy.

---

[42]See D.J. McCarthy, *Treaty and Covenant,* rev. ed. (Rome: Pontifical Biblical Institute, 1978), p. 23, for a list of ancient treaties.

[43]Mendenhall, "Covenant Forms."

[44]Kline, *Treaty,* pp. 42-43; K.A. Kitchen, *Ancient Orient and Old Testament* (Chicago: InterVarsity, 1966), pp. 91-92; idem, "The Patriarchal Age: Myth or History," *BAR* 21,2 (1995): 54-55.

[45]Moshe Weinfeld, *Deuteronomy and the Deuteronomic School* (Oxford: Oxford University Press, 1972), pp. 146-150. See Wenham, "Linch-pin," 10,3:19 for simple charts comparing the form of vassal treaties and law codes with Deuteronomy.

Vassal treaties from the first millennium have also been discovered.[46] Their structure is different in several respects from the earlier ones. Most conspicuous is the absence of an historical prologue, the detailed curse section with no corresponding blessing section, and no instructions for the preservation of the treaty. Nevertheless, several scholars, including Moshe Weinfeld, insist that Deuteronomy best resembles the seventh century Assyrian treaties. Weinfeld stresses the close parallel between some of the curses in Deuteronomy and the Assyrian treaties.[47] According to Weinfeld, the apparent parallels between Deuteronomy and the earlier treaties and law codes are based on the conservative persistence of treaty and legal traditions in the ancient Near East. The apparent changes of form merely reflect the accidents of discovery. However, his argument can cut both ways. Could not the parallels he has discovered between curses in Deuteronomy and the seventh century Assyrian treaties be due to the persistence of curse traditions in the ancient world? Could it not be that Deuteronomy, an old text, preserves the tradition that resurfaced in later Assyrian treaties?[48] It sometimes seems like the late seventh century date for Deuteronomy is assumed and any evidence for an earlier date is minimized or explained away.[49]

CONTENTS

The book of Deuteronomy is a repository of theological reflection that has deeply influenced the rest of the OT. The major themes will become apparent as one reads the book. But it will be useful to summarize some of the key thoughts.

1) The God of Israel is the only God and Lord of the covenant. There is no God beside him (4:35; 32:39). Compared to him the other gods are mere idols, made of wood and stone and utterly help-

---

[46]Specifically the Vassal Treaties of Esarhaddon from the seventh century are often referred to in the discussions.

[47]Weinfeld, *The Deuteronomic School*, pp. 116-146.

[48]Weinfeld does admit that Deuteronomy is influenced by the Hittite model, but it was an old tradition that Deuteronomy used at a later time (*Deuteronomy 1–11: A New Translation with Introduction and Commentary* [New York: Doubleday, 1991], p. 9).

[49]Wenham, "Linch-pin."

less (4:28; 32:37-38). He is God of gods and LORD of lords (10:17). The LORD is one and worthy of Israel's total allegiance (6:4-5). Because he is the only God and Israel is his people, he is zealous for their loyalty and obedience (5:9). He is sovereign over the whole world and over all nations.

2) God binds himself to his people by the covenant. This is an act of God's grace and love. He chooses Israel because he loves them (7:8). The covenant is an expression of his character, for through it he demonstrates his faithfulness, love, uprightness, and holiness. God's election of Israel is not based on their righteousness but on God's faithfulness to his promise to Abraham (9:5-6). The covenant is grounded in the past, it gave meaning to the present, and it promises hope for the future.

3) The covenant requires obedience from Israel (6:6,24,25; 11:13, 27; 13; 28:1,2; and often). Through obedience she would reap all the blessings of the covenant which included long life in the land (chapters 8 and 11). The simplicity of the demand is easily overlooked. Everything that God intends for his people is theirs if they would just obey the law. Every law is for their benefit. Obedience would protect Israel from pagan influence, provide her with good leadership, assure that justice was done in the land, and produce a wide range of other benefits. These benefits are concrete proof of God's love for Israel and his concern for her welfare.

4) God is the lord of history. Human history is the arena in which God chose to work out his will. Deuteronomy's constant references to the promise to the Patriarchs (1:8; 8:3; 9:5, etc.) and the Exodus (1:29; 4:37; 11:3, etc.) demonstrate that the reality of history is crucial to a relationship with God. Israel could trust God's promises and rely on his strength and power because he had proven himself over and over. Therefore, all of history (especially Israel's) is full of purpose and meaning. Under God's direction history is working out his will and plan (7:17-24).

5) The relationship between God and Israel could be described as one of love. God loves her (7:8) and he requires that she love him (6:5). Love could be commanded because it is based on decision not emotion. Love is often paralleled with obey (5:10), serve, and fear (10:12-13). God is portrayed as the father who loved the son enough to carry him (1:31) or discipline him (8:5). This love relationship is an important part of the covenant idea in the OT. It protects the

covenant from being viewed as merely a legal contract. Love is ground-ed in a relationship. Other OT writers, like the prophet Hosea, picked up on the theme. The command to love God is at the root of the New Testament call to love God. In fact any time the New Testament commands love for God it does so by quoting Deuteronomy 6:5.

6) The land is an important focus in Deuteronomy. Israel was sit-uated on the East bank of the Jordan River, ready to move into Canaan. This is the land promised to the forefathers (Gen 12:7). It is therefore a gift of God's grace (9:4-6). It is a good land (8:7-10) in which Israel could live a good life (28:3-6). It stands in sharp contrast to the wilderness through which the nation had come. The prospects for the future are bright, for God intended Israel to live a long and full life in the land. However, the promise of the land is conditional. If Israel disobeyed God, the land would become a place of sickness, famine, and disease. The blessings would turn into curs-es. Foreigners would come into the land, destroying and plunder-ing. Israel would eventually be taken out of the land and suffer under the dominance of evil nations (28:15-68).

7) Christopher J.H. Wright has argued that Deuteronomy has mis-siological significance.[50] It calls for loyalty in the midst of change and in the midst of the challenges of syncretism. The call to mission pres-ents a paradigm for how the people of God should conduct themselves in similar circumstances. God's people frequently find themselves in boundary situations and in the middle of temptations from idols. Faithfulness to God and his uniqueness are crucial at these times. Further, Israel is to be a model to the nations and a witness to the char-acter of God (4:6-8). Obedience to the covenant would witness to the character of the God Israel worshiped and exhibit the quality of life and justice possible under the sovereign God of the universe.

DEUTERONOMY AND THE PSALMS

The Psalms have been called the theological center of the Old Testament. The major themes found in them cover all the basic con-cepts that inform the rest of the Old Testament. The same could be

---

[50]Christopher J.H. Wright, *Deuteronomy*, New International Bible Com-mentary (Peabody, MA: Hendrickson, 1996), pp. 8-13.

said for the book of Deuteronomy. Recently, the close relationship between the two biblical books has begun to receive attention.[51]

Psalm 1 begins the Psalter by advocating meditation on the *torah* (v. 2). This meditation marks the righteous man and stands in contrast to the naïve man who gets trapped in the way of the wicked (v. 1).[52] Psalm 1 sets the stage for the entire collection of Psalms. The Psalms are reflections of the life of the righteous person who meditates on the law, a life in relationship to God characterized by lament and praise.

Several of the Psalms' themes are similar to Deuteronomy's.[53] 1) Israel's relationship to God is grounded in the covenant. Although only a few Psalms directly address the theme of covenant (25, 89, 132), the larger context for all the Psalms is covenant. The only reason Israel can speak to God and about him is because of the covenant relationship with him. 2) Israel can worship God and be assured that when they come to the temple they are in his presence. The hymns and laments both count on his response to the psalmist. 3) God's actions on behalf of his people were done in human history. Israel's history is a basis for both warning and praise (78, 136). 4) God was the true King who ruled over Israel and the whole earth (93, 96). Israel's king was under his rule and protection (2).[54] 5) God's law was central to his covenant relationship with Israel (1, 19, 119). 6) God's blessings were available to the righteous, but the wicked would fail (1). 7) The weak and oppressed were under the special care of God, and they could count on his help (9, 22, 72).

These themes in Deuteronomy will be uncovered as the book is studied. The close relationship between these two important biblical books attests to the theological integrity of the Old Testament.

---

[51]Patrick D. Miller, "Deuteronomy and Psalms: Evoking a Biblical Conversation," *JBL* 118 (1999): 3-18.

[52]Psalm 1:1 seems to be a direct contrast to Deut 6:7. Deuteronomy admonishes the Israelites to discuss the law at all times, including when they sit, walk, lie down, and get up. Psalm 1 warns against walking, standing, and sitting with the wicked. Two of the three verbs in Psalm 1 are the same words as in Deuteronomy, and "stand" is equivalent to "get up."

[53]For a brief summary of the major themes in the Psalms see Tremper Longman III, *How to Read the Psalms* (Downers Grove, IL: InterVarsity, 1988), pp. 51-62.

[54]James Mays, *The Lord Reigns: A Theological Handbook to the Psalms* (Louisville: Westminster John Knox, 1994).

OUTLINE

BIBLIOGRAPHY

I. COMMENTARIES

Brown, Raymond. *The Message of Deuteronomy: Not by Bread Alone.* Downers Grove, IL: InterVarsity, 1993.

Cairns, Ian. *Word and Presence: A Commentary on the Book of Deuteronomy.* Grand Rapids: Eerdmans, 1992.

Christensen, Duane L. *Deuteronomy 1–11.* Dallas: Word Books, 1991.

Craigie, Peter. *The Book of Deuteronomy.* Grand Rapids: Eerdmans, 1976.

Driver, S.R. *A Critical and Exegetical Commentary on Deuteronomy.* Edinburgh: T. & T. Clark, 1895.

Mayes, A.D.H. *Deuteronomy.* London: Oliphants, 1979.

Merrill, Eugene. *Deuteronomy.* Nashville: Broadman and Holman, 1994.

Miller, Patrick. *Deuteronomy: Interpretation, A Bible Commentary for Teaching and Preaching.* Louisville: John Knox Press, 1990.

Phillips, Anthony. *Deuteronomy.* Cambridge: Cambridge University Press, 1973.

Thompson, J.A. *Deuteronomy: An Introduction and Commentary.* Downers Grove, IL: InterVarsity, 1974.

Tigay, Jeffrey. *The JPS Torah Commentary: Deuteronomy.* Philadelphia: The Jewish Publication Society, 1996.

von Rad, Gerhard. *Deuteronomy.* London: SCM, 1966.

Walton, John H., and Victor H. Matthews. *Genesis–Deuteronomy.* The

IVP Bible Background Commentary. Downers Grove, IL: Inter-Varsity, 1997.

Weinfeld, Moshe. *Deuteronomy 1–11: A New Translation with Introduction and Commentary*. New York: Doubleday, 1991.

Wright, Christopher J.H. *Deuteronomy*. New International Biblical Commentary. Peabody, MA: Hendrickson, 1996.

Wright, G.E. "Deuteronomy." In *Interpreter's Bible*. Nashville: Abingdon, 1953. 2:307- 537.

II. SPECIAL STUDIES

Achtemeier, Elizabeth. *Deuteronomy, Jeremiah*. Philadelphia: Fortress, 1978.

Aharoni, Yohanan, and Michael Avi-Yonah. *The Macmillan Bible Atlas*. New York: Macmillan, 1968.

Christensen, Duane L., ed. *A Song of Power and The Power of Song*. Winona Lake: Eisenbrauns, 1993.

Clements, R.E. *Deuteronomy*. Sheffield: JSOT Press, 1989.

de Vaux, R. *Ancient Israel*. New York: McGraw Hill, 1961.

Enns, Peter. "Law of God." In *NIDOTTE*, 4:893-900.

Hall, Gary H. "Rhetorical Criticism, Chiasm, and Theme in Deuteronomy." *Stone-Campbell Journal* 1,1 (1998): 85-100.

Harrelson, W. *The Ten Commandments and Human Rights*. Philadelphia: Fortress, 1980.

Hoerth, Alfred J., Gerald L. Mattingly, and Edwin M. Yamauchi, eds. *People of the Old Testament World*. Grand Rapids: Baker, 1994.

Janzen, J.G. "On the Most Important Word in the Shema (Deuteronomy vi 4-5)." *VT* 37 (1987): 280-300.

Kitchen, K.A. *Ancient Orient and Old Testament*. Chicago: InterVarsity, 1966.

Kline, Meredith G. *The Treaty of the Great King: The Covenant Structure of Deuteronomy*. Grand Rapids: Eerdmans, 1963.

Lohfink, Norbert. *Das Deuteronomium*. Leuven, Belgium: Leuven University Press, 1985.

Manley, G.T. *The Book of the Law*. London: Tyndale, 1957.

Mayes, A.D.H. "Deuteronomy 4 and the Literary Criticism of Deuteronomy." *JBL* 100 (1981): 23-51.

McCarthy, D.J. "Notes on the Love of God in Deuteronomy and the Father-Son Relationship between Yahweh and Israel." *CBQ* 27 (1965): 144-147.

_____. *Treaty and Covenant*. Rev. ed. Rome: Pontifical Biblical Institute, 1978.

McConville, J.G. *Law and Theology in Deuteronomy*. Sheffield: JSOT Press, 1984.

_____. *Grace in the End: A Study in Deuteronomic Theology*. Grand Rapids: Zondervan, 1993.

_____, and J.G. Miller. *Time and Place in Deuteronomy*. Sheffield: JSOT Press, 1994.

Mendenhall, G.E. "Covenant Forms in Israelite Tradition." *BA* 17,3 (1954): 50-76.

Miller, J. Gary. *Now Choose Life: Theology and Ethics in Deuteronomy*. Grand Rapids: Eerdmans, 1998.

Miller, Patrick D. "The Gift of God: The Deuteronomic Theology of the Land." *Int* 23 (1969): 451-465.

_____. "Moses My Servant: A Deuteronomic Portrait of Moses." *Int* 41 (1987): 245-255.

Moran, W.L. "The Ancient Near Eastern Background of the Love of God in Deuteronomy." *CBQ* 25 (1963): 77-87.

Nicholson, E.W. *Deuteronomy and Tradition*. Philadelphia: Fortress, 1967.

Olson, Dennis. *Deuteronomy and the Death of Moses*. Minneapolis: Augsburg Fortress, 1994.

Polzin, R. *Moses and the Deuteronomist*. New York: Seabury, 1980.

Pritchard, J.B., ed. *Ancient Near Eastern Texts Relating to the Old Testament*. 3rd ed. Princeton: Princeton University Press, 1969.

von Rad, Gerhard. *Studies in Deuteronomy*. London: SCM, 1953.

──────────. *The Problem of the Hexateuch and Other Essays*. Philadelphia: Fortress, 1984.

Walton, John H. "Deuteronomy: An Exposition of the Spirit of the Law." *Grace Theological Journal* 8 (1987): 213-225.

Weinfeld, Moshe. *Deuteronomy and the Deuteronomic School*. Oxford: Oxford University Press, 1972.

Wenham, Gordon J. "The Date of Deuteronomy: Linch-pin of Old Testament Criticism." *Themelios* 10,3 and 11,1 (1985): 15-20, 15-18.

Wilson, Ian. *Out of the Midst of the Fire: Divine Presence in Deuteronomy*. Missoula: Scholars Press, 1996.

Wiseman, D.J., ed. *People of Old Testament Times*. Oxford: Clarendon Press, 1973.

Wright, C.J.H. *God's People in God's Land: Family, Land, and Property in the Old Testament*. Downers Grove, IL: InterVarsity, 1996.

DEUTERONOMY 1

I. THE FIRST SPEECH OF MOSES (1:1–4:43)

A. PREAMBLE (1:1-5)

These verses provide an introduction to the whole book as well as to the chapter. Some scholars see them as an introduction to what they call the Deuteronomistic history, which included the books of Joshua through 2 Kings.

The content of these verses foreshadows what Moses will cover in the first main section of the book. There is a threefold emphasis on Moses speaking to the people (vv. 1,3,5) interspersed with geographical references that reappear in chapters 1–3 (cf. v. 2 with 1:19-46 and v. 4 with 2:24–3:11).[1]

1:1 These are the words Moses spoke place the whole book in the context of prophetic speech. Moses, as the premier prophet (see 18:15-20), speaks the word of the LORD to the people. This fact is demonstrated throughout the Pentateuch, beginning in Exodus 3 with Moses' call. The words were not Moses' words but God's. This is the first of several references to Moses' speaking to the people (see 4:1; 5:1; 27:1; 29:2; 31:1,18; 32:45). Therefore, the book of Deuteronomy is set within the context of Moses' authority as God's spokesman. As is made plain throughout, it is God's word for the present generation as well as for all generations to come. The three references in verses 1,3, and 5 are not repetitious, but complementary. They demonstrate that the words are Moses' words (v. 1), but

---

[1] Jeffrey Tigay, *Deuteronomy* (Philadelphia: The Jewish Publication Society, 1996), p. 3, suggests a chiastic arrangement to the verses: A. The site of Moses' address, v. 1; B. The foreshadowing of the first message, v. 2; C. The date, v. 3; B'. The foreshadowing of the second message, v. 4; A'. The site of Moses' address, v. 5.

that God is the author (v. 3). Further, Moses is the mediator and teacher of these words.[2]

The recipients are **all Israel**. This is a very common designation for the nation in Deuteronomy which views Israel as a whole, both past and present generations (5:3-4; 29:10-17), and even future ones. The emphasis is on the unity of the people of God. They stand before God not merely as separate individuals or tribes, but as a whole nation.

The place of the speech is **in the desert east of the Jordan**. This geographical note ties the book closely with the preceding book of Numbers which places Israel at the same location (Num 22:1; 31:12; 33:48,50; 35:1; 36:13). The time they had spent in this location had been eventful as Numbers makes clear. It included the Baalam episode, the Moabite seduction, a census, the Midianite war, and the promulgation of various laws.

The Hebrew phrase translated by the NIV as **east of Jordan** could be understood as a proper name rather than a location — the Transjordan.[3] Verse 5 places this location in the "land of Moab." The area had a fluctuating border. Moab's southern boundary was always the Brook Zered, but its northern boundary was at times the Arnon River and at times several miles north. The general area in view here is that which was east of the Jordan River at the north edge of the Dead Sea.

The other place names carry an aura of specificity, but several have not been located for certain. **The Arabah** was part of the large rift valley that began north of the Sea of Galilee and continued south to the Gulf of Aqabah, a finger of the Red Sea. Mostly the name referred to the area between the south end of the Dead Sea and the Gulf, but it could refer to territory north of the Dead Sea as well. **Suph** is not mentioned elsewhere in the Bible, but it could refer to Supah in Numbers 21:14 which was a location in Moab. All other occurrences of Suph in the OT are paired with "sea" (□', *yam*) and most often refer to the Red Sea (or Sea of Reeds; Exod 13:18; 15:4,22; 23:31; Josh 2:10; etc.). However, in a few instances the phrase designated the Gulf of Aqabah (Num 14:25; 21:4; Deut 1:40;

---

[2]Patrick Miller, *Deuteronomy* (Louisville: John Knox Press, 1990), p. 24.

[3]Eugene Merrill, *Deuteronomy* (Nashville: Broadman and Holman, 1994), p. 62.

2:1; Judg 11:16; 1 Kgs 9:26). This latter meaning would be the most natural reference here since the other places that are known seem to be near the Gulf as well.[4] **Paran** was most likely the desert area in the eastern Sinai peninsula, just south of Kadesh Barnea. **Tophel, Laban,** and **Dizahab** occur only here in the Old Testament and their locations are not known for certain. **Hazeroth** could be the same Hazeroth as in Numbers 11:35, on the east side of the Sinai peninsula. If the above is true then the place names following the reference to the Jordan do not refer to unknown locations in the Plains of Moab, but rather rehearse in some way the wilderness wandering which led them to that place. Verse 2, then, would not be parenthetical as the NIV has it, but would identify the wandering through the Arabah as the Mt. Seir route.[5] The emphasis would be on the fact that although it was God's intention that they should enter the Promised Land soon after leaving Sinai (eleven days! see vv. 19-40), they were still in the wilderness after forty years.

1:2 Horeb is Deuteronomy's favorite name for Mt. Sinai (except in 33:2, a poetic text). The noun comes from a root that means to be dry or desolate, a fitting description of the southern end of the Sinai peninsula. The other Pentateuchal books prefer Sinai, though Exodus 3:1; 33:6 and 17:6 have Horeb. **Kadesh Barnea** is near the largest spring in northern Sinai and near the conjunction of two major ancient highways. It was the focus of much of Israel's stay in the wilderness. Eleven days for the journey from Horeb to Kadesh Barnea via the 'Aqaba/Mt. Seir route has been confirmed by modern explorers.[6]

1:3 In the fortieth year is the only precise date we find in Deuteronomy. It places Moses' speech as two and one-half months before the Passover of Joshua (Josh 4:19; 5:10) and six months after the death of Aaron (Num 33:38). The words of Moses were God's words and just as Moses had been obedient to all that God had told him to do, he expected Israel to be obedient to all that God commanded them to do. Hence we find throughout the book numerous

---

[4]The Greek translation of the Old Testament (LXX; c. 250 B.C.) and the Aramaic Targums have Yam Suph instead of Suph (Aramaic Targums are Aramaic paraphrases of the Hebrew text from 100 B.C. to 100 A.D.).

[5]Merrill, *Deuteronomy*, p. 63.

[6]Moshe Weinfeld, *Deuteronomy 1–11* (New York: Doubleday, 1991), p. 127.

references to commandments and numerous calls to obedience. This was Israel's covenant responsibility.

1:4 Even as Israel remembered the failures of the past and looked forward with fear to the future (v. 21), they were reminded of the recent victories that God had won for them. Moses here anticipates his longer recapitulation of the events surrounding the defeat of **Sihon** and **Og**.[7]

1:5 This statement rounds off the introductory preamble. It repeats the place and describes precisely what Moses was going to do. He would **expound this law**. Moses was going to do more than just speak (v. 1) or proclaim (v. 3) God's word. He was going to make it clear and plain by interpreting it. He was more than a lawgiver; he was a preacher and teacher. The verb בָּאַר, used here (*b'r*, "make distinct") emphasized the clarity of the message. The verb is also used in 27:8 for the act of writing clearly the words of the law and in Habakkuk 2:2 for writing down the revelation.

Christians often misunderstand the **law**. The Hebrew word תּוֹרָה (*tôrāh*) in its root meaning, and in its broadest sense means "instruction" or "teaching." It is often used of the regulations for cultic and ceremonial matters, especially in Leviticus, and for civil, social, and judicial matters, but that does not seem to be the nuance in this text.[8] Deuteronomy contains historical reminiscence and sermonic exhortation as well as law. Thus we are to understand *tôrāh* in its broadest sense here. God called Israel to be his people and graciously established a covenant with them (Exod 19). As a part of that covenant arrangement he revealed to them the way of life that would be pleasing to him (Deut 30:11-16) — his will for them grounded in his character. They were not left guessing about how to live their covenant obligations. As instruction *tôrāh* "deals with Israel's origin and the reason for her being, with her future and the fulfillment of her existence, with her attitude and her motivations for action."[9] Thus *tôrāh* was a delight and a wonder (Ps 119).

It was this full revelation of the will of God that Moses now set out to make plain. That is why we find in Deuteronomy more than

---

[7]See the commentary below on 2:24–3:11.

[8]Peter Enns, "Law of God," *NIDOTTE*, 4:893-900.

[9]Achtemeier, *Deuteronomy, Jeremiah*, p. 11.

legal regulations. It contains historical recapitulation, exposition, encouragement, warning, and profound theological reflection.

B. HISTORICAL PROLOGUE (1:6–3:29)

Ancient treaty forms included a brief historical section to recall the history of relations between the two parties. Accordingly Moses included in this introductory section of Deuteronomy an historical prologue in which he rehearsed some of the events in the forty years since Israel left Sinai. He especially focused on more recent events (chapters 2–3).

1. Instructions to Leave Horeb (1:6-8)

1:6-7 These verses begin the first major section of the book of Deuteronomy which is an historical review of several events of the last forty years, selected for their importance in teaching Israel what God had done for them. His redemptive deeds established his authority over Israel as his covenant community. Therefore, the law he will reveal was a gracious gift of a covenant-making, covenant-keeping God.

Israel had arrived at **Horeb** (Sinai) directly from Egypt in the third month after the exodus event (Exod 19:1). In the second month of the second year after the event they left Horeb and traveled northeast through the wilderness and desert to Kadesh-Barnea (Num 10:11ff). Moses, in his retelling of the story, picked up with the departure from Horeb. It was not God's intention that they should stay there long. He had a promise to keep. A similar command was given in 2:3 at the end of the wilderness era.

The geographical description of the Promised Land (v. 7) is a classical delineation of its dimensions (Gen 15:18; Exod 23:31; Deut 11:24; Josh 1:4). The **Amorites** were an ancient ethnic group that can be traced back as early as 2400 BC. They were at one time quite strong, controlling much of Mesopotamia. But in Moses' day they had only a tenuous control over part of the area, perhaps Syria and part of Palestine. They were associated with the **hill country** here, and the **Canaanites** with the lowlands (Num 13:29), though sometimes the Amorites and Canaanites seem to be interchangeable terms (Ezek 16:3).[10] In Egyptian texts of the period the term Canaan refers to the Phoenician coastal areas.

The **Arabah** marked the east and southeast border, the **Negev** the southern border, the **coast** (the Mediterranean Sea) the western border, and the northern sector of the **Euphrates River** in upper Mesopotamia was the northern border. It was an expanse to be realized only once, under Solomon (1 Kgs 4:21).

1:8 The promise of land was grounded in the promise to Abraham in Genesis 12:1-3 and 7 and involved not only land, but blessing and nation. The whole Pentateuch is shaped around the promise of the land but focuses on the difficulty of inheriting it.[11] Genesis even ends with Jacob and his family outside of the land. Beginning with the Exodus, the descendants of Jacob moved toward the land and at the end of forty years were poised to enter it. But only under Joshua did the nation take the land. Deuteronomy is full of references to the land because Israel was about to take it and was therefore given instructions on how to possess it and live in it.

Israel was confronted with the knowledge that God had **given** them the land, yet they had to **go in and take possession** of it (cf. v. 21). "To take possession" of the land was synonymous with inheriting it.[12] God's sovereignty and Israel's responsibility intertwined. God's gift was to be obtained by their obedience and faithful actions. Yet even as Israel advanced to dispossess the inhabitants, God was driving them out (7:1-2; 9:3).

Moses will come back again and again to these crucial themes, for they are at the heart of God's purpose for Israel. Israel was not to possess the land just for her own benefit. God still had his larger goal in view: the blessing of the nations (Gen 12:3). So the next step

---

[10]Keith Schoville, "Canaanites and Amorites," *People of the Old Testament World,* eds. Alfred J. Hoerth, Gerald L. Mattingly, and Edwin M. Yamauchi (Grand Rapids: Baker, 1994), pp. 157-182.

[11]Patrick D. Miller, Jr., "The Gift of God: The Deuteronomic Theology of the Land," *Int* 23 (1969): 451-465. The word "land" occurs 197 times in Deuteronomy.

[12]The verb, "to take possession" (ירשׁ, *yrš*) occurs 71 times in Deuteronomy; the verb "to give" (נתן, *ntn*) 176 times. "To take possession" also means "to dispossess," Deut 7:17; 9:1; 11:23. Both Deut 9 and 11 are extended reflections on taking the land.

of obedience was not just for Israel, it was for the "redemption of the world."[13]

2. Appointment of Leaders (1:9-18)

Because of the rapid growth of the people Moses needed assistance in the administration of justice. This selection is related twice elsewhere in the Pentateuch (Exod 18:13-29 and Num 11:11-17) and though details differ, all three seem to be referring to the same event. Proper leadership for God's covenant people was a major concern of the book of Deuteronomy (cf. 16:18–18:22). This section interrupts the account of leaving Horeb, for verse 19 chronologically follows directly on verse 8.

1:9 At that time introduces a look back to earlier events. In this section the events apparently preceded even Sinai (Exod 18:13ff). Moses originally tried to settle every dispute himself, but received wise advice from his father-in-law, Jethro.

1:10-11 The great increase of the number of Israelites was a direct result of the ancient promise to the patriarch Abraham (Gen 12:2; 15:5; 17:2; 18:18; 22:17; Exod 1:7; Deut 10:22; Josh 11:4). The word picture, **as many as the stars in the sky,** meant an uncountable number. At the time of the first promise it seemed like an impossibility for the childless Abraham. But now God's faithfulness to the promise was abundantly clear. This still was not enough for Moses and he wished for more. Another **thousand**-fold increase would be further assurance of God's **blessing.** Moses' complaint was not about the increasing number, but the increasing burden.

Despite all that had happened to Israel in Egypt and in the wilderness they were to know at this crucial stage that they still lived under the blessing of God. What Abraham never lived to see was theirs to receive.

1:12-14 The assistance that Moses needed was to come from the people. The qualities Moses required distinguished the men who were to be chosen as gifted and already proven leaders. They were to be **wise and understanding**, two qualities identified with the wisdom tradition of the Old Testament. This kind of insight came from

---

[13]Wright, *Deuteronomy*, p. 25.

study and experience and was grounded in the fear of God (Prov 2:5). It suggested ability in civil affairs and understanding of what was just and fair.[14] The two words could be taken together in a superlative sense to mean "very wise."[15] The leaders were also to be **respected**. They were to be well known among the people as men experienced in life, fair-minded and with a good reputation. In fact, a more accurate translation could be "experienced" if we understand the participle form as active rather than passive.[16] The people gladly followed Moses' wise instructions.

1:15 The organizational units **of thousands, of hundreds, of fifties and of tens** were basic military terms in the OT (Exod 18:21,25; Num 1:16; 31:4,5,14,48,52; Josh 22:21,30; 1 Sam 22:7, etc.) and are approximate terms for how to organize the people. The military terminology was appropriate at that time since the most immediate need for leadership under Joshua was military.

Commanders originally meant some sort of chieftain or clan leader (שַׂר, śar) and later came to mean one who assisted the king in some kind of official capacity. The word is often translated as "prince." The word translated **tribal officers** comes from the root, "to write" (שֹׁטֵר, šṭr). It literally means a record keeper, one who can write (Exod 5:6; Josh 1:10). He was someone with official, leadership functions that included record keeping and business affairs.

These were appointed to **have authority over** the people. The Hebrew text has "heads" (רֹאשׁ, rō'š, NIV "**leading men**") in the first part of the verse and also in the second half, which NIV translates as "have authority over." This is an attempt to clear up a seeming redundancy. How could Moses take the heads and appoint them as heads? Probably the people selected the leaders and then Moses confirmed that decision (vv. 13-14 and Exod 18:25). It seems best to keep "leaders" in both parts of the verse.[17]

---

[14]Gerald Wilson, "חכם," *NIDOTTE*, 2:130-134; Terrance Fretheim, "בִּין" *NIDOTTE*, 1:652-653.

[15]Merrill, *Deuteronomy*, p. 69.

[16]The root of the word is יָדַע (yd'), which carries the idea of knowing through relationships and experience. Weinfeld, *Deuteronomy*, p. 13, and others prefer "experienced."

[17]As do the NRSV and many commentators.

1:16 A new office is introduced, that of **judges**. This was both a judicial and military term as the book of Judges shows, but here the focus was on judicial matters. A judge's basic function was to listen (the Hebrew text has no word for the NIV **disputes**) to what their kinsmen were saying and make righteous decisions (צֶדֶק, *ṣedeq*) or **judge fairly**. There was a standard of justice and righteousness grounded in the character of God (Deut 16:18), and they were to make decisions based on that standard. **Brother** is a Deuteronomic term for members of the covenant community that reflected the strong family concept of the book (see Deut 1:28; 3:18,20; 15:2,3,7; 17:15; 22:1). Justice was to be also applied to the **alien**, that is, the foreigner who lived among them. These aliens were to be accepted into Israelite society with all the rights except access to religious practices (Exod 22:21; Deut 24:17,18; Lev 19:33,34). The basis for this compassion was Israel's experience as an alien in Egypt. Other alien laws are covered in Deut 14:29; 16:11 and 26:11.

1:17-18 The one human trait that has the greatest potential for injustice is showing partiality, especially based on social status. Such an evil practice was especially anathema in Israel whose system of justice was grounded in God's character. He was the ultimate Judge and perfectly just. Thus the judges were to reflect his character, not their own prejudices. Justice in Israel was divinely ordained; it was not a social construct. Ultimately legal affairs were a theological matter. Further instructions with similar language are given in Deuteronomy 16:18-20 and 17:8-13.

The difficult cases were to be brought to Moses whose unique role as mediator and prophet enabled him to convey serious matters to God and receive instruction (Num 27:1-11).

3. First Attempt to Take the Land (1:19–2:1)

This section has a symmetry that is reflected in two features: an interchange between God's word and the peoples' response, and a concentric arrangement of the material. The recapitulation of the first, abortive attempt to take the land is told in such a way as to focus on God's response in verses 34-39 and his anger with the people and Moses. This focus is demonstrated by the concentric arrangement of the events selected for retelling. It can be demonstrated in chart form.

   A. 1:19-20 – travel notice
      B. 1:21-25 – do not be afraid, possess the land; the spies go up
         C. 1:26-28 – Israel refuses to go up; spies bring bad report
            D. 1:29-31 – do not be afraid, God will fight for you
               E. 1:32-33 – they did not trust God who went ahead
                  F. 1:34-36 – God angry with Israel
                  F'. 1:37-39 – God angry with Moses
               E'. 1:40 – turn back
            C'. 1:41 - people confess sin; we will go up
               D'. 1:42 – do not go, God will not fight for you
      B'. 1:43-45 – in arrogance they rebel, go up and are defeated
   A'. 1:46–2:1 – travel notice

Although this is not a complete chiasm, the concentric structure is clear, and certain repetitions help us see the emphasis of the material. The section shows a movement back and forth between God's word and the peoples' response with an interplay between God's command to "go up" and Israel's refusal to "go up." When the people finally decided to "go up" God refused to go with them!

The characterization of God and the people stand in stark contrast: God was encouraging, commanding, supportive (do not be afraid, I will fight for you), and trustworthy; but he responded in anger to their disobedience and turned a deaf ear. The people refused to be obedient, rebelled, grumbled, did not trust God, and then in arrogance disobeyed by trying to go up into the land on their own.

The background for this section is Numbers 13–14. Moses followed the same order of events with only a minor variation or two.[18] But a comparison with Numbers shows significant selectivity of material. Much was left out. Scholars for years have resorted to hypothetical documents to explain the differences.[19] It is more fruitful to ask why there may be differences, and what the selectivity tells us about Moses' purpose in recounting these events. The answer lies in understanding the characterization of God and the people as noted above. Moses was retelling the story so as to emphasize God's

---

[18]See Driver, *Deuteronomy*, pp. 19, 24, and 29, for comparison charts.
[19]See ibid., pp. 22-32 for various suggestions, and A.D.H. Mayes, *Deuteronomy* (London: Oliphants, 1979), pp. 126-127.

faithfulness and Israel's lack of trust. The main problem was Israel's lack of faith in God.[20]

1:19-20 These verses are closely connected with verses 1-8 and continue the narration begun there. **The LORD our God command-ed us** refers back to verses 6-7 and the **hill country of the Amorites** continues the travel note in verse 7. They **set out** from Horeb. This verb is common in the travel narratives in the Pentateuch, 88 times in Numbers alone (in Deuteronomy see 1:7,19,40; 2:1,24; 10:6,7). It literally means to "break camp" (1:7, NIV) or pull up tent stakes. It underlined Israel's condition of being constantly on the move, of being sojourners and aliens in the land they were passing through, of the life of impermanence and wandering. They were forced to look forward to receiving the promised land, which was God's inten-tion from the first.[21]

Their journey was through a **vast and dreadful desert**. This was a graphic description of the area through which they had to travel to get from Horeb to **Kadesh Barnea.** Its desolation and intractable inhospitality to human life was described in the Pentateuch and has been confirmed by modern surveys.[22] Numbers 11:1–12:16 describes the trip and Numbers 33 gives the stopping places in the wilderness wanderings, from the Exodus to the plains of Moab. It was over 100 miles from Horeb to Kadesh Barnea and took 11 days according to verse 2. The experience was mentioned here to remind Israel of God's leading them safely through it (verse 31). In Deuteronomy the wilderness is a symbol for the dual emphasis of God's leading and providing, and of Israel's rebellion (8:15-16; 9:7. See also Amos 2:10; 5:25; Hos 13:5-6; Jer 2:6; Ezek 20:10-26; Ps 78:14-41). Both themes are evident in this section.

Kadesh Barnea, their destination, was an important place in the wilderness period. It was located forty miles south of Beersheba and in later years marked the southernmost boundary of the land of Israel. It is identified with the modern el-Qudeirat and the area has four springs. No permanent remains have been found from the period when Israel was there, but it seems unlikely that a nomadic

---

[20]Mayes, *Deueronomy,* p. 127.

[21]In a significant contrast, in Isa 33:20 the redeemed Zion will be like a tent that will never be moved, its stakes never pulled up.

[22]See K.A. Kitchen, "Wilderness of Wandering," *NBD,* pp. 1251-1254.

people would leave much behind. A fortress from King Solomon's time has been uncovered.[23] Israel was to stop at Kadesh Barnea briefly, for it was to be just the staging area for the conquest of the land. It was God's original intention that they enter from the south. This reprise is a bitter reminder to the new generation of their ancestors' failure.

1:21 See is a common expression in Deuteronomy (1:8; 2:24,31; 4:5; 11:26; 30:15; 32:39). It was a command to understand or pay attention to what God was doing. In this case Israel was to take notice that God **has given you the land**. Even though they still had to enter it, the reception from God was accomplished. What he promised to do he would do.[24]

This passage plays with the verb "see," contrasting what they should see, what they have seen, and what they would not see (cf. verses 19,21,28,31,33,35,36). Unfortunately, what they see is the might of the enemy and not God's power.[25]

The Hebrew text makes a change in this verse that cannot be reflected in English: it switches from the second person plural to the singular form of address. The same style recurs in verse 31. The significance of this phenomenon has been much discussed but no satisfactory solution has been proposed.[26] The phenomenon occurs throughout the book.

The reference to **the LORD your God** is in contrast to the LORD our God in verse 20. The latter is the overwhelming phrase of choice in Deuteronomy (over 260 times) and shows the identification of the speaker with the audience. But the former predominates in this section which stresses the rebellion of the people.

The admonition, **do not be afraid**, was a common assurance from God throughout the Old Testament. It seemed to come at times when there was every reason for the people of God to be afraid, whether it be uncertainty about the future or extreme danger. It was

---

[23]Dale Manor, "Kadesh Barnea," *ABD,* 4:1-3.

[24]On the giving of the land see remarks above on verse 8.

[25]Miller, *Deuteronomy,* p. 35.

[26]Christensen, *Deuteronomy 1-11,* pp. 33-34. He sees the switch as structural boundaries for a musical reading of the text. Other suggestions include seeing the plural passages as later additions or as signaling a switch between parenetic and historical material (Craigie, *Deuteronomy,* p. 101).

an exhortation from God meant to engender trust in him. It was often accompanied by some form of the phrase, "I will be with you." It is frequent in Deuteronomy (here and 1:29; 3:2,22; 7:18; 20:1; 31:6,8).[27] Here it is followed by **do not be discouraged**. These words are often a stock phrase (cf Deut 31:8; Josh 8:1; 10:25; 1 Chr 22:13; 28:20; Jer 23:4; 30:10, etc.) inviting faith and confidence in God. This should have been all the encouragement needed for Israel to move into the land promised to the fathers.

1:22 In Numbers 13 the spies were sent out at God's command, but here they were sent out at the people's request. Is this a contradiction or a reflection of the interplay between divine direction and human decisions in the affairs of God's people? Perhaps the people initiated the request and then Moses consulted with God and received his direction.[28] It was perhaps a concession by God, for although it would seem to betray a lack of trust, from Israel's and Moses' viewpoint it seemed like a good idea. Joshua did the same later (Josh 2:1; 7:2).[29]

The men were sent in to **spy out the land**. The same Hebrew word was used of Joshua's spies (Josh 2:2-3) and comes from a root that means "to dig out." The verb in verse 24 is different, meaning "to walk through, explore," while the verb used in Numbers 13 is still different, "to investigate, reconnoiter." These are apparently synonyms and are related to the idea of making a thorough investigation.

1:23-24 Numbers 13:21-24 lists other places the spies went, but it also concentrates on **the Valley of Eshcol**. The valley, more accurately "wadi," was apparently near Hebron though it has not been identified exactly. In Hebrew "Eshcol" means "cluster" which Numbers connects with the large cluster of grapes the spies cut and brought back. It was common back then to name wadis or valleys after plant life.[30] Even today there are vineyards near Hebron.

---

[27]The Hebrew phrase תִּירָא אַל ('al tayrā, "do not be afraid") occurs 75 times in the Old Testament. The equivalent occurs about 20 times in the New Testament. See Van Pelt and Kaiser, "יראָ," *NIDOTTE*, 2:527-533, and Fuhs, "יָרֵא," etc." *TDOT,* 6:290-315. The first occurrence is Gen 15:1.

[28]Merrill, *Deuteronomy,* p. 73. Even Driver (*Deuteronomy,* p. 22) accepts this explanation as a possibility, but he opts for different source documents as the best answer to the apparent contradiction.

[29]However, Mayes, *Deuteronomy,* p. 128, sees this as clear defiance of God.

[30]Weinfeld, *Deuteronomy,* p. 144.

1:25 Some of the fruit is not identified here but Numbers 13:23 specifically mentions grapes, figs, and pomegranates. It was a land that flowed with milk and honey, that is, at least the necessities of life if not more (Deut 6:3; 11:9; 26:5,15; 27:3; 31:20).

The report of the spies confirmed the promise of God. This gift that he was giving to them for an inheritance was indeed a **good land**. This concept was important to the theology of the land in Deuteronomy because it accentuated the fact that God's long awaited gift was valuable.[31]

Is giving us changes the completed action expressed in verse 21 to an incipient, continuing action here. The deed was as good as done, but it would take time and involve human effort as well as divine.[32]

1:26 This is a contravention of the direct command of God in verse 21. The verb "willing" was almost always used with a negative sense in the OT to indicate unwillingness (cf. 10:11). This unwillingness was defined as rebellion and understood as direct defiance. This rebellion was a conscious, intentional decision to disobey. This rebellious theme is found often in Deuteronomy (1:43; 9:7,23,24; 11:30; 21:18,20). In 31:27 Moses anticipated that their rebellious spirit would intensify. Their rebelliousness was a specific covenant-breaking act for they had committed themselves to obedience when they accepted the covenant offered by God.

1:27 You grumbled in your tents conveys a vivid picture. They were not courageous enough to rebel openly, but gathered in their tents to talk among themselves, as if what they did could be hidden from God. The word for grumble is used in Proverbs for the gossiper (Prov 18:8; 26:20,22; 16:28). They exchanged exaggerated stories that continued to drift further and further from the truth, inspired by the discouraging part of the spies' report (verse 28). The

---

[31]Compare the other references to the good land in Deut: 1:35; 3:25; 4:21,22; 6:18; 8:7,10; 9:6; 11:17. The phrase the "land flowing with milk and honey" appears first in Exod 3:8. It is a phrase used of Canaan in extrabiblical sources also: in the Tale of Sinuhe (*ANET*, pp. 18-23), and in the Annals of Thutmose III (*ANET*, pp. 237-238).

[32]The NT includes a similar concept in the kingdom of God, which has already come in the person of Jesus but whose full realization is still in the future.

further significance of doing this in their tents lies in the fact that in military terms, "to go to the tents" was a demobilization phrase, the very opposite of what they should have been doing (Josh 22:4; see also 1 Kgs 12:16; 2 Sam 10:1).

It is difficult to fathom how God's guidance and care through the wilderness could be ignored and how they could convince themselves that **the LORD hates us**. This stands in sharp contrast to God's love for Israel expressed in 4:37 and 7:9 (see Hos 3:1; 11:1; Jer 31:3). The despondent, depressed heart can turn any reality into the opposite. "It is sadly typical that even the people of God turn on God in accusation and blame when things go wrong, when obstacles seem insuperable, or when prolonged frustration leads to exhaustion."[33]

What God intended was to **deliver** them from the enemies and to **destroy** the inhabitants of the land. But Israel, unable to see the situation from God's perspective perceived the exact opposite – he was going to destroy them.

1:28 The report of the spies in Numbers 13:27-29 was divided into two parts in Moses' report here. Apparently he wished to contrast the goodness of the land with the negative response of the people. After the people's refusal to go, the reason was given for their action: the report of fearsome enemies in the land.

Where can we go? reflects the deep despair of the people. A literal translation of the Hebrew is, "Where can we go up/where are we going up." The NIV does not give the best sense here. The people seem to be asking how they could now go into the land. The route God had chosen was blocked by powerful enemies. The question implied that they saw no alternative; it was a hopeless situation. They were demoralized and paralyzed with fear, for the report **made us lose heart**. God said in verse 21, "do not be discouraged," but they were utterly discouraged.

What caused such fear? They gave two reasons: large people, **stronger and taller than we**, and large cities **with walls up to the sky**.

The large people were the **Anakites**, an apparently fearsome, tall race of people who inhabited the area around Hebron. The OT is consistent in portraying a group who were of giant proportions that inhabited the promised land. Numbers 13:22 names three of the

---

[33]Wright, *Deuteronomy*, p. 30.

famous ones. Numbers 13:33 equates them with the Nephilim. They were later defeated by Joshua and Caleb (Josh 11:21-23; 15:14) and driven out of the Hebron area. They moved to Gaza, Gath, and Ashdod in what later became the Philistine territory. Perhaps Goliath and other giant Philistines were descended from them.[34]

The cities in the land of Canaan sat on mounds or hills. Some, like Lachish, were as high as 70 feet. In the Middle Bronze Age (MBA: 2000–1550 BC) most of these cities were heavily fortified with high, thick walls. Most were destroyed in the Late Bronze Age (LBA: 1550–1200 BC), but some like Hazor continued to be fortified.[35]

The spies' report was true; they did not lie. But the issue was trusting God to give them the land as he said he would.

1:29 This verse is a repeat of verse 21b with the addition, **do not be terrified**. The same reassurance was repeated in 7:21; 20:3, and 31:6 in similar contexts. The exhortation always came with a motivation clause describing something about the character or action of God that was the basis for the assurance. God was "great and awesome" (7:21), he would fight for them (1:30; 20:4), or he would go with them (31:6).

1:30 The assurance recalled the past, for God was **going before** them from the very beginning in the pillar of cloud and the pillar of fire (verse 33; Exod 13:21). This "going before" happened even **in Egypt** and was a part of their own experience, and thus undeniable because it was **before your very eyes**. Moses continually reminded

---

[34]See Gerald Mattingly, "Anak," *ABD*, 1:222.

[35]Amahai Mazar, *Archaeology of the Land of the Bible: 10,000–586 B.C.E.* (New York: Doubleday, 1990), pp. 241-243. He believes most of the cities were not heavily fortified in LBA though at some sites the evidence is not clear, for the MBA walls apparently continued to be used into the LBA. Many of the sites show repeated destruction during the LBA. See also William Dever, "The Patriarchal Tradition," *Israelite and Judaean History*, eds., John H. Hayes and J. Maxwell Miller (Philadelphia: The Westminster Press, 1997), pp. 89-91, and J.M. Miller, "The Israelite Occupation of Canaan," ibid., pp. 254-262. An issue here is the time period this wilderness experience encompassed. This is tied to the date of the exodus from Egypt. Scholars give two possibilities, the fifteenth century and the thirteenth century. For detailed discussion see: W.H. Shea, "Exodus, Date of the," *ISBE*, 2:230-238 (a detailed consideration of both dates which favors the fifteenth century); K.A. Kitchen, "Exodus, The," *ABD*, 2:700-708 (who favors the thirteenth century); Merrill, *Deuteronomy*, pp. 23-26.

them of how much they had seen (4:6,34; 6:22; 9:17; 25:3,9; 28:31; 29:1; 31:7; 34:12).

The strongest assurance here was that God **will fight for you**. This assurance was repeated for Joshua (Deut 3:22) and later for Israel again (Deut 20:4). This is a concept difficult for Christians in the twentieth century to understand based on the teaching of Jesus.[36] However, it is an important OT concept crucial to understanding the nature of God and his relationship with Israel.[37]

First we must realize that this concept appears throughout the OT, from Exodus 15:3 (the LORD is a "man of war") to Psalm 24:8 (he is mighty in battle). Numbers 21:14 refers to "The Book of the Wars of the LORD." Secondly, the concept was carefully circumscribed: 1) God chose the battles, Israel did not; 2) God was present in the camp and the battlefield both; 3) preparation for battle involved sacrifice; 4) God provided the victory. Deuteronomy 20 provided the guidelines for Israelite warfare. It emphasized that the size of the army was not important and humane guidelines must be followed. Exodus 14:13-14 instructed Israel to stand still and do nothing while the LORD won the battle. Warfare presented God with an opportunity to demonstrate his care for his people and to manifest his power and presence in the world. When he fought, it was for his glory. This assurance should have calmed the fear of the people.

Holy war[38] language was appropriated in the New Testament also. The birth of Jesus was anticipated with war language of the OT prophets (Luke 1:51-52,68-71). The cloud-riding warrior in the OT came via Daniel 7:13-14 into Matthew 24 (and parallels in Mark 13 and Luke 21). Jesus' death and resurrection was a triumph over death (1 Cor 15:54-57) and over principalities and powers (Col 2:15).

---

[36]Objections to the concept based on the notion that modern mankind is somehow more sophisticated and less war-like is an illusion. The devastating wars in the twentieth century have given the lie to the idea that "modern" means in some way "less war-like."

[37]For a good overview see Tremper Longman III, "Divine Warrior," *NIDOTTE*, 5:545-559.

[38]Presently there is resistance to using "Holy War" language in these discussions. Many prefer "Yahweh war." What the OT was referring to was not the same as what modern proponents of "holy war" usually mean; Tigay, *Deuteronomy*, p. 430.

The Christian is in constant war with these same powers (Eph 6:10-18). Jesus comes in Revelation as the triumphant warrior (Rev 1:13-18; 12:7-11; 19:11-21), and the final victory between God and Satan is won.[39]

1:31 Again Moses reaches into the past to reassure the people. The great and terrible wilderness that was still so fresh in their minds (v. 19) was a place of God's loving care. The metaphor of the father and son was meant to express the tender provision of a gracious God. Israel was compared to a child too young to walk who was transported about in the strong arms of his father (in Exod 19:4 God bore them up on eagle's wings; cf. Deut 32:11). Carrying the child also conveyed the idea of a caring nursemaid (Num 11:12; Isa 46:3-4). The compassion and kindness of the caring father was expressed best in Hosea 11:1,3-4. This father-son image comes from the covenant concept that defined the relationship between God and Israel.[40]

1:32-33 Yet Israel could not bring herself to **trust** God. The Hebrew word comes from the root "to believe in." In this context it meant not just to trust, but to act in obedient response to what was heard. The same phrase was used of Abraham in Genesis 15:6, but he believed in and obeyed God. In Numbers 20:12 Moses was forbidden entrance to the promised land for the same reason that was given for Israel here, he did not trust (believe in and obey) God.[41]

Verse 33 functions as another motivating clause for why they should trust in God: his guidance in the past. Over and over Deuteronomy states that the past was the key to the present and the future. Ignorance of the past had serious consequences for the present, the most serious of which was lack of faith and trust in God. It was especially important for the new generation hearing these words to learn

---

[39]Mark Strom, *The Symphony of Scripture: Making Sense of the Bible's Many Themes* (Downers Grove, IL: InterVarsity, 1990), p. 79.

[40]D.J. McCarthy, "Notes on the Love of God in Deuteronomy and the Father-Son Relationship between Yahweh and Israel," *CBQ* 27 (1965): 144-147; C.J.H. Wright, *God's People in God's Land: Family, Land, and Property in the Old Testament* (Downers Grove, IL: InterVarsity, 1996), pp. 15-22. See also Deut 8:5 and 14:1 for different uses of the image.

[41]In a later text that shows a significant contrast, the pagan Ninevites did believe God, trust Him, and repent, Jonah 3:5.

from the past so that they would not replicate the failure of their ancestors. "One antidote to fear is a good memory."[42] Faith (trust) was not a leap in the dark but prudent action based on experience. Refusal to act was not realism but rebellion. However, Israel constantly failed to trust the providential care of God in every crisis.[43]

Verses 34-39 are the thematic center of chapter 1. They represent the main point Moses had been aiming for, the conclusion to the sad narrative: God's anger with Israel and God's anger with Moses. God's response to their unbelief showed the consequences of disobedience.

1:34 The thought of an **angry** God is disquieting to Christians, but it is firmly embedded in the OT.[44] Deuteronomy alone refers to his anger 26 times. Anger does not refer to a defective emotion that is a flaw in God's character, but to his just reaction to the willful disobedience of his covenant people. Disobedience became the basis for God's judgment on the sin of Israel. This anger was provoked by Israel (4:25; 9:18; 31:29; 32:16,21), an expression that eliminates any arbitrariness from the divine response. The consequence in this case was a solemn promise (he **solemnly swore**) from God to carry out his judgment. Ironically this was the same phrase used when God promised to give the land to Abraham and his descendants (Gen 50:24; Exod 33:1; Num 14:16). To swear in the OT was to assure that one would faithfully keep his word. Oaths were serious matters in the ancient world and were to be fulfilled.

In this case we learn God's promises were not unconditional. Disobedience nullified them and even resulted in a completely opposite promise.

1:35 The new promise from God was that the generation that took part in the rebellion would be completely cut off. Moses was addressing the children of the rebellious generation. The excruciating years in the wilderness watching their parents die would be vivid in their minds. Because the parents had refused to take the land at God's direction, he assured them they would not even **see** it.

---

[42]Wright, *Deuteronomy,* p. 31.

[43]Thompson, *Deuteronomy,* p. 88.

[44]The very first Christian to be branded a heretic, Marcion (mid-second century AD), rejected the OT because the angry, wrathful God portrayed there seemed so non-Christian.

It would have been a shock to have the first generation described as **evil** (compare Num 32:13).[45] There is a stark contrast between the good land (v. 25) and the evil people. The chilling results of God's sworn oath is stated in 2:14 — that entire generation had died. However, the oath to destroy was for just one generation. The oath of promise was for all the following generations.[46]

1:36 The exception was faithful **Caleb**. Moses here assumes familiarity with the narrative in Numbers 13:30 and 14:6-9 where Caleb and Joshua tried to persuade the people to trust God and go in and take the land. Their reward was a threat of being stoned.

But in contrast to the people, Caleb **will see** the land, that is he will actually go into it and receive his just inheritance. Where he **set his feet on** apparently refers to the exact area which he walked through on his spy mission. Joshua 15:13-19 details the land he received, which was Hebron, the very place where the large bunch of grapes had been found.

Caleb was distinguished from all the others because **he followed the LORD wholeheartedly**. The Hebrew expression meant to be "filled up after the LORD" and was used almost exclusively of Caleb (Solomon is noted for not finishing out his life with wholehearted obedience, 1 Kgs 11:6).

The **except** should not be taken too literally. In Numbers Joshua was also a faithful spy who supported Caleb (Num 14:6-9). He is omitted here because Moses introduces him in the next section to speak to the issue of succession.[47]

1:37 This verse raises two problems. First, it seems to contradict Numbers 20:1-13. There the reason for Moses not being able to go into the land was because he did not glorify God in the matter of the water at Meribah (reaffirmed in Deut 32:51). Secondly, the chronology implied here does not seem to fit the chronology in Numbers.

---

[45]See David Baker, "רעע," *NIDOTTE*, 3:1154-1158. The most common use of "evil" in Deuteronomy is in the two phrases, "to do evil in the eyes of the LORD," or "to purge the evil from your midst." The former refers to idolatry, the latter to the penalty for unlawful actions.

[46]Craigie, *Deuteronomy*, p. 104.

[47]Some again resort to separate documents to explain the differences: Driver, *Deuteronomy*, p. 26; Mayes, *Deuteronomy*, p. 132; Weinfeld, *Deuteronomy*, p. 150.

There the event in chapter 20 came near the end of the 38 year sojourn near Kadesh-Barnea, not near the beginning.

The first problem centers on the meaning of **because of you**. The Hebrew word בִּגְלַל (*big̱lal*) is rare, occurring only 10 times. It may mean cause here or occasion.[48] If it means cause, then Moses is blaming the people. If it means occasion, then we can understand Moses as implying that he was responsible for his sin, but it was occasioned by the rebellious nature of the people. A similar circumstance seemed to prevail when God blessed Laban because of Jacob (Gen 30:27) or when he blessed Potiphar because of Joseph (Gen 39:5).

The second problem of chronology can best be solved when we remember that Moses was not giving a complete account here, but was selecting certain items to make his point. Since he was speaking topically he disrupted the chronology to show that God's refusal to let him enter put him in the same situation as the people. They will not enter because of disobedience and neither will he.[49]

1:38 Joshua was the other faithful spy. His place in Israel's life is well-known. He was first introduced in Exodus 17:9 where he led in victory over the Amalekites. He was appointed Moses' successor in Numbers 27:18-23 (an event repeated in Deut 3:28 and chapter 31). Joshua's appointment as Moses' successor was crucial, for Moses was the only leader Israel had ever known. The enormous challenge Joshua faced required that Moses **encourage** him, or make him strong. This reference to Joshua is chronologically out of order, for he was not appointed as a replacement until later. However, the references here and in 31:1-8,14,23 and 34:9 bind the book together and add to the concept of this being Moses' last will.[50]

1:39 The irony of this verse would have been apparent to Moses' audience, for they were these same **little ones** that their fathers had said would become booty of the enemy in Numbers 14:3. Yet it is they that **will enter the land**. These were apparently the very young

---

[48]Merrill, *Deuteronomy*, p. 82.

[49]Driver, *Deuteronomy*, pp. 26-27, sees it referring to a different episode. He is supported by Craigie, *Deuteronomy*, p. 105, and Weinfeld, *Deuteronomy*, p. 150. Mayes, *Deuteronomy*, p. 147, suggests that Moses was innocent but must suffer with the people. Both Driver and Weinfeld posit different documents as well.

[50]Wright, *Deuteronomy*, p. 33.

since they **do not yet know good from bad** (compare Isa 7:15,16; 8:4; Jonah 4:11). The first generation of Israel's lack of faith was further demonstrated. Even though God had carried them as children (v. 31), they did not think he would take care of their children.[51]

When Israel heard she could not have the land, she became determined to take it. But the positive response came too late.

1:40 The immediate result of disobedience was to retrace their steps back toward Horeb, reversing the journey described in verse two. **The Red Sea** probably refers to the Gulf of Aqabah and not the Gulf of Suez near Egypt.

1:41 At last Israel acknowledged her sin, which had been described before as rebellion (v. 26). It is difficult to determine if they are acting out of guilt and shame, presumption, or adolescent selfishness.[52] They now thought the task was easy and they could do it, which was a miscalculation equal to the refusal to go. They were determined to **fight** although earlier God had said he would fight for them.

1:42 This word from the LORD reversed the previous word. Since they had rejected God's original help, he would not help them now. The window of opportunity had passed; the promise of verses 29-30 was no longer operative. **I will not be with you** is literally "I will not be among you." Since the Exodus, God had led them and had been in their midst with the ark and the tabernacle. But if this venture were undertaken, he would no longer be there. In Numbers 14:44 Moses and the Ark of the Covenant stayed in the camp when Israel went up to the promised land.

1:43 Israel was both rebellious and arrogant. It is ironic that they adopted the same attitude that Pharaoh did before the Exodus (Exod 7:13; 8:19,28-29,32, etc.). Israel assumed God would bless them and guide them when he had expressly said he would not. This was the height of presumption. To **not listen** was to not obey. After the judgment for disobedience was announced, disobedience was still the main issue.

---

[51]Craigie, *Deuteronomy*, 105. Numbers 14:29-30 explains that everyone over age 20 would die in the wilderness, a much broader range than suggested here.

[52]All motivations have been suggested by commentators; see Craigie, *Deuteronomy*, p. 106; Thompson, *Deuteronomy*, p. 89; Merrill, *Deuteronomy*, p. 85.

1:44 Israel's defeat was assured once God decided not to fight for them. The **Amorites** easily repulsed their attack. The vivid word picture, **they chased you like a swarm of bees**, portrays the headlong flight of Israel in front of their enemies. Bees were native to Canaan (Judg 14:8), and the simile was a powerful one (Isa 7:20; Ps 118:12). Numbers 14:43 relates that it was Amalekites and Canaanites who defeated Israel. Amorites was a more general term and is used often in Deuteronomy.[53] **From Seir all the way to Hormah** suggests the area west of Arad. In Numbers 21:3, Israel defeated the Canaanites near Hormah in another battle.

1:45 As Israel had earlier ignored God's words, he ignored their weeping. **But he paid no attention to your weeping** is literally "he did not listen to your voice." This seems like a deliberate attempt to contrast God's reaction to Israel with the many calls throughout the book for Israel to "listen to the voice of the LORD" which meant "obey the LORD" (4:30; 13:4[5]; 15:5; 26:17; 27:10; 28:1,2,15,45,62, etc.).

1:46 The result was a long stay in the vicinity of **Kadesh Barnea**. The Hebrew expression suggests an indeterminate amount of time. It may have been the whole 38 years of the wilderness period (2:14, until that generation died). The actual events recorded for this period are few (Num 16–17; 20).

2:1 This travel note rounds off the section begun in 1:19 with a travel note about their arrival at Kadesh Barnea. It completes the command of 1:40. The area designated was a dry, hostile place — the dreadful wilderness of verse 19. It was bounded on the east by the Arabah, the depression going south from the Dead Sea to the Gulf of Aqabah and on the west by a line from Kadesh southeast to the Gulf.

---

[53]Weinfeld, *Deuteronomy,* p. 152.

DEUTERONOMY 2

4. The Journey to the Transjordan (2:2–3:29)

This section is a detailed account of how Israel moved from the Arabah to their present position on the east side of the Jordan River. It was familiar information to the generation listening to Moses because they had experienced it. Yet it was important to recount the journey in order to encourage them as they stood poised to enter the Promised Land. Moses in this section deliberately contrasted the failure of the older generation and the victories already won by the new generation. This provided a paradigm for entering the land. The nation must learn to trust in the promises of God.[1] So far the new generation had trusted God and been successful.

The deliberate contrast of this section with chapter 1 can be observed in several subtle ways. God's promise to give the land into their hands (1:8,20) was repeated (2:32; 3:2) and successfully completed. Sihon and Og "come out to war" (2:32; 3:1) just as the Amorites did (1:44) but were defeated. The "do not be afraid" (3:2,22) echoes the same assurance to the forefathers (1:21,29) and is accepted as a true promise. The giants and large cities dismayed the forefathers (1:28), but the children defeated the giant Og and his heavily fortified cities (3:3-5,11). In every encounter God demonstrated his guidance and deliverance, contrary to the despairing cry of the forefathers (1:27). All the failures of the first generation were reversed by the second.[2]

---

[1]Miller, *Deuteronomy*, p. 39.

[2]See Tigay, *Deuteronomy*, p. 23, for these observations. William L. Moran has also shown how much indebted to Exodus 15 these chapters are, "The End of Unholy War and the Anti-Exodus," *A Song of Power and The Power of Song*, ed., Duane L. Christensen (Winona Lake: Eisenbrauns, 1993), pp. 147-155.

The structure of this section unfolds in five parts, each part recounting the situation with a different group of people: Edom, Moab, Ammon, Sihon of Heshbon, and Og of Bashan (2:2-8,9-16,17-30; 2:31-3:1, and 3:2-11). The narrative concludes with Moses' instructions to Israel and Joshua and his second plea to enter the land (3:12-29).[3] The geographical movement was from south to north. Three encounters were peaceful because of ethnic links, and two involved war. The three peaceful encounters are told in a similar way with several parallels between them. The two accounts of the military encounters also are similar.[4] However, the accounts are not geographically in order. Ammon, which was located north of Sihon's territory, comes in the middle of the narrative where the shift is made from peaceful to military encounters.

In addition, each narrative is introduced by divine speech addressed to Moses (2:2,9,17,31; 3:2). Some prehistory is given for the three peaceful encounters (2:10-12, concerning both Edom and Moab; 2:20-23). Three events are introduced by the phrase "and we turned" (2:1,8b; 3:1). Food is mentioned in two of the accounts (2:6,27) but probably assumed in the others. The two military encounters are told in very similar language as a close reading will show (2:32-37 and 3:1-7).

The structure is also marked by a somewhat regular alternation between narrative, command, and background information. Some find the background information irrelevant and from a later editor but a close study suggests the various segments are important to the overall narration.[5]

A key verb in this section is "pass through" (עבר, '*br*) which the NIV translates in six different ways: pass through/by (2:4,18,27-30),

---

[3]Casper Labuschagne has analyzed the book of Deuteronomy according to the passages phrased as words from God, that is, divine speech. He has found 30 divisions in the book, 10 of these in chapters 1–3. I found his discussion helpful and have based my structural analysis on his observations. See his essay, "Divine Speech in Deuteronomy," *Song of Power,* pp. 375-393. As usual, Christensen finds several chiasms in this section, some more convincing than others (*Deuteronomy,* 39, 52, 59, 62, 65). However, he does not take full account of the parallels between the five sections.

[4]W.A. Sumner, "Israel's Encounter with Edom, Moab, Ammon, Sihon, and Og according to the Deuteronomist," *VT* 18 (1968): 216-228.

[5]See comments below on 2:10-12,20-23.

went on past (2:8), cross/crossed (2:13,14,24; 3:18,27), across (3:20, 28), are going (3:21), and beyond (3:25). It strongly emphasizes the focus on Israel moving through the Transjordan toward the Promised Land in these narratives.[6] After 38 years they were once again on the way.

Passing through Seir (Edom) (2:2-8)

2:2-3 The phrasing of these two verses is almost identical to 1:6-7 where the forefathers were commanded to leave Horeb. This command marks a significant new step in Israel's history, a watershed change of purpose. The punishing wilderness experience was at an end. **Then the LORD said** gives this section a prophetic thrust and is one of the many divine speeches that mark chapters 2 and 3.

Numbers 20:14–21:35 record these events also. Understanding the relationship between the Numbers account and the one here, as well as the exact itinerary traveled, is a complex issue. Moses left out some details here including Edom's refusal to let them pass through (Num 20:14-21), the death of Aaron (Num 20:22-29), the defeat of the Canaanites at Hormah (Num 21:1-3) and the poisonous snake episode (Num 21:4-9).

Many find it impossible to harmonize the narratives recorded in Numbers and Deuteronomy.[7] First, according to Deuteronomy, Israel seemed to have left Kadesh Barnea in the second year after the exodus, moved southeast, and wandered around near the territory of Edom for 38 years, then bypassed Edom and Moab on the east side (1:46–2:25). According to Numbers Israel seems to have stayed at Kadesh most of the 40 years, then moved almost straight east directly into Moab (20:10; 21:10-20; 33:37-49). Second, according to Numbers, Israel requested safe passage through Edom, was refused and opposed by an Edomite army, and retreated (20:14-21). In Deuteronomy Israel requested safe passage, no opposition was given, and they passed by (2:3-8a). Third, Numbers seems to imply that Israel stopped at Ezion-Geber near the end of the 40 years

---

[6]The verb occurs around 60 times in the entire book of Deuteronomy which means one-third of the occurrences are in these two chapters. The verb is also found 81 times in the book of Joshua.

[7]Driver, *Deuteronomy*, pp. 31-33; Tigay, *Deuteronomy*, pp. 425-429; Weinfeld, *Deuteronomy*, pp. 165-167.

before they arrived at Kadesh (33:36-37). Deuteronomy seems to imply a great deal of time was spent in the vicinity of Ezion-Geber after they left Kadesh (1:46–2:8). Fourth, the entry into Edom in Deuteronomy is from the south, near 'Aqaba (2:1-3). Numbers lists stations that would suggest an entry from the west at the north end of Edom (20:10-13; 33:41-49).

Attempts to harmonize these difficulties are as old as the Dead Sea Scrolls where some Torah scrolls spliced verses of Deuteronomy 1–9 into Exodus and Numbers.[8] A few brief observations can be made.[9] First, the travel notes in Deuteronomy are summary and do not exclude more than one visit to Kadesh. Deuteronomy 2:14 does not necessarily mean that Israel left Kadesh never to return (though the NIV translation strongly implies such). As the primary water source in the whole wilderness region it would have been natural for Israel to return often. As pastoral nomads they would have been constantly on the move, looking for pasturage and water. In Numbers Israel first arrived at Kadesh in the second year (12:16; compare with 13:3,26) from where the spies were sent out. Therefore, their arrival in 20:1 in the "first month" was in the *fortieth* year, the year of Miriam and Aaron's death. This implies they did not stay there the whole 38 years.

Second, the relationship with Edom is difficult to assess. In each case the result was the same: Israel passed by Edom. Selectivity in the retelling cannot be ruled out (see below). Third, since neither Numbers or Deuteronomy gives complete details of the wilderness

---

[8]Tigay, *Deuteronomy*, p. 428. E. Tov, "The Nature and Background of Harmonizations in Biblical Manuscripts," *JSOT* 31 (1985): 8, 24-25, note 16.

[9]See Merrill, *Deuteronomy*, pp. 89-90. Tigay rejects single authorship and harmonization of the two accounts as special pleading (*Deuteronomy*, pp. 428-429). However, he does recognize that valid principles of interpretation require that, when faced with seemingly contradictory statements, "it is necessary to determine if the contradiction is real or only apparent: they may bear on different aspects of a matter." (428, quoting H.C. Hockett, *The Critical Method in Historical Research and Writing* [New York: Macmillan, 1955], p. 69). Tigay and others take a critical approach whose essence is to forgo presuppositions about authorship. However, both Numbers and Deuteronomy indicate that the author is Moses. It would seem appropriate to treat this fact seriously unless there was overwhelming evidence to the contrary. Are biblical texts the only ancient texts that are presumed guilty until proven innocent? Should not they be presumed innocent until proven guilty?

period, Israel could have been at Ezion-Geber more than once. Fourth, the entry into Edom and Moab in Deuteronomy is not clear. It is possible to interpret the account as referring to entry from the Arabah. The verb, '*br*, can mean "pass by" as well as "pass through." Therefore, if Israel was near Aqabah and turned north, they could have gone up the Arabah road on the west side of the Seir mountains and then turned east near the Dead Sea as Numbers indicates.[10] Part of the difficulty is that although Deuteronomy is generally selective in details, at this point it is more detailed about the travels of the people.[11]

It has been shown that the route described in Numbers 33:45-50 was a heavily traveled Egyptian highway through the Transjordan in the Late Bronze Age (1500–1200 B.C.).[12] Therefore, there was good reason why Israel would take that route.

2:4-5 Instructions were given for the peaceful treatment of the Edomites. In Numbers 20:14-21 the request to pass through Edom peacefully was met with resistance, and so Israel turned away. Moses omits that part of the episode here.[13]

An important consideration here is that the Edomites were **your brothers the descendants of Esau**. This reflected Genesis 25 and 36. Jacob and Esau were sons of Isaac but were constantly in conflict and parted ways. In Genesis 36 we learn of Esau settling in the mountain country of Seir and becoming patriarch of the Edomites. **Brothers** in Deuteronomy is used for the close community relationship within the nation.[14] The meaning is expanded here to include diplomatic relations with another ethnic group exhibiting a strong awareness of other nations and ancient connections.[15]

---

[10]Many scholars interpret Deuteronomy as suggesting that Israel passed on the east side of Edom: Wright, *Deuteronomy*, p. 35; Driver, *Deuteronomy*, p. 34.

[11]Gordon J. Wenham, *Numbers* (Downers Grove, IL: InterVarsity, 1981, p. 159. See Yohanan Aharoni and Michael Avi-Yonah, *The Macmillan Bible Atlas* (New York: Macmillan, 1968), p. 42 for a map that shows both routes.

[12]Charles R. Krahmalkov, "Exodus Itinerary Confirmed by Egyptian Evidence," *BAR* 20,5 (1994): 55-62.

[13]Weinfeld suggests the presentation here reflects a more patriotic attitude and is in line with the descriptions of the dealings with Moab and Ammon (*Deuteronomy*, p. 166).

[14]See comments on 1:16 above.

[15]The later prophets exhibited a great deal of hostility toward Edom: Jer 49:7-22; Ezek 25:12-14; Obad 8-21. This was probably because of the

When the Edomites settled in their land is unclear. Archaeological researches in the area have discovered little settled population until the Iron Age (1200 B.C.). However, if the earliest Edomites were nomads, they would have left little trace. The territory of ancient Edom is normally identified with the mountainous region southeast of the Dead Sea and the wadi Zered. However, there is some evidence that Edomite territory may have extended west of the Arabah on occasion. From the time of David Israel had several encounters with the Edomites and their land (2 Sam 8; 1 Kgs 3, 8).[16]

They will be afraid was anticipated in Exodus 15:15. Israel was not to take advantage of that fear. This called to mind God's admonitions for Israel not to fear (1:21,29) that the forefathers had ignored.

A better translation of the end of verse 4 and beginning of verse 5 is: "**be very careful** *and do not engage them in battle*" with no period after "careful." The care they were to exercise was about making war. Also the verb גרה (*grh*, "engage") carries more the idea of actual engagement in warfare (the NIV thus translates it in v. 24). The same expression is used for the Moabites (v. 9) and Ammonites (v. 19).[17]

God treated Edom the same as Israel for he had **given** Edom the land. Two of the words used here are typical of Deuteronomy's vocabulary for God's gift to Israel: "give" and "take possession of" (NIV, "**as his own**"). Also **put your foot on** is used in Deuteronomy 11:24 and Joshua 1:3 in possession contexts. Similar language is used of Moab (v. 9) and Ammon (v. 19). Therefore both Israel and these nations had received their land as gifts from God. This reflected an important theological concept: God was the lord of history, and he ordered the affairs of all nations. If he was sovereign over Israel as his covenant people, he was also sovereign over all nations.

---

history of hostilities between the two countries in later centuries (2 Kgs 8:20-22; 2 Chr 20:1; 28:17; Ps 137:7). This provides some evidence for an early date for Deuteronomy. See also Num 20:14; Amos 1:11; Mal 1:2.

[16]Deuteronomy prefers Seir as the name for the territory of Edom. Edom predominates in the rest of the OT though Seir occurs 29 times outside of Deuteronomy. For a summary discussion of the Edomites see J.R. Bartlett, "The Moabites and Edomites," *People of Old Testament Times*, ed., D.J. Wiseman (Oxford: Clarendon Press, 1973), pp. 229-258; and Kenneth G. Hoaglund, "Edomites," *Peoples of the Old Testament World*, pp. 335-347.

[17]See John M. Bracke, "גרה," *NIDOTTE*, 1:891.

Israel may be special in some ways (see Deuteronomy 7 and 9) but God's concern was for all peoples. He gifted them and they were accountable to him (Amos 1–2). Therefore, Israel must understand her position within this larger context. Later texts talk about God using other nations and kings for his purposes (Amos 9:7; Jer 18:1-10; 27:1-11; Isa 44:28; 45:1-3).

Israel's uniqueness was not in being gifted with the land, but in her covenant relationship with God. Israel could, in fact, lose the land if she was disobedient (Deuteronomy 9 and 28). The later prophets based their theology of exile on this precise point.

2:6 The Edomites feared that such a large group of people coming through their land would deplete the scarce food and water resources through theft or confiscation. God warned Israel against such mistreatment. They must **pay them in silver** for all their supplies, even water. These instructions were not repeated for Moab and Ammon but, perhaps, could be assumed. However, the ancestral relationship between Israel and Edom was different than that between Israel and Moab or Ammon. That may account for the different treatments. Later, Moses' offer of peace and compensation for food and water was refused by Sihon, which led to warfare (vv. 26-37).

2:7 This is an important summary statement about God's provision. The forefathers had failed to trust God to lead them in victory over the inhabitants of the Promised Land. The new generation now had **forty years'** experience with God's provision (representing a rounding off of the 38 years in the wilderness, v. 14). God had **blessed** them. He had taken care of all of their material needs while they were in the "vast and dreadful desert" (1:19). In the OT nothing was more important than to live under the blessing of God. The highest concentrations of the verb for "blessing" occur in Genesis, Numbers, Deuteronomy and Psalms.[18] This blessing included fertility and material well-being and was especially important in the theology of Deuteronomy (7:13; 14:24; 15:18). Blessing was especially promised to Israel if they took care of the poor and needy (14:29; 16:15-17; 24:19). Covenant blessing resulted from obedience (28:1-14). **The work of your hands** referred to their labor in food production, the most important focus of labor in ancient cultures.

---

[18]Michael L. Brown, "ברך," *NIDOTTE,* 1:267ff. See on 1:11 above.

Cairns suggests this might refer to their development of husbandry, agriculture, and even handicraft skills during the wilderness years.[19]

God had **watched over** them (יָדַע, *yd'*, "know"). That is, he had known them in the sense of caring for them, one of the many nuances of "to know" in the OT (Ps 1:6; 37:18; Neh 1:7-8; Hos 13:5; Jer 29:11). Perhaps he also knew them in the sense that he experienced their hardship with them (Exod 3:7; Ps 31:7; 69:19; 142:3).

These forty years includes the time from the exodus until the moment the new generation was standing on the east side of the Jordan River. This included one year for each of the forty days the spies were in the land (Num 14:33-34; cf. also Deut 8:2; 29:5; Exod 16:35; Num 12:13). Verse 14 gives the actual time in the wilderness: 38 years.[20]

You have not lacked anything has in view the manna, the quail, the water, and the clothes that did not wear out (Deut 8:3-4) which met all their basic needs (see 1:31). There is a subtle play on words here because the word "anything" in Hebrew is דָּבָר (*dābār*), a noun with a wide range of meanings (translated "word" most of the time). The usage here recalls the "words" (*dᵊbarîm*) of 1:1.

2:8 This verse records the response to the command in verse 3 to "turn north." The Hebrew preposition "from" (מִן, *min*) is used four times in this verse. They passed *from* **the descendants of Esau,** *from* **the Arabah road,** *from* **Elath and** *from* **Ezion Geber**. This was an emphatic statement that they were leaving behind one era and entering a new one, both chronologically and geographically. The new generation was now on the road to the Promised Land, leaving the wilderness and the last 40 years behind.[21]

The most natural reading of this verse is that they went up from the Gulf of Aqabah on the west side of the Seir mountains through the Arabah and then turned east and took the Egyptian road to Moabite territory.[22]

---

[19]Cairns, *Deuteronomy*, pp. 40-41.

[20]The math to reach this figure is the 40 years minus the one year at Sinai (Num 10:11), minus the time spent at Kadesh, and minus the time to travel through Edom and Moab and battle Sihon and Og.

[21]The same idea is expressed in vv. 14-16 also with the note on the death of the forefathers; Merrill, *Deuteronomy*, p. 96; Mayes, *Deuteronomy*, p. 138-139.

[22]See Harry T. Frank, *Atlas of the Bible Lands* (Maplewood, NJ: Hammond, 1990), p. 10; Mayes, *Deuteronomy*, p. 136.

The Hebrew Masoretic Text begins a new paragraph after **Ezion Geber**, suggesting that the section on the Moabites begins here and not with the divine speech in verse 9. Verse 8d is a transition to verses 9-13 and probably should be set off as a new sentence: "Then we turned and passed along through the desert road of Moab."

The locations of **Elath** and **Ezion Geber** are debated. Some have identified them as successive names for the same place.[23] Nelson Glueck identified Ezion Geber with the modern site of Tell el-Kheleifeh after his excavations in the 1930s.[24] The site is located about a mile north of the Gulf. However, recent reappraisal of the site indicates it was not occupied until the eighth century B.C.[25] More recent research has suggested Ezion Geber should be identified with Jeziret Faraum, an island in the north end of the Gulf on the west side, about seven miles south of modern Eilat. It has a natural harbor with man-made improvements, Phoenician style remains from the 10th century, and remains of jetties on the west coast of the Gulf opposite the harbor.[26]

Elath was closely connected with Ezion Geber but it was a separate place. It probably originated as an Egyptian port for the shipping of copper from the mines in Timna in the Seir mountains. It has been identified with a site just north of the coast and two and one-half miles west of Tell el-Kheleifeh.[27]

Passing through Moab (2:9-16)

This section contains much of the same language as verses 4-5 of the previous section on Edom. The Moabites inhabited an area between the Zered Brook at the south end of the Dead Sea and the

---

[23]Craigie, *Deuteronomy*, p. 109; Mayes, *Deuteronomy*, p. 136; Aharoni and Avi-Yonah, *Atlas*, p. 40 (map 48).

[24]Nelson Glueck, "The First Campaign at Tell el-Kheleifeh (Ezion-Geber)," *BASOR* 71 (1938): 3-17.

[25]Gary Pratico, "Nelson Glueck's 1938-1940 Excavations at Tell el-Kheleifeh: A Reappraisal," *BASOR* 259 (1985): 1-3; idem, "Where Is Ezion Geber: A Reappraisal of the Site Nelson Glueck Identified as King Solomon's Red Sea Port," *BAR* 12,5 (1986): 24-35; see also Meir Lubetski, "Ezion Geber," *ABD*, 2:723-726.

[26]Alexander Flinder, "Is This Solomon's Seaport?" *BAR* 15,4 (1989): 30-44; Meir Lubetski, "Ezion Geber," p. 725.

[27]Jeffrey Zorn, "Elath," *ABD*, 2:429-430.

Arnon Gorge, half-way up the east side.²⁸ The northern border, however, shifted from time to time further north. There were numerous contacts between later Israel and Moab (Judg 3; Ruth 1; 2 Sam 22; 2 Kgs 3; Isa 15–16; Jer 48; Amos 1).

2:9 Israel was to approach Moab in the same way as Edom for the same reason: family connections. Here the connection was through Lot the nephew of Abraham (Gen 19:30-38). The incestuous origin of Moab was ignored.

Ar was another name for Moab (also in verse 18 and Num 21:15).²⁹ Although in some texts (Deut 2:29; Isa 15:1) it seems to be the name of a city, we probably are to understand a figure of speech here (the part standing for the whole).³⁰

2:10-11 This explanatory note gives some historical background on the former inhabitants of Moab. A similar note occurs in verses 20-23. Most scholars understand these notes to be later additions.³¹ However, the placement of the two notes in the same part of each section, preceded and followed by identical phrasing (cf. vv. 9 and 19, and 13 and 23) suggests a deliberate rhetorical device.

These notes continued the fundamental theology of this chapter: God's sovereignty over all the nations. The nations surrounding Israel were just as dependent on God for the gift of their land as Israel was.

The **Emites** are unknown except for another reference in Genesis 14:5. They were a people living in Shaveh-kiriathiam and subdued by Chedorlaomer, along with the Rephaim, the Zuzim, and the Horites in Seir (other groups mentioned in these notes). They were part of a race of **Rephites** (KJV, "giants") who at one time inhabited the area east of the Jordan River and Dead Sea. The Ammonites called them Zamzumites (v. 20) and Og was a descendant (3:11; see Gen 15:20; Josh 12:4; 13:12; 17:15). Since the giants in David's time in the

---

²⁸For the latest research and understanding of ancient Moab see *BA* 60,4 (1997): 194-248 which includes six articles on Moab. The uncertainty about its geographical boundaries and the location of some of its cities persists, even after recent concentrated surveys and research.

²⁹Verse 18 in the NIV is not translated correctly. Ar is in apposition to Moab, not the object of a preposition.

³⁰Called synecdoche; Merrill, *Deuteronomy*, p. 92.

³¹Craigie, *Deuteronomy*, p. 110 et al.

Philistine territory were descendants of Rapha (2 Sam 2:16,18,20,22), it seems likely the Raphaim were driven out of the Transjordan and settled in the Philistine plains.[32] The Valley of Rephaim near Jerusalem is mentioned in Joshua (15:8; 18:16) and 2 Samuel (5:18,22; 23:13).[33]

2:12 This is a parallel historical note on the former inhabitants of Seir that we would have expected in the previous section. In this case also, the descendants of Esau were given the land by driving out the earlier people. The Horites are identified with the Hurrians, a Semitic people from Mesopotamia known from ancient texts.[34]

Just as Israel did is seen as clear proof of the later date for these historical notes. The phrase presupposes Israel settled in the land.[35] However, it is possible to understand the completed action of the verb as anticipatory of the future.[36]

2:13 The narrative is picked up from verse 9. Crossing **the Zered Valley** (the modern Wadi el-Hesa) took Israel into Moabite territory. The Zered extended about 40 miles east from the Dead Sea. It had a wide floor and steep cliffs and was a major geographical break between Edom and Moab.[37]

---

[32]Merrill, *Deuteronomy,* p. 93.

[33]The noun *rᵊpha'im* occurs in Ps 88:10; Prov 2:18; 9:18; 21:16; Job 26:5; Isa 14:9; 26:14,18 as a name for the shadowy inhabitants of Sheol. It occurs also in Ugaritic texts. The ethnic usage of the word is also found in Ugaritic texts where it seems to equal "hero" (R.F. Schnell, "Rephaim," *IDB,* 4:35). The Transjordan area was full of megalithic structures from the Neolithic age and the Early and Middle Bronze Age: Nelson Glueck, *The Other Side of the Jordan* (Cambridge, MA: BASOR, 1970), pp. 149ff. This volume is an excellent resource for descriptions of the Transjordan area. Glueck refers to an Arab legend of giants in Gilead (p. 10).

[34]H.A. Hoffner, "The Hittities and Hurrians," *Peoples of Old Testament Times,* pp. 221-226. Though the identification is widely accepted, it is not universal. Both Christensen, *Deuteronomy,* pp. 41-42, and Tigay, *Deuteronomy,* p. 27, express doubts.

[35]Christensen, *Deuteronomy,* p. 42; Tigay, *Deuteronomy,* p. 26; Driver, *Deuteronomy,* p. 38.

[36]The Hebrew "prophetic perfect." Merrill, *Deuteronomy,* p. 94. See Bruce K. Waltke and M. O'Connor, *An Introduction to Biblical Hebrew Syntax* (Winona Lake: Eisenbrauns, 1990), pp. 489-490. It is also possible to understand it as a later editorial gloss.

[37]See Yohanan Aharoni, *The Land of the Bible,* tr., A.F. Rainey (Philadelphia: Westminster, 1967), p. 186, for a convenient map.

2:14-16 The first generation died as promised in Numbers 14:20-35 and Deuteronomy 1:35 (cf. Josh 5:4-5). Deuteronomy and Joshua limited the deaths to the **entire generation of fighting men**. This was war language. But here God was not fighting for Israel, but against her to destroy her, for the **LORD's hand was against them**.

The phrase **from the camp** (Hebrew: "from the midst of the camp") is striking because it occurs only here (vv. 14,15) and in Numbers 14:44. In Numbers Moses and Aaron and the ark did not depart "from the midst of the camp" when the first generation went up to Canaan to fight. The phrase was deliberately used in Deuteronomy to call attention to the direct connection between the act of defiance and the deaths.[38]

There is a precise parallelism between verses 14c and 16 with the exception of "people" being substituted for "camp" in verse 16. The destruction of his own people was a part of God's plan for their ultimate victory. The new generation needed to understand that God would fight for them or against them. The decision was theirs. They could trust God, obey, and be victorious. Or they could disobey, fail, and perish.

Verse 16 is a transition to the next section and the next divine speech.

Passing through Ammonite Territory (2:17-30)

This section is not in geographical order. The Ammonites lived in the area around the Jabbok River, halfway between the Dead Sea and the Sea of Chinnereth (Galilee). This was some distance north of the Zered Brook. Verse 24 is the immediate sequel of verse 13 where Israel was instructed to cross the north border of Moab, the Arnon Gorge. The displacement of the Ammonites from a geographical order was deliberate because the arrangement of the material is topical. Moses wished to end the historical background part of his presentation with two successful military encounters in order to encourage the people for the task immediately ahead of them. He completed the accounts of the peaceful encounters before describing the successful battles (2:32–3:11).

---

[38]"Camp" is very frequent in Numbers, but rare in Deuteronomy (23:9-14; 29:11) because the latter anticipated permanent settlement in the land.

2:19 This verse uses the same language as verse 9. It also gives the same reason for not **harassing** the inhabitants — they were descendants of Lot (Gen 19:30-38).[39] Because of their proximity it is no surprise that the Ammonites and Israel experienced a history of interaction. It ranged from incursion during the time of the judges, to war with Saul, friendship with David, subjugation by Israel, and opposition to Nehemiah. Their capital was Rabbah Ammon, 21 miles east of the Jordan River. Today it is Amman, the capital of the modern state of Jordan.

2:20-21 These verses are another background note like verses 10-13 which explain who the former inhabitants were and how God had given the Ammonites the land.

The LORD destroyed them was part of the theology of God's sovereignty over all the nations. The verb "destroy" (שָׁמַד, *šāmad*) often has God as the subject. It is also part of the language used for Israel taking Canaan (Deut. 7:23-24). It indicated the destruction of the people who had come under the judgment of God.[40] If God's sovereignty included giving the land, it must also include taking the land from others. It meant that all nations were responsible to God for their conduct. Unrighteousness brought judgment (Gen 15:16; Amos 1-2).

2:22-23 Verse 22 basically reiterates verses 5 and 12, but verse 23 introduces a new geographical reflection. God's sovereignty included other nations not on the direct route, and **Gaza** is used as an example. Little is known about her original inhabitants, the **Avvites** (Josh 13:3; 2 Kgs 17:31). Gaza was one of the 5 major Philistine cities (Josh 11:22; 13:3) and was located on the Mediterranean coast. It marked the southern limit of Canaan and was in and out of Israelite control over the years. Gaza was on the major trade route that followed the coast and was mentioned often in Egyptian and Assyrian records.

Caphtorites apparently refers to the Philistines who moved into the southeast coastal area of Canaan in the twelfth century as a part of a larger wave of people who came from the Aegean. The Egyptians called them the "Sea Peoples." Caphtor probably referred to Crete. Though these people were not from Crete, they may have

---

[39]Randal W. Younker, "Ammonites," *Peoples of Old Testament Times*, pp. 293-316.

[40]Gary H. Hall, "שמד," *NIDOTTE*, 4:151-152.

come via Crete, or Crete in its ascendant period may have become the general name for the Aegean area.[41]

2:24-25 These verses are the continuation of verse 19 and parallel in language to verse 13. They recount the next stage in moving through the Transjordan and transition to the two following accounts that show Israel at war.

The **Arnon Gorge** was at the north edge of Moab proper, midway up the east side of the Dead Sea. Sometimes Moab control extended further north as the Mesha Stone shows.[42]

Again we find gifting language, only this time it was for Israel. Some land east of the Jordan River would be given to them and they could now begin to take possession of it. **Given into your hand** is the technical phrase for the conquest and was used often in Joshua (8:7,18; 10:8,19,30; Judg 1:2,4; 2:23; see Deut 7:24). The idiom means given into their power or control. It was the reverse of the negative fears of the forefathers (1:27).

Sihon the Amorite at this time controlled the territory north of the Arnon and south of the Jabbok River. This was between Moabite and Ammonite territory (v. 19). This area was given to the tribes of Reuben and Gad (see below on 3:12-17). Sihon had earlier taken over land belonging to the Moabites (Num 21:26). In this case Israel was not forbidden to engage in warfare (as in vv. 5,9,18) for the land would have to be taken by force.

God would begin to fulfill his promise of Exodus 23:27 by bringing **terror and fear** on Sihon and all the nations, already prefigured by the Edomites (v. 4; cf. Deut 11:25). The language was again divine war language. God fought on Israel's side not only through physical means, but through exciting the emotions as well. The conquest of Sihon was encouragement to later Israel (Josh 2:9-11,24). At this

---

[41]J.C. Greenfield, "Caphtor," *IDB*, 1:534. This statement does not seem connected to its context nor does it include the usual divine gift language. Mayes suggests that the author's purpose was to show that God did not give the Philistines their land and therefore Israel's later possession of it was acceptable (*Deuteronomy*, p. 140).

[42]Also called the Moabite Stone. It is an inscription on a black basalt stone commemorating the revolt of Mesha, king of Moab, in and after the days of Ahab (2 Kgs 3:4ff). Mesha tells of rebuilding several cities north of the Arnon; see Aharoni, *Land*, p. 306, for a helpful map.

point in the history of Israel God's work among them was a dreadful experience for non-Israelites.

Heshbon was Sihon's capital. It has been identified with the modern Tel Hesbon, about fifteen miles east of the Jordan River. Recent excavations have revealed no remains there prior to the twelfth century B.C., after the time of Sihon. Therefore, some scholars have suggested ancient Heshbon was at modern Jalul, one mile east of Madeba and southeast of Hesbon, where there are Late Bronze Age remains. Others have suggested that Sihon was a nomadic chieftain and therefore would not have left any material remains.[43]

2:26-30 These verses transition to the next divine speech in verse 31 and prepare the way for the details of the defeat of Sihon in verses 32ff. Though Israel had already been told they would have to fight Sihon, they offered a peaceful way first, just as they had done with the Edomites (Num 20:14-17; Judg 11:19-21). Their crossing of both Edom and Moab had proven their peaceful intentions. They were willing to pay for everything and stay on the road. Their object was not Sihon's land, but the land beyond the Jordan. Their desire to **pass through** was emphasized by the four uses of the verb (vv. 27,28,29,30). Nothing could seem more reasonable.

Incredibly **Sihon refused**. Literally, he "was unwilling" to let them through. It was a matter of his will against theirs and God's (the forefathers had also been unwilling, v. 26). Though Sihon was accountable for the consequences of his choice, God encouraged his unwillingness. He **had made his spirit stubborn and his heart obstinate**. This is the same language used of God's actions on Pharaoh's heart (Exod 7:3; 10:27). But Pharaoh had also hardened his own heart (Exod 9:34,35). These texts reflect the complexity of the interaction between God's sovereignty and human freedom. At the human level Pharaoh and Sihon resisted Israel. At the divine level God was at work. Both were operating at the same time and reflect the OT theology of history.[44] In these special cases God encouraged and strengthened the path Pharaoh and Sihon had chosen because of his larger purpose for Israel. These words were important encouragement for the new generation of Israel who had heard about the

---

[43]Lawrence T. Geraty, "Hesbon," *ABD*, 3:181-184.
[44]Craigie, *Deuteronomy*, p. 116; see also Wright, *Deuteronomy*, p. 38.

fathers' failure (chapter 1) and faced the daunting task of taking the land. The encounter with Sihon was their first test of opposition and their own military preparedness for battle. It was also God's reactivation of intervention on Israel's behalf. As he had been at work in the Exodus, so he was now again at work.

The Defeat of Sihon (2:31–3:1)

2:31 A new divine speech introduces the main narrative on the defeat of Sihon. The language is similar to verses 24-25. These verses form an inclusion around the transitional verses 26-30.

Now begin to conquer and possess is an emphatic imperative which could be rendered literally "begin, possess to possess" (or "dispossess to possess"[45]). The divine-human interaction is part of the events. God delivered the people and the land into Israel's hand but they had to take possession of it through military action. Israel still had to experience the vicissitudes of real life with all of its uncertainties and ambiguities. Yet God fought for them and assured them victory.

2:32 The battle occurred at **Jahaz**. Its location is uncertain, but it was north of the Arnon. The place is referenced only a few places in the OT with different spellings (Num 21:23; Josh 13:18; 21:36; Judg 11:20; Isa 15:4; Jer 48:34). According to the Mesha Stone, King Mesha retook it in the ninth century. It was still in Moabite hands in Jeremiah's time (Jer 48:34).

2:33 Just as God gave the land to Israel, he gave Sihon to her (NIV, **delivered him over**). Israel **struck him down**, a common verb for killing and often used for warfare. It is especially used in conquest contexts with the verb חרם (*ḥrm*, "completely destroy" [v. 34]). **His whole army** is literally "all his people." In war context the phrase indicates military fighting men (Exod 14:6; 17:13; Num 20:20; Deut 20:1, 2,5,9; 1 Sam 14:15, etc.; in v. 34 it includes women and children).

2:34 So Israel **took all his towns**. This verb is used often in Joshua and Judges for capturing cities, land, people, or animals as booty (Deut 2:35). Israel captured the cities and people, not for their own benefit, but for God. Therefore they **completely destroyed** them. The verb *ḥrm* means to banish or devote to the ban. It involves the consecration of something for a permanent offering for the

---

[45]Craigie, *Deuteronomy*, p. 116.

sanctuary, or the consecration of a city or people for destruction. Here it refers to the total destruction of the city and people because they had been devoted to God in this divine war. The capture of Jericho and its dedication to God is another example of the concept in a conquest narrative (Josh 6:17).[46]

These texts present problems to interpreters because they portray the biblical God as demanding the total destruction of the enemies of Israel. This violence strikes the Christian and non-Christian as repugnant. The non-Christian understandably decries divine sanction to such behavior, especially in an age that has become sensitive to violence and abuse. The Christian has learned from the New Testament that the proper treatment of the enemy is love.

Some scholars suggest that Deuteronomy (and Joshua and Judges) represents a later ideology of holy way that was imposed on earlier narratives. When Deuteronomy and the Deuteronomistic history were assembled in the seventh century B.C. a more militant perspective had developed from conflict with persistent Canaanite religion. The editors wished to undergird national identity and imposed this ideology on the ancient texts. A later ideal of what should have happened was added to the earlier stories about conquest.[47]

Others have suggested that we must understand the theology of Deuteronomy and place these texts within that context. The theology of Deuteronomy centers on Yahweh as one God, Israel as God's elect, and religious purity. Israel's existence can be fully understood only within the larger context of Yahweh's battle with other gods. Israel's purity as God's elect had to be maintained in order for him to have a witness among the nations. Threats to that purity and witness had to be eliminated because God's larger purpose was the salvation of the world. In this context the OT *ḥērem* was different from that practiced by other nations. It was not an ideology of conquest, but part of an effort to ultimately save the world.[48]

---

[46]J.U.P. Lilley, "Understanding ḤEREM," *TB* 44 (1993): 169-177.

[47]N. Lohfink believes that there were no *ḥerem* wars in ancient times in Israel; all the accounts are later systematization: "חרם," *TDOT,* 5:180-199, especially pp. 193-194. Miller believes that there may be at most only three valid *ḥerem* wars in the OT (based on an earlier study by Brekelmans), that is Num 21:1-4; Josh 6–7; 1 Sam 15 (*Deuteronomy,* pp. 40-42).

[48]See McConville, *Grace,* pp. 139-144; John W. Wenham, *The Goodness of God* (Downers Grove, IL: InterVarsity, 1972), pp. 119-147; Wright, *Deuteronomy,*

Furthermore, the Canaanites were condemned for their wickedness (Deut 9:4-5). Their destruction was a part of God's eschatological judgment executed upon them in the present. The way for this thinking was prepared in Genesis 15:16. The iniquity of the Amorites was now complete and merited judgment. Israel's war of conquest became the instrument. There was precedence for this type of judgment in the narrative of the flood in Genesis 6–8 and the destruction of Sodom and Gomorrah in Genesis 19.

Eschatological judgment is a strong biblical theme, even in the NT. The NT teaches that judgment will come at the end of history and mark the break between the old and the new. The *ḥērem* war in the OT indicated that at one point the future judgment broke into history and God used ancient Israel as his instrument.

2:35 Certain items were not under the *ḥrm*, the livestock and **the plunder**. Israel apparently left the cities standing and took what objects would be useful to her (Deut 6:10-11). In the rules of warfare in chapter 20:10-17 Israel could keep the booty of distant cities. It seems that that rule applied here although the tribe of Reuben later was given the land.[49]

2:36-37 Israel was successful and took all of Sihon's territory. **Gilead** was the territory of Og (3:10), so the area captured stretched north from the Arnon to the Jabbok River which was midway between the Dead Sea and the Sea of Chinnereth (Galilee). It was an area about 55 miles long and 20-25 miles wide. However, in obedience to the injunction in 2:19 they did not encroach on any Ammonite territory that lay further to the east.

3:1 This verse is a transition to the account of the defeat of Og. The wording is the same as 2:32 showing that the two accounts are being told in a similar way. There are also numerous parallels between 3:1-7 and 2:31-36 as well as between 3:1-7 and Numbers 21:33-35.

---

p. 231; John Goldingay, *Theological Diversity and the Authority of the Old Testament* (Grand Rapids: Eerdmans, 1987), pp. 141-153. Deuteronomy 7, 9 and 20 also deal with these issues. See comments on these texts below.

[49]Mayes (*Deuteronomy*, p. 141) suggests *none* of the rules of chapter 20 were applied, perhaps because Sihon and Og were outside the promised land.

Bashan was the high plateau area east of the Sea of Chinnereth. Israel would have to go through Gilead, the area between the Jabbok and Yarmuk Rivers, to reach it. Since Gilead was under the control of Og, he rallied to defend it.

Bashan was famous for its fertile pasturelands (Amos 4:1; Ps 22:12; Isa 2:13; Ezek 39:18). Later, Israel battled Syria and Assyria for control of it.[50]

---

[50]Bashan is now known as the Golan Heights and is once again a focus of serious conflict between Israel and Syria.

DEUTERONOMY 3

Defeat of Og (3:2-11)

3:2-7 This next divine speech introduced a word of encouragement as in 2:31. It gave the important assurance **Do not be afraid**.[1] The same wording is used here as for the account of Sihon. The promise of verse 2 was immediately realized in verse 3. Og and his people and cities were treated the same way Sihon was (2:34).

The exact location of **Argob** is unclear; perhaps it refers to the whole plateau east of the Sea of Galilee. The area was renamed Havvoth-Jair in 3:14.[2]

Even though the cities were **fortified with high walls and with gates and bars**, Israel was victorious. This deliberately recalls the lack of faith of the forefathers in 1:28.

3:8-11 These verses summarize the defeat of Sihon and Og to establish once again that Israel could trust in the power and faithfulness of God. Verses 8-10 summarize all the territory that was taken. **Mt. Hermon** was the mountain north of the Sea of Chinnereth that marked the ideal northern boundary of the Promised Land (Josh 11:17; 13:5). It was 9,232 feet high and snow capped most of the year. Its melting snows are a major source of the Jordan River. It was known by several different names in antiquity.

Verse 11 provides a later historical gloss as noted by the last sentence. **Og** was remembered as the last remnant of the giant Rephaites (2:11). His **bed** was remarkable for its size (13 by 6 feet) and its construction. Some scholars reinterpret the bed as a sarcophagus and point to basalt rocks with high iron content in the area.[3] However,

---

[1] For discussion see above on 1:21.

[2] There is some fluidity in the understanding of these geographical locations in the OT. In Solomon's administrative districts in 1 Kgs 4:13 the villages of Jair are in Gilead.

[3] Craigie, *Deuteronomy*, p. 120.

the bedstead was probably inlaid with iron, not made of iron. Since the Iron Age was just beginning, iron would have still been a precious metal and thus the bed a valuable and remarkable object.[4]

Apportioning of the Land (3:12-17)

This section completes the summary of the preconquest era that was covered in more detail in Numbers 32. The material is presented in a different order and with different emphasis than in Numbers. The giving of the land to some of the tribes presented a deposit on the assurance that God would indeed give them land that he had promised. It was a fitting end to the early success of the second generation and allowed them to see the fruit of their obedience to God. They trusted God to defeat their enemies and in return received the gift of the land. Therefore, they were spiritually prepared for the conquest under Joshua.

Moses' presentation is a good example of a concentric structure. The account begins and ends with information on Reuben and Gad (vv. 12 and 16-17). The geographical details in verse 12 run from the south to the north; in verses 16-17, north to south. The central section concentrates on Manasseh (Manasseh, v. 13; Jair and Makir, vv. 14 and 15).[5]

3:12 The territory given to **Reuben** and **Gad** was the territory won from Sihon (and apparently part of Og's).[6] The details of the allotment seem at odds with Numbers 32 and Joshua 13. It is possible that the lists in Joshua reflect more the reality of actual allotment, and Deuteronomy reflects more the ideal. There could have been flexibility in the details. It is also possible that the Reubenites ended up living among the Gadites.[7]

The Reubenites' ancestor, Reuben, was the first son of Jacob by his wife Leah (Gen 29:32). He was remembered for his illicit sex with the concubine Bilhah (Gen 49:3-4), but he pled for the life of Joseph

---

[4]Alan Millard, "King Og's Iron Bed — Fact or Fancy," *BRev* 6,2 (April 1990): 16-21, 44; Tigay, *Deuteronomy*, p. 35.

[5]Josh 13:8-13 also details the giving of this land.

[6]See on 2:36 above.

[7]Merrill, *Deuteronomy*, p. 108. See Aharoni, *Land of the Bible*, p. 196 for a convenient map.

and offered his two sons for Benjamin (Gen 37:21-22; 42:37). The tribe was involved in the rebellion of Numbers 16.

Gad was the son of Jacob by Leah's maid, Zilpah. He was remembered for his raiding ability (Gen 49:19, a distinct word play in Hebrew). The Gadites are mentioned on the Mesha Stone (840–830 B.C.) as long having dwelt in the land of Ataroth.

3:13 One half of the tribe of Manasseh received the territory of Og that included half of Gilead and all of Bashan. Again there are some differences in the various accounts. Perhaps the political and geographical boundaries were somewhat different.[8]

Manasseh was the oldest son of Joseph who lost the right of the firstborn to his brother, Ephraim (Gen 48:14ff). Half of the tribe's allotment was west of the Jordan, south of the Jezreel valley and going from the Jordan River to the Mediterranean Sea. It was the largest portion of any tribe (Josh 17:1-13). Two famous judges, Gideon and Jephthah came from this tribe (Judg 6–8; 11).

3:14-15 The next two verses detail more about the territory given to Manasseh, specifically which subtribal groups inherited which parts. In Numbers 32:41 we are told only that Jair took "their villages." The antecedent is unclear. The closest territory mentioned is Gilead in verse 40. Some see a conflict with the mention of the Bashan here.[9] The name change means "villages of Jair." Jair was the great-great-grandson of Manasseh (1 Chr 2:21; 7:14). **Geshur and Maacah** were small states south of Mt. Hermon and east of the Sea of Chinnereth (Galilee).

Makir (also spelled Machir) was a son of Manasseh and father of Gilead. His descendants captured the territory of Gilead (Numbers 32:39-40). Comparison with verse 13 suggests the impreciseness of some of the assignment language.

3:16-17 Moses returned to the territory given to the **Reubenities and the Gadites** but in more detail than before. He adds here the western border which was basically the Jordan River and Dead Sea.

This is the first mention of **Pisgah** in Deuteronomy. Its location is debated. Four times in the OT we find the "top of Pisgah" (Deut 3:27; 34:1; Num 21:20; 23:14) and four times the "slopes of Pisgah"

---

[8]Craigie, *Deuteronomy*, p. 122.
[9]Mays, *Deuteronomy*, p. 145.

(here and 4:49; Josh 12:3; 13:20). It was also associated with Mt. Nebo (34:1). Perhaps Mt. Nebo was the major mountain and Pisgah was a rocky promontory to the west. The slopes would then be the plateau area west of mountain. Or the slopes could refer to the entire edge of the Moabite plateau. Pisgah is identified with modern Ras es-Siyaghah, a few miles east of the north end of the Dead Sea, from which one can get an excellent view of the land of Israel.

Further Instructions (3:18-22)

Further instructions are given to the three tribes (vv. 18-20) and to Joshua (vv. 21-22), rhetorically set off by the expression **at that time** (vv. 18,21; also vv. 8 and 23).

3:18 Israel was a covenant community in which it was essential that the whole nation participate in the conquest. The land belonged to the entire nation and it must maintain its solidarity. The fact that some tribes had received their inheritance could lead them to resign as members of the community. There were strong geographical factors that would promote separation also. They were not to allow this to happen. As a part of the nation all the men must participate in the military campaigns to come.

Was this a test of their commitment to the nation? Though the nation was divided into tribal units, it was God's intention that they be united. Sadly this unity was an ideal often broken. Following the unified effort at conquest the nation settled into the land in disunity (Judges).[10] Only David was able to bring them together and that unity lasted only through the reign of Solomon (2 Sam 5; 1 Kgs 12).

3:19-20 Leaving their families in the territory unprotected would be a test of their commitment and trust (cf. Num 32:16-19). In 1:39 it was the perceived danger to the children that was an excuse for the forefathers to distrust God.

The conquest took seven years (compare Josh 14:6-15 and 22:1-4), a significant time span. However, since Joshua's headquarters for

---

[10]In Numbers 32 the request by the Reuben and Gad tribes to stay in the Transjordan area aroused Moses' suspicion. The fragility of the union was further illustrated by the episode of the altar in Joshua 22. The tribes west of the Jordan River immediately suspected apostasy. The Reuben and Gad tribes were fearful of future isolation. In Deborah's song, Judges 5:15b-16, the Reuben tribe was questioned because it stayed home.

the conquest were at Gilgal near Jericho the army was not far away
if danger threatened.

God promised them **rest**. This is a theologically loaded term.[11]
The rest that God offered included safety and security. Often it was
described by the phrase: "rest from his/their enemies on every side"
(Deut 12:10; 25:19; Josh 1:13,15; 23:1; 2 Sam 7:1,11; 2 Chr 14:7; Neh
9:28; Isa 14:3). It meant relief from threat of attack. The Promised
Land was not just a good land, it was a place of security. This was
ultimately a spiritual blessing, for once at peace in their own land
they could worship and serve God. Their failure to experience this
rest was due to disobedience (Judg 2:6ff; already anticipated in Deut
4:25-28; 31:16).

3:21-22 The words of encouragement to Joshua take up the command of God in 1:38. Again the victory over Sihon and Og was used
as an example of what God was able to do through those who trusted him. Joshua, as the new leader, could take courage. Again Moses
used familiar words of encouragement and divine war language (see
above on 1:21 and 1:30).[12]

Moses' Second Plea (3:23-29)

This section not only includes a very emotional plea from Moses,
it shows significant word play. Since God had begun to give victory
to Israel in the Transjordan, perhaps Moses began to think that he
may have relented in the decision to bar Moses from the promised
land. This is shown in the subtle play with עבר (*'br*), "to cross over,"
which occurs 14 times in chapters 2 and 3. Moses wanted to go
across the Jordan (v. 25), but God said he would not cross (v. 27).
Joshua would lead Israel across (v. 28). Further, God's anger was
expressed with a homonym of *'br* (*'abēr*, v. 26).[13]

3:23-24 Moses' pleading was not a single request. It had been an
ongoing conversation. The Hebrew verb הִתְחַנַּן (*hithḥanan*, from חנן,
ḥnn, "show favor, be gracious") indicates that Moses was specifically
asking for God to be gracious to him (see also 1 Kgs 8:33,47; Esth

---

[11]John N. Oswalt, "נוח," *NIDOTTE*, 3:56-59.

[12]These are very similar to Moses' words to Israel in Exod 14:13-14.

[13]Tigay, *Deuteronomy*, p. 38. Compare the British expression "went over
the top" in anger.

8:3; Ps 4:1; 30:8; 142:1; Hos 12:4). God was a gracious God (it was a part of his character, Exod 34:6-7), but he could extend grace or withhold it as he saw fit (Exod 33:19).

Moses' servant status was an important dimension of who he was (see 34:5). Here he took on almost the status of a suffering servant.[14] His failure to enter the land was on account of the people's failure to obey God. As God's servant he shared the failure of the people and suffered with them (1:37; 4:21-22).[15]

God's resumption of his mighty acts through his **strong hand** was encouragement to Moses. It had been many years since he had been at work. God's deed established his uniqueness (Exod 15:11; Deut 10:21–11:7). The "gods" here are probably the other heavenly hosts, not actual pagan gods (see Ps 89:7).[16]

3:25 The plea would be better translated "Please let me go over . . . ." Moses wanted to go over so he could **see** the land. God told him to go up to Pisgah, and he would see the land from there (v. 27). The good land was described by several phrases. The **fine hill country** here (Josh 9:1; 10:6,40; 11:3; 12:8, etc.) is equal to the "hill country of the Amorites" in other places (1:7,19,20,24,41; 2:3).

Lebanon was famous for its vegetation and beauty. It was often used in the description of the Promised Land as its northern border. The OT designation was a geographical area and was not equal to the political region of modern times. In ancient times Lebanon was famous for its dense forests, especially the cedar trees. The Phoenician cities on the coast such as Tyre and Sidon gave it its historical and cultural fame.[17]

3:26 That is enough is the same expression that was used in 1:6 and 2:2. It indicated that the situation had gone on sufficiently and it was time to end it.

3:27 On the location of **Pisgah** see on verse 17. From this rocky promontory on the east side and above the Dead Sea one could see 100 miles north to Mt. Hermon on a clear day. One could also see Mt. Gerizim and Mt. Ebal (Deut 27:12-13) and on down the central

---

[14]Miller, *Deuteronomy*, p. 43.

[15]This observation does not absolve his guilt (32:51). Moses' failure was caused by the people's rebellion, but he was accountable for his own sin.

[16]Tigay, *Deuteronomy*, p. 39.

[17]K.A. Kitchen and A.K. Cragg, "Lebanon," *NBD*, pp. 690-691.

mountain ridge to Hebron. That would have included all the Promised Land except the Negev and the western slopes of the hill country. This command recalls the command to Abraham in Genesis 13:14. There Abraham was on the west side of the Jordan near Bethel so he could also see the western slopes of the hill country (see also Gen 28:14).

3:28 The command to encourage Joshua summarizes Numbers 27:18-23. **Commission** comes from the verb צוה (ṣwh, "to command"). In Numbers this commissioning was accomplished by the laying on of hands. Joshua already had the spirit of God. The narrative is taken up again in Deuteronomy 31:1.[18] It is interesting how often Joshua is told to be strong and courageous (see Deut 31:6-7; Josh 1:7,9, and often). Joshua eventually became the encourager of Israel (Josh 10:25; 23:6).

3:29 This concluding geographical note sets off the first section of the book, chapters 1–3. It returns to the beginning geographical note in 1:5. In 4:46 **Beth Peor** is identified with more detail (see also 34:6; Josh 13:20). The term means "temple [lit., house] of Peor." It is probably the same as the Peor mentioned in Numbers 23:28 where Balaam built seven altars. Numbers 25 mentions a god, Baal Peor (Lord of Peor) who was worshiped by the Moabites (Deut 4:3). Beth Peor was evidently beneath Mt. Pisgah.

---

[18]See comments there.

DEUTERONOMY 4

C. EXHORTATION: IDOLATRY FORBIDDEN (4:1-40)

Many scholars recognize the unity of 4:1-40, though there is some dissent.[1] The sermon exhibits its unity by both subject matter and structure. Its teaching character has also long been recognized. It is clearly a sermonic exhortation to obedience and is a fitting conclusion to the introductory section of the book, the historical prologue, 1:6-3:29. At the end of the historical review Israel was encamped at Beth Peor, poised to cross the Jordan and take possession of the land. It was fitting that Moses should pause to reflect on the past and offer exhortation for the future, a future that would not include his leadership.

The passage serves as an introduction to the next major section of the book, chapters 5-11, and prepares the way for the Decalogue in chapter 5. Therefore, it is a transition chapter.[2] It also shares many themes with Deuteronomy 29-30, thus forming a frame around the main address of the book, chapters 5-28. Tigay asserts that chapter 4 is the theological heart of Deuteronomy.[3]

Its overall structure is simple: verses 1-8 and 32-40 share an emphasis on the uniqueness of God; verses 9-31 build on the second commandment (5:7-10) by warning against idolatry.[4] However, a more detailed outline will help us understand the development of Moses' sermon better.[5]

---

[1]A.D.H. Mayes, "Deuteronomy 4 and the Literary Criticism of Deuteronomy," *JBL* 100 (1981): 23-51; a dissenting voice is G. von Rad, *Deuteronomy*, p. 49.

[2]Christensen, *Deuteronomy*, p. 69, developed a concentric structure (chiasm) for chapters 4-11.

[3]Tigay, *Deuteronomy*, p. 41.

[4]Wright, *Deuteronomy*, p. 45.

[5]Olson, *Deuteronomy and the Death of Moses*, p. 31, and Mayes, "Deuteronomy 4,"

1. Exhortation: Obedience Brings Life (4:1-4)

4:1 Hear now, O Israel (NIV) masks the Hebrew discourse marker that indicates a new beginning (literally, "And now Israel, hear . . ."). This is a transition to the moral or religious lesson that is to be learned from what follows.[6] The lesson to be learned is based on history as we shall see.

The summons to Israel to hear is characteristic of didactic address (5:1; 6:4; 9:1; 20:3; 27:9). They were to hear God's instructions as given through Moses. This instruction was referred to in different ways. Here it is **decrees** and **laws** (חֻקִּים, *ḥuqqîm* and מִשְׁפָּטִים, *mišpāṭîm*). These are common words in Deuteronomy for the covenant requirements (4:5,8,14,45; 5:1; 6:20; 7:11; 11:32; 12:1), but other combinations of words were used (e.g., *miṣwāh* as in v. 40). Although each word seems to have its distinct meaning, when used together, there is little difference between them and their meanings overlap

---

p. 25, are the source of much of this outline, though I have added refinements.

[6]See Weinfeld, *Deuteronomy*, p. 199. "And now" occurs 6 times in Deuteronomy: 5:1; 10:12,22; 26:10; 31:19 and here, and 278 times in the OT. It is especially emphatic with the "and."

with *tôrāh* (law, instruction).[7] It was the total revealed covenant law Israel was to obey.

Moses' task was to **teach** this law. Instruction was an important part of the purpose of Deuteronomy and of this chapter (vv. 5,10,14; v. 9 uses a form of the verb "to know"; see also 5:1,31; 6:1; 11:19; 14:23; 17:19; 18:9; 31:12,13,19,22). Parents were an important part of the teaching process also (implied in vv. 9 and 10 and explicit in 6:2,7,20ff.; 11:19; 31:12-13). In later Judaism Moses was revered as the first great teacher and given the title Moses Rabbenu ("Moses our teacher"). First century BC and AD synagogues had the "chair of Moses" that designated the place of the preacher and teacher (Matt 23:2).

Teaching of and obedience to the law was crucial to Israel's future. Only by obedience could she be assured of advancing into the Promised Land and possessing it as God's gift. To **live** for Israel was to live in the land. There was no life for her apart from the land. It was the law that made this life possible (Lev 18:5; Deut 6:24; 11:8-10; 30:15-20) because the law was the revealed will of God graciously given to his people.[8]

4:2 The law was complete as given, and it was Israel's responsibility to obey it, not amend it at her whim. Such warnings appear also in ancient Near Eastern treaties between countries. The vassal nation was warned not to change anything in the treaty by adding to or taking away from it.[9] Perhaps we have a canonical principle beginning to take shape here. The word of God, when delivered, was not open to human manipulation (Deut 12:32; Prov 30:5-6; Jer 26:2; Rev 22:18-19).

4:3-4 The historical recital of chapters 1–3 was important background for the exhortation of chapter 4. What Moses had to say was

---

[7]Peter Enns, "קח," *NIDOTTE*, 2:250-251; H. Ringgren, "קקח," *TDOT*, 5:139-47.

[8]Even Jesus agreed, Matt 19:17. If this point sounds inaccurate to the Christian, it is because of the influence of Paul's negative comments on the law (Rom 7:10; 10:5; Gal 3 and other places). But we must realize Paul was combating a legalistic perversion of the law. He also made the point that the problem was not with the law but with the human heart (Rom 7:14).

[9]See Weinfeld, *Deuteronomy*, p. 200 for quotes. Primary material can be found in *ANET*, p. 161, and D. J. Wiseman, *The Vassal-Treaties of Esarhaddon* (London: British School of Archaeology, 1958), p. 60.

grounded in historical fact to which he also appealed in verses 9-31. It was still fresh in Israel's memory that obedience did indeed ensure life. Their **eyes saw** what God had done. On the other hand, the disobedient were dead (Num 25:1-9).

Moses juxtaposed two competing ideas. Israel could either follow (lit. "walk after") other gods (a strong warning theme in Deuteronomy: 6:14; 8:19; 11:28; 13:2; 28:14), or they could **hold fast** to the LORD. "To walk after" was a political idiom in the ancient Near East for giving allegiance to another.[10] To "hold fast to" indicated a single-minded honoring of God (10:20). The choice was clear-cut. The repetition of "live" in verse four (see v. 1) holds this beginning unit together.

2. Obedience Demonstrates Israel's Uniqueness and Greatness (4:5-8)

This unit is marked by the key words "great" and "nations" (vv. 6,7,8) as is the corresponding section, verses 32-39. Rhetorically it is closely connected to verses 1-4 by the repetition from verse one of "decrees," "laws," "teach," "possess," and "land" in verse five. Moses returned to these ideas often (see v. 14). Verse eight rounds off this section with "decrees," "laws," "great," and "nation." Moses intended to promote obedience by reflecting on the honor that would accrue to Israel and God.

4:5 The wording of this verse is very close to verse 1, though it begins with **see** rather than "hear," a good interjection to precede a declaration (1:8,21; 2:31; 11:26). In contrast to verse 1, Moses indicated he had already taught the people the law. The Hebrew verb form is ambiguous and relies on context for meaning. It could be translated "I am teaching," a formal declaration relating to the present or future. Perhaps both ideas are true: Moses was continually teaching the people in the wilderness, and he was continuing to teach them now with his final address to them.

4:6 The call to **observe** the law (lit., "keep to do") resounds throughout Deuteronomy (5:1,29; 6:3,25; 7:12; 11:32; 16:12; 17:10; 26:16; 28:13) as we might expect from Moses' opening exhortation

---

[10]Tigay, *Deuteronomy*, p. 44.

in chapter 4. In this verse we also catch a glimpse of another concern of Deuteronomy: Israel's influence on the nations.[11]

Obedience will be a demonstration of **wisdom and understanding**. Wisdom in Deuteronomy was conformity to the will of God. Obedience would bring a well-ordered life, as celebrated in Proverbs, and was the common sense thing to do.[12]

Why would this appeal to the nations? Because collecting and passing on wisdom was a major concern in the ancient Near East. The Mesopotamian countries and Egypt collected wisdom into literary texts for future reference. Solomon's reputation among the nations was due to his wisdom (1 Kgs 10:4-7,23-24).

There is a certain irony in the idea that the nations would recognize the **greatness** of Israel. Moses reminded Israel later that she was the smallest of nations (7:7) and warned that she could become smaller (4:27). Her greatness was probably to be understood in a spiritual sense which is made clear in the following statements.

4:7 One aspect of Israel's greatness was the nearness of the LORD. The polytheistic gods of the nations were noted for their distance. Though Israel's God was transcendent, he also offered his presence in the cloud at Sinai (Exod 19, 24) and in the Ark. Because of this nearness they could "call on him" (NIV **"pray"** is too narrow). This could include prayer, thanksgiving, praise, lament and cries for help (Ps 145:18: "The LORD is near to all who call on him").[13]

4:8 This verse is structured like verse 7 with the interrogative and the answer. In the ancient Near East the kings bragged about giving out righteous laws, for the king was wise, not the people. But in Israel the people were wise and the law was **righteous** because it

---

[11]This "missiological significance" is a major concern of Christopher Wright in his commentary; see *Deuteronomy*, pp. 8-17.

[12]This wisdom concern has led Weinfeld to believe that wisdom teachers were involved in the composition of Deuteronomy. He also notes that some laws in Deuteronomy have no counterpart in the Pentateuch, but they do in Proverbs. He compares Deut 19:14 and Prov 22:28; 23:10; 11:1; Deut 23:22-26 and Eccl 5:1-5; Prov 20:25; Deut 23:16 and Prov 30:10; Deut. 1:9-18 and the wisdom qualities of the leaders (*Deuteronomy*, pp. 62-65). However, the wisdom tradition was old and widespread in the ancient Near East and in Egypt. Moses, educated in Egypt, would have been exposed to it. It is not difficult to imagine that he baptized some of it into his covenant theology.

[13]See Louis Jonker, "קרא," *NIDOTTE*, 3:971-974.

came from God, not the king. Righteousness assumed a natural standard to which all behavior and laws were to conform. For Israel that
standard was God, and his standard was the highest of all (Ps
119:7,62,144,160,172).[14] Verse eight rounds off this section with parallels to verse five through the use of "decrees and laws."

3. Be Careful to Avoid Idolatry (4:9-31)

These verses are the heart of the chapter and are an extended
reflection on the second commandment ("You shall not make for
yourself an idol . . . ," 5:8-10). In Israel's cultural context the main
temptation was idolatry. Moses returns to the theme three times in
this section, using the past, present, and future as the grounds for
his lessons (see the outline above). Rhetorically the various sections
have several interconnections, evidence of the complex nature of
the sermon. Verses 9-14 and 25-28 are connected by "children" and
"grandchildren"; verses 15-20 and 23-24 are connected by "form"
and "idol."

Lesson from the Past (4:9-20)

The Events at Horeb (4:9-14)

The first section is an exhortation (vv. 9-10) and a background
narrative (vv. 11-14) about the events at Horeb. These serve as the
basis for the lesson in verses 15-20. The lesson also consists of exhortation (vv. 15-19) and background narrative (v. 20).

4:9 The call to **be careful** is frequent in Deuteronomy (v. 23; 6:2;
8:11; 11:16; 12:13,19,30; 15:9; 24:8) and emphasizes alertness in spiritual matters, and the consequences of not being alert. Often the
focus was idolatry as it is here. **Watch yourselves** is a double emphatic (lit. ,"guard yourself, guard yourself exceedingly"). They were to
guard against **forgetfulness**, a particular concern of Deuteronomy
(4:23; 6:12; 8:11,14,19; 9:7). What had happened forty years ago was

---

[14]Several of Israel's laws, especially concerning justice, were unique in the
ancient Near East, such as the just treatment of aliens and bondservants, the
prohibition of vicarious punishment, and noncapital economic crimes (Tigay,
Deuteronomy, p. 45).

crucial to their continued existence. To forget was to lose a way of life marked by obedience to God and his covenant and to turn to a life marked by idolatry. That was apostasy. Therefore, memory was crucial to keeping a relationship with God (8:18-19; 9:7).[15]

Passing on the faith was essential also. **Teach** here is not the same word as in verses 1 and 5, but it carries the same meaning. It literally means to "make known" which seems to emphasize the experiential side of the teaching. This is similar to the wisdom tradition (Prov 2:1; 3:1; 4:1, etc.) and is a concern elsewhere in Deuteronomy (v. 25; 6:2,7,20-25; 11:19; 12:25,28; 29:22,29; 30:2,19; 32:46).

4:10 The experience at Horeb was intended to incite the right mind-set for worship of God (fear or reverence; see Exod 19). Fear that produces worship is the polar opposite of fear that produces terror. Fear, or reverence, could be taught, was the natural response to a holy God, and was a proper component of a relationship with God. In Deuteronomy 10:12-13 the verbs fear, walk, love, serve, and obey are all used to describe what God required of his people. There were two aspects to this requirement: adoration and obedience. Obedience was the fundamental expression of the total dependence on God that could be expressed in adoration. The object was Israel's good. This type of fear was also a part of the wisdom tradition (Prov 1:7).[16]

4:11 This verse provides narrative background describing the event at Horeb. Contrasting **fire** and **black clouds and deep darkness** marked that event (see Exod 19:9,16,18; 20:18,21; 24:15-17). Fire and smoke are typical of divine theophanies in the OT and express both the ideas of revealing and concealing, transcendence and immanence. Concealment was necessary for no one could survive the full disclosure of God.[17] **Fire** is a major theme in this sermon (vv. 11,12,15,24,33,36). It both illuminates (v. 15) and consumes (v. 24). Such language illustrates the difficulty of trying to describe the glory and holiness of God (in 5:22 fire, deep darkness, and cloud are parallel).

4:12 There is a repeated emphasis on the spoken word of God in this sermon. God revealed himself through words, not **form** (Exod

---

[15]The NT assumes the same with its emphasis on the Lord's Supper that is to be done in "remembrance" of Christ.

[16]See M.V. Van Pelt and W.C. Kaiser, Jr., "יָרֵא," *NIDOTTE,* 2:527-533, especially 529-530.

[17]Jeffrey J. Niehaus, "Theophany, Theology of," *NIDOTTE,* 4:247-250.

19:9). His words came from the **fire** (v. 36), that is, from the physical manifestation of his presence (Deut 5:4,22).

God had no form, which distinguished him from the pagan gods (cf. v. 15-18). In Exodus the people were warned not to look at the mountain. Here they are reminded that there was nothing to see anyway. Since there was no form, an idol would not make sense, for what could it represent? Israel's God spoke with them but the visible gods of the nations could neither speak nor hear (v. 28)!

4:13 This is the first explicit reference to the **covenant** in Deuteronomy.[18] The covenant defined the relationship between God and Israel. Here it is explicitly limited to the **Ten Commandments** though the concept of covenant is much broader than the Decalogue. The Ten Commandments function as a summary or digest of the covenant law.[19]

Since ancient Near East treaties required two copies of the treaty, one for each party, the **two stone tablets** probably represented two copies of the Ten Commandments. One copy was for Israel and one was for God. Both were kept in the Ark of the Covenant.[20]

4:14 The themes of verses 1 and 5 are taken up again here. The task given to Moses to **teach** the **decrees and laws** was essential to the survival of the nation. Moses came back again and again to this responsibility. The book of Deuteronomy suggests that the essence of the law found in the Ten Commandments was understood to be also contained in the more extensive teaching in this book.[21]

Lesson: Do Not Make an Idol (4:15-20)

4:15-18 The crucial lesson to be learned from not seeing a **form** of God at Sinai is explained. Since Israel worshiped an invisible God, they should not attempt to construct a visible one (cf. 5:8-10). There was also a contrast between the visible idols, and the *audible* God of Israel.

---

[18]*Bᵉrith* occurs 28 times in the book. See the discussion on covenant in the Introduction above, and Gordon McConville, "ברית," *NIDOTTE*, 1:747-755.

[19]Actually reference to the "ten words" is rare in the OT, only here, 10:4, and Exod 34:28. Deut 12:28 refers to "all these words" (NIV, "all these regulations").

[20]See Meredith Kline, *Treaty of the Great King*, pp. 13-15.

[21]See further the comments on verses 1 and 5 above.

Verse 15 begins with the same warning as verse 9 (put in the middle of the verse by the NIV). Solid or graphic objects could not represent the transcendent God because idolatry was based on a contradictory worldview. Since the image or statue was linked with the deity in some way "spells, incantations and other magical arts could be performed on the image in order to threaten, bind or compel the deity."[22]

Idols would morally **corrupt** Israel (v. 16) because they represented a totally different way of viewing reality. If no one knew what God looked like, then how could an image be made of him? There was nothing in the created physical world that could represent the Creator. Verses 16-18 deliberately recall Genesis 1:20-27 but reverse the order of the created beings. Genesis 1:26-27 does teach that mankind was created in the image of God, but the two words used are different from the words used here in Deuteronomy. The "image of God" in Genesis was not intended to imply a physical representation.[23]

Egyptian culture represented her gods in many different animal and bird forms, and many mummified animals have been discovered there. The animals apparently aroused an awe in the Egyptians that they identified with deities, especially the fact that animals did not change over the years.[24] Mesopotamian cultures pictured their gods mostly as having human forms.[25] These cultures identified many of the gods with natural phenomena, such as the sun, moon, storm, mountain, waters, or wind.[26]

This instruction by Moses then stood in sharp contrast to those ancient cultures and is to be understood as a polemic against their worldview. The later prophets were notably satirical in their descriptions of the pagan propensity to manufacture their own gods (Isaiah 40–45; Jer 10:1-16; Hab 2:18-19).

---

[22]John Walton and Victor Matthews, *Genesis to Deuteronomy*, The IVP Bible Background Commentary (Downers Grove, IL: InterVarsity, 1997), p. 224.

[23]See Gordon J. Wenham, *Genesis 1–15* (Waco, TX: Word, 1987), pp. 27-32.

[24]Henri Frankfort, *Ancient Egyptian Religion* (New York: Harper and Row, 1961), pp. 8-14.

[25]Othmar Keel, *The Symbolism of the Biblical World* (New York: Seabury Press, 1978), pp. 47-56.

[26]Helmer Ringgren, *Religions of the Ancient Near East* (Philadelphia: The Westminster Press, 1973), pp. 5-6, 52-53.

No image of God has been unearthed from ancient Israel. Any idolatry that was practiced was borrowed through syncretism. The bull calf, for example, was a well-known Canaanite symbol (1 Kgs 12:28-38). The god portrayed as a bull was popular in Egypt as well (Exod 32:1-6).

4:19 Moses turned from making idols to the concept of worshiping something in nature. Without revelation of the true God, the nations filled their need for worship by honoring the most impressive heavenly objects. Genesis 1:14-18 is noticeably reticent when relating the creation of these objects. Only the stars were specifically named. Genesis deliberately downplayed the sun and the moon. God created them for service to humans by serving as time markers. They were not substitute deities that controlled human destiny. They were meant to glorify God (Ps 19:1). Therefore, there was a penalty for being drawn into astral worship: death (Deut 17:2-7). Tragically, astral worship proved too enticing and became rampant in Israel in the eighth and seventh centuries (2 Kgs 21:3,5; 23:4,5,12; Jer 7:18; 19:3).

It is unclear whether God **apportioned** the **heavenly array** to the nations for their worship (which seems unlikely) or for their benefit (which is probable).[27] God's sovereignty included his providential care for the nations as well as Israel. The world was created for everyone's benefit.

4:20 The real difference between Israel and the nations was that God had chosen Israel for his own people and rescued her from pagan Egypt. Yet the sojourn in Egypt was useful for it refined Israel in an **iron-smelting furnace**. The refining process was designed to take the rough ore and make it usable. Before Israel could be God's **inheritance**, they needed to be purified and tested. Consequently, they now stood ready for taking the land God had promised.

By God's grace the land was given to Israel as her inheritance, both to the nation and to families/clans within the nation (v. 21,38; 26:1; 19:14; Lev 25:14-28). It was, therefore, striking that Israel could be called God's inheritance. By purifying her, he made her his precious possession (7:6; 9:26,29; 14:2; 26:18; 32:9). Consequently, her privileged place among the nations required a very different level of conduct.

---

[27]Merrill, *Deuteronomy,* pp. 123-124.

Lesson from the Present (4:21-24)

Denial of Moses (4:21-22)

The second lesson of the sermon comes from an example from the present and is the same: idolatry is forbidden.

4:21-22 Although Moses had already dealt with this issue (1:37; 3:23-28), he raised it again for its exhortation value. If he could not escape the judgment of God for his disobedience (see Num 20:9-12; 27:12-14), then the nation should not think they could if they committed idolatry.[28]

Lesson: Do Not Make an Idol (4:23-24)

4:23-24 The same warning is repeated from previous sections of the sermon (v. 9). Again the nation is to take great care in her conduct and not mimic the nations. This danger could become acute after Moses' death. The specific covenant breaking act was the disobedience of idol making but the reasoning this time was new. God was a **consuming fire, a jealous God**.

Israel had already experienced God's consuming fire of judgment (Lev 10:2; Num 11:1-3; 16:35) and they had seen it visited on others (Exod 15:7).[29] The association of God with jealousy is common in the OT. God's jealousy was grounded in his zeal for his own honor and the purity of his people. There could be no rivals for allegiance. The LORD was the only God and had exclusive claim on Israel. His redemption of Israel required her utmost loyalty to the covenant. But idolatry was the preeminent violation of that loyalty (see 5:9; 6:15; 32:16,21; Exod 34:14).[30] The fire of God's redeeming love had brought Israel out of the fire of bondage (v. 20) to become his precious inheritance. To tolerate rivals was unthinkable.[31]

---

[28]Mayes' judgment that the substance of these verses have little relevance to the context is too negative (*Deuteronomy*, p. 154). Tigay guesses that Moses may have wanted to prevent posthumous worship of himself (*Deuteronomy*, p. 51).

[29]But this fire had a positive side also (Deut 9:3).

[30]H.G.L. Peels, "קנא," *NIDOTTE*, 3:937-940.

[31]The author of Hebrews in the NT reminded the early church that they worshiped the same God as Israel. Therefore, they must not refuse him, but must respond with "reverence and awe" for this God was "a consuming fire" (Heb 12:29).

But God's jealousy was not the whole story. There was another lesson to be learned. God was merciful. The next section of the sermon addresses this truth.[32]

Lesson from the Future (4:25-31)

Idolatry Will Result in Exile (4:25-28)

For the next lesson of the sermon Moses took a look into the future. With his understanding of human nature and his understanding of the heart of God he contemplated both Israel's apostasy and God's mercy.[33]

4:25 The look into the future spanned several generations, not necessarily just two as the NIV suggests (**grandchildren**). The conditional **if you become corrupt** (NIV) is one possible understanding of the Hebrew text. "When you become corrupt" is another possibility. "Should you" become corrupt (offered by Weinfeld)[34] seems better. The corruption was the moral corruption of idolatry (see v. 16; 9:12; 31:29; 32:5). From what Moses says elsewhere in Deuteronomy, this deviation seems almost a certainty, though it was the very thing forbidden in verses 15 and 23 (same words).

God was **provoked to anger** by apostasy through idolatry (32:16,21; 1 Kgs 14:9,15; 16:33; 22:53; 2 Kgs 17:11,17; Jer 7:18,19; Ps 78:58 – parallel with making God jealous[35]). From the past the golden calf incident was a prime example (Exod 32; Deut 9:18-19) of the people's disobedience and God's anger.

4:26 If such a thing should happen, God had witnesses to call to testify to his swift judgment. In ancient Near Eastern treaties, witnesses were called to authenticate and solemnize the agreement. They were usually the gods, but sometimes the heavens and earth. There could be no other gods as witnesses within Israel's worldview.

---

[32]Wright, *Deuteronomy*, p. 53: there are two ways to find God in verses 24 and 31. Through rebellion he is found as a consuming fire, but through repentance he is found as a merciful God.

[33]The covenant lawsuit pattern where God brings a charge against the covenant people seems to be presupposed here although the technical word *rîb* is not used (see Jer. 2:4-13). See Merrill, *Deuteronomy*, pp. 126-127.

[34]Weinfeld, *Deuteronomy*, p. 194.

[35]God's jealousy means his zeal for the faithfulness of his people, not a human emotion of possessiveness.

Therefore, the **heavens and earth** were called upon because they would endure forever and would testify in the future about past warnings and events (Deut 30:18-19; 31:28; Isa 1:2; Jer 2:12).

Disobedience would reverse the direction of their present history. Just as God was bringing them into the land to **possess** it, he could take them out of it. This would overthrow everything that made them the treasured possession of God.

4:27 Exile would be the consequence. **Scattering** as a divine judgment goes back to Genesis 10 and 11. The later covenant curses saw exile as the consequence of disobedience (28:36,64; 29:28; Lev 26:33). The seventh century prophets Jeremiah and Ezekiel lived to see the reality of these covenant curses (Jer 9:16; 10:20; 13:24; 23:1-2; Ezek 11:16; 12:15; 34:5,21).[36]

That only a **few . . . will survive** indicates a grim reversal of the promise to the patriarchs (Gen 15:5; 17:6). They had become great in number (Exod 1:7; Deut 1:10) and would continue to grow (Deut 7:13; 13:17) but not if they disobeyed.

4:28 The great tragedy was that in exile they would be forced to worship the pagan gods. It was as if God said, "You have chosen this path, now live with it." The exchange of gods is astounding. In the place of the God who was alive, who provided, led, saved, and spoke, they would serve inanimate pieces of **wood and stone** that possessed none of the senses.[37] The punishment fit the crime: if they ignored what they heard and saw, they would worship what could not see or hear.[38] Nor, Moses could have added for effect, could they speak. Because of the effect of the worshiped on the worshiper, Israel could become just like those gods, not hearing, seeing, or understanding (Isa 6:9-10).

Many scholars cannot see how this passage could come from any time other than after the exile. However, it is not difficult to understand how the wise Moses, who knew the covenant God better than

---

[36]Beyond the scattering there was the hope of "gathering" which also appears as a strong theme in Jeremiah (32:3-4) and Ezekiel (11:17; 20:34,41; 28:25).

[37]This sermon is far removed from the modern world where tolerance is the highest value and the mantra, "all gods/religions are the same" is often heard.

[38]Tigay, *Deuteronomy*, pp. 52-53.

any, could look into the future and contemplate the consequences of Israel not choosing to obey the covenant.[39] He had long years of experience with their rebelliousness already, and he was fully aware of the covenant curses yet to be explained. This sermon is his mature reflection on these crucial issues. Furthermore, he was the first and foremost of all the prophets (18:15; 34:10-12).

Lesson: You Can Return to God (4:29-31)

A future exile would not be the end of Israel. Even in those awful circumstances they could learn something about God. They could discover that a return to God was possible because of his nature. The present generation could learn this lesson as well.

4:29 The Hebrew text has only one **if**, in the second half of the verse. It seems to take the seeking as a given, "From there you will seek the LORD your God and you will find him if . . . ."

Seeking the LORD was foundational to having a proper relationship with him and is a consistent OT theme. Here it is united with repentance (v. 30; cf. Hos 3:5). To seek God properly they must turn around. The words **seek** and **look** are synonymous. In many texts seeking God is the way of identifying faithfulness (1 Chr 28:9; 2 Chr 15:2,15). Not seeking God is synonymous with breaking the covenant (1 Chr 10:13-14; Isa 8:19; Jer 8:2). If God were sought, he could be found (1 Chr 28:9; Jer 29:13). However, there might be a time when he could not be found (Isa 55:6). The seeking, however, must be wholehearted, that is, **with all your heart and with all your soul**. God demanded complete devotion from Israel (Deut 6:5; 11:13; 10:12-13; 30:1-3,10) and a return to him could demand no less. "Heart and soul" refers to the sincere, wholehearted turning of the intellect and will, with the deepest of inner desire and undivided devotion.[40]

4:30 The only true recourse for relief from the **distress** they would experience was rescue by God (2 Chr 15:3-4; Ps 106:40-46). This kind of distress was specifically caused by covenant breaking (Deut 31:17,21).

---

[39]In addition, Moses was inspired by God.

[40]"Soul" is not the best translation. "Life" or "inner being" would reflect the Hebrew more accurately. See Tigay, *Deuteronomy*, p. 77; D.C. Fredericks, "נֶפֶשׁ," *NIDOTTE*, 3:133-134. The modern idea of an immortal soul does not fit the Hebrew concept of *nepheš*.

So they must **return**, that is, repent. The word *šûb* used here is a theologically loaded term that refers both to turning away from God (apostasy) and returning to him (repentance). It is a concrete word that gives vivid meaning to the abstract idea of repentance (cf. Deut 30:1-10; Jer 29:11-14). Israel must make an abrupt about face and return to God.[41]

4:31 They could return to God because he was **merciful**. This was a major characteristic of God grounded in his very nature as first revealed in Exodus 34:6-7. "Merciful" is used 13 times of God in the OT, 11 of those connected with "gracious." It described the warm compassion of God who was ready to forgive and ready to replace judgment with grace.[42] This was a picture of a God who hangs on to his people even when they have rebelled and have broken the covenant.[43]

God could not himself **abandon** the **covenant** because he had promised with an **oath** that he would keep it (Gen 15:12-21; 17:1-8; Lev 26:40-45; Deut 1:8; 7:12). Israel might **forget** but he never would.

4. The Lord Is Unique (4:32-39)

This section ends the sermon by returning to the theme of verses 5-8, the uniqueness and greatness of the subject, in this case God (in the former text it was Israel). The two key words in the two sections are the same: "greatness" and "nations." This section functions as the climax to the first four chapters; the end toward which they have been moving. It is presented in three parts: the setting, marked by four rhetorical questions, verses 32-34; the main statement, verses 35-38; and the exhortation, verse 39. Similar concepts appear in Deuteronomy 7:6-11 and 10:12–11:19.

4:32 The first section is a series of questions intended to elicit a reflective answer from the audience. They were encouraged to compare their situation in relationship with their God with that of

---

[41]J.A. Thompson and Elmer A. Martens, "שׁוּב," *NIDOTTE,* 4:55-59. The classical study is by William Holliday, *The Root shûb in the Old Testament* (Leiden: Brill, 1958).

[42]Exodus 34:6-7 is repeatedly reflected in other parts of the OT: Ps 86:15; 103:8; 145:8; Joel 2:13; Jonah 4:2; Neh 9:17.

[43]Mike Butterworth, "רחם," *NIDOTTE,* 3:1093-1095.

the other nations. In every case they should discover the uniqueness of their situation.

They were to begin their search by reflecting on all of time and all of space. The **former days** refers not just to the days of the ancestors (as in 32:7) but to the very beginning, back to creation. They were to also search all of space known to them. The **ends of the heavens** included the universe as they could imagine it. The two phrases "the ends of the heavens" and "the ends of the earth" apparently meant the same (Deut 28:29; Isa 13:5). This was a phenomenological, not a scientific, way of speaking. In Genesis 1:1 the universe is referred to by the merism, heavens and earth.[44]

4:33 Moses returned to the emphasis on the **voice of God** (vv. 10, 12,30,36) which is a major theme of this chapter. There are texts that speak of the danger of seeing God (Exod 33:20), but here we learn for the first time that it was dangerous to hear the voice of God also. This question was easy for Israel to answer in the negative, for Moses had already established that the nation's idols could not even see, hear, eat, or smell (v. 28; cf. vv. 7-8).

4:34 These questions follow the macrostructure of the OT, for there was first a question about creation (32), and then revelation (33), and now redemption. The wonderful signs of God's acts in redeeming Israel from Egypt were proof of his superiority and victory over Pharaoh and his gods. These signs are used over and over in Deuteronomy as proof of God's power (6:22; 7:19; 11:2-3; 26:8). **A mighty hand and an outstretched arm** are common idioms in the Pentateuch for the display of God's power in the Exodus (Exod 3:20; 6:1,6; 7:4-5; 9:15; also see the Deuteronomy texts listed immediately above). This power of God was demonstrated before their **very eyes**. They could not see the LORD and live, but they could see his mighty acts on their behalf. Thus his greatness was manifested before them. These acts were visible and experiential, not abstract or mythological.

4:35 Verses 35-38 draw out the implications of the rhetorical questions: Israel's God was absolutely unique. Israel could **know** this in an experiential, not just intellectual, sense. Moses desired to deepen their conviction of God's power and presence in their lives.

---

[44]A merism is two opposite words used to stand for a totality.

There is no other is one of the strongest statements of monotheism in the Old Testament. This Hebrew phrase is found only in Deuteronomy, Isaiah (45:5,6,14,18,21,22; 46:9), 1 Kings (8:60), and Joel (2:27).[45] The affinity with the strong statements in Isaiah has led some scholars to think Deuteronomy's assertion is late.[46] But similar statements occur in early poetic texts such as Exodus 15:1-8 and Deuteronomy 32:1-43. "Monotheism in Israel was not the conclusion of an evolution of religious speculation, but an assertion generated out of historical experience and grounded there."[47]

4:36 The emphasis is on the spoken word of God again, expressed in two parallel expressions. Israel was made to **hear his voice** and they **heard his words**. These phrases are synonymous in meaning though one took place **from heaven** and the other **on earth**. Some find conflicting traditions here about how God spoke to Israel — it was either from heaven or on earth.[48] However, more likely these phrases reflect the difficulty of expressing God's transcendence and immanence at the same time. The **fire** from which he spoke is the language of theophany of chapter 3 and Exodus 19 and 24.

Knowing God meant more than mere intellectual knowledge. Thus God spoke to Israel for her **discipline**. This was not a negative concept as in some texts, but reflected the educational purpose of God's words (cf. 8:5). The consequence was a changed way of life, living in obedience to his commandments.

---

[45]For the same idea in Deuteronomy but different language see 6:4; 7:9; 32:12.

[46]Mayes, *Deuteronomy*, p. 158; Driver, *Deuteronomy*, pp. 90-91; Georg Braulik, "Deuteronomy and the Birth of Monotheism," in *The Theology of Deuteronomy*, ed., Georg Braulik (N. Richland Hills, TX: BIBAL Press, 1994), pp. 87-130. According to Alexander Rofe, Deut 4:32-40 was composed during the exile ("The Monotheism Argumentation in Deuteronomy IV:32-40: Contents, Composition, and Text," *VT* 35 [1985]: 434-445).

[47]Wright, *Deuteronomy*, p. 55. For Tigay, practical monotheism goes back to Moses (*Deuteronomy*, pp. 433-435). It was a "de facto" monotheism in which Israel understood that only the LORD was an independently effective power. The teacher of the law, who responded to Jesus' question about the two greatest commandments, alluded to this verse. God's oneness also meant his uniqueness (Mark 12:32).

[48]From investigating the texts about the experience at Sinai some scholars think one tradition has the LORD coming down to Sinai (Exod 19:11,20; 24) while the other tradition has him speaking from heaven only (Exod 20:22). See Weinfeld, *Deuteronomy*, pp. 212-213.

4:37 Two of the most important covenantal terms in the Old Testament are combined in this verse: **loved** and **chose**. It was God's love for their ancestors Abraham, Isaac, and Jacob that motivated the Exodus. This proved his election love even though covenant texts about the patriarchs in Genesis never used the word.

It was God's love that motivated everything he did for Israel. Christians are mistaken if they believe only the New Testament teaches God's love. The concept is firmly embedded in the teaching of Deuteronomy (7:8,12,13; 10:15; 23:5; 33:3) and elsewhere (Hos 11:1; Jer 31:3; Mal 1:2; 2:11). Of the thirty-two times in the Old Testament that God is the subject of love, Israel or Jerusalem is the object twenty-five times. The verb is also used for the people loving God twenty-two times, twelve times in Deuteronomy. The concept is the background to two important metaphors in the Old Testament, the father-son imagery (Hos 11:1) and the marriage imagery (Hos 2–3; Jer 2). The former image is common in Deuteronomy (8:5; 14:1; 32:5,19,20; cf. Exod 4:22, "Israel is my firstborn son"; Jer 3:19). This imagery, or course, carries through into the New Testament. This love was not an emotion but a product of the will that fostered commitment and loyalty. That is why it could be commanded (6:5). It was one of the most important foundations of the covenant.[49]

Bringing out from Egypt with **his great strength** is parallel to the idiom "mighty hand and outstretched arm" in verse 34. "Strength" is translated better as "power." It is a common term associated with the exodus (Exod 32:11; Num 14:13; Deut 9:29; Neh 1:10; 2 Kgs 17:36).

4:38 The purpose of God's love for and election of the descendants of the patriarchs was to give them the land. The technical language for receiving that land that has appeared before is used here also. The land was intended as the place where Israel should live in obedience to the covenant and experience peace and comfort.

Since it was a land full of **greater and stronger nations** than Israel (7:1; 9:1,14), it was only by God's power that she could hope to possess it. In fact, Moses suggested Israel was the smallest of nations (7:7).

---

[49]In ancient Near Eastern treaties love was required of the vassal, which was equal to loyalty; see W.L. Moran, "The Ancient Near Eastern Background to the Love of God in Deuteronomy," *CBQ* 25 (1963): 77-87. See also P.J.J.S. Els, "אהב," *NIDOTTE*, 1:277-299, especially pp. 279-283 and H. Seebass, "בחר," *TDOT*, 2:73-87.

But through God's sovereignty over all the nations, the new generation could stand poised to experience the same power of God that
brought their fathers out of Egypt. The land was clearly a gift of grace
and proof of Israel's unique relationship with her unique God.

4:39 Therefore, the conclusion was that Israel should **acknowledge** that their LORD was the only unique God. There were none like
him in the whole universe. This conviction was a heart issue. It
involved the whole person. It was not primarily intellectual. The consequence is spelled out in verse 40. It was not reflective essays that
should result, but obedience.

5. Exhortation to Obey (4:40)

4:40 The sermon in this chapter concludes where it began, with
a call for obedience so that Israel could live in the land (see verses
1-4). The promise was that things would **go well**. This is a common
phrase in Deuteronomy and refers to material well being (5:16,26;
6:3,18; 12:25,28, etc.). Rewards for obedience in the Old Testament
were both spiritual and physical: a significant relationship with God
and a good life in the good land (chapter 8). The further promise
was long life (see on 11:9; cf. 5:16,33; 6:2, etc.) and possession of the
land. Only the gracious, unique, sovereign, loving God of Israel
could make such promises because only he could carry them out.

D. CITIES OF REFUGE (4:41-43)

These verses take up an important aspect of Israel's life in the
land that was also addressed several other places (Num 35:6-34;
Deut 19:1-14; Josh 20:1-9). They seem out of place here since verse
40 ends the sermon quite well and verses 44-49 provide an introduction to chapter 5 and the Decalogue. However, to attribute them
to a later editor does not solve much, for on what basis would a later
scribe think they should be placed here?[50] On the positive side they
do take care of a piece of unfinished business concerning the two
and one-half tribes who were given the Transjordan area. Before he

---

[50]Driver, *Deuteronomy*, p. 78; Mayes, *Deuteronomy*, p. 159; von Rad, *Deuteronomy*, p. 51.

died, Moses made sure he provided for them the same refuge cities that were provided for the tribes in the promised land in Deuteronomy 19:1-14. In fact, the latter text seems to presuppose the former.[51] The promise of long life in the land (v. 40) included places of refuge and safety. From a rhetorical perspective, this is the first mention of Moses by name (v. 41) since 1:1-5. Therefore these verses nicely round off the first section in Deuteronomy (1:1–4:43).

4:41-42 The simple statement in Exodus 21:13 that refers to a place God will designate assumes the later appointment of cities of refuge (for fuller comment see the commentary on Deuteronomy 19:1-14). The cities were for those who had accidentally killed someone. The NIV **without malice aforethought** translates the Hebrew "he had not hated him before." (see 19:4). Thus a clear distinction was made between premeditated murder (5:17) and an accident. An example is given in chapter 19. The law was directed at the ancient practice of blood revenge in which the next of kin had a right to avenge a death, accidental or otherwise.[52]

4:43 The cities were named, but all three locations are uncertain. Scholars have, however, come to some basic agreement about them. They were in the south, central, and north regions of the Transjordan and were thus accessible to the transjordanian tribes.[53] The ninth century king of Moab, Mesha, says in his inscription on the Mesha stone that he rebuilt **Bezer**.[54]

Ramoth in Gilead was strategically located on the main road between Ammon and Damascus and was an area of major conflict between Israel and the Arameans (1 Kgs 22; 2 Kgs 9). It was also the capital of Solomon's sixth district (1 Kgs 4:13).

II. THE SECOND SPEECH OF MOSES (4:44–29:1)

We now come to Moses' second speech which includes the major portion of the book. This section is rounded off in 29:1 (which is

---

[51]Weinfeld, *Deuteronomy*, p. 233, against Mayes, *Deuteronomy*, p. 159.

[52]This principle still operates in many Middle Eastern countries and is a matter of honor. Once the cycle begins how can it be halted?

[53]See the discussion by Weinfeld, *Deuteronomy*, pp. 231-232.

[54]See D. Winton Thomas (ed.), *Documents from Old Testament Times* (New York: Harper and Row, 1958), pp. 196-197.

28:69 in the Hebrew text) with another reference to the covenant law, indicating that the section of additional laws was ending. This second speech can be divided into two subdivisions, chapters 5–11 and 12–29:1. The first part, chapters 5–11, contains the Decalogue, the people's immediate response (5), and then extended reflection on the first commandment (6–11). The second part, chapters 12–29:1, contains reflection on and expansion of the remainder of the ten commandments (see outline in Introduction). This part has its beginning in 12:1 marked with the stereotypical reference to the "decrees and laws" that we find in the first four chapters. A useful title for the second speech could be "Exposition of the Law."[55]

INTRODUCTION (4:44-49)

Verses 44-49 serve as an introduction to the second speech and also as a transition from the first speech. The verses use much of the formulaic language we have already encountered and repeat the geographical setting by briefly summarizing the narrative accounts in 2:24–3:11. In many ways these verses review 1:1-5 to remind the reader of the original introduction to the book after the long historical reflection in 1:6–4:40.

4:44 In 1:5 we are told that Moses began to "expound this law." Now he will **set the law before** them (see comments on *tôrāh* on 1:5), that is, present it to them. He refers here to the total teaching of God, not just the Decalogue.

4:45 The law is further defined with three technical terms adding here **stipulations** to the other two words Moses had already used in 4:1,5,14 (see 6:1; 11:1,32; 12:1, etc.;[56] see comments on 4:1).[57]

---

[55]Weinfeld, *Deuteronomy*, p. 234.

[56]The NIV translation is misleading. It translates both *tôrāh* and *mišpātîm* as "law." It would be clearer to translate the latter as "ordinances" (NRSV) or "judgments" or some such term.

[57]Weinfeld points out that it is the custom of Deuteronomy to make a general statement followed by a more specific one as here; see also Deut 5:28 (*Deuteronomy*, p. 235).

DEUTERONOMY 5

GENERAL STIPULATIONS

A. THE TEN COMMANDMENTS (5:1-21)

Ancient Near Eastern treaties included sections that laid obligations on the vassal nation. These were called stipulations. They could be general or specific. Chapter 5 initiates the stipulation portion of Deuteronomy, beginning with ten general laws. More specific legislation is presented in the second portion of Moses' second speech, chapters 12-29:1.

It was important that the divine origin of the laws be emphasized. In other ancient countries the laws were the products of the people. The king was often pictured as receiving the laws from the god (see the Code of Hammurabi stele) but he was still the one who turned what he received into law.

Since covenant preceded law, it was important that Moses begin with a statement about the covenant before getting to law. Therefore, the first verses in this section (v. 1-5) provide the setting for the Decalogue.

5:1 The people were called together into a solemn assembly (the technical meaning of **summon**; see Num 10:3; Deut 29:2) to hear the word of God. The language is very close to 4:1. The emphasis here, however, was on the people **learning** the law rather than Moses teaching it (though the Hebrew word is the same). The spoken word was central.[1] Israel was to **hear** it (4:1). Hear equals "obey" in this kind of context.

---

[1]The root, דבר (*dbr*, "speak") occurs 65 times in Deuteronomy while the corresponding noun, דָּבָר (*dābār*, "word, words") occurs 96 times. The other verb for "speak, say" (אמר, *'mr*) occurs 141 times with either God or man as the subject.

5:2-3 Ancient treaties were regularly renewed and updated. Likewise the covenant between the LORD and Israel must be renewed. The emphasis was on the present generation receiving the covenant as their own as if they had been at the original event at Sinai. This presentation could be effective because community solidarity was at work. The covenant was made with the whole nation, not particular individuals. Individuals may pass on, but the nation continued, providing the continuity (cf. 4:10; 11:2-7; 29:12-15). However, each generation must pledge its loyalty to the covenant stipulations. This concept has continued even today in the modern Jewish Passover celebration. The liturgy in the Passover Haggadah reads, "It was not only our fathers that the Holy One . . . redeemed, but us as well did he redeem along with them."[2]

Our fathers has been interpreted in two ways. Some view it as being the original generation that gathered at Mt. Horeb (Sinai).[3] Others understand the "fathers" to be the patriarchs of Genesis: Abraham, Isaac, and Jacob. Since every reference to "our/your fathers" in Deuteronomy (with the possible exception of 13:6) points to the patriarchs (cf. 1:8; 4:31,37; 7:8,12; 8:18; 9:5, etc.), the latter position seems correct. Therefore, a contrast is being made between a covenant of grace, dependent on the divine promise to give offspring, land, and blessing, and the Sinaitic (Mosaic) covenant which carried the obligation of obedience to the law.[4]

5:4-5 Are these verses in conflict? Did God speak directly to Israel, or through Moses? Verse 4 speaks of a direct encounter between God and Israel, **face to face.** Yet other texts tell us that only Moses had a face-to-face relationship with God (Exod 33:11; Deut 34:10). Also in the book of Exodus Israel did not go near Mt. Sinai; only Moses went up (Exod 19:12,20-23; 20:15).

Verse 5 seems to remove the discrepancy. Moses was the chosen mediator between God and Israel (5:23-31). Therefore, what God said to Moses he was in effect saying directly to Israel. The divine face-to-face encounter with Moses was as if the nation encountered

[2]Nahum Glazer, ed., *The Passover Haggadah* (New York: Schocken Books, 1969), p. 49.

[3]Mayes, *Deuteronomy*, p. 165; Wright, *Deuteronomy*, p. 62.

[4]Weinfeld, *Deuteronomy*, p. 239; Merrill, *Deuteronomy*, p. 141.

him in the same way, for Moses was a faithful, true mediator.[5] We cannot underestimate Moses' unique and profound place in God's plan for Israel. However, above all it was still the personal relationship between God and Israel that was being emphasized.

5:6 The Decalogue begins in verse 6 with a brief introduction. This verse in effect is another historical prologue, giving the bare minimum of historical information. God's redemption of Israel from **slavery** in Egypt was the greatest of all his salvation acts in history (until the death and resurrection of the Messiah) and marks the moment when they became his people. This event formed the foundation for God's claim on Israel and thus the basis for the covenant law that follows.

The Decalogue is never called "the Ten Commandments" in the Hebrew Bible. It is "the ten words" (Exod 34:28; Deut 4:13; 10:4), or "the words" (Deut 5:22; 9:10) or "these words" (Exod 20:1).[6] We can conclude that these ten statements were not understood in the same way as the rest of the covenant law. They were divine words by direct revelation, not legalistic formulations. They were not abstract moral principles, but a list of fundamental, concrete demands. Since they are in the second person singular they applied to every Israelite.[7]

There are two kinds of law formulations in the Pentateuch. One is called *apodictic* law and is characterized by a direct command, "you shall," or by a negative command, "you shall not." This is the type we find in the Decalogue.[8] It does not include a sanction for noncompliance. The second is called *casuistic* and is marked by an "if . . . then" style, what is sometimes called case-law. This kind predominates in Deuteronomy 12:1–26:19 (and Exod 22:1–23:33). It includes specific sanctions for noncompliance.[9] The apodictic emphasize the

---

[5]Some scholars find this harmonization too simple. They prefer to accept a contradiction between Deuteronomy and Exodus at this point. In this view verse 5 is a later gloss to resolve the problem, not an original explanation. See Weinfeld, *Deuteronomy*, pp. 240-241; Mayes, *Deuteronomy*, p. 166.

[6]They are never designated by one of the technical words such as statute, commandment, judgment, or decree. The NIV is misleading when it translates "words" as "Commandments" in several of the verses listed.

[7]Weinfeld, *Deuteronomy*, p. 250.

[8]There are other apodictic collections in the OT also: Exod 34:12-26; Lev 19:1-4,11-19,26-37; Deut 27:15-26; Ezek 18:5-9; Ps 15:2-5.

[9]See Merrill, *Deuteronomy*, pp. 144-145 and footnotes there for a conven-

absolute nature of the statement, the casuistic the conditional nature of the law. Apodictic type laws are almost unique to Israel. They are rarely found in ancient Near Eastern law codes.

The Decalogue is customarily divided into two parts. The first explicates the vertical relationship between God and his people and demands exclusive loyalty to God. The second half explicates the horizontal relationship between the people and is concerned with social and moral conduct. The division into two parts has usually been made between the fourth and fifth commandments. But a good case can be made for division between commandments five and six.[10] The first five contain the phrase "the LORD your God," the second five do not. The fifth commandment, verse 16 concerns honor for parents. This demand goes more readily with the first four which demand honor for God since parents (as was God) were in a superior position of authority in the community. The fifth commandment also functions as a transition commandment to the second five that deal with interpersonal relationships.[11]

The commandments also have received different enumeration in Jewish and Christian traditions. The early Jewish leaders Philo and Josephus, the church fathers, and Protestantism in general have understood verses 6-7 as the first commandment, verses 8-10 as the second, the others in order, and verse 21 as one, thus giving ten. Augustine, the Roman Catholic Church, and the Lutherans have understood the first commandment to be verses 6-10, and the 9th and 10th commandments to be found in verse 21. Coveting the neighbor's wife is separated from coveting the neighbor's possessions. Some Jewish traditions have taken verse 6 as the first and verses 7-10 as the second.[12]

---

ient discussion with documentation. A. Alt established this distinction only in the 20th century but it has been widely accepted.

[10]Weinfeld, *Deuteronomy*, p. 245; Tigay, *Deuteronomy*, p. 62.

[11]Often the motivation to divide the law into two halves comes from the mistaken belief that the two stone tablets contained one-half each. The two tablets represented two copies, one for Israel and one for God. Nevertheless, it is legitimate to recognize two different emphases in the Decalogue.

[12]See Walter Harrelson, *The Ten Commandments and Human Rights* (Philadelphia: Fortress, 1980), p. 47, for a convenient chart. To make matters even more complex the accentuation tradition in the Massoretic Text of the Hebrew Bible presents two different versifications. The alternate versification considers commandments 6 through 9 as one verse, verse 17.

A comparison with Exodus 20:2-17 reveals a few small differences and one significant difference between its wording and Deuteronomy 5:6-21. These will be noted as necessary below.

5:7 The first word is grounded in the uniqueness of God already expressed in 4:33-35,39. It is a simple statement of God's exclusive claim on Israel. He alone was Israel's God. The commandment implies a positive side: they were to be totally faithful to God. This was a relationship based on their prior experience with God who had proven his loyalty to them.

This prohibition is unique to Israel. Polytheism accepted other gods and worshiped them side by side, an impossibility in Israel (the most likely meaning of **before me** is "at the side of me"). Israel's God was not part of a pantheon. Therefore, pluralism was not possible. There was only one God who had done what the Lord had done for Israel, therefore there was no possibility that some other deity could be a different, but similar, god.[13] **Other gods** included the Canaanite fertility gods that so severely tempted Israel after she moved into the land.[14]

This word is the foundation of all the other words (commandments). It is the essential formulation for building up the community of God's people.

5:8-10[15] The second "word" forms the basis for the extensive discussion already presented in 4:9-24 (see comments there). God could not be represented in any way, for he was the Creator, not a part of the created world. He was also invisible. The polytheistic world was again quite different, having no reservations about representing their deities in both human and animal form.

---

[13]In the New Testament, God is defined by Jesus Christ, who calls himself the "I am." Therefore, he is the only way to God for no one has ever done what he did.

[14]"Other gods" is a favorite term of Deuteronomy and Deuteronomy-influenced texts for referring to the false/no gods to whom Israel was willing to bow down. Just a sampling of the numerous references includes: Deut 6:14; 7:4; 11:16; 13:2; 28:14; 30:17; Josh 23:16; Judg 2:17; 1 Kgs 9:9; 11:4; 2 Kgs 17:7; Jer 1:16; 7:6; 11:10; 22:9.

[15]There is good textual evidence for seeing two prohibitions here: do "not make for yourself an idol *or* the form of anything . . ." based on several ancient Hebrew manuscripts, a Deuteronomy manuscript from Qumran and two ancient translations.

God's jealousy was a function of his exclusive covenant loyalty to Israel. He deeply cared for his people and expected exclusive loyalty in return.

Because of his loyalty, God rewarded loyalty in Israel or punished disloyalty. Verses 9 and 10 are not stating some inexorable law of divine determinism, but expressing the greatness of God's mercy and love. Punishment for disloyalty was limited (**third or fourth generation**) while the reward for faithfulness was lengthy (**to thousands**; cf. 7:9, "to thousands of generations"). Family solidarity concepts inform our understanding of these statements. Extended families included three generations or more. If the patriarch rejected God, the entire family would suffer guilt. Further, the younger generations would suffer from the lack of education in the covenant law and from the godless environment. It was likely also that the deprived generations would continue in the sins of the fathers. In contrast faithfulness carried its reward and made covenant faithfulness and blessing possible for generations.[16] The **love** that God would show was his special covenant loyalty (חֶסֶד, ḥesed) or covenant faithfulness that he demonstrated toward Israel. This is a theologically loaded word. It describes God's grace or unmerited favor he demonstrated to Israel by choosing them as his people. It also describes his continuing grace he will show toward them; a grace necessary for their survival. It is the kind of covenant love that overcomes wrath as well (cf. Deut 9:10 with 10:10 and Isa 54:8; Micah 7:18).[17]

5:11 The first two words were in the first person. The text now switches to the third person. It is difficult to tell if this command deals with making false oaths or with making empty (vain) oaths (literally, "lift up his name for a lie"). The former seems more likely since the ninth commandment, which deals with false testimony (v. 20), uses the same word for **false**.

It was not forbidden to swear by God's name (Deut 6:13; 10:20), but it was forbidden to make a false oath in his name (Lev 19:12). Jeremiah 7:9 certainly understood this commandment to mean taking a false oath (NIV, "perjury").

---

[16]However, Deut 7:10; Jer 31:28; and Ezek 18 oppose the idea of an intergenerational personal guilt that could be passed on.

[17]See D.A. Baer and R.R. Gordon, "חסד," *NIDOTTE*, 2:211-18.

Further, since the **name** of the LORD carried the same weight as reference to the Lord himself, the commandment could refer to misusing his name for personal gain. In the ancient Near East this would have meant using his name for magical arts or divination, both common practices among the nations.[18]

5:12-15[19] The Deuteronomic version of this word contains the most significant difference from the Exodus version of any of the commandments. That difference is contained in the reason for observing the Sabbath (cf. v. 15 with Exod 20:11). In Exodus the reason was grounded in creation, here it is grounded in the Exodus. These are not contradictory reasons, but complementary, and suggest the Sabbath reflected multiple purposes. It was a day to contemplate both divine creation and divine redemption. There is no parallel to this kind of day in ancient Near Eastern cultures. Other nations had special days but they were usually bound up with rhythms in nature and were not work-free.

Israel was to honor God by keeping the Sabbath day holy. God had consecrated the day (set it apart) in Genesis 2:3 and had rested. The word Sabbath derives from a root שׁבת (*šbt*) that means "to stop, cease, rest." It was a day not only for Israel but also for servants and aliens. All the people should rest in imitation of God, not just Israelites. Further, Israelites must be compassionate to their servants because they had experienced God's compassion (see also 15:15; 16:12; 24:18,22). The command thus served as a brake on socioeconomic oppression and exploitation. That is why when the classical prophets condemned Sabbath breaking, they also attacked economic exploitation (Amos 8:4-6; Isa 58:13-14). The Sabbath year, which built on the Sabbath concept and occurred every seventh year, was a year for canceling debts and freeing slaves, that is, a year for reversing economic oppression (Deut 15:1-18).

---

[18]The commandment could probably be stretched even further to refer to vain worship of God, that is, worship that was corrupt or empty. The modern practice of associating this commandment with cursing or swearing by using God's name was not a part of the ancient concept. Israel and other nations took their gods too seriously to engage in that kind of blasphemy. However, it does not violate an expanded meaning to apply the commandment to such modern profanity.

[19]The fourth and fifth commandments, which center on honor of God and parents are the only two stated positively.

Work is not defined here or elsewhere in the Old Testament though there are a few texts that offer hints (Exod 16:23-26: gathering manna; 34:21: plowing and harvesting; 35:3: kindling a fire; Amos 8:5 and Jer 17:19-27: doing business; Isa 58:13: personal pleasure). In ancient agrarian societies every facet of life, even providing daily food, required intensive labor. A day to cease from those labors would have been a welcome relief.[20]

Work and what it produces were intended for the benefit of God's people. But both could become idolatrous if they became an end in themselves.[21]

Permitted activities on the Sabbath were offering sacrifices (Num 28:9-10; Lev 24:8), visiting sanctuaries (Isa 1:13), singing (Ps 92), and expressing joy (Isa 58:13). The Sabbath could be profaned by desecrating it with work (Exod 31:14), offering sacrifices while living in sin (Isa 1:10-17), doing evil (Isa 56:2), or being disobedient (Ezek 20:13,21).

Jesus took on the legalistic interpretation of the Sabbath in his day in order to restore it to its rightful use (Matt 12:1-13; John 7:21-24). It was a day made for people, not vice versa (Mark 2:27). Under the new covenant, observing special days was an individual choice (Rom 14:5-9; Col 2:16). The church gathering to worship on Sunday is appropriate, for the first day of the week looks back to Jesus' redemptive act, his resurrection. However, to observe Sunday as a Christian Sabbath violates freedom in Christ.[22] The look back to redemption occasioned by the Sabbath is balanced in the New

---

[20]Since the instructions for building the tabernacle in Exod 25:1–31:11 were followed immediately by instructions for the Sabbath in 31:12-17, the Jewish Rabbis concluded that the 39 classes of work needed to build the tabernacle were what was forbidden (Mishna Shab. 7:2-4). See Miller, *Deuteronomy*, pp. 80-83 for helpful reflections on the Sabbath idea.

[21]This has occurred in the modern American culture where people are defined by their work ("What do you do?") and workaholism is a recognized behavior.

[22]However, the Sabbath idea as a day of personal rest and refreshment for the Christian can be an important part of the Christian life. See the work of Eugene Peterson: "Confessions of a Former Sabbath Breaker," *CT* 32 (Sept 2, 1988): 25-28; "Rhythm of Grace," *Weavings* 8 (Mar-Apr 1993): 14-19; "The Good-for-nothing Sabbath," *CT* 38 (Apr 4, 1994): 34-36. *Perspectives* 11 (Mar 1996) has several articles on the Sabbath from the perspective of different Christian and Jewish traditions.

Testament by a look ahead to the ultimate rest that God's people will inherit (Heb 4:1-11).

5:16 The fifth "word" is the only one with a promise attached (Eph 6:2): long life. But the promise was also an implied threat of short life if not obeyed. This commandment, as all the others, was addressed to the adults in Israel. It is to be understood within the social context of the extended family structure of that culture. The elder patriarch and matriarch were to be given their rightful places of respect. This honor was to be expressed in tangible ways, though few guidelines were spelled out. Obedience was most often mentioned (Deut 21:18-21; Prov 1:8-9; 30:17). The parallel law in Leviticus 19:3 uses "respect" (lit. "fear") in place of **honor** indicating the terms are synonymous.

This commandment was important because the family was the basic social, economic, and spiritual unit in Israel. A threat to the family meant a threat to the covenant relationship and national survival. Therefore, rebellious children were punished with death (Deut 21:18-21; 22:20-21).

The promise meant that those who cared for their parents would live long enough to experience the same care by their children. The promise of long life in the **land** provides a fitting conclusion to the first five commandments (see on 11:9; cf. 4:40; 5:33; 6:2, etc.). Life in the Promised Land was contrasted to life in the "land of slavery" in verse 6 thus providing an envelope for the first half of the Decalogue.

The commandment offers a paradigm for the social health of a nation that Christians must take seriously. Social policies that threaten to undermine the economic and physical well-being of families need to be critically assessed.[23]

5:17 This word begins the second half of the Decalogue. Deuteronomy connects all of the second five with "and." The first three have no objects and consist of just two words each in Hebrew.

The NIV correctly translated this commandment **You shall not murder.** The prohibition was against premeditated killing, not just any killing. This commandment is grounded in Genesis 1:26-27 and 9:6. God was the creator of life and thus the only one allowed to take it. Thus God was absolute, not the sanctity of life.[24]

---

[23]Wright, *Deuteronomy*, p. 78.

[24]Wright, *Deuteronomy*, p. 79. The point is that it is not life as an ultimate,

Murder was a capital crime, for which the penalty was death (Exod 21:12; Lev 24:17; Num 35:30). There were other capital crimes as well (Exod 21:15-17). However, not all taking of human life was of the same order and not all was forbidden. A distinction was made between murder and accidental killing (Deut 19:4-6). The cities of refuge were provided for this latter crime (4:41-43; 19:1-13). In Israel the victim's family could not be monetarily compensated for the death (Num 35:31) as in other cultures, for life was a priceless gift from God.[25]

The narrative sections of the Old Testament relate several murders that illuminate the kind of emotions that could cause such an act. They record jealousy (Gen 4), lust (2 Sam 11), rage (1 Sam 25), and greed (Prov 1:10-19). It is interesting that the law (Lev 19:17-18) anticipated the teaching of Jesus (Matt 5:21-22) by forbidding such emotions as hate and grudge bearing and commanding love (Lev 19:17-18).

5:18 Adultery was referred to in the ancient Near East and in the Old Testament as the "great sin" (Gen 20:9; Exod 32:21). Joseph declared it a "sin against God" (Gen 39:9). It was also a capital crime (Deut 22:23-27). Adultery was sexual relations between a man and a married woman outside of marriage. It was not a private matter, but threatened the integrity of the foundational family unit (see comments on v. 16). Even the ancient Near Eastern law codes agreed on this point. It was also a breach of a covenant relationship, the marriage bond (Gen 2:24; Mal 2:14). It violated the commitment between the husband and wife. Even sexual relations with members of the extended family were forbidden (Lev 18:6-18). There were also laws to protect the innocent wife from false accusation (Num 5:11-31; Deut 22:13-19). The wisdom literature recognized the dangers of sexual infidelity (Prov 2:16-19; 5:1-23; 7:1-27), even to the condemnation of lust (Prov 6:25; Job 31:9-10). On the other hand the joys of physical love in marriage were celebrated in the Song of Solomon.[26]

---

abstract principle that is sacred. Rather, the sacredness of life is grounded in the sovereign God who created life.

[25]For a contrasting view see the Quran 2:178, which allows for compensation as a sign of mercy.

[26]Jackie A. Naudé, "Sexual Ordinances," *NIDOTTE*, 4:1198-1211.

The marriage covenant was of such a nature that marriage could be used as a metaphor for the relationship between God and Israel. God was the husband and Israel was the wife. Therefore, when Israel turned to other gods, they committed spiritual adultery (Hos 2, Jer 2–3, and Ezek 16 and 23).[27]

5:19 Stealing addressed the right to personal property. Each one in the covenant community had that right, so to steal was to injure the community. The penalty for stealing was restitution (Exod 22:1-13), often two to five times the value of the stolen goods. Prohibitions against stealing were also common in other ancient law codes. However, the penalties in these codes differed from the Old Testament, ranging from death to mutilation to fines. Penalties also differed by class.

Since Exodus 21:16 uses the same word to refer to kidnapping, some have suggested that this commandment actually referred to the theft of a person. That would put it in the same category of the previous two commandments which were capital crimes. However, this speculation is not compelling. There is no direct object in the text and the second half of the Decalogue seems to be arranged in a descending order of severity.[28]

Stealing was not just the taking of property. It violated the person as well since one's property in some sense was an extension of the self. In the Old Testament world, goods were a limited resource. Property was allocated by God and was intended for each person's good. To steal was to attempt to gain some kind of control over the other, a direct violation of the covenant community. Even kings could not legally steal (1 Kgs 21).

Stealing can have broader implications than the simple theft of property. John Calvin included for consideration such things as usury, bribes, incorrect weights and measures, negligence, oppression of the poor, and barring the poor from access to necessities of life.[29]

5:20 This word assumes the legal setting of the court and the perversion of justice. The **neighbor** was not just anyone but a person

---

[27]See Gary H. Hall, "נאף," *NIDOTTE*, 3:2-5.

[28]See V. Hamp, "גנב," *TDOT*, 3:39-45 and Merrill, *Deuteronomy*, p. 155.

[29]Miller, *Deuteronomy*, p. 92. What would Calvin say to our era which has witnessed flagrant examples of fraud, bribery, economic exploitation, usury, and negligence by the government, corporations, and individuals?

with whom one had a reciprocal relationship. Deuteronomy differs here from Exodus by using "nothingness" (שָׁוְא, *šw'*) instead of "false" (שֶׁקֶר, *šeqer*) (see also Exod 23:1). The usage connects this commandment with the third one (v. 11). Thus breaking the ninth included breaking the third. The penalty was severe. The person who brought a false charge suffered the penalty of the crime involved (Deut 19:18-21). Also two witnesses were needed for cases to guard against false witnessing (Deut 19:15). The famous case of Naboth's vineyard demonstrated how kings could subvert these laws (1 Kgs 21). The many Psalmists' complaints against false accusations were not imaginary (Ps 4:2; 5:6,9-10; 7:14; 10:7-9, etc.). Though addressing the judicial process, this commandment has a wider application to truthfulness in general.

5:21 The last word has to do with the inner disposition, not an outward act and thus differs from the first nine. This commandment was not open to community censure since only God knows the heart. However, violation of this one was the first step to violating the others, especially the last three. To covet a person's life, wife, or property could eventuate in murder, adultery, or theft. David's life provided an example of how coveting a wife led to adultery and murder (1 Sam 11-12).

Deuteronomy's formulation differs from Exodus in a few minor areas. Deuteronomy uses two words for coveting rather than one as reflected in the NIV. There is probably little difference in meaning between them although חמד (*ḥmd*, "covet") may indicate more of the wish to appropriate property while אוה (*'wh*, "desire") may include the lust and inner desire for wealth.[30] Desire seems to be a continuous lusting after something.

Deuteronomy also reverses "house" and "wife" and adds "land." Both these changes reflect the concerns of Deuteronomy for the fair treatment of women (15:12-18; 22:28-29) and for the proper allocation of land.

This last commandment forms a fitting conclusion to the other nine for it raised the important issues of desire, attitude, and will. The state of the heart of each Israelite was crucial to the well-being of the covenant community (Deut 10:16; 30:6). If the tenth commandment

---

[30]Compare Weinfeld, *Deuteronomy*, p. 318, with Merrill, *Deuteronomy*, p. 156.

were kept, all the others would be as well. If the tenth were not observed, any or all others would be violated. In fact to break the tenth was to be in grave jeopardy of breaking the first. To wish for anything to have first place in one's life except God was to break both.

B. THE PEOPLE'S RESPONSE (5:22-28)

This section is very similar to Exodus 20:18-21 (see also Exod 19:16-24; 24:3-4,7,12). The people, afraid of God, asked Moses to be a mediator for them.

Several repetitions of key words bind this section together as a unit. Verb and noun forms of "word/speak" occur nine times; "voice" occurs seven times, "hear" occurs eight times, "say" occurs three times. These words are not repeated in 5:29ff with the same intensity. However, many commentators and translations do not recognize a break between verses 28 and 29.[31]

5:22 These are the commandments the LORD proclaimed is literally "These words the LORD spoke . . .", a somewhat stronger meaning. The emphasis was on the uniqueness of the Decalogue. They were complete and special. God added more laws after delivering the Decalogue (cf. 4:2), but Moses only received the Decalogue on the mountain. The rest of the covenant law was given later in a variety of ways. Consequently, it was only these commandments that were on the tablets of stone.

5:23-27 The details of the fearful response by the people are summarized succinctly here from the book of Exodus. The same language of theophany is used that we have seen in 4:12. After experiencing the reception of only the Decalogue directly from God, the people were afraid for their lives. They lived through that experience, but they were not certain they could live through another. They understood the difference between themselves as **mortal man**

---

[31]Gary H. Hall, "Rhetorical Criticism, Chiasm and Theme in Deuteronomy," *Stone-Campbell Journal* 1 (1998): 98. Norbert Lohfink and Christensen prefer a section 5:27 to 6:3 while others see 5:22-6:3 as a unit (N. Lohfink, *Das Hauptgebot: Eine Untersuchung literarischer Einleitungs-fragan zu Dtn 5–11* [Rome: Pontifical Institute, 1963], pp. 67-68; Christensen, *Deuteronomy*, pp. 132-133; Wright, *Deuteronomy*, p. 90; the NIV and NRSV).

("flesh", בָּשָׂר, *bśr*) and the holy God who spoke out of the darkness and fire. Any direct contact could be fatal. Their God was a **living God**, not mere wood and stone like the idols (4:28). Therefore, contact with such a God was not a benign experience. He was totally different from a god who could be clothed, fed, carried around in procession, touched, handled and manipulated (Isa 10:3-10). The truth of Moses' assertions in chapter 4 and in the first two commandments had been reinforced by their brief encounter (see 18:16).

This reverence for God was his goal for them (4:10). But they had to learn it and choose it themselves. Exodus 20:20 explains that the giving of the Decalogue was a test so that the fear of the LORD would keep them from sinning. They had passed the test.

They also pledged to **listen and obey** (v. 27). Literally they pledged to "hear (obey) and do." It is impossible to merely to listen to God's word. Action is implied and is vital to a proper relationship with God. Interestingly, in Exodus 24:7 the people pledged to "do and obey," the reverse of here. Just as obedience must issue in action, action was a proof of obedience.[32] Israel was committing herself to heed the numerous demands by Moses in Deuteronomy to "keep and do" the commandments (see on 4:6).

5:28 God's response was positive and warm. They pledged to *hear* God and he **heard** their pledge.[33] Usually in Deuteronomy **good** refers to something God had given Israel, like the land or life, but what Israel had done here is "good." They had earned divine approval.

C. EXHORTATIONS TO OBEY (5:29-33)

Sections 5:29-33 and 6:1-3 are closely related and provide a transition from the Decalogue and its sequel (5:1-28) to the "Great Shema" and its sequel (6:4-25). However, since there are several verbal affinities between 6:1-3 and 6:4ff we will deal with 5:29-33 as a unit.[34]

---

[32]James understood this principle, James 1:22-25.

[33]Forms of דבר, "speak/word" occur five times in this verse and "hear" twice.

[34]See below on chapter 6 and Hall, "Rhetorical Criticism," pp. 93-94.

5:29 God allowed Israel to see the deepest desire of his heart, expressed in the strongest terms. **Oh** translates an idiom expressing a strong wish, "Who would give . . .", sometimes translated as "If only . . . ."[35] God desired their response but he could not force them to serve him; they had to choose.[36] However, in circumstances like this, God did try to influence the decision (Eccl. 3:14). The blessings God gave them would seem to weigh the issue in his favor. The historical fact that Israel often resisted such influence could only be ascribed to her stubbornness (Deut 9:6,13; 10:16; 31:27; Exod 32:9). At the end of Israel's history, which was a history of disobedience, Jeremiah promised that God would give them a heart for him (Jer 32:39-40).

The **fear** that God desired was the kind expressed in reverence and worship, which was intended to prompt obedient hearts. The people's earlier response in fear (vv. 24-27) was of a different kind, a fearful anxiety that caused them to be concerned for their lives.

5:30-31 Moses' role as mediator was confirmed, first by the people (v. 27) and then by God. The language is from 4:1 and provides a frame around chapters 4-5 (see comments on 4:1). According to Exod 24:18, Moses stayed on the mountain 40 days and nights, presumably receiving the rest of the law. The narrative of verses 22-31 provided the background for the exhortation that followed.

5:32-33 Chapter 5 ends with an exhortation to obedience and loyalty, using language typical of Deuteronomy and comparable to 5:1. To **not turn aside . . .** and to **walk in the way** were common phrases for loyalty and obedience (the former, Deut 17:11,20; 28:14; Josh 1:7; 23:6; 2 Kgs 22:2; the latter, Deut 10:12; 11:22; Prov 4:27; 8:20; 9:6). They were equal to "obey and do." "To walk in the way" was the antidote or safeguard to "going after other gods" (6:14; 8:19; 11:28; 13:2; etc.) which often tempted Israel. The rewards of faithfulness were immediate and material (**live and prosper**) which is typical of the theology of Deuteronomy. The promise to the patriarchs was land specific, and promised blessing in a broad sense (Gen 12:1-7). The OT concept of blessing was concrete, not otherworldly or

---

[35]This idiom occurs 25 times in the OT. For other strong statements see Exod 16:3; Deut 28:67; 2 Sam 18:33[34]; Ps 14:7; 55:7; Job 6:8 (11 times in Job).

[36]Talmud Ber. 33b, "All is under the control of heaven except for the fear of heaven," quoted by Tigay, *Deuteronomy*, p. 74.

immaterial (spiritual?). The rewards were a gift of God's grace, but they were appropriated through obedience. They were not a claim Israel had on God to be accessed through some kind of manipulation. It was the desire of God's heart that Israel live long in the Promised Land as a faithful witness to him among the nations. Therefore, the material blessings were not an end in themselves but a part of this larger purpose. Deuteronomy returns to these ideas again and again.

EXCURSUS: THE CHRISTIAN AND THE LAW

A difficult issue for Christianity that deserves further reflection is the relationship of the OT *Torah* (law) to the Christian life. There are a variety of different opinions on this subject, some strongly held, that have developed over the centuries.[37] The main issue focuses on the nature of the authority the law has for the Christian: Is the Christian obligated to obey the whole law, part of it, or none of it?[38]

Christian scholars have developed various ways of understanding the law over the years. An early effort was dividing the law into three categories: civil, moral, and ceremonial (Aquinas, 1235–1274 AD; maybe going back to Augustine, 354–430 AD). The Reformers isolated three functions of the law: 1) to bring knowledge of sin (Rom 3:20) in order to move one to seek grace (emphasized by Luther); 2) to restrain evildoers with the fear of punishment; 3) to help one learn better the nature of God's will and thus arouse to obedience and good works (emphasized by Calvin).

Calvin argued that whoever wanted to do away with the law misunderstood. Jesus did not come to end the law but to remedy transgressions of it. Therefore, the law was abrogated to the extent that it no longer condemned the Christian. Jesus bore the curse of the moral law for us. The ceremonial laws were different. They have

---

[37]For a brief overview see my essay, "The Christian and the Old Testament," *Essentials of Christian Faith*, ed. Steve Burris (Joplin, MO: College Press, 1992), pp. 251-272.

[38]*Law* in this essay is interpreted as the whole *torah*, or the entire instruction that came from God for the covenant people of Israel. It is found in various parts of the Pentateuch, especially parts of Exodus 20–40, Numbers, Deuteronomy 5–26, and most of Leviticus.

been abrogated only in use, not in effect. They were shadows of Christ. Colossians 2:13-14 refers only to the ceremonial law.[39]

Calvin's position has wide influence today. The practical outcome of this approach is that the law is still binding on the Christian, especially its moral aspects. Some of its ceremonial aspects, especially circumcision and the Sabbath, are shifted to Christian ceremonies (infant baptism and Sunday), while other aspects are regarded as nonbinding. A small group of Reformed Christians believe that even the civil laws should be enforced (called the Theonomy movement).[40] An excellent guide to the array of perspectives is: Willem VanGemeren, ed., *The Law, The Gospel and the Modern Christian: Five Views*.[41] The five essays include perspectives from Reformed, Theonomy, modified Reformed, Dispensationalist, and modified Lutheran views. Only the last is not a variation of a Calvinist approach.

The following perspective is the one adopted in this commentary. It has been developed over two and one-half decades of teaching the OT in college and seminary. It is applicable to the whole OT, not just the law, although that is where the remarks will be focused.[42]

I have already remarked that in the OT, covenant preceded law and was a gift of God's grace. Therefore, the law was understood as God's instruction for how the covenant people should live out their lives under his will. Law was not understood in a specific legal sense as some external code, but a revelation of the will of God to be internalized and applied to all of life. The OT does not make a neat distinction between moral, civil, and ceremonial law (nor does the NT). The law was a whole, all of equal importance.

---

[39]See John Calvin, *Institutes of the Christian Religion*, Book II: VII, 7-17.

[40]This movement is grounded in the writings of R.J. Rushdoony, for example his *Institutes of Biblical Law* (Nutley, NJ: Craig, 1973). For a brief introduction see Kenneth L. Gentry, Jr., *God's Law in the Modern World* (Phillipsburg, NJ: P. and R. Publishing, 1993).

[41]Willem VanGemeren, ed., *The Law, The Gospel and the Modern Christian: Five Views* (Grand Rapids: Zondervan, 1993).

[42]Some readers will recognize affinities with Alexander Campbell's "Sermon on the Law." However, my view was developed through the years under the influence of various Restoration scholars before I had occasion to study Campbell's sermon. A college course decades ago with Cameron Sinclair on the book of Galatians was a powerful formative influence on my thinking.

The NT teaching on the law is very complex. Jesus taught that he came to fulfill the law, to bring it to fruition (Matt 5:17-20). He also reaffirmed some of the Decalogue, but probed deeper behind it to the intentions of the heart (Matt 5:21-48). In his day the law had been hedged with many protective traditions. Jesus' controversies with the Pharisees often centered on these restrictions. Jesus affirmed that the law was for Israel's good, not a burden to be imposed on them. Many of his conflicts with the Pharisees arose over the observance of the Sabbath. Jesus affirmed that doing good works on the Sabbath was right, and that the Sabbath was made for people, not vice versa (Matthew 12; Luke 13; John 5; Mark 2:27). Jesus affirmed that the law could be summed up in two basic formulations: to love God wholeheartedly and to love one's neighbor (Mark 12:28-34). By this he seemed to be saying there was an essential foundation upon which the whole law was based.

Paul's views on the law must be understood in the context of his struggle with Jewish Christians who took a legalistic stance on the law and wanted to require its observance by Gentile Christians as a means to salvation. Paul had positive things to say about the law understood as *torah*, but negative things to say about it understood as a legal external code necessary for salvation. The law was holy, righteous, and good (Rom 7:12). But the law (legalistically understood, Gal 3–4; 5:1-12) could not justify anyone. Christ's death canceled the written code (Col 2:14), and the law was a shadow destined to perish (Col 2:16-23). But there was a righteousness apart from the law that upheld it (Rom 3:21-31). It was designed to lead us to Christ (Gal 3:24). The writer of Hebrews sees the law foreshadowing Jesus Christ, especially the "ceremonial" sections (Heb 4:14-15; 7–8; 9; 10).

Since the law revealed God's will to his covenant people, it was grounded in his character of holiness, righteousness, justice, love, graciousness, faithfulness, etc. The law was therefore an application of his character to the life of his people in a specific cultural and historical situation. The specific laws reflected the deeper reality — a foundation grounded in God. It is the task of the Christian interpreter to seek to understand the foundational principles underlying the specific laws. Even the OT prophets did this when they addressed issues of justice and covenant loyalty (Isa 1:10-17; Micah 6:1-8). It is these principles that are valid for all time, not the context specific formulation of the principle (though we must remember that the principles we deduce are not the Scripture themselves). With the aid of the Holy Spirit we apply the principles we have discerned (especially their theological underpinning) to our specific situation. As God's people we are expected to reflect God's character in our lives just as Israel was expected to do.

The law, as a covenantal demand, is no longer applicable to the Christian in its specific form. However, it is still the revealed will of God, so it has authority for us in the form of instruction and guidance. A Christian perspective on any issue, moral, civil, or otherwise, must begin with an intense study of the OT to discern God's will revealed there. Foundational principles will carry forward into the NT and undergird its teaching. Only in that manner could we say that we have developed a biblical view of the issue. There will be both continuities and discontinuities that will need to be explored.[43]

The Christian is free in Christ and not encumbered with an external code. But he is not free from the authority of the OT and what it reveals to us about the nature and character of God and his will for his people.[44]

---

[43]Wright's three-point hermeneutical strategy is similar: ascertain the function of the particular law, articulate the objective of the law within the ancient Israelite context, and seek to preserve the object in our modern sociocultural context (*Deuteronomy*, pp. 13-14).

[44]Further significant insights and detail can be gleaned from Douglas Moo, "A Modified Lutheran View" in *Five Views*; D. Brent Sandy and Ronald L. Giese, Jr, *Cracking Old Testament Codes* (Nashville: Broadman and Holman, 1995); George L. Klein, ed., *Reclaiming the Prophetic Mantle* (Nashville: Broadman Press, 1992); Elizabeth Achtemeier, *Preaching from the Old Testament* (Louisville: Westminster/John Knox, 1989); David Baker, *Two Testaments, One Bible* (Downers Grove, IL: InterVarsity, 1991); and especially Sidney Greidanus, *Preaching Christ from the Old Testament* (Grand Rapids: Eerdmans, 1999).

DEUTERONOMY 6

D. REFLECTIONS ON THE FIRST COMMANDMENT (6:1–11:32)

1. The Great Commandment (6:1-25)

The first verses of chapter 6 are often included with the last verses of chapter 5 to form a separate unit, 5:22–6:3. However, as I have briefly shown earlier, it seems better to follow the usual break with the traditional chapter divisions.[1] Nonetheless, the close relationship between 5:29-33 and 6:1-3 and the transitional character of the material should be recognized. Moses is deliberately moving from the presentation of the Decalogue to an important series of sermons on the first commandment. The two sections repeat familiar words and themes as a part of this transition. Repetition of such key words as "do" (5:31,32; 6:1,3) and "keep" (5:29,32; 6:2,3) bind them together.

On the other hand many affinities between 6:1-3 and 4-25 compel us to acknowledge 6:1-3 as an introduction to the latter section as well. "Fear" is repeated in verses 2,13, and 24; "son" in verses 2-3,20-21; "do" in verses 1,3,18,24,28; and "keep" in verses 2,3,17,25. The three words for the laws ("commandment," "statute," and "judgment") occur in verses 1-2,20,24, and 25 suggesting an inclusio for the chapter.

Structurally 6:4-9 provides the fundamental statement of the sermon. The rest of the chapter is a commentary on the statement, specifically answering the question, how does one live out whole-hearted love for God? One loves God by not forgetting God (vv. 10-15), by not testing God (vv. 16-19) and by instructing the children (vv. 20-15). The last section adroitly sums up the whole sermon by incorporating ideas from all of the sections of the chapter.

---

[1]Hall, "Rhetorical Criticism," pp. 92-94; see on 5:22-28 and 29-33 above.

Introduction (6:1-3)

6:1-2 Language and themes are repeated from previous sermons in Deuteronomy. There are close connections to 5:31. The emphasis on **teach** is reiterated from 4:1,9, and 10 and will be taken up in a significant way in this chapter.

Children and **their children** are the focus of these verses, for they are the next generations. The effective passing on of the central components of the covenant was crucial to the continuance and health of the covenant community in its relationship with God. The covenant law's purpose was not only to offer directions for covenant life, but also to promote proper respect (**fear**) for God. God's greatest desire (5:29) could be accomplished through this simple task of teaching the law.

6:3 The summons to **hear** prepared the way for the most important summons of the whole book in verse four.[2] The language is familiar to us from previous texts, but two new ideas are added to the reward. That they **may increase greatly** replaces the usual promise of "long life" (4:40; 5:16,33; 6:3). This promise is picked up in 7:13; 8:1; 13:17; and 30:16. Also the land is now described for the first time in Deuteronomy as **a land flowing with milk and honey** instead of the "good land" (1:25,35; 3:25; 4:21,22). This phrase first appeared in Exodus 3:8,17 and appears later in Deuteronomy (11:9; 26:9,15; 27:3; 31:20; cf. also Josh 5:6; Jer 11:6; 32:22; Ezek 20:6,15). It reflects the natural bounty of the land with its abundant supply of food, domesticated livestock, and natural resources.[3] The variety of expressions was Moses' attempt to persuade the people to obey. They were encouraged to follow up on their pledge given in 5:29.

---

[2]In the Hebrew, the imperative force is not as strong as in v. 4. Verse 3 does not have an actual imperative verb form although grammatically the verb can be understood as an imperative.

[3]Milk was probably goat's milk. The honey could be bees' honey, but it could also mean the sweet syrup from fruit and thus refer to dates, figs, and grapes. There was both a literal and metaphorical aspect to the phrase, referring to fertility in general. In Greek literature milk and honey were the food of the gods. For one familiar with modern Palestine this description may seem puzzling. However, there is much evidence from archaeology and ancient literary sources that in OT times the land was much more fertile than it is today. See Tigay, *Deuteronomy*, pp. 437-438.

The Great Shema (6:4-9)

6:4 The second summons to **hear** was a call to the nation to both pay attention and to obey (see 4:1; 5:1; 9:1; 20:3), and is tied directly to 5:1. The nation was addressed as an individual (the imperative is in the second masculine singular) and was expected to respond as a whole. The close tie to 5:1 lends support to the observation, often made, that verses 4-5 were intended to be a summary of the essence of the Decalogue (which is affirmed by Jesus in the NT). These verses also function as the foundational principle of the decrees and laws that follow in chapters 12–26. The later chapters explicate how absolute loyalty to God and love for him should be lived out in everyday life.[4]

Verse 4 is the primary declaration of faith for Judaism, called "The Great Shema."[5] This title comes from the transliteration of the imperative form of the verb "hear" (*šema'*). The declaration is four words in the Hebrew, usually construed as two nominal clauses.[6] How should it be translated? The NIV offers one possibility in the text and three alternatives in the footnote. The first two Hebrew words are certainly to be translated as in the NIV. **The LORD our God**, rather than "the LORD *is* our God." The simple reason is that in Deuteronomy when "LORD" and "our God" appear together "our God" is always in apposition to "LORD" (that is, it describes LORD). It never is a predicate nominative (to be translated as "the LORD *is* our God") (1:6,19,20; 2:33,36; 4:7; 5:2; 6:24,25; 29:14,17,28).[7] The

---

[4]For a detailed exposition of Deut 6:4-5 with many references to Jewish sources see S. Dean McBride, "The Yoke of the Kingdom: An Exposition of Deut 6:4-5," *Int* 27 (1973): 273-306.

[5]Though verses 6-9 were incorporated into the morning and evening prayers, it was understood as a declaration of faith according to Rabbi Hayim Halevy Donin (*To Be a Jew* [New York: Basic Books, 1972], pp. 163-164). See also Josephus, *Ant.* 4:212-213; Tigay, *Deuteronomy*, p. 440; Marvin Wilson, "Shema," *NIDOTTE*, 4:1217-1218.

[6]Hebrew grammar does not require an expressed verb as the English does. Thus Hebrew can juxtapose nouns, adjectives and adverbs without a verb. The reader is expected to put the verb in the proper place based on context. The verb is usually some form of "to be" in the present tense.

[7]There are 313 occurrences of this idiom in Deuteronomy including the one here. It would be extremely inconsistent for this text to be the only exception. See R.W.L. Moberly, "'Yahweh Is One': The Translation of the Shema," *Studies in the Pentateuch*, ed., J.A. Emerton (Leiden: Brill, 1990), pp. 209-215.

translation of the second two Hebrew words is less certain because the Hebrew word אֶחָד (*'eḥād*) is ambiguous. It can mean either a oneness that expresses a unity, or it can mean uniqueness. So is the LORD **one** (NIV) or is he LORD alone?

If the LORD is one, then he is a unity in plan and purpose. There is a singularity about who he is and his ability to do what he says. He is consistent, faithful, and reliable. Therefore, Israel could trust him and have confidence in him. This assertion was important in the light of some occasions in Israel's history when it appeared that God would not be willing or able to do what he said (Exod 32–34; Num 14; Hos 11; Jer 32:36-44; see Deut 9:7-29; Job). The Shema, then, would be about God's unchangeableness and integrity.[8]

If he is LORD alone, then the emphasis is upon his uniqueness; his being wholly different from the other gods. It would be a polemic against the other gods who were mere stone and wood (4:28) and a further affirmation of the first and second commandments. Since Israel frequently found other gods attractive, as 4:25-28 anticipates, then it was important to assert the LORD's uniqueness for Israel. For Israel there were no other gods. The one and only God demanded their total devotion and loyalty (v. 5).

Each option is supported from the OT. Perhaps the ambiguity was deliberate, and the emphasis shifted as circumstances required.[9] The implications of the Shema are drawn out in other OT texts. The prayers of both David (2 Sam 7:22-26) and Solomon (1 Kgs 8:60) affirm that the LORD is the only God and that all nations hopefully will come to know him. Psalm 97 affirms the LORD's uniqueness as does Malachi 2:10. Zechariah 14:9 portrays the eschatological future when the LORD will truly be one (the only exact quote of Deut 6:4 in the OT), that is, he will be the only deity over the whole earth.

---

[8]J. Gerald Janzen, "On the Most Important Word in the Shema," *VT* 37 (1987): 180-200 and Miller, *Deuteronomy*, pp. 99-101; Moberly, "'Yahweh Is One,'" pp. 212-213.

[9]Rabbi Eugene Borowitz edited a volume of 26 essays on the meaning of *'eḥād*. Each author had a different idea for its meaning such as coherent, unique, exclusive, singular, incomparable, comprehensive, primary (*Echad: The Many Meanings of God Is One* [Port Washington, NY: Shma, 1988]). The Jewish Publication Society's translation of the Hebrew Bible has "the LORD is one God, the LORD alone," but the Jewish Union Prayerbook has "the LORD is our God, the LORD is One."

The affirmation of the Shema is about Yahweh, the one, unique God of Israel. This has implications for modern theistic pluralism that affirms that all religions are essentially headed in the same direction and believe in the same deity. This projected deity usually ends up being some sort of monistic idea which by definition eludes any precise description and floats off into nothingness.

Yahweh of the OT is incompatible with such theistic pluralism (as is Jesus Christ in the NT) and those who affirm the opposite are misinformed or willfully misleading.

[T]he sharp precision of the Shema cannot be evaporated into a philosophical abstraction or relegated to a penultimate level of truth. Its majestic declaration of monotheism defined by the history-laden, character-rich, covenant-related, dynamic person of "Yahweh our God," shows that the abstract and definitionally undefinable "being" of religious pluralism is really a monism without meaning or message."[10]

6:5 The declaration of faith explicating God's uniqueness and oneness is followed by a demand for total and complete devotion to him. Since God loved Israel (4:37), he expected love in return. The demand to love God occurs almost exclusively in Deuteronomy or Deuteronomy -influenced texts in the OT. This reflects the influence of ancient Near Eastern treaty forms on the book. In the treaties and in the Egyptian Amarna letters of the fourteenth century B.C. "love" was used as a term for loyalty. The overlord loved the vassal, and the vassal was to love the overlord.

Love in this context was not an emotion. It involved the behavior becoming to love (loyalty and obedience) and so could be commanded.[11] The command to love occurs seven other times in Deuteronomy and is often associated with obedience to the commands. It also appears in contexts with fear, serve, cling, walk, and keep and is parallel in meaning to those concepts (10:12; 11:1,13,22;

---

[10]Wright, *Deuteronomy*, p. 98.

[11]Several studies emphasize this point; J.W. McKay, "Man's Love for God in Deuteronomy and the Father/Teacher–Son/Pupil Relationship," *VT* 22 (1972): 426-435; and D.J. McCarthy, "Notes on the Love of God in Deuteronomy and the Father-Son Relationship between Yahweh and Israel," *CBQ* 27 (1965): 144-147. See also on 4:37 above.

19:9; 30:16,20). "Total self-entrusting and faithful love for God, then, is at the heart of what the OT regards as genuine piety and a love that necessarily includes an attitude of gratitude . . . trust . . . and consistent solidarity."[12] Obeying the covenant law then was not a burden but a privilege and a joy (Ps 119).

Love for God involved the whole person — **heart, soul, and strength**. In the Hebrew mentality "heart" was equal to what we associate with the mind, that is, the intellect, the will, and the intentions. "The soul" is better translated as "life" or "self." This included the whole inner self with all its emotions, desires, and personal character (Ps 103:1).[13] **Strength** is a rare meaning for a common Hebrew adverb, מְאֹד (m²'ōd), which is usually translated as "very, exceedingly." Here, however, it is apparently a noun (and in the parallel text, 2 Kgs 23:25). The love required involved the uttermost of personal devotion, a total commitment.[14] The oneness of God was to be matched by the oneness of devotion to him.[15] It was this devotion that would protect Israel from apostasy (13:3-4). Josiah was the only OT figure to achieve this ideal (1 Kgs 23:25).

Jesus in the NT affirmed the centrality of Deuteronomy 6:4-5 to the faith of Israel. In answer to a lawyer's question he stated that verse 5 was "the greatest and first commandment." The second commandment he referred to was a quote from Leviticus 19:18, "You shall love your neighbor as yourself." (Matt 22:34-40; Mark 12:29-30). In a different setting, another lawyer asked about eternal life. When Jesus questioned him about the law, the lawyer quoted both Deuteronomy 6:5 and Leviticus 19:18 in answer (Luke 10:25-28). This attests to the fact that the Jews in the first century also had already discerned that the Shema was the fundamental principle of their law. This almost certainly arose from the fact that by this time

---

[12]P.J.J.S. Els, "אהב," *NIDOTTE*, 1:286. This is parallel to the concept of love in the New Testament.

[13]For heart and soul elsewhere in Deuteronomy see 4:29; 10:12; 11:13; 13:4; 26:16; 30:2,6,10. For the anthropological data see H.W. Wolff, *Anthropology of the Old Testament* (Phildelphia: Fortress, 1974), pp. 17-22, 46-55.

[14]Later Judaism interpreted "soul" (*nepheš*) to include the possibility of martyrdom, and "strength" to mean one's material wealth (Prov 3:9). Therefore, the command required everything of the person.

[15]Miller, *Deuteronomy*, p. 103.

the Shema was a part of morning and evening prayers as a part of Jewish devotion.[16]

It is interesting that the quotes in Mark and Luke add "mind" to heart, soul, and strength, whereas Matthew substitutes "mind" for strength. Evidently, Mark and Luke divided the Hebrew "heart" into the categories of emotions and intellect to clear up any confusion about the precise meaning of the word.[17]

6:6 These commandments are variously interpreted as referring to either the Shema and the Decalogue from the immediate context, or as referring to all the law and teaching in Deuteronomy (cf. similar phrases in 4:2; 6:1-2; 19:9; 28:1,14,15). Modern Jewish scholars prefer the latter.[18]

The law was to be internalized, memorized, and made a part of the will (11:18; 30:14; 32:46). Since obedience was to come from the **heart**, it was necessary that the law be placed there. It was no external code to be legalistically followed but a way of life to be internalized. This internalization of teaching was a part of the wisdom tradition as well (Prov 3:1; 4:4; 6:21) which suggests Moses' role as a teacher was being emphasized.

6:7 Impress is better translated as "repeat, recount." This word is parallel with **talk** and refers to the constant repetition for the benefit of the children (Ps 119:13). The law was to be repeated wherever they went and wherever they were, which is the force of the double merism[19] (**when you sit . . . when you walk; when you lie down . . . when you get up**). In the parallel passage in 11:19 the verb "to teach" replaces "impress/repeat" confirming the nuance here (see on 4:1 and references there). The covenant community had an obligation to pass on the covenant requirements to the next generation. Failure to do so jeopardized the people of God, and God's witness in the world faced extinction. Therefore, educating the **children** (literally "sons")

---

[16]Tigay, *Deuteronomy*, p. 440.

[17]Merrill, *Deuteronomy*, pp. 165-166, has an extended discussion of the issues raised by these changes.

[18]Tigay and Weinfeld are in agreement on this point.

[19]A merism is an abbreviated way of expressing a totality. Two words or phrases are used to indicate a complete, larger idea. The individual parts are not in view but the whole ("body and soul" = the whole person).

was crucial (vv. 2,20-26; 4:9-10).[20] In Proverbs "sons" means "pupils." The implementation of this requirement was crucial for any future king (Deut 17:19) and for Joshua (Josh 1:8). It was also the mark of the righteous man (Ps 1:2).

6:8-9 Visible reminders were required for the implementation of the command of verse 6. A similar method was introduced in Exodus 13:1-16 where the observance of the feast of unleavened bread was a sign and reminder of the exodus event (v. 9). The dedication of the firstborn was to serve the same purpose (v. 16).

In Exodus the language is clearly metaphorical.[21] However, is the language here in Deuteronomy intended literally or metaphorically? Scholars have argued both sides. Several factors argue in favor of a metaphorical understanding: the use of the word **symbol**, the same word as is used in Exodus 13:9 and 16; the seeming impracticality of actually wearing objects on the head and arm daily; and the inconsistencies of those who do take it literally.[22] The "symbol" or "sign" was a mnemonic device to remind one of the past divine actions. These reminders could take many forms, such as feast days, solemn assemblies, piles of stone, and such.[23]

However, since it was "words" (v. 6) that were to be bound on the forehead and arm, the literal interpretation has prevailed in Judaism.[24] The custom developed of writing certain verses on scraps of parchment (especially Exod 13:1-16; Deut 6:4-9 and 11:13-21), placing them in little boxes and strapping them to the forehead and arm ("hands" is

---

[20]Although the evidence is scarce, it seems that education of the children in early Israel was the father's responsibility. It is uncertain when scribal schools may have begun (reflected in Proverbs?). Still there was a great diversity in ancient Israel: see James L. Crenshaw, "Education in Ancient Israel," *JBL* 100 (1985): 601-615.

[21]Tigay, *Deuteronomy*, p. 78.

[22]Merrill, *Deuteronomy*, pp. 167-168. Furthermore, Proverbs speaks of metaphorically writing wisdom teaching on the tablets of the heart and binding them on the neck or fingers (Prov 3:3; 6:21; 7:3). One would expect Christian commentators to lean toward the metaphorical, but Driver (*Deuteronomy*, p. 93) interprets the passage literally. Further, there is a long Jewish tradition of teaching that emphasizes the metaphorical; see Weinfeld, *Deuteronomy*, pp. 341-343.

[23]Paul A. Kruger, "אוֹת," *NIDOTTE*, 1:331-333.

[24]Tigay, *Deuteronomy*, p. 78; Weinfeld, *Deuteronomy*, p. 342.

understood to mean "arm" here[25]). This continues today. The boxes are called *tefillin* ("phylactaries" in the NT).[26] By analogy this practice imitated the instruction to the high priest to wear a frontlet of gold with the words, "Holy to the LORD" (Exod 28:36-38). Wearing Scripture texts inscribed on objects is apparently ancient. Miniature silver scrolls were found in a seventh century B.C. tomb near Jerusalem with Numbers 6:24-25 engraved on them. They were to be worn tied to the body.[27] Also, there is some evidence from the ancient world that various peoples wore amulets to indicate devotion to their deity.

However, the debate over literal or metaphorical meaning is less important than the significance of this command. The words of the law were to be continually before the people and also embedded deep in their hearts so that the whole community would be constantly reminded of its love commitment to God.

The "words" were also to be on the houses, the places where the people lived. From this commandment arose the tradition of the *mezuzah,* a little box by the door with the scripture texts in it.[28] They were also to be placed on the **gates**. This probably meant the city gates, for houses rarely had courtyards or gates. The city gate was the most public place in the city. It was the town square, where commerce, socializing, and judicial proceedings took place (Ruth 4). It was a perfect place to remind the covenant community of God's laws and its obligations. The progression implied in verses 6-9 (heart, children, houses, gates) enlarged the sphere of the covenant claim in an ever-growing circle of responsibility, from the father, to the extended family, to the entire village.

Explication (6:10-25)

The material that follows the Shema was designed to help the people safeguard their wholehearted devotion to the Lord. It took the form of two warnings common to the book of Deuteronomy (vv. 10-15,16-19) and further direction for instructing the children

---

[25]P.R. Ackroyd, "ד," *TDOT,* 5:400.

[26]For a good discussion see Tigay, *Deuteronomy,* pp. 441-444; *EncyJud* 15:898-904, s.v. "Tefillin."

[27]Walton and Matthews, *Genesis–Deuteronomy,* p. 228; Weinfeld, *Deuteronomy,* p. 342.

[28]*EncyJud* 11:1474-477, s.v. "Mezuzah."

(vv. 20-25). The first two sections share themes with 4:1-40. Three warnings are given (vv. 12,14,16) that are expanded in chapters 7 and 8. This passage is of particular interest to Christians because of the support it provided for Jesus when he encountered Satan (Matt 4).

Do Not Forget (6:10-15)

6:10-11 The gift of the Promised Land had been kept before Israel as proof of God's faithfulness to his promises. Yet its reception as a gift included some negative possibilities. The dangers were real enough that this brief passage was not sufficient warning. Moses returns to this subject with a long exhortation in chapter 8.

The land that God would give Israel would already be full of the necessities of life: **houses, wells, vineyards, and olive groves.** Food and shelter would be theirs with little effort on their part. Vineyards and olive groves must grow for years before they produce, but Israel would inherit mature plants. Grapes provided several kinds of food and drink, and olive oil was indispensable for cooking, lamps, and medicinal purposes. Springs and rivers were scarce in Palestine, but there would be wells or cisterns for them. God's gift to them was this richness of abundance that would meet all their needs (they would be **satisfied**; see 31:20; 32:13-16). This is the OT corollary to Matthew 6:25-34.[29]

Many scholars have observed that the book of Joshua suggests a complete and destructive conquest of Canaan. However, since archaeological research has not turned up any evidence of such widespread destruction from the suggested time of Joshua, these scholars suggest the conquest could not and did not happen, and the Bible is in error. But Deuteronomy 6:10-11 and other texts provide a perspective that shows such a simplistic interpretation of the OT is misleading. First, only three cities were destroyed by Joshua: Jericho, Ai, and Hazor (Josh 6:24; 8:19; 10:11,13).[30] The other cities were spared (Josh 24:13). Second, populations were decimated but buildings and crops were

---

[29]Miller rightly observes that Israel lives by God's grace. He suggests that Deuteronomy 6–9 anticipate Eph 2:8-9 (*Deuteronomy*, p. 106).

[30]On the recent finds at Hazor and their significance for Joshua's campaign see: Amnon Ben-Tor, "Excavating Hazor, Part One: Solomon's City Rises from the Ashes," *BAR* 25,2 (1999): 26-37, 60; and Amnon Ben-Tor and Maria Teresa Rubiato, "Excavating Hazor, Part Two: Did the Israelites Destroy the Canaanite City?" *BAR* 25,3 (1999): 22-39.

not (Deut 2:24–3:11 reflect the policy for the trans-Jordan area; the policy was similar in Canaan). Third, this passage and Deuteronomy 19:1 support the first two points. Therefore, we should not expect to find much archaeological evidence of a supposed violent conquest of the land. The lack of such evidence does not call the reliability of the OT into question, but supports it (see also on 7:2-3,22 below).

6:12 The danger is now addressed. Material well-being, even though a blessing from God, could lead to a sense of self-sufficiency, a false feeling of autonomy. This in turn could lead to a lessening of dependence on God, a turning away from him. Apathy toward God could set in, as well as a feeling of worthiness ("I deserve this"), and a sense of achievement ("I earned this on my own"). The result would be apostasy, a complete turning against God. To **forget** God amounted to such a turning away (see on 4:9,23). The central antidote was to remember their history (5:6; see on vv. 21-23 below).

6:13 Another antidote to apostasy was to **fear God**, to relate to him with proper reverence and awe (see on 4:10,23-27 above). On the one hand God's people were not to be afraid or anxious in time of trouble (Deut 3:2; 20:3; 31:6,8 and often in the OT). On the other hand they were to show respect for God. Fear was about focus and relationship and part of the language of covenant loyalty. Awe of God would result in obedience and faithfulness. Covenant ceremonial duties such as worship and sacrifice were built on a foundation of reverence for the covenant God.

The Hebrew grammar in this verse emphasized the word LORD by putting it first (lit., "the LORD your God, fear him . . ."). Fear was proper in the context of 6:5 since in Deuteronomy fear of God and love of God are synonymous in meaning.

By **serving** God **only** Israel's focus would be protected from distraction. To serve God involved obedience and worship. "Serve" is from the same root as "slavery" in verse 12. God had rescued Israel from her hard service in Egypt so that she could devote her energies to serving him. This was not a new slavery but a road to freedom. By serving God the people could fulfill their potential to become what God desired them to be (5:29) and place themselves in a position to receive his blessings.[31]

---

[31]Jesus found in this verse an answer for the crafty seduction of Satan (Matt 4:10; Luke 4:8) though he changes "fear" to "worship," a legitimate interpretation.

Fear of God would also enable Israel to avoid the destructive path of idolatry and the temptation to acknowledge the bogus power of other gods by **swearing** by them. Only God could guarantee an **oath**, because he was the only one who had the power.[32]

6:14 Following other gods (lit., "to walk after other gods") is a phrase for apostasy common to Deuteronomy (7:4; 8:19; 11:16,28; 13:3,7,14; 17:3; 28:14,36,64; 30:17; 31:18,20). It addressed not merely intellectual interest or curiosity but a real abandonment of God and active service to idols, non-gods who had done nothing for Israel. Seduction by the Canaanite gods and goddesses was the strongest temptation Israel faced in Canaan.

6:15 God was **among** his people in order to bless or judge. His zeal for them would not allow him to overlook apostasy (see on 4:24). This is the first time Deuteronomy mentions God's judgmental wrath, expressed as his **burning anger** (cf. 7:4; 11:17; 31:17; 29:26). God's anger was never arbitrary, nor was it merely an emotion. It was kindled because of real acts of covenant disloyalty, especially apostasy to other gods. Therefore, it was a legitimate response of a just and holy God (Exod 34:6-7).[33]

The consequence of God's anger would be the reversal of the whole exodus-conquest sequence. Israel would be **destroyed** rather than living in peace in the Promised Land (Deut 28:63; Lev 26:43). God intended to destroy the Canaanites in war (Deut 7:23-24) if Israel remained obedient. But if Israel turned against God, he would turn the war against them.[34]

If this text offends one's view of a "loving God" then the nature of the biblical God has been misunderstood. Love is compatible with anger and judgment because God is holy, just, and righteous. Therefore, he could not allow covenant disloyalty and unfaithfulness to go unnoticed. Otherwise he would only be some harmless, man-made

---

[32]Verse 13 is a commentary on the third commandment. Swearing an oath in God's name for the right reasons was legitimate. Only Israel's God could be a standard for fidelity.

[33]Jerome F.D. Creach, "חרה," *NIDOTTE,* 2:265-268.

[34]Wright suggests this is a reversal of Rom 8:35-39. Nothing can separate God's people from his love, but many things can separate God from the love of his people (*Deuteronomy*, p. 100).

deity susceptible to manipulation and not worthy of respect and worship. Such a deity could be neither just nor good.[35]

Do Not Test God (6:16-19)

6:16 The third admonition was based on the event at Massah in Exodus 17:1-8.[36] The people needed water and quarreled with Moses. Moses warned them not to test God. They should not question God's faithfulness to his promises, as if he were not able to keep them. They should not doubt the divine word (Ps 106:13-15). Testing was the consequence of forgetting God's past action, so this warning was a natural sequel to verse 12. Israel also tested God by disobedience, which was the same as doubting God's authority (Ps 78:41,56). Since God had proven himself over and over, testing showed a serious lack of trust.[37]

6:17-19 The negative warning of verse 16 is followed by positive directions. Obeying the law would keep Israel from affronting God by testing him.

Do what is right and good is a new variation on the Deuteronomic theme of obedience. What is right and good? Doing God's will. What is God's will? Obeying the law (Deut 12:28, ". . . obey . . . and you will be doing what is righteous . . . ."; 13:18; Exod 15:26). The force of the idiom seems to be focused on ethical conduct that would result from obedience since "doing right" is usually associated with proper conduct (Deut 12:25; 21:9).[38] Many of the kings of Judah were commended for doing the right and good. The standard for them was the obedient David (1 Kgs 15:5).[39] The kings who were seduced into idolatry did not do right (1 Kgs 11:33; 2 Kgs 16:2).

---

[35]The ancient Near East law codes are noted for their class distinctions and lack of justice.

[36]The name Massah comes from the root for "test," נסה (*nsh*).

[37]Gerry L. Brensinger, "נסה," *NIDOTTE,* 3:111-112. God often tested Israel to measure obedience, or to instill fear, or to prevent sinning, or to discern the heart, or to ensure future prosperity. For a few examples see Gen 22:1; Exod 15:25; 16:4; 20:20; Deut 8:2,16; 13:3; Judg 2:22. Jesus also puts the authority of this text to use in his confrontation with the devil in Matt 4:7.

[38]Hannes Olivier, "ישר," *NIDOTTE,* 2:563-568.

[39]Besides David, eight kings were commended: Asa, Jehu, Joash, Amaziah, Azariah, Jotham, Hezekiah, and Josiah.

The consequence of doing right was to finally be benefactors of the **promise** to the **forefathers**: taking over the Promised Land. Usually Moses said that the nations would be dispossessed, but in verse 19 he used a much stronger expression. The nations would be thrust out with a violent physical action (9:4). God's control was emphasized for he would do the driving out (Josh 23:5).

Instruct the Children (6:20-25)

This section is an expansion of 6:7, providing greater detail for the instruction to be given to the children. It brings together several themes in Deuteronomy.

6:20 The commands of the law would raise questions in the minds of the children. **"When** the children asked" anticipates the fact that they would. The children's concern would be about purpose. Parental conduct as lived out in obedience to the law was to be so obvious that it would arouse questions. The law in this case had the same function as other practices and symbols that were intended as teaching tools for learning about the Exodus (the Passover, Exod 12:26-27; the rite of the firstborn, Exod 13:14-15; the stone memorial, Josh 4:6-7,20-24).

6:21-23 The lesson to be taught expanded on the set formula in verse 12. The law was grounded in the redemptive act in which God's intervention was clearly attested by signs and wonders. No Exodus meant no redemption and no proof of God's faithfulness to his promise to the patriarchs. History mattered, and knowing the history mattered to the survival of the nation. It was this redemptive action of God that gave him the authority to make demands on Israel through the covenant law.

Von Rad called this passage a creedal statement and compared it to Dueteronomy 26:5-9.[40] If it can be called a creed, it is noteworthy for its emphasis on events and not on abstract dogma.

---

[40]Gerhard von Rad, *The Problem of the Hexateuch and Other Essays* (London: Oliver and Boyd, 1966), pp. 4-6. Since the "creed" did not mention the events at Sinai, von Rad came to the conclusion that the giving of the law was not an important part of Israel's early history. However, von Rad undervalues the context in Deuteronmy 6:20-24 and 26:5-9. The "creed" was a response to the fact that laws had been given, so the Sinai event was assumed by the "creed" even if not made explicit.

6:24 Only after the foundation was laid in God's redemptive acts was the parent to talk about obedience. The children were to be given reasons for obeying, not just a demand. It was especially important for the children to understand that obedience was the means to an end. The end was living under the blessings of God in prosperity and peace (6:1-2,13; 10:12-13,20; 31:12).

6:25 A significant new concept is added here. Obedience would bring **righteousness**. In the Hebrew text "righteousness" is the first word in the verse, and thus emphasized. This verse is similar to the profound statement made about Abraham in Genesis 15:6, "Abraham believed the LORD, and he credited it to him as righteousness."

Righteousness was usually understood as conformity to a standard, but it also was a relational word, especially involving being in right relationship with God. The LORD was the faithful, upright, and righteous one (Deut 34:4). Therefore, one could be righteous and in relationship with him only as a gift from him. Obedience did not achieve redemption. Obedience was in response to redemption and was the only proper response to a gift of grace. The relationship that God desired for Israel could come only from obedience. This was a profound promise, the results of faithfulness and loyalty.[41] Therefore, this righteousness had the same content as the blessing for obedience that occurs so often in Deuteronomy. It meant that Israel "shall have, experience, enjoy the blessing of, everything being right — in our family, in our society, and in our relationship with God."[42] Wright finds in this section the OT "gospel" in a nutshell. It contained the story of redemption (21-23), the blessings of redemption (24), and the fruit of obeying (25).[43]

---

[41]It is the same perspective of James in the NT: faith had to result in works or it was not legitimate (2:14-26).

[42]Wright, *Deuteronomy*, pp. 106-107. Compare Ps 24:3-5. The NRSV translation "being in the right" carries a legal, forensic sense that does not seem to fit the context.

[43]Wright, *Deuteronomy*, p. 104.

DEUTERONOMY 7

2. In Faithfulness to His Promises
God Has Chosen Israel (7:1-26)

The structure of chapter seven and its relationship to chapters six and eight are disputed. Scholars cannot agree whether there are three or four paragraphs in the chapter. This commentary follows the Massoretic tradition of four paragraphs, 7:1-6,7-11,12-16,17-26. It appears they are arranged in a chiastic order:

A. Destroy the Canaanites from the land — 1-6
B. God chose Israel out of love — 7-11
B'. God will bless obedient Israel — 12-16
A'. God will drive out the Canaanites — 17-26[1]

Scholars do not agree on the theme of the chapter either. The following have been suggested: the meaning of Israel's selection, warning against alliances, holiness and holy war, divine love and grace, Israel's policy of holy war, and the conquest of Canaan.[2] It seems to me that the chiastic structure focuses the theme on the election of Israel by God's love and grace. How the nation is to deal with the Canaanites flows out of that election. The Canaanites must

---

[1] Robert O'Connell has developed a detailed, thirteen tier concentric structure for chapter 7 which suggests that verses 11-12 are at the center of the chapter. His minutely detailed outline demonstrates the unity of the chapter and its similarity in structure and rhetorical design to chapter 8 (see the commentary on chapter 8 below). Chapters 7 and 8 are at the heart of the larger unit, chapters 4–11. ("Deuteronomy VII 1-26: Asymmetrical Concentricity and the Rhetoric of Conquest," *VT* 42 [1992]: 248-265).

[2] O'Connell's analysis leads him to conclude that the primary focus of chapter 7 is "on appeals to human activity deemed necessary to the successful conquest and continued possession of the land" ("Deuteronomy VII 1-26," pp. 264-265).

be cleared from the land promised to the fathers so that chosen Israel can maintain her purity. The structure also shows that the chapter is a unit and should not be divided up and connected with other chapters.[3]

Furthermore, each of the parallel units is related to the other by repetition of key words. The first and last sections share "destroy totally" (vv. 2 and 26), "many; nations; clear away" (vv. 1 and 22), "possess" (vv. 1 and 17), "give" (vv. 2-3 and 23-24), "destroy" (vv. 4 and 23-24), and "quickly" (vv. 4 and 22). The two middle sections share "swore to the fathers" (vv. 8, 12, and 13), "covenant, loyalty" (vv. 9 and 12), "keep" (vv. 8, 9, 11, and 12), "love" (vv. 8, 9, and 13) and "do; ordinances" (vv. 11 and 12).[4]

Destroy the Canaanites from the Land (7:1-6)

7:1. When introduces a real condition in the future — it will happen. It is not some hypothetical possibility (cf. similar construction in 6:10). Moses uses familiar language for God giving Israel the land. God **brings** Israel into the land to **possess** it and **drive out** the **nations**. "Drive out" is a new and rare word but is parallel to "dispossess" used in verse 17 (cf. v. 22; 28:40; 1 Kgs 16:6).

The nations who inhabit the land and are the object of God's actions are listed. They are seven in number, probably a whole number intended to reflect completeness, that is, these seven represent all the people in Canaan who will be driven out. There are 27 places in the OT where these nations are listed, with the number ranging from two to twelve. Only two other times are the seven listed as here (Josh 3:10 and 29:11). Eleven times, six nations are listed (omitting the Girgashites; Deut 20:17; Exod 3:10,17; 23:23; 34:11; Josh 9:1; 11:3; 12:8; Judg 3:5; Neh 9:8).[5] The **Hittites, Amorites,** and **Canaanites** are often the first three listed, but sometimes in different order.[6] The last three names also often occur in lists in the same

---

[3]Contra Christensen, *Deuteronomy*, pp. 137,161. He connects verses 1-11 with chapter 6.

[4]For more detailed discussion see Hall, "Rhetoric," pp. 95-97.

[5]Tomoo Ishida, "The Structure and Historical Implications of the Lists of Pre-Israelite Nations," *Biblica* 60 (1978): 461-490.

[6]Weinfeld (*Deuteronomy*, pp. 362-363), following Ishida, uses the different orders as a dating scheme. Lists with Canaanites first are early (15th century

order. This method of listing was probably an ancient traditional, stylized way of noting the early inhabitants of Canaan (Exod 23:23 has six names in a different order).

Little is known about the **Girgashites** and **Perizzites** ("villagers"). The **Hivites** were in Canaan over a long period of time, both in the central area (Gen 34:2; Josh 9:7; 11:19) and in the north in the Lebanon hills (Judg 3:3; Josh 11:3). Some equate them with the Horites.[7]

The other four nations are better known. The Hittites founded an empire around 1800 BC in Asia Minor. They were Indo-Europeans who took their name from the Hatti, the earlier inhabitants of the region. They extended their control East and South and collided with Egypt for control of Palestine in the fourteenth century. After the collapse of the empire in 1200 BC, two dozen city-states became heir to the territory, some in Syria. These persisted until their overthrow in the eighth century. The Hittites mentioned in the OT may or may not be related to this northern group. In Genesis 23 Abraham bought a burial ground from Hittites in Hebron. Esau married two Hittite women (Gen 27:46). The Araunah of 2 Samuel 24:16ff is thought to have been Hittite. The ill-fated Uriah, David's body guard, was also a Hittite, probably from Jerusalem. All the Hittites mentioned in the OT probably come from the southern hill-country, rather than Asia Minor.[8]

The Amorites were an ancient Mesopotamian group who occupied the central hill country when Israel moved into the land (see on 1:7 above and Num 13:29; Josh 11:3). Amorites and Canaanites were names sometimes applied to the same groups.

Canaanites referred to the inhabitants of the coastal area (1:7; Num 13:29; Josh 11:3). However, the word had a broader meaning at times, especially in the Table of Nations in Genesis 10:15-19

BC when the land was commonly called Canaan). Lists with the Amorites first are ninth century (when inscriptions show Amurru was the name for the land). Lists with Hittites first are seventh century (when Hattai was the name for Palestine).

[7]*NBD*, p. 486, s.v. "Hivites."

[8]Harry A. Hoffner, Jr., "Some Contributions of Hittology to Old Testament Study," *TB* 20 (1969): 27-55, especially pp. 28-37; idem, "Hittites," *People of the OT World*, pp. 127-155; *NBD*, pp. 485-486, s.v. , "Hittites."

where their territory was all the land of Palestine. According to Genesis 10 the descendants of Canaan included the Jebusites, the Amorites, the Girgashites and the Hivites among others.[9]

The Jebusites dwelt mostly in the hill country around Jerusalem (Josh 15:8; 18:16). Jebus was an early name for the city (Judg 19:10-11). They were a minor group, yet Israel was unsuccessful in dislodging them permanently from Jerusalem until David's time (Josh 15:63; Judg 1:8,21; 19:11).[10]

These nations were **larger and stronger** than Israel (9:1). Thus there was little prospect that Israel could drive them out on her own. She would have to rely on the power and might of God (4:38; 11:23; Josh 23:9) which is the point of verse 2 (see v. 17 also)[11]

7:2 The defeat of the nations would be the work of God and Israel would be delivered (see vv. 20-24), but Israel would have to do battle with them and defeat them. Israel was also to treat these nations under the *ḥērem* principle (see 2:34 and comments there). However, *ḥērem* in this passage seems to convey a nuance different from **destroy them totally**. Verses 3-4 indicate that there would still be people alive in the land. Verse 22 indicates that the elimination would be gradual. Therefore, we either have a policy that was never carried out or a later ideal that was never implemented.[12] Or possibly verse five offers a commentary on how extensively the principle was to be applied; all that was to be utterly destroyed was the religious paraphernalia. Wright offers a middle ground. The root *ḥrm* should be understood here as meaning "renounce" in the sense of refusing to gain or profit by anything in the land. Thus Israel was commanded to utterly renounce any attempt to profit by establishing a relationship with the nations. The relationships they were to

---

[9]*NBD*, pp. 163-166, s.v. "Canaanites"; Keith Schoville, "Canaanites and Amorites," *Peoples of the OT World*, pp. 157-182. Also see below on 9:3.

[10]*NBD*, p. 553, s.v. "Jebusites."

[11]In Exod 1:9 Israel's size had the opposite effect, for the Egyptians perceived that Israel's rapid growth made them a threat. This dramatic growth was God's creation blessing at work.

[12]See Merrill, *Deuteronomy*, p. 180, and Judg 1:21-34 and I Kgs 9:20-21 for the former interpretation, and Weinfeld, *Deuteronomy*, p. 365, for the latter. Weinfeld calls this verse "wishful thinking" from the seventh century authors.

renounce were political alliances (v. 2b), social contacts (v. 3), and religious contacts (v. 5).[13]

Make no treaty forbade any political alliance through formal means. The Hebrew word for covenant (*bᵉrît*) has its secular meaning here (cf. Gen 21:27,32; 2 Sam 3:13), but the contrast was intended between the covenant Israel had with God and the one she was not to make with the nations.

7:3-4 Israel was to refuse social contact also. **Intermarriage** would involve the extended family and lead to compromise with the idolatrous religion of the spouse. That would threaten Israel's distinctiveness, loyalty to the only God, and violate the first two commandments. In the parallel text in Exodus 34:15-16, intermarriage would lead Israel to commit *prostitution* with the foreign gods. This reflects both the marriage metaphor used for the covenant between God and Israel and the fertility cult of the Canaanites.[14] Similar intermarriage, which involved political alliances as well, was one cause of Solomon's downfall (1 Kgs 11).

Intermarriage would earn God's wrath (burning **anger**) and the destruction they were to visit on the nations would come upon them instead. Israel would find herself treated just like the other nations because she would have become just like them.

7:5 Israel was also to refuse religious contact. This was the greatest of all the dangers for her and was addressed repeatedly as we have seen (4:15-20,23; 5:7,8-10; 6:14). The danger was so great because of the attractiveness of the Canaanite fertility cult. It promised fertility of the land and guaranteed it through sexually oriented cultic rites, including sacred prostitution. Through sexual intercourse, which the worshiper could imitate, the gods assured rain and crops. **Sacred stones** (*maṣṣibōth*) that were erected to represent the god marked the cultic sites. Many such stones have been found in ancient remains at Gezer, Hazor, Shechem and Arad. The sites also included **Asherah poles** — live trees or wooden poles representing the fertility goddess

---

[13]Wright, *Deuteronomy*, p. 109. The context here supports Wright. Also the root *ḥrm* does not always mean "destroy," (Lilley, "Understanding," pp. 176-177).

[14]These ideas were developed extensively by Hosea, Jeremiah, and Ezekiel. See comments on 5:18 above.

Asherah. The poles also may have had an image of the goddess on them (1 Kgs 15:13; 2 Kgs 23:7; Deut 16:21-22).[15]

7:6 Israel was not to participate in any way because she was different. She was **holy to the LORD**, set apart for service solely to God. Israel was holy because God was holy and her life was to imitate his (Lev 11:44-45; 19:2; 20:7-8,26; 21:6,8; Deut 14:2,21; 26:19; 28:9). Israel was to live in God's world as his witness, but she could not be a true witness to the world if she became a part of it. Syncretism[16] was the major danger to Israel. It involved an assimilation that would have been slow and unnoticed. Tragically, Israel did not heed Moses, and by the eighth century she was trapped in the fertility cult (Hos 1-4).

Of course Israel was not different from the nations in many ways, in such things as material culture, some laws, certain morals. But she was totally different in her theological foundation and her concept of God (Deut 4-6). Since God was unlike any other deity, Israel could not let religious differences become blurred.

Israel was also different because she was **chosen** (4:37; 10:15; 14:2) by God, elected out of all the nations to be his people. This choice was totally unmerited (v. 7) and was grounded only in God's love. She was chosen for God's purpose, elected for his service.[17] This made Israel God's **treasured possession**, a special word used six times for Israel to show her special status (Exod 19:5; Deut 14:2; 26:18; Ps 135:4; Mal 3:17, and here). She was his "crown jewel" from all of the nations.[18]

God Chose Israel Out of Love (7:7-11)

This section is intended to blunt any idea that Israel might have gleaned from verse 6 that she merited her election in any way.

7:7 God **set his affection** on Israel (10:15) and thus chose her. He was drawn to her because he loved her (v. 8). The word suggests

---

[15]Ringgren, *Religion*, p. 158.

[16]Syncretism is combining different religions or philosophical beliefs.

[17]H.H. Rowley, *The Biblical Doctrine of Election* (London: Lutterworth Press, 1950), ch. 1.

[18]*S e gullāh* refers to the special treasure of kings in 1 Chr 29:3 and Eccl 2:8. The NT applies the concept to Christians also but uses the phrase "people belonging to God": Titus 2:14 and 1 Pet 2:9 (quoting Exod 19:5).

both emotion and reasoned decision. It referred to the desire of a young man for a woman in Genesis 34:8 and Deuteronomy 21:11.

The affection was not because Israel deserved it. She was a small, ineffective people (not **numerous**). In fact Israel was an oppressed, enslaved people when God delivered her from Egypt. She was the **fewest** of people (or smallest), that is, she had no worth or attractiveness. She was not some nation that by its importance or strength could advance God's cause.[19] Anything that would be done would have to be done through God's power. This theme is continued in succeeding sermons. In 8:17 Israel had no economic power or expertise; in 9:4-6 she had no righteousness. Election was based totally on God's grace.

Though Israel was evaluated as being small here, elsewhere her large size was celebrated (Deut 26:5-10; 1:10; 10:22; 28:62; Exod 1:9). Her size seems to vary according to what the writer wanted to emphasize. Perhaps there is a figurative sense to the expression here, meaning that Israel was small (not important) on the international stage.[20]

7:8 The sole reason for Israel's election was God's love. God loved her because he loved her.[21] Moses had expressed this idea already (see on 4:34,37) and would later also (v. 13; 10:15; 23:5). God chose Israel because of his character and his promise to Abraham (1:8; 4:31; 6:18,23).

To the familiar language about the exodus Moses now added the idea of **redemption**. This carried the concept of paying a price for deliverance from evil. It was more than simple deliverance from danger or whatever. It was grounded in Exodus 13 and Numbers 18. In Deuteronomy the LORD is always the subject of this verb (9:26; 13:5; 15:5; 21:8; 24:18) and Israel's redemption from slavery is the object. It was on this historical foundation that the OT could build a theology of redemption. Subsequently, the prophets used the concept for both judgment and hope (Hos 7:13; 13:14; Isa 29:22; 35:10; Jer 15:21; 31:11). Because Israel refused to respond to God's redemption, he would punish them. But his desire was still to redeem them, although

---

[19]Paul gives the NT version of the concept in 1 Cor 1:26-29.

[20]According to Weinfeld the Rabbis took the verse to refer to humility versus pride (*Deuteronomy*, p. 369).

[21]This is a "wonderful tautology" according to Cairns (*Deuteronomy*, p. 91).

it would be after judgment. The Psalms also could affirm trust in God because of his redemption (Ps 31:5[6]; 55:18[19]; 71:23; 130:8). Everything that Israel was she owed to God.[22]

7:9 Keeping his covenant of love is a misleading translation. "Keeping" has a double direct object in the Hebrew. The LORD keeps the "covenant" *and* "love" (*ḥesed*, covenant love, loyalty). The covenant was a covenant of grace which was sustained by God's unrelenting loyalty to it, which was another aspect of his reliability (see v. 12). The focus was the uncontested trustworthiness of God, demonstrated in every aspect of his relationship with Israel.[23]

This loyalty was shown toward those who **love him** and **keep his commands**. Obedience and love are synonyms in this verse (as elsewhere in Deuteronomy). Israel, as the recipient of the covenant based on God's love, had an obligation to love him back, which was to be demonstrated through obedience (5:10; Exod 20:5).

7:10 But Israel could choose to make herself an enemy of God. The nation or the individual could "hate" God, that is, they could choose to disobey the covenant. There was no middle ground – it was obey or disobey. There were consequences for each choice. God would **repay** his enemies, bringing just retribution on them (cf. Isa 65:6; 59:18; 66:6; Jer 16:18; 25:14). Retribution was his action designed to restore order in the world. God would also "repay" to *his* face (literal Hebrew), not **their** face (NIV). In other words the retribution would be to the individual sinner (NRSV, "in their own person"), not to the family unit or future generation as suggested in 5:9.[24]

7:11 The **therefore** concludes this section with a typical Deuteronomic admonition (4:6,9,23; 5:1,10,32; 6:3,17,25). Based on God's love and promises, Israel should obey. The repetition of **commands, decrees and laws** is often used as a rhetorical device to mark breaks in the text (4:1,40; 5:1; 6:1,20; 8:11; 10:12-13, etc.).

---

[22]See Robert L. Hubbard, "פדה," *NIDOTTE,* 3:578-582. Of course in the NT redemption is grounded in Jesus Christ: Rom 3:24-25; Mark 10:45; 1 Cor 6:19-20,22-23; Heb 9:15.

[23]Some commentators take "covenant" and "love" as an hendiadys, two terms expressing a complete idea. So they translate it as "gracious covenant" (Weinfeld, *Deuteronomy*, p. 370) or "loyalty to covenant" (Merrill, *Deuteronomy*, p. 181).

[24]Wright, *Deuteronomy*, pp. 116-117, sees vv. 9-10 as the core of the chapter and close to the NT "God is love."

God Will Bless Obedient Israel (7:12-16)

This section corresponds to the previous one (vv. 7-11) by laying out in further detail the blessings that will accrue to Israel if she obeys the covenant law (expanding verse 9). The result of obedience was God's desire to bless. The rhetorical style is prediction, a portrayal of the future possibilities for an obedient nation. בָּרַךְ (*brk,* "to bless") occurs three times in vv. 13-14, setting the tone for the unit. This section is a more detailed version of Exod 23:25-26.

7:12 A rare word combination appears in v. 12 and 8:20, suggesting a rhetorical connection between the two verses. "Because" (עֵקֶב, *'eqeb*) plus "you obey" (NIV, **If you pay attention**) holds out the promise of blessing. The same phrase with the negative in 8:20 promises destruction. The two options before Israel could not be more starkly put — blessing or destruction, life with God or death (30:15). The word play in this verse provides a motivation. If Israel will "keep" (NIV, **are careful**) the commands God **will keep his covenant**. God had established his covenant with Israel out of love, but he expected reciprocity.

7:13 The resulting blessing was materialistic. It included God's love (*'hb,* not *ḥēsed* as in v. 12) and fruitfulness. First of all they would **increase** as a people, in contrast to their original smallness (v. 7). This would fulfill the creation blessing of Genesis 1 and 9. Secondly, all their crops and livestock would experience fertility (see on 6:11). All the necessities of life would be provided and then some.[25]

This promise was crucial to Israel for it emphasized that the destruction of the Canaanite fertility gods would have no effect on Israel's actual fertility. Those false gods were totally powerless to influence fertility and their demise would be meaningless. There is also ironic satire here, for each of the Hebrew words used for the different products were also names of Semitic deities. The Israelites may or may not have understood the wordplay.[26]

These blessings would be to Israel further tangible proof of God's grace and reliability, providing further grounding for their ability to "know God" (v. 9). They would experience God not just through the Exodus but in their daily life in the land (see chapter 8).

---

[25]See the listing in 28:1-11. Because of disobedience the blessings could be reversed, 28:15ff.

[26]Grain = Dagon; wine = Tiresh; calves = Sheqer; lambs = 'Ashtorot.

7:14 The specific emphasis on children recalls the Genesis patri-archal narratives in two ways. It reverses the barrenness of the matri-archs (Sarah, Rebekah, and Rachel) and it fulfills the promise to Abraham in Genesis 15:5. Israel may have been the least of all nations (v. 7), but through God's covenant love they would **be blessed more than** all others.[27]

7:15 The ancient world did not understand basic sanitation and was disease-ridden. Therefore, a significant blessing would be to be free from **disease**. These diseases have been variously interpreted as the diseases of the plagues (Exod 9:9) or the typical diseases found in Egypt. The latter included especially smallpox, malaria, polio, TB, eye diseases, dysentery, and elephantiasis.[28] Just as freedom from dis-ease was a blessing of the covenant, the onslaught of disease was a possible curse or judgment (Lev 26:16; Deut 28:22,27,59).[29]

7:16 This verse concludes the section with a reprise of verses 1-7 and a look ahead to the next section. To keep Israel from allowing emotions to get in the way of carrying out God's command, she is warned to show no **pity** (cf. v. 2). God required justice under the law and in his treatment of the nations. While compassion was appro-priate in certain circumstances, it was not in this situation (cf. Deut 13:8[9]; 19:13,21; 25:12). The threat of the Canaanite gods was suf-ficient reason. Though nothing but wood and stone, they could allure and entrap Israel. The metaphor of **be a snare** was inspired by the use of the bird net or animal net. The bird would be enticed into the range of the net by some lure and unwittingly be trapped. Therefore, everything was to be destroyed or denounced so that the enticement would not even be present. The very existence of the covenant people was at stake.[30]

---

[27]Human barrenness offers God the opportunity to exhibit his power and blessing; cf. Isa 54:1-3.

[28]Walton and Matthews, *Genesis–Deuteronomy*, p. 230; Tigay, *Deuteronomy*, p. 89; cf. Exod 15:26.

[29]The role of the suffering servant (Isa 53:4), the healing ministry of Jesus, and the healing in the early church reveal further God's desire to eliminate these plagues of human existence. Although ultimate relief awaits the new heaven and earth (Rev 21:4; 22:3), God still can use the church for healing (Jas 5:14-15).

[30]Cf. W.R. Domeris, "יָקֹשׁ," *NIDOTTE*, 2:525-527.

God Will Drive Out the Canaanites (7:17-26)

This section returns to the subject of the first unit (vv. 1-6) and repeats many of the same ideas. Israel's small number was not to be a reason for concern.

7:17-19 Israel's smallness could become a reason for lack of confidence. It was for the former generations (1:26-28) and led to their rebellion. The current generation must not emulate their fathers. The antidote to such fear was a good memory of what God had already done (1:21,29-38; 4:9,29; 6:12; 8:17-18). He had taken care of the Egyptians and exhibited his power and might against them. Consequently, the nations in the land would pose no threat. As Moses had already stated many times, the key to the present and the future was the past (2:21-22; 4:34; 6:22).

7:20 Part of God's demonstration of power would be to **send a hornet** among the nations. The significance of this "hornet" is uncertain. Is it intended literally or metaphorically? Besides a literal hornet, the Hebrew word צִרְעָה (ṣir'āh) can mean "destruction, fear, or discouragement." The difficulty comes from the fact that the word occurs only three times in the OT, all in similar contexts (Exod 23:28; Josh 24:12).[31] It could mean that just as a hornet caused chaos and panic, God's intervention would also cause panic (see v. 23 and 1:44). For example, a report of what God had done for Israel discouraged the people of Jericho in Joshua 2:10-11. The related root (ṣr') refers to suffering from a skin disease (Lev 13:44f; 2 Kgs 5:1). Merrill suggests the hornet could be God himself.[32] Perhaps it was an obscure reference to the angel who would go before Israel (Exod 23:20).

7:21 The basis for Israel's confidence was that the **LORD your God who is among you** was **great and awesome**. Moses had already established this point (4:33-37) and needed only to remind Israel. Since God was the one who struck terror in others, Israel's fear was unfounded. Joshua assured the people that they could be certain God was among them when he drove out the nations before them (Josh 3:9-10).[33]

---

[31]The LXX translates the word as "wasp's nest" all three times. First century Judaism also interpreted the word literally.

[32]Merrill, *Deuteronomy*, p. 183.

[33]Actually God was among Israel from the earliest time in the cloud and fire and in the tabernacle, in order to lead and assure. It was possible, how-

7:22 This verse expands on verse 1 with the introduction of a new idea. God would **drive out** the nations, but not all at once. It would be a gradual process, **little by little**. The purpose would be for the protection of Israel. So the promise of verse 13 would take some time for its fulfillment. Joshua and Judges show that inhabiting the land was a lengthy, confused, and incomplete process. In the book of Joshua we find general descriptions of total destruction (Josh 10:29–11:23) followed in subsequent texts by qualifying statements (Josh 11:18; Judg 1–2). According to Judges some of the original inhabitants were left to test Israel (2:20–3:6). All the texts must be examined to give us the true picture of Israel taking and settling the land.[34]

7:23-24 Canaan was a land of small city-states in the Late Bronze Age (1550–1200 B.C.). Therefore, an invading army could defeat them one by one. Joshua 12:7-24 lists 31 kings who were conquered by Israel.

For the ancient Semite, survival of the **name** was important. After death the only thing that remained was fame in the form of the persistent memory of the person's name. To wipe out the memory was the worst thing that could happen.

7:25-26 The repeated command to destroy the idols here adds a new possibility. Israel might be in danger of **coveting the silver and gold** (the same word as in 5:21). The idols were inlaid with precious metals, which would naturally appeal to the greed of Israelites.[35] Therefore, to eliminate the temptation, the metals were reserved for God.

The strongest possible language was used for God's attitude toward the idols. They were **detestable** and **abhorrent**. The practices of the Canaanites was regularly referred to by these strong

---

ever, that God's presence could be a threat to them as well (see Deut 6:15; 23:14[15]; 31:17).

[34]Deuteronomy 9:3 seems to contradict this verse. In 7:22 the nations will not be driven out "quickly" (*mahēr*, NIV "all at once") but in 9:3 God will drive them out "quickly"(same Hebrew word). Weinfeld suggests the solution is to understand *mahēr* in 9:3 as "easily" (*Deuteronomy*, p. 376). Also Jewish commentators have suggested 9:3 referred to the wars of conquest, not the settlement in the land. Different perspectives on the actual events of the conquest are certainly possible in these two passages.

[35]Achan is the case study in disobedience to this command (Josh 7). He was seduced by the silver and gold (v. 21).

words (Lev 18:26,27,29,30; Deut 18:12,19; 20:18; 1 Kgs 14:24; 2 Kgs 16:3; 21:2; 2 Chr 33:2; 36:14).[36] Other practices were classified as detestable also: cheating, perverse sexual relations, impure foods and defective sacrifices. All these made God's holy people unclean and unfit for God. The danger lay in the ability they had to make Israel detestable to God as well. Therefore, utter destruction in this case was crucial to Israel's survival.

Invoking the *ḥērem* ends the sermon where it began (v. 2). Perhaps its application to the idols sheds some light on its use for the nations in the first section. Joshua 6:19 indicates that the "devoted things," the silver and gold and other valuable objects, were to be eliminated from Israel's private usage by giving them to God. Since these verses here deal with gold and silver inlaid idols, perhaps the principle was to be understood in the same sense as Joshua 6. Thus the idols would not have been totally destroyed (despite the NIV translation). It is also possible then that the total destruction of the inhabitants (NIV) did not mean annihilation (as vv. 3 and 22 suggest). A clear translation of this complex term in these texts is difficult.[37]

---

[36]Ezekiel uses *tô'ăbāh* "detestable" 43 times for cultic impurity and aberrant practices such as idolatry. See Michael A. Grisanti, "תעב," *NIDOTTE,* 4:314-318.

[37]Since Weinfeld and others think that Deuteronomy is from the seventh century, they see this passage as a later idealization, creating a picture of the past that never existed.

DEUTERONOMY 8

3. Warning: Do Not Forget God (8:1-20)

Deuteronomy 8 is one of the most carefully constructed sermons in the entire book, making the most of the rhetorical device of chiastic structure. The sermon clearly develops a line of thought up to verse 11, which states the main idea and marks the focus of the chiasm. The second half develops away from the focal point through a repetition of the same details as found in the first half. Though a more detailed progression could be provided, the following simple outline will be used in this commentary for clarity and ease of treatment.[1]

Introduction: 1
A. Manna to test you, so remember — 2-3
   B. God led you in the wilderness — 4-5
      C. The blessings of the land — 6-9
         D. Satisfaction brings praise — 10
           E. Do not forget — 11
         D'. Satisfaction brings a warning — 12a
      C'. The blessings of the good land — 12b-14
   B'. Leading in the wilderness — 15
A'. The manna to test you, so remember — 16-18
           E'. Do not forget — 19-20

---

[1]For more detail see Hall, "Rhetoric," pp. 88-90. Norbert Lohfink was the first to publish a chiastic structure for Deuteronomy 8 (*Das Hauptgebot*, p. 195). Robert O'Connell followed three decades later with a more detailed study, done without knowledge of Lohfink's work ("Deuteronomy VIII 1-20: Asymmetrical Concentricity and the Rhetoric of Providence," *VT* 40 [1990]: 437-453). The major redactional study of Deuteronomy 8 posits 3 strata in the chapter, thus nullifying the structural symmetry of the sermon (F. Garcia Lopez, "Yahve, fuente ultima de vida: analisis de Deuteronomy 8," *Bib* 62 [1981]: 21-54).

Sections c, e, c', and e' have the same themes. The last section has sometimes been seen as a later redactional addition because it does not seem to fit the sermon. But more likely Moses put it at the end to emphasize the main theme of the sermon from verse 11 and round off an emphatic conclusion. The repetition of forget (vv. 11, 14,19) and remember (vv. 1 and 18) highlight the theme of the chapter and hold it together. Israel should not let the blessing of God and resulting wealth distract her from her dependence on God and loyalty to him.

Introduction (8:1)

8:1 This sermon begins with all the familiar admonitions. The emphasis was on **every command** that God was *commanding* (NIV, **giving**) Israel. The singular "command" was intended in a collective sense to represent all of the commands, statutes, and decrees that were given in the *Torah* (see also 5:31; 6:1,25; 11:8,22; 15:5; 19:9; 27:1). Obedience (6:1-3) was the road to **life** (4:1; 5:33), to **increase** (6:3; 7:13-14), and to **possession** of the land (4:1,5). Obedience would allow Israel to reap the benefits of God's promise to the fathers (1:8; 4:31; 6:23; see v. 18).

Remember, the Manna Was a Test (8:2-3)

8:2-3 To prepare for the main admonition in verse 11 (do not forget) Moses appealed to Israel's memory, for the past was the key to the present (as he had so often taught). In this case, Israel should **remember** that God led them in **the desert** and the purpose of that experience. This emphasis complemented Moses' previous commands in 5:15 (remember servitude in Egypt) and 7:18 (remember God's power over Pharaoh). In 6:20-23 the past was the foundation for instructing the children. Here the past becomes an occasion for reflecting on the purpose of the experience. It was a time of **humbling** and **testing.**

For Moses the wilderness had a twofold function. It was a time of punishment for rebellion (1:19-46), but it was also a time for Israel to learn submission through enduring hardship. The latter was intended as a positive experience. It was an opportunity for Israel to discover the gracious provision of God. But they could do so only through realizing their total dependency on him. Thus it became an opportunity for Israel to live up to her promise of 5:27. God wanted to **know** if he could count on her. Would she be reliable and faithful and keep her integrity?[2]

God's method for humbling Israel was to cause her to be **hungry**. From this she was to realize she was totally dependent on God for everything (7:16). The exact nature of the test was spelled out in Exodus 16:1-5. The people longed for the meat of Egypt, so the manna was given as a test to see if Israel would follow God's instructions (some people failed the test, Exod 16:20,27).

The **manna** was a mysterious substance. Many have tried to give its origin a naturalistic explanation. For example, it has been likened to the honeydew-like excretion of certain insects that feed on tamarisk twigs every June. But this explanation does not account for the large amount and its abundance for forty years.[3]

The naming of the manna was derived from a pun. When the Israelites saw the white droplets they asked, "הוּא מָן [*mān hû'*]," "What is it?" (Exod 16:15). So the substance was called "*mān*," equivalent perhaps to a slang word like "Whatszit."

The manna also had another lesson to teach. It was to remind the people that there was more to life than just food. They were dependent on God for everything. Although the NIV and other translations render the phrase **every word that comes from the mouth of the LORD**, the literal Hebrew is "*everything* that comes from the mouth of the LORD," a different concept. Many commentators spiritualize the lesson and reflect on the spiritual word of God that sustains life (which in Deuteronomy is the decrees and statutes). Other texts such as Isaiah 55 provide a cogent commentary.[4] However, other things than just words come from God's mouth (2 Sam 22:9 [fire]; Job 37:2 [rumbling]; Lam 3:38 [calamities and good things]). Therefore, since "the mouth of God" probably means God himself, the significance of the lesson was to be comprehensive. Israel was to learn from the manna that they were dependent on

---

[2]At Massah Israel had tested God's faithfulness (6:16). How misguided and arrogant that was is clarified here. Israel's faithfulness needed testing, not God's.

[3]*NBD*, s.v., "Manna"; John Durham, *Exodus*. Word Biblical Commentary (Waco: Word, 1987), pp. 224-225.

[4]Merrill, *Deuteronomy*, p. 186.

God for everything needed for life, physical and spiritual, and that God would provide it.[5]

Moses had already addressed this issue in 6:3,11,18 but here he is more explicit. A major lesson of this sermon was that Israel could not rely on her own power and wealth, but must rely on God. Moses returns to this theme in vv. 12-17.

God Led You in the Wilderness (8:4-5)

8:4-5 God sustained Israel in the wilderness not only with food but with clothing and health. The similar statement in 29:5 refers to the sandals that did not wear out, rather than **feet** that **did not swell**. The parallel verse in 8:15 concentrates on Israel's safe passage through the wilderness. It was waterless and full of deadly creatures but God provided water and protection (see Jer 2:6 and Hos 11:1-2 for different interpretations of the wilderness experience).

The humbling and testing period of the wilderness was also a time of **discipline**. Moses resorted to the father-son metaphor to emphasize that the discipline was motivated by love (7:8; Prov 3:11-12). Although the OT often spoke of God chastising Israel for disobedience to the covenant (Lev 26:18; Ps 6:1; 94:10; Hos 10:10), that

---

[5]John Willis, "Man Does Not Live by Bread Alone," *RestQ* 16 (1973): 141-149. Jesus' use of this verse quotes the LXX which adds "word." The fact that in his most serious encounter with Satan, Jesus relied on Deuteronomy reflects his deep meditation on the book (cf. on 6:13,16). It obviously had a significant place in his life. The temptation for Jesus was whether he was going to be a real human or play at it. He took the human path, relying on Scripture and the Holy Spirit, not divine power (see A.B. Taylor, "Decision in the Desert: The Temptation of Jesus in the Light of Deuteronomy," *Int* 14 [1960]: 300-309). The parallels between Jesus and Israel presented in the Gospels also testify to the profound grounding of the life of the Messiah in the OT, especially Deuteronomy (Wright, *Deuteronomy*, p. 125). Thus Jesus was the son God loved (Matt 3:17; Deut 7:6,8) who spent forty days in the wilderness (Matt 4:2; Deut 8:2,14) and became hungry. Jesus was also the true bread of life (John 6:32-40) come down from heaven and the living water from whom anyone could drink (John 7:37-39). These parallels go to the very heart of the unity of God's purpose that is so profoundly expressed in the unity of the Scripture, the Old and New Testament. For further study see Mark Strom, *The Symphony of Scripture: Making Sense of the Bible's Many Themes* (Downers Grove, IL: InterVarsity, 1990), and Christopher J.H. Wright, *Knowing Jesus through the Old Testament* (Downers Grove, IL: InterVarsity, 1992).

was not the sole purpose of discipline. Suffering could also be educative. In this case it was an opportunity for Israel to learn the providential care of God. In Deuteronomy 1:31, God the father was carrying the infant Israel. In 4:36 and here Israel was the young child who was being shaped and educated by the loving father so that he could become what God intended him to become.

The Blessings of the Land (8:6-9)

8:6 Verse six transitions to the next section by picking up themes from verse one. If Israel were to pass the testing, she must exhibit covenant loyalty by obedience. This would enable her to **walk** in God's **way** (cf. v. 2: God caused Israel to *walk* [NIV, "led"] all the *way* in the desert) and **fear** him (5:29; 6:13). Walking in God's way meant doing what was just and right (Gen 18:19).[6]

8:7-9 Here Moses turned to a description of the promised land that contrasted it with the wilderness (**land** occurs six times in these verses). The impact of the verses is heightened in the Hebrew by their poetic quality. **For** (v. 7) is better translated "when" because it opens a long conditional clause that culminates in verse 11. The **good land** had already been noted several times (1:25,35; 3:25; 4:21,22; 6:18) but its goodness is given more detail here, beyond the "milk and honey" of 6:3.

Verse seven describes the water resources. There were **streams**, or rivers, such as the Jordan River, which was surface water. In addition there was subterranean water — both **springs** that bubbled up and deeper ground water.[7] In the Near East reliable water sources were (and are) crucial to survival. Cisterns were also an important resource for ancient Israel, though not mentioned here.[8]

Verse eight lists the foodstuffs available. **Pomegranate** (an addition to the list from 6:11) was a popular fruit, fresh or dried. It had juice that could be drunk. The pomegranate was a popular subject

---

[6]See also 5:33; 10:12; 11:22; 19:4; 26:17. In Judaism the entire collected tradition of Jewish practice is called *halakha*, from הלך (*hlk*, "walk").

[7]These three categories are not made clear in the NIV translation.

[8]NBD, s.v., "Cistern," has a detailed drawing of a large cistern from ancient Ta'anak. Dan Cole, "How Water Tunnels Worked," *BAR* 6,2 (1980): 8-29, has a fascinating study of the water systems at Hazor, Megiddo, Gibeon, and Jerusalem. Today availability of water is a major source of tension in the Middle East.

for religious art (Exod 28:33-34; 1 Kgs 7:18,20,42) and was used for sensual overtones in poetry (S of S 4:3,13).[9] The corresponding verse, verse 13, also listed flocks and herds, completing the picture of abundance. According to Ezekiel 27:17, Israel had surpluses to export on occasion. Excavations at ancient Ekron have uncovered Israelite **olive oil** production complexes from the seventh century BC unparalleled in the ancient world.

Verse nine lists the mineral resources, **iron** and **copper**. Copper was mined in the Arabah, near Timnah, as early as the thirteenth century BC. It was in wide use for daily utensils. It was also mixed with tin to form bronze.[10]

Iron products were rare until about 1200 BC. Iron was first refined by the Hittites in Anatolia (modern Turkey). The Philistines brought the technology to Palestine. Earlier references in ancient written sources perhaps refer to meteorite iron. The technology was not common in Israel until Solomon's time (1 Sam 13:19-22). Iron ore was found in the Arabah, near Mt. Carmel, below Mt. Hermon, and in the Transjordan area (though not in large amounts or of high quality). The only high quality iron today is found near the Jabbok River.[11] Iron was easier to mine than copper, but the technology to produce hard, usable iron implements was more difficult than that to produce copper implements. Thus bronze and copper were widely used until upheavals across the whole Mediterranean world and the Middle East in the thirteenth century BC cut off trade. Then iron working became a necessity.[12]

---

[9]André Lemaire describes a small ivory pomegranate shaped piece from the eighth century BC that was apparently used on the scepter of a priest who served in the temple: "Probable Head of Priestly Scepter From Solomon's Temple Surfaces in Jerusalem," *BAR* 10,1 (1984): 24-29. Also several pomegranate-shaped vessels and pomegranate-inscribed seals from the Israelite period have been found in Palestine.

[10]Scholars designate 3100–1200 BC as the Bronze Age in the ancient Near East.

[11]The Israelites entered the land as a major shift was being made in ancient Near East material culture, that is from the Bronze Age to the Iron Age. Israel entered during the Late Bronze Age, 1550–1200 BC. The beginning of the Iron Age, which is set at 1200 BC, parallels the time of the Judges. David's reign as king began around 1000 BC. Job 28:1-11 describes the mining process. See also Isa 44:12; 1 Kgs 8:51; Job 40:18; Dan 2:40.

[12]See Jerome D. Muhly, "How Iron Technology Changed the World — And Gave the Philistines a Military Edge," *BAR* 8,6 (1982): 40-52.

The Promised Land had everything Israel needed for living in it. It was truly to be proof of God's blessing and his providential care.

Satisfaction Brings Peace (8:10)

8:10 The productive land would satisfy every need of Israel, even to excess. It would be a wonderful change from the wilderness (6:11). God's gifts were intended to satisfy and even give pleasure (11:15; 14:29; 26:12; 31:20; Ps 42:4; 67:4; Isa 12:3; 61:3). The proper response to God's blessings was to return blessing by **praise** ("bless" in the Hebrew). To bless God was to praise him (Ps 28:6; 31:21; 66:20; 145:1-2). However, because of the human propensity to twist everything about the divine, God's blessing could yield pride (vv. 12-15), which Moses will address.[13]

Do Not Forget (8:11)

8:11 This verse is the focal point of the sermon. **Be careful** is the only inflected imperative in the whole chapter, calling attention to this warning and completing the sentence begun in verse seven.[14] When Israel had experienced all of God's blessings, they should not, through some perverse thought process, forget where all their good fortune came from and begin to go their own way.

It is difficult to overemphasize the importance Moses puts on obedience in Deuteronomy. It was obedience to the covenant law that demonstrated Israel's love for God, her fear of God, her loyalty to the covenant, and her wholehearted devotion to God. Obedience would remind Israel of God's grace, love, and faithfulness. It would also protect her against apostasy (the real impact of "forgetting"; see on 4:9 and cf. 4:23,31; 6:12; 9:7).

The "remember" of verses two and eighteen was an important antithesis to **forget** of verse eleven (cf. v. 14) as well as a clue to the sermon structure. A good memory was critical to an obedient relationship with God. A slide into syncretism with pagan idolatry would not be innocent or harmless. It would take a deliberate act. The covenant Lord demanded single-hearted devotion. A loss of focus would be fatal.

---

[13]Deuteronomy speaks often of God's blessing: 1:11; 2:7; 7:13,14; 14:24, 29; 15:4,10; 16:10,15; 28:3-6.

[14]The other imperatives noted in the NIV are implied by the grammar.

Satisfaction Brings Warning (8:12a)

8:12a Verse 12 begins the second half of the chiasm (and sermon) in which Moses retreats from the focal point via the same subject path that he used to advance to it. In the first half he stressed that sufficiency *should* generate praise (vv. 2-10). In the second half he warns that sufficiency *could* generate pride (vv. 12-17). Verse 12a, as verse seven, begins a long phrase which ends in verse 17. It repeats verse 10: if they forget God, they will have misunderstood the blessings in the good land.

The Blessings of the Good Land (8:12b-14)

8:12b-14 The situation assumed here seems to be that Israel had been settled in the land for some time (as opposed to 6:10-11) and had made productive use of the resources of the land. But even that growth would be a product of God's blessing, not their effort (cf. 7:13). Still such productivity could lead to pride and a loss of the sense of dependency (cf. 17:14-20 where the same warning is given for the king; see Hos 13:6). Such loss could in turn lead to the apostasy Moses so feared (v. 14). Pride was the cause of the first sin (Gen 3) and rebellion against God was the result. Israel could find herself in the same situation. God had given ample proof of his provision (vv. 15-16), but would it be enough?

Leading in the Wilderness (8:15)

8:15 This verse matches verses 4-5 but emphasizes the dangerous aspects of the wilderness, rather than God's leading and discipline. The **venomous snakes** were literally "fiery (שָׂרָף, *śārāph*) snakes" (compare the seraphs of Isa 6:2,6).[15] This recalls the attack of the snakes in Numbers 21:6-9. The provision of water recalls Exodus 17:6 and Numbers 10:8,11.

---

[15]Some have suggested the translation "flying snakes," but there is little support in the ancient sources for such an idea, despite the early Greek historian Herodotus who talked about them. Based on comparison with an Akkadian cognate the word refers to "piercing" snakes, meaning deadly poisonous snakes. See D.J. Wiseman, "Flying Serpants?" *TB* 23 (1972): 108-110.

The Manna Was to Test, so Remember (8:16-18)

8:16-17 Moses returned to where he began the sermon by recalling the provision and purpose of manna again. There was no better proof of God's blessing. Verse 17 concludes the thought begun in verse 12. When Israel was satisfied, she might say that everything was really the production of her own efforts. She would be in danger of confusing her own effort with God's blessing.

The road from dependency to self-centered sufficiency is paved with material wealth. The frequent admonitions in Deuteronomy to care for the alien, widow, and orphan (10:18-19; 24:19-21; 26:12-13; 27:19) called Israel to responsible use of wealth. Amos the prophet is rightly noted for his preaching on the dangers of wealth. It generated oppression of the poor (4:1; 5:11), perversion of justice through bribery (5:12), self-indulgence (6:1-6), and dishonesty in business (8:4-8). Unless one's labor was done for the Lord, it was done in vain (Ps 127:1-2).

This sermon raised for ancient Israel an important issue: the concept of retributive justice. People, ancient and modern, have a tendency to turn the concept into a purely anthropological one. Everything happens according to a human perspective. However, Moses affirms two crucial points. First, some suffering may not be the result of sin, but may fit into God's educative purposes (vv. 2,5, 16). Secondly, material wealth may not be a reward for good behavior but be a result of God's grace. In 9:4-5 Moses further affirmed this second point. Israel did not receive the land because her righteousness merited it. It was only because of the wickedness of the nations that she received it. God was a just God (32:4) and was committed to justice in the human sphere. But his justice was much more complex than the simplistic formulation favored by humans: sin merits punishment and goodness merits reward.[16]

8:18 The sermon comes to a climax with repetition of the main point — remember what God had done (so you will not forget him, v. 11). God's blessing of wealth confirmed the covenant. It proved his faithfulness to his promise to the patriarchs.

---

[16]See John Gammie, "The Theology of Retribution in the Book of Deuteronomy," *CBQ* 32 (1970): 1-12; Andrew Hill and John Walton, *Survey of the Old Testament* (Grand Rapids: Zondervan, 1991), pp. 271-272, 281-282, 290-291.

Do Not Forget (8:19-20)

8:19-20 These two verses are outside of the chiastic structure to emphasize the main theme from verse 11. Via a conditional sentence they pose the possible consequence of forgetting. Moses had not spelled it out so vividly before (cf. 6:14-15; 7:4).[17]

I testify against you is better translated "I warn you" (cf. Exod 19:21; 1 Sam 8:9; Jer 6:10 and NRSV). Israel will suffer divine judgment and will be treated just as the seven nations in the land were to be treated (7:1-2,17-26). In other words, Israel would become an enemy of God just like every other nation. Such a development would be a reversal of God's election of Israel through the covenant as so tenderly portrayed in 7:6-8.

Moses had taught that Israel was to learn to live by everything that came from the mouth of God (v. 3). He ends the sermon by a similar warning. Destruction would come to Israel if they "did not listen to the voice of the LORD" (NIV, **for not obeying the LORD**). First and last Israel was totally dependent on God. It was a lesson she needed to thoroughly learn.

---

[17]The verses also provide commentary on the first commandment, 5:7.

DEUTERONOMY 9

4. Warning: There Is No Basis for Self-righteousness (9:1–10:11)

This section, which begins at 9:1, concludes at 10:11 (cf. the emphasis on possessing the land in 9:1 and 10:11). Chapter 10:12-22 is a final admonition connected thematically to 9:1–10:11. The development of thought can be seen in the structure of this lengthy sermon.

- a. 9:1-6: God will drive the nations out, but not because of Israel's merit
- b. 9:7-24: Israel was rebellious from the first, as seen in the golden calf incident
- c. 9:25-29: Moses' intercessory prayer
- d. 10:1-11: The new tablets of stone
- e. 10:12-22: Final admonition: love, fear, and serve the one and only God

The central portion of the sermon, 9:7–10:11 is a summary of the events recorded in Exodus 32 and 34. It is offered as support for the assertion in 9:1-6 that the wickedness of the nations did not automatically prove the righteousness of Israel. In fact, history proved just the opposite. Israel had always been stubborn and rebellious. Nevertheless, God would still give her the land because of his graciousness, love, and faithfulness to the promise to the forefathers. This sermon thus expands on the lesson of 7:1-7: it was God's love that prompted Israel's election, not her merit. However, God expected a specific response from Israel (10:12-22) as the covenant people. Israel did not earn the covenant through her behavior, but it could only be maintained through obedience.

This text also has an interesting relationship to 5:2-23a, the giving of the Ten Commandments. Chapter five related the first giving of the commandments within the context of admonitions to Israel to obey (4:32-40 and 5:23b-31) and their promise to obey (5:27). Chapters nine and ten related both the first giving and the second giving of the commandments within the context of Israel's repeated failure to heed the admonitions or to obey.[1]

God Will Drive Out the Nations but Not because of Israel's Merit (9:1-6)

This section builds on the warnings to Israel in the previous two chapters. She should not think that there was some inherent greatness in her that merited her election (7:7-8), nor was she to think her affluence came from her own efforts (8:12-17). Now she is cautioned against thinking that she had a righteousness that merited the land.

9:1-2 Hear, O Israel is a strong introductory statement used to call attention to the importance of what follows (4:1; 5:1; 6:4). The address that follows was as important as the Great Shema. The focus in the first two verses was on Israel, "you."

The setting is similar to chapters 1-3. Israel was still poised to enter the Promised Land and must go in and possess it (1:8). The nations were still **greater** and stronger than Israel (4:38; 11:23; 7:1: "larger and stronger"). The cities were still **large** with **walls to the sky**. The evaluation of the first generation was in fact accurate (cf. 1:28 which serves as a basis for 9:1; cf. also Num 13:28). The **Anakites** were still there as they had certainly heard from their fathers.[2] Nothing had changed from when the first generation, intimidated by the Anakites, had refused to try to take the land. Even the proverbial **Who can stand up against the Anakites?** was true. Moses did not try to minimize what Israel was facing. By themselves they were incapable of conquest.

9:3 By shifting the focus to the third person, that is to God, Moses could affirm that the threat of the Anakites was not serious before the power and might of the LORD. Israel could **be assured** or

---

[1]Robert O'Connell, "Deuteronomy IX 7–X 7,10-11: Panelled Structure, Double Rehearsal and the Rhetoric of Covenant Rebuke," *VT* 42 (1992): 492-493.

[2]See the footnote on 1:28. The Middle Bronze Age city defenses were formidable. They consisted of sloping, earth-packed mounds with trenches at the bottom dug to bedrock. The mounds were topped by walls 20-25 feet thick and up to 30 feet high. Some of these certainly persisted into the Late Bronze Age; cf. Walton and Matthews, *Genesis–Deuteronomy*, p. 231.

"know, be informed, learn from this" (see same use in verse 6, "Understand"; cf. 4:39; 7:9; 8:5; 11:2) that their God was going before them to destroy the inhabitants. Israel knew that God was a "devouring fire" (see on 4:24). But it was a threat to her if she failed to remain faithful. Here Israel learned that the LORD could also be a threat to her enemies.[3]

Israel's cooperation with God in destroying the Canaanites was again stressed. Four verbs divide the task evenly between God and Israel. God would **destroy** and **subdue**; Israel would **drive out** and **annihilate**. For the first time Israel was told that the LORD would "subdue" her enemies. He would humble them through military defeat (Judg 3:30; 4:23; 8:28; 11:33; 1 Sam 7:13).[4] This message of assurance was not believed by the first generation and resulted in the terrible sojourn in the wilderness (1:34-36; 2:1; 8:2,15). It would be further disaster if the current generation did not believe the message either.

9:4 This verse is the crux of the sermon. It reflects what Israel might be tempted to think once they had received the gift of the land. The perspective is that of having already taken the land, then reflecting on the past and drawing unwarranted conclusions. Israel was not to think that somehow she had merited the blessing of God.

It was very common in the ancient world (and modern for that matter) to think that military victory somehow established the moral superiority of the victor. Consequently the vanquished were considered morally inferior and deserving of defeat and whatever consequences might follow. A victory justified the actions of the winner,

---

[3]The motif of God as a consuming fire is common in the OT: Exod 15:7; 24:17; Isa 29:6; 30:27,30; Ps 18:8; 50:3; 59:13. Israel also had firsthand knowledge of this judging fire in her life, Num 11:1-3; as did Abraham, Gen 19:24.

[4]This verb seems to have been deliberately chosen for its punning value. The root is כנע (kāna‘), which sounds similar to kana‘an, that is Canaan. The latter proper noun seems to be formed from the root by an addition of a common suffix, (a)n (Schoville, "Canaanites," p. 159). However, the connection between the root and the meaning of the proper noun is uncertain. Astour suggests that since kn‘ means "sink, be low," the noun Canaan refers to the direction in which the sun sets, and thus means something like "Sundowners/Westerners" (Michael C. Astour, "The Origin of the Terms 'Canaan,' 'Phoenician,' and 'Purple,'" *JNES* 4[1965]: 346-350).

no matter how reprehensible they might be, for the victor was carrying out just retribution. Israel could easily fall into that trap, and Moses wanted to present the true picture.[5]

Righteousness and **wickedness** here should be understood in a juridical sense, that is, as "innocence" and "guilt." Israel should not think she gained the land because she was innocent before God and deserved it. To be sure, the nations stood guilty before God and deserved judgment, but Israel could not think that automatically indicated her lack of guilt. A legal case at the human level in Deuteronomy 25:1 illustrates the point. A case was to be brought before the judge who decided, based on the evidence, the guilt or innocence of the accused. By assuming her own innocence Israel was usurping the place of the judge, who was the LORD.

9:5 God's judgment on the guilty (wicked) nations did not automatically prove the innocence (righteousness) of Israel. They could not go by the common folk-theology that military victory equaled superiority.

God had early foreseen that the wickedness of the inhabitants of Canaan would be the basis for their ouster (Gen 15:16; cf. Lev 18:24-25; 20:23). The justification for their destruction was grounded in God's character. His sovereignty extended over all nations and those that did not measure up to universal standards of human conduct were subject to his judgment (Amos 1:3–2:3). This was not arbitrary, nor done in haste. The destruction of the nations involved the use of Israel as God's instrument of judgment, but it implied nothing about Israel's character.

---

[5]By placing "no" in the middle of the verse the NIV has created a redundancy with verse 5. The whole of verse 4, after "yourself" is to be understood as a quote. It should read, "The LORD has brought me here to take possession of this land because of my righteousness, *and* it is on account of the wickedness of these nations . . . ." The "no" should be eliminated. Then verse 5 becomes Moses' response in which he disputes half of the assertion but agrees with the other half. Understood this way the "you" at the end of the verse means "me," the Israelites. Cf. Weinfeld, *Deuteronomy*, p. 406; he accepts an earlier suggestion by Ehrlich that the *ka* (you) on the last word in verse 4 is a misplaced *ki* from verse 5. If so, then the last word in verse 4 would end in the first person singular, "before me." This textual emendation fits the context though there is no support for it in other Hebrew manuscripts or the ancient versions.

There were two reasons for Israel receiving the land: the inhabiting nations had exhausted God's patience, and God was keeping his promise to the patriarchs. Both reasons were grounded in Genesis 15 and had nothing to do with Israel deserving the gift.[6]

The reasoning here used by Moses is similar to the argument Paul advances in the NT in Romans 1-3. No one was righteous, either Gentile or Jew. Therefore, it was only God's mercy and grace that provided salvation, not merit.[7]

Moral self-righteousness is one of the most persistent of all human self-delusions, following closely on delusions of self-sufficiency (Deut 8). These delusions continue unabated today.

9:6 Israel could be assured (the same word that begins verse 3; NIV, **Understand**) that it was not their character that merited God's gift, for the truth was that she was **stiff-necked**, more stubborn than a rebellious animal (cf. Isa 1:2-3). The phrase is a particularly vivid term for stubbornness and is used eighteen times in the OT. The image is of a person deliberately making the neck rigid in order to resist suggestions or correction (or the discipline of 8:5). Isaiah 48:4 explains, "For I knew how stubborn you were; the sinews of your neck were iron . . . ." (cf. Deut 10:16; 31:27; 2 Kgs 17:14; Jer 7:26). It was a common description for those who resisted God's will. There was plenty of proof in Israel's history of her resistance to God. Moses turned to an early example to prove his point.

Remember the Rebellion at Horeb (9:7-24)

Moses turned to history to support his contention that Israel was stiff-necked. In fact he asserted they had been rebellious from the earliest times and more than once. This section parallels Exodus 32 in several ways but with modifications traceable to Moses' theological

---

[6]As we have already seen, the wickedness of the Canaanites was particularly apparent in her religious life with its sexual immorality and child sacrifice. These religious practices could only reflect a value system and way of life that had completely sold itself out to the most base of human impulses. Therefore, God's use of Israel to destroy the Canaanites was not in violation of his character or of a high moral value system.

[7]Cf. Wright, *Deuteronomy*, pp. 131-132; Miller, *Deuteronomy*, pp. 121-122; George Braulik, "Law as Gospel: Justification as Pardon According to the Deuteronomic Torah," *Int* 38 (1984): 5-14.

interests. It was a summary to highlight Israel's rebellious spirit. The parallel is specifically noticeable in the common sequence of events between Exodus 32:7-20 and Deuteronomy 9:12-21 though Deuteronomy has no sequential counterpart for Exodus 32:11-14 and 16-18. However, the gist of Exodus 32:11-14 is picked up in Deuteronomy 9:25-29 (see comments below).

This section is unified by its content which supports the main theme: Israel's rebellious nature.[8] It is also unified by its concentric (chiastic) structure. The chiasm has some displacement and repetition that adds to its overall effect.

A. 7-8: Israel's rebellion at Horeb made God angry
    B. 9-11: Moses spent 40 days and nights on the mountain and received the tablets
        C. 12: Moses told to go down; Israel made an idol
            D. 13-14: God wanted to destroy Israel
        C'. 15-16: Moses goes down and sees the idol
    B'. 17-18: Moses destroyed the tablets and spent another 40 days and nights on the mountain
A'. 19-20: Moses feared God's anger to destroy Israel
    C". 21: the idol destroyed
A". 22-24: Israel provoked God to anger by her history of rebellion[9]

9:7-8 We might expect Moses to outline the wickedness of the nations since that was the reason Israel was getting the Promised Land. But he executed a telling switch and focused on the wickedness of Israel.

---

[8]Against Mayes, *Deuteronomy*, pp. 195-196, and with Miller, *Deuteronomy*, p. 118, and others.

[9]Christensen also suggests a chiasm, but from vv. 8-29, which is based on his prosodic analysis (theory of poetic structure) (*Deuteronomy*, 188). The above is based on key words and thus sees Moses' prayer in vv. 25-29 as standing apart from the historical review. O'Connell offers what he calls a parallel panel construction: A: 9:7-8a; B: 9:8b-21; A': 9:22-24; B': 9:25-10:7, 10-11 which mimics the two receptions of the Ten Commandments. The A sections focus on Israel's provocations and the B sections on Moses' reception of the commandments. His detailed outline connecting all the interrelated words and phrases illustrate the tightly focused unity of the passage. Rhetorically he understands the section as rebuking Israel and, by repetition, retarding the flow of the text to emphasize how disobedience has slowed her progress ("Deuteronomy IX 7-X 7,10-11," 493-498, 507).

Remember this and never forget is a familiar admonition in Deuteronomy usually calling Israel to focus on what God had done for them in bringing them out of Egypt into the good land (1:19; 4:9; 6:12; 8:2,11). Memory was to be a motivation for faithfulness and obedience. But this call to remember stands in sharp contrast to the other exhortations, for they were now called to remember their own history, a history of conduct in sharp contrast to God's conduct. God had called them to wholehearted devotion (6:4-5), but their history was just the opposite. They had been **rebellious** (מרה, *mrh*, vv. 7,23,24) and had **provoked** God's **anger** (קצף, *qṣp*, vv. 7,8,19,22).[10]

The golden calf incident was the rebellion that provoked God's anger at **Horeb** (vv. 12ff). In the larger context of Deuteronomy it should come as no surprise that idolatry would be characterized so harshly. The many admonitions already given were a sure indicator of its grave danger to Israel (chapter 4; 5:8-10; 6:13ff). There were other post-Horeb events Moses could have also listed, such as Korah's rebellion (Num 16) or the refusal to enter the land (Num 14; Deut 1:34).

The LORD's **anger** threatened the very existence of Israel (v. 8). Israel was in the same danger as the nations, for the destruction that God was going to visit on them (2:21-23; 4:3; 7:24; 9:3) he was going to visit on Israel (cf. 4:26; 6:15; 7:4; 9:14,19,25). Israel's refusal to obey God placed them in the same status before God as the godless nations.

9:9-11 Moses moved to recounting the calf episode to prove his point. Moses had gone up Mt. Horeb to receive the law (Exod 24:12-18; cf. especially vv. 12a and 18b). The mountain was covered with a cloud and the glory of the LORD looked like a consuming fire (cf. Deut 9:10,15).

Moses' stay of **forty days and forty nights** produced anxiety in the people and they requested that Aaron make them something tangible (Exod 32:1). Forty days has symbolic significance in the Bible. It was often understood as a time of testing or judgment (Gen 7:4,12,17; Exod 34:28; 1 Kgs 19:18; Jonah 3:4; 1 Sam 17:16; Matt 4:4-11). In this case it represented a significant time for interchange between Moses and God, but a time of testing for Israel.

---

[10]Moses returns to these accusations in vv. 22-24, thus providing a frame around the historical portion of the sermon.

The tablets of stone (see on 4:13; 5:19) probably contained two copies of the Ten Commandments. They were expressly designated here as the **tablets of the covenant** (vv. 11,15 also) which signified their importance in establishing the relationship between God and Israel.

The fact that Moses **ate no bread and drank no water** is a detail not found in Exodus 32, although it was included in the account of Moses' second ascent to receive the stone tablets (Exod 34:28). It is well known that a person cannot survive without water past a few days. Forty-day fasts on the other hand are not uncommon. Does Moses' additional reference here illustrate the truth of Deuteronomy 8:3 ("man does not live on bread alone") and point to divine provision? Or is it rather a symbolic expression for an intense fast, though not necessarily forty days?[11] However explained, we must admit that in the presence of God Moses was beyond normal human experience. The fast was in sharp contrast to the feast Moses and the elders enjoyed in the presence of God just prior to Moses' ascent to the top (Exod 24:9-11).

The first set of stone tablets was given to Moses by God (Exod 24:12), but the second set was made by Moses (Deut 10:1; Exod 34:1). The first set was also special in that it was written by **the finger of God** (v. 10; Exod 31:18).[12] This is the only occasion when God is said to have written something directly by his finger, although other texts refer to him writing (Exod 32:16; 34:1,28). Most often in the OT God spoke to his prophets or spokesmen who then repeated his words and wrote them down. These "words" (NIV, **commandments**) were distinctive because they came directly from God with no human agency. The exact mechanics of how God wrote on the tablets is not clear. The anthropomorphism is an analogy, not a factual statement. The origin of the law with God is the important point.[13]

---

[11]The conservative commentator Wright suggests symbolism (*Deuteronomy*, p. 142) while Merrill (*Deuteronomy*, p. 192) and Tigay (*Deuteronomy*, p. 99) see divine provision. The Rabbis taught that the total fast was necessary to eliminate all normal bodily functions. Otherwise Moses would have become ritually impure and dishonored God (cf. Deut 23:12-14).

[12]See also Exod 8:19 where the plague of gnats was ascribed to the finger of God (= the power of God) by the Egyptian magicians.

[13]R.W. Wall suggests that Jesus' use of the "finger of God" phrase in Luke 11:20 is evidence that Luke ordered part of his gospel as a midrash (com-

The **LORD proclaimed . . . out of the fire** is the usual way the interaction between God and his people was portrayed at Sinai. God's glory was like a fire (Exod 19:18; 24:17; 40:38) and so it was out of his glory (presence) that he spoke (Deut 4:12,15,33,36; 10:4). It was this fire which the people feared would consume them (5:24-25). Fire could be both a purifying agent and a destructive force (Num 11:1,3). It thus provided a significant symbol for describing God's appearances to Israel. The covenant God was gracious and merciful in giving the covenant law, but he was also dangerous and inspired fear (6:13).

The **day of assembly** (v. 10) referred to the official gathering of the nation before God. Here they were at the foot of the mountain waiting for Moses' return to receive the covenant law. The assembly (קָהָל, *qāhāl*) of God was the same community as the people of God. But Israel was an "assembly" when gathered to participate in a specific function before God (Lev 16:17; Deut 31:30; Ps 22:22[23]; 35:18). At the end of the forty days Moses received the tablets (v. 11).

9:12 But all was not well (Exod 32:7-8a). Events had transpired throughout the forty days at the foot of the mountain as well as on the top. The people had requested Aaron to make something tangible for them (Exod 32:1-6). Since this was unknown to Moses, God told him to descend "quickly" (NIV, **at once**), because **your people** had **become corrupt**. The idol-making changed Israel's relationship with God significantly. Now they were "your people," or Moses' people. They were no longer God's people. He deliberately dissociated himself from them. The profound theological fact that God had brought Israel out of Egypt to be his people (1:27; 4:20,37; 5:6; 6:12,21; 8:14) and even his "treasured possession" (7:6) was nullified. God refused now to be known as the God of this people. This provoked a personal crisis for Moses. As mediator would he be willing to identify with the people in their rebellious state? In his prayer to God, recorded later in verses 26-29, Moses refused to accept this new designation, but rather reminded God that Israel was still his people.[14]

---

mentary) on Deuteronomy 9:1–26 ("'The Finger of God': Deuteronomy 9:10 and Luke 11:20," *NTS* 33 [1987]: 144-150). Wall overstates his case, but he does illustrate the influence Deuteronomy had on Jesus and the Gospels.

[14]In the development of the events in Exodus 32–34 a lengthy dialogue occurs between God and Moses about the necessity of God going with Israel

Israel's **corruption** was a moral corruption, brought on by idolatry (cf. Gen 6:11-12). Exodus 32:6 indicates that morally reprehensible behavior accompanied the adoration of the golden calf. Substituting an image for God automatically resulted in practices that dishonored him as well. This corruption had turned them **quickly** (cf. on 8:6) from the "way" (NIV, **from what**).[15]

Exodus 32 relates that the result of Israel's rebellion was an idol in the shape of a calf made from the jewelry of the people (vv. 4,24). Deuteronomy omits the details of its formation and calls it a **cast idol** (מַסֵּכָה, *massēkāh*) or a "calf cast idol" (v. 16). The fact that the image was a calf places it in its ancient Near Eastern context. In Egypt the bull or calf was a symbol of fertility and physical strength, and perhaps had connections with the host of heaven. In Canaan the bull or calf represented Baal or Hadad, the gods of storm, fertility, and vegetation, thus symbolizing fertility and strength. In this cultural setting, it was natural for the Israelites, when they desired a physical representation of God, to choose a calf image. But by doing so they reduced God to the status of nature and equated him with the gods of other nations.[16] Whether the calf was intended as an idol, as a representation of God, or as some sort of figure that served as a pedestal for God has been debated. Certainty is impossible. However, the very fact that a material image was constructed broke the second commandment against making images of God (5:8) and presented a real possibility of drawing the people into the vortex of idol worship.

A connection between the calf of Exodus 32 and the calves of Jeroboam I has long been noted. It is made explicit in the texts when

---

(ch. 33). He eventually responded positively and pledged to go with Israel (vv. 12-17).

[15]It is interesting how the word "quickly" appears in this chapter. Israel would drive out the inhabitants quickly (3); Moses was to go down quickly (12) for the people had turned quickly away (12,16). The event that happened quickly was not the one anticipated in verse 3.

[16]Tigay, *Deuteronomy*, Excursus 12, "The Golden Calf," pp. 445-446. One small bull figure has been found in an ancient Israelite site; see A. Mazer, "The 'Bull Site' — An Iron Age Open Cult Place," *BASOR* 247 (1982): 27-42; idem., "Bronze Bull Found in Israelite 'High Place' from the Time of the Judges," *BAR* 9,5 (1983): 34-40. Also a small silver bull has been found in Canaanite Ashkelon: Lawrence E. Stager, "When Canaanites and Philistines Ruled Ashkelon," *BAR* 17,2 (1991): 24-43.

the exact phraseology of Exodus 32:4 is used in 1 Kings 12:28. The connection illustrates vividly how susceptible Israel was to the enticements to conceptualize God just like the nations around them.[17] This reduction of God was as evil as abandoning him.

9:13-14 According to the concentric structure of verses 7-24, these two verses stand at the center, focusing our attention on them as the main thought. Moses' intention in reviewing the calf episode was to pinpoint how Israel's rebellious nature endangered the covenant relationship with God. God's reaction was to desire the total destruction of the nation so that he could begin again with a totally new people.

This people is intended in a demeaning way and expresses God's attitude. Israel was no longer his people, or even Moses' people. They were just another nation, like any other. The calf incident proved the accusation of verse 6; Israel was **indeed stiff-necked**, resistant to God's grace.

Therefore God intended to utterly annihilate Israel until no memory of her was left on the earth (**blot out their name from under heaven**). What he had planned to do to the wicked nations (7:23-24), he would do to Israel. And he wanted no interference from Moses (**Let me alone**, v. 14). Moses as mediator between God and Israel occupied a powerful position (cf. 5:24-25). This was the mediatorial position to which God had earlier called a reluctant Moses. But now God wanted Moses to abandon that position so he could execute his judgment. God's request reflects the fact that he expected Moses to attempt mediation. And if Moses did, God, because of his nature, would be required to respond. However, God did not at this time wish anyone to attempt to change his mind.

In fact God made a very attractive proposal to Moses. He would make a totally new beginning and Moses would become the new Abraham, the father of a whole new nation. The father of a nation was a better position than mediator within a nation. The new nation would even exceed the present descendants of Abraham. Moses' nation would be **stronger and more numerous** than Israel. This designation had been used of the other nations (7:1; 4:38; 11:23 —

---

[17]See John I. Durham, *Exodus,* Word Biblical Commentary (Waco: Word, 1987), p. 420, for fuller discussion.

greater and stronger) to indicate their superior strength. Thus Moses' descendants would be far beyond what Israel was now, and a match even for the nations. Moses' response to this enticement was not recorded in Deuteronomy for it would have sidetracked him from the main point.[18]

9:15-16 Moses' responded to the command in verse 12 and went down to see what Israel had done (cf. Exod 32:15,19a). These verses repeat almost exactly verse 12, adding only a further reference to the fire (v. 10) and the tablets of the covenant (v. 11). Also, "become corrupt" was replaced by **had sinned** (חטא, ḥṭʿ, v. 16; also vv. 18,21), a more common word for deviation from God's covenant demands.

9:17-18 Moses' reaction was quick and drastic. He smashed the tablets of the covenant in front of the people (Exod 32:19b). This was not just an impulsive, angry response. It was a deliberate act signifying that the covenant between Israel and God was broken. Israel's apostasy had canceled the relationship. They were witnesses to the formal declaration of that dissolution by seeing Moses smash the physical symbols of the covenant law. This followed ancient Near East custom where destroying the documents of the treaty dissolved the relationship.[19]

The calf incident demonstrated that Israel had a long way to go in understanding all the spiritual implications of their relationship with God. That was why it was so important for Moses to continue to warn the second generation in the plains of Moab about the necessity of obedient, wholehearted devotion to God.

Moses himself understood the significance of the situation and once again prostrated himself before God for forty days and nights

---

[18]A negative response is implied in his later prayer of intercession, verses 25-29. In Exod 32:12ff Moses ignored God's offer and sought to change his mind. Later in the dialogue (32:32ff) Moses requested that his name be blotted out if God could not forgive Israel, thus offering himself as a substitute for their guilt. By this he distinguished himself as the selfless servant of his people.

[19]Weinfeld, *Deuteronomy*, p. 410. He cites an Akkadian expression, "Breaking a tablet." In Exodus 32 the drastic change in Moses' attitude toward Israel was portrayed. God's *anger burned* against Israel and he wished to destroy her (v. 10) but Moses interceded and appealed to God to relent (vv. 11-14). However, when Moses approached the camp and actually saw what was happening, his *anger burned* against Israel, and he smashed the tablets (v. 19). Then Aaron tried to intercede with him and assuage his anger (v. 22).

(v. 18). This time it was for intercession (vv. 25-29), not to receive the law. The nation's future and God's covenant promises were at stake. Could anything be salvaged from the debris of the shattered covenant?

9:19-20 These two verses repeat three key words from verses 7-8 (שׁמד, קצף, אנף/אף; *šmd, qṣp, 'np/'p;* "destroy," "provoke to anger," "anger") rhetorically rounding off this historical section. Moses was very aware of the nature of God. He knew that the calf-making was a direct affront to the holy God who loved Israel and required wholehearted devotion and obedience. The only just response could be punishment, described here in terms of anger and wrath.

Moses' **fear** was not the fear of the LORD required by covenant loyalty (6:13) but a dread of what God could do. Just as Israel's obedience could unleash God's blessing, Israel's disobedience could unleash God's destruction. But Moses' intercession was successful. God **listened** to him **again**.

Though in the Deuteronomy summary Moses had not mentioned the role of Aaron, he included him here because of Aaron's need for intercessory prayer also. Aaron had been left with the people to provide direction while Moses was on the mountain (Exod 24:14). His place of leadership in Israel was second only to Moses'. He was Moses' mouthpiece to Pharaoh (Exod 14:14ff), had ascended Mt. Sinai with Moses (Exod 19:24; 24:9ff), and was installed as high priest (Exod 28; Lev 8; Deut 10:6). As patriarch of the priests he was in a sensitive position. Therefore, his failure at Sinai was especially grave.

The anger and wrath of God was the righteous indignation of a just and holy God who was zealous for the holiness, purity, and faithfulness of his people. It was aroused when they flaunted the covenant, disobeyed, and offered their allegiance to other gods. By this they turned their backs on the One who had freed them from slavery and given them the Promised Land in faithfulness to his oath to the patriarchs. The worship of other gods also involved immorality and gross sin. Thus this "anger" was totally justified. It was not arbitrary but consistent with the character of the Creator of the universe.

This portrayal of God's "anger and wrath" is often used as the basis for denigrating or rejecting the OT God. The ancient heretic Marcion, some Christians, and many non-Christians strongly object to a God like this. However, this objection is misguided and not well thought out.[20]

To conceive of a loving, merciful, and gracious God who does not justly treat evil and rebellion as it ought to be treated is to posit a deity not worthy of worship or respect. It is rather to posit a deity who is no more impressive than a kindly grandfather who chuckles at the antics of his grandchildren but never does anything. Such a deity is of no help or use to the oppressed of the world or to the sensitive souls who clearly see the injustice in the world and rail against it. People rightly reject such an incompetent deity.

Only the biblical God as so clearly portrayed in the OT can satisfy the deepest yearnings for justice and provide hope that just retribution will be executed. It is that kind of God that confronted Israel.[21]

9:21 Moses returned to the topic of verses 15-16 to complete the account of what he did with the calf (Exod 32:20). The **sinful thing** was **burned, ground** into **fine dust**, and **thrown** into a **stream**.[22] In Exodus the people were made to drink the water, perhaps reflecting some kind of ordeal (cf. Num 5:5-31). Drinking the water containing the dust illustrated the total destruction and worthlessness of the idol. Moses was following his own instruction for the treatment of idols (Deut 7:5,25; 12:3; cf. 2 Kgs 23:6,15).[23] Rhetorically this verse functions as a parenthesis outside of the concentric structure and by such displacement calls attention to its subject matter. Its inclusion earlier would also have disrupted the chiasm.

9:22-24 These verses provide a second, expanded conclusion to the historical section of the lesson. By repeating the key words

---

[20]In fact Marcion not only eliminated the OT, but part of the NT as well; see on 1:34 above.

[21]Consider the pilgrimage of a university lecturer in chemistry in India. He began his university studies as a Marxist, committed to fighting for justice. Given a Bible by some Christians he began to casually read in the OT and suddenly discovered a God committed to justice as much he was. He was especially overwhelmed by the details in the law directed toward the care for the poor and vulnerable. He became a Christian before he got to the NT! (see Chris Wright, "I Never Knew Such a God Existed," *Themelios* 17,2 [1992]: 3).

[22]"Sinful thing" is a phrase used of Jeroboam's calf also: 1 Kgs 12:30; 13:34; 14:16, etc.

[23]For a parallel see Micah 7:19: all sins will be cast into the sea.

"made the LORD angry," "rebellion," and "from the day/ever since" (same Hebrew words) from verses 7-8 they provide an envelope around the intervening verses as well. They also provide further reasons for God's anger reflected in verses 19-20. The calf incident at Horeb was only one of many cases of rebellion that Moses could have reiterated. It was the most flagrant of the early examples, but it was not a fluke as Moses shows by listing several more.

Two of the episodes are detailed in Numbers 11. Sometime after leaving Sinai the people complained about their hardships. Consequently a fire from God came down and burned (בער, *b'r*) some of the camp. Thus the place was called **Taberah** ("burning," Num 11:1-3). Later when the people wanted meat in addition to the manna, God gave them quail. Yet this still was not enough to satisfy their cravings. Some died in punishment so the place was named **Kibroth-Hattaavah** ("graves of craving," Num 11:34).

The testing of God at **Massah** (cf. on Deut 6:16; 8:2) occurred even before Israel arrived at Sinai (Exod 17:1-7) and was one of the most often cited early rebellions. The refusal of Israel to go up to take the land when encamped at **Kadesh Barnea** had already been reviewed by Moses (Deut 1:19-46) and was familiar to the second generation.

Thus Moses' conclusion (v. 24) was not an exaggeration. Even before the LORD orchestrated the plagues on the Egyptians to win her freedom, Israel complained because the Egyptians made their work more difficult (Exod 5). The grumbling began again soon after leaving Egypt and never ceased for long (Exod 14:10-12; 16:2-3; 17:1-2, etc.). Moses had supported his summary statement in verse 7. It was abundantly clear that Israel was no more righteous than the nations in the land and could not regard the land as merited (vv. 1-6). Israel's lack of **trust** (confidence in the reliability of God) and **disobedience** was beyond question (v. 23).[24]

Moses' Intercessory Prayer (9:25-29)

Moses now completes the reprise of Exodus 32 by relating his intercessory prayer that was implied at verses 18-19 (and which came

---

[24]A textual variant in the Samaritan Pentateuch and the LXX at the end of v. 24 suggests "ever since *he* (i.e. God) knew you" rather than "ever since I (Moses) knew you."

where expected in Exod 32:11-13). It also explains verse 19b, "the LORD listened to me." It is a part of Hebrew style to provide a unified account to make an important point, then to back up and fill in the details. If this prayer were earlier, it would have interrupted the flow of thought.[25] The prayer exhibits rhetorical devices that we expect from Moses, reflecting similarities between the beginning and end (vv. 26 and 29).

9:25 Moses' position as **prostrate before the LORD** recalls verse 18 and is the proper position for intercessory prayer. Moses refused to accept God's designation of Israel as Moses' people (v. 12) and called them, as he does throughout Deuteronomy, God's **people** and **inheritance** (v. 26; see on 4:20; cf. v. 29).

9:26-27 Moses' appeal picked up themes he had already covered, but he inverted their significance. Throughout Deuteronomy he supported his calls for Israel's obedience by appeals to not forget or to remember what God had done for her by keeping his promises to the fathers and bringing her out of Egypt. However, Moses here reminded God of the same events and promises. They could serve as reasons for God to be forgiving as well as Israel to be faithful. They were reminders to God that he should not go back on his promises. The display of God's **power** and **redemption** and mighty hand was an event he should **remember** along with Israel. Was his deliverance to come to nothing? He should remember also his centuries' old promise and commitment to faithfulness. If God broke the promise, to what could he later appeal as proof of his trustworthiness?

Moses' audacity is breathtaking. He asked God to **overlook** or pay no attention to (NRSV, "concern yourself with") Israel's **stubbornness** ("stiff-neck," vv. 6,13), **wickedness** (vv. 4-5,18), and **sin** (v. 16). Moses used each of these characteristics earlier as proof of Israel's rebellious spirit which had aroused the anger of God. Moses shattered the tablets because of these defects, signaling the shattering of the covenant (v. 17). But now he requested that God overlook them. He suggested that the very actions of Israel that justified God's anger should be ignored. This request goes to the very heart of the nature of God and the purpose of mediation. Moses assumed that the love and devotion of God for Israel would mitigate his justice and judgment.

---

[25]Cf. Weinfeld, *Deuteronomy*, p. 414, and other commentators.

9:28 However, Moses was not satisfied with just an appeal to God's nature. He had what he felt was a clinching argument (v. 28). If God destroyed Israel, it would destroy his reputation among the nations. One purpose of the Exodus was to prove that God was sovereign over all the nations and gods and thus to create respect (fear) among the nations (cf. Deut 2:25; 11:25; Josh 2:10-11; 7:7-9; Ps 79:9-10; 115:1-2; Jer 14:7; Ezek 20:44; 36:22). If God now failed to follow through, it would be proof that he was not able or willing to do what he said, and he would become just like the other gods, ineffective and powerless. In fact the nations would see the Exodus not as proof of God's power but of his hatred for Israel. Consequently God's whole purpose for rescuing Israel would be reversed, his redemptive work nullified (Exod 32:12; Num 14:15-16).

9:29 This verse rounds off the prayer where it began, reminding God of who Israel was and what he had done. Often "mighty hand" (v. 26) and **outstretched arm** are paired together (4:34; 5:15; 7:19; 11:2; 26:8), but they are separated here to provide, along with "your people, your inheritance," an inclusio for the prayer.[26] A positive answer to Moses' prayer was implied in verse 19b, but a fuller account of God's response is left until 10:10-11 (see comments below).

Moses' role as intercessor highlights this passage. He was a leader who prayed for his people. Though he was fully aware of the great sin of the people, he prayed for God's mercy. This was a daring plea as if the greater the sin, the greater occasion for God's mercy (Rom 5:20). Moses was not afraid to appeal to God's character and concerns in his appeal, especially to his integrity.

As mediator, Moses had to place himself between his sinful people and his God and trust in God's love and faithfulness. It was this same trust in God that caused Amos to cry out on Israel's behalf when he saw the judgment coming (Amos 7:1-6). Both Moses' and Amos's intercessory prayers were successful, but not because of Israel's merit or Moses' or Amos's merit. It was only because of the grace of God.

Intercessory prayer is an important part of biblical leadership (note all of Paul's prayers for his people, Eph 3:14ff; Phil 1:4; Col 1:3; 1 Thess 3:10). But it is not to be undertaken lightly. However,

---

[26]"Mighty hand" by itself predominates in the book of Exodus: 3:19; 6:1; 13:3,9,16, etc.

when it is practiced, it is to be practiced boldly, trusting in the grace of God.[27]

---

[27]See the excellent discussion in Patrick Miller, *They Cried to the Lord: The Form and Theology of Biblical Prayer* (Minneapolis: Fortress, 1994), chapter 8, especially pp. 270-274.

DEUTERONOMY 10

The New Tablets of Stone (10:1-11)

This section is the conclusion of the historical reprise that began in 9:7. It relates the renewal of the covenant through the giving of the commandments on stone tablets a second time (cf. Exod 34). Moses had shattered the original tablets, signifying the covenant was broken. The response of God to his intercessory prayer required new symbols of the restored covenant in the form of new stone tablets. This section is also concerned with the Ark of the Covenant as the repository of the tablets and the responsibility of the Levites in the care of the ark.

There are verbal links with Deuteronomy 31:9-29, which is also concerned with a proper treatment of the tablets of the covenant law and Israel's rebellious nature. These two sections are the only places in Deuteronomy that certain phrases occur: "ark of the covenant of the LORD" (10:8; 31:9,25,26) and "tribe of Levi/Levites" (10:8; 31:9,25). The description of the tablets of the law is also similar (10:4-5; 31:9,26).[1]

10:1-2 At that time sets the following within a specific time frame, in this case following the calf incident. Moses omitted the extended dialogue between himself and God recorded in Exodus 33. The issues treated there, God's willingness to go before Israel and his freedom to deal with them as he wished, apparently were not relevant to Moses' presentation here.

Moses had to make the second set of stone tablets himself. The tablets on which the words of God were written were intended to stand in contrast to the idols. **Chisel** (פסל, *psl*) is a rare verb (6 times in the OT) that almost exclusively refers to the carving of the tablets

---

[1] See Christopher Begg, "The Tables (Deuteronomy X) and the Lawbook (Deuteronomy XXXI)," *VT* 33 (1983): 96-97.

(Exod 34:1,4; Deut 10:1,3; Hab 2:18). The idols (פֶּסֶל, *pesel*) were formed ("chiseled out") from wood and stone (Deut 4:16; 5:8; 7:25; 12:3) and were to be destroyed. The only appropriate chiseled object for Israel was that which carried the word of God.

God was also concerned with where the tablets would be kept. A **wooden chest** was appropriate. It is only briefly mentioned here. More details were given to Moses in Exodus 25:10-20 (cf. 37:1-9). The Hebrew אֲרוֹן (*'ărôn*) is often translated "ark" but it is not to be confused with Noah's ark or the ark made for baby Moses (תֵּבָת, *tēbath*). This wooden chest is referred to in the OT with over 20 different expressions including: "the ark of the covenant," "the ark of God/the LORD/the Lord Yahweh [NIV Sovereign LORD]," "the ark of testimony," and "the ark of your might." The ark is conceptualized here in Deuteronomy in its simplest function — as a place for the stone tablets. Other texts had different interest (as a place to meet God, Exod 25:22; as the symbol of God's presence, Num 10:35,36; Josh 3-6; as God's earthly throne, 1 Sam 4:4; 2 Sam 6:2), but they are not necessarily contradictory interests as modern scholarship asserts.[2]

10:3-4 The ark was made from **acacia wood** (שִׁטִּים, *šiṭṭîm*). Acacia wood was common in the Sinai peninsula and Palestine as evidenced by the several place names that have *shittim* as a component ("Beth Shittah," Judg 7:22; "Shittim," Num 25:1; Josh 2:1; 3:1; "valley of acacia/shittim," Joel 3:18[4:18]).

It was important that the second set of tablets be exactly as the first. So God **wrote** on them the ten words (**commandments**) again (cf. 9:10; Exod 34:28b) signifying it was the same covenant and the same instruction.[3]

---

[2]Mayes, *Deuteronomy*, pp. 203-204. See Stephan T. Hague, "אֲרוֹן," *NIDOTTE*, 1:500-510. There was a surge of interest in the ark in the later 20th century, prompted by the movie, "Raiders of the Lost Ark." There is even a lengthy investigation of legends that the ark ended up in Ethiopia: Graham Hancock, *The Sign and the Seal: The Quest for the Lost Ark of the Covenant* (New York: Simon and Schuster, 1993). Very little in this modern quest has much relationship to the biblical Ark of the Covenant.

[3]Exodus 34:5-28a includes an important basic description of the character of God (vv. 5-7) and another summary of the covenant law (vv. 10-26). In v. 27 Moses was commanded to write the words down, but who wrote on the tablets is ambiguous from the text (v. 28b). Durham argues that it was God, referring back to vv. 1 and 10 (*Exodus*, 462-469).

10:5 This verse concludes the brief account of the second pair of stone tablets with the acknowledgement that Moses did as he was told. Verse 10 picks up with this episode again and fills in the information that Moses was on the mountain 40 days and 40 nights.

10:6-9 This is another one of those seeming parenthetical sections that challenge the interpreter. It has two parts to exhibit its two concerns: verses 6-7 are an itinerary that sandwiches a notice of Aaron's death; verses 8-9 note the functions of the Levites vis à vis the ark of the covenant. Israel is referred to in the third person in these verses, not in the usual second person. Apparently the previous reference to the ark triggered Moses' desire to offer more complete information on it, especially the relationship of the Levites to it. The addition of a note on Aaron's death completes the thought of 9:20.

The itinerary of verses 6-7 is related to Numbers 33:30-34 in some way, though the order of names is different. Numbers 33 is a long, formulaic list of places where Israel camped in the wilderness. Although Moses uses the language of itinerary,[4] the concern is different. Here he wished to place the death of Aaron and Eleazar's succession within the historical context only in a general way. Thus the references to the **well of the Jaakanites** and **Jotbathah, a land with streams of water** focused on water resources and was a different emphasis than Numbers 33. Numbers 20:23-29 and 33:37-39 place Aaron's death at Mt. Hor, near Kadesh Barnea, which seems to be a different locale than indicated here. But the places here are unknown (except perhaps Jotbathah). Further, **Moserah** means "chastisement" (Moseroth in Num 33:31) which may be emphasizing the purpose of Aaron's death, not the place.[5]

Aaron was succeeded by his son **Eleazer**, the third of his four sons (Exod 6:23). The two oldest had died because of disobedience (Lev 10; Num 3:2-4). Aaron died outside of the Promised Land because of his rebellion with Moses at Meribah (Num 20:22-25; Exod 17). Eleazar and Joshua took over the leadership of Israel after the

---

[4]Especially through the use of the verb נָסַע (ns', "encamp").

[5]Cf. G.T. Manley, "A Problem in Deuteronomy," *EvQ* 27 (1955): 201-204. Weinfeld accredits the differences to different sources (*Deuteronomy*, p. 419). Thompson suggests a nonitinerary purpose for them (*Deuteronomy*, p. 145). The places could be located near Kadesh Barnea and thus Mt. Hor.

deaths of Aaron and Moses, and on occasion acted in concert (Josh 14:1).

The consecration of the **Levites** took place in Exodus 32:29 in connection with the calf incident. Therefore, the brief note in verses 8-9 fits the historical context of this section in Deuteronomy. The Levites were chosen, according to these verses, for three reasons. They were to carry the ark (Num 3:31; 4:15), to minister before the LORD (**to stand before the LORD** was the idiom for ministry; Deut 1:38; 17:12; 18:7; 21:5) and to bless his name, which meant bless the people on God's behalf (Deut 21:5; Num 6:22-27). In these functions they were to assist Aaron, or the current high priest (Num 3:6-10). They had an important theological function also, because God accepted them as a substitute for the firstborn (Num 3:11-13,40-48).

Deuteronomy 18:1-8 also addresses the priestly and Levitical allotments. The Pentateuch recognizes a threefold hierarchy of priests and Levites drawn from the tribe of Levi: the high priest (Aaron and successors), the priests (Aaron's sons), and the other Levites. However, most modern scholars do not accept this view. Since Julius Wellhausen,[6] a radical reorientation has been accepted, namely, that precise delineation of the differing duties of priests and Levites was a late development in Israel. Originally all priests and Levites shared functions, but after the late sixth century the Levites were demoted and the priests elevated to be the only ones to serve at the centralized cult center in Jerusalem. Thus Deuteronomy is alleged to know of no distinction between the priests and Levites.[7] This reconstruction has been contested. Both Deuteronomy 10 and 18 seem to make a distinction between the priests ("Levitical priests," 17:9; 18:1) and the rest of the Levites (10:8; 31:9,25).[8]

Since the Levites had a special commission from the LORD they were not to share in receiving a designated part of the Promised

---

[6]See his *Prolegomena to the History of Ancient Israel* which first appeared in 1878.

[7]Weinfeld, *Deuteronomy*, p. 422.

[8]See further the commentary on 18:1-8. The issue has been covered in detail in numerous places. For convenience see: Phillip Jensen, "לֵוִי," *NIDOTTE*, 2:772-778; idem., "Priests and Levites," *NIDOTTE*, 5:1066-1067; Raymond Abba, "Priests and Levites in Deuteronomy," *VT* 27 (1977): 257-267; J. Gordon McConville, "Priests and Levites in Ezekiel: A Crux in the Interpretation of Israelite History," *TB* 34 (1983): 3-31.

Land (v. 9; 12:12b; 18:1-2). Their special relationship with God was their **inheritance**. They also received the tithes that the people gave to the LORD as a part of that inheritance (Num 18:24; Deut 26:12).

10:10-11 Moses concluded the account he began in verses 1-5 by giving the data about the length of his stay on the mountain. Actually Moses *stood* on the mountain (NIV, **stayed**), a deliberate reference to verse 8 where the Levites were to "stand" before the LORD (that is, serve). Earlier Moses had lain prostrate before God in intercessory prayer (9:25) but this time he served the LORD. In Exodus 34:5 God was said to have come down and stood with Moses.[9]

God **listened** to Moses (Exod 32:11: God "relented" at Moses' prayer). This simple statement has great significance (cf. 9:19). If God did not listen to prayer and have the potential of responding, prayer would be useless, an exercise in self-deception. If God was not being receptive to Moses' intercession, it would have been a game. Unfortunately some have conceptualized the biblical God as being totally unchangeable (immutable) to such a degree that he seems impervious to human requests and incapable of interaction with his creation. They import Greek philosophical abstractions into Christianity rather than depending on the biblical description of God's relational qualities. Thus John Calvin could deny that Genesis 6:6, which attributes changeableness to God, means what it says.[10] The Old Testament makes it clear that indeed God is reliable and trustworthy and his character does not change. Yet he operates in a living relationship with his people and with the world and responds to both repentance and apostasy.[11] Otherwise intercessory prayer would be a sham.

---

[9]Though not the same word in Hebrew, but a synonym, *yṣb*.

[10]*Institutes*, 1.17.1ff. The same word "relent" is used in Genesis 6:6, Exodus 32:14 and other places. J.I. Packer's discussion of this topic in his widely used book is inadequate (*Knowing God* [Downers Grove, IL: InterVarsity, 1993], ch. 7). For an excellent discussion of the issues see chapters 1 and 2 in Clark Pinnock et al, *The Openness of God* (Downers Grove, IL: InterVarsity, 1994). See also Miller, *They Cried*, ch. 8.

[11]Jeremiah 18:6-10 is the clearest statement. There is of course a difference between God's eternal purpose for the universe worked out through his Son and his ongoing relationship with his people. God's purpose never changes. But a relationship implies give and take between the two parties. God responds to his people and they respond to him. Both Num 23:19 and

God responded to Moses' prayer because of his character. **It was not his will to destroy** Israel. It was not within his pleasure to follow through on the threatened judgment. This unwillingness was grounded in his character as revealed in Exodus 34:6-7 and Deuteronomy 7:8-9. The covenant was established on the foundation of God's love, mercy, and grace. Forgiveness was possible and intercession prompted it.[12]

Verse 11 returns to the theme of 9:1 and rounds off the larger section. Deuteronomy was preparing Israel for the next major step in her history, possessing the land. Moses was given a key role. He was to **lead** her on the journey (NIV, **on the way**) to the land (1:7). It was usually the cloud that went before Israel, directing their travels to the land (Exod 40:36,38; Num 9:22-23; 10:12). Was Moses in some way equal in importance to the cloud, which represented God's presence going before Israel?

Final Admonition (10:12-22)

This section forms the conclusion to the sermon begun in 9:1. In light of the past sins as described in the historical review a fresh admonition was needed in order that the past not be repeated. For this appeal Moses chose many of the key words of the preceding sermons and gathered them together into a succinct exhortation to obedience.[13] It is "one of the richest texts in the Hebrew Bible."[14]

The structure of the passage shows a symmetry and repetition that we have come to expect from Moses. Verse 12 thematically and verbally generates the rest of the section. A verbal inclusion marks its beginning and end ("And now," "fear the LORD," and "serve him" in vv. 12 and 20-22). "Love the LORD" in verse 12 provides the theme

---

1 Sam 15:29 (contrast v. 11) must be understood within their immediate contexts and then within the context of the whole OT.

[12]See 1:26 for the same idiom referring to the people's unwillingness to go up into the land.

[13]See footnote 18 below. It is possible to understand these verses as connected directly to chapter 11 as the final segment of chapters 4–11 and paralleling 4:1-40 (Christensen, *Deuteronomy*, p. 201). However, it seems preferable to see them as a transition to chapter 11 and allow them to provide a relevant conclusion to the preceding sermon, while providing a text for the preaching in chapter 11 (Tigay, *Deuteronomy*, p. 109).

[14]Wright, *Deuteronomy*, p. 144.

for God's love for the forefathers and aliens in verses 15 and 18, and the admonition to love the alien in verse 19. This symmetry suggests that verses 16-17 are the focal point.[15] Rather than a chiasm, the structure is more of an envelope device with verses 12-13 and 20-22 surrounding verses 14-19.[16] Verses 14-19 have a complex interrelationship. The development of thought in verses 14-16 is paralleled in verses 17-19 in which 14 and 17, 16 and 18, and 15 and 19 are related.[17]

10:12-13 These verses resound with phrases from the earlier chapters. The most important words exhorting Israel to obedience are gathered together as a foundation for a fresh perspective on Israel's relationship to God. **And now** transitions from the historical review to the practical lessons that are to follow which require a decision. It is identical in function to 4:1 (cf. Exod 19:5; Josh 24:14). However, the repeated "and now" in verse 22, while providing a connection with verse 12, has a different function.

What does the LORD ask of you is a rhetorical device to gain attention and emphasize the answer. What the LORD requires is what he seeks or desires from his people. What he requires is obedience to his moral demands. The five demands he makes have all appeared before in Deuteronomy. The fact that they can all be brought together here indicates they are closely interrelated ideas. Each one on its own or in combination expresses the similar thought: God requires wholehearted devotion from his people. The demands are actions (**walk, serve,** and **observe**) and attitudes (**fear** and **love**) that mark off Israel from everyone else. They emphasize behavior and relationship.[18] Their substance is briefly detailed in verses 18-19. Love and fear of God must be demonstrated by practicing justice in Israel (see below). This important admonition is reinforced in the Psalms and prophets. Thus Psalm 40:6(7), Hosea

---

[15]Christensen's chiasm is plausible but seems somewhat forced: he relates vv. 12-13 to 20-22 and vv. 14-16 to 17-19 (*Deuteronomy*, p. 205).

[16]Merrill, *Deuteronomy*, p. 201.

[17]Wright, *Deuteronomy*, pp. 145-146.

[18]For "fear the LORD" see on 4:10; 6:2,13,24; 5:29; for "walk in all his ways" see on 5:33; 6:14 (11:22); for "to love him" see on 6:5 (11:1,13,22); for "serve the LORD" see on 6:13; 10:8 (11:13); for "observe the commands" see on 4:6,40; 6:1; 8:6,11 (11:1,9,13,22).

6:6 and Micah 6:8 all agree that what God desires most of all from his people are not the sacrifices (that is religious ritual) but justice and loyalty.[19] All of this was to be done with the total will and life (**heart** and **soul**), a requirement elucidated in 4:29 and 6:5. This appeal to the heart prepared for the demand of verse 16. Obedience to the **commands and decrees** was an issue of the will (heart), not merely a behavioral matter. Moses understood that the core of Israel's relationship with God was not contained in ritual or cult, but flowed out of reverence for and devotion to God. Without the latter, the former was useless.

All of this was for Israel's **good** (cf. on 4:40). God would bestow the best blessings of life on his obedient people. What he desired for Israel was their welfare (*shalom*), the best for them he could give (5:33; 6:24 — NIV "prosper" translates the Hebrew "good"; Ps 34:8-10[9-11]). Obedience was the key (4:6-8). It was unfortunate how often Israel missed this fundamental principle.[20]

10:14 Moses inserted here the first of two motivational clauses into his admonition (see also v. 17). He draws attention to it by using a Hebrew expression that could be translated "Look!" (omitted in the NIV).[21] God had ownership over the whole universe, the **heavens** and the **earth** (Gen 1:1; Ps 24:1). But beyond that, the universe could not contain him for he was even above the **highest heaven** (a Hebrew idiom indicating the highest degree; 1 Kgs 8:27; Neh 9:6). He was unlike the pagan gods in a fundamental way (granting, for the moment, their existence). Those gods were contained within the heavens and were a part of the heavens; they had no sovereignty over them.[22] In contrast to them God's glory was above the heavens (Ps 113:4; 148:13) and covered the heavens (Hab 3:3). Moses was setting the stage for the amazing contrast of the next statement.

---

[19]These passages employ various synonyms to reflect on the demands of God. Thus the text here uses שׁאל (*š'l*), Ps 40:6 uses חפץ (*ḥpṣ*) and *š'l*, Micah 6:8 uses דרשׁ (*drš*), and Hos 6:6 uses *ḥpṣ*. They can be variously translated as: demand, seek, require, desire.

[20]It is also unfortunate how often Christian readers of the OT miss this point.

[21]*hēn* which is often translated as "behold" or "indeed."

[22]The ancient Mesopotamians conceived of three superimposed heavens, but Moses did not share that view.

10:15 Yet (an emphatic "in spite of, nonetheless") God concerned himself with Israel. The astounding fact was that the sovereign LORD of the universe had decided to bestow his favor on Israel, a point already made from different perspectives in chapters 7–9. He deliberately **set his affection** on their ancestors in that he committed himself to become involved with them in a personal relationship (see on 7:7-8). This unmerited affection and **love** led to Israel's election as God's people through their **forefathers**. By returning to this theme, Moses brought to conclusion his line of reasoning in the prior sermons. Though he had made it clear that Israel did not merit the Promised Land or God's blessings in any way, they still needed to remember that God had **chosen** them from **all the nations**. There was still something special about them – their unique relationship with God. The universality of God and the particularity of his love are complementary, not contradictory.[23]

10:16 Israel must deal directly with her rebellious spirit that Moses had so vividly described. The only way to do that was through a change of heart. Apparently, the reference to the forefathers triggered thoughts about circumcision as the premier covenant sign. But Moses realized that the physical sign was only a sign, and unless it reflected an inner, spiritual condition, it was of limited value in producing the kind of relationship God desired (v. 12). Physical circumcision was the mark of Abraham's covenant (Gen 17:10-14), a sign required of all males, including foreigners. It was also a necessity for observing the Passover (Exod 12:44,48; Josh 5:2-28). However, literal circumcision of the flesh did not assure a faithful people. What was needed was a changed will (heart). So Moses applied the metaphorical idea to the heart. A drastic operation on the will was needed to assure obedience and faithfulness.[24]

The opposite meaning of the metaphor could also be applied to Israel. If they were unrepentant and sinful they were uncircumcised in heart (Lev 26:41). Jeremiah saw no difference between rebellious

---

[23]Wright warns against extrapolating either unbiblical universalism or a narrow exclusivism from this text (*Deuteronomy*, p. 147).

[24]Jer 4:4 agrees. Jeremiah's admonition followed his strongly worded call for repentance in chapter 3. For a full discussion on circumcision see R.G. Hall, "Circumcision," *ABD*, 1:1025-1031.

Israel and the foreign nations who were also circumcised in the flesh but not in the heart (Jer 9:25-26).[25]

Was such a change of heart possible without divine assistance? Moses returns to the subject in 30:16 and seems to recognize this difficulty. He affirmed God would circumcise the heart.[26] Stubbornness was a heart problem and needed a heart-centered solution. The circumcised heart was the pure heart and the broken and contrite spirit of Psalm 51 (vv. 10,17). The contrast between past Israel and what God desired was the contrast of an obstinate, rebellious spirit, and a compliant, obedient will.

Segments of first century Judaism recognized the force of the metaphorical sense of circumcision. Thus the Qumran community's *Manual of Discipline* emphasized the need to circumcise the foreskin of the evil inclination and stiff-neck.[27]

10:17 Moses provided a motivation for changing the heart: the nature of God. He used hymnic language and superlative expressions to illustrate just who this God was who had chosen Israel. He was the greatest God and the greatest Lord. He was far beyond the other gods (who were nothings, 4:28). No other language was capable of expressing how God exceeded everything in the universe in might, power, and character. The Old Testament in several places tries to express the same and can only use the language used by Moses (Ps 136:2-3; Dan 2:47; Ps 135:5; Dan 11:36).[28]

God was not only a superlative God in name, but also in action. Thus he was **great, mighty**, and **awesome**. Moses had already used this language in 7:21 (see comments there) in the context of assuring Israel that she had nothing to fear from the strong nations living in the land. These terms are also used throughout the Old Testament

---

[25]For other metaphorical uses see Exod 6:12,30 (uncircumcised lips) and Jer 6:10 (uncircumcised ears).

[26]The prophets also recognized that the fundamental problem for Israel was the will. Therefore, Jeremiah anticipated that the *Torah* would ultimately be written directly on the heart (31:31-34). Ezekiel went further and asserted that God would give his people a new heart, a heart of flesh (responsive heart: 11:19; 36:26).

[27]1QS 5.5. 1Q Hab 11:13 also refers to circumcision of the foreskin of the heart. See Leslie Allen, "Circumcision," *NIDOTTE*, 4:474-476.

[28]The NT also must use the same language of God (1 Tim 6:15) and of the Lamb (Rev 17:14; 19:16).

as the only fitting language to describe God.[29] This language was used to describe the all-powerful king in the ancient Near East. Perhaps Moses selected these terms to underscore that Israel's God was the only proper one to receive these accolades. "Mighty" is often used in war contexts and stresses the warrior aspect of God's character. He was the one who fought on their behalf and saved them (3:22,24; Zeph 3:17; Ps 24:8). God confirmed his superiority through his demonstration of power over Israel's enemies, especially Egypt and the nations in the Promised Land. "Awesome" is often used in contexts that highlight worship of God. God is awe-inspiring (Hebrew, "fearful," cf. v. 12) and worthy of honor through praise and adoration (Exod 15:11; Ps 47:2[3]; 68:35[36]; 76:7[8]).

From this lofty language Moses descended quickly to the practical. God was also impartial and just. He was not only a deity to be honored from afar. He was concerned about and involved in the practical, everyday activities of his people. His major impact on daily life was his concern for justice, because justice was at the very heart of who he was. In the ancient Near East the kings were the ultimate arbiters of justice in the land. However, these kings were notorious for showing partiality and being open to bribes, the two most human and widespread causes of injustice in human society. In fact ancient Near Eastern law collections, such as the Code of Hammurabi, legalized partiality. A violation of the law carried a more severe punishment for the lower class, common citizen.

However, particularity was forbidden in Israel for her covenant law was grounded in God, who was totally just and righteous. The leaders and judges in Israel were to imitate God (1:17) and favoritism was forbidden (16:19; 27:25; Lev 19:15). "Follow justice and justice alone, so that you may live and possess the land the LORD your God is giving you" (Deut 16:20).[30]

10:18-19 Proof of this aspect of God's character was in his concern for the oppressed of the society. In Israel the **fatherless**[31] **and the**

---

[29]Neh 9:32 uses all three terms; Ps 4:3 uses two.

[30]It took a special revelation to convince Peter of this OT truth (Acts 10:34).

[31]The fatherless, not the orphan, is in view as Exod 22:24 shows (cf. Ps 109:9). God himself is their special protector (Exod 22:21-24). The protection of the widow, orphan, and poor was a part of ancient Near Eastern cus-

widow had the least security because they would not have access to the extended family. The family group provided housing and food for its members and the overall social structure was built on the assumption that every individual was a part of a family.[32] Lack of access to the family group meant deprivation and maybe starvation (see Ruth and Naomi's experience). To this grouping Moses added the **alien** (foreigner). Aliens were especially despised because they were outside of the community. But God had a special concern for them, even **loving** them, just as he had loved the ancestors (v. 15). This encompassing love of God condemned all ethnic pride and exclusivity.

The three classes of people grouped together here is a common Old Testament classification that symbolizes all oppressed groups. God's concern was for justice for all, no matter what the social status. This concern was codified in the law (Exod 22:20-21; 23:7-9; Lev 19:33-35; Deut 14:29; 16:11; 24:14-22; 26:11-13).[33]

As God's people, Israel was obligated to **love those who are alien** (v. 19) also. They must imitate God's concerns. They must love as God loved. God loved Israel (4:37; 7:8; 23:5; Hos 11:1) and Israel was to love God (6:5; 1:1,22). God loved the aliens, so Israel was to love them.[34] The motivation was to remember their experience. Israel had once been foreigners in a strange land where she had ended up suffering oppression. She had no access to power or influence and was at the mercy of the Egyptians who enslaved her. That experience should have made her especially empathetic to foreigners in her midst (Exod 23:9). Moses offered a very practical test for assessing Israel's obedience to and love for God. Would they imitate his passion for justice?

---

tom and law in Mesopotamia, Egypt, and Syro-Palestine. See F.C. Fensham, "Widow, Orphan and the Poor in Ancient Near Eastern Legal and Wisdom Literature," *JNES* 21 (1962): 129-139 and Richard D. Patterson, "The Widow, the Orphan and the Poor in the Old Testament and in the Extra-Biblical Literature," *BibSac* 130 (1973): 123-134.

[32]See Victor H. Matthews and Don C. Benjamin, *Social World of Ancient Israel: 1250–587 BCE* (Peabody, MA: Hendrickson, 1993), chapters 1, 2, and 10.

[33]The prophets also reflected this concept of justice: Isa 11:4; Jer 9:23-24; 22:15-16; Micah 6:8; Hos 12:6; Ps 7:1,2; 146:7-10.

[34]The NT counterpart is Jesus' admonition to love one's enemies (Matt 5:43-48).

10:20-22 These verses end the admonition by returning to the themes of verses 12-13. Moses picks up only two of the verbs: **fear** and **serve** the LORD. There could be no question as to how service was defined after the explanation in verses 18-19. True devotion and service could be guaranteed if Israel would **hold fast** to God, cling to him with loyalty and affection (cf. Gen 2:24; Ruth 1:14). Psalm 63 is a meditation on the full significance of holding fast to God. In the Psalm, Israel's devotion (v. 8) is matched by God's covenant loyalty and love (*ḥesed*, v. 4).

Israel's loyalty was also exhibited by how she guaranteed truth (cf. on 5:11,20). It was acceptable to appeal to God to verify truth by taking oaths in his name. It was not acceptable to swear by pagan gods (Josh 23:7-8).[35]

Moses provided further motivation in his closing comments (v. 21). He recalled God's **great and awesome wonders** of bringing Israel out of Egypt (cf. on 4:34 and 9:26,29). Because of his work, he was praiseworthy, One who could be praised with integrity.[36] God's praiseworthiness is, of course, celebrated throughout the Psalms (18:3[4]; 48:2; 96:4; 78:4). Praise was the adoration rendered to God because of who he was and what he had done. What he had done was no secret, it was done right before Israel's **own eyes** (cf. on 4:9; 7:19). Astonishingly, praise could even come from the nations to Israel because of what God would do for them (Deut 26:19).

Moses adds one final reason for praising God (v. 22), his expansion of Israel from **seventy** people to being as **numerous as the stars in the sky**. This was not a natural growth but a miraculous one.[37] "Seventy" was both a literal number (Gen 46:26-27; Exod 1:5) and symbolic for Israel's insignificant smallness (7:7; 26:5).[38] The miracle was that Israel would become uncountable (cf. on 1:10; 28:62). This

---

[35]The Joshua passage offers an important parallel to Deuteronomy. Joshua exhorted Israel to not swear by pagan gods, not *serve* them, but to *hold fast* to God.

[36]The New JPS version translates *tᵉhillāh* as "glory."

[37]Seventy is in the emphatic first position in the Hebrew sentence which equals "You were only seventy . . . ."

[38]Groups of 70 occur throughout the OT in various contexts: Genesis 10 (nations); Exod 24:1 (elders); Judg 1:7 (kings); Judg 8:30 (sons of Gideon); 2 Kgs 10:1 (princes of Ahab).

was part of the promise to Abraham (Gen 12:2; 15:5; 22:17; 26:4, etc.).[39]

God's faithfulness was beyond question, thus Israel's should be exemplary also. The admonition of verse 12 was grounded in the reality of God's character and his actions. To fear, love, and serve God was not a burdensome demand, but the proper response of praise from a grateful and devoted people.

As a summary of Deuteronomy 9:1–10:11, verses 12-22 underscore two major points: the antidote to stubbornness and rebellion was wholehearted devotion to God, and such devotion must be demonstrated by imitation of God's love for the oppressed. Praise of God and service to the downtrodden would be evidence of a circumcised heart.

---

[39]The comparison with the sand on the seashore was also used: Gen 22:17; 32:12; Isa 10:22; Hos 1:10. According to Carl Sagan there are more stars in the universe than grains of sand on the earth. The expressions in the Bible are hyperbole.

DEUTERONOMY 11

5. Exhortation: Obey God and Live (11:1-32)

Chapter 11 completes the first major section of the second speech of Moses (chapters 4:44–11:32). It includes reflections and exhortations based on the second commandment that began in chapter 6. It also rounds off what Christensen calls the "Inner Frame" (with chapters 27–30 being the corresponding frame at the end of book)[1] and shares certain themes with chapter 4.[2] It contains echoes of chapters 5 and 6, especially the wording of 5:1 and 11:32 (forming an inclusion) and the commands of 6:6-9 and 11:18-20. Furthermore, 11:5-7 repeat 5:3. Therefore, this section functions as a summary of chapters 5-10. The main emphasis is twofold: exhortation to keep the commandments today, and the giving of the land. These two themes have been repeated over and over in Deuteronomy as we have seen. Before Moses moves on to a new section (chapters 12-26) in which he explicates the rest of the commandments, he pauses to one more time draw Israel back to the fundamental requirement for maintaining covenant faithfulness and insuring reception of God's promise.

Chapter 11 also prepares for the second half of the "Inner Frame" (chapters 27–30) by adding a new theme at its end — the blessings and curses of the covenant which were to be announced at Mounts Ebal and Gerizim after entrance into the land. Chapters 27–30 then expound at some length on these themes.

The structure of chapter 11 is not as clear as other sermonic units in chapters 5-10. However, there are the usual repetitions of key words in various sections that point us to the interrelated ideas and themes. The sermon develops something like the following:

---

[1]Christensen, *Deuteronomy 1-11*, pp. 69, 201.
[2]Mayes, "Deuteronomy 4," p. 41.

a. 1-7: Remember the acts of God
b. 8-17: Obey so that you may live in the land
c. 18-21: Teach the commandments
d. 22-25: Keep the commandments and possess the land
e. 26-32: Obey so that you may live in the land under blessing

The power of choice comes to the foreground: the right choice will bring blessing and the wrong choice will bring disaster.[3] Chapter 30, in the second part of the "Inner Frame" makes this choice even more explicit.

Remember the Acts of God (11:1-7)

These verses provide the foundation for the rest of the sermon by stressing two things: the current generation should remember clearly the work of God because they had experienced it, and the work of God should serve as a warning to them to be faithful. The work of God is referred to seven times in these verses through use of both the noun and verb of עשֹׁה ('śh, translated in the NIV as "things" or forms of the verb "to do"). In chapters 9 and 10 God's works were for redemption and were a blessing to be thankful for (9:3,26,29; 10:21-22) but here they are used as a warning.

11:1 The call to **love the LORD your God** is identical to 6:5 (see comments there). To love God is to **obey** him (see vv. 13,22; 15:3; 30:6,16 and on 10:12-13) and to **keep his requirements**. This particular word, "requirements," occurs only here in Deuteronomy and sums up the **decrees, laws, and commands** that have been referred to so often (see on 4:1-2). It emphasizes the obligations or duties associated with the commands. It occurs often in Numbers and Leviticus, though in a more technical sense.[4] Verse 1 connects chapter 11 with chapter 10 and shows that the love of God and the fear of God (10:20) are synonymous.[5]

---

[3]Wright, *Deuteronomy*, p. 153

[4]In Numbers it refers often to the guard duty for the tabernacle: 3:7-8,25, etc.

[5]In chapter 6 the call to love God in verse 5 is followed immediately by the instruction to teach the children the commandments, verses 6-9. However, in chapter 11 this instruction does not come until verses 18-21. This was perhaps a deliberate rhetorical move to provide a sort of inclusion for chapters 6–11.

11:2 Though **remember** is an important theme in Deuteronomy, it is not זכר (*zkr*) that is used here but the verb for know, ידע (*yd'*), which can be translated "acknowledge" (see 4:39; 7:9; 8:5; 9:3,6). The current generation should be clear in their thinking: they must learn from their experiences (v. 7). God had acted in the past to redeem them from Egypt in order to **discipline** them (see on 8:2-5). It was their experience not their children's. If they did not learn from the past and transfer the lessons on to their descendants (vv. 18-21), then Israel as a covenant people would vanish.

The second generation, who did not experience the mighty deeds of God in Egypt and the wilderness, would struggle for faith even if carefully taught (cf. Judges 2:7ff). Israel's relationship to God was not just based on the covenant law, an objective standard of conduct. It was also experiential and emotional. God had been at work in their lives both saving and punishing them. Their vivid memories should motivate them.

11:3-4 The acts of God in delivering Israel from Egypt were especially powerful. They should be etched in the memory even if the current adult population had been young at the time (Exodus 14–15). The work of God was the primary basis for Israel's trust in him (see on 4:32-35) and the Exodus theme permeated all of the Old Testament, providing even a basis for anticipating the future.[6]

11:5-6 Events during the wilderness journey were important examples of God at work also. Moses mentions just one to serve as a warning. The event is recorded in Numbers 16:1-35. **Dathan** and **Abiram** joined Korah and 250 others in rebellion against Moses and Aaron's authority. Dathan and Abiram specifically accused Moses of taking advantage of the people. After the deaths of the rebels the people complained. Only Aaron's quick action halted the plague which God brought on them as punishment.

---

[6]See Leland Ryken et al., eds., *Dictionary of Biblical Images* (Downers Grove, IL: InterVarsity, 1998), s.v. "Exodus, Second Exodus," pp. 253-255. The grammar of verses 2-7 that holds this material together is quite striking. Verses 2b and 3a mark the fivefold direct object of "see" and "experience" with five direct object markers. The last direct object is God's "deeds." Verses 3b,4,5 and 6 state the four great acts God did by marking them with *'ăšer 'āśāh* ("what he did"; NIV: "the things he did" in 3b, and "what he did" in 4,5, and 6). Verse 7 is the climax with the contrastive "But" plus "your eyes saw" the "great deeds" of the Lord "which he did."

God's great deeds were both redemptive and punishing. The choice this generation and each succeeding generation would make would have enormous consequences. Therefore, they must learn from their experiences. This current generation should be motivated more than any other to love and serve God. They should be intellectually and spiritually ready to obey.[7]

Obey so That You May Live in the Land (11:8-17)

These verses form the heart of the sermon. To experience the blessings of God in the land, especially the rain, Israel must live in obedience. Nine references to the land and nine references to taking possession of it or the giving of it dominate this section.[8]

11:8-9 These verses are the heart of the sermon, picking up the theme from verse 1. Obedience was required for two reasons: to ensure possession of the land and to ensure long life in the fruitful, Promised Land. Moses comes back to this theme again and again because it was crucial to Israel's survival, and because Israel had already exhibited tendencies to rebellion (9:7-24). Long life in the land was a consistent promise of God and is repeated in verse 21 (see on 4:40; 5:16,33; 6:2 and also 17:20; 22:7; 25:15; 32:47).[9]

11:10-11 The land God was giving Israel was quite different from what they had experienced in Egypt. In Egypt the annual flooding of the Nile River inundated the neighboring fields. When the Nile had subsided the fields were watered by irrigation via canals and mechanical conveyors that would lift the water from the Nile. The system involved a great deal of ingenuity and hard work. The desert was continually threatening the narrow strip of fertile soil along the

---

[7]Unfortunately the next generation failed. The reason given in Judges 2:7,10 uses the language of Deuteronomy 11. Only the generation that served with Joshua remembered the great deeds of God. The next generation forgot both God and his deeds.

[8]The beginning of the section is disputed. Tigay (*Deuteronomy*, p. 111); the MT and others prefer extending the first section through verse 9. However because of the shared language and the coordinate use of *ki* in verse 10, verses 8-9 seem to go better with verses 10-17.

[9]On the land of "milk and honey" see on 6:3. In Numbers 16, Dathan and Abiram longed for Egypt as the land of milk and honey and denied that the new land was fruitful. Perhaps Moses includes the phrase here as a deliberate response to their denial.

river. Little rain fell in Egypt itself and so the clever irrigation system could easily lead to ideas of self-sufficiency because growing crops depended on how hard the farmer worked.

The Promised Land was different. Rain, rivers, and springs (8:7) watered it and its terrain was mountainous, not flat. Therefore, the people living in Canaan would be more dependent on divine providence, for the rain was seen as a gift from God. Life in the two lands would be different in a theological sense. Israel living in the Promised Land would be aware of her absolute dependence on God and should therefore maintain a close relationship with him.[10]

11:12 The Promised Land was a special land because God provided special care for it; he sought out its welfare. He concentrated attention on it for protection and assistance. It was therefore a good land in which to live (cf. 2 Chr 16:9 where the eyes of the LORD range throughout the earth to strengthen those committed to him; cf. also Prov 15:3; Zech 4:10; Ps 33:18; 34:15[16]).

11:13-15 The key to the good life in the good land was obedience in the truest and fullest sense. The only proper response to such a gracious God was love and service (vv. 1 and 22; 10:12; cf. 8:6ff). Obedience had a very practical consequence: rain and fertility. Any agriculturally based economy is sensitive to both. Without them, famine and death lurk nearby. The enticement to Israel in the land of Canaan would be the Canaanite fertility gods. They were attractive but powerless (cf. v. 16; ch. 4).

---

[10]Scholars have generated a complex debate over the meaning of "irrigated it by foot." Traditionally the phrase has been taken to refer to the physical labor involved in the canal system in Egypt in which water direction was sometimes changed by digging the foot into the canal wall (Tigay, *Deuteronomy*, p. 112). Or it has been taken as a reference to the foot-operated water wheel, the *shaduf* (Merrill, *Deuteronomy*, p. 208). Other scholars have suggested Moses was being sarcastic to contrast the desirability of the Promised Land with the undesirability of Egypt. This interpretation understands "foot" here, as in 2 Kgs 17:2; Isa 36:12, as a scribal euphemism for the genitals. So Moses was contrasting the garden plots Israel had in Egypt which they would water with urine (impure water) to the wonderful land in Canaan watered by God's rain (L. Eslinger, "Watering Egypt (Deut XI 10-11)," *VT* 37 [1987]: 85-90; and Walton and Matthews, *Genesis–Deuteronomy*, p. 233). Another scholar sees hyperbole. The plots in Egypt, so small they could be watered by urine, were contrasted to the spacious land of Canaan (G. Nicol, "Watering Egypt (Deut xi 10-11) Again," *VT* 38 [1988]: 347-348).

Palestine had (and has) two rainy periods, the fall and spring. The fall (Oct., Nov.) rains softened the ground for plowing and then watered the newly planted cereal crops like barley and wheat. Intermittent rains continued during the winter. In the spring (Apr., early May; Hos 6:3; Joel 2:23; Zech 10:1; Prov 16:15) rain enabled those crops to head out to provide a good harvest in June. Spring rain also watered the vineyards and fruit trees as they blossomed and set fruit. The benefits extended to animals as well.[11]

11:16-17 The middle section of the sermon ends with a warning.[12] The warning was necessary because Israel could be self-deceived or seduced by outside influences. The result of the obedience encouraged by Moses would be fertility, food, and prosperity. But these very blessings could lead to ideas of self-sufficiency, which could lead to forgetfulness and disobedience (this was already addressed in chapter 8). By such a process the rewards of obedience carried the seeds of disobedience, not because of any defect in God, but because of the perverse character of sinful humanity.

On the other hand Israel could be **enticed** (or seduced) away by outside pressures. They could become like the simple-minded and be deceived. The noun related to the verb here occurs in Proverbs to refer to the simpleton who lacks prudence or wisdom (1:4; 8:5; 9:6; 19:25; 21:11). The Canaanite fertility cult would be the seducer, for it spoke in very concrete terms to fertility concerns.

Hosea 2 describes in detail later Israel's confusion when she succumbed to syncretism with the fertility cult. She came to think that her grain, new wine, and oil came from the gods, not God. Therefore, God threatened to take all that away so she would come to her senses and return to him.

Such drastic measures would have been unnecessary if Israel had paid attention to Moses. The covenant God was the originator of all

---

[11]In Palestine rain falls a total of 40 to 60 days over a growing season of 7-8 months. In temperate zones rain falls around 180 days over a 12 month period; *EncyJud*, s.v. "Israel, Land of. Climate," 9:185-186.

[12]Chapter 11 uses the prevalent verb, *šmr*, "to keep, guard," five times in initial position in five verses to call attention to Israel's need to take great care to be obedient. These appear in verses 1,8,16,22,32. The NIV translates the word in five different ways: "Keep, Observe, Be careful, Carefully observe, Be sure." Sensitivity to this use of *šmr* helps us to see the flow of the sermon.

Israel's food and necessities. There was no need to look to another and become confused. Yet Israel did both.

The consequence would be famine and drought. Without rain the crops could not grow. Famine was common in Palestine (1 Kgs 17:7; Jer 17:8; Joel 1:10-12,17-20), often as a consequence of judgment. In this regard Egypt was in fact a better place for it was not dependent on rain.[13] However, the issue was not which was the best land, but whether Israel was willing to be obedient and trust God's providential care to provide for her needs.[14]

Teach the Commandments (11:18-21)

11:18-21 This segment parallels 6:6-9 and perhaps should come immediately following 11:1. However, it could have been placed here to provide a rhetorical balance with 6:6-9 and provide a frame around chapters 6–11. This would suggest that the chapters were intended as one sermon.[15] The major difference is that 6:6-9 is written in the second person singular and 11:18-21 is written in the second person plural (except 19b). There are also a few other minor variations in the use of words and the order of the commands (6:7 and 8 appear in reversed order in 11:18b-19). Also 11:21 adds a promise of long life to the instruction comparable to 11:9 and 6:18 (for further discussion see above on 6:6-9). The promise of long life in 11:9 and 21 form a frame around the main section of chapter 11.

The promise of long life is expressed in typical ancient Near Eastern language. The **many days of the heavens** is an idiom that means as long as the world exists. Many similar phrases are found in the Old Testament and contemporary documents from other countries.[16]

Keep the Commandments and Possess the Land: 11:22-25

The two conclusions of chapter 11 function as two conclusions to the larger section, chapters 5–11. The first conclusion, verses 22-

---

[13]In many OT texts Egypt is regarded as a fruitful land: Gen 13:10; Exod 16:3; Num 20:5.

[14]Similar warnings about giving and withholding rain occur in Lev 26:3-5,9-10,19-20,26 and Deut 28:12,22-24.

[15]Weinfeld, *Deuteronomy i–ii*, p. 448.

[16]Cf. Ps 89:30; 72:5,7 and S.M. Paul, "Psalm 72:5, A Traditional Blessing for the Long Life of the King," *JNES* 31 (1972): 351-355.

25, summarizes the major themes of the larger section. The second conclusion, verses 26-32, prepares for the corresponding "Inner Frame" section in chapters 27-30.

11:22 The first conclusion is framed in conditional language.[17] *If* they are obedient to all of the demands so often repeated, then blessing will result. The various commands are summarized in three phrases here (cf. the five phrases of 10:12-13) and are similar to 11:1 and 13. **Command** is in the singular which indicates that they are all considered as of one piece and cannot be separated out. God's will was to be lived out in totality, not in a piecemeal fashion. **To hold fast** is taken from 10:20 (see comments there).

11:23 The consequence is spelled out here, **then** . . . . Possession of the land had always been God's steadfast promise from the time of Abraham. The only possible barrier to receiving the promise was disobedience (cf. vv. 8,10,11,29,31, and many other places in chapters 1-11). God's power, at work on Israel's behalf, would overcome the power of the nations. God had already demonstrated his power over Egypt and her gods (vv. 3-4), so there could be little doubt he could follow through in the Promised Land as well (see on 4:38 and 9:1).

11:24 As Israel literally marched through the land, they would stake claim to it. To **set your foot** on the land was a legal procedure resulting in legal title to the land. The promise had already been given to Caleb (1:36; cf. Josh 14:9) and was repeated to Joshua (Josh 1:3, referring back to this text). To tread on the land was also to assert dominion or conquest (Isa 62:1-3).[18] The outline of the Promised Land goes back to Genesis 15:18 (see on 1:7-8 above; cf. Josh 1:4; Exod 23:31; Num 34:1-12).

11:25 Israel would be invincible with God on her side (cf. 7:24). This was a promise given often to Joshua (Josh 1:5; 10:8; 23:9). Further, God's desire from the first was to use Israel to create awe among the nations (Exod 23:27). This could only come as a result of their obedience (see on 2:25). Therefore, Israel's inclination to mistrust God and be fearful (1:26-28; 7:19-21, etc.) was from a lack of faith and frustrated the plan of God. Israel's disobedience had consequences not only for her life and future, but could effectively

---

[17]The Hebrew *kî 'im*, "Indeed if" is emphatic. Either particle alone can express the conditional; together they strengthen it.

[18]See Eugene Merrill, "דרך," *NIDOTTE*, 1:992.

curtail her important witness to God who desired to be honored among the nations.

Obey so That You May Live in the Land under Blessing (11:26-32)

The second conclusion, verses 26-32, introduces a crucial new element from the treaty/covenant formula — the blessing and curses. The ancient treaties always carried promises and warnings to the recipient nation. If the vassal remained faithful to the stipulations, it could expect the favor of the ruling king, but if it violated the treaty in any way, it could expect retribution. These warnings were couched in language of blessing and curse. The idea is only briefly introduced in this section. More detail is given in chapter 27 about the ceremony at Mounts Ebal and Gerizim, and chapter 28 details the precise blessings and curses Israel could expect. So this second conclusion prepares the reader for the second half of the "Inner Frame" which functions as an envelope around the central portion of the book, chapters 12–26. These latter chapters lay out in detail the stipulations of the covenant. All that Moses had said so far offered two choices for Israel: obedience or rebellion. Each had its consequence, blessing and life or cursing and death (30:15-20).

The phrase **I am setting before you today** (vv. 26 and 32) provides a frame around the section and stresses the immediacy of the exhortation. Moses functions more as a pastor/teacher here before he turns to the law-giving of chapters 12–26.

11:26-28 God had always intended that the world live under his **blessing** (Gen 1:22,28; 2:3; 5:2; 9:1, etc.).[19] He also intended that Israel live under his blessing. Moses had already listed several benefits of covenant obedience (6:10-11; 8:6-9,12-13; 11:14-15) and adds more in chapter 28:1-12. It is clear that the commandments are more than legislation for the covenant community, they are intended to be a **way** of life (*derek*). To turn from that way means not that Israel may have broken a commandment or two, it means that they had taken on a totally new way of living. Thus **following other gods** was adopting a new way of life.[20]

---

[19]See Claus Westermann, *Elements of Old Testament Theology* (Atlanta: John Knox, 1982), Part III, "The Blessing God and Creation."

[20]The earliest Christians were often referred to as followers of the Way: Acts 9:2; 19:9,23; 22:4; 24:14,22!

The opposite of blessing was curse, and this too had been possible from the very beginning of creation (Gen 3:14,17; 4:11; 9:25; 5:29). God made blessing and curse available through Abraham (Gen 12:1-3). The curses that threatened Israel were extensive and devastating (see on chapters 27:14-26; 28:16-68).

11:29 The following verses shift to the future. When Israel finally arrived in the land, the first thing the people had to do was gather at the center of the land to announce the blessings and curses (see on chapter 27). **Mounts Gerizim and Ebal** are in the central hill country and flank the ancient site of Shechem (modern Nablus). Ebal is on the north and stands 3,077 feet high; Gerizim is on the south and is 2,849 feet high. A narrow valley between them (one-quarter mile wide at the east end) provided a natural amphitheater from which the proclamation of blessings and curses could be easily heard. In chapter 27 we learn that six of the tribes were to gather on each of the mountains and call out the blessings and curses.[21] This command was carried out in Joshua 8:30-35. Some scholars speculate that this command reflects that a yearly covenant renewal ceremony was held at these mountains near Shechem.[22]

11:30 The mountains are located more precisely from the perspective of the people who are gathered at the foot of Mt. Pisgah east of the Jordan. **In the vicinity of Gilgal** has created debate since the well-known Gilgal of Joshua 5 is east of Jericho and about 30 miles from the mountains. Another, unknown, Gilgal has been proposed. It has also been proposed that Gilgal is a directional marker, pointing the people to the road that leads to the mountains up the Jordan Valley and into the central hill country.[23]

11:31-32 The concluding verses of the larger section, chapters 5–11, restate the central themes of the section and the book. This is one of the most succinct summations of Moses' message. It assumes

---

[21]A study of various places in Palestine mentioned in the OT and NT as sites of addresses to large crowds concluded that these sites had excellent acoustical properties. These sites included Ebal and Gerizim. See B. Cobbey Crisler, "The Acoustics and Crowd Capacity of Natural Theaters in Palestine," *BA* 39,4 (1976): 128-141, especially 138-139.

[22]von Rad, *Problem of the Hexateuch*, pp. 37-38.

[23]See Merrill, *Deuteronomy*, p. 215; Driver, *Deuteronomy*, p. 133; Tigay, *Deuteronomy*, p. 117; and Weinfeld, *Deuteronomy 1-11*, pp. 452-453, for the conflicting views.

that God's grace will prevail and that Israel will move into the Promised Land. It also restates Israel's covenant obligation to be obedient. Grace and law are put together in their proper order with grace first. Therefore, obedience is not an onerous demand, but a grateful response to a gracious God.

These verses also prepare the way for chapters 12–26. Moses will proceed in the main section of the treaty/covenant to explicate the law. But it will not be a law devoid of theology. Rather it will be a law derived from and full of theological reflection grounded in God's gift of the covenant.

DEUTERONOMY 12

SPECIFIC STIPULATIONS

E. ELABORATION OF THE TEN COMMANDMENTS
(12:1–26:15)

Chapter 12 begins the second half of Moses' second speech which continues through 26:15. These chapters are an elaboration of the Ten Commandments in chapter 5. The various laws promulgated are specific applications of the ten general statements in the Decalogue. The chapters are often referred to as the "Code of Deuteronomy" and are compared to the "Book of the Covenant" in Exodus 20:22–23:19. However, a careful examination will show that although many of the same laws are dealt with, Deuteronomy is not legal genre, but an homiletical expansion of the commandments. Moreover, laws that are not listed in the Book of the Covenant are included in Deuteronomy. Moses anticipated settlement in the Promised Land and therefore dealt with issues not found in earlier legislation. The intention was to apply the broad principles of the Ten Commandments to everyday life in the land. Because of this focus Deuteronomy had a continuing relevance for the people of Israel and each new generation could hear it afresh. It is because of this nature of the material that it lends itself to reflection and meaning for God's people through the ages.

From a form-critical perspective, chapters 12–26 conform to the ancient treaty pattern. Ancient Near Eastern treaties included a section that stipulated what the vassal nation was to do to maintain the treaty. Observance of the stipulations would bring the blessing of the ruling nation. In the same manner, chapters 12–26 provide the stipulations for Israel's life as the covenant people of God. The laws and judgments that required obedience and were so often referred to in chapters 1–11 are recorded here.

We must not draw too sharp a distinction between chapters 1–11 and 12–26 as many scholars are inclined to do. There are many close thematic and verbal connections between the two sections as noted below. Chapters 12–26 are not some new or second law but a continuation of legislation already in place. Further, the recognition that chapters 12–26 serve as commentary on the Decalogue reinforces the continuity between the chapters. In addition to the laws some of the connecting themes are references to the gift of the land, God's acts of deliverance, blessings for obedience, and curses for disobedience.[1]

The arrangement of chapters 12–26, though sometimes thought to follow no logical order,[2] has been carefully studied in relationship to the Ten Commandments. It now appears that the material has been topically arranged, following the order of the Decalogue. Though some breaks between sections are not clear, the presentation is logical. The outline followed in this commentary (see Outline at beginning) is that of Dennis Olson.[3]

1. Elaboration of the First and Second Commandments (12:1–13:18)

Chapter 12, as the commencement of the stipulations, is grounded in the first and second commandments. The chapter is concerned with the *where* and *how* of the worship of the one God, thus building on the more basic *who* of chapters 5 and 6. In the context of ancient Israel this was a radical claim for the Lordship of God (see below). Chapter 13 continues the theme with concern for the one God. There were to be no rivals to him in Israel. The temptation to worship other gods, no matter the source, was to be sternly resisted.

The contents of chapter 12 illustrate the essential unity of the two halves of Moses' second speech, chapters 5–11 and 12–26. It follows chapter 7 in both theme and structure.[4] There is the command to

---

[1]The close connection of the two sections in words and themes has been demonstrated by McConville, *Law and Theology*. See also Wright, *Deuteronomy*, pp. 158-159, and Thompson, *Deuteronomy*, pp. 160-161.

[2]So Thompson, *Deuteronomy*, p. 161.

[3]Olson, *The Death of Moses*, pp. vii-ix.

[4]McConville, *Law and Theology*, pp. 60-64.

destroy the peoples and religion of Canaan (7:1-5 and 12:1-4). God's choice of Israel as a holy people is reflected in the command to worship in one place (7:6-11 and 12:5-12). Enjoying the abundance of the land in chapter 7 is a corollary to the law for the slaughter of nonsacrificial animals in chapter 12 (7:12-16 and 12:13-28). There is a warning against ensnarement by foreign religion (7:17-26 and 12:29-32).

The basic structure of chapter 12 has elicited little controversy. However, the ending of the chapter has been marked at different places by English translations and the Hebrew Bible, with 12:32 of the English being 13:1 of the Hebrew. Though the verse in question is clearly transitional, because of its relationship to 12:1 the English versions will be followed here.

McConville has made a minute analysis of the Hebrew text of chapter 12 and has revealed a detailed interrelationship among the various paragraphs.[5] He suggests that the chapter can be divided into two main parts: 5-12 and 13-28 with verses 1-4 and 29-32 functioning as an inclusio.[6] My analysis of the structure builds on McConville with the following outline:

A. Destroy the Canaanite Religion: 1-4
   B. Bring sacrifices and gifts to the chosen place and rejoice: 5-7
   B'. Bring sacrifices and gifts to the chosen place and rejoice: 8-12
      C. Take care to offer only at the chosen place: 13-14
         D. Eating regulations: 15-19
         D'. Eating regulations: 20-25
      C'. Take care to offer only at the chosen place: 26-28
A'. Avoid Canaanite religion: 29-32[7]

Destroy the Canaanite Religion (12:1-4)

12:1 Verse one forms both an inclusio with verse 32 (13:1 in Hebrew) with its stress on obedience and provides a transition from chapter 11. It repeats the key phrases "statutes and judgments,"

---

[5]Ibid., p. 67.

[6]These two halves are also marked in the Hebrew by verses 1-12 using the second person plural and verses 13-28 using the second person singular.

[7]See Gary Hall, "Rhetorical Criticism," pp. 98-99.

"keep to do," and "give" from 11:32. However, the verb "give" reflects completed action in 12:1, not the ongoing action of 11:32. Moses anticipated the settling in the land as already done. Furthermore, 11:32 emphasizes "today" while 12:1 looks to the time "in the land" (see 4:10,40; 5:16,33; 6:2; 11:9,21). Also 12:1 shares similar wording with other introductory sections in 4:44-45; 5:1; 6:1-2 and 29:1.

12:2-4 The first order of business when Israel entered the Promised Land was the utter destruction of the artifacts of the Canaanite religion. The only, unique God of Israel could not be worshiped in the same way or at the same places as the Canaanite gods (v. 4). This was not the first time Israel had heard these strong words (7:24; 9:3). It was God's intention that Israel should not be put in a position of temptation to become like the pagans. **All the places** where the Canaanites worshiped were to be destroyed. This phrase stands in the chapter in key contrast to **the place** (v. 5) which the LORD will choose. The chapter is then not so much about centralization of worship, as popularly assumed, but about the *place* God will choose. It will differ in purpose and location from all the places now being used in the land. Thus God's uniqueness will be protected, and Israel will be sheltered from syncretism.

The Canaanite worship places were easily identifiable and fit the nature of their religious beliefs. The **high mountains and hills** were apparently thought to be closer to the gods, so altars and idols were placed there. **Spreading trees** (or green, luxuriant trees) perhaps had fertility associations as part of a sacred grove. **Stones** and **poles** represented the idols.[8] The stones apparently represented the male god Baal and the poles represented the goddess **Asherah**.[9]

---

[8]Many of the phrases in these verses are used separately or together in the prophets and Kings to refer to the idolatrous Canaanite worship which so strongly tempted Israel. See Hos 4:13; Isa 57:5; Jer 2:20; 3:6,13,23; 13:27; 17:2; Ezek 6:13; 1 Kgs 14:23; 2 Kgs 16:4; 17:10 and William L. Holladay, "On Every High Hill and under Every Green Tree," *VT* 11 (1961): 170-176.

[9]For a description of the Canaanite sacred sites see on 7:5 and Walton and Matthews, *Genesis–Deuteronomy*, pp. 229-230, 233-234. Archaeologists have found apparent examples of the standing stones at Gezer, Shechem, Hazor, and Arad.

The instructions in these verses point to a radical discontinuity between Israel and her surroundings. There was to be no compromise when it came to worship of God. He could not be honored with the trappings of the pagan cult. However, it is a sad fact that these instructions seemed to have been honored more in the breach than in the observance. The prophets' condemnation of Israel's assimilation of the Canaanite cult vividly illustrates Israel's apostasy (Hos 1–2; Jer 2–3; Ezek 16, 23). Various kings' reforming efforts also suggest fundamental disobedience by Israel.[10]

To prepare the way for God's **name** to be placed in his chosen location the **names** of the Canaanite idols were to be utterly removed from the land. Their presence and power were to be totally repudiated. Only one God could be served in the land. The literal Hebrew at the end of verse 3 is "that place" (NIV, "**those places**"). But clearly multiple places were meant. It is possible then that in the following verses when "the place" is used to refer to where the LORD will choose, it is not referring to a *single* sanctuary, but a *central* sanctuary that may move from place to place.

Verse 31 expands on verse four, informing Israel why they cannot worship God in **their way**. Pagan worship involved practices that were detestable to God and incompatible with his character (see below).

Bring Sacrifices and Gifts to the Chosen Place and Rejoice (12:5-7)

Verses 5-12 form a unit that parallels chapter 7:6-11. The thought is developed in two parallel paragraphs, with the second paragraph, verses 8-12, expanding on the first, verses 5-7.

12:5 This verse has generated an enormous amount of discussion because of its central place in the formulation of the critical theory about the origin of Deuteronomy (see Introduction). Before reflecting on that discussion we must first understand the verse in its context. It begins with a strong contrast to verse four. **But** (NIV) renders the Hebrew *kî 'im*, which marks a strong exception after a

---

[10]For Asa's efforts see 1 Kgs 15:11-14; for Hezekiah see 2 Kgs 18:3-4,22 (which was short-lived since his son Manasseh revived paganism, 2 Kgs 21:3ff); for Josiah see 2 Kgs 23:4ff. The full force of Deuteronomy's ideal seemed to have had only sporadic influence.

negative. This is to be expected, for Israel was to make radical changes in the cultic sites in the land. Since Israelites could not worship at the pagan places, there had to be a designated place for them. It was to be a special place because God would personally **choose** it. The stress was on God's choosing, not on the place. Just as God had chosen Israel (4:37; 7:6-7; 10:15; 14:2) and the priests (18:5; 21:5), so he would chose a place for his name (12:5,11,14,18, 21,26; 14:23-25; 16:2,6,7; 17:8,10, etc.). Throughout Deuteronomy the place where Israel was to worship was consistently referred to in this way. Furthermore, God would place his **name** there.[11] The use of "name" was appropriate because Deuteronomy focuses on worship. It was through God's name that Israel had access to him. The "glory" of God referred to dramatic divine manifestations and was used when his might and majesty were in view. God's glory threatened Israel and would be inappropriate in general worship contexts (Exod 33:18ff).[12] "Name" denotes both presence and ownership. His presence was in the tabernacle and Ark of the Covenant (Exod 29:43-46). But since he was also the sovereign God, to place his name in the land was symbolic of his ownership of the land.[13]

In light of the view that Deuteronomy was addressed to cult reform in seventh-century Judah, two omissions from chapter 12 seem striking. First, the normal word for "high place," (בָּמָה/בָּמוֹת, *bāmāh/bāmôth*) as an (mostly) idolatrous cultic center for worship

---

[11]Von Rad's contention that Deuteronomy represents a late demythologizing of God's immediate presence (his "glory" in the Ark for example) to a more distant "Name" theology is opposed by the book of Deuteronomy itself. The people appear before the LORD at the chosen place (16:10,16; 26:10,13) and God is among his people (23:15). Also in chapter 26 the people speak before the LORD. (See von Rad, *Studies in Deuteronomy*, pp. 37-44, and *Deuteronomy*, p. 90). For a full rebuttal of von Rad see Ian Wilson, *Out of the Midst of the Fire: Divine Presence in Deuteronomy* (Atlanta: Scholars Press, 1995).

[12]J. Gordon McConville, "God's 'Name' and God's 'Glory,'" *TB* 30 (1979): 149-163.

[13]See G.J. Wenham, "Deuteronomy and the Central Sanctuary," *TB* 22 (1971): 112-114; Thompson, *Deuteronomy*, p. 166. See passages where God's ownership is established by use of the phrase "called by my (your) name": 1 Kgs 8:43; 2 Chr 7:14; Jer 7:10,11,14, etc.; and passages where he asserts his sovereignty over Israel: Deut 28:10; 2 Chr 7:14; Isa 63:19; Jer 14:9.

does not appear in this chapter, nor in all of Deuteronomy except 32:13 and 33:29. However, Kings, Chronicles, and the prophets are replete with condemnations of high places as illicit places of worship.[14] It would seem that if Deuteronomy 12–26 was specifically directed to the eradication of the high places in the seventh century B.C., we should expect to find references to high places in Deuteronomy, especially in chapter 12.

Secondly, the place where worship was to be centralized is not named anywhere in Deuteronomy. This omission suggests that the focus was more on the LORD whose name was there and who had chosen the place than on the place itself. The place was only important because of who was there. It was the LORD, not the many whose names had been there in the past. And it was the chosen place, not the many places where worship had been done. If God did not receive the honor he should, then the place would not make any difference.

There is a certain reticence in Deuteronomy about the place that is not always recognized. The chosen place did not become a holy site on its own with independent sacredness. God chose the place in opposition to all the Canaanite sites there and it had God's name rather than other gods' names. The precise place remains unnamed. The historical books support this reserve about the place. God would not and could not be confined to one place (2 Sam 7:5-7; 1 Kgs 8:27). Places that were chosen could in fact receive censure (Shiloh — Jer 7:12-15; Jerusalem — Micah 3:4-6; 7; Jer 7). Therefore it would be misleading to concentrate too much on the theme of centralization in one place.[15]

From the time of David onward Jerusalem was without doubt the intended central sanctuary (1 Kgs 8:44,45; 11:13,32,36; 14:21, etc.; Ps 87; 122; 132). But prior to David's time other places seem to have served as central sanctuaries.[16] In fact the early history of

---

[14]K-D. Schunck, "בָּמָה," *TDOT,* 2:139-145.

[15]As Clements does, *Deuteronomy,* pp. 27-30. See J. Gordon McConville, "Jerusalem in the Old Testament," *Jerusalem Past and Present in the Purposes of God,* ed., P.W.L. Walker (Grand Rapids: Baker, 1994), pp. 21-51.

[16]If Jerusalem were the place in view and high places were to be eradicated, as the critical theory assumes, it would not have been difficult for the author/editor to say so. The standard response is the assertion that the

Israel suggests that the first place where God was to be worshiped was Shiloh (Josh 22; 1 Sam 1–3; Jer 7:12) because the tabernacle and Ark were there. Other sites such as Shechem (Josh 8:30ff), Gilgal (Josh 5) and Bethel have also been mentioned but with less textual support.[17] The book of Deuteronomy itself commands worship at Mounts Ebal and Gerizim (Deut 27; cf. Josh 8:30ff).

12:6 The various offerings that were to be brought are listed. Since some well-known ones, like the guilt offerings, sin offerings, and cereal offering, are not included, the list is probably representative, not exhaustive (cf. verses 11 and 17). The emphasis was on the place (NIV **there**). Israel was to **bring** her offerings to the chosen place (often commanded in chapters 12–26) in response to the fact that God had *brought* them into the land (often stated in chapters 1–11).[18]

Offerings were the whole burnt offering in which everything was consumed on the altar. **Sacrifices** included several kinds in which the fat was burned. The priest and the worshiper ate the remainder of the animal. These were the two most common types of sacrifice and often occur together in Leviticus 1–7. The **tithes** were a required offering and included grain, wine, oil, and the first of the flocks and herds (see on 14:22-29). **Special gifts** (literally "what your hand contributes") referred to special portions taken from larger amounts and dedicated to the use of the priests (it may refer to the first fruits – Deut 26:4). The gifts from **vows** and **freewill offerings** were voluntary sacrifices, either from a vow made to God in some situation, or as a free offering out of gratitude (Lev 7:16-17; 22:18-23). The **firstborn of** the **herds and flocks** was that which was to be given to God in order to redeem the rest (Num 18:15-18; Deut 15:19-23).

---

author was aware that such references would have been obvious anachronisms (Clements, *Deuteronomy*, p. 28; Moshe Weinfeld, *Deuteronomy and the Deuteronomic School* [Oxford: Oxford Press, 1972], p. 6). However, Clements finds in Deuteronomy direct interaction with seventh-century ideas in its views on the Ark, the central sanctuary, the election of Israel, and the gift of the land (R.E. Clements, "Deuteronomy and the Jerusalem Cult Tradition," *VT* 15 [1965]: 300-312). Von Rad admits that attaching the central sanctuary to Jerusalem was too hasty. The fact that the idea was later applied to Jerusalem proves nothing about its origin (*Deuteronomy*, p. 94).

[17]See McConville, *Law and Theology*, pp. 23-28.

[18]This is another important parallel that ties the two major sections together; McConville, *Law and Theology*, pp. 33-34.

This law apparently did not forbid all sacrifices at other places. Special occasions might call for an offering to God. Exodus 20:24-25 states the fundamental law: sacrifices should be made on an altar of earth or unhewn stone "wherever I cause my name to be honored." The circumstances of battle and theophany were the most important special occasions. The various sacrifices and offerings recorded in Joshua, Judges, Samuel, and Kings that were not condemned fit this pattern and were permitted by Deuteronomy 12:5.[19]

12:7 Bringing the offerings and sacrifices had several purposes. It was done in the **presence of the LORD your God**. God was present with the Ark but he was also accessible because his Name had been pronounced on the place. "Before the LORD" (NIV, "presence") corresponds to the many acts of God which he did before Israel as recorded in chapters 1–11 (1:8,30; 2:23; 4:8; 11:26,32, etc.).[20] The LORD did his work before them, so now they could and should worship before him. The worship was comprehensive for it involved the extended family. The sacrifices and offerings were community celebrations, not individual (verse 12 gives more detail of the household components: it included all the servants also; cf. 5:14). It was to be done with **rejoicing**. Worship and joyful times go together in the Old Testament according to numerous references in Deuteronomy, the Psalms, and elsewhere (Deut 12:12,18; 14:26; 16:11; 26:11; Ps 9:2; 32:11; 33:21; 104:34, etc.; Lev 23:40; 2 Chr 30:21,23,25-26, etc.).[21] The orgies of the pagans were forbidden, but they were replaced by joyful celebration, usually accompanied by music, dancing, and exuberance (David before the Ark in 2 Sam 6). There is no hint here that God disapproved of his people enjoying their blessings from him. The worship was a consequence of **blessing**. To live under blessing was to experience material well-being and joy. The offerings Israel brought presupposed her living in the land and benefiting from its riches (see chapter 8).

---

[19]See Jeffrey Niehaus, "The Central Sanctuary: Where and When?" *TB* 43 (1992): 3-30, especially 8-16.

[20]McConville, *Law and Theology*, pp. 35-36.

[21]See Michael A. Grisanti, "שׂמח," *NIDOTTE*, 3:1251-1254.

Bring Sacrifices and Gifts to the Chosen Place and Rejoice (12:8-12)

This paragraph addressed the same issues as the previous but with more detail in some areas. It also addressed directly the situation of Israel in the plains of Moab east of the Jordan.

12:8-10 When Israel arrived in the Promised Land, the situation would be different than the present. **Everyone as he sees fit** referred here to cultic anarchy (cf. Judg 17:6; 21:25 = political anarchy). There was a certain ad hoc quality to worship during the wilderness period. The Ark of the Covenant and tabernacle were always there, but there was no chosen location like Moses now envisions. A central sanctuary would change the situation. The change is reflected in verse 28. If they followed the regulations Moses was expounding, they would then be **doing what is right in the eyes of the LORD** (cf. 13:18). The situation would be radically turned around.

Israel could live in peace and experience the **rest** of God and **safety** in the land only when the hostilities of the conquest were complete. In those circumstances they could worship God according to the directives in this chapter.[22]

12:11-12 These verses repeat verses 5-6. **Levites** were added to those to be included in the worship. They had no land or income from the land so the bounty of food was to be shared with them (v. 19). Part of the tithe was for them and for the widow and orphan (14:28-29) and the great feasts were to include them (16:11,14). God's concern for the downtrodden had already been expressed (10:18-19). Therefore, worship that fully honored God and was genuine included all of those that God loved.

Profane Slaughter (12:13-28)

The center section of chapter 12 covers the laws for what is called "profane slaughter." The laws of sacrifice naturally raised the question: Was the only meat that could be eaten sacrificial meat? The answer was no. Nonsacrificial meat could be eaten, but certain regulations must be followed, especially the proper draining of the blood.

This section has two parallel halves arranged in chiastic order

---

[22]See the references to that rest in Josh 22:4; 23:1; 2 Sam 7:1,11; 1 Kgs 8:56.

(see outline above). The theme of the chapter is continued: the importance of worship at the place **God will choose.**

The instructions given here are related to Leviticus 17. Its law required all animals that were eaten to be sacrificed in front of the tabernacle with the assistance of a priest. Israelites were forbidden to slaughter animals outside of the camp. This was to protect them from offering sacrifices to pagan desert gods (v. 7). However, hunted animals or birds could be killed and eaten anywhere (v. 13) as long as the blood was properly drained. The proper draining of the blood was a focal point of Leviticus 17 (vv. 10-12,14). Those regulations prevailed in the desert wandering when every Israelite lived in proximity to the tabernacle.[23]

However, Deuteronomy anticipated Israel's entrance into and settling of the land. When that happened and a central sanctuary was established, it would be an extreme hardship for everyone scattered about the land to bring any animal they wanted to eat to the central sanctuary. Therefore adjustments in the law had to be made.[24]

12:13-14 The regulations begin with a warning about the whole **burnt offering;** it was to be offered only at the central sanctuary since it was totally consumed as an offering to God.

Verse 14 has been interpreted to refer to "any" of your tribes (NIV, **one**) and thus in support of the idea that the chapter is about a central sanctuary, not a sole sanctuary. A central sanctuary could change location from time to time.[25]

---

[23]See G.J. Wenahm, *The Book of Leviticus* (Grand Rapids: Eerdmans, 1979), pp. 240-248.

[24]For a proper perspective on this law we must recognize that eating meat in ancient cultures was not a daily event. Israelites probably rarely attained such a wealth of animals that they could slaughter them indiscriminately. Thus the killing and eating of an animal would be a solemn and sacred occasion. Lack of refrigeration also meant that any animal killed had to be consumed immediately before it could spoil. Verse 20 refers to the "craving" of meat, suggesting it was not a regular practice. The Jewish Talmud regarded the daily consumption of meat an extravagance that could reduce the wealthy to poverty (Tigay, *Deuteronomy*, p. 124).

[25]Scholars who support the sole sanctuary theory have to interpret verse 5 as an adjustment by a later editor to limit the ambiguity of verse 14 (Mayes, *Deuteronomy*, p. 227). However, if a later editor worked on verse 5, why did he not remove the ambiguity from verse 14 also?

12:15-19 An important exception was provided.[26] Animals that were to be eaten as food could be slaughtered like hunted animals, the **gazelle or deer**. They did not have to be treated as sacrificial as before (Lev 17) and both **the unclean and the clean** persons could eat. However, the main concern of Leviticus 17 must be observed, the proper pouring out of the blood onto the ground (Lev 17:10-12; Gen 9:4ff).[27]

However, sacrifices and offerings that were specifically given over to the LORD could not be treated like the "profane slaughter" (the classes of offering listed are similar to v. 6). They were to be eaten **in the presence of the LORD at the place the LORD will choose**. These were to be properly shared with the whole household and the Levites as already commanded (vv. 16-19, cf. vv. 7,11-12).

12:20-25 To the repetition from verses 15-19 is added the concern that the blood be treated properly, a chief concern of Leviticus 17. Since the life was in the blood it had to be poured out onto the ground and not eaten. Obedience would bring blessing, and it would **go well with** them (cf. on 4:40; 5:16,29,33). By being obedient Israel would reverse the cultic anarchy reflected in verse 8 and please God (v. 25b).[28]

12:26-28 Several earlier themes are repeated as part of the sermonic style.

Avoid Canaanite Religion (12:29-32)

12:29-32 The final paragraph returns to the concern of verses 1-4 with its warning against Canaanite cultic practice. It also serves as

---

[26]Verse 15 begins with the particle רַק (*raq*), "only, yet" (NIV, **Nevertheless**), as do verses 16,23, and 26.

[27]This commentary assumes the chronological priority of Leviticus 17, contrary to modern critical scholarship. This priority has been cogently defended by McConville, *Law and Theology*, pp. 48-52. The episode of Saul and the Israelites in 1 Sam 14:31-35 seems to presuppose both Leviticus 17 and Deuteronomy 12. The army could eat animals taken as booty of war if properly killed by draining the blood on to the ground.

[28]The Jehovah's Witnesses use Leviticus 17 and Gen 9:4 as authority for refusing blood transfusions, because the life is in the blood. Such an interpretation ignores both the biblical context and the historical setting of the texts. See Leonard and Marjorie Chretien, *Witnesses of Jehovah* (Eugene, OR: Harvest House, 1988), pp. 182-190, for a description of how this doctrine developed.

a transition to chapter 13.[29] The admonition of verse 32 to not add anything to the commandments leads into the prohibition of chapter 13 to not add any gods.

Verses 1-4 were stated in imperative language — Israel was to destroy all the Canaanite cultic apparatus so she would not be tempted to worship God in that way. This paragraph is stated in language that envisions the future intermingling of divine and human activity. God would destroy the Canaanites but Israel would drive them out. After that happened Israel was to protect herself.

The reprehensible Canaanite act of child sacrifice drew the strongest divine censure. It was an act of appeasement to the gods that was radically counter to the nature of the true God. Child sacrifice was a grisly part of ancient Near East pagan worship that persisted at various times and places throughout the Mediterranean world.[30] The practice was strongly condemned in the Old Testament (Lev 18:21; Jer 7:31; 19:4; 32:35; Ezek 23:37; Ps 106:37-38) though unfortunately it was practiced in Israel (Ahaz — 2 Kgs 16:3; Manasseh — 2 Kgs 21:6). It was called the shedding of "innocent blood."

This important chapter in Deuteronomy invites reflection in more than one direction. First, its emphasis on the radical nature of the worship of the one God in one place fits well the central theological core of the book. It is a theme that has been noticed often already. Israel lived in an environment of religious pluralism. All ancient religions tolerated others and were open to new gods and new beliefs. It was easy for them to assimilate new ideas. Israel stood in radical tension with those religions just as Christians stand in relation to their culture. It is ironic to the extreme that pluralism, in its expressed respect for all religions, actually denigrates every faith. It, in effect, says that the beliefs of each religion are not important. Pluralism further denigrates religious faith by assigning all beliefs to

---

[29]Thompson, *Deuteronomy*, p. 172, places these verses with chapter 13, not chapter 12.

[30]L.E. Stager and S.R. Wolff, "Child Sacrifice at Carthage," *BAR* 10,1 (1984): 30-51; Tigay, *Deuteronomy*, pp. 464-465; John Day, *Molech: A God of Human Sacrifice in the Old Testament* (Cambridge: Cambridge University Press, 1989).

the creative matrix of human culture and history. All beliefs are merely a product of time and place.[31]

Secondly, the emphasis on worship at the place God will choose had a strong impact on the history of Israel and Judaism. It led to reforms by Asa, Hezekiah, and Josiah. It impacted postexilic Israel and resulted in the centrality of Jerusalem and the temple for Judaism. With the New Covenant, as Jesus taught the Samaritan woman (John 4; cf. Acts 7:44-50), the place of worship would not be important, but the manner of worship would be central, "in spirit and in truth." These words have liberated the church to worship in any place in which the gospel is spread. Nonetheless, the central theology of Deuteronomy remains in that the focus of God's choosing and presence has become Jesus Christ. Just any worship will not do. The word of God and salvation can come through no other. The person who responds to the gospel is called to radical decision, to come to God through Jesus Christ and him alone.[32]

---

[31]It is a further irony that pluralism fails to reveal what supreme confluence of culture and history gave rise to its absolute certainty that everything is the result of culture and history! See also the discussion in Wright, *Deuteronomy*, pp. 160-162.

[32]Ronald Nash, *Is Jesus the Only Savior?* (Grand Rapids: Zondervan, 1994). For a presentation of another point of view that accepts pluralism and finds witness to the "sacred" in all religions see Marcus Borg, *The God We Never Knew* (New York: Harper Collins/HarperSanFrancisco, 1997).

DEUTERONOMY 13

Worship One God (13:1-18)

Chapter 13 continues the theme of chapter 12 as it further reflects on the implications of the first two commandments. It complements the emphasis of chapter 12 which detailed how Israel was to worship at one place as opposed to the Canaanites who worshiped everywhere. Chapter 13 stresses that Israel should also be different from the Canaanites by whom they worship. They must worship only one God, not the numerous gods of the pagans. This point had been made already, especially in chapter 4, but it is now explicated in the context of the temptations that may come to deviate from faithfulness.

Chapter 13 has a simple threefold structure, marked by the use of the conditional particle "if" (*kî*) at verses 1,6 and 12.[1] Therefore, the three paragraphs are verses 1-5,6-11, and 12-18. The paragraphs are bound together by a common theme and common wording. The theme is the warning to resist being led astray after other gods, no matter who the instigator may be. One common catch phrase is "Let us follow other gods (gods you have not known) and worship them" or some variation (vv. 2,6,13). Another common theme relates to the penalty for the crime: death. In each paragraph the penalty is described in more detail and with intensification. The wording of paragraphs 1 and 2 are especially close.

There were three possible sources for the temptation to turn against God: a prophet (vv. 1-5), a family member or close associate (vv. 6-11), or a popular movement in another village (vv. 12-18). All were to be resisted. Deuteronomy has further reflections on these

---

[1]The English versification differs from the Hebrew in chapter 13. English verse 1 is verse 2 in Hebrew since English 12:32 is 13:1 in the Hebrew text. The English versification will be followed in this commentary.

matters in chapter 18:14-22 (related to the first paragraph) and 16:21–17:7 (related to the second paragraph and in some ways to all of chapter 13).

Each of the paragraphs is case law; it provides instructions for what Israel was to do if certain conditions developed. Case law is distinct from the unconditional demands of the Decalogue and is the predominate type in the Pentateuch (cf. Exod 21:2–22:16; Lev 20; Deut 22).

Resist (False) Prophets (13:1-5)

Chapter 12:32 (Hebrew 13:1) provides a transition verse between the two chapters. Nothing was to be taken away from God's words as spoken by Moses. What follows are descriptions of three occasions when additions might be made to God's word. None were to be tolerated. We must keep in mind that the stress throughout is on the content of the spoken word. It takes precedence over all else.

13:1 The first situation concerns the prophet. There is nothing unorthodox about his appearance, the source of his message, or the signs offered. God often communicated messages in dreams to warn, to give assurance, to reveal the future, or to show his superiority over other gods.[2] The NIV here offers too narrow of an interpretation with its **foretells by dreams.** "Divine by dreams" (NRSV) is more accurate. Prophets of God could also do a **miraculous sign or wonder.** Moses, as he led the people out of Egypt, is a good example. In Deuteronomy, signs and wonders are associated with the Exodus (4:34; 6:22; 7:19; 26:8; 29:3; 34:11). However, they could not only be a special display of God's power, they could also be a token or sign of a future event (1 Kgs 13:3,5; Isa 8:18; 20:3). In the case in view here, they would be a pledge or attestation of God's presence (cf. Exod 4:8,9; 7:3; Judg 6:17; 1 Kgs 19:28; 20:8,9) or approval.

13:2 It was the usual expectation that if a true prophet spoke of the future, what was spoken would come to pass. Deuteronomy

---

[2]For these various messages see Gen 20:3,6; 28:12; 31:10; 37:5,7; 41; Judg 7:13-15; 1 Kgs 3:5; Dan 2; Joel 2:28. The recipients could be Israelites or non-Israelites. However, at a later period, Jeremiah, in the context of a plethora of false prophets, warned against those who prophesied by dreams — Jer 23:27-32; 27:9; 29:8-9. See Gary V. Smith, "חלם," *NIDOTTE,* 2:153-155.

18:22 uses this factor as a way to distinguish between a true prophet and a presumptuous (false) one. However, for chapter 13 that is not the foundational test. The most crucial test is the content of the message. In Israel's historical context of religious polytheism, pluralism, and syncretism, loyalty to the one God was foundational (see 5:7-8). Therefore, the content of the message of the prophet was more important than the actions. No matter what the messenger was able to do, if the referent of the spoken word was not the God of the Exodus, the message was false. It was false because, among other things, Israel had had no experience with those other gods. Those gods had done nothing for the nation and were therefore not suitable for worship (cf. ch. 4).[3]

13:3 The appearance of such a prophet was not a random event. It was a **test** from God so that he could discover if Israel had internalized the Shema, Deuteronomy 6:5. God had done a great many things so that Israel might know that he was God (4:39; 7:9; 8:5; 9:3,6; 11:2). But he also wanted to know if they were going to be loyal. In light of the history of the nation as Moses outlined in chapters 1–3 it was not certain that Israel would pass the test.[4] They were not to even listen to the **words** of the prophet. They could too easily be dazzled by the signs and ignore the message but it was the content of the message that was crucial.

13:4 The LORD **your God** and **him** are in emphatic position in the Hebrew text, which stresses the importance of the admonition. In sharp contrast to the temptation to follow other gods, Israel must **follow** God alone. Wholehearted devotion was required.[5]

13:5 There were consequences for the prophet who came with a wrong message. In this case it was death. To **put to death** in legal texts is the language of capital crimes (for example Exod 19:12; 21:12,15; Lev 20:2,9,10,11; 24:16,17, etc.). The consequence was so severe because tempting God's people to follow other gods was no innocuous or idle message. It was **rebellion** against the covenant

---

[3]A common designation for the Canaanite and other gods was "gods they had not known" which meant that Israel had no experiential knowledge of them (see 11:28; 28:33,36,64; 29:26; 32:17).

[4]On the matter of testing see on 4:34; 8:2,16; 6:16. In the biblical narrative this kind of testing begins in Genesis 22 with Abraham.

[5]For comment on the words used here see on 10:12-13,20.

LORD and redeemer (cf. 11:28; Exod 32:8). The prophet had **tried to turn** Israel away from God or "seduce" her into a false faith (cf. 4:19; 30:17). This was an **evil** that had to be **purged** (literally "burned") out of the nation.

Evil had to be burned out because it was incompatible with the presence of God who was holy, just, and good. The evil here refers to people who practice evil. Only the righteous and good could live in God's presence (Psalm 15). If the evil were not burned out, it itself could consume everything like a fire (Isa 9:18).

Other evil persons condemned in Deuteronomy that had to be burned out were those who held the priest in contempt (17:12), the malicious witness (19:19), the rebellious son (21:21), the adulterer (22:21), and the kidnapper (24:7).[6]

Resist Family Members (13:6-11)

13:6-11 This paragraph carries the same warning against being led astray after other gods, but it raises the possibility that the temptation may come from family or close friends. These were the precise people who were likely to have the most influence on a person. In the context of the extended family unit in Israel, it would be extremely difficult to resist such powerful forces. A person who broke with a family would give up security, livelihood, home, and future. Yet Moses suggested that loyalty to God superseded personal relationships and security.

There would be a natural tendency to shield the family member from the harsh penalty or show them more grace. But Moses used harsh language to forestall such mercy. They were to **show no pity**, feel no compassion (**spare him**), nor try to cover up (**shield**) for the miscreant (v. 8).

The penalty for a family member was the same as for a prophet – death. In this paragraph the death penalty is spelled out – it must be by stoning (vv. 9-10). Stoning to death (literally "stone with stones") was the death penalty of choice in ancient Israel, probably partly because of the abundance of stones in the land. To accent personal responsibility for the sentence, the family member was to cast

---

[6]See also 4:25; 9:18-21; and 31:17-18,29 which refer to idolatry as an evil.

the first stones, then the community joined in.[7] This procedure involved the community in both the discovery of the breaking of the covenant law and the punishment of the violator. The public execution was to serve as a deterrent (v. 11) by creating fear among the people (cf. 17:3; 19:20; 21:21). This was in addition to the prime motive of removing the evil from the nation (v. 5).

Resist Popular Movements (13:12-18)

13:12 The third possible case involved a strong movement toward apostasy in another village. It was conceivable that a movement to apostasy could occur, orchestrated by charismatic leaders who could sway the masses. If such an event occurred, it was to be investigated thoroughly. No decisions were to be made on the basis of rumor.

13:13-14 The leaders are described by the unusual phrase בְּנֵי־בְלִיַּעַל (bᵉnê bᵉliyya'al, that is, "sons of beliaal"; NIV, **wicked men**, NRSV, "scoundrels"). The root of the word is uncertain, but it normally refers to worthless persons who are a detriment to society. Besides turning people away from God, as here, they also were the kind involved in sexual deviation (Judg 19:22; 20:13; 1 Sam 2:12), in treating others harshly (Deut 15:9; 1 Sam 30:22), in rebelling against authority (2 Sam 20:1), and in giving false testimony (1 Kgs 21:10; Prov 19:28). In other words, they were a general category of people who engaged in activity that destroyed the community.[8]

13:15-18 The penalty in this case was total destruction of the village and its people, that is, the application of the ḥērem principle, an action normally used only against the enemies of Israel (see on Deut

---

[7]Stoning as the penalty was also applied to the idolater (17:5), the non-virgin bride (22:21), the male and female adulterers (22:24), the Israelite who touched Sinai (Exod 19:13), and the goring ox (Exod 21:27-32). In the OT this penalty was carried out against Achan (Josh 7:25) and Naboth (illegally; 1 Kgs 21:13-15). It was threatened against Moses (Exod 17:4) and David (1 Sam 30:6).

[8]In the Jewish intertestamental literature the noun came to be used as a proper name for Satan (Jub 1:20; T. Levi 18:12; T. Dan 5:10-11); and in the Qumran documents (the *Manual of Discipline* and the *War Scroll*). See also 2 Cor 6:15 and 2 Thess 2:3. For the debate on meaning see Paul D. Wegner, "בלה," *NIDOTTE,* 1:661-662.

2:34; 3:6; 7:2,26). As the evil was to be purged out by burning (v. 5), so the town and all its material remains were to be burned, thus purifying the nation from the terrible evil done (v. 16). This purging action would earn the blessings of God, which included **mercy, compassion, and increase** in **numbers** (cf. 1:10; 7:13; Gen 17:6) because it was considered **right in** God's **eyes** (v. 18; cf. 12:25).

In Israel's historical and cultural context prophets exerted great influence. Their ministry was enhanced if accompanied by powerful signs. Elijah and Elisha are two good examples (1 Kgs 17–2 Kgs 9). But their power was not in the signs. It was in the message: the LORD is God, serve him (1 Kgs 18:21,39). Without the message their powerful signs would have been empty. They were models of true prophets who opposed the hundreds of false prophets who did not proclaim a message of loyalty to the one God of Israel.

DEUTERONOMY 14

2. Elaboration of the Third Commandment (14:1-21)

The relationship of this section to the third commandment is rather subtle. The third commandment limited the people's use of God's name. Deuteronomy has another name theology that also imposes limits on the people. God's name was holy in contrast to the other gods' names (6:13; 10:20). Furthermore, the place where his name would dwell was set apart from all other places (12:5,11,21). Finally, Israel was set apart to God and, therefore, from the names of other gods (6:13-14).[1] In this respect then Deuteronomy carried on the theology of the limits of the use of God's name.

Chapter 14:1-21 also deals with limits, the limits on diet. The foundation for these limits imposed on Israel was the truth that Israel was holy, set apart for God. Thus her holiness imposed boundaries on every aspect of her life, including food. It is in this respect that 14:1-21 elaborates on the third commandment. Chapter 14 also continues the theme of chapters 12–13 — Israel must be separate from her pagan neighbors.

Furthermore Deuteronomy 14 fits into the larger context of purity and holiness in the Torah. Purity (cleanness and uncleanness) was applied not only to food, but to an array of social relationships such as sex and marriage, family relationships, business practices, physical anomalies, dwellings, and abhorrent worship practices (cf. Lev 11–15; 17–20; Num 19). In each of these areas boundaries were established. The danger before Israel was that she might drift into uncleanness and thus become unacceptable to her covenant God. We will return to this issue below.

---

[1]See Olson, *Deuteronomy*, p. 72.

Chapter 14:1-21 consists of two sections, verses 1-2 that describe Israel's special status with God and verses 3-21 that illustrate how that special status impacts her diet. **You are a people holy to the LORD your God** (vv. 2a,21c) forms an inclusio for the material and provides both the rhetorical and theological parameters of the section.

Israel's Special Status (14:1-2)

The chapter shifts from the case law style of previous sections back to the apodictic command format of the Decalogue.

14:1 God could make demands on Israel because she had a special relationship with him. Moses introduced the Decalogue in a similar way (5:1-5). Israel's special status required her to be different from other nations for she was the only one chosen by God (ch. 7). In fact this is the only text in the Old Testament that calls Israel **the children of the LORD your God.** Other texts imply such a relationship but do not state it directly (Isa 1:2; 30:1,9; 63:8; Hos 11:10; Jer 3:14,22; Ezek 16:21). Deuteronomy 32, a poem from the end of Moses' career, also refers to such a status (32:5 ["his children"], 19,20). The earlier statements that God was Israel's father (Deut 1:31; 8:5) had already implied an intimate relationship. The power of the analogy comes from the child's status in the Old Testament. Children had special privileges as well as special obligations and responsibilities. It was an honorable status, but the child was still under the control of the father. Therefore, God had every right to expect obedience from his people.[2]

Their special status meant that the Israelites were not to conduct themselves like the other nations. In this case special mourning rites were singled out: **cutting** and **shaving . . . for the dead** was forbidden. This was a pagan practice apparently associated with magic and polytheism. To engage in such rites would blur the distinction between Israel and the nations.[3]

---

[2]Compare other texts that conceive of Israel as sons: Hos 1:11; 11:1; Jer 3:19; 31:9; Ezek 4:22; Mal 2:10. See Victor Matthews and Don C. Benjamin, *Social World of Ancient Israel: 1250–587 BCE* (Peabody, MA: Hendrickson, 1993), chapter 1, "The Father."

[3]The OT refers to these practices elsewhere also: 1 Kgs 18:28 (the prophets of Baal); Jer 16:6; 41:5; Isa 15:2; Jer 48:37; 22:12; 47:5; Amos 8:10; Micah 1:16; Ezek 7:18; 27:31.

14:2 Israel's further special status was as God's **treasured possession** (repeated from 7:6). God had a distinctive love for Israel and exercised a special covenant loyalty toward her. Therefore the demands God made on Israel were grounded in his prior actions of making her his chosen nation.

The most important assertion for the immediate context however was the pronouncement that Israel was a people holy to the LORD. This established them as set apart to a holy God who himself was separate from the world and above it. Of all the worthy attributes of God his holiness was the premier one out of which the others flowed. Israel, as his people, was to reflect his character in their lives. In fact everything dedicated to God was holy, whether it was a person, place, or thing. This theological theme was the keystone of Leviticus (11:44,45; 19:2; 20:7,26). In fact Leviticus 20:24-26 seems to provide the foundation for Deuteronomy 14. In Leviticus 20 the separation between clean and unclean animals mimicked the separation between Israel and other peoples.

The theme of Israel as God's holy people is strong in Deuteronomy also (7:6; 23:14[15]; 26:19; 28:9; 33:3).[4] Both Leviticus and Deuteronomy demand that Israel's holiness even extend to the nature of her diet.

Clean and Unclean Food (14:3-21)

14:3 This section is dominated by the word "eat." What was acceptable for food to a holy people was described in both positive and negative terms. Verse 3 provides the fundamental prohibition, using the same wording as the Decalogue. The following verses provide the explication with a threefold classification of food sources: land animals (vv. 4-8), sea animals (vv. 9-10), and flying creatures (vv. 11-20). The latter were of two types: birds (vv. 11-18) and flying insects (vv. 19-20). A brief note on dead carcasses concludes the explication (v. 21a,b). The classification was apparently based on the threefold domain classification of Genesis 1:6-13 though presented in reverse order.

The connection of this material to Leviticus 11 is apparent. The threefold classification system and the order in which it is presented

---

[4]See also Deut 5:12; 12:26; 15:19; 22:9; 23:18; 26:13,15; 32:51; 33:2.

are identical. However, Deuteronomy presents an abbreviated form of the law.[5]

14:4-8 Land animals acceptable as food were detailed first, encompassing both domesticated (v. 4) and nondomesticated species (v. 5). The acceptable, domesticated animals were the same as used for sacrifice. Thus there was an obvious parallel between diet and worship. Acceptable animals had to have a split hoof and chew the cud (v. 6). This was considered the "normal" standard for animals and marked those most common in a pastoral economy. Though only ten species are mentioned the list is probably not exhaustive.

The unacceptable land animals were listed because they did not fit the norm (vv. 7-8). Creatures about which there might be some confusion were specifically mentioned. There is debate why the pig was singled out. The reason may have been cultic as it was apparently used in some pagan rites (cf. Isa 65:4; 66:3,17). The reason may have been economic also. Pigs were not generally raised in pastoral economies because they required large amounts of water and shade and could not live off pastureland.[6]

14:9-10 Water and sea creatures with fins and scales were acceptable. No specific species are named. In fact no fish species are named in the Old Testament (cf. Gen 2:19-20) except the great creatures of Genesis 1:21 (cf. Isa 51:9; Ps 74:13) and the leviathan (Ps 74:14; 104:26; Job 3:8; 40:25). However, postexilic Jerusalem had a

---

[5]The nature of the relationship is debated. W.L Moran contends that the author of Deuteronomy depended on Leviticus 11, especially for verses 12-18 ("The Literary Connection Between Lv 11,13-19 and Dt 14,12-18," *CBQ* 28 [1966]: 271-277). J. Milgrom thinks the author had the entire copy of Leviticus before him (*Leviticus 1-16* [New York: Doubleday, 1991], pp. 698-704). However, von Rad (*Deuteronomy*, p. 102) and Mayes (*Deuteronomy*, p. 237) think both go back to a common source.

[6]Mayes thinks the reason was cultic (*Deuteronomy*, pp. 240-241). Walter Houston presents a lengthy argument for economic reasons (*Purity and Monotheism: Clean and Unclean Animals in Biblical Law* [Sheffield: JSOT Press, 1993]). Houston notes that although pig bone fragments are not prominent in the remains found in excavated sites in the ancient Near East, they decline sharply in Palestinian village sites in the Iron I period (the Israelite period) but not at Philistine sites. This is circumstantial evidence to suggest that the prohibition of pigs in ancient Israel was early, not late (tenth or ninth century, not sixth or fifth century B.C.).

fish gate which implied a market nearby (Neh 3:3; 12:39) but the fish trade was controlled by Tyrian merchants (Neh 13:16). There is no evidence the ancient Israelites were fishermen at any time in their history. Part of the reason was geographic. The Mediterranean coast of Palestine offered no natural harbors and much of the coastal terrain was marshy.[7]

14:11-18 Flying creatures merited a lengthy section. There were two kinds: birds (vv. 11-18) and insects (vv. 19-20). Distinguishing characteristics for clean and unclean birds were not given, but the unclean birds were listed (twenty plus the bat).[8] Most of the forbidden birds seem to be carnivorous and would have had a diet of animals with the blood in them or dead animals. Ancient Israel was forbidden to eat meat with blood in it (Gen 9:4; Lev 7:26-27) or dead animals (Lev 11:39-40; Deut 14:21). Therefore the rationale could have been that Israel could not eat anything that violated her own food laws. Though no clean birds were listed, the Old Testament elsewhere does mention a few kinds of birds that could be eaten (quail, Exod 16; doves and pigeons, Lev 5:7; choice/fatted fowl, 1 Kgs 4:23 [5:3]).[9]

14:19-20 The unclean insects were the **swarming** kind, while the clean were the **winged** kind. Leviticus 11:20-22 is more precise. Those that mimicked animals by walking on all fours were unclean. Those that had jointed legs for hopping were clean. Specific clean insects were listed (Lev 11:22).[10]

The debate over the underlying rationale for the distinction between clean and unclean animals has been detailed and lengthy. We can only briefly list the important proposals here.

---

[7]Milgrom refers to a study that suggested that in ancient times the eastern Mediterranean had few fish at all because the silt from Nile River floods flowed counterclockwise along the Palestinian coast and robbed the sea of its nutrients (*Leviticus 1–16*, p. 660).

[8]Leviticus 11:13-19 listed 20 including the bat. It does not have the falcon (*dayyā*, Deut 14:13; Lev 11:14). There is perhaps a scribal addition in MT of Deuteronomy since some Hebrew manuscripts, the LXX, and the Samaritan Pentateuch do not have *dayyā*.

[9]Later Jewish tradition developed a list of acceptable birds and criteria for forbidden birds (see Tigay, *Deuteronomy*, p. 139).

[10]Joel 1:4 lists several different kinds of locusts.

1. Hygienic theories go back as far as Maimonides, the eleventh century Jewish scholar. This theory proposes that the unclean animals were mostly of the carrion type (eaters of dead flesh) and thus most likely to carry disease. Though Israel may or may not have understood the reasoning, God knew what was healthy and unhealthy for her diet.[11] However, this logic is not an obvious basis for all the animals forbidden and thus does not provide a comprehensive explanation. Well-cooked flesh of any animal is safe and flesh of animals other than the pig could be disease filled (anthrax in cows for example).

2. Cultic explanations go as far back as the early Christian scholar Origen (*Contra Celsum* 4:93).[12] He reasoned that animals used in pagan worship practices were forbidden. There is some evidence that pigs may have been used in magical pagan rites, but again the rationale is not comprehensive enough. Furthermore, the theory does not fit the facts well. Ancient pagan cultures and Israel used the bull, sheep, and goat in sacrifices, but they were clean.

3. Traditional Judaism taught that the laws were arbitrary demands from God to teach Israel obedience. Some Christian scholars have supported this view.[13]

4. An ancient Jewish view was that the underlying principle for the laws was ethical. The laws expressed a moral point of view and described a way of life designed to discipline the appetite and prevent the human from being dehumanized through the violence involved in killing animals (Philo, first century BC; Maimonides). This inculcated

---

[11]Many conservative scholars accept this view: R.K. Harrison, *Leviticus* (Downers Grove, IL: InterVarsity, 1980), pp. 124-125; Thompson, *Deuteronomy*, p. 178 (for the pig); R.V.G. Tasker, "Clean and Unclean," *NBD* (2nd ed.), pp. 219-220; S.L. McMillen, *None of These Diseases* (Westwood, NJ: Fleming Revell, 1963); W.F. Albright, *Yahweh and the Gods of Canaan* (Garden City, NY: Doubleday, 1968), pp. 154-155.

[12]See also Martin Noth, *The Laws of the Pentateuch and Other Studies* (Edinburgh: Oliver and Boyd, 1966), pp. 56ff; Thompson, *Deuteronomy*, p. 178 (for some). On the pig see Roland de Vaux, "The Sacrifice of Pigs in Palestine and the Ancient Near East," in de Vaux, *The Bible and the Ancient Near East* (Garden City, NY: Doubleday, 1971), pp. 252-269.

[13]For Jewish thinking see Tigay, *Deuteronomy*, p. 138; for Christian see Merrill, *Deuteronomy*, p. 236.

reverence for life in imitation of God. It was also grounded in the blood prohibition and the laws for ritual slaughter.[14]

5. A sociological/anthropological approach has been advanced in recent years. The underlying logic was that there was a wholeness to life that extended to the animal world. The animals that inhabit each of the three spheres (land, water, and air) have standard pure types. Clean animals must conform to the standard (whole) type. Those that transgress the boundaries are unclean. The social background of the laws explains the forbidden nature of the pig and camel. They did not conform to the ordinary norm of the cattle and sheep favored by a pastoral economy. Further, there was a threefold division in Israelite society: the unclean, the clean (most Israelites) and the priests. This was reflected in the animal world: unclean, clean, and sacrificial. Thus there was a symbolic connection between the human and animal world. Israel's entire world fit into a whole. Even their diet reflected purity and integrity. This conformed to the concept of holiness.[15]

6. A more recent sociological theory builds on the pastoral economy of ancient societies. Traditionally those types of cultures developed various reasons for taboos on animals. Certain animals were proper for sacrifice and others were not. Out of this the priests devised the lists for sacrifice. Further, only animals fit for sacrifice were fit for food. Consequently there was a close connection between diet and cult, and between human and divine "diet." So even Israel's eating habits exhibited loyalty to God and separation from other people.[16] This theory attempts to explain the rationale as a purely anthropological development.

14:21 The section on clean and unclean concludes with two further commands and the motivation from verse 2. Eating dead animals made the person unclean according to Leviticus 17:15. This was

---

[14]Milgrom, *Leviticus*, pp. 725-735. Andrew Bonar suggested a similar, but more allegorical, reasoning. Each forbidden animal reminded Israel of some sinful conduct they should avoid (*A Commentary on the Book of Leviticus* [Grand Rapids: Baker, 1978 {1852}], pp. 207-210).

[15]Mary Douglas, *Purity and Danger* (London: Routledge and Kegan Paul, 1966); Wenham, *Leviticus*, pp. 18-24, 169-171.

[16]Houston, *Purity and Monotheism*; Walton and Matthews, *Genesis–Deuteronomy*, call this viewpoint a promising suggestion (p. 237).

probably because the blood had not been properly drained from the carcass (Deut 12:16; Lev 11:40; 17:10-15). However, it could be given to the **alien** who was probably poor or sold to the **foreigner**, who was probably an independent businessman living among them and not poor. Israelite food laws were not binding on these groups.

The prohibition of cooking **a young goat in its mother's milk** appears also in Exodus 23:19 and 34:36. In Exodus it is in the context of proper observance of the festival and first fruits and is apparently related to proper worship. Therefore, some scholars have suggested that the prohibition was grounded in pagan cultic or fertility rites.[17] Others suggest a humanitarian purpose — young kids should not be taken from their mothers and eaten for pleasure.[18] Others see the prohibition grounded in the separation between life and death. Life-giving milk should not be used to cause death. This would carry on the theme of separation of the clean/unclean laws.[19]

Certainty about the logic of the food laws may never be achieved. However, the explicit statements in the text affirm that they involve the special life that God's covenant people were to live because they were to imitate him in holiness. Israel was to be separate from and different from her neighbors. Since her life was a seamless whole, this difference even applied to diet. The diet then reflected in real and symbolic ways Israel's holiness. "Holiness was woven into everyday life. Every meal should have reminded the Israelite family of God's commitment to them and their commitment to God. A God who governs the kitchen should be not easily forgotten in the rest of life."[20]

3. Elaboration of the Fourth Commandment (14:22–16:17)

The fourth commandment required the regular observance of the Sabbath, the day of rest, every seven days. This section, 14:22–16:17, describes several religious activities that require a regular observance also. Collected here are the regulations for the tithe (14:22-

---

[17]Craigie, *Deuteronomy*, p. 232; Cairns, *Deuteronomy*, p. 143.

[18]Tigay, *Deuteronomy*, p. 140. It is in line with the prohibition to slay the mother and its offspring on the same day, Lev 22:27-28, or to take a mother bird and its young at the same time, Deut 22:6-7.

[19]Milgrom, *Leviticus 1–16*, pp. 737-742.

[20]Wright, *Deuteronomy*, p. 182.

29), the Sabbatical year with remission of debts and release of slaves (15:1-18), the firstlings (15:19-23), and the three yearly pilgrim festivals (16:1-17).

The Tithe (14:22-29)

The paragraph on the tithe addresses two practices, the yearly tithe (vv. 22-27) and the triennial tithe (vv. 28-29). Though this paragraph begins a new section, it is tied to the preceding section by 14:21 and by the emphasis on eating. In 14:2-20 Israel was admonished to not eat unclean food (vv. 3,8,10,12,19,21) but only clean food (vv. 4,6,9,11,20). It was a mark of their holiness before God (vv. 2 and 21). A further mark of their holiness was that they could also eat the tithe (vv. 22,26,29). Therefore it is likely that 14:1-2 control the whole chapter. The tithe, as well as the diet, reflected Israel's special status before God as his chosen people. Another transitional feature of verse 21 is the reference to the alien which is picked up in verse 29. God's concern for this particular group of outsiders was an important part of many of the exhortations of Deuteronomy.[21]

The earliest mention of tithe in the Old Testament is Abram's tithe to Melchizedek (Gen 14:20; cf. also Jacob in Gen 28:22). This fits in with the well-known ancient Near Eastern custom of tithing to both god and country, usually as a tax (cf. 1 Sam 8:15). There was little difference between a tithe and a tax in ancient Near Eastern countries. Both were required by the government and stored in the temple complexes. The king was divinely chosen and so the line between sacred and secular was blurred. In ancient Israel, God was the real King (1 Sam 8:7), so the tithe could be understood as the tenth required by the Ruler. However, Samuel warned that an earthly king would take a tenth (tax) to maintain the government (1 Sam 8:16-17). This was not in God's plan nor was it desirable.

14:22-27 The tithe Israel was supposed to save for the LORD was a tenth. It was an expression of thankfulness for the blessings that God had given them in the land. The increase of grains, vineyards, flocks and herds was a witness to God's largesse and a consequence of his love for them. The same items were listed as special blessings for obedience in 7:13. When the people brought the tithe, they

---

[21]See McConville, *Law and Theology*, pp. 80-81.

acknowledged that God owned everything and was graciously allowing them nine-tenths of the produce. The assumed situation is the same as that reflected in chapter 12 as evident by the key phrase **at the place the LORD your God will choose** (or some variant; vv. 23,24,25; cf. 12:5,11,14). God would choose a place for the sacrifice (12:4-7) to which they must bring the tithe also (14:23). As with the sacrifice they were to eat the tithe in the presence of the LORD (v. 23; cf. 12:7). But if the chosen place was too far away, they could convert the produce into money, carry the money to the sanctuary, and then buy food there to eat as part of the tithe offering (as they could do with the sacrifices, cf. 12:11,17-18,21-23). It is evident that Deuteronomy understood the function of the sacrifice and the tithe in worship to be identical.

The purpose of the tithe was educative, so that Israel might learn to fear God, that is, to relate to him with proper respect and honor (23b). In other words the tithe was for the ultimate spiritual benefit of Israel, not to meet a need of God. This was further illustrated by the fact that, after carrying the tithe to the worship center, the Israelite could then eat it. He also was to share it with the Levite. It was to be a communal meal eaten in the presence of God and with God as a reflection of the covenant relationship with God (as was the sacrifice, 12:11-12).

14:28-29 The tithe was intended to benefit others also. Every third year it was to be deposited in storage in the home village and used to feed the poor and the Levite (cf. 26:12-14). This reflects again the fact that God's concern for the poor and oppressed was to be reflected in the life of his covenant people (cf. 10:18-19). The result of this generosity would be more blessings (v. 29c), which in Deuteronomy meant more goods to share with God and the poor.

The theology of the tithe law recognized that the LORD owned everything including the land that he had given Israel. The proper response was to bring part of the produce of the land to God. By giving up some of the produce Israel would receive more. But even what the Israelites gave up they would not lose because they would eat it as a shared meal with the poor and the Levite. Therefore, obedience and sacrifice could result in joyful celebration (14:26).

Two other texts in the Pentateuch also address the issue of the tithe: Leviticus 27:30-33 and Numbers 18:21-32. Leviticus 27:30-33 is the last paragraph in the book of Leviticus. It comes in the context of other things that have been specially dedicated to God such as special vows (27:2-13), a house (27:14-45), and land or a field (16-21,22-25). The underlying principle was that everything was holy to the LORD. That included the tithe (27:32,33). Substitution was allowed for grain products (v. 31) but not for animals (v. 33). The concern of this passage for holiness reflects the larger theme of Leviticus.

Numbers 18:21-32 occurs in a context that explains the duties of the priests and Levites and the parts of the offerings that were for their use. The tithes were for the use of the Levites as compensation for their service since they had no inheritance in the land (18:21-24). From the tithe of the people given them the Levites had to present a tithe to the priests (18:25-29). The rest of the tithe then belonged to them and their families for food (18:30-32).

Each of the three texts in Leviticus, Numbers, and Deuteronomy has different details. The Leviticus and Numbers texts do not mention either the participation of the worshiper in eating the tithe nor the triennial tithe for the poor. Therefore, the relationship of the three texts to each other has been debated. Some scholars have seen clear contradictions between the texts while others understand a development to have occurred over the years, with Deuteronomy showing innovation.[22]

Those who see development explain the differences between the texts cited above as evidence of that development. Deuteronomy would be the earliest text, emphasizing the gift of the people. Numbers and Leviticus would be later, reflecting the postexilic period when the priests gained control and turned the tithe to their advantage (cf. Neh 10:37-39; 13:10-12).

However, the texts can be better understood in their contexts. Each tithe law is case specific to the circumstances and concerns of their context. Deuteronomy was addressed to the people of Israel and was concerned with their faithful obedience. It concentrated on their responsibilities, which were to bring the tithe to the sanctuary, eat it there, and share it with the Levites. The people were also to take care of the poor by sharing it with them every third year. The Leviticus and Numbers texts were concerned with the Levites' conduct when they

---

[22]Driver: Serious and irreconcilable conflict (*Deuteronomy*, p. 169); Cairns and Mayes: Development and innovation (*Deuteronomy*, pp. 144-145; *Deuteronomy*, pp. 245-246).

received the tithe. The tithe was their source of income since they did not have an inheritance in the land. They were also to share it with the Priesthood. Deuteronomy is a natural follow-up on Numbers. The texts are therefore complementary not conflicting, nor is there significant development in the laws.[23]

Considering the strong emphasis on tithe in the Old Testament it is somewhat surprising that the New Testament does not enjoin a tithe on Christians. Jesus condemned the legalistic Pharisees for paying attention to the minutia of the law for tithes but ignoring weightier matters such as justice, mercy, and faithfulness (Matt 23:23). They should have done both. In this teaching Jesus agreed with Micah 6:8b on God's basic expectations for his people. But Jesus never required his disciples to tithe.

Paul had a great deal to say about giving, but he never required a tithe of the people (Rom 15:25-28; 1 Cor 9:6-18; 16:1-3; 2 Cor 8–9; Eph 4:28). Paul urged that material possessions be shared to meet the needs of the poor and to support spiritual ministry. He based his appeal on generosity. The Christian was to give voluntarily as he determined in his mind to give. He was to give as God had prospered him realizing that what he had was not his own.

In the early church tithing was also rejected in favor of voluntary giving by those who prospered. Giving was to take care of the needy and orphans and widows. Origen thought that Christian giving would far exceed any tithing.[24]

We can see the theology of the tithe at work in the New Testament. Everything belonged to God (Ps 24:1), and his people lived under his blessing. It was a natural response to this blessing for Christians to share what they had with others. The Christian was responding to God's greatest blessing, the crucified, resurrected Messiah. Therefore, generosity would be the norm. Imposing limits on this generosity would be inappropriate.

---

[23]For detailed overview of the issues see R. Averbeck, ,"מַעֲשֵׂר," *NIDOTTE,* 2:1035-1055; McConville, *Law and Theology,* pp. 70-78. In order to harmonize perceived conflicts between the texts early Judaism posited that there were two or three different tithes. Tobit 1:7-8 and the Mishnah specifically mention three tithes. The Qumran Temple Scroll and the Book of Jubilees seem to refer to two tithes.

[24]See G.F. Hawthorne, "Tithe," *NIDNTT,* 3:854-855.

DEUTERONOMY 15

Canceling of Debts (15:1-11)

Deuteronomy 15:1-18 continues the expansion of the fourth commandment on the Sabbath (5:12-14). Its references to the seven-year time span in verses 1,9, and 12 clearly build on the Sabbath concept. The law of the Sabbath year in Exodus 23:10-11, which is followed by the law on the Sabbath in verse 12 makes the connection between the Sabbath commandment and the Sabbatical year law explicit (cf. Lev 25:1-7). Furthermore, the motivation for the Sabbath day, God's redemption from Egypt, and the same concern for the dependent classes exhibited in the Sabbath commandment are strikingly present in Deuteronomy 15. These concerns in Deuteronomy are grounded in the monotheistic claims of chapters 6–11. Chapter 15 also continues the sequence of laws that began in 14:22 that focus on alleviating the burden of the poor. The sequence ends with 15:12-18 and the release of the slave, the class that suffered the most misery.

Chapter 15 has four main paragraphs: 1-6,7-11,12-18 and 19-23. The second paragraph expands on the first and thus they should be considered together. The third is also closely related by content to the first. The fourth paragraph, the setting apart of the firstborn, introduces a topic that is related to the tithe of 14:22-29 and functions as a transition to chapter 16, which details the feast days.

The overall structure of chapters 15 and 16 suggests an expansion of the brief laws in Exodus 23:10-16 on the Sabbath year and the three major feasts. In addition 15:1-18 seems to be related to Leviticus 25. Chapter 15:1-11 and Leviticus 25:8-38 cover the Jubilee year, and 15:12-18 is related to Leviticus 25:39-55. Furthermore 15:1-11 is very similar to Exodus 21:2-6. It is reasonable to conclude that the laws of Deuteronomy 15 are grounded in and expand on previous laws.

249

The structure of the two laws in verses 1-11 and 12-18 is similar. Each has a heading (vv. 1 and 12), a warrant for the law (vv. 2-3 and 13-14), a call to obedience (vv. 4-6 and 15), and a reward for obedience and/or negative outcomes for disobedience (vv. 7-11 and 16-18).[1]

15:1 A literal rendering of verse 1 shows its close relationship to Exodus 23:11. Both texts refer to the seventh year as the year of "release" (שָׁמֹט, *šmṭ*) (the NIV in verse 1 interprets the word as **cancel debts**, apparently under the influence of verse 2). However, the Exodus text refers to the land being released from plowing and sowing rather than the debtor being released from debt. This aspect of the Sabbatical year is unique to Deuteronomy. Apparently Deuteronomy's concern for the poor led to this expansion of the law which had not been previously explained. This further application presupposes a settled, growing economy, when for various reasons the people would have contracted debts.[2]

15:2-3 The giver of the loan (lit., "lord of the loan of his hand" which emphasized the power of the loaner) was to relinquish his control (power) over the debtor. The loaner gained control by taking over personal property, such as land, clothing, or even in extremity, family members (vv. 12-18) as guarantee for a loan (cf. Deut 24:10-13; Exod 22:25-26). He was to give up this control. Such generosity was a fitting climax to the three-year cycle in which the tithe was used locally for the poor (Deut 14:28-29). In the seventh year, after two three-year cycles, a much more significant contribution was offered to the poor — release from debt. It was an act grounded in the character of God, therefore the loaner was constrained by loyalty to his covenant God to offer the canceling of the debt. God was by his nature "open-handed" (Ps 104:28) and generous; the Israelite should follow suit.[3]

However, this generosity was to be extended only to the **fellow Israelites or brothers**. This commitment to the community is a strong

---

[1]See Jeffries M. Hamilton, *Social Justice and Deuteronomy: The Case of Deuteronomy 15* (Atlanta: Scholars Press, 1992).

[2]Deut 31:10-13 also requires that during this year the law be read publicly at the annual Feast of the Tabernacles.

[3]The phrase at the end of verse 3 translated by the NIV as "cancel any debt" is literally "release your hand," which has the same meaning as "be open-handed" in verses 8 and 11.

theme in Deuteronomy. Non-Israelites were to be treated differently. They were not a part of the community and had no stake in the
covenant land. Moreover their presence in Israel was most likely to
be for business reasons, to make money from Israel. Therefore, they
did not come under the protection of this law. These **foreigners**
were not the same as the "aliens" of Deuteronomy 14:29; 16:11 and
other texts. The aliens were in Israel for noneconomic reasons and
were to be protected.

15:4-5 God intended that Israel live in the land he had given
them under his blessing. Because his blessing would include generous outlays of the necessities of life (7:12-16; 8:7-9,12-13), ideally
there would be no poor in Israel and therefore no need for anyone
to take out loans. This passage is marked by the theme of blessing
(vv. 4,6,10) because it was the nature of God to be a blessing God.
His deepest desire was to be generous to his covenant people.

There should be no poor among you seems to contradict verses
7 and 11, especially the latter. However, understanding the connection of verse 4 to verse 5 resolves the apparent discrepancy. It was
God's intention that there be no poor because of his blessing the
people. There would be more than enough in the land that he was
giving Israel for everyone to live in security because it was a good
land full of everything they would need (ch. 8). But there was a condition: **If only you fully obey.**

This demand surfaces again and again in Deuteronomy. Only if
Israel fully obeyed God would they receive his blessing. This was not
an obedience that earned Israel her redemption. Israel was already
God's chosen people. The obedience required here and elsewhere
in Deuteronomy was the grateful response of a saved people whose
greatest desire should be to please their covenant God. This obedience would result in the general economic well-being of everyone.
Verse 11, then, seems to presuppose that total obedience would not
occur (see below).

15:6 The result of obedience would be that God's blessing would
lead to international dominance (cf. 28:12-13). The future was open.
The only obstacle that could thwart God's desire was an obstinate
nation. The consequences of disobedience were clearly spelled out
later in the covenant curses that picture the reverse of verse 6 (see
28:43-44).

15:7-10 A proviso to the law was added. This paragraph is in typical case law style. **If there is a poor man** (and there should not be), then this was what they were to do. Deuteronomy is not naive about Israel's disobedient nature. The forefathers' failure (Deut 1) and the likelihood of failure in the future (Deut 4:25ff) had already been addressed. Therefore, the recognition of possible disobedience was a part of the realism of the book.

The admonition was necessary, for the disobedient heart could also be a hard, nongenerous heart. The **tight fist** was the opposite of the open hand of God. Israel was to emulate his open hand (vv. 7-8).

A Sabbath year when debts were released could produce some cunning calculations (v. 9). If the year was near, then loans might be withheld because the prospect of total repayment would be slight. Such economic practicality was considered evil by Deuteronomy and would incur **guilt**. The purpose of the loan to a fellow Israelite was not to get a return on investment but to provide generously for a needy brother.

A materialistically oriented culture will condemn this law as foolish and unworkable. Many arguments can be marshaled against its implementation. However, such arguments would miss the theological orientation of the law. Deuteronomy's law was not driven by practicality or economic necessity but by God's character. Justice and generosity were its hallmarks.

The operant theological factor was the blessing of God (v. 10). If Israel gave generously, she would be blessed generously and she would experience proper success in everything. The loans were in fact to be more like gifts of charity. From an economic perspective it made no sense, but from a theological perspective it was fundamental. The basic issue was trust in the provision of God.[4]

The two paragraphs (vv. 1-6,7-11) are marked by references to human anatomy, especially the eyes, hand, and heart. Israel's response to poverty was to be holistic, involving both her intentions and her actions. She was to be openhanded, not closehanded (vv. 3, 7,8,11). Such generosity could only come from a right heart, not a hard or evil heart (vv. 7,9,10). Unselfishness could only flow from the will (heart) that was committed to loving God. Obviously the poor could

---

[4]See Wright's excellent discussion, *Deuteronomy*, pp. 189-192.

be taken care of in some fashion through grudging obedience, but without a willing heart it would be only a show and would eventually degrade the recipient.

15:11 Verse 11 seems to contradict the whole passage. How could there **always be poor** when its eradication was possible through both God's desire and Israel's obedience? As a solution to this apparent contradiction some have suggested that **land** had two different meanings in this verse. The first occurrence refers to the whole earth, but the second occurrence refers to Israel.[5] However, such a significant switch in meaning seems unlikely.[6]

The verse seems to recognize the sad fact that Israel could not totally obey this law, and therefore there would always be poor. A further factor to consider is that the poor in Deuteronomy were often classified as the widow and orphan (14:29, etc.). These were classes of people who through no fault of their own lost the protection of a husband or father (through death by disease, accident, or war). This verse also adds another class of poor, the afflicted/needy (עָנִי, 'anî). These were the dispossessed, without landed property, who were in the same social situation as widows and orphans (cf. Exod 22:25[24]; Lev 19:10; 23:22; Deut 24:12,14,15; Isa 10:2 and throughout the Psalms).

Some debate revolves around the intention of verses 1-11. Did the law instruct the Israelites to cancel all the debts every seven years (NIV translation) or to only suspend payment for the Sabbatical year? The Hebrew text of verses 1-6 is not as clear on the issue as the NIV suggests.

On the side of total debt cancellation is the context. The release of the debt-slave in verses 12-18 suggests that "release" in verse 1 must mean more than suspension. Also the language of verses 2-3 seem to indicate permanent release from payment. An Old Babylonian custom allowed kings to forgive debts at their pleasure. Therefore, the custom of total release from debts would not have

---

[5]Miller, *Deuteronomy*, p. 137; NRSV.

[6]Jeffries M. Hamilton, "hā'āres in the Shemitta law," *VT* 42 (1992): 214-222. Most of the uses of the word "land" in Deuteronomy refer to the land of Israel. Furthermore, the logic of the passage suggests that verses 7-11 are contrary examples of the law of verses 1-6 and therefore is dealing with Israel.

been unique to Israel. Consequently the NIV translation seems to reflect accurately the sense of the text.[7]

However, some scholars object that total cancellation of the debt would have been self-defeating.[8] Who would be willing to make a loan on this basis? These scholars use the analogy of the Sabbatical year. It required the land to lie fallow for a year and the landowner gave up his income, so also the creditor would give up his claims for a year. Further, since the land was to lie fallow, there would be no income for the poor landowner. Therefore payment was suspended.

Freeing of Slaves (15:12-18)

This paragraph parallels Exodus 21:2-6 and is related to Leviticus 25:39-55. It continues the theme of the Sabbath year by addressing the issue of freeing bondservants. It is a natural sequel to the first two paragraphs. Poverty or default on a loan could easily lead into indentured servitude.

15:12 The law treats the possibility that an Israelite would have to sell himself or herself into slavery because of dire financial need. Second Kings 4:1 relates a widow's appeal to Elisha on behalf of her two sons who were about to be sold into slavery (Exod 22:3b; Lev 25:47 and Neh 5 list other circumstances).[9] Exodus 21 does not specifically mention women, though it does refer to the wife who was to go free with her husband (v. 3). The Deuteronomy law seems to be more precise about the status of the woman.[10]

---

[7]Total cancellation of the debt is the oldest Jewish interpretation (Philo, the Mishnah) and is supported by many modern commentators: Merrill, Mayes, Thompson, Miller, Cairns, and Walter & Matthews

[8]Driver, *Deuteronomy*, p. 179; cf. also Craigie, *Deuteronomy*, p. 236 and C.J.H. Wright, *God's People in God's Land* (Grand Rapids: Eerdmans, 1990), pp. 172-173.

[9]The chief source of slaves in the ancient Near East was war. Prisoners were enslaved for life (20:10ff; 21:10ff). The second major source was exorbitant interest loans on debt (forbidden for Israel, Exod 22:24; Deut 23:20). See I. Mendelsohn, "Slavery in the Ancient Near East," *BA* 9 (1946): 74-88.

[10]Thompson, *Deuteronomy*, p. 189. Cairns suggests that Deuteronomy reflects a later time when the position of women had changed. They were no longer a man's household property but could own property themselves and incur debt (*Deuteronomy*, p. 149).

The seventh year here is not the same as the Sabbatical year of verse 1. The bondservant had to serve for the full 6 years, so his freedom would come at an individually calculated interval, unrelated to the set, universal seven-year period.[11]

How often this law was observed is uncertain. The prophet Jeremiah hints that it was not observed very much. During the last days of Jerusalem when the city was under siege by the Babylonians, King Zedekiah proclaimed freedom for the debt slaves, but then rescinded the order. Jeremiah condemned this hypocrisy and asserted that the forefathers had regularly ignored the seven-year release law (Jer 34:8-16).[12]

15:13-14 The principle of generosity also continues in this law. The bondservant was to be given a new chance at a free life by being provided with the necessities to make a new beginning. Without such largesse many would perhaps find themselves compelled to enter servanthood again. They needed resources to live independently. Therefore, the master was to send him out with a generous supply of food. This was the same generosity that was shown to the poor (v. 8) and was presented as an emphatic demand ("Be sure to provide . . .").

---

[11]In the Hammuribi code, #117, the debt slave was freed after three years of service.

[12]A technical debate has arisen over the meaning of "Hebrew" in verse 12. The Hebrew word (עִבְרִי, *'ibrî*) occurs 34 times in the Old Testament, first in Gen 14:13 of Abraham. It appears also in Gen 39–41; Exod 1–10; 21:2; Deut 15:12; 1 Sam 4–14; 29:3; Jer 34:9 and Jonah 1:9. The question is, is it an ethnic term, or does it refer to a social class? In the ancient Near East there was a social class called the *habiru* who were usually hired helpers or servants. Therefore, some have suggested that the "Hebrew" in Deut 15:12 is actually referring to a social class of "non-ethnic Israelites" (Wright, *Deuteronomy*, pp. 192, 197). However, the majority of scholars seem to agree that *'ibrî* has an ethnic meaning in almost all, if not all of the Old Testament uses. The phonetic relationship of *'ibrî* and *habiru* is highly questionable. Furthermore, the context of Deuteronomy 15 suggests strongly that an ethnic Israelite is understood. Verse 12 in fact has "your brother, the Hebrew." (NIV, "a fellow Hebrew"). "Your brother" is the usual designation in Deuteronomy for an ethnic Israelite. See especially Meredith Kline, "Hebrews," *NBD*, 2nd ed., pp. 466-467; Nahum Sarna, *Genesis*, Jewish Publication Society Torah Commentary (New York: JPS, 1989), Excursus 4; Tigay, *Deuteronomy*, p. 148.

These gifts would not be a burden on the master because they were grounded in God's blessings (vv. 4,6,10,14). The Israelite master was sharing God's resources, not his own. Furthermore, when Israel left Egypt, she went out with gifts from the Egyptians (Exod 3:21,22; 11:2; 12:35-36). Therefore, it was a matter of doing for others what God had done for them.

15:15 The motivation for this generous bondservant law was the memory of Israel's own slavery in Egypt and God granting them freedom by bringing them out from there (cf. 16:12; 24:18,22 and 5:15). Their own experience should make them more sympathetic to others.

15:16-17 However, it was conceivable that the servant might find the experience a positive one and to his benefit, and therefore wish to remain a servant. Under a beneficent master there could be significant security. Some may have had little to go back to, others may, because of age, find starting over again too taxing. Affection between the parties could also develop.[13]

Therefore, voluntary, lifelong servitude was possible. It was to be visibly marked by putting a hole through the ear lobe. Perhaps the ear was chosen because it was associated with hearing, and hearing in Deuteronomy is associated with obedience.[14]

15:18 If the servant did want to go free, the master was to remember that the arrangement had been financially beneficial. The service of the servant had been worth the cost to the master, and he should let him go. The Hebrew of this verse is difficult, especially the precise meaning of the word *mišneh*. A comparison of recent translations confirms this point. The NIV has **worth twice as much**; the NRSV, "worth the wages"; the RSV, "at half the cost." The

---

[13]In Exodus 21:4-5 the motivation for staying was the fact that the man may have gained a family while serving. If the wife were a gift from the master, the family would have to stay with him.

[14]Often "hear the voice/word of the LORD" equals "obey the LORD" and is translated thusly: Deut 13:4,18; 21:18,20; 26:27, etc. (see also Ps 40:6-8). In Exodus 21:6 the punching of the hole in the ear was to be done "before God." This could suggest at the door of the tabernacle. The NIV interprets the word as meaning the tribal judges. Deuteronomy probably eliminates the phrase "before God" because Moses envisions a central sanctuary after Israel moves into the land (ch. 12) which might be some distance from where people lived.

Hebrew word can mean "double," "equal to," or "second." Some scholars agree that "double" is the best meaning here based on similar use in Genesis 43:12, Exodus 16:5,22, Isaiah 61:7, etc. In this sense the text would affirm that a bondservant was worth twice what a hired hand would be paid, perhaps because he or she was available 24 hours a day, not 10 or 12.[15] However, others argue that the meaning here is "equal to," in agreement with the use of *mišneh* in three passages where it clearly means "duplicate" (Deuteronomy 17:18, Joshua 8:32, and Ezra 1:10). From the context of Deuteronomy 15 this seems to be the preferable translation. The focus was not just on the benefits to the master, but also on the labor of the servant. He had already worked for six years and should not be exploited further. The master had received full payment and should give the servant his freedom.[16]

The two laws in Deuteronomy 15 require reflection on the interplay between community and economics. The fundamental principle was the health of the community as exhibited in the concern for the poor, not in the accumulation of individual wealth. Actions that benefited the oppressed were to take precedence over financial gain. Human existence was not to be governed by greed but by generosity. Economic gain was not as important as relief of the poor. Profit was not as important as protection of freedom from want. Debt was to be repaid but not at the cost of permanent poverty. Life was lived out under the watchful eye of God who was prepared to bless generously those who were generous themselves. For our modern culture these are radical ideas, but the people of God were always expected to be distinct. Wright's conclusion is pointed:

---

[15]Driver, *Deuteronomy*, p. 185; Richard Hess, "מִשְׁנֶה," *NIDOTTE*, 2:1138-1139; James Lenderberger, "How Much for a Hebrew Slave? The Meaning of *mišneh* in Deuteronomy 15:18," *JBL* 110 (1991): 479-482.

[16]Matitiahu Tsevat, "The Hebrew Slave According to Deuteronomy 15:12-18: His Lot and the Value of His Work, with Special Attention to the Meaning of mshnh," *JBL* 113 (1994): 587-595. Some scholars concluded *mišneh* meant "equal to" based on an earlier article by Tsevat in which he pointed to a cognate word in the Alalah texts (Craigie, *Deuteronomy*, p. 239; Mayes, *Deuteronomy*, pp. 252-253). Tsevat now considers the earlier article to be in error on the cognate word. But he still argues for the same point based now on the meaning of *mišneh*.

First, social justice in Deuteronomy was no mere abstract ideal, but a matter of detailed practical legislation on behalf of the dependent. Secondly, the justness and health of any society is measurable in terms of the quality of its care for the weakest and most vulnerable members of it. Thirdly, the laws aim their rhetorical weaponry at those who have the power to effect change. Fourthly, God is portrayed as the advocate of the powerless, a role that the church can and should take on in God's name.[17]

The sabbatical principle also stands in sharp contrast to modern market-driven culture. It provides a mechanism for overcoming slavery in an economic system that ties people to debt, that allows ownership to belong forever to the wealthy, that grinds people into poverty. It says there is a time for release from all this, a release required by God himself.[18] The principles of Deuteronomy, if applied, would transform modern culture.

Firstborn Animals (15:19-23)

The final paragraph of chapter 15 addresses the regulations for the sacrificial offering of the firstborn animals. The firstborn had already been included in the list of offerings to be given at the central sanctuary (12:6,17) and as a part of the tithe (14:23). This law defines the physical qualities of the animal (vv. 19,21) and how it was to be eaten (v. 20). Nonqualified animals could also be eaten (vv. 22-23).

The paragraph is connected to its context in several subtle ways. The reference to redemption from Egypt (v. 15) would have recalled Exodus 12 and the use of the firstborn in the original Passover meal. The paragraph also returns to the topic of 14:22-28 with some of the same language and thus forms a frame around the laws of release in chapter 15:1-18. Further, the release of the debtor and slave in 15:1-18 parallels in some fashion the release of the firstborn. Finally, the paragraph provides a transition to the following sections on the three annual feasts, beginning with the Passover (16:1-17).[19]

---

[17]Wright, *Deuteronomy*, p. 195, summarizing from Jeffries Hamilton, *Social Justice*, pp. 135-138.

[18]Miller, *Deuteronomy*, pp. 138-139.

[19]Other subtle connections are elaborated by McConville, *Law and Theology*, pp. 93-95.

The foundation for this law is given in Exodus 13:2: "Consecrate to me every firstborn male. The first offspring of every womb among the Israelites belongs to me, whether man or animal." This demand was connected with the Exodus events and especially the last plague that took the life of every firstborn in Egypt (Exod 11). Setting apart the firstborn recalled the cost to the Egyptians of Israel's redemption and commemorated the sparing of the Israelite firstborn (Exod 13:11-16; 22:29b[28b]). The firstborn sons were not sacrificed, but redeemed (Exod 13:13; 34:20) by the substitution of the Levites (Num 3:40-41). The sacrifice of the firstborn animals was a recognition of God's ownership and blessing on the herdsman just as the giving of the first fruits recognized God's ownership of and blessing on the land for the farmer (Lev 25:23; Deut 8:10-18).

15:19 Set apart translates the Hebrew verb "to make holy, consecrate." In the ancient Near East the firstborn had preeminent status but there is little evidence of the consecration of the firstborn to the gods.[20] This consecration of the firstborn required a sacrifice from the owner. He not only had to give up the animal, he had to give up any benefit from the animal, whether it was work from the oxen or the fine, first shearing from the sheep. The owner was to suffer a real loss.

15:20 These instructions are identical to the instructions for the offering of the tithe in chapter 14:23 (cf. 12:11-14). The sacrifice was to be eaten as part of the fellowship offering at the central sanctuary.

15:21 The animal must not only be a firstborn, it had to be in perfect physical condition, without any defect. The defects are specifically two, being **lame or blind**. Leviticus 22:22-24 gives a much longer list that can be used to fill out the general phrase here, **any serious flaw**.

God required a perfect animal for two reasons: he was perfect and therefore the sacrifice must be as fit for him as possible. Also the sacrifice had to cost the worshiper something. If the owner offered an animal with little market value, there would be little cost to the worshiper. Violation of this requirement was an abomination (Deut 17:1) and showed contempt for God (Mal 1:6-9).

---

[20]Walton and Matthews, *Genesis–Deuteronomy*, p. 239.

15:22-23 The defective animal that could not be offered was given to the owner for food and was to be available to everyone. It could be treated just like the normal animal slaughtered for food. Thus this law is identical to the law for the profane slaughter of meat in 12:15-16 (see comments there).

The law on the firstborn appears in several Pentateuchal texts (Exod 13:11-16; 22:29b-30; 34:19-20; Lev 27:26-27; Num 18:15-18, and Deut 15:19-23). A cursory reading of these texts reveals several differences, the most obvious being the disposal of the sacrificed animal. In Exodus it is a sacrifice to the LORD, in Numbers it provides food for the priest and his family, and in Deuteronomy it is to be eaten by the owner. Many scholars see the differences as contradictory and the law as undergoing development.[21] However, the various versions can be understood as complementary. Each one fits into the specific concerns of the context in which it was given. Exodus states the basic law. Numbers is concerned about food for the priests and Levites and addresses only that issue. Deuteronomy shows more concern for the common person. Since most sacrifices were fellowship meals involving the worshiper and the priest, such an interpretation fits well the larger theology of sacrifice in the Pentateuch.

---

[21]Tigay, *Deuteronomy*, p. 151; Cairns, *Deuteronomy*, p. 151.

DEUTERONOMY 16

The Three Annual Feasts (16:1-17)

Chapter 16 moves on to the regulations for the three annual festivals that were to be celebrated as a part of the rhythm of Israel's religious life. They were akin to the regular tithes and sabbatical years and so continue the theme of the fourth commandment, "Observe the Sabbath day by keeping it holy" (5:12). Elsewhere in the Pentateuch it was customary to place the regulations for the Sabbath and the festivals together.[1] The order of description here, Passover, Feast of Weeks and Feast of Tabernacles, varies from the other texts.

The Passover and Unleavened Bread (16:1-8)

This section begins with the Passover because the Passover forms a natural connection with the regulations on the firstborn of 15:19-23. The mention there of the firstborn would naturally call to mind the Exodus event and the original Passover when Israel's firstborn were saved from the last, devastating plague.

The brief regulations here presuppose the extensive historical account in Exodus 12:1-13,21-30 and involve some apparent updating. They also incorporate a few comments about the Feast of Unleavened Bread which was celebrated immediately following the Passover (Exod 12:14-20; 13:3-10).[2] The close interspersing of instructions show that the two festivals were considered a unit. Verses 1-3a explain the time, place, and ritual of the Passover. Verses 3b-4a

---

[1]Exod 23:10-17; 34:21-25; Lev 23 and Num 28–29.

[2]In Exodus 13 the instruction for the Unleavened Bread is sandwiched by instructions for consecrating the firstborn (vv. 1-2 and 11-13) which helps explain the logic of the connection between Deut 15 and 16 as pointed out above.

address the Feast of Unleavened Bread. Verses 4b-7 return to the ritual, place, and time of the Passover (in reverse order of verses 1-3a). Verse 8 concludes instructions for the Unleavened Bread.[3]

16:1 The language commanding the keeping of the Passover is that of the fourth commandment (5:12), **observe** (cf. 6:17; 11:22; 27:1). It underscores the importance of this particular festival that commemorated the foundational salvation event in Israel's history, the Exodus. It was celebrated in the first month of the religious year, the month **Abib**. This was in the spring of the year near the time of the latter rains and the barley and flax harvest (March–April). Very few of the names of the months in preexilic Israel have survived. Most were designated in the biblical texts numerically as first, second, third, etc. The first month, Abib, was named Nisan in the postexilic period, evidently under the influence of Babylonian culture.[4]

Deuteronomy seems to presuppose the day of the celebration (which was the 14th day of the month, Exod 12:18) and mentions only the month.[5] The feast was called the **Passover** (*pesaḥ*). The root meaning of the word is uncertain. The verb is used in Exodus 12:13,23, and 27 and translated in the NIV as "pass through" or "pass over." Others suggest "skip by, spare." The root means "leap, jump" in 2 Samuel 4:4 and 1 Kings 18:21.

The noun always refers to the Passover event or the feast, so its meaning is clear. The feast recalls the time when God bypassed the Israelite households in Egypt as he executed the tenth plague, the death of the firstborn. The blood of the lamb spread on the doorposts marked the homes to be spared. The celebration of the Passover marked that decisive moment when God decimated Israel's taskmasters and delivered her from bondage. Every part of the celebration recalled some part of that defining event. The lamb was eaten with

---

[3]Mayes considers vv. 1-7 a chiasm and v. 8 to be a later addition (*Deuteronomy*, p. 254).

[4]"Abib" literally means "ears of grain" in Exod 9:31 and Lev 2:14. As the name of the month it also occurs in Exod 13:4; 23:15; and 34:18. Nisan occurs in Esth 3:7 and Neh 2:1.

[5]It seems unlikely that there would not be a fixed day for the festival despite R. de Vaux's assertion (*Ancient Israel* [New York: McGraw-Hill, 1965], p. 485). Deuteronomy is customarily less concerned about cultic details than Exodus or Leviticus.

unleavened bread and bitter herbs to recall the haste of the departure and the bitterness of the service in Egypt (Exod 12:8-11).

16:2 A lamb was the animal selected to be sacrificed. This represented the original lamb that was killed so that its blood could be used to mark the homes. Deuteronomy expanded the possible victims to the **herd** as well as the **flock.** This possibly reflects the changing circumstances. As Israel moved into the Promised Land, they would begin to accumulate cattle as well as sheep. The tribes that inherited the Transjordan already had large herds (Deut 3:19). The addition probably also includes the sacrifices that would be offered as a part of the seven-day festival of Unleavened Bread.

In agreement with chapter 12, the Passover was to be celebrated at the **place the LORD will choose as a dwelling for his Name.** The original Passover was a family event, eaten in the home, awaiting the order to go out of Egypt. Deuteronomy understood it was to be celebrated as a national event at the central sanctuary. These two aspects are complementary, not contradictory as often thought. Families could travel to the central sanctuary and celebrate it together. Second Chronicles 35 records just such a practice (vv. 4,12). Verse 7 (see below) confirms the family nature of the feast. The dual nature of the celebration is consistent with Deuteronomic legislation for the central sanctuary (12:7) and the tithe (14:23).[6]

16:3 The bread eaten at the meal also reflected the urgency of the historical Exodus. It was to be **unleavened** (מַצָּה, *maṣṣāh*, pl. מַצֹּת, *maṣṣoth*), that is, bread made quickly without putting yeast in the dough and waiting for it to rise.[7]

To provide an emphatic reminder of the Exodus event the Israelites were to continue to eat the unleavened bread for another **seven days** after the Passover. In their continuing relationship with their covenant God it was important for the people to remember the hard service from which he had saved them. Therefore, the hard,

---

[6]Cf. McConville, *Law and Theology,* p. 109. The NT indicates the Passover in the first century incorporated both aspects also. People gathered at the temple in Jerusalem, but the meal was eaten with a small group in a residence. So Jesus ate the Passover with his disciples in the upper room.

[7]Modern Bedouins still fix unleavened bread for unexpected guests because it is quick. Modern Judaism defines grain that has been in contact with water for 18 minutes or over as leavened (Donin, *To Be a Jew,* p. 220).

crusty bread was called **the bread of affliction**, a term used of their slavery in Exodus 3:7,17; 4:31 (translated as "misery" in the NIV).

The bread was also to remind the Israelites that they had left Egypt **in haste** (Exod 12:11). The Hebrew word implies haste with alarm or fear as the use of the verb shows in Deuteronomy 20:3 and elsewhere (1 Sam 23:26; 2 Sam 4:4; 2 Kgs 7:15; Ps 48:5[6]; 31:22[23]).

The combination of the Passover and the Feast of Unleavened Bread reminded Israel in several ways of the transforming event in their history. The particular aspects of the feasts enabled the nation to actualize its salvation experience for each new generation. Every aspect was loaded with meaning and intimately tied to the Exodus. If faithfully observed, the feasts would accomplish their purpose of bringing freshly to mind what God had done. Throughout Deuteronomy Israel was warned not to forget what God had done because they could easily be diverted into idolatry. God himself provided the memory joggers she needed to prompt her faithfulness.

16:4 The Unleavened Bread festival included the exclusion of **yeast** from the homes for the seven days, but the theology of the prohibition was not made explicit. In the law of sacrifice, yeast was forbidden in the bread offered to the LORD because it was to be fresh and pure, not old or contaminated (Lev 2:11; 7:12; 8:2). Yeast came to symbolize corruption in the Bible, though not in a uniform way (1 Cor 5:7).[8] So there was some sort of purity symbolism in the feast as well as the reminder of the Exodus.

The second half of the verse returns to the instructions for the Passover. All the **meat** that was sacrificed was to be consumed or burned (Exod 12:8-10). This feature reminded Israel of the need for haste unencumbered by leftover food.

16:5-7 The instructions for the Passover were repeated. The meat was to be **roasted** not boiled (Exod 12:8-9). These instructions seem to contradict Exodus for the Hebrew word used here, בשל (*bšl*), is used in Exodus 12 for boiling the meat in water (which was forbidden, v. 9). However, the word by itself apparently means "cook." The context determines if it means to boil in water or in pots and pans (Exod 12:9; Lev 6:28; 1 Sam 13, 15). Without such

---

[8]Allen Ross, "Bread, Cake," *NIDOTTE*, 4:448-453.

specification it can mean cooking without the precise method stipulated (Exod 29:31; Lev 8:31; 2 Chr 35:13). Therefore, "to cook" here could include "roast" as the NIV has.

Then in the morning return to your tents has been variously interpreted. It seems to presume a nomadic existence but the phrase lingered on in Israel's culture long after the settlement into the land. It was a stock phrase for going home (2 Sam 20:1; 1 Kgs 12:16). However, here it probably refers to the worshipers returning to their temporary shelters in Jerusalem where they stayed during the festivals.[9]

16:8 This section ends with a return to more instructions for the Feast of Unleavened Bread. Besides continuing for seven days (v. 3) the last day was to be a designated holy or Sabbath day and observed as one.[10]

The Passover was foundational to Israel's life according to the Pentateuch, but records of its observance are rare in the rest of the Old Testament. Its celebration is recorded only in Joshua 5:10-12; 2 Chronicles 30 (under Hezekiah); 2 Kings 23:21-23 (2 Chr 35:1-18 — under Josiah), and Ezra 6:19-22 (after the exile). The celebration under Josiah was prompted by the discovery of the Book of the Law (Deuteronomy?) in the temple. The writer observed that such a Passover had not been celebrated since the days of the judges (2 Kgs 23:22). Did this mean that it had not been celebrated at all since then (as many scholars suggest) or that it had not been celebrated with such ceremony and prominence? Second Chronicles 30:26 likewise described the Passover celebrated in Hezekiah's time as extraordinary, going back to the time of David (there is no parallel account of this event in 2 Kings).

It seems unlikely that such an important feast would have been completely ignored. It is not difficult to imagine, however, that a

---

[9]Merrill, *Deuteronomy*, p. 253; Mayes, *Deuteronomy*, p. 259. For a dissenting view see Driver, *Deuteronomy*, p. 194.

[10]The origins of the Passover and the Feast of Unleavened Bread are debated. R. de Vaux offers a thorough discussion of the standard critical view (*Ancient Israel*, pp. 485-493). However, his contention that the Unleavened Bread was originally an agricultural feast in Canaan can be challenged on several grounds (McConville, *Law and Theology*, pp. 102-103). Whatever their origin, they were thoroughly baptized by Israel and associated with each other from the earliest time. As Deuteronomy makes clear, they both were significant reminders of the Exodus.

wayward nation would celebrate it in a perfunctory manner with no existential sense of its importance. Certainly part of the exuberance of the celebration in the time of Josiah reflected the almost certain absence of the feast in the dark days of Manasseh, Josiah's grandfather who reigned for 55 years.

The Feast of Weeks (16:9-12)

The second major pilgrim festival is called the Feast of Weeks here. It has two other names: The Feast of Harvest (Exod 23:16) and The Day of First Fruits (Num 28:26). Its agricultural nature is made explicit by this alternate terminology. Its name here comes from counting off the seven weeks from the beginning of the spring harvest. The most detailed instructions for the relevant sacrifices are given in Leviticus 23:15-22 (see also Exod 23:16; 34:22; Num 28:26-31). The celebration began on the day after the seventh Sabbath (a Sunday) which made it fifty days after the wave offering (as the first fruits of the harvest; Lev 23:9-14 and 15) from which comes the later name, Pentecost (Greek, *pentēkostē*, fifty; Acts 2:1; 20:16). The offerings included two loaves of bread made with fine flour and yeast, the typical food of the farmer (not the unleavened bread of the previous feast).

16:9 The exact time when the counting was to begin is not given. Since it was associated with the harvest, tradition took it to mean sometime during the Feast of Unleavened Bread.[11] The seven weeks would allow enough time for the harvest throughout the land, though it might begin at different times in the different areas.[12] A tenth-century BC Hebrew inscription that appears to be a calendar

---

[11]Tigay, *Deuteronomy*, p. 157. In Leviticus 23 the feast follows directly the instructions for the First Fruits. In Deuteronomy the law of first fruits is delayed until chapter 26 where it forms a part of the conclusion to the larger section of laws, chapters 12–26.

[12]Because of this lack of specificity Jewish tradition developed competing methods for determining the date. The Pharisees began with the day after Passover and celebrated the feast on the 6th of Sivan. The Sadducees began with the day after the Sabbath after the Passover so that the feast fell on the 8th Sunday after Passover. The Christian observance of Pentecost follows their pattern. The Jewish *Book of Jubilees* began counting after the whole week of Unleavened Bread and ended up celebrating it on the 15th of Sivan (Bruce H. Charnov, "Shavuot, 'Matam Torah,' and the Triennial Cycle," *Judaism* 23 (1974): 332-333.

provides one month in the Spring for barley harvest, and one month for harvesting (wheat) and measuring, which equals two months for harvest.[13] The Jewish name, *Shavuoth*, comes from the Hebrew for "weeks" (שָׁבֻעֹת, *šābu'ōth*).[14]

16:10 The **Feast** is more properly understood as a pilgrimage festival (cf. vv. 13,14,16). The Hebrew word (חַג, *ḥag*) is related to several Semitic cognates that carry the idea of pilgrimage, including the Arabic *ḥagg* or *ḥajj*.[15] The three festivals in this section of Deuteronomy were the three which required the attendance of all males at the central sanctuary (Exod 23:17; 34:23; v. 16 below). Therefore, its significance goes beyond just another feast day.

The celebration was to be accompanied by a **freewill offering** which was understood as an appropriate response to God's blessing (see v. 17). The amount was not specified as it was with other offerings. Thus it provided an opportunity for the worshiper to be generous, especially since the offering was to be shared with the priest, Levites, and the poor. God's blessings are referred to at least fifty times in Deuteronomy and underline the principle that everything Israel did was a response to God's prior action.

16:11-12 The circumstances made it a time of **rejoicing** (see v. 14), a common theme in Deuteronomy (12:7,12,28; 14:26; 26:11) especially in the contexts of sacrifice. This response was appropriate since no sacrifices or gifts would have been possible without God's goodness.

The celebration was not just for the one who could afford the gift. It was to include all the servants as did the Sabbath observance (5:12-15) and all the poor as did the law of the tithe (14:28-29). In other words honoring God was a community affair and could be properly done only when reflecting his concerns (as spelled out in 10:18-19). There is no concept of a purely vertical, individualistic response to God in Deuteronomy.

Israel's slavery in Egypt was a motivating factor as well. They knew what oppression and deprivation were like. But God had rescued them from their suffering and had brought them into a good land

---

[13]Klaas A.D. Smelik, *Writings from Ancient Israel* (Louisville: Westminster/ John Knox, 1991), pp. 21-25.

[14]Since soon after the exile the feast has also commemorated the giving of the Torah at Sinai based on Exod 19:1 (Tigay, *Deuteronomy*, p. 156).

[15]The *ḥajj* is one of the Five Pillars of Islam and requires a journey to Mecca at least once during the believer's lifetime (see the Quran 2:185-195).

where they would experience freedom, prosperity, food, shelter, and a multitude of other blessings (ch. 8). How could they not then be joyful and generous when they responded to his blessings?

The Feast of Tabernacles (16:13-15)

The third major feast, the Feast of the Tabernacles, is somewhat misnamed in English. The Hebrew is סֻכָּה (*sukkāh;* pl. *sukkôt*) which can refer to a lion's den (Job 38:40), a livestock shelter (Gen 33:17), or a temporary hut in a vegetable garden (Isa 1:8). The plural form is most commonly used in reference to this feast. What is in view is a temporary shelter made out of branches and foliage similar to the temporary huts put up in the vineyards and fields by the harvesters. The NIV "tabernacle" is misleading and in this context almost meaningless (cf. the NRSV "booths").[16]

The festival is called the Feast of Ingathering in Exodus 23:16 which shows that it was a harvest festival at the end of the agricultural year, just prior to the fall rains. The fruit crops were harvested and processed during the summer (dates, figs, olives, and grapes) and the feast celebrated the completion of that task. The extensive guidelines for the sacrifices were given in Leviticus 23:33-42 and Numbers 29:12-38.

16:13 It was a seven-day feast celebrated from the 15th to the 22nd day of the seventh month (September/October; Lev 23:34-36). The day after was considered a sacred day also, so the actual celebration lasted eight days. Perhaps the most famous celebration was when Solomon dedicated the temple during the Feast (1 Kgs 8:2). Moses also stipulated this feast as the time for public reading of the Torah every seven years (Deut 31:10-13).

Leviticus 23:43 associated the feast with Israel's salvation history. It was supposed to remind them of the time when they lived in the wilderness in temporary shelters and under divine protection.

16:14-15 The festival was perhaps the most joyous of all of the Israelite feasts. The fall harvest time itself was an occasion for great rejoicing (Judg 21:21; Isa 16:9-10; Jer 25:30) as were the festivals themselves (Isa 30:29; Ps 42:4[5]). The harvest was complete and

---

[16]The Greek translation of the OT, the LXX, translated *sukkôt* 26 times as "tent" (*skênê*).

food for another winter was secured. It was a time of thanksgiving and praise to God for his blessings.[17]

Jesus appeared in Jerusalem at the Feast of the Tabernacles and engaged the crowds in controversy through his teaching (John 7). It had become the custom by New Testament times to include in the celebration drawing water from the Pool of Siloam and carrying it to the temple to pour it out over the altar. It is likely that it was during this time that Jesus spoke of streams of living water (John 7:37-38). The Babylonian Talmud records that Zechariah 14 was read at the Feast of Tabernacles. The chapter looks forward to living water flowing out of Jerusalem (v. 8) and to all nations coming to Jerusalem to worship God at the Feast (v. 16).

Concluding Admonition (16:16-17)

16:16-17 The law on the three major feasts concludes with a final exhortation taken from Exodus 23:14,17; 34:23-24. These feasts were mandatory for every male. The law provided that at least three times during the year the nation would gather as one to celebrate the blessings of God and to remember his grace and power in freeing them from Egypt. These feasts were not a burden but a privilege and an occasion to exhibit thanksgiving by bringing gifts to God. How could they appear **empty-handed** when God had done so much (cf. 15:13)?

In light of the above, the prophetic protest against these festivals comes as a surprise (Isa 1:11-15; Amos 5:21-23; Mal 2:3). It is the sad fact that what was intended to reflect devotion, loyalty, and joyous thanksgiving became a sham, a dry formality devoted only to show. They became detached from ministry to the poor and obedience to the law. Consequently, God hated them because they had become a cover for sin.

---

[17]Scholars have wanted to turn the Feast of Tabernacles/Booths into something more than a joyous harvest festival. Mowinckel saw a yearly festival in which God was enthroned anew on his heavenly throne as King over Israel. Weiser suggested it was the occasion for a yearly covenant renewal ceremony. Kraus understood it as a celebration of the election of the Davidic dynasty over Israel. Each theory suffers from lack of biblical evidence. See Hendrik L. Bosman, "סֻכּוֹת," *NIDOTTE*, 3:249-251. There is no direct connection between this festival and the NT theology. Peter's misguided offer to build three shelters/booths (*skênê*) at the transfiguration may be related to the customs of the Feast (Mark 9:5).

However, the prophet Zechariah offers hope. In his look to the future he anticipates all nations coming to God and celebrating together the Feast of Tabernacles (Zech 14:16-18). The time will come, he asserts, when God's plan for Israel and all nations will be accomplished as they all gather together in worship and praise (cf. Rev 5).

Wright offers several profound observations on the theological implications of the festivals.[18] First, they emphasized Israel's history and wedded her thanksgiving for harvest with God's saving acts. Second, they emphasized joy and rejoicing as a part of the core of Israel's faith. This was a deliberate choice they made. Third, they emphasized a social inclusiveness and awareness for the economically and socially vulnerable that Jesus also taught (Luke 14:12-14). Finally, they emphasized the reciprocal nature of God's blessing and people's giving. Each prompted the other in dynamic reciprocity.

4. Elaboration of the Fifth Commandment (16:18–18:22)

A new, major section begins with 16:18 and continues through 18:22. The purpose was to enlarge on the implications of the fifth commandment, "Honor your father and mother" (5:16). The key issue is leadership and authority. In the Israelite family structure the parents were the proper authority and were to be accorded respect and honor. In the larger Israelite society there were several different orders of authority as spelled out in this section: judges and the related law courts (16:18–17:13), kings (17:14-25), priests and Levites (18:1-13), and prophets (18:14-22). The implication is that authorities who implement their leadership under the rules of God's law were also to be accorded honor.

The laws carefully outline and delimit a variety of offices that were to operate in Israel. Authority was decentralized by providing for four offices, each one legitimated by a different basis, heredity (king and priest), human appointment (judge), or divine appointment (prophet). This distribution of power provided a "checks and balances" system for Israel and was grounded in one fundamental concept, the primacy of God's rule of Israel based on the first com-

---

[18]Wright, *Deuteronomy*, p. 201.

mandment.[19] Faithful adherence to the laws would prevent tyranni-
cal power from being concentrated in one office.

Judges and the Judicial Court (16:18–17:13)

From the early period judges played an important role in Israel's
life. Moses had already addressed the issue of the selection and qual-
ification of judges in the wilderness period (see 1:9-18 and comments there). As Israel looked forward to a settled life in villages
scattered throughout the land, further instructions were needed.
The law is presented in three steps: the selection of judges (16:18-
20), a case study of how to handle a difficult case of apostate worship (16:21–17:7), and the settling of difficult cases at the central
judicial court (17:8-13). The linking word for the three sections is
"town, village." The judges were chosen for each town (16:18), the
forbidden pagan rites occurred in a town (17:2,5), and the difficult
case is one that took place in a town (17:8). In other words this law
is directed at the proper administration of village life.

Choosing Judges (16:18-20)

16:18 We are not to think of **judges** in the modern, Western
sense. Israelite judges were responsible for maintaining order and
protecting justice in each village and were responsible for a variety of
situations, not just the narrow administration of a legal system. The
primary function was to undertake whatever action was needed to
restore order to the community so that justice, especially social justice, was guaranteed (Lev 19:15; Isa 1:17; cf. also Deut 19:17-18; 21:2;
25:1-2). Judges were probably selected from the elders of the villages
who were the leading patriarchs of the large families that made up
the villages. The book of Ruth illustrates how the elders functioned
in legal matters. In Deuteronomy 1:13 judges were to be "wise,
understanding and respected." Second Chronicles 19:4-7 reports that
King Jehoshaphat (873–849 BC), as a part of his reform, appointed
judges in the cities, following some of Deuteronomy's guidelines.

This office of judge is to be distinguished from the more familiar "Judge" who appears in the book of Judges. The latter are divine-

---

[19]See Olson, *Deuteronomy*, pp. 78-79.

ly appointed leaders who often functioned as a military leader to deliver the nation, or a portion of the nation, from oppression.[20]

The **officials** were probably subofficers who assisted the judge. They are found in a variety of situations in the Old Testament including administrative and military settings. The word probably originally referred to a scribe or record keeper.

16:19-20 Instructions for how to **judge the people fairly** (v. 18; cf. 1:16) are given in verse 19 with three apodictic, negative commands taken from Exodus 23:6 and 8. If justice was to be fair, it had to be evenhanded and impartial. No party in a dispute should have an advantage for any reason. In a small village, personal relationships and social status could easily impede just decisions. Exodus 23:6 explicitly places the perversion of justice in the context of preference against the poor. But Exodus 23:3 also recognized the possibility of favoring the poor. Neither was appropriate. Nor was following popular opinion acceptable (Exodus 23:2).[21]

Taking a **bribe** or gift (שֹׁחַד, šōḥad) was no doubt a common temptation. Samuel's sons in 1 Samuel 8:3 provide a good case study of officials who perverted justice by taking bribes. Bribes transformed the concept of blind justice (impartial) to blinding the judge to what was just (Exodus 23:8 uses the phrase "those who see"). This admonition was grounded in the character of God for he did not accept bribes (Deut 10:17). It was the wicked who accepted bribes (Prov 17:23).[22] Unfortunately, as the prophets make clear, this command was often violated (Isa 1:23; 5:23; Micah 3:11). Job 29:7-25 provides a detailed description of the honor that accrued to a village

---

[20]See Richard Schultz, "שֹׁפֵט," *NIDOTTE,* 4:213-220 and the survey by Robert Wilson, "Israel's Judicial System in the Preexilic Period," *JQR* 74 (1983): 229-248.

[21]The phrase translated as "show partiality" is literally "recognize faces" indicating the high level of personal relationships in the village.

[22]Some scholars suggest that the difference between a bribe and a gift was subtle at times, e.g., the wise used it to avert anger, Prov 21:14 (Tigay, *Deuteronomy*, p. 161; M. Greenberg, *IDB* 1:465, s.v. "Bribery, Bribe"). However, all the ancient Near Eastern law codes are silent on bribes. Reciprocity in gift giving was a common practice. Judges taking gifts was considered perfectly moral. On the other hand, the *Hammurabi Code* had stiff fines for judges who altered decisions (because of a bribe? Walton and Matthews,

elder (judge) who was committed to impartial justice and defended the poor (in this case, Job).

Israel was commanded in the strongest terms to execute justice (**Follow justice and justice alone**, v. 20) because they were to live in imitation of God. God's concern for the poor in Deuteronomy is pervasive (see 10:17-18 and comments there). It was usually the poor and oppressed that suffered first and most in an unjust society. Their welfare was the standard for evaluating social fairness. For Israel, the reward for justice was inheritance of the Promised Land. This put social justice at the same level of importance in Deuteronomy as obedience to the law (4:1; 8:1) and the honoring of parents (5:16).

The instructions for selecting the judges are followed by a case study on carrying out the duties of a judge. The section has two parts: the presentation of three laws (16:21-17:1) and the specific function of the village judge when the law is violated (17:2-7). It is interesting that the case is in the realm of Israel's religious life, a violation of the second commandment, illustrating that judges had authority in religious affairs also.[23]

Presentation of Three Laws (16:21-17:1)

16:21-22 Israel was not to adopt any of the paraphernalia of Canaanite worship. It would lead to idolatry. This issue had been addressed forcefully in chapter 4 already. Therefore, the prohibition is stated only briefly to provide background for the case study. The **wooden Asherah pole** (or "tree," NIV footnote) represented the Canaanite fertility goddess and the **sacred stone** represented their

---

Genesis–Deuteronomy, p. 241). Israel was set apart from the nations by the fact that she was to be holy as God was holy, and therefore her judges were to imitate God (Michael Goldberg, "The Story of the Moral: Gifts or Bribes in Deuteronomy?" *Int* 38 [1984]: 15-25). Goldberg notes that the law forbidding the taking of bribes follows directly the law of gifts to God in 16:16-17. But they were not gifts intended to provoke reciprocity from God as among the nations. They were gifts resulting from the harvest and thus after the fact. Therefore, they represented thanksgiving, not bribery.

[23]Although this explanation of the order of the material seems clear, some commentators have been unable to see a rationale for the inclusion of 16:21-22 (Craigie, *Deuteronomy*, p. 248). In fact Driver contends the verses are totally unrelated to 16:18-20 and have been misplaced from their original position, perhaps belonging before 13:1 (*Deuteronomy*, p. 201).

male god. The Israelites had already been instructed to destroy the idols they would find in the land (see 7:5 and 12:3 and comments there). Now Moses commands that they were not to construct any of their own either. In other words, Israel was not to "baptize" any of the pagan symbols and bring them into her worship. Because of God's uniqueness as reflected in the first two commandments, syncretism was spiritually debilitating and would be a sure sign of apostasy. Unfortunately, Asherah poles were adopted in the period of the monarchy (2 Kgs 13:6; 21:7; 23:6-7) and reflected occasions of terrible apostasy under Ahab and Manasseh.[24]

Hates in this context was a covenant term. It was the opposite of love and indicated a situation that made it impossible for God to maintain a relationship with his people (cf. 12:31). It is a parallel term to **detestable** in 17:1.[25] Moses had made it clear often before that idolatry was a covenant breaking practice (cf. 17:2).

17:1 A law on defective sacrifices at this point indicated that there was no difference between violating laws of sacrifice and idolatry. They both signaled carelessness toward the covenant. Pure sacrifices and pure worship were both grounded in the holiness of God's people, who were to reflect his holiness (Lev 22:19-25,31-32). This concern goes back to the earliest instructions for the Passover lamb (Exod 12:5). The brief statement here also builds on the law of the firstborn in Deuteronomy 15:19-23 with the use of "defect" (מוּם, *mûm*) and "flaw" (רָע דָּבָר, *dābār rā‘* paralleled to *mûm rā‘*) from 15:21. Deuteronomy 17:1 also connects to the case study in 17:2-7 with the repetition of "detestable" (v. 4) and "evil deed" (הָרָע הַדָּבָר, *haddābār hārā‘*, v. 5). Thus 17:1 has been carefully placed in its context. Offering defective animals resulted from despising God according to Malachi 1:6-8.

---

[24]Sacred stones were at one time accepted and put up by Jacob, Moses, and Joshua (Gen 28:16-22; Exod 24:4; Josh 24:26), but under the circumstances of the conquest and settlement their presence would have been devastating to faith in God. Hos 1-2 illustrate how soon syncretism set in and how subtly it led Israel away from God. The average Israelite may not have noticed the drift away from God and may have indeed thought Canaanite concepts and practices had been adequately "baptized."

[25]Everything that God hates in the OT can be understood in terms of actions and attitudes that violate the covenant (Hos 9:15; Amos 5:12; 6:8; Isa 1:14; Zech 8:17; Mal 2:16; Ps 11:5).

DEUTERONOMY 17

Function of the Village Judge (17:2-7)

This case study was an application of the law in Exodus 22:20(19). It is closely associated with the situations addressed in chapter 13 and provided the judicial procedure for implementing those laws. The law applied equally to men and women.

17:2 The **evil in the eyes of the LORD** is a characteristic phrase for idolatry in Deuteronomy (4:25; 9:18; 31:29) and throughout Kings (1 Kgs 11:6; 14:22; 2 Kgs 3:2; 8:18; 13:2,11, etc.; see on Deut 6:18; 12:25 for "doing what is right in the eyes of the LORD"). Idolatry involved actions toward the false gods (bowing down to, serving, and worshiping them) that were reserved for God alone (see the warnings in 4:19; 5:9; 7:4; 8:19; 11:16, etc.). It was a **violation of his covenant** and equal to political treason (see the similar phrasing in Josh 7:11,15; 23:16; Judg 2:20; 2 Kgs 15:19; Hos 6:7; 8:1).[1]

17:3 Pagans were not only involved in idolatry but in worship of astral bodies. The **sun** (Shamash; Hebrew, שֶׁמֶשׁ, *šemeš*) was in all the ancient Semitic pantheons. Its popularity in early Palestine is attested by the place names Beth-shemesh (Josh 15:10; 1 Sam 6:9) and En-shemesh (Josh 15:7; 18:17). Adoption of such worship in Israel would have violated the second commandment and elevated the sun beyond its created purpose (Gen 1:14-18). The same was true of the **moon** (Hebrew, יָרֵחַ, *yārēaḥ*). In both early Palestine and Syria the moon was regarded as a male deity, Yaraḥ. The ancient city of Jericho was named for this god.[2] The later Assyrian cult of astral deities was a part of evil Manasseh's reign (2 Kgs 21:2-6), and its remnants continued for most of the century (Jer 7:18; 44:17-19).

---

[1] On the terminology for breaking the covenant used in the OT see M. Weinfeld, "בְּרִית *bᵉrîth*," *TDOT*, 2:261-262.

[2] See *IDB*, 4:464, s.v. "Sun," and 3:436, s.v. "Moon."

17:4-6 The procedure for dealing with suspected idolatry was precise and thorough. The judges had to **investigate it thoroughly** to determine if it were **true**. Innocence was presumed and protected. Hearsay was not enough. A case based solely on the word of one person against another was not accepted. Guilt could be established only on the **testimony of two or three witnesses** (v. 6), eliminating the chance of personal vendetta. If the guilt was proven, the case required the death penalty (vv. 4-5) by stoning in the **city gate**. The penalty, and presumably the trial (Ruth 4), was public, thus forestalling secret tribunals and their attendant abuses. The witnesses and the community both had to accept full responsibility for capital cases by participating together in the stoning (v. 7).[3] Since the setting was the village, this public aspect would provide a deterrent to false testimony. Furthermore, everyone would know the person being stoned. Deuteronomy 19:15-21 provided further protection against false witnesses: they must suffer the penalty of the crime of which they falsely accused the person. Unfortunately, some instances in Israel's history demonstrated that the courts could be so corrupted that these laws were useless.[4]

17:7 To **purge the evil from among you** was an important aspect of the theology of Deuteronomy. It literally meant to "burn" it out (13:5; 17:12; 19:19; 24:7). The concept was grounded in Israel's status as God's holy people and treasured possession (7:6). Evil of any sort that tainted her character would destroy her relationship with the holy God. Therefore, it was crucial to purge out the cancer of sinful individuals so that the community could survive.

Respect for Courts (17:8-13)

The concluding section on the judges, 17:8-13, provided the procedure for dealing with difficult cases. It was recognized that some cases would be intractable for the local judges and guilt or inno-

---

[3]Death by stoning was a common way of executing capital punishment in ancient Israel. It provided a sobering moment in the community by requiring everyone to have a role in the death of the guilty party. Cairns thinks it was practiced because it avoided contact with the dead (*Deuteronomy*, p. 163). See on 13:6-11.

[4]Naboth was condemned on the testimony of two false witnesses because the court had been co-opted by the evil monarchy (1 Kgs 21:1-16).

cence would be difficult to determine. Therefore, provision was made for a central tribunal that would hear these cases and provide the final decision. This was similar to Moses' role as the final arbitrator in the wilderness period (Exod 18:13-26; Deut 1:13-18).

17:8 Three kinds of cases might present serious difficulties: homicide (literally, "blood for blood"; see Exod 21:12-14), **lawsuits** ("claim for claim"; see Exod 22:6-15) and **assault** ("blow for blow"; see Exod 21:22-26; Lev 24:19-20). Hard cases might include homicide cases where the intentionality was unclear. The central authority also prevented a type of regional anarchy where different judicial decisions might pit one region against another (as different state laws do in the United States).[5]

17:9 The tribunal consisted of **priests** and a **judge** (or "judges" if the word is understood in a collective sense; cf. 19:17). It is not clear whether there was a leading priest and a leading judge, or if the priests concentrated on religious matters and the judge on civil matters. In the Pentateuch it seems the priests only had judicial roles in unusual cases when there were no witnesses (Num 5:11-31; Deut 21:1-9) unless "before the LORD" means before the priests (Exod 22:11; cf. Num 27:5; Deut 19:17). In the case of false witnesses the accused came before both priests and judges, but the judges investigated the matter (Deut 19:15-21; see below).[6]

17:10-11 The decision of the tribunal carried the same authority as the revealed laws of God. This seems indicated by the fact that in Deuteronomy the same words are used for both: **law** and **decisions** (*tôrāh* and *mišpaṭ*). Numbers 27:1-11 and Numbers 36 record an exceptional situation regarding Zelophehad's daughters and inheritance laws that was brought before Moses. Out of it came new statutes.

17:12-13 The authority of the decisions was paralleled to the authority of the court. **Contempt** for the court would be demonstrated by an arrogant and angry rejection of the legal decision (cf.

---

[5]Craigie, *Deuteronomy*, p. 252. In ancient Near Eastern countries hard cases were decided by divination such as reading livers and interpreting dreams.

[6]Jewish tradition connected this text with Num 11:16-17 and concluded that the high court had 71 members. It also saw this court as the prototype for the Great Sanhedrin in first century Jerusalem (Tigay, *Deuteronomy*, pp. 163-164).

1 Sam 17:28 and Prov 21:24 for use of the word). To show contempt for the decision was tantamount to showing contempt for God and was equal to the apostasy described in verses 2-7. Therefore, the penalty was **death** in order to **purge the evil** out (v. 7).

The laws in this section 16:18–17:13 reflected the fundamental concern in Israel for fairness and justice. The regulations to produce justice are detailed and to the point: careful investigation of the facts, sufficient testimony to guard against error, respect for the laws and the authorities, an advanced court for difficult matters, accountability, and acknowledgment of the authority of the decisions of the court.[7]

These laws could be violated and subverted as the prophets and the case of Naboth show (Isa 1:17,21; 5:23; Amos 2:5; 5:7,12; Jer 2:8; 5:31; Hos 5:1, etc.). But the laws were there and expressed the central concern of the covenant God for justice among his covenant people.

The King and Covenant Law (17:14-20)

These paragraphs have generated an enormous amount of discussion among scholars. Some understand that Moses was anticipating Israel's desire for human leadership later and was placing parameters on it.[8] Others, impressed by the intimate knowledge of later kings' excesses, see this passage as an attack on a well-entrenched institution.[9] Consequently, the latter scholars find support for a later date for Deuteronomy here (see Introduction). They assume that the law came in response to historical conditions, especially Solomon's kingship, and was an attempt to reform excessive practices.

However, it is legitimate to ask if the correspondence between the law of Deuteronomy and the historical accounts can be explained differently. Is it possible that the historical texts were written in such a way as to make violations of an earlier law explicit?[10]

---

[7]Miller, *Detueronomy*, pp. 144-145. Jeremiah's trial in chapter 26 was not a careful investigation of the facts, but justice prevailed through the intervention of elders and a politician.

[8]Merrill, *Deuteronomy*, pp. 264-265; Wright, *Deuteronomy*, p. 211; Thompson, *Deuteronomy*, p. 204.

[9]Cairns, *Deuteronomy*, p. 166; von Rad, *Deuteronomy*, pp. 118-119; Mann, *Deuteronomy*, p. 125.

[10]Weinfeld makes the point that the redactor of 1 Kings arranged the account of Solomon's kingship in such a way as to show the violations of the law of Deuteronomy 17 (*Deuteronomy and the Deuteronomic School*, p. 168).

Several lines of reasoning can be drawn upon to support the priority of the law. 1) Kingship was an old and prevalent institution in the ancient Near East, and Israel had already had experience with it. 2) Moses would have been especially familiar with kingship as practiced in Egypt and therefore was well aware of the extremes that could result. Texts from Ugarit and elsewhere detail the excesses that both Moses and Samuel warned against (1 Sam 8).[11] 3) Israel was already a theocracy and understood the concept of God as king (Exod 15:18). The idea that mankind would rule God's creation went back to Genesis 1:26-28. Kingship in Israel was in fact anticipated as far back as Genesis 17:6,16. It would therefore be a simple extension to apply the concept to the Promised Land.

This paragraph continues the theme of the section that began at 16:16, the limiting of human authorities in Israel. It is probably not accidental that the law on the king follows the law on the judges. The judge reflected the way of God; the king reflected the way of human leadership and was to function as a model for Israel.[12] The major duty of the king was to follow the law of the LORD. This requirement made Israel's king unique in the ancient world. In other ancient Near Eastern countries of the time the king was divinely appointed, accorded divine status, and accountable only to the gods. He was the lawgiver and, in Egypt, the law. He was practically indispensable for the welfare of society.[13] However, in Israel the law was from God and the king was required to obey it the same as the common person. The king was, in fact, an optional leader and the prophets felt quite free to criticize him (1 Sam 13:13-4; 2 Sam 12; Jer 22:13-19). Although the law allowed a king, it overthrew all pagan notions of kingship.

17:14 The law differs from the others in this section in that it is permissive, not a command or an initiative of God (cf. 16:18; 18:1;

However, he does not hold to an early date for the book of Deuteronomy. Olson, in fact, holds that much of the whole history of 1 and 2 Kings is concerned with documenting the abuses of the kings along the lines of the law of Deuteronomy (*Deuteronomy*, p. 83).

[11]I. Mendelsohn, "Samuel's Denunciation of Kingship in the Light of Akkadian Documents from Ugarit," *BASOR* 143 (1956): 17ff.

[12]Miller, *Deuteronomy*, p. 147.

[13]Tigay, *Deuteronomy*, p. 166.

18:15). When the people would begin to eye the other nations with envy and chafe under the uncertainties of charismatic leadership, they could select a king, but they must adhere to certain requirements.

Later in Samuel's day when the people campaigned for a king, imitation of the nations was the main reason they gave (1 Sam 8:5,19-20). They were especially concerned about someone to fight their battles for them.[14]

The desire to be **like all the nations** (1 Sam 8:20) was especially pernicious in the context of Deuteronomy. For Moses, the nations were wicked (9:4,5) and stronger than Israel (7:17; 9:1). Yet God would drive them out of the land and destroy them (4:38; 7:22; 8:20). So why would Israel want to be like them? In fact God would elevate Israel above the nations (8:20; 9:14). But a threat hung over Israel's head. Disobedience could result in exile among the nations or destruction at their hands (4:27; 28:49; 30:1).

17:15 Though the king was established because of Israel's desires, he would have to be one **chosen** by God. This meant selection by a prophet of God. The first two kings, Saul and David, were anointed by the prophet Samuel (1 Sam 10:1; 16:13). The third, Solomon, was chosen through the influence of Nathan (2 Sam 12:25; 1 Kgs 1).

The king could not be a **foreigner**. No reason is stated but within the context of Deuteronomy the danger that a foreigner might lead

---

[14]Wellhausen proposed years ago that there were two contradictory perspectives on the institution of kingship in the historical books. An early source was pro-king (1 Sam 9:1–10:16; 11:1-11,15; 13–14) and a later source was anti-king (1 Sam 7:3-17; 8; 10:17-27; 11:12-14). These views can be traced to the book of Judges also. Gideon's refusal to accept kingship (Judges 8:22-23), Abimelech's abortive attempt (ch. 9) and Jotham's fable (9:7-15) show opposition to kingship. However, the cryptic comment that there "was no king in Israel" seems to support kingship (17:6; 18:1; 19:1; 21:25) (*ABD*, 4:40-48, s.v. "King and Kingship."). However, recent research has concluded that rather than two conflicting sources, the author of Samuel has allowed conflicting viewpoints on kingship to be represented. As a new institution in Israel, kingship certainly aroused differing opinions. Ultimately Israel accepted the office with Samuel providing warnings against apostasy (1 Sam 12:19-25). God as ultimate king continued his providential control. He appropriated the institution and guided it toward his redemptive purposes. He subsequently made a covenant with David (2 Sam 7) and revealed his plans through the Royal (and thus Messianic) Psalms (2, 45, 72, 101, 110).

Israel into idolatry was certainly in the forefront. The law was not pointless as some hold, but its wisdom was proven by future events.[15] During the time of the Judges Gideon's son Abimelech, a half-Israelite, aspired to be king and was rejected. Later the power and influence of Jezebel, the foreign wife of Ahab, almost obliterated the faithful in Israel. Only the heroic actions of Elijah averted disaster.

The law must be understood in its theological context. It is not a statement about ethnic exclusivity in Israel. Deuteronomy was very concerned about just treatment of the non-Israelite (*gēr*) who, for economic or political reasons, had settled in the land (5:14; 14:29; 16:11,14; 24:17,19-21, etc.). However, the foreigner (*nokrî*) was an outsider who did not plan to settle in Israel but came in to conduct business or politics (cf. 14:21; 15:3; 23:20; 29:22[21]) and was to be treated differently.

17:16-17 The king was bound by three restrictions. Moses, or anyone, did not have to be particularly insightful to understand the propensity of absolute rulers. The conduct of ancient oriental potentates would have been fresh on Israel's memory. The urge to power would manifest itself in typical ways. One was the accumulation of war implements and an army, which in the ancient world meant **horses**, mainly for chariots.[16]

Through much of Israel's history **Egypt** was the most ready source of chariots and horses. It was an indicator of Solomon's power that he could at one time control that trade (1 Kgs 10:28-29). The worst part of such trade for Moses was the prospect that the king might use men in the trade, perhaps providing Israelite mercenaries as barter.[17] Samuel echoed this warning, concentrating on the conscription of sons for the army (1 Sam 8:11-12). David's sons,

---

[15]David Daube, "One from among Your Brethren Shall You Set King over You," *JBL* 90 (1971): 480-481. Daube thinks the situation with Abimelech in Judg 8:29–9:57 is in view.

[16]For the use of horses in the ancient Near East see D.R. Ap-Thomas, "All the King's Horses," *Proclamation and Presence*, eds., J.I. Durhan and J.R. Porter (Richmond: John Knox Press, 1970), pp. 135-151.

[17]At least that seems to make the best sense out of the last half of verse 16; see von Rad, *Deuteronomy*, p. 119; Craigie, *Deuteronomy*, pp. 255-256. The last statement in the verse, "You are not to go back that way again," sounds like a quote although there is no precise command like that elsewhere in the Pentateuch. It may be loosely based on Exod 14:13b which seems to be

Absalom and Adonijah, signaled their desire to seize the throne by acquiring chariots and horses (2 Sam 15:1; 1 Kgs 1:5). For Isaiah the degeneration of Israel's trust in God was graphically exhibited by the build-up of military forces and turning to Egypt for help (2:7b; 31:1). The Psalmist reminded Israel, "Some trust in chariots and some in horses, but we trust in the name of the LORD our God." (Ps 20:7[8]). The impulse to accumulate armies and make war is ancient and has characterized human history up to the present. Its motivation has never changed: power, self-aggrandizement, and the false illusion of national security.

Accumulation of **wives** was also a mark of ancient kingship. In many cases marriage between a king and the daughter of his counterpart in a foreign country ratified a treaty between the two countries. Solomon married the Pharaoh's daughter for that very reason (1 Kgs 3:1), and doubtless many of his other wives reflected the practice. However, these wives were his downfall because of their foreign religious influence (1 Kgs 11:1-8). His experience, and kings after him, illustrated the gravity of the warning in Deuteronomy 7:3-4 (cf. Exod 34:16). The heart that was to be devoted to God (Deut 6:5) could be easily "turned aside" (NIV, **led astray**). Only careful obedience to the law could keep the king on the narrow path (see vv. 19-20).

Accumulation of **silver and gold** (wealth) characterized ancient centralized government also. Through taxation and confiscation the king could end up owning much of the land and the people end up being serfs, taking care of his holdings. Samuel warned about the taxation the king would exact (1 Sam 8:14-17). Again Solomon reflected the apex of wealth in ancient Israel (1 Kgs 10:7,14-29). Moses had already warned that wealth could make the nation arrogant and ungrateful (6:11-12; 8:12-17).

17:18-20 One positive command was given to the king: he was to make his own personal copy of the **law** and consult it constantly. By doing this he would provide a model for the people. In other instructions in Deuteronomy the people also were directed to keep a copy of the law and read it regularly (27:2-8; 31:9-13,24-26). In

---

referred to in Deut 28:68. See David J. Reimer, "Concerning Return to Egypt: Deuteronomy xvii 16 and xxviii 68 Reconsidered," *Studies in the Pentateuch*, ed. J.A. Emerton (Brill: Leiden, 1990), pp. 217-229.

chapter 27 Moses told them to have the law written on plastered stones. But they were also to have a copy made, given to the Levites and placed in the Ark of the Covenant for safe-keeping. It was to be read in public every seven years at the Feast of the Tabernacles.

This law is no doubt the book of Deuteronomy.[18] Adhering to it placed the king at the same level as the people. He was subject to the same laws. He did not have his own laws or special privileges as was often the case in the ancient Near East.[19] Therefore, the Israelite king was a "constitutional monarch." Obedience to the law was to promote the same fear of the LORD for the king as for the people. It was also a safeguard against idolatry and apostasy. David's instruction to Solomon was a model of advice based on this law that was seldom followed (1 Kgs 2:3-4).

The law was to be **read** aloud as was the ancient custom. Ideally the king was to fit the role of the righteous man of Psalm 1 who meditated (read aloud) on the law day and night, meaning all the time (Ps 1:2). Joshua was given the same instruction (Josh 1:8). The law is apparently reflected in 1 Samuel 10:25 where Samuel wrote down the regulations for the king.

The most important ramification of this law was that the king was not to **consider himself better than his brother**. He was a common member of the community with no special status or honor. His kingship was to be marked by humility before God and narrow focus on the will of God through obedience. This admonition was intended to counter the most common maladies of kingship: letting power and prestige corrupt character and actions.

The promise to an obedient king was dynastic succession (v. 20). This was a reward from God, not a divine right of the king. The common impulse in monarchies is to pass on the kingship to family. It is a custom that can lead to abuse. The Deuteronomy law was intended to counter this impulse.

---

[18]For references to "this law" elsewhere see 1:5; 4:44; 27:3,8,26; 29:21,29; 30:10; and throughout chapter 31. As explained in the Introduction, Christendom's name for the book comes from the Greek translation of this verse which translates "copy" as *deuteronomion*, that is, this "repetition of the law." The translation is inaccurate.

[19]In Egypt and Mesopotamia the king was the source of the law and only the gods could bring him to justice. His purpose was to maintain the order built into the universe (Walton and Matthews, *Genesis–Deuteronomy*, p. 243).

The implications of this passage are far reaching. Human leadership is under God and owes its first allegiance to God. It brings no special privileges, but is to be marked by obedience. It is to provide a model of God's leadership for the people. An accumulation of power or prestige is not a sign of God's blessings but a sign of disobedience.

DEUTERONOMY 18

The Priests and Levites (18:1-8)

After two passages on "secular" leadership, the judges and kings, there are now two passages on "spiritual" leadership, the Levites (vv. 1-8) and prophets (vv. 9-22). The repeated phrase "among your/ their brothers" (2,15,18) holds the chapter together.

This paragraph is not concerned about the duties of the priests or Levites, but about their allotment as a part of the Israelite nation. God had set them apart to minister to him through service at the sanctuary and the ark of covenant. Their responsibilities were often intense and afforded little time for agricultural pursuits. Consequently, provision for their welfare was important. This legislation addresses that issue, building on laws from Leviticus and Numbers. The passage has three subsections: Levites in general (1-2), the priests' share (4-6), Levites who want to serve at the central sanctuary (6-8).

18:1-2 Terminology used for the Levites is typical of Deuteronomy but is ambiguous. The NIV is only one way of translating the Hebrew. **The priests, who are Levites—indeed the whole tribe of Levi** can also be translated "The Levitical priests, the whole tribe of Levi" (NRSV, NASB). The literal Hebrew is "to the priests the Levites, all the tribe of Levi." This ambiguity has fueled the debate about the relationship between the priests and Levites in the book of Deuteronomy.[1]

---

[1]See on 10:6-9 above. Since the time of Wellhausen a distinction has been made between how Deuteronomy understood the Levites in contrast to Leviticus and Numbers (Wellhausen, *Prolegomena*, pp. 121-151). According to his reconstruction in the early period almost anyone could preside at sacrifices. Later the tribe of Levi was designated for that office. Josiah's reform, reflected in our text here, confined priestly activity to Jerusalem. Only after the exile did a distinct class of priests arise that traced its ancestry back to

"To the priests the Levites" occurs five times in Deuteronomy and is to be translated "the Levitical priests."[2] The second phrase, "the whole tribe of Levi," is an explanatory appositional phrase. It expands the more limited group, Levitical priests, to include the whole tribe. Since Moses' concern was with the prerogatives of the whole class, the Levites, he wanted to make sure that it was clear. Therefore, Deuteronomy recognizes that priests are Levites, but not all Levites are priests.[3] Since Moses' emphasis in Deuteronomy was on the unity of Israel, he downplayed distinctions in order to legislate for the entire tribe of Levi.[4]

The **allotment** of the Levites was not land, but a share in the offerings of the people (Num 18:21-32).[5] **Offering made to the LORD by fire** is one possible translation of the rather obscure Hebrew text, which reads literally "fire of the LORD."[6] A better understanding of the text is probably that the referent is gifts in general that the people brought to God. This could include all kinds of offerings presented to the LORD, including sacrifices consumed by the families and priests and Levites.[7]

The fact that the Levites did not receive an inheritance of land did not make them a lesser member of the nation. They had their own **inheritance** that was a gift from God. As he prospered the nation through blessings (ch. 8) the Levites would also prosper from the gifts the people bought for sacrifices and offerings (Num 18 has the details). Therefore, the Levites received the blessings of the covenant along with **their brothers**. The unity of the nation was

---

Aaron through Zadok. Thus the book of Deuteronomy is midway in this historical development. Tigay, *Deuteronomy*, p. 170, offers a brief summary of this reconstruction and the various biblical texts used to support it.

[2]17:9,18; 24:8; 27:9 and here.

[3]See Rodney K. Duke, "The Portion of the Levite: Another Reading of Deuteronomy 18:6-8," *JBL* 106 (1987): 193-201.

[4]McConville, *Law and Theology*, p. 148. See on 10:6-9 and verse 5 below for the various functions of the Levites.

[5]The connection of "allotment" with the land is especially focused in Josh 14-19 where each tribe is given its allotment or share of land.

[6]If the Hebrew אִשֶּׁה is to be related to אֵשׁ, "fire."

[7]Richard Averbeck, "אִשֶּׁה," *NIDOTTE*, 1:540-549; J.E. Hartley, *Leviticus* (Waco: Word, 1992), pp. 13-14. Deut 12:17 refers to freewill offerings and special gifts in addition to tithes and firstfruits.

maintained. As long as the tribes lived together in covenant faithfulness, each one could live in economic security.[8]

More important than the gifts the Levites would receive was the promise that **the LORD is their inheritance** (10:9), a promise already made to Aaron (Num 18:20). This promise reflected the unique relationship that existed between the Levites or priests and God (see on v. 5 below) and the special blessings they had from God. Just as Israel was God's most treasured possession (7:6; Exod 8:22), the Levites had God as their most treasured possession, an inheritance better than any land.

18:3-4 This subsection turns specifically to the Levites who were priests and the portion of the sacrifices they would receive (see Exod 29:26-28; Lev 7:31-34; Num 18:11-12,18). General provisions had already been addressed in 14:27-29. The portion of the animals to be provided to the priests here is more detailed and somewhat different from Leviticus and Numbers. In the earlier legislation it was the breast and right thigh that was to be given to the priest. Here it is the shoulder, the two cheeks and part of the stomach. One possible explanation for the difference is that Leviticus is referring to the peace offering, whereas Deuteronomy seems to be referring to sacrifices in general.[9] The practices may have changed over time as well. The custom in Samuel's time seemed to be that the priest took whatever he could grab in the pot (1 Sam 2:13-14) though the author's language and the context suggests disapproval of the practice.

The **firstfruits of your grain, new wine and oil** were the gifts brought to the altar at the harvest festivals (16:10,13,17; 26:1-11). The combination of these three items was a standard cliché throughout the Old Testament to reflect the abundance with which God had blessed his people (cf. 12:17; 7:13; 11:14; 14:23 and Hos 2:8,21-22;

---

[8]The Levites were not entirely landless. They were given 48 cities with the surrounding pastureland as their inheritance also (Num 35:1-5; Josh 21:41-42).

[9]Though the shoulder of the wave offering of the Nazirite belonged to the priest (Num 6:19). Excavations at Lachish uncovered a pit from the Late Bronze Age (between 1500 and 1200 BC) with numerous right shoulder bones of young sheep and goats that had been sacrificed (O. Tufnell, "Lachish," *Archaeology and Old Testament Study,* ed., D. Winton Thomas (Oxford: Oxford University Press, 1967], p. 301). Therefore, the custom predated Israel's settlement in the area.

Jer 31:12).[10] The third year tithe given to the Levites no doubt contained these foodstuffs also (cf. 12:17). If the people were faithful in bringing their tithes and offerings to the central sanctuary the priests would have ample provision.

18:5 Just as God has chosen Israel from among the nations to be representative of them (7:6), so he had **chosen** the priests and Levites out of Israel to be representative for them. As Israel stood before God on behalf of the nations so that through her blessing could come upon the nations (Gen 12:1-3), so the Levites stood before God on Israel's behalf so that blessing could come to her (10:8). To **stand and minister** before God was a special privilege. Ministering to the LORD in this sense involved worship through thanksgiving and praise (1 Chr 16:4; Ps 135:1-2), sacrifices (Exod 30:20), and caring for the place of worship (Num 1:50; 3:31).[11] The Levites were commissioned to care for the Ark of the Covenant (10:8) and the whole tabernacle (Num 3:1-13).

18:6-8 This subsection applies to a specific circumstance of a Levite who did not live near the central sanctuary but might want to serve there. A clear understanding of the force of this passage is not provided by the NIV. Verse 6 introduces the conditional clause, **if a Levite moves.** The condition continues through verse 6, **and comes,** and into verse 7 "and ministers" (not **he may minister**), with the final clause in verse 8, "then" **he is to share equally.** The force of the regulation is that a Levite who lives in one of the outside towns (one of the 48, **one of your towns**) may wish to come to the central sanctuary **in all earnestness** (literally, "his own desire") to minister (probably temporarily). If that is the case, he was not to be considered inferior but was to **share equally** (literally "to eat") in the portion designated for the Levites at the central sanctuary.[12]

---

[10]The lack thereof was a sign of judgment (Deut 28:38-40; Joel 1:10). This list of abundance became a picture of eschatological plenty and blessing (Amos 9:13; Joel 2:19,24). See further on the comments on the law of first fruits in ch. 26:1-11.

[11]The combination of "stand" and "minister" is rare in the Pentateuch, used of Levites in Num 16:9, Deut 10:8, and here, and of the priest in Deut 17:12. That 18:5 is referring to the Levites and not just the Levitical priests is indicated by the phrase, "out of all your tribes" which infers Moses' interest in the entire tribe of Levi, not just one portion.

[12]These verses are considered by some as strong support for the Well-

This legislation recognized the practical situation that not all Levites would be involved in ministry at the central sanctuary. They would be living in their own towns, teaching and ministering in other ways. However, it was their privilege to minister at the central sanctuary as well.[13]

Prophets (18:9-22)

The last section on leadership in Israel is the most important. Prophets were the only leaders chosen directly by God. The others were appointed or followed family succession. Prophets were also the leaders of last resort in a sense. If the previous classes of leaders failed, God could still raise up the prophet who would speak God's words to the people (cf. v. 18 below).

The legislation is developed in two steps. First, pagan methods of controlling the future are described and condemned (vv. 9-13), then instructions for the true prophet are given (vv. 14-22). As in so much of Moses' instruction in Deuteronomy, a sharp contrast is made between the practices of the pagan Canaanites who are in the land and what Israel's conduct was to be. Two totally incompatible

---

hausen position that Josiah's reform has strong echoes in Deuteronomy. On this view the legislation makes provisions for the Levitical priests who served at the altars that Josiah demolished in the countryside. These priests were allowed to come and serve at the temple in Jerusalem. This interpretation is unlikely. First the law is for Levites, not priests (2 Kgs 23:89 specifically refers to priests). Secondly, if it were about priests from abolished sanctuaries, they would have hardly been considered fit to serve in Jerusalem (Mayes, *Deuteronomy*, pp. 278-279; also Duke, "The Portion of the Levite," p. 198).

The parallelism of vv. 1 and 8 needs to be noted. "Allotment" of verse 1 and "benefits" of verse 8 translate the same Hebrew word.

[13]The phrase translated by the NIV as "the sale of family possessions" in verse 8 is one of the most difficult translation problems in Deuteronomy (see A.R. Hulst, *Old Testament Translation Problems* [Leiden: E.J. Brill, 1960], p. 15). The common translation seems suspect since family inheritances were seldom for sale and the Levites had no inherited property. The literal Hebrew is "his selling according to the fathers." L.S. Wright has suggested translating "selling according to custom." The selling would then refer to the sale of carcasses of animals sacrificed as sin and guilt offerings which provided income for the Levitical priests (Lev 5:15,18; 6:6 compared with 2 Kgs 12:16) ("MKR in 2 Kings vii 5-17 and Deuteronomy 18:8," *VT* 39 [1989]: 438-448).

worldviews are represented. Human efforts to know and control the future violate the character of the only true God of the universe.

18:9 Throughout Deuteronomy Moses had exhorted Israel to learn to fear the LORD (4:10; 14:23; 17:19; 31:12-13) and to learn the commandments (5:1) so that they would do them (4:1; 5:1; 6:1,3; 7:11-12; 8:1, etc.). However, there are some things they should not learn. All knowledge is not equal, and some can be lethal. To **learn to imitate** (literally, "to learn to do") the pagan Canaanites would constitute a violation of her covenant with God for their practices were the exact opposite of reverence for and obedience to God.

A common desire among all peoples is to know the future and in some way establish some control over it. This desire comes out of the insecurity common to the human experience. Even though the ancient cultures believed in gods, they did not believe these gods were in total control of the universe. The very multiplicity of gods prevented the ascendancy of an all-powerful high god. Therefore, they looked for some other power outside of the gods and developed numerous methods of getting in touch with this power. The basic methods involved some form of divination or magic. Moses, in the most comprehensive list in the Old Testament, addressed most of these methods. They were all **detestable**, that is utterly repulsive, to the holy God. "Detestable" is the most common word applied to Canaanite idolatrous religious practices which sets this section firmly in a religious context (7:25-26; 12:31; 13:14[15]; 20:18, etc.).

18:10-11 The list begins with strictures against child sacrifice (see on 12:31). This was not an occult practice as such, but some have suggested it may have divination overtones (2 Kgs 17:17).[14] It was a practice mentioned often in the Old Testament (2 Kgs 3:27; 16:3; 21:6; 23:10; Jer 19:4-5; 32:35; Ezek 16:21; 20:26,31; 23:37) because it was such a common part of the ancient world and even infiltrated into Israel. The connection of this practice with what follows puts divination and its related practices in a moral context. Pursuing the occult was not an innocent pastime for Israel, for it violated the

---

[14]Merrill, *Deuteronomy*, p. 271. The literal Hebrew here is "pass through the fire." It is not clear whether this refers to actual child sacrifice or to some magic rite. Scholars are divided on the issue. See Tigay, *Deuteronomy*, pp. 464-465, for a full discussion; also see the discussion in *Archaeology Odyssey* 3,6 (Nov/Dec 2000): 28-31, on whether the Phoenicians practiced child sacrifice.

character of God. Everything that concerned her relationship to God had moral implications.

Divination involved a variety of practices designed to predict the future or discover the unknown. These included the examination of animal entrails such as livers, reading omens of various kinds, and interpreting various natural and unnatural phenomena. Divination is something of a general term that included some of the other practices listed.[15]

Sorcery involved the use of magic of which there were two kinds, black magic and white magic. Black magic involved potions and curses to bring harm or death on the victim, and in ancient Mesopotamian laws, was punishable by death. White magic was used in medical aid and to bring good fortune on religious endeavors. Isaiah found eighth century Judah full of these practices (Isa 2:6), and Jeremiah had to confront them a century later (Jer 27:9).

Interpreting omens was an important part of ancient life; almost any important task was never undertaken without consulting the omens. A vast literature on omen interpretation developed for consultation. Interpretation often was not clear and required several efforts before a decision was made.[16]

Witchcraft (see Exod 7:11; Dan 2:2; 2 Kgs 9:22; Mal 3:5), or black magic, involved the negative use of magic to destroy an enemy. Practitioners were condemned to death in the law (Exod 22:17). Closely related is the one who **casts spells** (cf. Ps 58:5[6]; Isa 47:9,12).

A medium or spiritist or one **who consults the dead** are terms that refer to the belief that, somehow, the dead had superhuman knowledge about the future and could share it with the living (necromancy; see Isa 8:19-20). The key was adopting the correct method. This belief has a folk-religion status and is widespread in the world, even today. The most vivid example in the Old Testament

---

[15]Consulting various English translations will demonstrate the overlap of terms. For example both the NRSV and the NASB vary from the NIV in the English words they use for the various Hebrew terms. However, the major point is still clear.

[16]Joseph under the direction of God and in a pagan environment practiced the art of interpreting omens of mixed liquids in a cup (Gen 44:5,15). Ezekiel mentions the use of arrows and livers (Ezek 21:21). A. Leo Oppenheim describes the practices from the ancient literature (*Ancient Mesopotamia* [Chicago: University of Chicago Press, 1964], pp. 206-227).

is the case of King Saul in 1 Samuel 28. He had outlawed the practice in obedience to the law. But when in great distress, he consulted the witch of Endor who was successful in arousing the ghost of Samuel. The penalty for a medium was death (Lev 20:27).

It was believed in the ancient Near East that if the dead were not honored properly with ongoing gifts, the ghost or spirit could become dangerous. Consequently, ancestor worship was an important part of the occult practices in Mesopotamia.[17]

18:12-13 The listed practices clashed with the holistic worldview of the Old Testament and are condemned not only in the laws but also in the prophets. Attempts to gain control over others or to control the future apart from God were crass denials of his sufficiency. As creator and redeemer he was not only in control of the universe he was faithful to care for his people. Their responsibility was not to use superstitious attempts to control their neighbors and the future, but to trust in the faithful, trustworthy God who was Lord over all. The only true word from God came through the prophet (vv. 15,18).

God's judgment on the Canaanites, which he would demonstrate in his **driving** them **out,** had a moral base. Their religious life violated the very core nature of God. They could not be allowed to persist in such evil. Therefore, the command throughout Deuteronomy to purge or drive out the Canaanites was not arbitrary or wicked. It was an example of God's judgment being manifested in human history.

God's expectations for Israel were that she was to be quite different from the rest of the nations, especially the Canaanites. She was to be **blameless** (תָּמִים, *tāmîm*), that is, she was to maintain her integrity before God through genuine loyalty to him.[18]

This section is dominated by the words "hear/listen" (שָׁמַע, 5 times, vv. 14,15,16,19,20) and "speak"(verb) or "word" (noun; דָּבַר, 10 times, vv. 17,18,19,20[3×],21,22[3×]). The issue revolves around who or what is going to control Israel and her future, the word of

---

[17]See Walton and Matthews, *Genesis–Deuteronomy*, pp. 244-245; Malcolm J.A. Horsnell, "קֶסֶם," *NIDOTTE*, 3:945-951; *NBD* s.v., "Magic and Sorcery," pp. 723-727; *Dictionary of Biblical Imagery*, s.v., "Magic," pp. 524-528; C. Brown and J. Stafford Wright, "Magic," *NIDNTT*, 2:552-562.

[18]This adjective is used most of the time in the cultic law for the offerings that were to be brought to God: they were to be without blemish, perfect (Lev 1:3,10; 3:1,6,9, etc.). For its use in the human sphere see Gen 6:9; 17:1; Josh 24:14; Ps 18:23(24).

the impostor or the word of God. In a certain sense this passage brings into sharp focus all the calls to Israel to "hear" in the book of Deuteronomy (4:1,10,30,36; 5:1,27; 6:3,4; 11:13; 12:28, etc.). It also brings to focus the overarching theme of the "word" of the LORD (see ch. 4). There is more than one word Israel could listen to. The popular methods were real possibilities. However, all but the word of God was spurious, and it was only through his divine word that Israel was to understand the present and the future.

As with kingship, Israel's prophets were to be different from those of the nations. Magic and accumulation of human wisdom were forbidden. The sole source of authority for the prophet was the word of God. Furthermore, the prophet mediated between God and the people and spoke directly to them. He was not under the authority of the king nor responsible to him.

18:14 Israel could not resort to the practices of the pagan nations when seized with a desire to know the future. The command is doubly emphasized in the Hebrew with the unusual order of object and implied subject with verb before the expressed subject (literally "but you, he did not permit you, the LORD your God."). What were they then to do? They were to listen to the prophet of God, a person whom God would raise up and through whom he would speak (v. 15). They would not have to resort to charlatans or their imagination.

18:15-16 The prohibition of divination was balanced by a provision. God would not leave Israel leaderless when Moses died, but he would raise up his own spokesman like Moses. The nation would not be thrust into the future with no direction.

The emphasis of verse 15 is **a prophet like me**. Moses becomes the model for ensuing prophets. That meant that future prophets would be characterized by at least the following qualities: 1) Moses was specifically called by God and commissioned (Exod 3). There was no hereditary right to the office of prophet in Israel. Therefore, God would call each succeeding prophet (Isa 6; Jer 1; Amos 7). 2) Moses had an intimate relationship with God even talking with him face to face (Num 12:6-8). Therefore prophets would expect a similar encounter (Isa 6). 3) Moses received his words directly from God (Exod 24; 34). Therefore the prophets would continually refer to a "Thus says the LORD." 4) Moses faithfully spoke the word of the LORD despite opposition from the people and his own family. So the prophets would often not be well received (Jer 20, 26; Amos 7).

5) Moses was directed by the Spirit (Num 11:17). So the prophets would be under the control of the spirit (1 Sam 19:20; Ezek 3:12,14) and their compulsion to speak would come from God (Amos 3:7-8; Jer 20:9).[19]

The focus in this passage and in these criteria is on God. God would raise up a prophet, put his words in the prophet's mouth, and command him (v. 18). This is consistent with other passages in Deuteronomy that emphasize the contrast between the pagans and God's people. For example, in chapter 12 Israel will worship where God decides, not at the pagan places.

In some ways, however, Moses was a unique prophet (34:10-12). He was the mediator of the covenant and the giver of the law. He had a unique relationship with God and stood as a fountainhead of all Old Testament prophets.[20] Therefore, succeeding prophets did not offer a new law but grounded their preaching in the Mosaic covenant and called the people to repentance and faithfulness.

18:17 God sent a prophet in response to the people's request. In one of those rare insights Israel realized that continued exposure to God's presence endangered her life, and she requested a mediator (Exod 20:18-21; Deut 5:23-27). Therefore, Moses was both a mediator and shielded the people from God's holiness.

18:18-19 The true prophet had the very words of God **put in his mouth**. Therefore, the successors of Moses would be just like him in that respect (cf. Exod 4:15-16), and the people could be confident they were still being led by God. Thus the prophet Isaiah had the coals touch his lips to purify them (Isa 6:7), and God touched Jeremiah's mouth to put his (God's) words in it (Jer 1:9).

Consequently, to not **listen** to the words of God through the prophet was the same as disobeying God. It could even mean

---

[19]"A prophet like me," though in the singular, apparently was intended in a collective sense (Tigay, *Deuteronomy*, p. 175). Out of Israel arose many prophets to carry on the tradition of Moses and call the people back to the covenant. Likewise the king in 17:14-20 is in the singular but has a collective sense and means all succeeding kings. However, since prophet is in the singular, the interpretation given this verse by the early church as pointing to Jesus Christ is legitimate (Acts 3:22).

[20]W. VanGemeren, *Interpreting the Prophetic Word* (Grand Rapids: Zondervan, 1990), p. 28.

death.[21] This established the authority of the prophet as the highest in the land, even higher than the king.

18:20 The reassurance of leadership directly under God's influence still raised some issues. How could the people know that a prophet was speaking God's word? Two criteria for judging the prophets were offered. One who had spoken presumptuously or arrogantly (v. 23) in God's name and one **who speaks in the name of other gods** would not be God's prophets and should **be put to death** (see ch. 13). The latter case would be easy to assess, but the former case would be more difficult.

18:21-22 It was important that Israel know that not everyone who claimed to be a prophet from God was one. But since a false prophet could make the same claims and use the same formula as a true prophet, how could Israel tell the difference? This was not just a theoretical problem as the history of prophetism in Israel makes clear (see 1 Kgs 22, Jer 28). Many prophets flourished in Israel. However, not all were given divine sanction. Deuteronomy 13 suggests that "false" prophets could even perform signs and wonders.[22]

The test for a true prophet was simple. Since God's word controlled the present and the future, if a prophet spoke a word about the future and it did not happen, he was not from God. Of all the gods, only the LORD declared beforehand what was to happen (Isa 41:21-29). The true prophet spoke truth. There was a correspondence between his word and historical reality.[23] It was said of Samuel that everything he said happened (1 Sam 3:19-20, "none of his words fell to the ground"). His words to Saul came true immediately (1 Sam 10:2-9). Eljah accurately predicted a drought (1 Kgs 17:1-7) and the demise of Jezebel (1 Kgs 21:23; 2 Kgs 9:32-36). Micaiah, when faced with 400 other prophets opposing his message and a king who hated him, staked his life on the accuracy of his word (1 Kgs 22). This kind

---

[21]A possible meaning of "call to account" is to invoke the death penalty. The history of Israel contains a number of examples of disobedience to the prophetic word resulting in death: Saul (1 Sam 28:17-18), an unnamed prophet (1 Kgs 20:35-36), the king's captain (2 Kgs 7:17-20). Even a prophet who spoke God's word could die because of disobedience (1 Kgs 13:20-24).

[22]The Old Testament never refers to illegitimate prophets as "false." Only the Greek translation adds the word false before prophet at appropriate places.

[23]Miller, *Deuteronomy*, p. 153.

of prediction-fulfillment schema forms a strong subplot in the structure of the books of Samuel through Kings.[24]

However, this criterion had an obvious limit. The people could not make an immediate evaluation of the prophetic word but had to wait. How long should they have to wait, and what if the predictions were long range? For example, the prophet Jeremiah was faced with two related dilemmas. When the prophet Hananiah gave a word opposed to Jeremiah's message, Jeremiah could only reply, "I hope your word is true, but the prophets before us have never said such things." Only when Jeremiah received a further word from God did he respond with condemnation of Hananiah's false message (Jer 27). The other dilemma was that many of Jeremiah's words were long-range, concerning the coming destruction of Jerusalem. His intention was to motivate his contemporaries to repent. However, if they had to wait until that event occurred, it would then be too late, and Jeremiah's message would be rendered ineffective.

It is important to note that Moses stated the test in the negative (if the prophet's word did not come true). The text does not suggest that if what the prophet said came true he was speaking for God. Moses had already pointed out that a false prophet could predict the future (13:1-2). Therefore, this test was not definitive but has to be understood within the context of the larger picture. A prophet must be like Moses (v. 17). He must excel in moral authority, challenge the sin and rebellion of the people (Lam 2:14, the false prophet did not expose the sin of the people), remain faithful in the face of opposition, and remain steadfast in devotion to God. Any prophetic word that contradicted Deuteronomy 6:4-5 was false.[25] Jeremiah reflected on these same issues in his attack on prophets in chapter 23. The bottom line was that the people had to be extremely diligent and not listen only to those that pleased them (Jer 5:31; 23:17).[26]

---

[24]G. von Rad, "The Deuteronomic Theology of History in I and II Kings," *The Problem of the Hexateuch*, pp. 205-221.

[25]Gene Tucker, "Deuteronomy 18:15-22," *Int* 41 (1987): 292-297.

[26]There is considerable evidence that Jeremiah took as his model for ministry the life of Moses (William L. Holladay, "The Background of Jeremiah's Self-understanding: Moses, Samuel and Psalm 22," *JBL* 83 [1964]: 153-164; idem, "Jeremiah and Moses: Further Observations," *JBL* 85 [1966]: 17-27); Achtemeier, *Deuteronomy, Jeremiah*, ch. 6).

DEUTERONOMY 19

5. Elaboration of the Sixth Commandment (19:1–22:8)

The first five of the Ten Commandments concerned the vertical relationship with God and were elaborated in chapters 12–18. The second five were concerned with the horizontal relationships between people and are elaborated in chapters 19–26. This next major section in Deuteronomy (19:1–22:8) provides explanatory details on the sixth commandment, do not murder (5:17).

Olson suggests four subunits in this section:[1] 19:1-21 which is concerned with the protection of innocent life; 20:1-20 which addresses rules for warfare; 21:1-23 which covers laws for unsolved murder as well as other issues of life and death; 22:1-8 which provides laws that enhance life.

A cursory reading of the section reveals some material that is only loosely tied to the main theme, for example 19:14 on boundary markers, 21:10-14 on marriage, and 22:1-5 with miscellaneous laws. Olson suggests all the material fits under the general theme of matters concerning life and death. However, a few verses actually anticipate the next section on sexual misconduct and were deliberately put where they are as rhetorical devices (e.g., 22:5).[2] A related theme is the concern with either removing bloodguilt or avoiding actions that incur bloodguilt.[3] This theme was anticipated in the previous section in 17:8.[4]

The variety of laws are held together by the repetition of several key words or ideas: "bloodguilt" (דָּם/דָּמִים, *dām/dāmîm* — 19:6,10,

---

[1]Olson, *Deuteronomy*, p. 89.
[2]Ibid.
[3]Tigay, *Deuteronomy*, p. 178.
[4]Although Tigay ends the section on bloodguilt at 21:9, the fact that 22:8 also deals with the issue supports Olson's analysis of the larger unit rather than Tigay's.

12,13; 21:7,8,9; 22:8); "death" (מֹות, *môth* — 19:5,6,11,12; 20:5,6,7; 21:21,22); "tree or wood" (עֵץ, *'ēṣ* — 19:5; 20:19,20; 21:22-23; 22:6); various words for the authorities who are to apply the laws such as "elders" (19:12; 21:2-6,20), "priests" (19:17; 20:2; 21:5), "judges" (19:17,18; 21:2), and "officials" (20:5,8,9); and the location where much of the action will take place, the "cities" (19:1,2,5,7,9,11-12; 20:10,14-16,19-20; 21:2-6,19-21). There are more subtle connections that will be noted in the comments that follow.

Cities of Refuge (19:1-13)

The sixth commandment, "you shall not murder/kill" was ambiguous for there are different kinds of murder.[5] The law on the cities of refuge makes a distinction between deliberate, premeditated killing and accidental killing. The distinction was crucial because Deuteronomy was concerned about the protection of innocent life. The concern went in two directions: vengeance for the innocent life taken, and protection for the innocent person who killed accidentally. In each case bloodguilt was or could be incurred. The law was grounded in both Genesis 9:5-6 and Exodus 21:13-14. God was the giver of life and anyone who took life was accountable to him. But since there was such a thing as accidental killing, the killer could take temporary sanctuary at the altar until the authorities had an opportunity to determine guilt.

19:1-3 This law anticipates the settlement into the Promised Land similar to chapter 8 and the whole book. Three cities of refuge had already been set aside east of the Jordan (4:41-43), and the three in view here were to match them on the west side.[6] Numbers 35 is the more detailed law about the six cities and how due process should be worked out. The original law of sanctuary is in Exodus 21:13-14 which addressed the issue of taking asylum at the central altar. Deuteronomy seems to presuppose both laws and offers only the details that fit into the overall theme of covenant obedience and protection of the innocent.[7]

---

[5]The verb *rṣḥ* was not restricted to just premeditated murder (see on 5:17 above). However, it is to be distinguished from sanctioned killing in the law which included capital punishment, sanctioned war (ch. 20), and the *ḥērem*.

[6]The cities are called cities of "refuge" (*miklāṭ*) in Numbers 35 and Joshua 20, 21 but not in Deuteronomy.

[7]Contra Cairns, *Deuteronomy*, p. 176, and deVaux, *Ancient Israel*, pp. 160-163.

Joshua 21:7 relates the actual setting aside of the three cities and names them. They were Kadesh in Galilee in the north, Shechem in the central hill country, and Kiriath Arba (Hebron) in the Judean hill country in the south. These three cities met the criteria of being **centrally located** in each of the three main geographical areas of the Promised Land. They corresponded to the three cities set apart east of the Jordan that were also located in the north, central, and south areas of the land.

The three cities were to be strategically located geographically so that the manslayer might have ready access to them. **Build roads** was part of the procedure to give access. If the distance was too far or the cities were not easily accessed, the manslayer might be caught by the avenger of blood before he got there (v. 6).[8]

The concept of sanctuary was common in the ancient Near East and quite old. It is attested in Hittite, old Babylonian, and Egyptian documents. It represents a social structure that was still tribal but moving toward a more centralized form of government. Such a situation fits the Mosaic era when Israel was preparing to settle into the land.[9] There are very few examples of blood revenge in the Old Testament. The one apparent case, Joab's murder of Abner, had political motivation as well (2 Sam 3:27,30).[10] Two examples of sanctuary at the central altar, based on Exodus 21:13-14, are recorded, only one of which was honored (1 Kgs 1:50-53 and 2:28-34).[11] However, asylum at the central sanctuary could have been only a temporary situation, so the cities of refuge provided for the long-term needs.

19:4-13 The main section of the law has three subunits. The details are given in verses 4-7 (unintentional killing) and 11-13 (intentional killing). Verses 8-10 interrupt the presentation with a

---

[8]The phrase "build roads to them" is unclear in the Hebrew. It could be translated "determine the road" which some translators have taken to mean "calculate the distance" (NRSV) or "fix the distance of the road" (Hulst, *Old Testament Translation Problems*, p. 15). However, either translation provides the same emphasis which was easy access.

[9]Walton and Matthews, *Genesis–Deuteronomy*, p. 247.

[10]Since Abner was a principle rival of Joab for general of David's army, the latter's motives are suspect.

[11]Joab's request was not honored because his killing of Abner was considered the shedding of innocent blood. Sanctuary at the central altar was similar in conceptualization to the cities of refuge but different in practice.

glance to the future expansion of the nation and the need for more cities of refuge (a situation that apparently never came to pass). The first words of verse 2 and the last words of verse 7 are identical, perhaps setting off verses 1-7 as a subunit.

In the context of ancient Israel, errors in murder cases could happen. The innocent could be unjustly killed, and the guilty could unjustly be given asylum. Innocent killing was defined as accidental, such as a flying ax head (v. 5) or accidental pushing, or accidental hitting with a thrown or dropped object (Num 35:22-23). For this offense the killer was given refuge in one of the cities. The intentional killer, one who had animosity toward the victim (v. 11; Num 35:20-21) or approached him with murder weapon in hand (Num 35:16-18), could also flee to the city. The function of the cities was to allow the judicial process to have time to work so that both types of cases could be decided apart from the heat of the moment (v. 6). In both cases the elders of the home village, no doubt in cooperation with the elders of the city of refuge, were to deliberate the case to determine guilt.[12] If the case was deliberate murder, the person was handed over for execution (vv. 11-12). As an important safeguard a person could not be convicted of murder without at least two witnesses (vv. 10,13; Num 35:30; see comments below on 19:15ff).[13]

The process outlined was designed to protect the nation against the shedding of **innocent blood** (vv. 10,13). The innocent victim was avenged by the death of the killer, and the innocent killer was protected from unwarranted vengeance. However, Numbers 35:26-28 makes it clear that there was a penalty for the manslayer and expiation for an innocent life taken. Thus the manslayer was confined to the city of refuge until the death of the contemporary high priest. The death of the high priest provided for the expiation of the guilt and the manslayer could go free. The fundamental principle of a life for a life was maintained.

No compensation for the taking of a life (Num 35:31-32) was allowed in either of the cases. This made Israel unique in the ancient world. Babylonian laws allowed for payment to be made to the victim's family for either intentional or unintentional murder.[14]

---

[12]Num 35:25 and Josh 20:6 refer to the "assembly."

[13]Hos 6:8-9 seems to reflect violation of this due process.

[14]Walton and Matthews, *Genesis–Deuteronomy*, p. 214.

The phrase **shedding of innocent blood** (v. 13) or **bloodshed** (v. 10) points to the foundational principle behind this law. The killing of an innocent person involved the spilling of his blood on the ground (Gen 4:10; 9:5). Such an act polluted the ground.[15] The holy God could not live among his people if the land were polluted. Therefore, the spilled blood must be atoned for in some way.[16]

The **avenger of blood** (v. 6) had the responsibility of carrying out justice in murder cases. This person was usually the nearest of kin, possibly an eldest son, brother, uncle, or cousin, depending on who fit the criteria.[17] Their function was not absolute or unilateral however since the elders of the village were to carry out due process (cf. 13:14; 17:2-7; 21:1-10). It has been suggested the avenger was in fact an elder who represented the village where the killing took place, not the next of kin.[18] Whichever is the case, justice was served in determining guilt.

Carrying out objective, nonemotional justice (**show no pity**) earned a common Deuteronomy blessing, **so that it will go well with you** (v. 13; cf. 4:40; 5:16,29,33; 6:3,18; 8:16, etc.). Living under the blessing of God entailed promoting justice in the land by protecting the innocent and convicting the guilty. God's holy land must remain pure so that he could dwell among his people as he promised.

Boundary Stones (19:14)

19:14 The verse is widely held to poorly fit the context. What

---

[15]The most common use of "blood" (*dām*) in the Old Testament is in the context of bloodshed through violence which often resulted in death (cf. Hos 4:2; Isa 1:15; 4:4; Jer 2:34; 2 Kgs 21:16; 24:4). The combination of "innocent" (נָקִי, *nāqî*) with "blood" (v. 13) occurs 21 times, referring to someone killed without cause, especially the powerless and blameless (Jer 2:34; 7:6; 22:3; Ps 106:38). It was a wicked act that characterized some of the most evil people and times in Israel, especially the reign of King Manasseh (2 Kgs 21).

[16]Wenham, *Numbers*, p. 236. Numerous other acts polluted the land including idolatry (spiritual adultery), covenant breaking, sexual misconduct, divorce and remarriage to the same person, etc.

[17]See Lev 25 and 27; 2 Sam 14:4-10. Ruth 4 is a different case that doesn't fit the circumstances in view in Deuteronomy.

[18]Anthony Phillips, *Ancient Israel's Criminal Law* (Oxford: Blackwell, 1970), p. 103. His strongest arguments are that there is no evidence of blood revenge in the Old Testament and that the phrase occurs only in the context of the cities of refuge. However, there does not seem to be enough evidence to come to a decisive conclusion. Craigie suggests the truth may be somewhere in between (*Deuteronomy*, p. 266).

connection is there between laws on killing and property rights? Of the many reasons offered, two make the most sense and are complementary. The law on the cities of refuge (19:1-13) recalls both Deuteronomy 4:41-43 and 3:12-17, the cities of refuge and the territorial division of the land east of the Jordan. Thus by association, a law on the sanctity of land boundaries is placed here. Furthermore, it is a common occurrence in many cultures and times that land disputes lead to conflict and often full-scale war.[19]

The law reflects the fact that the ownership of inherited land was crucial to the economic well-being and security of the family in Israel. The wisdom tradition also condemned violation of boundary lines (Prov 15:25; 22:28; 23:10-11; Job 24:2-4) implying that God was the defender of the defenseless. It was a mark of greed and abuse of power. It violated God's gift of land to each family, a gift given in sacred trust. In one famous case land grabbing included murder and earned Ahab the death sentence (1 Kgs 21:10; 22:38). Prophets made the violation of this law part of the basis for their condemnation of the nation (Hos 5:10; Isa 5:8; Micah 2:2-4).[20]

Witnesses (19:15-21)

This unit has two concerns that reflect on both the sixth and ninth commandments (5:17,20). The procedures laid out for the cities of refuge lead naturally to issues of witnesses: how many are needed for conviction (v. 15) and what about dishonest witnesses (vv. 16-21).

19:15 This law is in the same style as that of the Decalogue. It is a negative command, "One witness shall not rise up against a person . . . ." At least two witnesses were needed for conviction of any crime. This law expands the law of 17:6 that addressed only capital cases (see comments there) and agrees with its precursor in Numbers 35:30 (in the same context). Related texts forbid being a malicious witness (Exod 23:1) and condemn reluctance to be a witness (Lev 5:1). The ancient Code of Hammurabi also relied heavily on witnesses in

---

[19]For the former suggestion see Wright, *God's Land*, pp. 128-131; for the latter see Olson, *Deuteronomy*, p. 92.

[20]Land theft was a problem elsewhere as reflected in the Egyptian wisdom tradition, especially in the 11th century B.C. composition, *The Instruction of Amem-em-opet*, ch. 6 (*ANET*, p. 422; Victor H. Matthews and Don C. Benjamin, *Old Testament Parallels* [New York: Paulist Press, 1991], p. 192).

criminal cases (see below on verse 20). The importance of such a law is evident. It avoided the possibility that it would be the word of one person against another for conviction. It also was designed to prevent a powerful person from taking advantage of a weaker. The law was ingrained enough in Israelite society that even the non-Israelite queen, Jezebel, recognized she needed two witnesses to orchestrate the death of Naboth (1 Kgs 21:13).[21]

19:16-20 It was possible that a witness could try to deliberately bring a false charge against another so that it would be the word of one person against another. The person in view here is one who has a distinct animosity against another, setting out to do him deliberate harm with cold-blooded intent and hate. The act is also called **false testimony** (v. 18) and **an evil thing** (v. 20).

Many of the Psalms reveal how often this kind of thing happened (Ps 27:12; 7:14-16[15-17]; 25:19; 55). The wisdom tradition's strong words against lying witnesses (Prov 12:17; 19:5,28; 21:28; 24:28; 25:18) agree with the Psalms. On both a legal and a practical level such behavior destroyed community and violated justice.

Technically the person in view in these verses was not a witness but more like a plaintiff. He was bringing a charge that the other had to defend against.

The procedure for dealing with the situation was similar to that outlined for the judges and priests in 17:8-13. A **thorough investigation** (v. 18) had to be made by the officials to determine the truth.[22] This is consistent with the procedures outlined already in 13:14 and 17:4. The law was concerned about careful, deliberate, and nonarbitrary decisions.

---

[21]The fact that Jezebel was successful with two false witnesses shows how the justice system could be perverted by the powerful. But God intervened and pronounced a death sentence on both Jezebel and Ahab for their evil because he is on the side of the oppressed as stated in Deuteronomy. Note too the efforts of the Sanhedrin at Jesus' trial. After many tries they were able to get two of the witnesses to agree on a charge (Matt 26:59-61).

[22]To "stand in the presence of the LORD" probably means the person should come before the priests. Elsewhere in Deuteronomy it signifies appearing at the central sanctuary that God would designate (12:7,12,18; 14:23; 15:20, etc.) or being at Sinai (4:20; 9:18). But here the grammar suggests that "before the priests . . ." is in apposition to "the presence of the LORD" so that the sense is "stand in the presence of the LORD, that is, before the priests." See Deut 1:17 where the decisions of the judges are the judgment if God. However, some

The penalty was completely just. If the accusation was proven false, the perpetrator suffered the penalty of the crime with which he had charged the defendant. What he **intended to do** was turned back on him (v. 19; cf. 21). The objective was justice and deterrence (v. 20). This was a common penalty in the ancient Near East law codes. The first four laws in the Code of Hammurabi proscribe due process for false accusations and a penalty equal to the false charge, for example, death in capital cases.

19:21 Life for life, eye for eye or the *lex talionis* (exact retribution) is widely known and probably often misunderstood. It often is used as an example of the vengeful type of legal system exhibited in the Old Testament. But that is not an accurate interpretation. The intent was to guide the judge in determining the just penalty. The punishment should fit the crime, no more and no less. Therefore, it is better to translate as "Only life for life, eye for eye . . . ."[23] **Show no pity** balanced the law on the other side. There were certainly circumstances when the judge may be tempted to temper the judgment in favor of the guilty for a variety of reasons (cf. 13:8; 7:2,16). That was not just either. Only strict fairness was just.[24] Scholars debate whether compensation or fines were ever permitted. The evidence is only suggestive. Exodus 21:22 allows a fine for an unspecified injury, and Numbers 35:31 suggests that in nonmurder cases a ransom could be paid.

The laws in this chapter speak to several issues. The fundamental concerns for justice and for protection of the innocent are an important foundation for any society. It is also important for a just society that conviction of crimes not be arbitrary or open to outside influence. If it is, then justice is subverted and becomes a meaningless concept. Further, there is strong support in the Old Testament for capital punishment, but there is no support for convictions based on circumstantial evidence or lack of multiple witnesses.

---

think here the phrase also means to appear at the central sanctuary (Craigie, *Deuteronomy*, p. 270; Driver, *Deuteronomy*, p. 236).

[23]See Lamech's vengeful boast in Gen 4:23-24. That was a normal human inclination. The law protects against such excess. Revenge was forbidden in Lev 19:8.

[24]The ancient Code of Hammurabi also had similar provisions as the *lex talionis*. But it made distinctions between the upper and lower classes. If a person from the lower classes was the victim, a fine was sufficient. Later Rabbinic exegesis of this law soften it to allow for compensation (Tigay, *Deuteronomy*, p. 185).

DEUTERONOMY 20

Policies for War (20:1-20)

Chapter 20 focuses on warfare and continues the elaboration of the sixth commandment. The sixth commandment forbade premeditated murder (5:17), but killing during warfare was not forbidden. Apparently it was not considered premeditated murder. Warfare was a state-sanctioned act, not personal criminal conduct. Therefore, this text does not use the word for murder, רצח (*rṣḥ*), of the sixth commandment. It uses words like "strike down" with a sword (v. 13, נכה, *nkh*; NIV, "put to the sword") and "completely destroy" (v. 17, *ḥērem*).

The chapter is marked by the exhortation style of the sermon as seen in the admonitions to "not be afraid" (vv. 1,3). The thought is developed in four paragraphs: 1-4, the priest's assurance; 5-9, exemptions from service; 10-18, exemptions for cities; 19-20, exemptions for trees.[1]

The sermon shows the compassionate side of God. The material is not as much rules for warfare as it is fundamental principles for governing conduct in war. It concerns those who do not have to fight and those who should be spared in battle. Utter, wanton destruction in warfare is forbidden. War is still war (the verb and noun occur eleven times in the chapter), but concern for people and plants takes precedence. Deuteronomy realized that in the grim reality of human affairs one sometimes had to work for the humane among the inhumane.[2]

---

[1]The MT marks three paragraphs: 1-9, 10-18, 19-20, following the placement of the rhetorical marker "when" (*kî*).

[2]Wright, *Deuteronomy*, p. 227. Other Deuteronomy texts that deal with war issues are 21:10-14 (captive women), 23:9-14[10-15] (purity in the camp), 24:5 (similar to 20:7). The overall features of all these texts are devotion to

The chapter raises important ethical issues about the relationship of God to warfare in ancient Israel. Some of these issues have already been addressed (see above on 2:34 and ch. 7).

Do Not Be Afraid (20:1-4)

20:1 When you go to war begins exactly as case law sections. "If you go to war . . ." is grammatically possible also. The Hebrew *kî* can be translated as a conditional particle "if," or a temporal particle "when." From the context the latter seems more appropriate here. In the course of human affairs there was little doubt that Israel would be involved in warfare, especially as they moved into the Promised Land.

Moving into the land would involve conflict with armies more powerful than Israel (7:1; 9:1). One element of enemy power would be their superiority in warfare technology. The **chariot** was introduced into the ancient Near East somewhere in the middle of the second millennium B.C. In comparison to the common foot soldier based armies, chariots were high tech. They were a lightweight, swift moving platform from which warriors could fight. Most of the Syrio-Palestine city-states had them by the time Israel appeared (Josh 17:16; Judg 1:19; 1 Sam 13:5).[3] They were most useful on the flat plains. They did not become a part of Israel's arsenal until the time of David, but Solomon was the one who actually utilized them in his army.[4] Chariots coupled with superior armies provided plenty of reason for Israel to be fearful as they engaged in battle.

The message, **do not be afraid** is common in Deuteronomy, especially in the context of entering and taking the land (1:21,29; 3:2,22; 7:18). The call was for absolute trust in God because he was **with you.** It was not a call for blind faith. It was for trust in God who had already proven himself by his victory over the gods and armies of Egypt (3:22; 7:18-24; 31:6,8). The implication was that God would

---

the LORD, purity, and manifestation of humaneness (Miller, *Deuteronomy*, p. 157). These are the only instructions for war in the Old Testament.

[3]The Egyptians had them earlier (Exod 14; 15:5,19; Deut 11:4).

[4]David kept some chariots but hamstrung the horses (2 Sam 8:4). Solomon built stables and engaged in international horse and chariot trading (1 Kgs 4:26; 9:19; 10:26-29).

fight for them (1:29-33). He was not a God who performed only once. He would continue to fight on their side (v. 4).[5]

20:2-3 In ancient Mesopotamia the armies were blessed by the priests on behalf of the gods, making the wars a religious enterprise. The priests carried images of the gods, performed sacrifices and rituals and probably interpreted the omens.[6] There is none of that in the Old Testament. The **priest** here was to function as a prophet with a message from God. It was the same message that Moses gave in his introductory exhortation: trust God.

The priest's form of address, **Hear, O Israel**, was to mimic Moses' introductory words to the shema (Deut 6:3,4), a signal that the ensuing message was crucial to the people. The crux of the message was reinforced by four negative admonitions on the theme "don't be afraid" and covers the range of meaning from timidity (**fainthearted**) to **panic** (cf. 1:29; 7:21; 31:6; Josh 1:9). **Terrified** carries the idea of running away in fear. The opposite would be steadfast courage exhibited by standing anchored in place in the face of overwhelming odds. In fact Moses had already assured Israel that God would put the fear of Israel in their enemies (11:25; 7:18-21), a convincing reason why Israel should not fear.

20:4 The reason to be fearless and trusting was simple: **the LORD your God . . . will fight for you.** As he did in Egypt, he would continue to do. What Israel needed was to stand firm and watch God give them **victory** (literally, "salvation").[7] This assurance was at the heart of the concept of warfare in the Old Testament. God was a Warrior (Exod 15:3; Josh 5:13-15) and present with the army to provide the victory (1 Sam 17:47 — David's words to Goliath, "the battle is the LORD's"). The later Psalmist captured the thought, "Some trust in horses, some trust in chariots, but we trust in the name of the LORD our God" (Ps 20:7). This was not Holy War in the modern sense, but rather Yahweh war in which there was a strong judicial

---

[5]It was Israel's lack of trust that led to the first defeat when they tried to take the land from the south (1:29-33). When they finally decided they should go in, it was too late; God would no longer fight for them (1:41-42).

[6]Walton and Matthews, *Genesis–Deuteronomy*, p. 248.

[7]יָשַׁע (yš‘) is rare in Deuteronomy (28:31; 33:29) but occurs often in the Psalms in expressions of confidence that God will save his people (6:4; 18:3; 20:6; 28:9; 31:2, etc.) or in pleas for him to save (54:1; 60:5; 106:47, etc.).

element. War was one means by which the sovereign God of the universe held the nations accountable. Yahweh wars were just wars because Yahweh was a righteous judge. Nations were expected to capitulate to his control and come under his judgment.[8] This legal aspect is more prominent in some texts than in others, but it is a basic assumption behind war in the Old Testament.[9] The Canaanites were to be destroyed because they had a long history of sin and were a long-term threat to Israel's holiness. Israel had one task in these types of war, trust in God.[10]

Exemptions (20:5-9)

20:5-7 After the priests finished their exhortation, then certain **officials** were to offer exemptions to the people. These officials were apparently tribal leaders (cf. 1:15; 16:18; 29:10; 31:28) who were given leadership in the militia. The **army** was literally the "people,"

---

[8]Merrill, *Deuteronomy*, p. 282.

[9]Some clear examples are Judg 5:9-11,13; 11:15-27; Amos 1:3-5; Joel 4:1-3,9-13; 2 Chr 20:6-12. Exodus 15 suggests a water ordeal in which the guilty sink into the sea (see Robert M. Good, "The Just War in Ancient Israel," *JBL* 104 [1985]: 385-400). Yahweh's wars had the following elements: God chose the battles; he was present in the camp and in the battle; the battle required spiritual preparation and cultic purity; the ark of the covenant represented God in the battle; there was no doubt of the outcome; and God used nature to fight on his side (see Tremper Longman, "לחם," *NIDOTTE*, 2:785-789).

[10]The issue of Holy War in Israel has been debated for decades. It presents a particularly serious problem in Old Testament interpretation. Some of the issues have been discussed in the commentary already in the comments on chapters 1, 2 and 7. It is commonplace for scholars to understand Holy War as a late ideology projected back onto earlier texts (see the survey by Ben C. Ollenburger, "Gerhard von Rad's Theology of Holy War," in Gerhard von Rad, *Holy War in Ancient Israel*, tr. and ed., Marva Dawn [Grand Rapids: Eerdmans, 1991], pp. 1-33; and Millard Lind, *Yahweh Is a Warrior* [Scottdale, PA: Herald Press, 1980], pp. 23-34). However, the grounding for the concept as understood in the comments already made here is in Exodus 15. Craigie thinks there may be a certain idealistic character about this chapter though it has what he calls a thoroughly realistic theory of war (*Deuteronomy*, pp. 270-271, 57). A key, it seems to me, to gaining a proper perspective is to understand the judicial grounding behind the texts on war. Yahweh wars were not a ploy by the king and state to enlarge territory and control. They were about establishing God's people in his land and executing salvation and justice.

so it was not a standing army that was in view, but ordinary citizens called out for military service. Each new war would require a new summons.

It is significant that the king was not included in the rules for warfare at all. In the ancient Near East the main function of the king was to protect the nation from external danger by warfare, but not in Israel. That is one reason why Samuel so opposed the people's request for a king in 1 Samuel 8. They wanted a king precisely so he could lead them into war (v. 20). This request was in direct violation of Deuteronomy's theology of war.[11]

Three exemptions were offered. They demonstrate that several facets of life took precedence over war. Compassion and human freedom were to be controlling factors. In each case the qualified person was exempt to enjoy the blessings of God. The concern in each case was also that **someone else** might be able to take advantage of the house, crop, or wife. A nonrelative should not be able to gain access to the family inheritance. The reversal of these circumstances was a part of the curse language in 28:30, thus suggesting that part of the reasoning behind the law was that one could appear to be under a curse if deprived of home, crops, or wife (cf. Ps 109:9-11). The three areas were those of normal life. If that ceased, then what was the point of war?[12] The people released would be the most likely to be the ones distracted by their new responsibilities. The exemptions would probably take some of the youngest and fittest warriors. In 24:5 the new husband could stay with his wife for one year. The law on new plantings (Lev 19:23-25) forbade eating the new fruit until the fifth year, which meant the owner of a new vineyard may have received a lengthy exception. Clearly, family and community life stood above military requirements.[13]

20:8 The subject of fear is revisited. If by chance there were those who did not respond positively to the admonitions of the priest, then they were to be exempt from the army also. The reasoning seems

---

[11]See also vv. 11-12. It is difficult to see how this text of Deuteronomy could have been composed late in Israel's history and ignore the whole history of kingship which was focused on warfare in the books of Kings. See Millard Lind, *Yahweh Is a Warrior*, pp. 101-102, 154-155.

[12]Craigie, *Deuteronomy*, p. 274.

[13]Perhaps Luke 14:16-24 alludes to this text but with a negative application.

clear: the fearful or **fainthearted** would cause morale problems with the troops. This had the potential of being a significant number of people (it reduced Gideon's army from 32,000 to 10,000). Israel was not to become **disheartened** (literally, "hearts melt") because that was to be the response of the enemy (Josh 2:11; 5:1; 7:5).

An underlying principle behind these exemptions also seems to be that the army needed to be reduced enough so that the victory was clearly God's. Gideon's militia was ultimately reduced to less than ten percent of the original size (Judg 7:2, "You have too many men for me to deliver Midian into their hands.").[14]

20:9 Only at this point were military leaders appointed (**commanders**, שַׂר, *śar*). These were probably the same as those commanders over thousands, hundreds, fifties, and tens in 1:15 (Num 31:14,48). They are mentioned often in military contexts (1 Sam 8:12; 17:18; 22:7; 2 Kgs 1:9,11). As with the officials, these were not permanent positions.

Treatment of Distant Cities (20:10-15)

Directions were also given for the treatment of the enemy in war. Cities at a distance that were outside of the Promised Land were to be treated differently (vv. 10-15) than those within the land (vv. 16-18).

20:10-11 When Israel first approached a city that was distant (v. 15), it was to offer the opportunity to **make . . . peace**. This was understood in terms of surrender and submission to vassal status.[15] The objective was peaceful integration, not destructive conquest. The incident of the Gibeonites in Joshua 9 (though they deceived Joshua) illustrates the law put into effect. If the city submitted as a vassal, then they would also have to submit to **forced labor**.

20:12-15 Refusal to make peace would lead to a siege of the city and its conquest. God would do the conquering. Only the men were to be killed. There was to be no wanton destruction of people as was customary in the ancient Near East. The Assyrians were especially known for their cruelty: impaling people, skinning them alive, and leading them into captivity with hooks. A common custom appar-

---

[14]In fact one aim of Judges 7 may be to illustrate the practicality of this verse.

[15]Donald J. Wiseman, "Is It Peace? Covenant and Diplomacy," *VT* 32 (1982): 311-326.

ently was violent slaughter of pregnant women (Amos 1:3,13; Hos 13:16; 2 Kgs 8:12). Israel's treatment of captive women, on the other hand, was to be quite restrained (cf. 21:10-14).

This law on siege and killing the men was not rigorously applied in Israel's history. In fact Israel's kings earned a reputation for mercy (1 Kgs 20:31). Further, Elisha once counseled a king to feed and release his prisoners of war (2 Kgs 6:20-23). Perhaps this law was understood as a concession and was to be applied only in rare cases.[16]

Treatment of Canaanite Cities (20:16-18)

20:16-18 Cities in the Promised Land were to be treated differently. They were to be subjected to total destruction by instituting the ḥērem (see on 2:34 and 7:2).[17] The reasoning (v. 18) is the same that has been advanced elsewhere in Deuteronomy: the spiritual danger the Canaanites would pose to Israel with the temptation to idolatry and syncretism (12:31; 14:1; 18:9-13). Because of the Canaanites' wickedness God was going to use Israel as his instrument of judgment on them.

Treatment of Fruit Trees (20:19-20)

20:19-20 The law takes a surprising turn, allowing for exemptions even for trees. In ancient warfare the siege of cities took a great deal of wood. Armies needed to build siege machines, siege towers, ladders, ramps for the machines, and support for tunneling (cf. 2 Sam 20:15; Jer 6:6; Ezek 4:12; 21:22).[18] The Assyrians would customarily clear the entire area around a city of its trees during a siege. It was also common practice to destroy the fields and render

---

[16]See Derek Kidner, "Old Testament Perspectives on War," *EvQ* 57 (1985): 99-113.

[17]The principle was applied in the cases of Jericho (Josh 6), Ai (Josh 8:25-27) and Hazor (Josh 11:10-11). Judges 1:27 and 35 imply that it was not consistently carried out in the conquest period. Rather some inhabitants of the Promised Land were subjected to forced labor instead. This was interpreted as God testing Israel (2:22; 3:1). Saul's pattern of disobedience included violating Samuel's command of ḥērem for the Amalekites (1 Sam 15).

[18]The article by Hershel Shanks, "Destruction of Judean Fortress Portrayed in Dramatic Eighth-Century B.C. Pictures,"*BAR* 10, 2 (1984): 48-65, has pictures of Assyrian reliefs showing the conquest of Lachish.

them unusable.[19] There was a very practical reason for the law: Why should Israel destroy something they would benefit from later? But there was a theological reason as well. The land was God's gift and should be treated with respect. There was to be no wanton destruction of the people, so there should be no wanton destruction of the land or its vegetation. Further, fruit trees were in a different category than people, incapable of rebellion and a gift of God for their benefit. Therefore, they should also be treated well.[20] The ecological restraint of this law is remarkable. It pronounces a condemnation on many military practices through the ages into modern times.[21]

The theology of warfare in Deuteronomy 20 was intended to prevent assimilation to the common ancient Near Eastern standards. Israel was powerless and called to trust totally in God's miraculous intervention. Yahweh did not work through her army to win battles, but won them himself. Consequently, a standing army was not required and only a few fearless volunteers were needed. Yahweh as true king was the only savior of Israel, not the earthly king or army. The Exodus event was the paradigm of victory and salvation. Therefore, Israel was required only to obey God and trust in him.[22]

---

[19]The Egyptian Pharaoh Thutmosis III (15th century B.C.) described the siege of Megiddo in detail (*ANET*, pp. 234-238).

[20]The meaning of the text of the last part of verse 19 is unclear as is reflected in the NIV footnote. It is not clear whether the text is a question. Further, other ancient versions have a negative with "man" suggesting that trees are not men that threaten cities or people. The law was set aside when God commanded Israel through Elisha to destroy everything in Moab (2 Kgs 3:19,25).

[21]The text raises ecological concerns too complex to address here. See such works as Tony Campolo, *How to Rescue the Earth without Worshiping Nature* (Nashville: Thomas Nelson, 1991), and Lionel Basney, *An Earth-Careful Way of Life* (Downers Grove, IL: InterVarsity, 1994).

[22]Lind, *Yahweh Is a Warrior*, pp. 156-157.

DEUTERONOMY 21

Issues of Death and Life (21:1-23)

This section continues to expand on the implications of the sixth commandment, "You shall not murder" (Deut 5:17). It consists of five paragraphs of case law, each paragraph beginning with the conditional particle כִּי (*kî*). The paragraphs are 1) 1-9, 2) 10-14, 3) 15-17, 4) 18-21, and 5) 22-23).[1] The case laws continue into chapter 22 (vv. 4,6,13, etc.).

Though some scholars are unable to find an orderly arrangement in the chapter,[2] there are some rhetorical clues to suggest careful work. The section is marked by an inclusio in verses 1 and 23, "the land the LORD your God is giving you to possess (as an inheritance)." There is a repeated admonition at the end of the laws in the first paragraph and the fourth paragraph (vv. 9 and 21), "you must purge" the guilt or the evil. The overriding theme is the juxtaposition of death and life. The issue of death is obvious in paragraphs 1, 4, and 5. It is more subtle in paragraphs 2 and 3. The captive woman (para. 2, vv. 10-14) must be allowed to mourn for her parents (v. 13) as if they were dead, for she will likely never see them again. The law of the firstborn (vv. 15-17) brings together the impending death of the father and the right of the firstborn to carry on his life. It was an issue that should have been settled at the birth of the son.[3]

Wenham and McConville have suggested a chiastic arrangement to the chapter: a dead body polluting the LORD's land (vv. 1-9 and 22-23); a captive slave girl mourning her parents and a rebellious

---

[1]There are four other *kî* particles in the chapter but they have different meanings (vv. 5,9,17, and 23).

[2]Thompson, *Deuteronomy*, pp. 224-225.

[3]See Calum M. Carmichael, "A Common Element in Five Supposedly Disparate Laws," *VT* 29 (1979): 129-142.

son executed by parents (vv. 10-13 and 18-21); and an unloved captive girl receiving freedom and an unloved firstborn son receiving inheritance (vv. 14 and 15-17).[4] Though the analysis may be weak in some details (breaking v. 14 off from its paragraph), it demonstrates the chapter was given careful thought. There is a direct link between paragraphs 1 and 4 with their several references to the "elders of the village" (vv. 2,3,4,19,20) and "purging" (vv. 9,21).

Atoning for an Unsolved Murder (21:1-9)

21:1 This first paragraph provided guidelines for dealing with a case of homicide or manslaughter without witnesses. Previous instructions had assumed witnesses were present (ch. 19; Num 35). But this law makes it clear that even if the killer was unknown the case could not be left open. Bloodshed defiled the land and the people (Gen 9:5-6; Num 35:33), and expiation had to take place.

If a man is found slain refers to a person who was struck in such a way that blood was shed. Furthermore, the person was "struck down" (NIV, **killed**).[5] The violent nature of the death is emphasized. The body was found in a **field**, out in open country away from villages and people. The word could refer to either cultivated land or uninhabited open country. The point is that the death occurred where no one saw it.

It is not known presumes that an investigation took place according to the instructions of 17:4. Probably the law could have covered a similar situation in town (cf. 22:23-27) though it was very likely there would have always been witnesses.

Two assumptions underlie this law, one stated, one implied. First, the **land** was God's land that he was **giving** Israel **to possess**. Therefore, what happened anywhere in the land was of great importance. Cases of violent human death were especially serious (Gen 9:5-6). Secondly, corporate responsibility in ancient Israel meant

---

[4]G.J. Wenham and J.C. McConville, "Drafting Techniques in Deuteronomy Laws," *VT* 30 (1980): 251.

[5]The noun translated "man" by the NIV comes from the Hebrew חלל (*ḥll*) which comes from a root meaning "to pierce," most commonly referring to those slain in battle by the sword (Isa 22:2; Jer 14:18; Ezek 32:20,21,25). The NRSV provides a more literal rendering of the verse: "If . . . a body is found lying in open country and it is not known who struck the person down . . . ."

that the community of Israel was responsible for everything that occurred, even a crime for which individual guilt could not be ascertained.

21:2 The **elders and judges** were probably a group from surrounding towns (16:18) though it has been suggested that they were the central tribunal of 17:8-13.[6] The nearest town was held responsible under the assumption that the perpetrator was most likely to come from there. The involvement of the elders and judges, and later the priests (v. 5), indicated the serious nature of the situation.

21:3-4 The details of the ceremony to atone for the shed blood are clear. However, their significance is unclear and widely debated. There are two main possibilities. The ceremony could have represented vicarious execution of the unknown criminal and therefore the heifer would function as a substitute. On the other hand it could signify a symbolic reenactment of the murder in an uninhabited place. The guilt was removed and washed away. This would identify it as an "elimination rite" similar to the released bird (Lev 14:17) and the scapegoat (Lev 16:20-27). These kinds of rites were widely performed in ancient Hittite and Mesopotamian cultures.[7]

The chosen animal was a **heifer** or cow that had never been used for work and was uncontaminated by humans (cf. Gen 15:9; Num 19:2; 1 Sam 16:2; Isa 7:21). She was taken into a wadi (**valley**) that also had not been contaminated by human activity (**plowed or planted**). The wadi was also to have **flowing** water (cf. Amos 5:24; Ps 74:15). This instruction seems unusual since there were few constantly flowing streams in Israel.[8] Therefore it would seem to have limited the

---

[6]Compare Tigay, *Deuteronomy*, p. 191, with Craigie, *Deuteronomy*, p. 279.

[7]Cf. Wright, *Deuteronomy*, pp. 232-233; Tigay, *Deuteronomy*, pp. 473-474; and David P. Wright, "Deuteronomy 21:1-9 as a Rite of Elimination," *CBQ* 49 (1987): 387-403. Hittite and Babylonian laws also addressed unsolved crimes. Their concern was not with blood guilt, but with the compensation of the victim's family. See H.A. Hoffner, Jr., "Some Contributions of Hittitology to Old Testament Study," *TB* 20 (1969): 39; Anthony Phillips, "Another Look at Murder," *JJS* 28 (1977): 125; and Craigie, *Deuteronomy*, p. 279, note 1. The relevant laws are Hittite law # 6 (*ANET*, p. 189) and Hammurabi Code, # 23 and 24 (*ANET*, p. 167).

[8]See Denis Baly, *The Geography of the Bible*, rev. ed. (New York: Harper and Row, 1974), pp. 13-14. Most streams were in Galilee and almost none were in Samaria and Judah. Tigay gives the number as 18 (*Deuteronomy*, p. 381, note 15).

places where the ceremony could have been conducted. Apparently the water was necessary to symbolically carry away the guilt.[9]

The **heifer's neck** was to be broken;[10] so it was not a sacrifice that was to be performed. Sacrifices required slaughtering the animal and draining the blood (Leviticus 1, 3–4). Breaking the neck would not result in bloodshed, which would have only further polluted the ground.[11]

21:5 The priests were involved because of the cultic nature of the ceremony. Also since the case was a difficult one, perhaps they were present as a part of the higher court that was to decide difficult cases (Deut 17:8-13).[12]

21:6-8 The focus of this law was the ceremony performed by **the elders of the town nearest the body**. The shedding of blood that brought pollution upon the people and the land had to be atoned for in order to restore purity to the land. The purification was achieved by the washing of the hands which symbolized both a declaration of innocence (Ps 26:6; 73:13) and an acceptance of the responsibility for the dead.[13] The act was similar to laying on of hands on the scapegoat or the sacrificial animal. In a symbolic way the washing transferred the guilt to the running water which floated it away.[14] The necessity of such an act was grounded in the theology of Genesis 9:5-6. Life was God's and the shedding of any blood had to be addressed. According to Numbers 35:33 shedding of the blood of the guilty was the only way atonement for shed blood could be made. It was impossible in this case, but still a life had to be given for a life.

---

[9]Wright, "Deuteronomy 21:1-9," pp. 397-398.

[10]The only other situation calling for a breaking of the neck was the case of the unredeemed, firstborn donkey (Exod 13:13; 34:20). It would have been done away from the altar.

[11]I agree here with Carmichael, "A Common Element," pp. 132-133, rather than with Wright, "Deuteronomy 21:1-9," p. 394. Wright thinks the flowing water was needed to carry away the shed blood of the heifer and that "this blood" of verse 7 referred to both the blood of the heifer and the victim. However, it seems more likely that the breaking of the heifer's neck was the chosen means of killing because it would not shed blood.

[12]For other duties of priests as portrayed in Deuteronomy see 18:1-8; 20:2; 24:8; 26:1-11; 31:9.

[13]The word for "washing" (רחץ, *rḥṣ*) is often used in Leviticus in contexts of purification rites, Lev 14–16.

[14]For the use of water in purification rites see Lev 14:5; 15:13 and 19:17.

Our hands did not shed this blood referred to the blood of the murder victim, not the blood of the heifer. The statement would make no sense if referring to the heifer since the elders were the ones who killed it (v. 4). The statement also included the assurance that they did not know who did it.

The **atonement** brought about the reconciliation of the people to God, a relationship that had been disrupted by the guilt of the shed blood. The appeal to God for cleansing was grounded solely in the mercy of God. Israel was God's people who were inheriting the land only because he had **redeemed** them from Egypt (1:27; 4:34,37; 5:6; 6:12), a redemption of grace. Because of God's grace Israel could have confidence that her appeal would be heard and honored.

21:9 The ceremony would be effective and restore the people and land to the right relationship with God. It would **purge** ("burn out") the **innocent blood** (17:7,12; 19:13; 21:21).[15] To do **what is right** is generally understood in Deuteronomy to refer to being obedient to the law, to know what to do and to do it.

Maintaining the purity of the whole community in order to be holy before God (7:6; 14:2) required that even an unsolved murder be dealt with. The total community was involved, for the moral guilt was not individual but nationwide. Therefore, ultimately it did not matter who had done the deed, the guilt still had to be removed. This way of thinking is far removed from modern cultures and their obsession with individual rights.

Treatment of a Captive Girl (21:10-14)

21:10 The second paragraph begins exactly as chapter 20:1 with the addition of a phrase from verse 13, and is a further reflection on that law. It is perhaps placed here because it does not deal directly with rules for warfare, but rather with a possible domestic situation arising from warfare.[16] It assumes that the war was successful and

---

[15] For other situations where innocent blood is the issue see Deut 19:1-13; Jer 26:15; Jonah 1:14.

[16] In fact many commentators understand 20:10-14 to be the first of a series of laws related to domestic or family life and civil affairs that goes through chapter 25 (see Tigay, Mayes, Merrill, and Driver).

presupposes that the situation of 20:10-15 applied. The war in question was against a distant city and not a Canaanite city.[17]

21:11 The NIV translation suggests the law is conditional (**if you notice . . . you may take her**), but it is better to understand it as concessive (see NRSV, "suppose you see . . . and so bring her "[v. 12]).[18] It is assumed that both the captive woman and the soldier were unmarried. Although Deuteronomy law recognizes polygamy (see following section, vv. 15-17), it does not promote it.

Most captives taken in warfare in the ancient Near East were subjected to slavery (cf. 20:14; Judg 5:30). Rulers sometimes took women captives as concubines.[19] This law required that any such practice within Israel be conducted with compassion and concern for the woman. She was to be married, not raped and abused.[20]

A young soldier may be **attracted to** a captive. It would be too strong to suggest that the passion involved was lust. The word חשק (ḥšq) denotes a desire for or love that could be genuine. The closest parallel to this text is Shechem's love for Dinah that developed after he raped her (Gen 34:8). Shechem's love became the basis for his willingness to submit to circumcision in order to marry her. The word is also used in Deuteronomy of God's desire or love for Israel (7:7; 10:15).

21:12-13 The woman was allowed time to make the adjustment to her new situation. It included time to properly **mourn** her parents who may have been killed in the war. If not, they were as good as dead to her for she would not see them again.[21]

She was to **shave her head, trim her nails, and put aside the clothes she was wearing when captured**. Probably these were signs of mourning and transformation to her totally new life. A shaved head was a sign of mourning in Israel (cf. Amos 8:10; Micah 1:16; Jer 41:5; 48:37 [of Moab]; Ezek 7:18). It was also a part of cleansing rites

---

[17]The law does not conflict with the admonition of 7:3 as Mayes thinks (*Deuteronomy*, p. 303).

[18]There is a subtle hint in the text that the practice is disapproved of but grudgingly allowed. See the discussion below.

[19]Tigay, *Deuteronomy*, p. 194. Later Jewish teachers took a dim view of marrying a captive woman. It was allowed only if she converted to Judaism.

[20]Wright, *Deuteronomy*, p. 234.

[21]See Ps 45:10(11) where the bride is called upon to forget her parents.

after being healed of a disease or taking a vow (Lev 13 and 14; Num 6). Shaving the front of the head for the dead, on the other hand, was a pagan practice forbidden in Deuteronomy 14:1. The discarding of the old clothes perhaps signaled her incorporation into her new community.[22] The thirty-day mourning period was customary, and was identical to the thirty days set aside to mourn for Aaron (Num 20:29) and Moses (Deut 34:8).[23]

21:14 It was possible that not every marriage under these circumstances would be successful. Therefore, divorce was allowed.[24] The young man's initial desire for the woman could wane.[25] If so, he could not treat her as a slave or concubine but had to treat her as a woman with her own dignity and rights. This instruction was important for the well being of the woman, for the man had almost absolute power over the woman.[26] This case is similar to the law protecting the daughter who was sold as a servant and then taken into the family as a wife (Exod 21:7-11). She too had her rights and could win her freedom if mistreated.

The **dishonor** the man would bring on the woman by wanting to divorce her was akin to the dishonor Shechem brought on Dinah with his initial rape (Gen 34:2).[27] The charge was a serious one and

---

[22]Mayes, *Deuteronomy*, p. 303. It seems somewhat unusual that there are no strictures against pagan religious influence, especially in the light of the previous warnings in 7:3-4 (as Thompson has pointed out [*Deuteronomy*, p. 228]). One possible response is that the law at this point is primarily concerned about the humane treatment of the woman. The book of Ruth illustrates the fact that foreign women might readily convert.

[23]According to Jewish teaching shaving the head would make her more unattractive to the young man. Also the month in his house may discourage him even further (Tigay, *Deuteronomy*, p. 194).

[24]"Let her go" (NIV) translates the Hebrew word usually used for divorce (שׁלח, *šlḥ* – send away; Deut 24:1).

[25]The Hebrew word translated "pleased" is a synonym for "attracted" in verse 11.

[26]The word translated "treat her as a slave" is rare (only here and in Deut 24:7) but apparently refers to either exercising undue force or treating her as a commodity and not as a person (see Mayes, *Deuteronomy*, pp. 303-304, and Craigie, *Deuteronomy*, p. 282).

[27]For the use of the verb ענה (*'nh*) in similar contexts in which a woman has been dishonored see Judg 19:24; 20:5; 2 Sam 13:12,14,22; Ezek 22:10,11.

could bring dishonor on the man as well. There was perhaps a subtle disapproval of the whole arrangement by the rather obscure parallels to the Shechem/Dinah narrative of Genesis 34 (see verse 11 above). The law was a concession, but Moses disapproved of the practice and tried to direct as many negative comments toward it as possible. The law's subtle hints through word choice and the careful concern for the captive woman may have become a significant factor in discouraging such a practice.

The Right of the Firstborn (21:15-17)

The third paragraph in this chapter concerns the inheritance right of the firstborn son. It has several possible connections to its contexts. Wenham's chiastic structure (see above) connects it to verse 14; both parties received the freedom and inheritance due them. Carmichael sees the issue of life and death continued here. As the father faces death, he is reminded of the life force that he produced.[28] Some have suggested that the unloved wife of this section may be the captive wife of the previous law after the husband eventually married an Israelite woman.[29] There is a close connection to the law that follows (vv. 18-21) also. This law protects the rights of the son against an unfair father. The next law protects the rights of the parents against a rebellious son.

The law protects a custom that went back to Patriarchal times (Gen 25:31-34, Jacob and Esau; Gen 48:8-22, Manasseh and Ephraim). The custom of the oldest son inheriting the first portion of his father's estate becomes law here (v. 17 — *mišpat*).[30]

21:15 The law accepts bigamy but does not sanction it. Monogamy was God's intention for marriage from the beginning (Gen 2:24), but polygamy (bigamy) was soon practiced in the line of Cain (Gen 4:19). Later, Jacob the patriarch had two wives, and two con-

---

[28]Carmichael, "A Common Element," p. 136.

[29]Merrill, *Deuteronomy*, p. 292.

[30]Carmichael has offered the interesting suggestion that the law functions as a negative comment on Jacob's treatment of his firstborn son, Reuben. Because of his conduct Reuben did not receive his rightful inheritance (cf. Gen 35:22; 49:3-4) (Calum M. Carmichael, "Uncovering a Major Source of Mosaic Law: The Evidence of Deuteronomy 21:15–22:5," *JBL* 101 [1982]: 506-508).

cubines given him by his wives (Gen 29–30). The kings, including David (2 Sam 3:2-5) and Solomon (1 Kgs 11:3), had multiple wives as well. Although polygamy may have been accepted, its cost would have limited it to the wealthy, such as royalty.[31] Also, as this law recognizes, more than one wife created considerable tension in the home (1 Sam 1:6-7).

If there were more than one wife, it would no doubt be common that one might be preferred over the other. The Hebrew text uses the idiom of loving one and hating the other (see Gen 29:30-33) which the NIV has softened to **he loves one and not the other**. This translation gives the sense of the idiom for it refers to preferring one over the other (cf. Mal 1:2-3, referring to election) not to actual hatred.[32]

The place of the **firstborn** (בְּכוֹר, *bekôr*) was important to Israelite society. The firstborn son became the next head of the family, embodying its character and spirit. He also became responsible for its continuance and welfare. The genealogical lists show this importance. The firstborn was first on the list, the family line continued through him, and all other family members were listed in relationship to him. The firstborn also held sacred status in Israel. He was holy to the LORD and needed to be redeemed (Num 3:11-13,40-51; 18:14-16).[33]

21:16 It was absolutely crucial then that the firstborn be given his rightful inheritance (**property**).[34] The father could not arbitrarily

---

[31]See R. de Vaux, *Ancient Israel*, 1:24-26. Muslim law allows four wives, but in modern Arab cultures there is rarely more than one. A contributing factor for polygamy in the ancient cultures could have been the barrenness of the first wife (though not for this law), the desire for more children, or the desire for more help in the household. These reasons reflect a patriarchal system in a fallen world in which lust and power pervert God's plan.

[32]See Jesus' use of the idiom in Luke 14:26. To put Jesus first was to hate the family, that is, to prefer Jesus before them.

[33]See *IDB* 2:270-272, s.v. "Firstborn," and *IDBS*, pp. 337-338, s.v. "Firstborn." It is interesting that the laws of redemption in Numbers refer to the firstborn of the woman. A related issue of how to handle inheritance if there were no sons was precipitated early when Zelophehad died with five daughters as his only heirs (Num 27:1-11). The result was a new law governing dispersal of the inheritance under several contingencies.

[34]This verse is the only reference in Deuteronomy to personal inheritance. Every other reference is to the land that God was giving as a free gift to Israel (1:38; 3:28; 12:10; 19:3; 31:7; cf. Jer 3:18; 12:14).

choose someone else (that such a law was needed suggests fathers were doing so). The frequent theme in Genesis of the younger gaining ascendancy over the older (Isaac over Ishmael, Jacob over Esau, Joseph over his brothers, Ephraim over Manasseh) provides a dissonant background to this law. However, in each case in Genesis it was a divine decision.

21:17 The rightful inheritance was a **double share** to the firstborn. Apparently the inheritance was divided up into one more share than there were sons and the oldest was given two shares.[35] This was no doubt an economic necessity considering the extra responsibilities the oldest had after the father died. The firstborn's importance was tied to the fact that his birth had been proof of the father's generative **strength,** which assured the passing on of the family line. This phrase ties the law directly to Genesis 49:3. Though Reuben did not get his rightful inheritance, he was still proof of Jacob's fertility.

Treatment of a Rebellious Son (21:18-21)

The law on the rebellious son fits into its context in a variety of complementary ways. According to Wenham's chiastic structure it corresponds to the captive wife in that it anticipates separation and death.[36] It is tied to the previous law in that both limit parental authority.[37] The law on inheritance does not allow the father to play favorites, and this law restricts absolute authority of the parent over

---

[35]The expression translated "double share" is literally "mouth of two." The idiom also appears with the same meaning in 1 Kgs 2:9 (Elisha's request for a double share of Elijah's spirit). It occurs in these two places without any other numbers. However, it also appears in Zech 13:8 in conjunction with another number and means two-thirds. E.W. Davies has established that the former situation means multiplication but the latter indicates a fraction (Eryl W. Davies, "The Meaning of *pî suenayim* in Deuteronomy 21:17," *VT* 36 [1986]: 341-347). The Greek translation (the LXX) and other old versions also understood the idiom to mean double portion. Therefore, though there has been some debate about the term, it seems to clearly mean "double share" here (for a dissenting opinion see P. Watson, "A Note on the 'Double Portion' of Deuteronomy 21:17 and II Kings 2:9," *RestQ* 8 [1965]: 70-75).

[36]See also Carmichael, "Common Elements," p. 137.

[37]Tigay, *Deuteronomy*, p. 196.

the child. The matter must be brought to the village elders for resolution. This law also answers a question that might have been raised by the previous law: was there ever a circumstance when a son could lose the inheritance? The answer is yes. The case of Esau in Genesis 26:35 would seem to fit this law.[38]

This law provides additional comment on both the fifth and sixth commandments. It provides the penalty for dishonoring parents but is placed in the context of comments on the sixth commandment because rebellion against parents was a capital case. It is also closely related to Exodus 21:15,17; Lev 20:9 (cf. Deut 27:16).

Ancient Near Eastern law codes addressed children's treatment of parents, from outright rebellion to physical assault. The penalty was normally disinheritance or some type of mutilation such as cutting out the tongue or cutting off the hand. None required the death penalty, and in this regard the Deuteronomy law is more stringent.[39]

21:18 The setting for the case implies an ongoing attempt by the parents to correct a child with a persistent character flaw. The son was **stubborn and rebellious** (סרר, *srr*, and מרה, *mrh*). These two words together indicate an outright rejection of the authority of and a relationship to the parent. The object of the law was an adult son or one approaching adulthood who had rejected the family altogether.[40]

The mindset of the son can be gauged by the use of similar terminology applied to Israel in Deuteronomy and throughout the Old Testament. Israel was a stubborn and rebellious nation (Ps 78:8; Jer 5:23 — same two words) which meant that they had turned against God and broken the covenant. Deuteronomy often refers to Israel's rebellious nature (1:26,43; 9:7,23,24), a rebellion that prevented them from receiving the Promised Land the first time and jeopardized their future life in it.[41] Because of this rebellion Israel stood under the judgment of God.

---

[38]Carmichael, "Uncovering," pp. 508-511.

[39]See the Code of Hammurabi, # 168, 169, 192, 195 (*ANET*, pp. 173, 175).

[40]It is not addressing the occasional ornery child or rebellious two-year-old. The law is less harsh than it appears to the modern eye. See Elizabeth Bellefontaine, "Deuteronomy 21:18-21: Reviewing the Case of the Rebellious Son," *JSOT* 13 (1979): 13-31.

[41]For *srr* used of Israel elsewhere see Isa 30:1; 65:2; Jer 6:28; Hos 4:16; Zech 7:11; Neh 9:29. For *mrh* used of Israel elsewhere see Isa 3:8; 63:10; Jer 4:17; Lam 1:18,20; Ezek 5:6; 20:8,13,21.

The metaphorical picture of God as father and Israel as rebellious son is also instructive. Hosea 11 presents the most extended reflection. Israel the son rebelled against the loving father and earned judgment. Isaiah 1:2 used a court setting in which the father charged the son with rebellion.

Within the above context the nature of the rebellious son comes into focus. He was one who had persistently rejected both parental authority and the family. He had, by intent and actions, broken the family covenant. He had perhaps stated, "You are not my parents," or at least indicated so by his actions.[42]

Furthermore, the son had repeatedly resisted the **discipline** of the parents. He rejected their early efforts to instill values and norms of conduct by verbal instruction, and later rebukes and physical chastisements. Nothing they had done over his lifetime had been effective. They had apparently followed the admonitions found in the book of Proverbs but with no result (Prov 19:18; 29:15,17; 13:24; 23:13).

21:19 As a last resort the **father and mother** were to take the son to the **elders of the gate of his town**.[43] Both parents were responsible to take the son (two witnesses?) to the village leaders who would decide the case. In other words, the parents did not have absolute authority over the son. The family matter became a civil matter.[44]

In ancient Israel the family was the foundation of authority and the social structure for the village and ultimately the nation. Dysfunction in the family endangered the larger society. Therefore, the rebellious son was not just a concern for the family, he was a concern for the village. He threatened a host of structures which kept the social fabric intact, including family inheritance, family name, care for widows and orphans, and leadership in the village. As a rebellious covenant breaker he also ultimately threatened the covenant with God. Under these circumstances family dysfunction could not be a private affair.

---

[42]See the statement of divorce in Hosea 2:2 ("you are not my wife") which is the opposite of 2:19-20. The Code of Hammurabi no. 192 provides a penalty for the adopted son who later said "You are not my father, You are not my mother."

[43]On the importance of the city gate see on 17:5 and Ruth 4.

[44]In contrast to Judah who could condemn his daughter-in-law to death without trial (Gen 38:24; see also Gen 42:37; Judg 11:34-40).

21:20 In addition to being rebellious the son was also charged with reprehensible behavior, being a glutton (NIV, **profligate**) and a **drunkard**. It is curious why these two additional charges were made. They were in themselves not capital crimes. Perhaps they are offered as further evidence of the absolutely derelict character of the son.[45] There is probably another connection to the nation, for Israel's rebellious sins in the wilderness had to do with food (Exod 16; Num 11; Deut 8:3,16) and drink (Exod 17:1-7; Num 20:2-13; Deut 8:15). Such subtle hints reinforce the impression that the rebellious son was a microcosm of the rebellious nation.

21:21 Though the brief law does not mention an investigation, we are probably to assume one was undertaken following the law in 17:4 and 19:18. The penalty was to be carried out by the entire village though the parents apparently did not take part (contrary to 17:7). The admonition to **purge out the evil from among you** underscores the seriousness of the situation (cf v. 9; 13:5; 17:7,12; 19:19; 22:21,24; 24:7). The case of the rebellious son was equal to a host of other cases that threatened the purity of the holy people of God. Evil had to be eradicated to maintain the covenant relationship with a holy God.

Commentators debate if the penalty was meant literally or only as a rhetorical device for motivation. The intended fear could be engendered just by the threat without any actual occurrences. There are no records of this penalty ever being enforced in the Old Testament.[46]

Proper Burial of a Criminal's Body (21:22-23)

The final paragraph in chapter 21 is a brief law about leaving a body hung on a tree. In the chiastic structure noted for this chapter this paragraph parallels the first paragraph, verses 1-9.[47] Both sec-

---

[45]See the same phrases in Prov 23:20-21.

[46]Jewish rabbinic teaching put so many strictures on the law that it could hardly be carried out (Tigay, *Deuteronomy*, p. 382, n. 50). Some have pointed out David's reluctance to discipline his sons, but his behavior seems more of a parental defect than any commentary on this law. Proverbs 30:17 sees this kind of son coming to a natural bad end (by the wrath of God?).

[47]For another view see Merrill (*Deuteronomy*, p. 295) who puts this paragraph with 22:1-8 with the title "Laws Concerning Preservation of Life."

tions are concerned with a dead body defiling the land. This law is also case law like the other paragraphs in the chapter.

21:22 The law is concerned with the disposition of the body of those who had been convicted of a capital crime and executed.[48] Execution was customarily by stoning, not hanging (Lev 22:2,27; Num 15:35; Deut 13:10; 17:5; 21:21; 22:21). Apparently in some cases (all cases?) after execution the body was hung up on a tree as a way to both dishonor the body and deter others from such criminal activity. The law did not require hanging up the body, but dealt with its disposition **if** it was hung up.

Old Testament history records a few instances of bodies being hung up, mostly in military contexts and mostly to degrade the person (Josh 8:29; 10:26-27; 2 Sam 4 and 21). One case involved idolatry (Num 25:4). It also records the practice among the Egyptians (Gen 40:19) and the Philistines (1 Sam 31:8-10). It was an Assyrian custom to impale the bodies of inhabitants of conquered cities.[49]

21:23 The hanging up of the body was for a brief time. It could not be left **on the tree overnight**. This requirement effectively curtailed any extensive exposure that would have allowed the body to decay or be eaten by birds or animals. Joshua acted in obedience to this law in the conquest period (Josh 8:29 and 10:26).

Although this law does not clarify why a body hanging up is under a curse of God, elsewhere exposure of the body was intimately connected with covenant curses. Thus part of the punishment, foretold in the curse section of Deuteronomy, was the dead bodies of the people being left for wild animals to eat (Deut 28:26). Jeremiah announced the curse of unburied bodies for disobedient Israel (9:22; 16:4; 19:7; 34:20; 36:30). This law, however, differs from the covenant curses in the limited exposure the body was to receive. Nevertheless, the criminal, as a breaker of the law and therefore the covenant, was **under God's curse**. He had lived as though the covenant did not matter.[50]

---

[48]The NIV is somewhat inconsistent in translating the Hebrew here as "capital offense." The almost identical Hebrew phrase also occurs in Deuteronomy 19:6 and 22:26 where the NIV translates "deserving death." In Jeremiah 26:11,16 the NIV translates the phrase as "sentenced to death."

[49]See the reliefs from Sennacherib's palace of his defeat of Lachish (Shanks, "Destruction of Judean Fortress," pp. 48-65).

[50]Craigie, *Deuteronomy*, p. 285.

Overnight exposure would somehow **desecrate** the land. According to the law, touching dead bodies made one unclean (Lev 11:39; Num 19:11-13). Bloodshed also polluted the land and defiled it (Num 35:33-34). Therefore, perhaps the body was to be buried soon to avoid parts of it being scattered about and bringing uncleanness to the land.[51]

---

[51]Ezekiel seems to reflect the same idea by requiring the burial of Gog's army to cleanse the land (Ezek 39:11-16; see Tigay, *Deuteronomy*, p. 198).

DEUTERONOMY 22

Issues of Life and Death Continued (22:1-8)

The first verses in chapter 22 complete the section that began in 19:1 as an elaboration of the sixth commandment, "You shall not murder" (5:17). These laws however are brief, loosely connected, and address more directly issues of life. They fit into the larger context because they demonstrate that the sixth commandment also had a positive side. Life was to be protected and enhanced. The law in verse 8, which comes at the end of the larger section (19:1–22:8), rounds the section off by recalling the concern for blood guilt in the law in 19:1-13. The law in verse 5 seems out of place, but it is to be understood as anticipatory, transitioning to the laws related to the seventh commandment in 22:9 to 23:18.[1]

22:1 Verses 1-4 are closely related to each other with their concern for a neighbor's property. The emphasis was on taking responsibility for someone else's possessions. The command, **"Do not ignore it"** (vv. 1,3,5) both binds the verses together and lays a demand on the Israelite. In an agricultural economy like ancient Israel, loose and runaway animals would have been commonplace.[2]

The version of this law in Exodus 23:4-5 refers to the enemies' stray animals. Deuteronomy's main focus throughout is on the covenant community, so the law here only mentions the **brother's** animals.[3]

---

[1]Olson, *Deuteronomy*, p. 98.

[2]The NIV translation is misleading. The law is not expressed in the familiar conditional language with "if" as the translation has it. Rather the law is stated as a negative command, "Do not watch . . . and ignore them . . . ." It was not an issue if animals would stray. They would. What to do about them was the issue. The most important event in Saul's early life occurred as he was searching for his father's lost animals (1 Sam 9). Poetic references to Israel as a lost or stray animal are common – Isa 53:6; Jer 23:1-4; 50:6,7; Ezek 34:4,16; Micah 4:6; Zeph 3:19; Ps 119:176.

[3]References to the covenant community via the use of the word "brother" occur 48 times in Deuteronomy.

22:2-3 Since Deuteronomy anticipated life in the land, the law expanded on the Exodus version by explaining what was to be done with the animal if for some reason it could not be returned right away. The finder was to take full responsibility for caring for the animal. Not only was the finder to take the animal home, he was to take it "into the midst of the house." Most Israelite homes, especially two-story ones, included a courtyard which served as shelter for the livestock at night. Presumably the finder bore any expense involved.

The law applied not only to stray animals, but to **anything** that the neighbor lost. A threefold repetition in the Hebrew text of **do the same** highlights the responsibility the Israelite had for another's property.[4]

22:4 Another similar circumstance would be encountering a fallen pack animal on the road. Assistance should be provided to it as well.[5] We probably are to assume that the owner was present but needed help to get the animal back on its feet.

22:5 This law seems out of place, but from a literary perspective it anticipates both the laws on forbidden mixtures in verses 8-11 and the laws on sexual behavior between men and women in verses 13-30.

The English translations are somewhat misleading. In the first clause the word translated **clothing** is not the usual Hebrew word for clothing but means first of all "implement or vessel." Therefore, it could refer to weapons or anything worn that is a symbol of maleness. In the second clause the normal word for clothing is used.

The law was apparently aimed at deliberate attempts to confuse genders, that is transvestitism. It would be a violation of the clear sexual distinctions created by God (Gen 1:27; 2:21-24). Perhaps there were other reasons for the law as well. Disguises could be used to mingle with the opposite sex and engage in immorality. Or perhaps transvestitism was a part of some pagan cultic rite. The fact that the LORD **detests** the act puts it in the same category as idolatry and homosexual behavior (Deut 7:25; 18:12; Lev 18:22; 20:13).

---

[4]The single occurrence of the phrase in the NIV (replaced by **or**) is smoother English but masks the emphasis. Laws elsewhere deal with the issues of someone making a false claim about losing property or not finding property (Exod 22:9[8]; Lev 6:3,4[5:22,23]).

[5]Again this parallel law is not a case law ("**if**") but a negative command using the identical wording of verse 1.

22:6-7 The next two laws return to the concern to protect life. Both are case laws introduced by **if**. The law on the mother bird shows God's concern for even the smallest creatures.[6]

Leviticus 22:27-28 expressed concern for the mother and her young. The newborn must remain with its mother for at least seven days, and they were not to be offered as a sacrifice on the same day. This law seems aimed in a different direction, however. The concern here is for protection of a long-term food source. If the mother bird were slaughtered for food with the eggs or young, she would not be available for further production.[7] The law is similar to 20:19-20 that mandated the preservation of fruit trees. Short-term needs for food were to be balanced by long term planning.

The promise that comes with this law, **so that . . . you may have long life**, puts it on equal footing with the fifth commandment (honoring parents). Generally in Deuteronomy this promise is given as the result of obedience to the law (4:40; 5:33; 6:2; 11:9, etc.). Only three laws are specifically singled out: this one, honoring parents, and honest weights (25:15). This signals that the laws that might seem the least important, are as significant as all others. In fact the rabbis called this law the least of the commandments (cf. Matt 5:19) and paired it with the fifth commandment as the weightiest.[8]

22:8 The flat roofs of houses were routinely used for many activities including drying farm produce, socializing, sleeping, and pagan worship. (Josh 2:6; 1 Sam 9:25; 2 Sam 11:2; 16:22; Isa 22:1; Jer 19:13). Therefore, lack of some sort of protective railing or wall around the edge presented a real danger. A house owner's failure to take the necessary precautions to protect his family and friends exposed him to serious charges. **Guilt of bloodshed** puts negligence in the same category as murder or manslaughter (cf. 19:1-13). Personal responsibility for the safety of others highlights this law. This was perhaps a paradigm law that set the precedent for any negligence that brought harm to another.[9]

---

[6]Is this law and its concern behind Jesus' selection of the bird as an example of God's gracious provision (Matt 6:26)?

[7]Modern game laws that forbid the killing of the female of the species reflect the same concern.

[8]Robert M. Johnston, "The Least of the Commandments: Deuteronomy 22:6-7 in Rabbinic Judaism and Early Christianity," *AUSS* 20 (1982): 205-215.

[9]Exodus 21:8-36 deals with negligence in other areas.

6. Elaboration of the Seventh Commandment (22:9-23:18)

The section that elaborates on the seventh commandment, "You shall not commit adultery," (5:18) begins with admonitions about improper mixing of seeds, animals, and cloth and ends with strictures on cult prostitution. The central focus is on several laws on sexual behavior and marriage (22:13-30). The theme of sexual purity is carried thoughout by the application of purity (separation) in other areas of life. Proper boundaries are to be maintained in nature (22:9-12), in sexual relations (22:13-30), in membership in the assembly (23:1-8), and in conduct in the camp (23:9-14).[10]

Laws of Separation (22:9-12)

22:9-11 Three laws about the improper mixture of certain items are put together as the first unit in the section (cf. Lev 19:19). The theme of keeping certain things separate corresponds to the theme of keeping separate from sexual impurity.[11] There is also a similarity to the clean/unclean food laws of chapter 14:1-21 (and Lev 11:1-23) in that there were distinctions in the created order that had to be maintained. These laws might also be related to the created order of plant and animal life of Genesis 1.[12]

The reason for not planting **two kinds of seed in your vineyard** is unclear. The law in Leviticus 19:19 forbids mating two different kinds of animals. Mixing seed would violate the same principle. Merrill suggests a theological principle was at work. Since Israel was referred to metaphorically as a vineyard in some texts (Isa 5:1-7; Jer 2:10), the law had application to her status. She was not to allow alien religion to be mixed into her life (Deut 7) so that even her farming practice reflected her purity.[13]

---

[10]Olson, *Deuteronomy*, p. 99.

[11]C.M. Carmichael, "Forbidden Mixtures," *VT* 32 (1982): 394-415.

[12]C. Houtman, "Another Look at Forbidden Mixtures," *VT* 34 (1984): 226-228.

[13]Merrill, *Deuteronomy*, p. 300. Merrill is dependent on Calum M. Carmichael's view that these laws are more like proverbial comments on early Israelite behavior. Thus Carmichael finds extended allusions in these three laws to the patriarch Judah's behavior in Genesis 30–38 and Jacob's words about him in Genesis 49:8-12. They are not to be interpreted literally but metaphorically to refer to intermingling with foreigners, through marriage

The forbidding of plowing **with an ox and a donkey yoked together** seems more understandable. Not only were they of unequal strength, the ox was a clean animal while the donkey was unclean according to Deuteronomy 14. Again the separation principle was emphasized. Paul perhaps alluded to this text when he commanded the Corinthians to not be yoked together with unbelievers (2 Cor 6:14). It would be an unequal yoking, mixing believers with unbelievers and defiling the believer. Merrill insists that the spiritual lesson was the main point of this law. It was especially aimed at rejecting any syncretism with Canaanite religion.[14]

The forbidding of the wearing of **clothes of wool and linen woven together** is the most obscure of the three laws.[15] However, it seems most likely that this type of clothing was forbidden because it was reserved for the garments for the priests (Exod 28:6ff) just as the sacred anointing oil was only for use by the priest (Exod 30:22-37).[16] The material for the tabernacle was also made of yarn and linen (Exod 26:1ff) making the material even more sacred. Craigie has suggested it might refer to some sort of Egyptian practice since the word for "cloth" is not a Hebrew term.[17]

22:12 The final law in this section is also about clothing but is positive. Like the laws immediately preceding, it was to remind Israel of her special status before God. More detail is given in Numbers 15:37-41 where the **tassels** are called "fringes." The reason

---

or otherwise. The argument is interesting and subtle, but in the end unconvincing. See Carmichael, "Forbidden Mixtures," and "Forbidden Mixtures in Deuteronomy XXII 9-11 and Leviticus XIX 9," *VT* 45 (1995): 433-448.

[14]Merrill, *Deuteronomy*, p. 300. J.D.M. Derrett thinks Paul's use of this law was to forbid business associations with unbelievers, not marriage with unbelievers as is commonly thought ("2 Cor 6,14ff, A Midrash on Dt 22,10," *Biblica* 59 [1978]: 231-250).

[15]According to Tigay, even the Jewish Rabbis, who were extremely resourceful, could not think of a reason for this law (*Deuteronomy*, p. 203).

[16]It is assumed that the dyed yarn of Exodus 28 was wool since linen did not take dye well. The priest's ephod, breastpiece, and robe were of colored yarn and linen (vv. 6-35), the tunic, turban, and undergarments were of linen (vv. 39,42). For helpful discussions see *IDB*, 1:654, s.v. "Cloth"; and Jacob Milgrom, "Of Hems and Tassels," *BAR* 9,3 (1983): 61-65. Tassels (see v. 12) dating from AD 135 have been found that were made of white linen cords and blue woolen cords woven together.

[17]Craigie, *Deuteronomy*, p. 291.

given there for the tassels was that they were to be reminders of the covenant. In turn the reminder would keep Israel from religious apostasy, specifically idolatry. So the very clothing the Israelites wore reminded them of God's promises, his faithfulness to them, and the necessity of their loyalty to him.[18]

Laws on Sexual Conduct (22:13-30)

These verses are the major section on illicit sexual conduct in the larger unit of 22:9–23:18. It is composed of six laws intentionally arranged in a symmetrical order, united by a common theme. Each law contains similar elements: definition of a woman's status, circumstances surrounding the offense, the evidence required, appropriate punishment, and a comment on the punishment. G.J. Wenham and J.G. McConville have established the careful drafting of the arrangement.[19] The laws are set in two "parallel panels."

    a. Offenses of married women: 13-22
       1) Offense in father's house ("if," "gate of city"): 13-19
       2) Offense in father's house ("if not"): 20-21
       3) Adultery ("if," "caught in the act"): 22

    b. Offenses by unmarried girls: 23-28
       1) Betrothed girl in city ("if," "gate of city"): 23-24
       2) Betrothed girl in field ("if not"): 25-27
       3) Unbetrothed girl ("if," "caught in the act"): 28-29[20]

The laws are also arranged in chiastic order according to the punishment of each.

    A. 19 – damages of 100 shekels to girl's father; no divorce
      B. 21 – woman executed
        C. 22 – man and woman executed
        C'. 24 – man and woman executed

---

[18]The tassels, called "tallit katan," are still worn by orthodox Jews today. However, they are attached to an undershirt-type piece worn under the outer garment with only the tassels showing. In the Middle Ages when the tassels made Jews too conspicuous, the custom developed to attach them to a smaller inner garment.

[19]Wenham and McConville, "Drafting," pp. 248-252.

[20]Ibid., p. 250.

     B'. 25 — man executed
     A'. 29 — damages of 50 shekels to girl's father; no divorce.[21]

The laws are all presented from a patriarchal perspective, with men as the primary actors, either fathers, husbands, or single males. This is to be expected within the context of ancient Israel. However, it must also be noted that there was a genuine concern for the welfare of the woman. The new wife or the vulnerable female was not subject to the whim of males with no recourse. The laws were designed to protect the integrity and social security of innocent women. Males, including husbands, were held accountable for false accusations or sexual abuse. The wronged woman was assured social and economic security and vindication.

The first law in the group involves the most detail. It seems to deal with the most complex of the situations. A somewhat parallel law is found in Numbers 5:5-31 that deals with the case of suspected infidelity later in the marriage.

22:13 According to the marriage customs of the Old Testament times girls were betrothed at an early age and remained in their father's house until the wedding ceremony. The parents of the two parties usually arranged the betrothal, and the prospective groom paid a bride-price to the father. It was possible that the two young people would have had little time together before the ceremony.[22]

Therefore, the initial response of **dislike** would not have been unheard of, though why it occurred is not considered. The Hebrew word is "hate" (שָׂנֵא, śn') which can indicate feelings ranging from outright hate to a mild aversion or preference. Amnon's drastic change of feeling toward Tamar after he raped her shows the extreme contrast of prior love turning to hate (2 Sam 16:21). Jacob's preference for Rachel over Leah involves a mild meaning of the word "hate" (Gen 29:31-33). The law in Deuteronomy 21:15,17 reflects the preference of one wife over another.

The initial law is formulated from the perspective of a false accusation. The possibility of a truthful accusation is addressed in verses 20-21.

---

[21]Ibid., p. 250.
[22]See deVaux, *Ancient Israel*, pp. 24-34, for an extended description of marriage in ancient Israel.

22:14 The accusation was adultery (**I did not find proof of her virginity**). The virginity of the new bride was crucial to the integrity of the family. The husband had to be able to know that any children born to the marriage were his. Sexual misconduct during the betrothal time was considered adultery (see verses 23-24). Since the bride was under the care of her father prior to the wedding, he would have been responsible for her conduct.

22:15-17 Both the mother and father (the two witnesses needed [19:15]?) were required to defend their daughter against the **slander**.[23]

The significance of the **cloth** as **proof of her virginity** has been debated. Traditionally, the cloth has been interpreted as a bed covering from the wedding night when the marriage was consummated. If the bride were a virgin, the cloth would normally have blood-stains on it.[24] This explanation suffers from a major weakness. It seems likely the groom would be aware of the existence of the wedding cloth. Why, then, would he bring a charge that he knew could be proven false, especially in the light of the penalties?[25]

Wenham has argued that the word translated **proof of virginity** (בְּתוּלִים, *bᵉtûlîm*) is more accurately understood as an abstract noun referring to virgins as a class of young women in Israel. The charge then would have been that she was not a virgin. As proof of the falseness of the charge, the parents would bring forth the menstrual cloths to show that the girl was not pregnant when married and thus truly a virgin.[26] This explanation seems to make more sense in the context.

---

[23]The word in this context means some legal misdeed. The husband was charging the bride with a capital crime that would go beyond mere slander.

[24]According to Tigay, *Deuteronomy*, p. 205, it was a widespread practice in the Jewish and Arab communities for the parents to keep the bedcloths from the wedding night. See also Craigie, *Deuteronomy*, p. 292. On the other hand there are no examples of such a practice in the Old Testament.

[25]If his main motive was divorce or annulment, a false accusation achieved the very opposite (verse 19).

[26]G.J. Wenham, "Betulah — A Girl of Marriageable Age," *VT* 22 (1972): 326-348. See also Wright, *Deuteronomy*, p. 246. However, a book length study of this passage supports the more traditional interpretation. See Clemens Locher, *Die Ehre einer Frau in Israel: Exegetische und Rechtsvergleichende Studien zu Deuteronomium 22:13-21* (Freibourg: Vandenhoeck und Ruprecht, 1986), chapter 3 (for a convenient summary see the review by John F. Craghan, *CBQ* 51 [1989]: 527-528).

22:18-19 Elders of the village were responsible for hearing the evidence and deciding the case (similar to the case of the rebellious son in 21:18-21).[27] However, the expected punishment, death, was not prescribed.[28] Rather, the punishment was twofold.[29] The groom was fined **one hundred shekels of silver** (two and one-half pounds) which was twice the fine of verse 29. His accusation was an effort to force the father to return the bride-price, so the punishment fit the crime.[30] The groom was also denied the right of divorce, the objective of his accusation in the first place. Continued marriage to such a man sounds like a grim prospect for a young woman. But it provided her with economic security and the prospect of legitimate children, as opposed to a return to her father's house and greatly diminished chances of another marriage.

22:20-21 The law also dealt with the possibility that the charge could be true. In that case the crime would be adultery, and the girl would be subject to the death penalty.[31] The girl had been **promiscuous** (literally, "acted like a prostitute") and had brought shame and dishonor on her father and her father's house. Her illicit action declared her father was irresponsible and not in control of his household. Her **grave sexual sin** was in the same class as rape by a male (Gen 34:7; Judg 19:23; 20:6; 2 Sam 13:12). It was an **evil** to be **purged** which put it on the same level as several other offenses in Deuteronomy, such as the false prophet, idolatry, and murder (13:5; 17:7,12; 19:13,19; 21:9,21).

22:22 This law addresses a clear and simple case of adultery. It is the case law equivalent of the seventh commandment.[32] A man was

---

[27]This legal process was the same as the law required for the judges in Deut 17:2-7.

[28]According to Deut 19:16-19 a false witness was to suffer the penalty of the crime of which the innocent was accused. Perhaps the mitigating factor here was that the accuser was not technically a witness.

[29]Unless "punish" or "chastise" was a separate act of punishment (so Tigay, *Deuteronomy*, p. 205; he suggests flogging was the chastisement).

[30]Exod 22:16 refers to the bride-price of a virgin but gives no amount. Many assume the 50 shekels of verse 29 represent that bride-price, but the text does not make a direct connection. The 50 shekels are a fine and may or may not be the same amount as the bride-price.

[31]On stoning for capital crimes see the commentary on 13:10 and 17:5.

[32]See comments on 5:18.

caught having sexual relations with another man's wife.[33] The law assumed the act was consensual, probably based on the same reasoning exhibited in verses 23-27. The law also assumed eyewitness, **If a man is found . . . .** Adultery was a capital crime and the penalty was death, presumably by stoning at the city gate after an investigation by the elders of the village (see also Lev 20:10).[34] Numbers 5 augments this law by providing a procedure for the husband who suspected the wife of unfaithfulness but had no proof.[35]

There are no cases of execution for adultery in the Old Testament though the prophet Ezekiel speaks of stoning (16:38-40 — by the lovers!). Hosea 2:2 and Jeremiah 3:8 describe the wife being divorced.[36] The prophets speak of stripping the adulterer (Hos 2:5; Ezek 16:37,39; 23:26; Jer 13:26-27) and of adultery being one of the causes of the exile (Hos 4:2-3; Jer 5:7-9; cf. Lev 18:24-28).

A series of brief laws is collected together in the following verses to deal with other situations that would be classified as or be equal to adulterous acts.

22:23-24 The period of engagement or betrothal was considered the same as marriage (v. 24, **another man's wife**). The marriage contract[37] set the bride price, guaranteed that the bride would be a virgin on the wedding day (cf. vv. 13-19), and required complete fideli-

---

[33]A very unusual and strong phrase is used to underscore the married status of the woman. She is described as a "wife lorded over by a husband," a phrase occurring elsewhere only in Gen 20:3 when God informs Abimelech that Sarah is Abraham's wife.

[34]The Pharisees who brought the woman caught in adultery to Jesus violated this law by not bringing the man (John 7:53–8:11).

[35]Ancient Near Eastern laws also condemned adultery and prescribed the death penalty. However, since it was considered a sin against the king or husband, but not God, the sentence could be softened if the husband desired. See the Code of Hammurabi # 129 (*ANET*, p. 171) and Middle Assyrian Laws # 13-15 (*ANET*, p. 181). There was some tendency in these laws to ascribe the evil initiative to the woman.

[36]All three prophets are actually describing the relationship between Israel and God by the metaphorical use of marriage language. Spiritual adultery (idolatry) broke the covenant with God. Perhaps the law provided for the ultimate penalty, death, but divorce was acceptable (Mayes, *Deuteronomy*, p. 170).

[37]The marriage contract was comparable to Israel's covenant with God (Ezek 16:8).

ty of both parties.[38] Therefore, sexual misconduct was treated the same as adultery. This law also assumed that the act was consensual. If it was not, the girl would have **screamed for help** and would have been heard by someone in the village. This assumption is strengthened by the fact that the language of violence used in rape cases in verses 25 and 28 is missing.

22:25-27 The situation of an engaged girl caught in the country was treated differently. It was assumed the girl would have **screamed** for help, but since it was in the country there would have been no one nearby to hear her. The law also supposed that the man would have used force. He "seized her" and "lay with her."[39] This was a capital crime for the man and was equal to premeditated murder. Of course the event could have been consensual even if in the country, but the girl is given the benefit of the doubt and thus protected by the law. This law probably would have been applied to the married woman as well.[40]

22:28-29 If the girl who was violated was not married or engaged, the penalty was not death but a fine and the loss of the right of divorce. The law protected both the girl (economic security) and the father (loss of bride price). The girl's loss of virginity would have made her virtually unmarriageable. In Exodus 22:16 the father could refuse to let the girl marry the seducer.

There is some question whether the act in view here was **rape** (NIV) or consensual. The word of verse 25 ("seize") was not used but an apparently more mild word which meant "take hold of."[41] However, the explanation that the man had **violated** the girl points toward rape. The expression was also used of Shechem's treatment of Dinah (Gen 34:2).

---

[38]Walton and Matthews, *Genesis–Deuteronomy*, p. 253.

[39]The parallel phrases are translated in the NIV by the one word, "rape." The account of the rape of Tamar by Amnon uses the same two verbs (2 Sam 13:11).

[40]Hittite Law 197 applied guilt only to the man if the crime occurred in the mountains, but only to the woman if it occurred in the house (*ANET*, p. 196).

[41]The Hebrew word is תפש (*tps*) rather than חזק (*ḥzq*). The parallel law in Exod 22:16 uses פתה (*pth*), "seduce." However, תפש carries a sense of seizing or grabbing ahold of in order to overpower in Deut 21:19; 1 Kgs 13:4; 18:40; Ps 71:11 and Isa 3:6.

The man was fined and denied the right of divorce. This penalty was very similar to that of the new husband who brought a false accusation (v. 19), but the fine was half as much. Some have suggested that the **fifty shekels of silver** was the normal bride price, but this law does not make it clear (the word for bride price, *môhār*, does not appear). There probably was some sort of fine included in the amount. Since the normal yearly wages at that time was ten shekels, a bride price of fifty shekels would be high.[42]

22:30(23:1) This law provides a bridge to the next section. It still addresses sexual misconduct, but it is in the negative command form of the following laws, not in the case law form of the preceding ones.

The law was apparently directed to forbidding an eldest son from marrying his stepmother after the death of his father (see 27:20). It seemed to presuppose the early death of his mother and his father's remarriage. Perhaps the father would marry a much younger woman, who could have been nearly the age of the son. Marriage between a son and stepmother **dishonors his father's bed**. The NIV translation masks a Hebrew idiom that has widespread usage in contexts of fornication, shame, and great insult. The phrase involves the use of the verb "uncover" (גלה, *glh*) in combination with such words as "shame, nakedness, bed, legs." Here the literal phrase is "uncover the skirt" of the father.[43]

---

[42]Lev 27:1-8 sets the value of men and women for special vows according to age. Women ages 20 to 60 were valued at 30 shekels; woman ages 5 to 20 and over 60 at 10 shekels. Poor people could appeal to the priest who would set the value according to what the person could afford. The price of a slave was 30 shekels (Exod 21:32). Perhaps the bride price varied according to economic status (Weinfeld, *Deuteronomic School*, pp, 285-286). In the Middle Assyrian Laws the father had several choices. If the rapist was married, he could have the rapist's wife raped and keep her. He could also refuse to give the daughter in marriage, in which case he would receive triple the bride price (*ANET*, p. 185, # 55).

[43]Therefore, although this law is not technically dealing with incest, it seems related to the many laws limiting interfamily sexual contacts in Lev 18. See also passages such as Ezek 16:36,37; 23:10,29; Isa 57:8; Hos 2:12(12); Jer 13:22. There are several examples in the Old Testament of violation of this law: Gen 35:22(49:4); 2 Sam 3:7; 16:22; 1 Kgs 2:22. All are in the context of a son attempting to usurp the position or authority of the father.

The laws on adultery and illicit sexual conduct are not arbitrary but firmly grounded in core Old Testament thought. Adultery was sinful on theological grounds and had serious sociological implications. It threatened the stability of the Israelite family that was the cornerstone of Israelite society. It shattered the sexual integrity of the marriage that was God ordained (Gen 2). Sexual misconduct violated the covenant relationship between the man and woman that was energized and maintained by faithfulness, loyalty, and trust. Gender and sexuality were integral components of humanness. The unity of a man and woman into one under God included total fidelity at the emotional, spiritual, and physical level. It could not be violated without serious consequences (David and Bathsheba provide a good example, 2 Sam 11–12). Adultery also violated personal integrity, for it was ultimately a sin against God (Gen 39).

Therefore, the Old Testament prophets could appropriate marriage as a metaphor for the relationship between God and Israel. Its covenantal character provided rich images for conceptualizing the divine-human relationship. Three prophets, Hosea, Jeremiah, and Ezekiel, exploited the marriage metaphor. They used the imagery to address the spiritual unfaithfulness of Israel as exhibited in her idolatry and her trust in political alliances with foreign countries. This spiritual unfaithfulness was described with the sexual terms, adultery and prostitution. In fact fully one-third of the occurrences of the word for adultery (נאף, n'p) and two-thirds of the occurrences of the word for prostitution (זנה, znh) occur in these three prophets in a metaphorical sense (Hos 1–2; Jer 2–3; Ezek 16 and 23).[44]

Ezekiel includes the sin among a long list of evil perpetrated in Israel (22:10).

[44]See Gary H. Hall, "נאף," *NIDOTTE,* 3:2-5, and "זנה," *NIDOTTE,* 1:1122-1125.

DEUTERONOMY 23

Laws on Membership in the Assembly (23:1-8)

Chapter 23:1-18[2-19][1] is a disparate group of laws that are connected by the shared theme of establishing boundaries. The theme began in 22:9 and elaborates the seventh commandment forbidding adultery (5:18). A case law related to the theme and dealing with remarriage appears in 24:1-4. However, it is embedded in the next major section of the book which elaborates on the eighth commandment (23:19–24:7, see below).[2]

Verses 1-8 define various classes of people who were not accepted into the **assembly of the LORD**. This is a phrase that occurs six times in Deuteronomy, all in these verses. The word "assembly" (קָהָל, *qāhāl*) can have a wide range of meanings ("assembly, community, horde, army, congregation, mob, people"). But it is limited here by the phrase "of the LORD" which suggests a specific occasion or function of the people gathered together. On various occasions the people as the assembly of the LORD gathered to conduct business (Micah 2:5), crown a king (1 Kgs 12:3), do war (Judg 21:5,8), adjudicate legal cases (Jer 26:17), or worship (Joel 2:16). In these

---

[1]The Hebrew text begins chapter 23 one verse before our English translations. It counts English 22:30 as 23:1 and English 23:1 as 23:2 and so on. For simplicity's sake the English versification will be given without further reference to the difference. The student of Hebrew should note the variation when consulting the Hebrew Bible.

[2]This analysis follows Olson, *Deuteronomy*, pp. 103-106. However, there is little agreement among commentators on the unity or diversity of chapters 23, 24, and 25. For example, Merrill understands Deuteronomy 23:1-18 as "Laws of Purity" and 23:19–25:19 as "Laws of Interpersonal Relationships" (*Deuteronomy*, pp. 299 and 314). On the other hand Tigay calls 23:1-9 "Forbidden Relationships" and 23:10–25:19, "Miscellaneous Laws," (*Deuteronomy*, pp. 209 and 213).

situations the assembly was not synonymous with the whole nation of Israel but referred specifically to those people who were full-fledged members of the covenant community. On the other hand the term Israel, understood as a whole nation and as a political unit, could include aliens and other nonproselytes.

The assembly referred to here is likely the community of Israel gathered in worship at festivals and other special occasions,[3] or a similar assembly gathered to make public decisions.[4] This law is not addressing the issue of who may be a member of the nation, but the issue of who **may enter** the community as it was gathered to worship the holy God.[5]

23:1 The first disqualified person was the one who was **emasculated,** one who was defective in the genitals by (literally) the crushing of the testicles or the cutting of the male organ. It is not clear whether this prohibition was to apply to every case, whether caused by genetics, accident or intention.[6] The reasoning seems to be the same as for the priests in Leviticus 21:17-20. Eunuchs, for whatever reason, were not whole as created by God, and were therefore not qualified to be in the presence of God.

Perhaps self-mutilation was a feature of certain pagan religions. We know eunuchs were a part of foreign courts (2 Kgs 20:18; 23:11, and often) and that castration was a punishment in Middle Assyrian Laws.[7] However, there is no clear evidence that intentional emasculation was ever practiced in Israel. It is possible the objects of this law, as in the following verses, were non-Israelites.[8]

23:2 The second class excluded from the assembly were those **born of forbidden marriages**. Based on 22:30 in the immediately preceding law and the law in the following verses 3-6, this very likely

---

[3]Merrill, *Deuteronomy*, p. 307.

[4]Tigay, *Deuteronomy*, p. 210.

[5]It is akin to the law that lists defects that disqualified the sons of Aaron from serving as priests before God (Lev 21:16-23). The defective persons were not eliminated from the nation, but they could not appear before God.

[6]Applies to all cases (Merrill, *Deuteronomy*, p. 307); applies only to intentional cases (Craigie, *Deuteronomy*, p. 296).

[7]*ANET*, p. 181, #19, 20.

[8]Tigay, *Deuteronomy*, p. 210. Part of Isaiah's vision of the future was that eunuchs and foreigners would have access to fellowship with God and all the associated blessings (Isa 56:3-5).

refs to children of incest or of mixed marriages (see Zech 9:6).[9] Perhaps it referred to children who were the result of prostitution as well (v. 17). The reasoning seems to be the same as verse 1, the imperfect were excluded from worship.

In this case the penalty continued on to the descendants as well, until the **tenth generation**. Since ten is a "complete" number, it is likely that the phrase meant the descendants could never participate in the assembly. The same phrase occurs in verse 3 in parallel with "forever."[10]

23:3 The terminology from verse 2 is used of two more classes of people who were excluded from the assembly. These verses perhaps illustrate what the forbidden marriages of verse 2 were. The **Ammonites and Moabites** were close geographical neighbors of Israel who had many interactions with her. This law could be a subtle reflection of Genesis 19:37-38 that portrays the origins of the two nations as the product of the incest of Lot and his two daughters.

23:4-5 The reason for the exclusion of these two ethnic groups from the assembly of the LORD was their treatment of Israel as she advanced through the Transjordan lands on her way to Canaan. They were censored here for their lack of hospitality and their attempts to get Balaam to curse Israel (Num 22–24).

Moses had already given a brief account of this interaction in his summary in chapter 2 (see 2:8-9,18 [Moabites] and 19,37 [Ammonites]). But the Moabites' lack of hospitality had not been mentioned in chapter 2. In fact in 2:28-29 the Moabites in Ar were said to have sold Israel food and water.

In this law Moses seems to be taking a more general view of relationships between the three nations typified by the Balaam incident.[11] Balak, King of Moab, hired Balaam to curse Israel, but

---

[9]The Hebrew word, (מַמְזֵר, *mamzēr*) occurs only here and in Zech 9:6. In the latter text it clearly means "foreigner." The range of incestuous relationships was described in Lev 18:6-20.

[10]Merrill, *Deuteronomy*, p. 308. The NIV omits the "forever" in verse 3 thus masking the clarity of the Hebrew text. For the idiom "ten times" meaning countless times see Gen 31:7; Num 14:22; Job 19:3.

[11]Some scholars think that the Numbers and Deuteronomy accounts of interaction between Israel and Moab represent two separate traditions (Tigay, *Deuteronomy*, p. 211; David Frankel, "The Deuteronomic Portrayal of Balaam," *VT* 46 (1996): 30-42. For a full discussion see *ABD*, s.v. "Balaam."

through God's intervention Balaam refused to curse Israel and blessed her instead. This revealed the sovereign power of God who could control even pagan diviners (Num 22–24). Moses' view of Balaam here is somewhat more negative than the view in Numbers. Joshua 24:9-10 agrees with Deuteronomy's perspective on Balaam. Nehemiah 13:1-2 refers to this law and applies it to the postexilic situation in Judah.

Both Moab and Ammon occupy a large place in the condemnations of the later prophets.[12] Over the years one or the other nations might have ascendancy. Under David, Israel became the most powerful nation in the area and subdued Moab and Ammon (2 Sam 8 and 10). Moab did not gain independence until after Ahab's death (2 Kgs 3). However, individual Moabites could be accepted into the nation as the case of Ruth shows.

23:6 The prohibition of relationships with the Ammonites and Moabites extended beyond allowing individuals into the assembly to relations between the nations themselves. Israel was not to have any sort of international agreement or treaty with them.[13] After the fall of Jerusalem in 586 B.C. the book of Lamentations bemoans the fact

---

A reference to Balaam has been discovered in a nonbiblical inscription at a site called Deir 'Allā. The site is in the Jordan River Valley near the mouth of the Jabbok River. The inscription on a plastered wall from a temple dates from the eighth century B.C. and refers to Balaam as a seer from ancient times who founded a pagan cult. This confirms the biblical perspective on Balaam. Micah, the Judean prophet who mentions Balaam (Micah 6:5), prophesied in the eighth century, perhaps contemporary with the founding of the temple. For a translation of the Balaam inscription see J. Milgrom, *Numbers*, Excursus 60.

[12]For Moab see Isa 15–16; Jer 48; Ezek 25:8-11; Amos 2:1-2. For Ammon see Jer 49; Ezek 25:2-10; Amos 1:13. Zeph 2:8-9 mentions them together. This later censoring was for the conduct of the nations when Judah was under siege by Babylon.

[13]"Seek a treaty of friendship" is the idiomatic translation of "seek their peace and their good." Older versions of the NIV had "seek peace and good relations" (see also the NASB, "peace or prosperity"). Research has shown that the two words, peace and good, following the verb "seek" are ancient Near Eastern treaty terminology. For details see W.L. Moran, "A Note on the Treaty Terminology of the Sefire Steles," *JNES* 22 (1963): 173-176; and D.R. Hillars, "A Note on Some Treaty Terminology in the Old Testament," *BASOR* 176 (1964): 46-47. For the same idiom see Jer 29:7; Neh 2:10; Esth 10:3.

that these nations forbidden to enter the assembly actually entered the temple (Lam 1:10).

23:7-8 Israel was to have a different relationship with the Edomites who inhabited the territory south and east of the Dead Sea (see on 2:1-8) and the Egyptians. The relationship between Edom and Israel was considered one of kinship because the ancestors who gave their names to each nation were brothers (Gen 25:19-26; 32:3; 36). The relationship of the two nations, however, was one of intermittent conflict. David conquered the country (2 Sam 8:12-14), Solomon had trouble with Edom rebelling (1 Kgs 11:14-16), and she finally gained her freedom during the time of Jehoram (2 Kgs 8:20-22). Relations after that were poor, and Jeremiah condemned the nation (Jer 49:7-22; see also Ps 137:7-9; Ezek 25:12-14; Obadiah).

It is surprising that Egypt was given a favorable status, but apparently the preslave period was in view when Israel lived there as welcomed guests. The descendants of the Edomite and Egyptian nations had to wait for a period to enter the assembly, but it was brief, to the **third generation**. After this wait the descendant apparently could become a full member of Israel. Perhaps part of the reasoning behind this provision was that by the third generation the desire of the descendants to live permanently in Israel would have been clear.[14]

Purity in the Camp (23:9-14)

This section continues the theme of separation, addressing the issue of certain behavior that would violate purity in the army camp. The particular behavior was the proper disposal of bodily emissions, especially excrement. The background is in the laws of purity and cleanliness in Leviticus and Numbers. The immediate background law would be Leviticus 15 which details regulations about various bodily discharges that make the Israelite man or woman unclean (see also Num 5:1-4). The governing principle was stated in Leviticus

---

[14]This law did not apply to the class referred to throughout Deuteronomy as the "alien." This class consisted of resident foreigners who had equal protection under the law and could share in many of the religious observances including the Sabbath (Deut 5:14; 10:18; 14:21,29; 16:11,14, etc.). Probably full membership was open to them. Tigay points out that later Jewish teaching modified this law when a procedure for accepting proselytes was developed (*Deuteronomy*, p. 211).

15:31 — uncleanness defiled the tabernacle that was in Israel. Impurity could not be tolerated because God was present among his people.

23:9-11 The law presumed the men of Israel were gathered in the army camp preparing for war (ch. 20). It was a setting that required purity. Therefore they were to avoid every "evil thing" (NIV, **everything impure**). Though the phrase is used elsewhere in Deuteronomy to refer to defective sacrificial animals (17:1; cf. 15:21), idolatry (13:12; 17:5), or a malicious witness (19:20), the context here related to proper conduct in God's presence requires connecting the phrase with purity laws. The phrase is probably parallel with the phrase in verse 14, "anything indecent." In that case these two phrases form an inclusio around this paragraph and the earlier phrase helps define the latter, more obscure phrase (see below on verse 14).

The offense is described in general terms as any "event in the night" (NIV, **nocturnal emission**). Leviticus 15:16, a somewhat similar law, states specifically the offense in view was an "emission of semen." However, the law here is more general and could refer to even the unwillingness of the man to exit the camp for the usual bodily functions (v. 12).

The result was being **unclean.** But the state lasted only until **evening.** Then the man could cleanse himself through the normal procedure prescribed in Leviticus 14–16, which was washing with water. Afterwards he could reenter the camp.

23:12-13 A special site outside the camp was designated as a latrine. Perhaps it was even marked by a sign so that everyone used the same place.[15] The **equipment** they were to have included a tent peg like stick to dig the hole with (cf. Judg 4:21-22).

The reason for this facet of the law seems to be mainly hygienic. But hygienic cleanliness (health) and ritual purity were closely related.[16] Digging a hole for excrement and covering it up eliminated several potential health problems. There was no accompanying statement about purity since normal defecation, if done properly outside the camp, did not make a person impure.

---

[15]The literal Hebrew is "A hand shall be for you . . . ." Hand sometimes means a monument or sign in the Old Testament (1 Sam 15:12; 2 Sam 18:18; Isa 56:5)

[16]Craigie, *Deuteronomy*, p. 299.

23:14 The presence of God in the camp was the reason for purity. It is not clear whether this refers to God traveling with the army as described in 20:4, or to God actually moving about within the camp. The verb is the same used in Genesis 3:8 of God moving about in the Garden of Eden. Several times God went with Israel (1:30,33; 20:4; 31:6,8) in some way. Usually God's presence among Israel was designated by the presence of the ark. But the ark is not mentioned here or in chapter 20 although its presence in Israel is indicated in Deuteronomy 10. God's leading and the presence of the ark are included within the same context in chapter 31 (cf. vv. 9,25,26 with 6 and 8). Therefore, this passage probably assumes the presence of the ark in the camp.[17]

However we interpret the verse, it was God's real presence in some way in the military camp that required its purity. His presence made it **holy**.

Anything indecent is parallel to "any evil thing" (NIV, "everything impure") of verse 9. This indicates that the two cases mentioned in verses 10-13 are only examples and the application of the law would be much broader.

The word translated "indecent" (עֶרְוָה, *'ervāh*) has the primary meaning of "nakedness, genital area" and by extension "shame, dishonor." It is used with the verb "to uncover" to signify sexual relations with someone (Lev 18). It means shame in 1 Samuel 20:30. Perhaps in this law it means anything shameful or offensive, especially in the area of sexual conduct. But it could also be extended to include other areas of shameful conduct from the Old Testament perspective (see on 24:1 below).

The possible consequence of uncleanness in the camp was that God would **turn away**. This would have been tantamount to God abandoning the covenant. Throughout Deuteronomy God's loyalty and faithfulness to the covenant with Israel is emphasized. It would seem to run counter to his character to reverse himself. Yet this verb is used elsewhere in the Old Testament to describe Israel's apostasy and turning away from God and the covenant. Therefore impurity in the camp was no trifling matter for it jeopardized the covenant relationship with God.

---

[17]The Israelites, without divine approval, took the Ark into battle during the time of Eli and lost it to the Philistines (1 Sam 4).

Escaped Slaves (23:15-16)

This law does not seem to fit the overall theme of 22:13–23:18 which is separation and purity. But it does go with the following section that enlarges on the eighth commandment. Its placement here seems to follow the principle of composition that we have seen before in which a law in one major section anticipates laws in the next.

It is not clear whether this law refers only to slaves from foreign nations around Israel who might seek asylum in Israel (most commentators) or if it also applies to Israelite slaves. In ancient Near Eastern law harboring runaway slaves was a capital crime.[18] Therefore, Israel stood in sharp contrast to the surrounding culture in her care for and protection of this class of people.[19]

23:15-16 There seems to be a deliberate catchword connection with the previous law and verse 14. God was in the camp to protect Israel (נצל, *nṣl*). Likewise the Israelite was to care for the slave who had **taken refuge** (נצל) within Israel. This wordplay agrees with a common theme in Deuteronomy: Israel was to imitate God (see on 10:17-19). Although the motivation for the generous act here was not given, elsewhere Israel was to recall her slavery in Egypt as a reason for gratitude toward God and kind treatment of others (10:19; 15:15; 23:7; 24:17-18). The grace God extended to her was to be extended to others.[20]

Slavery because of debt was recognized in Israel (see on 15:12-18) although it was not intended to be permanent as the law of the Sabbatical year showed. On the other hand, an Israelite could voluntarily become a permanent debt slave (15:16-17). If the Sabbatical year were observed, it would have likely ameliorated pressure for slaves to run away. However, all debt holders would not have been kind to the debt slave. Therefore, we find in the history books cases of slaves running away (1 Sam 22:2; 25:10; 1 Kgs 2:39-40). Consequently it seems possible that the law could have included the Israelite slave as well as the foreign slave.[21]

---

[18]Code of Hammurabi, #15-20 (*ANET*, pp. 166-167). In the Hittite Laws a reward was offered for returning runaway slaves (#22-24 [*ANET*, p. 190]).

[19]Compare 22:5 above.

[20]This was the precise point of Jesus' parable about the unforgiving servant, Matt 18:21-35. Jesus was saturated with the theology of Deuteronomy.

[21]Weinfeld, *Deuteronomy*, pp. 272-273, note 5. Tigay observes that if this

On Wages of a Prostitute (23:17-18)

23:17 The law in these verses completes the section that expands on the seventh commandment by commenting on forbidden sexual behavior. Israelites were not to become **shrine prostitutes**. They were not to indulge in illicit sex as a part of religious activity. Nor were they to use any earnings from such activity to pay for any vows they might make.[22]

23:18 The words understood to refer to male and female shrine prostitutes (v. 17) are from the root קָדֵשׁ (*qdš*) "to be holy, sacred" (the masculine and feminine noun forms). These noun forms occur eleven times in the Old Testament.[23] Since the parallel statement in verse 18 uses the regular Hebrew word for prostitute (*zōnāh*) the interpretation of *qādēš* in verse 17 as prostitute seems assured.[24] In 1 and 2 Kings this class of people was associated with the pagan religious centers and sacrifices. Most commentators regard this practice as that of sacred prostitution that was a part of pagan fertility cults among the Canaanites and others.[25] However, a few scholars have suggested that there is no unambiguous evidence from the ancient Near East that sacred prostitution ever existed.[26] According to this perspective what these texts refer to is an individual using sex as an act of devotion or as a means to earn a fee with which to honor the god. Therefore, the act referred to here was common prostitution, not sacred sex, and was perhaps mostly indulged in as a part of revelry on the feast days.[27] Perhaps *qādēš* then was a technical euphemism for prostitute.[28] The phrase in verse 18, **earnings of a . . . prostitute** lends some support to this latter

---

law was just for the foreign slaves, it is odd there was not a similar law for the Hebrew slave (*Deuteronomy*, p. 215).

[22]For the law on making vows see on vv. 21-23 below.

[23]Three occurrences refer to Tamar (Gen 38:21-22), two appear here, four appear in Kings (1 Kgs 14:24; 15:12; 22:46; 2 Kgs 23:7), one in Job (36:14) and one in Hosea (4:14).

[24]The noun is paired with *zōnāh* in Gen 38:15 and Hos 4:14 also.

[25]Jackie Naude, "קָדֵשׁ," *NIDOTTE*, 3:886; Merrill, *Deuteronomy*, p. 313. See J.G. Westenholz, "Tamar, *qedeša*, *qadištu*, and Sacred Prostitution in Mesopotamia," *HTR* 82 (1989): 245-265.

[26]By this phrase it is meant a practice in which men and women were specifically assigned to sacred places to engage in sex with worshipers as a part of the regular worship experience.

[27]Tigay, *Deuteronomy*, pp. 215-216, 480-481.

[28]Tigay, *Deuteronomy*, p. 387, note 65.

position (see also Isa 23:17-18; Ezek 16:31,34,41; Hos 9:1; Micah 1:7). Whatever the practice was, any funds earned were not acceptable as a way to honor God.

Ambiguity also surrounds the meaning of the Hebrew word "dog" (NIV, **male prostitute**; Hebrew כֶּלֶב, *keleb*). In the ancient world dogs were not pets but scavengers who lived a disgusting and squalid life, even eating corpses (1 Kgs 21:23-24; 2 Kgs 9:35-36). To refer to oneself as a dog was to call attention to one's miserable condition or lowly status (1 Sam 24:14; 2 Sam 3:8; 9:8; 16:9; 2 Kgs 8:13). To refer to another as a dog was an insult.[29] The NIV takes the term in a derogatory sense and, based on verse 17, understands dog to refer to a male prostitute. This translation reflects the parallelism with the unambiguous reference to female prostitutes in the first half of verse 18.[30]

Another possibility is that dogs were actually used in some pagan cultic rites and what was forbidden was the payment for this practice. In that case dog would be meant in a literal sense. However, the evidence for this practice is uncertain and from a later period, and it does not seem to fit the context well.[31]

7. Elaboration on the Eighth Commandment (23:19–24:7)

A new section that elaborates on the eighth commandment, "you shall not steal," (5:19) begins at 23:19. Chapter 23:15-16, dealing

---

[29]See *Dictionary of Biblical Imagery*, s.v. "Dogs" and "Animals." The word "dog" is used in the New Testament in a negative metaphorical sense also: Phil 3:2; Rev 22:15.

[30]James DeYoung, "The Contribution of the Septuagint in Biblical Sanctions against Homosexuality," *JETS* 34 (1991): 157-177. D.W. Thomas has shown that "dog" is also used in Akkadian texts in the sense of "faithful servants." Such an interpretation would not alter the meaning of this law. The targeted practice or person would still be a devotee of foreign gods. The biblical name Caleb surely has a positive meaning. (See D.W. Thomas, "Kelebh, 'Dog': Its Origin and Some Usages of It in the Old Testament," *VT* 10 [1960]: 410-427).

[31]See L.A. Stager, "Why Were Hundreds of Dogs Buried at Askelon?" *BAR* 17/3 (May/June 1991): 26-42. Archaeologists found a large fifth-century B.C. cemetery of dogs at Askelon. Stager speculates that the dogs (mostly puppies) were part of a healing cult.

with escaped slaves (another's property), anticipated this section. The laws in this new section deal with money or stealing in a variety of settings. The laws placed limits on what could be taken from neighbors or from God. The section is bracketed by laws on human freedom: slavery and kidnappings (23:15-16 and 24:17).[32]

On Charging Interest (23:19-20)

The interrelated issues of debt, loans, interest, and concern for the poor received considerable attention in Deuteronomy. The law here forbade charging interest on loans. It is grounded in previous laws that forbade interest on loaning money (Exod 22:25[24]; Lev 25:35-37). But it expands on them by forbidding interest on food or anything else. Exodus 22:25 specifically directed that interest should not be charged to the poor as they would be the ones most in need of loans.

There is no evidence in the Old Testament for what the going interest rate may have been. However, in other ancient Near Eastern countries rates as high as 50% were charged.[33]

23:19 Charging interest on a loan to a fellow Israelite would have been the same as stealing. The covenant bond within the nation required generosity to the needy and poor. Such loans would not have been in the category of commercial transactions but in the realm of charity. The Sabbatical year, which called for the canceling of debts (15:1-11), required an unusual spirit of generosity. God's material blessings on an individual or family were to be shared with the less fortunate, enabling them to experience economic security also. The prophets and the Psalms affirmed this law (Ezek 18:8,13,17; Ps 15:5)[34] but there is evidence the law was ignored (Prov 28:8; Ezek 22:12).

23:20 However, a foreigner (cf. 15:3) could be charged interest. These foreigners were not the aliens in other texts who were to be protected from economic exploitation (cf. 10:18-19) but were

---

[32]That is, stealing freedom from people (Olson, *Deuteronomy*, p. 108).

[33]See below on 24:10-18, the law concerning making loans. Pledges for the loans could be taken from the borrower but that was different from interest.

[34]The NIV translation in Ezek 18:8,13, and 17 which reads "excessive interest" is unwarranted. The same word used in the Deuteronomy law is used in Ezekiel. The NIV footnote, "take interest," is more accurate.

probably foreign businessmen and traders who were in Israel for commercial purposes.[35]

On Keeping Vows (23:21-23)

Making vows to God was a voluntary act (v. 23), but if they were made, they were to be kept as a matter of personal integrity and honor. Not to keep them would be robbing God. Making vows was treated elsewhere in the Pentateuch (Num 6:1-20; 30:2-25) with more detail. Individuals could make vows to God, but God never made vows to individuals. Individuals could also make vows on behalf of the nation. Vows were made to secure protection, aid, or success (Gen 28:20-22), to ensure birth or harvest, for deliverance (Ps 61:5[6]; 8[9]), or for recovery from illness (Job 22:27; Ps 22:25[26]). For example, Jephthah made a vow to secure victory in battle (Judg 11), Hannah made a vow to secure a son (1 Sam 1), and Absalom used the pretense of a vow to escape confinement to Jerusalem (2 Sam 15).

23:21-23 The most common setting for vows was some sort of distress. Therefore, this and other warnings to repay them were necessary (Prov 20:22; Eccl 5:4-5[3-4]; Ps 50:14).[36]

Sacrifices offered in fulfillment of vows were to be without blemish (Lev 22:17-25; Mal 1:14). Vows could also include dedicating people to the LORD (besides the Nazirite vow of Numbers 6) for which a set sum of money was then given (Lev 27:1-8). Property such as a house or land could also be vowed to God. If the person changed his mind, he had to pay a premium of 20% to get it back (Lev 22:14-25), thus limiting rash vows.

Many Psalms mention vows as expressions of hope or thanksgiving (Ps 56:12-13; 66:13-15). Vows, or promises, could also be expressed without the word "vow" being used (Ps 79:13; 20:6).

---

[35]This class is called נָכְרִי, nokrî (cf. 14:21; 15:3; 17:15; 29:22[21]) whereas the aliens are called גֵּר, gēr (5:14; 10:18-19; 14:21,29; 16:11,14; 24:14, etc.).

[36]Since vows seem like some sort of bargaining for the favor of God, some scholars prefer to see this law as misplaced. Tigay sees it as a remnant of pre-Israelite religion (Deuteronomy, p. 218). Weinfeld thinks it is misplaced in Deuteronomy from wisdom literature (Deuteronomy, p. 271).

Vows were different from oaths. Oaths were promises between two people secured by a formula of self-cursing. Vows were directed to God and not secured with an oath.[37]

Provision for Traveling (23:24-25)

23:24-25 In keeping with the concern of Deuteronomy for providing for the poor and needy, a law is included here to provide for the hungry under certain circumstances. Travelers might find themselves in a field or vineyard when hungry. They could take what they could eat at the time but no more. They could not abuse the practice. To take more would be taking advantage of the landowner and equal to stealing, especially if they entered the field with a basket or sickle. The underlying principle for the landowner was perhaps the truth of Deuteronomy 6:11. God had given them the land that included vineyards they had not planted. His generosity was to be matched by theirs.

This law fits the pattern of other laws dealing with the sharing of the crops. Harvesters should not clean up what was missed or dropped but leave it for the poor (Lev 19:10; Deut 24:19-21). In the Sabbatical year the land was left fallow so the poor could eat from the volunteer produce (Lev 25:3-11).

---

[37]For further discussion see Robin Wakely, "נדר," *NIDOTTE*, 3:37-42; *IDB*, s.v. "Vows," and *IDB*, s.v. "Vow, Oath."

DEUTERONOMY 24

On Remarriage (24:1-4)

This law appears to be out of place here since it deals with matters related to the seventh commandment, not the eighth. Specifically it looks back to 22:13-30 that addressed the issues of marriage fidelity and illicit sexual conduct. The issue of divorce was introduced in 22:19 and 28-29. False accusations against a wife by her husband and rape of an unmarried woman created circumstances in which divorce was forbidden. The law in 24:1-4 assumes divorce was possible; it does not legalize it. In fact there is no specific law in the Old Testament that prescribes divorce. Its practice has to be inferred from other texts. The right of divorce is taken for granted in the laws in Leviticus 21:7,14; 22:13; Numbers 30:10[9], and in the prophet Ezekiel (44:22).

This law is case law, introduced by **if,** in which the conditions for the legal statement are presented in detail in verses 1-3. The law itself comes only in verse 4 and is introduced by **then.** Briefly the law addresses the case of a woman who had been married, divorced, married again, and either divorced again or widowed. Under those circumstances she could not remarry the first husband. Such a remarriage would be a serious breach of God's will, **detestable** to him[1] and a serious **sin** (verse 4).

24:1-3 The law seems quite straightforward but it has raised several controversial issues. The grounds for the man being able to divorce his wife are described by two phrases connected with the causal particle **because**. The first phrase is **the woman becomes displeasing to him** (literally, "the woman did not find favor in his eyes").[2] This exact

---

[1]Equal to idolatry, child sacrifice, and detestable practices catalogued in Deuteronomy: 7:25-26; 12:31; 13:14; 14:3; 23:18[19].

[2]Even though Deuteronomy stresses God's love and gracious acts toward

phrase is found only one other place in the Old Testament, Numbers 11:11.[3] Its exact meaning is not immediately clear. A common phrase used in supplications to authority figures was, "if I have found favor in your eyes . . . ." (or other similar wording, Gen 18:3; 19:19; 34:11; Judg 6:17; 1 Sam 20:29).[4] The plea was for the granting of a favor to develop the relationship. Granting favor was an act of generosity, an active kindness that contributed to the well-being of the other. It was given freely and could not be demanded.[5] It was a concept that certainly fit the ideal marriage. The good marriage would be one in which the husband granted favor to the wife and she responded in kind giving rise to a mutual kindness and close relationship. If the wife lost that favor, it would have had to be because of some serious breach of the relationship.

The serious breach was described by the second phrase. The husband **finds something indecent about her**. The Hebrew is עֶרְוַת דָּבָר (*'ervath dābār*, literally, "a naked thing"). The same phrase was used in 23:14 where it refered to activities that inflict uncleanness on the camp and was parallel to "every evil thing" of verse 9 (see comments on 23:14 above). *'ervāh* by itself refers to nakedness (1 Sam 20:30 [=shame]; Ezek 23:10; Hos 2:9[11]; Micah 1:11) and is used often in Leviticus 18 in an idiomatic phrase that refers to incestuous relationships in the family ("uncover the nakedness of" = have sexual relations with). It would seem then that the phrase would have overtones of some sort of sexual misconduct by the wife. This would not be adultery (for which the penalty was death, 22:22) but would include a wide variety of other acts from indecent exposure to shameless interaction with another man (Ezek 23:29; Hos 2:10).[6]

Israel, this is the only occurrence of the Hebrew word for favor/grace (חֵן, *ḥēn*) in the book.

[3]There Moses appeals to God, "Why have I not found favor in your eyes," in the context of the people grumbling about the manna and lack of meat. He continues, " and you put the burden of all these people on me?" Moses interpreted his having to deal with such obstreperous people as a sign of losing God's favor.

[4]This phrase occurs 34 times in the Old Testament.

[5]See Terence Fretheim, "חנן,"*NIDOTTE,* 2:203-206.

[6]Wright, *Deuteronomy*, p. 262; Merrill, *Deuteronomy*, p. 317; Fishbane, *Biblical Interpretation*, p. 309, "there is little doubt it carries a clear sexual component." However, Mayes thinks it refers to some impurity rather than

Therefore, the marriage bond could be broken only by some serious misconduct by the wife. In verse 3 the second husband could divorce if he **dislikes her** (literally, "hates her"). This is not to be taken as a lesser reason than for the first divorce but must be understood within the context of verse 1.

The divorce procedure was apparently conducted within the family social unit and was not subject to the administration of the village elders.[7] It was a three-step process. The husband **writes her a certificate of divorce, gives it to her and sends her from his house** (v. 1). The certificate given to the wife was crucial to protect her status. It was proof she was divorced and eligible for remarriage, not a loose woman or a runaway wife. Without the legal right to remarry the woman could have easily been forced to join the economically deprived social classes of widows, orphans, and aliens, or become a prostitute. The sending out or away was the crucial last step of the procedure. It signified complete separation from the husband's home, family, and economic protection.[8]

24:4 A return to the first husband was forbidden because the woman had **been defiled** (v. 4). "Defiled" (טמא, *ṭm'*) was used of adultery in Leviticus 18:20 and Numbers 5:13,14,20. Therefore, it seems likely that the law perceived the remarriage of the woman to

---

indecency (*Deuteronomy*, p. 322), and Tigay prefers a broad meaning of something intolerable with no particular sexual overtones (*Deuteronomy*, p. 221). For a detailed discussion of all the issues being considered here see Robin Wakely, "כְּרִיתוּת," *NIDOTTE*, 2:718-22. John Walton has argued in an entirely different direction. Based on the unusual verb form for "unclean" Walton suggests the woman had a condition that made her perpetually unclean and therefore unavailable to conceive children (based on the law in Lev 15:25). This then became grounds for divorce but was humiliating to the woman. The second husband was willing to accept her. The first husband was prohibited further contact with her because he had publicly degraded her by the divorce (John H. Walton, "The Place of the hutqattel within the D-stem Group and Its Implications in Deuteronomy 24:4," *Hebrew Studies* 32 [1991]: 7-17).

[7]Wright, *Deuteronomy*, p. 255, but Driver disagrees (*Deuteronomy*, p. 272). See also the discussion by William Heth, "Divorce, but No Remarriage," in *Divorce and Remarriage: Four Christian Views*, ed., William House [Downers Grove, IL: InterVarsity, 1990], pp. 82-87.

[8]This use of the verb send (שלח, *šlḥ*) became a technical expression for divorce in the Old Testament (Deut 22:19,29; Jer 3:1; Mal 2:15).

the first husband as constituting technical (not legal) adultery. Her defilement was not in a general cultic sense but only from the perspective of her first husband.

The purpose of the law then was not to forbid or allow divorce, but to circumscribe some possible consequences of divorce in order to prevent total anarchy in the family. Perhaps the law was aimed at forcing the first husband to think seriously before divorcing his wife. He could not divorce and remarry her just on a whim.[9] The cause had to be a serious breach of marriage loyalty. In addition the law would protect the second marriage. If the wife had second thoughts or compared the two husbands and wanted to return to the first husband, she could not, and therefore would not have an incentive to sabotage the second marriage.[10] However, uncertainty about the purpose precludes any dogmatic conclusions.[11]

Sometimes the case of David and Michal is cited as evidence that this law was not known in the early monarchy period. But the situation of David does not fit the case of the law here. He deserted Michal; he did not divorce her. Also it is not clear if Saul was within his rights to give her to another man (1 Sam 18:27; 25:44; 2 Sam 3:14-15).[12]

This law is reflected in three prophets: Jeremiah 3:1-5; Hosea 1–3 and Isaiah 50:1. Jeremiah, within the context of his extended metaphorical use of marriage to describe the relationship between God and Judah, contemplated the impossibility of a reunion between God and his unfaithful wife. But what was legally impossible God made possible if his people would repent (Jer 3:6-14). Hosea 2:2 apparently reflects the legal divorce procedure with the husband's declaration that the two parties were no longer husband and wife. Yet in chapter 3 Hosea took his wife back as a demonstration of

---

[9]Cairns, *Deuteronomy*, p. 210; Driver, *Deuteronomy*, p. 272.

[10]Driver, *Deuteronomy*, p. 272; R. Yaron, "The Restoration of Marriage," *JJS* 17 (1966): 1-11: the situation is not the same as, but has the same aim as the laws on incest; G. Wenham, "The Restoration of Marriage Reconsidered," *JJS* 30 (1979): 36-40.

[11]J. Carl Laney has catalogued six different reasons for the law advanced by scholars ("Deuteronomy 24:1-4 and the Issue of Divorce," *BibSac* 149 (1992): 8-13.

[12]J.D. Martin, "The Forensic Background to Jeremiah III:1," *VT* 19 (1969): 82-92.

God's love for Israel. Isaiah responded to apparent claims that God's punishment was permanent (49:8-26) by asking rhetorically if the certificate of divorce for the wife could be found (that is proof of permanent separation; 50:1). Since it could not be found (implied), the punishment for iniquity was temporary.

On Military Exemption (24:5)

24:5 This law is connected to the preceding law by the identical introductory phrase, "If a man takes a wife."[13] Both laws deal with marriage situations. However, this law is more closely connected to the laws for military exemption already covered in 20:5-8, especially verse 7. Its placement here counters the negative focus of the preceding law with a positive note on marriage. Wright calls this a generous and compassionate law.[14]

The exemption in 20:7 was for the benefit of the man. He should have opportunity to produce descendants. The focus of this law was to firmly establish the marriage and **to bring happiness to** the wife. The two laws were complementary. Furthermore, this law prevented the wife from becoming an immediate widow, and it allowed time for the couple to become parents.

The husband was not only to **be free** from military service but from any required government or public service (**any other duty**). In some sense government requirements on the newlywed man were considered the same as stealing time from him. That is perhaps why this law was included among those that expand on the eighth commandment.[15]

However, the exemption may not have been absolute. In an emergency King Asa ordered all men into the army, with no exemptions (1 Kgs 15:22). A Ugaritic text also mentions a national emergency when those normally exempt such as the blind, sick, and new husbands were mobilized for a campaign.[16]

---

[13]The NIV translation obscures this important verbal symmetry.

[14]Wright, *Deuteronomy*, p. 256. Tigay suggests that perhaps emphasis should also be placed on the phrase "new wife." Could it have been that some men were divorcing (vv. 1-4) and remarrying their wives in order to avoid military service? If so, this law would disqualify them from exemption (*Deuteronomy*, p. 222).

[15]Merrill, *Deuteronomy*, p. 319.

[16]Tigay, *Deuteronomy*, p. 222; Craigie, *Deuteronomy*, p. 306. This Ugaritic text provides an ancient Near East context for the OT law.

Forbidden Security for Loans (24:6)

Previous laws had forbidden charging interest on loans (23:19-20) and had commanded the canceling of debts every seven years (15:1-11). This law and ones following (vv. 10-13,17) define the procedure for collecting collateral for loans. It is clear from the details that the underlying concern was for the welfare of the poor, a common theme in Deuteronomy.

These laws are based on the premise that the poor man would have few possessions to use for collateral. What he would have would be the bare necessities for life, such as implements for food production (millstones, v. 7) or clothing (vv. 10-13,17). A creditor had a legal right to take something of the debtor to ensure payment of the loan. However, in doing so the creditor was required to respect the situation of the debtor and not make a difficult situation worse. As pointed out above, the nature of loans was more akin to charitable gifts (see on 15:1-11), and the creditor was to treat the debtor with respect. People were more important than money or property.

24:6 The particular item that was forbidden here was the **millstone,** a common implement essential to daily life. It consisted of a substantial bottom piece (up to 90 pounds, called a quern) which provided the base on which the grain was deposited. It was usually of basalt that had to be imported, although it could be of limestone. There was a much smaller upper piece (less than 10 pounds, called a "rider") which the woman would use to grind the grain to flour for bread.[17] Grinding grain was a daily task and the sound of the women at work were the familiar sounds of life in Israel (Jer 25:10). Taking the millstone was forbidden because it was a source of the man's **livelihood** (literally, it was his "life"). To take it would be akin to stealing his life.[18]

---

[17]The unfortunate Abimelech, who aspired to be king, suffered a fatal wound when a woman dropped an upper millstone on his head (Judg 9:50-53). The circumstances of his demise remained a part of Israelite folklore for centuries (2 Sam 11:21). There are many Egyptian statuettes representing women grinding grain. There is significant evidence of establishments that ground grain on a large scale. The Western Palace at Ebla had 16 grindstones in one room. Often slaves or prisoners of war would be used to do the grinding as the case of Samson attests (Judg 16:21). See *ABD,* s.v. "Mill, Millstone," 4:831-832.

[18]Tigay argues that this law and those following do not address the issue of collateral taken for the loan, but the issue of taking a lien on the property

Kidnapping (24:7)

24:7 Kidnapping is literally "stealing a life." The emphasis on life ties this law to the previous one and continues the stealing theme. Verse 6 is about stealing property, verse 7 is about stealing life. There is perhaps a further subtle connection between the two laws. There is some evidence that children could be taken as payment for a loan (2 Kgs 4:1). In an extensive catalogue of sins, Job paralleled kidnapping a child and seizing an infant of the poor for debt (24:9). This law is grounded in Exodus 21:16 and differs only in making explicit that the kidnapping in view is of a fellow Israelite.[19] It seems to be assumed that the kidnapped person would be sold into slavery to foreigners. Craigie calls this "social murder" because the Israelite would be cut off from the covenant community and the blessings of God.[20] The penalty for kidnapping was death. It was among the several classes of conduct that earned the epithet, **you must purge the evil from among you** (see 13:5; 17:7,12; 19:19).[21]

8. Elaboration on the Ninth Commandment (24:8–25:4)

According to the analysis followed in this commentary a new major section begins here expanding on the ninth commandment, "You shall not bear false witness" (5:20). The aim of the series of ten laws in this section is to protect and preserve the reputation, dignity and respect of the people in the community.[22]

(*Deuteronomy*, p. 223). However, the plainest meaning of the text seems to indicate accepting property as collateral.

[19]Tigay's effort to see this as a serious discrepancy between the two laws seems forced (*Deuteronomy*, p. 224).

[20]Craigie, *Deuteronomy*, p. 307.

[21]In the Hammurabi Law, kidnapping the son of another brought the death penalty (# 14; *ANET* 166). The Hittite Law prescribed a fine, not death for kidnapping (I: 19; *ANET* 190).

[22]Olson, *Deuteronomy*, 108. This structure becomes more tenuous as we near the end of the large section of stipulations, chapters 12–26. For example some of the laws after 24:8 would seem to fit better into the previous section that expanded on the concept of stealing. One thinks especially of verses 10-13 and 17-18 that deal with taking pledges again (cf. v. 6) and verses 14-15 on the paying of wages. However, Merrill points out that a

On Leprosy (24:8-9)

A law on leprosy to begin the section comes as a surprise. The connection with false witness is not readily apparent. However, the mention of the example of Miriam in verse 9 clarifies the reasoning for the placement here. The event referred to is recorded in Numbers 12. Miriam and Aaron, Moses' sister and brother, began to talk against Moses because of his Cushite wife. This was a case of slander (false witness). Instead of humbly accepting Moses' authority, Miriam and Aaron arrogantly elevated themselves to his level. For this offense both were reprimanded and Miriam was struck with leprosy.

24:8-9 The Levitical priests had authority in cases of leprosy (Lev 13) and the law commanded submission to their authority. The language, **be very careful to do** and **you must follow carefully**, was common Deuteronomic language for obedience to the covenant law. The brief law then operates in two directions: concern for proper treatment of a disease, and concern for respect for authority through obedience. **Remember** is a key word throughout Deuteronomy as a call to recall the past in order to prompt obedience in the present. Therefore, the past serves here as a warning against false witnessing.

The disease described as **leprosy** in the Old Testament is probably not what is understood today as Hansen's disease. The extensive descriptions in Leviticus 13–14 refer to a wide variety of scaly skin infections.[23]

On Taking a Pledge (24:10-13)

Ancient Israel was forbidden to charge interest on loans (23:19-20), but they were allowed to receive collateral for the loan.[24] This law provided guidelines for how the exchange of collateral was to be

---

connection can be seen between the laws in this new section when we see them as focused on the offended party (*Deuteronomy*, 321).

[23]See *IDB*, s.v. "Leprosy," 3:111-113; *ABD*, s.v. "Leprosy," 4:277-282. The Hebrew word probably refers to various skin lesions and diseases such as psoriasis, eczema, seborrhea, and conditions such as boils. Walton and Matthews (*Genesis–Deuteronomy*, p. 157) insist that "Clinical leprosy (Hansen's disease) has not been attested in the ancient Near East prior to the time of Alexander the Great." This disagrees with R.K. Harrison in *IDB*.

handled. The creditor was to do everything he could to respect the honor and dignity of the debtor. Debtors suffered from humiliation already, and there was little that they controlled. Therefore, the law required the creditor to allow the debtor to select the item for collateral (v. 11). The creditor could not barge into the house and rummage through what few things the person owned.

24:10-12 The law consists of two related sections. Verses 10-11 address all creditor-debtor situations. Verses 12-13 refer explicitly to the **poor** debtor. In this case it was assumed that the collateral the debtor had was a few necessities of life, and he would have to give over one of those items. The most likely personal possession was a **cloak**. This was the large outer cloak used both for warmth during cold weather and as a covering in the night.[25] It was an essential personal possession, and the poor were not to be deprived of its use. Frequent references to the violation of this law in other parts of the Old Testament are proof its importance (Amos 2:8; Prov 20:16 // 27:13; Job 22:6; cf. Job 24:3). Similar concern for the creditor's fair treatment of the debtor occurs in other ancient Near Eastern laws.[26]

24:13 The motivation for obedience was negative in Exodus 22:27 ("when he cries out to me, I will hear"). But here in Deuteronomy the motivation was positive. The debtor would bless (בָּרַךְ, *brk*) the creditor (NIV, **thank you**) and bring **righteousness** to the creditor.[27] There was a vertical as well as a horizontal dimension to just treatment of the poor. Not only did obedience result in compassion and dignity for the debtor, it resulted in a special blessing

---

[24]This law is apparently an expansion of Exod 22:26-27 with verses 10-11 adding further requirements.

[25]It was a garment with a large number of utilitarian applications also. In 1 Sam 21:9[10] the sword of Goliath was wrapped in a cloak. A late seventh-century Hebrew text from the time of Josiah from western Judah contains an appeal of a workman to an official for the return of his cloak that was taken from him while he was working (*ANET*, p. 568).

[26]Hammurabi Code # 113: a creditor who took a debtor's grain without his consent had to return it. Also the Code allowed a person to be held as collateral for debt (# 115, 116; *ANET*, p. 170).

[27]In the light of the context the NIV translation is weak and misleading. Of the 327 occurrences of *brk* in the Old Testament, this is the only place NIV translates it as thank. Most of the occurrences in Deuteronomy of *brk* refer to God's blessings on Israel. The few exceptions include chapter 33

from God. The righteousness attributed to the creditor was acknowledgment that the act of generosity conformed to the covenant
expectations of conduct. The debtor was invested with special spiritual power in this section of the legal material. In verse 15 (see
below) his cry of distress could bring guilt on another. So the creditor was credited with righteousness or sin depending on his treatment of the poor.

Paying the Hired Man (24:14-15)

24:14-15 Concern for the poor was extended to the **hired man**.
This refers to the **Israelite** who had lost family land or other means
of independent income and was reduced to hiring himself out as a
laborer.[28] The poor man, reduced to this condition, was in precarious economic circumstances. He needed **his wages each day**, or he
would not be able to provide daily food for his family. This situation
clearly illustrates how desperate the situation of the poor could
become. The wage was his very livelihood; his life depended on it. It
was the same sort of situation pictured in the law of the millstone
(v. 6). The hard life of the day laborer is reflected in Job 7:1-2.

The strongest possible language was used for this crime,
"defraud or oppress" (עָשַׁק, *'šq*).[29] It was a word synonymous with
"rob" according to the parallel law in Leviticus 19:13. The law
reflected the possibility that the rich could use their position to steal
from the poor or defraud them in some way. The law was broad
enough to include the **alien** also (cf. vv. 17,19,20,21).

The employer has countless ways that he can take advantage of
the employee if he so desires. In the ancient world it was to withhold
the daily wage. In today's world it could be lack of reasonable benefits, forced part-time work, unsafe working conditions, unpaid over-
time, or company mergers without regard to workers, to name a few
practices.

---

which is Moses' blessing on Israel and the priests who pronounce blessings
in God's name (10:8; 21:5). The blessing of the debtor should be understood in the context of these human examples of blessing. It carried significant weight.

[28]Jacob was described by the same term when he worked for Laban (Gen
29:15; 30:38; 31:7).

[29]The NIV "take advantage of" is much too mild.

The blessing of the poor man in verse 13 led to crediting the compassionate creditor with righteousness. Here the complaint of the poor man (**cry to**) could lead to the employer being found guilty of sin (cf. 23:21). This cry to the LORD was not some mild utterance but the desperate outcry of the oppressed who had no other recourse for assistance and rescue but God.[30] This was the same guilt incurred if aid for the needy was withheld because of the approach of the Sabbatical year (15:9). In the covenant community the vertical relationship with God was intertwined with the horizontal relationship with members of the community. Since the God of the covenant was a compassionate God (10:17-18) who was passionately concerned about justice, his covenant people were expected to practice that compassion and justice. Therefore, laws such as the ones in this chapter addressed those areas most open to abuse: loans, hired help, and feeding the poor (vv. 6,10-13,14-15,17-22).

Individual Responsibility (24:16)

This forthright statement about individual responsibility seems out of place in a section related to the ninth commandment. But to execute a person for something he did not do would be a serious miscarriage of justice and a false witness in the extreme.

24:16 In ancient Israel and in the ancient Near East in general the corporate solidarity of the family and larger community was assumed. Deuteronomy was grounded on the concept of the responsibility of the members of the covenant community to each other. However, in terms of justice under the law, each individual was responsible for his own actions. This law dealt with human administration of justice in a legal setting, not with divine justice. Deuteronomy 5:9 dealt with a different arena, that of offenses against God. It also addressed the theological and social consequences of the father's sins. Children might be affected by the sins of the fathers, but they were not to be held responsible for them (see Deut 7:10 also and the individual responsibility assumed in Exod 21–23).

Both Jeremiah (31:34) and Ezekiel (18) post strong statements undergirding the principle of individual responsibility. Though much later than the law in Deuteronomy, their restatement was apparently

---

[30]See Exod 22:22-24.

required both because of popular Israelite belief and by the attitude of the exiles. Many of the exiles apparently thought they were suffering for the sins of the fathers.

The episodes recorded in Joshua 7 (Achan's sin) and 2 Samuel 21:1-8 were not criminal cases covered by the law. The crime was committed against God in both situations and he ordered the executions.

There are several accounts in the historical books that detail the slaughter of whole families. But these were all royal cases, and there is no evidence they were approved (1 Sam 22:16-19; 1 Kgs 15:29; 16:11-12; 2 Kgs 10:6-8,11,17). King Amaziah of Judah, in obedience to this law (2 Kgs 14:6), executed some assassins but not their sons. Such royal conduct was rare.

In the ancient cultures all members of the family shared in the disgrace and shame if one member committed a crime. It would have been a natural conclusion that all members should be held responsible for it. The practice outside of Israel reflected such a premise. The Persian custom was described in Esther 9:13-14 and Daniel 6:24[25]. Ancient Near Eastern Laws in general stand in contrast with the biblical law. In Hammurabi's code if a man killed the daughter of another, his daughter was killed. If a son were killed in the collapse of a house, the builder's son was executed.[31]

Justice for the Poor (24:17-22)

Though often taken separately, verses 17-18 and 19-22 are closely bound by shared concerns, shared recipients of justice, and shared motivation. The shared concern is justice and care for the poor. The shared recipients are **the alien, the fatherless and the widow** (vv. 17,19,20,21). The shared motivation is the divine rescue from **Egypt** (vv. 18,22). Consequently, these verses will be considered together.[32]

24:17 The venue is the same as the law in verse 16, the administration of justice in the court. Justice was not to be "turned aside," or perverted. The law had already addressed one way that could happen,

---

[31]#210 and 230 (*ANET,* pp. 175, 176). See also # 116 and Middle Assyrian Law # 55 (*ANET,* pp. 175 and 185). However Middle Assyrian Law #2 established that a woman who committed blasphemy should be punished but not her family (*ANET,* p. 180).

[32]See Wright, *Deuteronomy,* p. 260. For prior laws that address the same concerns see Exod 22:21-22[20-21]; 23:6; Lev 19:9-10; 23:22.

through bribes (16:19).[33] The three classes of people mentioned would have been at a disadvantage because they would have had no one to represent them in the court. Other ancient Near Eastern societies were concerned for the widow and orphan also, but not for the alien.[34]

Previous law had dealt with the process by which collateral could be taken for a loan (vv. 10-13). But the case addressed here was that of extreme poverty, the widow. In the former law the cloak could be taken, but was to be returned at night. In the case of the widow her **cloak** was not even to be taken, because it may have been all that she had and her ability to repay would have been very limited.[35] The loan would have been more like a gift.

24:18 The motivation for this compassion was the compassion God had shown Israel in Egypt (cf. 10:19). God, because of his love (ch. 7), had **redeemed** Israel from bondage and servitude. His action demonstrated what was at the core of his heart: concern for the oppressed. His redemption of Israel from Egypt was motivation for other laws also (5:15; 15:15; 21:8) and at the heart of several other affirmations in Deuteronomy (7:8; 9:26; 13:6). A shorter version of the motivation statement in verse 22 forms a frame around the laws on gleaning for the poor in verses 19-21. The emphasis was on **remember**. If Israel forgot her history, she was also in danger of forgetting to care for the poor. The prophets had to remind Israel of both the need to care for the poor (Amos 2,5,8) and her history (Hos 11).

24:19-21 The laws on gleaning (cf. Lev 19:9-10) demonstrated in a practical way how justice for the poor could be achieved. The poor had a right to participate in the bounty of the land. Gleaning provided them a means for doing this by their own labor, which allowed them to maintain their dignity and not have to ask for a handout.

---

[33]The NIV is inconsistent in translating the phrase. It has "pervert justice" in 16:19, but "deprive . . . of justice" here. The former is better. The law in 16:19 suggests a legal process was initiated but it was a sham. The plaintiff would think he was getting justice because the case was taken to court, but he was not.

[34]See the *Tale of Aqhat*, V, epilogue to the *Code of Hammurabi, The Instruction of King Merikere,* and *The Instruction of Amenemopet,* ch. 28 in *ANET,* pp. 151, 178, 415 and 424.

[35]The more general word בֶּגֶד (*beged*) is used here referring to any kind of robe or garment.

The three crops were representative of the main food crops for Israel.[36] Harvesting the grain field (wheat and barley) was done with a hand sickle. It was easy to overlook some when picking it up or to drop some. This grain was to be left. Leviticus 19:9 instructed the farmer not to cut the grain all the way to the edge of the field. Olives were beaten from the branches by a long stick (Isa 17:6; 24:13). Unripe ones would remain, and some that fell on the ground would be overlooked. These were to be left also. Grapes did not ripen all at once, and ordinarily the vines would have to be picked over a second time. This was not to be done.

What was left or overlooked was for the poor. The language indicates ownership; it belonged to them (literally, "it is for . . .").[37] It was not charity. In a similar way the poor were the only ones who had access to the fallow fields during the Sabbatical year (Exod 23:10-11; Lev 25:2-7).

The book of Ruth offers a practical illustration of the implementation of these laws. Ruth was both an alien and a widow. Boaz was an exemplary landlord, for he even ordered his workers to leave more than normal in the fields. He understood the spirit of the law (Ruth 2). However, there is a slight hint that not everyone was willing to obey the law. Ruth would glean where she could "find favor" (2:2).

---

[36]See Gower, *New Manners*, pp. 87-119.

[37]The combination לְ יִהְיֶה (*yihyeh l⁾*) suggests ownership. The text does not say "leave it" as the NIV translation has.

DEUTERONOMY 25

Limits on Punishment (25:1-3)

This particular law addresses the form of punishment required for noncapital crimes, or cases for which there was no specific penalty prescribed. The case presented was probably only one of many possible ones that could have been used. It was intended as a sample situation.

This law fits the general context of chapter 24 for it provides for protection of the vulnerable in Israelite society, in this case the criminal. Excessive flogging could easily have led to brutality and degradation of the criminal, dehumanizing him. In that respect it could be understood as equal to false testimony which devalued the person as well.

25:1 The subject of the law was very broad, **a dispute** which is not further defined. The word used (רִיב, *rîb*) refers to a legal dispute (lawsuit) under jurisdiction of the courts. It has appeared already in Deuteronomy (1:12; 17:8; 19:17; 21:5; cf. Exod 23:2).[1] The procedure for such legal cases was covered in 17:8-12 and 19:16-19 (see comments there). The judges were to carry out a careful investigation. That procedure is assumed here. The legal process would result in a determination of innocence or guilt (literally, "pronounce as innocent the innocent and pronounce as guilty the guilty"). This was the goal of the judicial process.

25:2-3 If the accused party was found **guilty** of a crime that required corporeal punishment then the sentence was imposed. The sentence was **flogging**. It was to be carried out with two restrictions.

---

[1] The prophets used the concept of a lawsuit or court case to describe the action that God would take against Israel, against whom he brought charges (Jer 2:5-9; Hos 2:4-25; 4:1-3; Micah 6:1-8). The consequence was divine judgment for sin.

The punishment was to be done in front of the judge, and the miscreant was not to be given **more than forty lashes**. This made the sentence public and conducted under the watchful eye of the judge. In a situation where brutality and emotion could easily gain the upper hand, this provision was important. The presence of the judge also meant that he would carefully count the number of lashes to assure the limit was not exceeded.

The number of lashes was limited in order to protect the human dignity of the criminal. More was considered **degrading**, a dishonor to the person, and a violation of his human value and dignity. Forty lashes were the limit, not the legal amount. Thus the judge apparently had the authority to prescribe the number of lashes up to forty (**the number of lashes his crime deserves**). He had freedom to fit the punishment to the crime.

This is the only law in Deuteronomy on flogging, although some scholars think the punishment of the husband who falsely accused his wife was flogging (22:18; see comments there). Exodus provided a penalty for the man who beat a slave to death (21:20) suggesting flogging may have been a common way to punish slaves. Proverbs refers to the practice of flogging (17:10,26; 19:25c) and approves the use of the rod for parental discipline (23:13-14).

Ancient Near Eastern laws prescribed flogging for a wide variety of crimes including assault, false accusations, causing a miscarriage, encroaching on another's property, destroying another's house, not sharing water rights, fraud, and selling a person who was taken as security for a loan. Other penalties were often imposed as well. There was no limit on the flogging in these laws, with the number of lashes going as high as 100. The average was fifty.[2] These laws did not share Deuteronomy's concern for the dignity of the criminal.

Later Jewish legal experts defined specific offenses that required flogging and erected limits on the severity of flogging. By New Testament times a limit of thirty-nine lashes was imposed in order not to violate the forty allowed (2 Cor 11:24), and physical examination of the criminal was required to assess how well he could handle the punishment.[3]

---

[2]See *Code of Hammurabi*, #202, *Middle Assyrian Laws*, A, 7, 18, 19, 21, 40; B, 7-10, 14-15, 18; C + G, 2-3, 8, 11; F, 1; N, 1-2 (*ANET*, pp. 175, 181, 186-188).

[3]Mishna *Makkott* 3:1-11. See *EncJud*, s.v. "Flogging," 6:1348-1349.

The thrust of this law reflects the strong Deuteronomic concern for the protection of the less fortunate in Israelite society. The covenant community was bound together under God. Thus **your brother** could not be dishonored even if convicted of a crime. He was still a person who deserved honor, not dishonor. This powerful concern imbued the laws with a humaneness that could transform the legal system.[4] It is a concern often overlooked in negative assessments of the Old Testament law.

Respect for Animals (25:4)

25:4 At first glance this law seems completely out of place. But further reflection will suggest why it was put here. Deuteronomy consistently grounds its laws in the compassionate heart of God. The laws at the end of chapter 24 demonstrate how divine compassion was to be extended to the poor of Israelite society. Their dignity and honor was to be respected as provisions for their needs were made. This law on the ox fits into that pattern. God's compassion extended even to the animals and who were to be shown care as well. To employ the ox in grain production without allowing it access to some of the grain would be cruel. Thus gleaning rights were extended to animals (24:19-22). Deuteronomy had already shown this concern by forbidding the unequal yoking of animals for work (22:10). According to Proverbs a righteous man cared for his animals (Prov 12:10).

In ancient Israel grain was threshed by laying the grain stalks out on a threshing floor of packed earth or rock. The stalks were then flailed with a long rod (probably the method used in Judg 6:11; Ruth 2:17). Oxen were also employed to walk over the grain pulling a wooden sledge with sharp rock or metal attached to the bottom. The stalks were cut up and the grain knocked off. Then winnowing and sieving separated the straw, chaff, and grain. Since many farmers may not have owned oxen, they would hire them, and feeding them grain would be part of the fee.[5] Ancient Near Eastern laws required grain as payment for the hire of oxen and other animals. Carved reliefs from Egypt show oxen and donkeys threshing.[6]

---

[4]Wright, *Deuteronomy*, p. 265; Cairns, *Deuteronomy*, p. 215

[5]See Gower, *New Manners and Customs*, p. 97 (with a picture on page 96); Walton and Matthews, *Genesis–Deuteronomy*, p. 258.

[6]*Code of Hammurabi*, #268-270 (*ANET*, p. 177); *ANEP*, figs. 89 and 122.

9. Elaboration of the Tenth Commandment (25:5–26:15)

We come now to the last major unit of the stipulation section of Deuteronomy, 25:5–26:15. It contains a variety of laws that are related to the tenth commandment, "You shall not covet" (5:21). The commandment specifies several categories of forbidden coveting related to the "neighbor," that is, a fellow Israelite. The laws in this section reflect the complexity of Israelite life by dealing with several issues tied to the concept of coveting, including interfamily relationships, honesty, and devotion to the LORD. Although coveting is essentially an internal matter of the heart, the negative and positive laws in this section constructed some parameters for conduct and thus for curbing coveting. The laws were not intended to be exhaustive, but only representative of the sorts of issues Israel should be concerned about.

The Case of Levirate Marriage (25:5-10)

The first case involved a situation within the family that addressed an important social issue, the family line of a deceased Israelite. It dealt specifically with the first admonition of the commandment, the relationship to the neighbor's wife, or in this case the brother's wife. There was a circumstance when the wife of a brother could be married ("coveted"?).

The law anticipates the case of a man dying and leaving no son. In such a circumstance the brother who lived in the same household was obligated to marry the widow and produce a male heir for the deceased to carry on his name. However, the brother could refuse to accept the responsibility.

25:5-6 This situation is called levirate marriage (from the Latin, *levir*, "brother-in-law"). The Hebrew uses the rare word יבם (*ybm*) which carries the meaning of fulfilling the duties of a brother-in-law by consummating the marriage. The related nouns are translated as brother- or sister-in-law.[7]

The law is case law and the situation is that of **brothers living together and one of them dies without a son.** "Living together" probably is intended to mean that the brothers were living in the same

---

[7]The verb and noun forms (masculine and feminine) of the word occur only in this text and in the related texts, Gen 38:8 and Ruth 1:15, a total of ten times for all three words.

household or on the same family land, so that the potential merging of two inheritances would not be difficult.[8] The law is silent both about the marital status of the brother and whether he is the brother next in line. In the related situation of Tamar, albeit from a different era, the responsible brother was next youngest (Gen 38).

The widow was not to **marry outside the family**, presumably to keep the family land intact. However, the main reason for the arrangement was so that **the name of the dead brother** would **not be blotted out from Israel**.[9] Memory as carried on in the family name was the only way an Israelite man achieved immortality. To have one's name cut off from memory was a terrible thing. Both Saul and Absalom set up memorials for themselves (1 Sam 15:12; 2 Sam 18:18). Absalom did it because he had no son to carry on his name.[10] To have one's name **blotted out** often was the consequence of God's judgment against sinners (Exod 17:14 and Deut 25:19 [the Amalekites]; Exod 32:33; Ps 9:5). Without a male heir it could look like the Israelite man was suffering such a consequence.

This law stands in tension with Leviticus 18:16 and 20:21 that forbids a man from having sexual relations with his brother's wife or marrying her. Leviticus however gave the general principle while Deuteronomy dealt with a specific and exceptional case.[11]

---

[8]"Brothers living together" is a rare phrase. The three words occur together in Ps 133:1 and perhaps refer to a similar situation. The Psalm suggests a congenial family community was not common. Similar language is used to describe the proximity of Abram and Lot (Gen 13:6) and Jacob and Esau (Gen 36:7). In both cases increase of flocks and family necessitated a geographical separation. See Wright, *God's People*, pp. 54-55; Tigay, *Deuteronomy*, p. 231. Jephthah was driven away by his half-brothers because his mother was a prostitute (Judg 11:1-2). On the other hand Gideon went back home to live after his exploits even though he had a large family (Judg 8:29-30).

[9]Despite the clear statement in the text Mayes thinks the purpose was to avoid loss of property to the family (*Deuteronomy*, p. 328).

[10]1 Sam 14:27 reports that Absalom had three sons. They all must have died rather young.

[11]Ancient Hittite and Assyrian laws also provided for levirate marriages. Hittite law specified the brother had first obligation, then the father-in-law. Hittite law also agreed with Leviticus that sleeping with a brother's wife while he was alive was anathema (#193, 195; *ANET*, p. 196). Middle Assyrian Laws included the betrothal time under the levirate umbrella (# A, 30, 33, 43; *ANET*, pp. 182, 184).

The book of Ruth appears to illustrate the application of this law, but the cases were not entirely analogous. The story of Ruth describes the function of the *goel*, the kinsman-redeemer. The situation did not involve a brother of her husband (there were none), but a distant relative of Naomi and the possession of ancestral land. Both the redemption of the family property and the continuation of the family name were the focus (Ruth 4:5,10).

25:7 The brother could refuse. The acceptable reasons were not specified but there could be several. Perhaps he did not care for the widow, or he had a wife already and thought two would be too expensive, or she would be a rival to the first. Perhaps he thought he could get a larger share of the family estate for himself if he did not marry her. In the case of Tamar, she appeared to be bad luck to Judah, and he did not want to lose another son (Gen 38:11). If the brother refused to marry her, the widow was to **go to the elders at the town gate** and report his refusal. Thus the matter became a community affair to be settled by the community leaders (see 19:12; 21:2; 22:15).

25:8-10 The elders were to investigate the matter thoroughly (1:17; 13:14; 17:4). If the man **persisted** in refusing to meet his obligation then the widow was to symbolically declare her independence of him and the family. She did this by removing **one of his sandals** and **spitting in his face**. This action has generated considerable discussion. It apparently had something to do with property transactions. In Ruth 4:7 the author included a note that the exchange of a sandal ratified the sale of property. But in the case here in Deuteronomy no property exchanged hands. Furthermore, no sandal exchange took place. Rather the widow removed the sandal of the brother. Therefore, Ruth 4 is not an exact parallel.[12] The action

---

[12]In several texts ownership of land was attested by walking through or around it (Gen 13:17; Deut 1:36; 11:24; Josh 1:3; 1 Kgs 21:16-17). So the association with the sandal was made. In the Psalms God lays claim to Edom through sandal imagery (60:8[9]; 108:9). See Mayes, *Deuteronomy*, p. 328; Cairns, *Deuteronomy*, p. 217. Carmichael proposed that since "foot" sometimes is a euphemism for genitals in the Old Testament, this law refers to the widow exposing the brother in order to shame him (C.M. Carmichael, "A Ceremonial Crux: Removing a Man's Sandal as a Female Gesture of Contempt," *JBL* 96 [1977]: 321-336). Though this explanation helps provide a reason for the juxtaposition of the following law, it seems somewhat tenuous. Would the original audience have made all the euphemistic connections?

reflected negatively on the brother for his family gained a name that must have carried a sense of shame with it (the **Family of the Un-sandaled**). Public disgrace seemed to be its main intent. Public stigmatization by removing a sandal was a part of ancient Hittite law.[13] Further the act may have symbolized that the widow was free from obligation to the family of her dead husband, and was allowed to seek her own security, perhaps in another marriage.[14]

Spitting in his face was apparently a way of insulting the brother (cf. Isa 50:6; Job 30:10). In the Old Testament, bodily fluids could have serious effects on a person. A man with a bodily discharge who spit on another made the recipient unclean (Lev 15:8; cf. Num 12:14). Therefore, the punishment fit the crime. The brother insulted the household of his brother and degraded his own with a stigma.

This law further demonstrates Deuteronomy's strong concern for the family and justice for the widow. Even though the brother could refuse, he was branded with shame for his lack of concern.

A Wife's Intervention in a Fight (25:11-12)

This law is unique and has elicited much discussion about its connection to its context. It is the only law that mentions genitals and the only law that prescribes bodily mutilation. It is also one of the few laws that counsels no pity.

25:11 Scholars differ on its connection to its context,[15] but it is related to the previous law by verbal and thematic parallels. Verbally the introduction in verse 11 shares three important words with the introduction to the preceding law in verse 5 — the words "man," "brother," and "together." The NIV translation, **If two men are fighting,** does not reveal this connection. The Hebrew text reads: "If two men are fighting together, a man and his brother . . . ."[16] Thus,

---

[13]H.A. Hoffner, Jr., "Some Contributions of Hittitology to O.T. Study," *TB* 20 (1969): 42-44.

[14]Paul Kruger, "The Removal of the Sandal in Deuteronomy xxv 9: 'A Rite of Passage'?" *VT* 46 (1996): 534-539.

[15]According to Thompson it is one of three distinct and unrelated laws at the end of chapter 25 (*Deuteronomy*, p. 252). However, other commentators have tried to find some tie to the context.

[16]"Brother" in Deuteronomy usually indicates a fellow Israelite except in verse 5 when it refers to an actual brother. Because of the parallelism it

the two laws are linked by similar beginnings. They are also connected by similar themes. The previous law gave freedom to a wife to degrade her brother-in-law. This law made it clear that that freedom was severely limited. The wife could not normally injure or insult another man even in defense of her husband. Further, both laws deal with the issue of procreation and progeny. In the first case, death threatened a man's progeny, in the second case injury of the genitals threatened the same. Neither was to be allowed.[17]

Laws on men fighting, and related injuries, occur in the Book of the Covenant in Exodus 21:18-19,22-25. The law in verses 22-25 prescribed the *lex telionis* as a penalty. This may be the background to the penalty in the law here in Deuteronomy.

The wife had a good reason for coming to the aid of her husband, for the text indicates he was in serious danger. The word for **assailant** comes from the verb "to strike, to kill" (נכה, *nkh*). The verb was used to refer to death in every occurrence in Deuteronomy except in chapter 25:2,3,11. Verses 2 and 3 refer to flogging. Therefore, the fight in this law was conceived to have taken a serious turn and the wife used the most extreme measure to rescue her husband.[18]

25:12 The penalty for the wife's assult was severe: **you shall cut off her hand**. No other Old Testament law carries physical mutilation as a penalty, except that suggested by the *lex talionis* (if it was intended literally).[19] On the other hand ancient Mesopotamian laws often prescribed mutilation. In fact the Middle Assyrian Laws addressed this same situation. The penalty was the cutting off of a finger, or gouging out the eyes (assumed).[20]

---

seems that the latter meaning was intended in verse 11 also although English translations do not construe it that way.

[17]The context and verbal parallels do not support the opinion that the law deals only with female modesty violations (Walton and Matthews, *Genesis–Deuteronomy*, p. 259; Weinfeld, *Deuteronomic School*, pp. 292-293). It has a much more serious grounding.

[18]The word for "rescue" (נצל, *nṣl*) is a common word for deliverance or rescue and is often used of God's rescue of the psalmist from trouble or an enemy.

[19]See above on 19:21.

[20]MAL A, 8 (*ANET*, p. 181). The Hebrew text does not use the usual word for hand (*yad*) but the word for the palm or hollow of the hand (*kap*). Building on this fact L.M. Eslinger has suggested parallels with the use of

Show no pity puts this law in a select category of laws that carry that admonition (7:16; 13:8[9]; 19:13,21). It was applied to situations where the judges might be tempted to be lenient to the defendant as in this case where the wife's motive would have elicited great sympathy.[21]

Honest Weights and Measures (25:13-16)

The connection of this law with the tenth commandment is clear. Coveting was an attitude of the heart, an inner desire that, if allowed to grow, would result in action. If coveting property was not curbed, the result would eventually be stealing. Although it is impossible to write laws that could prevent thoughts, this law ingeniously attacked the problem by prohibiting the ownership of implements that could be used for stealing. Thus even the temptation to steal was removed.

25:13-14 Two items essential to commerce were in view, **weights and measures**. Weights refers to objects, usually stones (which is the Hebrew word), used on a balance scale to weigh out produce for trade or purchase. A dishonest merchant would have two different weights, a light one for selling the produce and a heavy one for buying it. Measures were baskets or jars used for the trading of liquid produce such as wine or olive oil. Large or small jars could be used in the same way.[22]

25:15 The law required **accurate and honest** weights and measures (literally "complete and righteous"). The parallel law in Leviticus

---

kap in Genesis 32:25-33 (Jacob's wrestling with the divine figure) where he understands *kap* to refer to the genitals, not the hollow of the thigh as usually understood. Thus he understands the penalty here to be a true *lex talionis*. The woman's genitals were to be mutilated in some way ("The Case of an Immodest Lady Wrestler in Deut 25:11-12," *VT* 31 [1981]: 269-281). The biblical penalty of loss of a hand suggests the woman's action was shameful and possibly resulted in emasculation.

[21]Because of its many difficulties Jewish scholars debated the meaning and intent of this law extensively. See Tigay's discussion (*Deuteronomy*, pp. 484-486, Excursus 23).

[22]Weights and measures took many forms in the ancient world. Standardization made commerce possible but was difficult without a strong central authority (cf. the effort mentioned during David's reign in 2 Sam 14:26). Archaeologists have uncovered numerous weights; many of them are inscribed. There is no uniformity among them. For a detailed discussion and pictures see IDB, 4:828-839, s.v. "Weights and Measures."

19:35-36 provided the rationale that this was the word of the LORD God who had led Israel out of Egypt. It was this theological grounding that distinguished the Deuteronomy law from similar laws and concerns in the ancient Near East.[23]

25:16 Both a covenant blessing and a covenant sanction accompanied this law. Obedience would bring long life in the land that God was giving them. That promise put the law on a par with a small number of similar admonitions in Deuteronomy (4:40; 5:16,33; 6:2; 11:9; 22:7; 30:20) and elevated it to a high level of importance. The sanction, **the LORD your God detests anyone who does these things**, also put the law in a select group (7:25; 12:31; 17:1; 18:12; 22:5; 23:19; 27:15). Most of the other laws that carry this sanction dealt with idolatry. Therefore, to defraud others was the same as idolatry because money took the place of God.[24]

The foundation for the law was the character of God. Israel should not deal **dishonestly** because there was no dishonesty in God (32:4, "who does no wrong" [NIV] translates the same word). The frequent references to dishonest weights and measures in the prophets and in Proverbs suggests the problem was a serious one in Israel (Hos 12:7[8]; Amos 8:5; Micah 6:10-11; Prov 11:1; 16:11; 20:10,23).

Dishonesty in commerce was rejected so strongly because the most common result of such cheating was further oppression of the poor. Concern for the poor is a major theme in the book.

The Amalekites (25:17-19)

This paragraph seems out of place. It is written neither as a case law nor in the direct command style (apodictic) of the other laws in the stipulation section, chapters 12–26. Its subject matter also seems foreign to the context. It would fit more properly into chapter 20 that deals with Yahweh war.

---

[23]Laws or admonitions about dishonest weights can be found in a wide variety of Mesopotamian and Egyptian sources. See the *Code of Hammurabi*, #94 (*ANET*, p.. 169), the Babylonian "Hymn to the Sungod," ii, 51-52 (*ANET*, p. 388), the Egyptian "Instruction of Amem-em-opet," ch. 16 (*ANET*, p. 423), "The Protestation of Guiltlessness," A22-26 (*ANET*, p. 34), and "The Protest of the Eloquent Peasant," (*ANET*, pp. 407-410).

[24]The particular phrase "it is an abomination to the LORD your God" appears only in the book of Deuteronomy and the book of Proverbs.

However, it is possible to discern connections between this admonition and its immediate context. Chapter 25 addresses relationships between brothers in Israel, both other Israelites and family members. According to Genesis 36:12 the Amalekites were related to Israel through Esau. Amalek was the son of Eliphaz and the grandson of Esau. Therefore, the law continues the theme of relationships between brothers.

Furthermore, the description of the offenses of the Amalekites in verse 18 places their actions within the realm of the tenth commandment. Coveting was to desire what the weak and powerless had. The Amalekites were depicted as mistreating the weak and powerless of Israel because they lacked a relationship with God (verse 19).[25]

The Amalekites were apparently a nomadic tribe that inhabited the desert areas of the Sinai Peninsula, the Negev, and sometimes the Arabah and areas east of the Jordan River. They are first introduced in Genesis 14:7 which is historically prior to Esau, and may be an editorial explanation. Israel first encountered the Amalekites near Rephidim in the wilderness of Sinai and defeated them in battle (Exod 17:8-15). However, a year later, the Amalekites defeated Israel in Israel's abortive attempt to take the Promised Land (Num 14:44-45). The Amalekites were a consistent thorn in Israel's side during the time of the judges (Judg 3:13; 6:3-5,33; 7:12; 10:12). One reason Saul was chosen as king was to defeat the Amalekites (1 Sam 15). Saul's failure in this led to his rejection as king (1 Sam 28:18). David apparently was more successful against them (1 Sam 30:18; 2 Sam 1:1; 8:12). There were still a few survivors in Hezekiah's day who were finally eliminated by a small band of Simeonites (1 Chr 4:43).

25:17-18 Deuteronomy condemns the Amalekites for a different action than Exodus 17. The harassment of stragglers was more important to Deuteronomy than the battle itself as in Exodus. The stragglers would have been mostly women, children, and the elderly who could not keep up. Such action demonstrated a vicious lack of concern for the most rudimentary of humane conduct. According to Deuteronomy it was because the Amalekites had **no fear of God**. Usually "fear of God" in Deuteronomy refers to the

---

[25]Olson, *Deuteronomy*, p. 114. Kaufman in his insightful article failed to see these connections ("Structure," p. 144).

proper relationship of the covenant people to her God which entailed love, obedience, loyalty and service. It exhibited itself in concern for the helpless (6:2,13; 10:12-20). However, in this case it was the Amalekites' lack of knowledge of God (any god) that led to absence of fear. A result was no normal humane consideration for others. They had no conscience and thus no moral parameters for treatment of others. They were cruel and inhuman. For this they were held accountable to the sovereign God (as were other nations, Amos 1–2) and earned their destruction at the hands of Israel.[26]

25:19 The time would come when Israel would carry out God's mandate. Their task was to **blot out the memory of Amalek from under heaven.**[27] This was the same task, worded in the same way, that God had set for himself in Exodus 17:14. This task is the main purpose of the paragraph. It is emphasized by the call to **remember** in verse 17 that is matched by the last words in verse 19, **Do not forget.** Israel was to remember to wipe out the memory of Amalek.[28]

This last paragraph in chapter 25 took care of some unfinished business for Israel. It also forms with chapter 26 a transition section to the future when Israel will be in the land.[29]

This paragraph is a reminder that all nations answer to the sovereign God of the universe for their actions. It agrees in principle with Paul that no one is without excuse before God, for he has provided in creation evidence of himself (Rom 1:18-20). He has also

---

[26]Such condemnation of unbelief and inhumanity is found in an ancient Sumerian text also. According to a document from ancient Uruk the god Enlil commanded the king to destroy the memory of the Gutians, cruel mountain invaders. They were a people "who were never shown how to worship a god, who do not know how to properly perform the rites and observances." (Tigay, *Deuteronomy*, p. 236). The truth of this ancient observation has been demonstrated again and again in the twentieth century as atheists in places such as Russia and China have exacted untold brutality on millions.

[27]This stands in contrast with the law in verses 5-10. There God's concern was that the name of the Israelite man not be blotted out.

[28]This paragraph is read by the Jews in the Synagogue on the Sabbath before Purim because Haman in Esther 3:1 is described as an Agagite. By implication he was a descendant of Agag the Amalekite (1 Sam 15:8). Purim celebrates the victory of Esther and the Jews over the anti-Semitic plot of Haman, another unprincipled foe of Israel.

[29]Craigie, *Deuteronomy*, pp. 317-318.

created humans in his image with a conscience to guide them in humane treatment of others. Failure to live by the basic requirements of humaneness will ultimately earn God's judgment. In a time when evil and cruelty seem widespread, it is difficult to be comforted by this assurance. Christians know that the way of Christ is not extermination, but everyone still wishes for justice. However, understanding the big picture from God's perspective is crucial.

> Yet we affirm the reality of God's sovereign historical justice and the reality of judgment to come on those who persist, with no fear of God, in trampling on other human beings made in God's image. If the crimes of Amalek were "written in a book," then we know that there will come a day when "the books will be opened" (Rev. 21:11-15) and the judge of all the earth will do right.[30]

---

[30]Wright, *Deuteronomy*, p. 268

DEUTERONOMY 26

Firstfruits and Tithes (26:1-15)

The law on firstfruits and tithes has at least two functions in its placement here. First, it continues the commentary on the tenth commandment, "You shall not covet" (5:21). The law required the people's stewardship as an antidote to coveting material wealth, for stewardship recognized God's ownership of everything. What properly belonged to God could not be kept, but was to be given to him and shared with the poor.[1] Secondly, since stewardship was put in the context of worship and confession at the central sanctuary, the law provided a fitting conclusion to the stipulation section of Deuteronomy (ch. 12–26). Chapter 12 began the unit with directions for worship, and chapter 26 ends it here with the same theme.[2]

The law has two parts: offering of the firstfruits (vv. 1-11) and bringing the three-year tithe (vv. 12-15). It functions as an expansion of previous regulations in 18:4 and 14:22-29. Theologically this law, plus verses 16-19, ties together the major covenant themes of Deuteronomy: grace, obedience, and blessing.[3] Offering the firstfruits was a response to God's gifts (vv. 1-11), the bringing of tithes to share with the Levites and poor was an obedient response to God's grace (vv. 12-15), and the blessing was the divine response to obedience (vv. 16-19).

---

[1]Olson, *Deuteronomy*, p. 115. However, others find the placement of these laws puzzling (Mayes, *Deuteronomy*, p. 331).

[2]Miller, *Detueronomy*, p. 178.

[3]Wright, *Deuteronomy*, p. 270. Verses 16-19 form the conclusion to the larger section of chapters 4–26 and lie outside of the scheme of commentary on the Ten Commandments. They will be considered separately below.

Firstfruits (26:1-11)

26:1 The law anticipated Israel's conquest and settlement in the Promised Land and applies specifically to those circumstances. Other admonitions and laws shared this perspective as well (8:12f; 11:31; 12:10; 17:14; 19:1). It further anticipates the successful initiation of farming the land that was pictured so well in chapter 8.[4]

The foundational theme of verses 1-11 is giving. God gave the land and its produce to Israel (vv. 1,2,3,9,10,11), so in return the Israelite was to bring (give back) some of the produce to God (vv. 2,11). The following law on the tithe continues the theme with the emphasis on giving the tithe to the Levite and poor (vv. 12,13). This theme is reinforced by the repetition of the verb "to go, enter, produce" (בוא, *bô'*) in verses 1,2,3,9, and 10. God brought Israel into the land so they could bring to him what they had brought (produced) out of the ground.

26:2 The event was still some years in the future. Only after Israel had conquered the land, settled in, and produced the first harvest could this law be obeyed. The **firstfruits** would be the very first of every crop produced.[5] Chapter 8 described the abundance that would be available to Israel. It included wheat, barley, vineyards, fig trees, pomegranates, olive trees, herds, and flocks (8:8,13).[6] These crops ripened at different times, so there probably would have been a number of occasions when the offering was brought.

God owned the land (Lev 25:23) and its fertility was a blessing from him (Deut 28:4-12). The offering of the firstfruits recognized this fact and gave thanks for his provision. In 18:3-4 the firstfruits belonged to the priests in honor of their ministering before the LORD. The firstborn of the flocks and herds belonged to the LORD also. The firstfruits was a way of redeeming the crops so that Israel could use the rest for themselves.

---

[4]For more on the significance of the language used here see commentary on 1:8.

[5]The word is רֵאשִׁית, *rē'šît*, "first, best" (Lev 1:12; Num 18:12; 1 Chr 31:5, etc.). In Jer 2:3 Israel is God's holy nation and the firstfruit of his harvest. A synonym is בִּכּוּרִים, *bᵉkûrîm* which is used in Exod 23:16,19; 34:22,26. See Bill Arnold, "בכר," *NIDOTTE*, 1:658-659.

[6]See also 7:13; 12:17; 14:23; 18:4; 28:51 for a briefer, more stylized description: "grain, new wine, and oil."

The basic law on firstfruits appears in Exodus 23:19 (cf. Exod 34:26). Leviticus 23:9-14 gave specific instructions for how the grain was to be offered as a sacrifice. Numbers 18:11-14 detailed what belonged to the priests and Levites.

The firstfruits were associated with the Feast of Weeks (Exod 34:22; Lev 23:15-22; Num 28:26) although some of the other major feasts also included offerings of the first of the harvest. The first sheaf of grain was a part of the Feast of Unleavened Bread (Lev 23:4-14,15) and the Feast of Tabernacles had new wine associated with it (Deut 16:13). This is logical since the crops had different ripening times.[7] The grains ripened at different times in the spring and the vineyards ripened in the fall. But apparently the major firstfruit offering was presented at the Feast of Weeks.[8]

The produce was to be offered in a **basket** at the **place** that God would **choose as a dwelling for his Name.** This language comes out of chapter 12 and verbally connects the two passages. The designated place had several locations until it finally became Jerusalem (see comments on ch. 12).

26:3-4 The presentation of the firstfruits was accompanied by two recitations by the farmer who brought the offering (here and verses 5-10). They both had a historical focus. The first recitation emphasized that what God had been promising for generations had now come to pass. The Israelite had actually settled into the **land that the LORD swore to our forefathers to give us.** This was a triumphant declaration of God's faithfulness and great blessing on the Israelite because he was the beneficiary of this faithfulness.

---

[7]The later Qumran community in the first century before Christ developed a calendar that had provision for four different firstfruit offerings: barley right after Passover, wheat at Pentecost, new wine seven weeks later, and new oil seven weeks after that (J. Milgrom, "First Fruits, O.T.," *IDBS*, pp. 336-337).

[8]deVaux, *Ancient Israel*, 2:493-494. The Feast of Weeks in later times became associated with the giving of the law on Sinai. The association was based on the statement in Exod 19:1 that Israel arrived at Sinai in the third month after the Exodus. The Feast of Weeks, coming 50 days after Passover, fit the chronology. The first direct connection was apparently not made until the intertestamental times in the Book of Jubilees. However, 2 Chr 15:10 mentions a religious feast under Asa in the third month.

It is significant that the statement focused on God's faithfulness, not his causing fertility. Israel was not to confuse God and the fertility gods and goddesses of the Canaanites (7:1-6; 12:1-3) who were credited, even by Israel at times (Hosea 2), with causing the bounty of the land. This shift from nature to history was unique to Israel and crucial to her identity and theology. Of course the LORD was the Creator of the universe and thus responsible for the produce of the land. But it was crucial for Israel to understand that God had been at work in history since Abraham to create for himself a nation, and provide a place for them to live.

26:5-10 The second recitation was considerably longer. It pulled together several important events from the past to undergird the joyful pronouncement of verse 3. It provided a six-part summary of Israel's past, a series of interconnected events that accounted for how Israel came to be in the land. The recitation included Jacob's wanderings, the descent into Egypt, the oppression in Egypt, Israel's outcry and God's deliverance, and divine guidance through the wilderness. The language and expressions relied heavily on previous accounts in Exodus and Numbers.

The first important event was the fact that **my father was a wandering Aramean**. This was evidently a reference to Jacob who was an Aramean by birth and association. His mother was Aramean and Jacob lived twenty years with his uncle Laban in Aram (Aram Naharaim in Gen 24:10). He also married Laban's two daughters.[9] Aram was apparently a term for northwest Mesopotamia or some of its inhabitants in the second millennium B.C. In the first millennium, the word came to be applied in a more restricted sense to the area of Syria, and Israelite kings had several contacts with its rulers.[10]

"Wandering" is one possible interpretation of a verb that means "to perish, to be lost."[11] A more literal translation is, "A perishing

---

[9]See Genesis 24, 28–29. Aram was also the origin of Baalam (Num 23:7; Deut 23:4).

[10]See *NBD*, s.v. "Aram, Aramaeans," pp. 67-68; Wayne Pitard, "Arameans," *Peoples of the Old Testament World*, pp. 207-230. For contacts in the time of the monarchy see 1 Kgs 11:25; 15:18; 20:1; 2 Kgs 5:1; 6:8; 12:17, etc. The language of the Arameans, Aramaic, became the international language of diplomacy and commerce in the ancient Near East by the 9th–8th centuries B.C. (cf. 2 Kgs 18:26, dated at 701 B.C.).

[11]Benedikt Otzen, "אבד, 'ābhadh," *TDOT*, 2:20.

Aramean was my father." "Wandering" points to Jacob's rootless and landless existence as compared with Israel settled firmly in the land. "Perishing," the preferred translation, points to Jacob's precarious existence because of the famine that drove him from Canaan into Egypt (Gen 42:1-2; 43:1-2; 47:4). The recitation at the time of harvest was to call attention to the sharp contrast between Israel's experience in the land and Jacob's. The rich bounty of the land was proof of God's blessing and his faithfulness to his promises to Jacob (Gen 46:3-6).[12]

The remainder of the recitation uses language borrowed from earlier accounts of events in the early history of Israel. Jacob and his family were small (v. 5, **a few people**) when they went into Egypt (Gen 48:8-27, seventy in all; see Deut 10:22), but God increased them and made them **powerful and numerous** (Exod 1:9, "much too numerous" are the same Hebrew words). This growth threatened the Egyptians and they oppressed the Israelites by enslaving them (v. 6; Exod 1:11-12,14). The Israelites cried out to God, and he heard them (v. 7; Exod 2:23-25; see also Num 20:15-16). God came to their rescue and delivered them from Egypt by showing his mighty power through the plagues on the Egyptians (v. 8). **Mighty hand and outstretched arm** is typical language describing God's powerful intervention (see on 4:34; also 5:15; 6:21; 7:8; 9:26; 34:11; Exod 3:20; 6:1,6; 7:4-5; 9:15, etc.). The plagues were the **miraculous signs and wonders** (4:34; Exod 4:17; 7:9-21; 8:5,16; 9:22; 10:12-15,21-23; 14:15-18,26).

The recitation ends with the same affirmation that the first one did (v. 3). God had brought Israel into the bountiful land of promise **flowing with milk and honey** (6:3; 11:9; 27:3), and the worshiper was now bringing the **firstfruits of the soil** (vv. 9-10). The blessing of provision came from the God of history.

26:11 The experience of God's blessing was to be shared with the **Levites and the aliens** with rejoicing (see 12:10-12,18; 14:28-29). The aliens were specifically mentioned because they were sojourners in Israel (*gēr*) just as Israel had been sojourners in Egypt (v. 5, *gûr*; NIV, "lived"). Israel was to understand that God's grace shown to them in

---

[12]See J. Gerald Janzen, "The 'Wandering Aramean' Reconsidered," *VT* 44 (1994): 359-375. Still some prefer the NIV, "wandering" (Merrill, *Deuteronomy*, p. 334).

the past was to be reflected in their treatment of the less fortunate among them (cf. 10:19). Sharing God's blessings horizontally exhibits the same theology behind the care for the poor in 24:6,10-22.[13]

The Triennial Tithe (26:12-15)

The second part of the law continues the same themes of the first eleven verses: Israel was to share the produce of the land that God had given them.[14] It also contains a recitation or confession by the Israelite. It is certainly of great significance that the last legal prescription in the main stipulation section, chapters 12–26, concludes with requirements concerning the tithe and care for the poor. Obedience to God and provision for the poor of Israelite society are major themes in Deuteronomy. The covenant community was to be characterized above all by loyalty to the covenant God and the covenant community. A vertical relationship with God and a horizontal relationship with others were inseparable. This was to be

---

[13]A scholarly debate has centered on verses 5-10 since G. von Rad argued that they represent an early Israelite creed ("The Form-Critical Problem of the Hexateuch," *The Problem of the Hexateuch and Other Essays* [London: SCM, 1966]: pp. 3-8). He found shorter and longer versions in Deut 6:20-24 and Josh 24:2-13. Since this "creed" did not contain any reference to the giving of the law at Sinai, von Rad surmised that the tradition about Sinai was not a major Israelite tradition. Rather it was local and minor and only later was expanded into the importance it seems to have in the Pentateuch. The issue has been widely debated. The recitation was time and event specific, which calls into question its creedal status (Craigie, *Deuteronomy*, p. 321) even though it was certainly an important statement of Israelite faith. It also seems incredible that the Sinai "tradition" was minor and late. Much of Exodus and the whole book of Deuteronomy presuppose the giving of the law as central to Israel's existence and identity. It was not mentioned in this recitation because it was not one of the specific mighty acts of God that were the focus of the occasion (H.B. Huffmon, "The Exodus, Sinai, and the Credo," *CBQ* 27 [1965]: 101-113). It was also probably omitted because the giving of the law was one of the primary reasons for celebrating the Feast of Weeks and any reference to it would be superfluous (Merrill, *Deuteronomy*, p. 333; Cairns, *Deuteronomy*, p. 223). For a brief, but insightful presentation with evidence from several early texts for the connection of land and covenant see Wright, *God's People*, pp. 13-15, 24-43.

[14]"Give" (*ntn*) occurs four times. The Israelite had given the produce to the poor (vv. 12,13) but had not given it to the dead (v. 14) because God had given them the land (v. 15).

demonstrated at the very practical level of sharing material blessings. All of Israel was to benefit in concrete ways from God's care
for them.

The tithe and triennial tithe was the subject of the law in chapter
14:22-29.[15] The law here in chapter 26 adds the confession of cultic
purity. This law also clarifies that the firstfruit and tithe were not the
same offerings. The firstfruit did not specify an amount while the
tithe was clearly one-tenth.[16]

26:12-13 The tithe was called the **sacred portion** because it was
set apart for God. According to Leviticus 27:30 all tithes were holy
and belonged to the LORD. Even though the triennial tithe was kept
in the villages rather than being taken to the central sanctuary
(14:28), it still belonged to the same category.[17] It had been properly **removed** from the house. This verb is the same one used elsewhere of purging out evil from the nation (13:5; 17:7,12; 19:13,19;
21:9) and thus reflects the total and absolute obedience to the law.
Nothing of the tithe had been kept back.

The assertion of faithfulness in keeping the law of the tithe was
tied to obedience to all the commandments. The worshiper asserted both that he had "kept every commandment which you commanded me,"[18] and that he had **not turned aside from your commands**. The Hebrew text makes the distinction between the singular in the first phrase and the plural in the second phrase. Thus the
worshiper seems to be confessing obedience both to the specific triennial tithe law and to all the commandments in the law. In some
way obedience to the tithe law signified obedience to the whole law.
If care of the poor was not practiced, obedience to the rest of the

---

[15]See commentary there for detailed consideration of the subject as well
as reflections on the New Testament texts.

[16]Cairns takes a developmental view of the tithe and understands the tithe
and firstfruits to be the same (*Deuteronomy*, pp. 223, 144).

[17]"Then say to the LORD your God" or "before the LORD your God" is
often taken to mean this was done at the central sanctuary of chapter 12
(Cairns, *Deuteronomy*, p. 224; Mayes, *Deuteronomy*, p. 336). But in Deuteronomy the phrase "the place the LORD your God will choose as a dwelling for
his name" (v. 2) is usually used when the central sanctuary is meant. Moses
was aware that access to God was not limited to one place (see 19:17).

[18]A literal translation of the phrase the NIV renders, "according to all you
commanded."

law was negated. The prophets vigorously argued this point as well (Isa 1; Micah 6; Jer 7).[19]

26:14 The confession included three negatives in addition to the positive of verse 13. The confession established the ritual purity of the Israelite, which placed bringing the tithe firmly within the arena of worship. Touching a dead body or anything that had contact with a dead body made one unclean (Num 22:11-13; Lev 22:4), and whatever an unclean person touched was unclean (Lev 9:19-21). Therefore, nonparticipation in **mourning** rites and not touching the tithe while **unclean** were important to ritual purity.[20]

Offering to the dead may refer to pagan rites in which food and drink were left at the grave for the deceased. On the other hand it might be a veiled reference to the "Dead One," that is, Baal, the Canaanite dying and rising god.[21] In either case the practice would have reflected relying on someone other than God.

The tithe required that the worshiper be both ritually and spiritually pure. The confession guided the Israelite to the proper attitude in which to share his blessing with the poor.

26:15 The confession ends with a remarkable prayer, an appeal to God in **heaven** which is his **holy dwelling place**. This stands in contrast to the concern in other places for the place that God would choose on earth to put his name. According to chapter 12 the central sanctuary was the place to meet God. But this prayer recognizes that God is in heaven. It was specifically intended to emphasize the contrast between the pagan gods who were on earth, or even under it when they died, and the covenant God. Israel's God was transcendent. Yet the Israelite could still appeal to him. He was transcendent over all others, but not inaccessible.[22] This appeal to the transcendent God for blessing provides a fitting end to the legal portion of Deuteronomy.

---

[19]"Sacred rites are no atonement for social wrongs," (Wright, *Deuteronomy*, p. 272).

[20]Some scholars suggest the possibility that the mourning may refer to pagan fertility rites or sympathetic magic that would include weeping and lamentation for the god that died in the autumn (see Hos 9:4; Ezek 8:14) (Merrill, *Deuteronomy*, p. 336).

[21]Craigie, *Deuteronomy*, p. 323. See comments on 14:1.

[22]Solomon's prayer at the completion of the temple, which was God's dwelling on earth, included a section on God's transcendence (1 Kgs 8).

F. CONCLUDING EXHORTATION (26:16-19)

26:16 This brief paragraph concludes the long stipulation section of the book of Deuteronomy that began at chapter 12:1. This fact is signaled both by the covenant renewal language of the paragraph and by the deliberate verbal parallels between verse 16 and 11:32–12:1. But verse 16 also has verbal parallels with 5:1,31-32; 6:1 and 6:5. This strengthens its summary force by relating it to the larger unit of chapter 5:1 through 26:15. The verse's concentration of several key words is one final, powerful exhortation at the end of the law.[23]

This day, with its threefold repetition (vv. 16,17,18), emphasized Moses' presentation of the covenant law in the plains of Moab East of the Jordan. The reference also tied in with the crucial affirmation in 5:3 (see also "this day" in 4:8; 15:5; 19:9). The covenant was for the current generation, not a former or future one. When the covenant would have been reaffirmed and repeated down through the generations, "this day" would have taken on significant weight. Each rereading would have been a "re-presentation"[24] of the covenant to the people. It would also have involved a reaffirmation of the community's commitment to the covenant. Thus its abiding importance continued on, not unlike the Christian celebration of the Lord's Supper.

26:17-19 These verses, although somewhat difficult to translate, seem to reflect a formal covenant ratification ceremony. Ancient Near Eastern treaties were ratified when both parties swore by an oath to observe the terms of the treaty. The declaration in these three verses apparently had the same function. No ratification ceremony was described, but the two statements seem to assume one.[25]

By a formal statement Israel declared her commitment to the LORD, and through Moses the LORD declared his commitment to Israel.[26] Israel made one affirmation, **that the LORD is your God**, and three commitments. They promised to **walk in his ways, keep his**

---

[23]These key words are decrees (*ḥūq*), laws (*mišpāt*), carefully (*'śh*), observe (*šmr*), heart (*lēb*), and soul (*nepeš*).

[24]Cairns, *Deuteronomy*, p. 227.

[25]Craigie, *Deuteronomy*, p. 324. Josiah's renewal of the covenant in 2 Kgs 23:3 is described with much of the same language. Deut 29:12-15 asserts that the covenant was confirmed with an oath.

[26]The technical nature of these declarations is reinforced by the rare

decrees, commands and laws, and obey him. These promises correspond to the many times throughout Deuteronomy that Israel was
exhorted to do just those things. They were to walk in God's ways
(5:33; 8:6; 10:12; 11:22) rather than in the ways of other gods (6:14;
8:19; 11:28; 13:2). They were to be careful to keep all the commands
of God (4:6; 6:3), and they were to obey (11:13,27; 12:28; 13:18).
Therefore, this affirmation represented a wholehearted obedient
response to God's will for the covenant community, a response that
promised to bring blessing and life (28:1-14; 30:15-16).

In response God accepted their commitment **to keep all his
commands** (v. 18) and affirmed three consequences for Israel. The
LORD promised that Israel would be **his treasured possession, set
. . . high above all the nations, and a people holy to** him. This was
a promise that God had made at Sinai (Exod 19:4-6; see on Deut 7:6;
14:2; 28:9). There was no doubt about God's faithfulness to the
covenant promises. His commitment to Israel was nothing new. But
in the context of covenant ratification it represented a renewed
emphasis on what Israel would receive for obedience. As God's
covenant people they were objects of great blessing. The only thing
that prevented blessing was their disobedience.

Israel's special status in the world as God's covenant people
would bring **praise, fame and honor high above all nations**. It is
possible to interpret the praise, fame, and honor as referring to that
which would accrue to God not Israel.[27] God's elevation of Israel

---

usage of the common verb אָמַר (*'mr*) which occurs here in the causitive
Hiphil stem. These are the only two occurrences of that stem for the verb
in the Hebrew Bible (out of its 5300 occurrences). The syntax with the fol-
lowing infinitive of "to be" equals "to proclaim or vow to do something"
(David J.A. Clines, ed., *The Dictionary of Classical Hebrew* [Sheffield: Sheffield
Academic Press, 1993], 1:325). The NRSV translation provides a totally different perspective. It understands verse 17 to state God's commitment to
Israel and verse 18 to state Israel's commitment to God. Thus verse 17
begins, "Today you have obtained the LORD's agreement: to be your
God; . . ." Verse 18 reads, "Today the LORD has obtained your agreement:
to be his treasured people. . . ." The translation still sees three commitments
by Israel in verse 17 and three promises to Israel by God in verses 18-19, so
the ultimate meaning is the same.

[27]The NIV translation removes the ambiguity of the Hebrew text. There
is no "you" preceding "in praise" in the Hebrew.

would result in praise and honor to God, not Israel (see 4:6-8). Jeremiah 13:11 and 33:9, using the same three words, affirmed that God's purpose for choosing Israel was for his glory. Israel's purpose was to be a witness to God among the nations so that the nations would recognize who God was and respond to him in awe and praise. On the other hand Israel's elevation above the other nations was the consequence of blessing from God (28:1,10,12-13).[28]

Thus the legal section of Deuteronomy ends with an emphasis on the ultimate purposes of God. He had chosen Israel and was going to establish them as his covenant people in the land, so that as his holy people they would elicit praise and honor to him from the nations. The law was not to be understood apart from God's grace, and Israel's election was not to be understood apart from his larger purposes.

---

[28]To avoid the possibility of pride on Israel's part Moses had already affirmed that God's election of Israel was because of his love, not because of their worth or righteousness (7:6-8; 9:4-6).

DEUTERONOMY 27

G. COVENANT RENEWAL (27:1-13)

Chapter 27 moves into a new major section of the covenant-treaty document: the ceremony for covenant renewal. The general and specific stipulations were ended. The next step was to articulate the proper response.

According to Christensen's chiastic outline of the whole book, chapter 27 is the initial chapter in part 2 of the Inner Frame, chapters 27–30, that corresponds to part 1 of the Inner Frame, chapters 4–11.[1] More specifically chapter 27:1-13 takes up the theme of chapter 11:26-32 where Mounts Ebal and Gerizim were first introduced. Thus these two passages form a literary enclosure around chapters 12–26.

Several scholars think chapter 27 is misplaced. It seems to interrupt the smoothness of movement from chapter 26 to chapter 28, and it separates covenant curses from their proper place in chapter 28.[2] In response Merrill has pointed out that chapter 27 would not fit well after 29:1 (which is the conclusion of ch. 28). Furthermore, the covenant sanctions of 27:14–28:68 make sense only within the context of the covenant renewal ceremony of chapter 27:1-13.[3]

Chapter 27 has four sections: verses 1-8,9-10,11-13, and 14-26.[4] The unifying theme of the first three sections is the covenant ceremony

---

[1]Christensen, *Deuteronomy*, p. 6.

[2]Driver, *Deuteronomy*, p. 295; Tigay, *Deuteronomy*, p. 246. Even the conservative M. Kline thinks chapter 27 may not have come at this precise point in the ancient covenant renewal ceremony (*Treaty*, p. 121).

[3]Merrill, *Deuteronomy*, p. 341.

[4]The MT marks the first three paragraphs as 1-8,9-10, and 11-14. It then marks each verse in 15-26 as a separate paragraph. Tigay prefers three sections: verses 1-8,9-10,11-26 (*Deuteronomy*, p. 246).

on Mounts Ebal and Gerizim.[5] The tone is optimistic and grounded in the grace of God that called Israel to be his people. Verses 14-26, with the pronunciation of curses, introduce a more pessimistic tone that continues through chapter 30.[6]

The literary artistry and inner connections of verses 1-13 are complex but help us see the emphasis and development of thought. The whole section is held together by the time references. We find "crossing the Jordan" (vv. 1,4,12) and "the day" or "in the day" (vv. 1, 2,4,9,10,11). The references to Moses (vv. 1,9,11) also unify the section. The repetitions in verses 2 and 4 serve to highlight verse 3 that commands the writing of **this law** on the stones. The command in verse 3 is then repeated in verse 8 for emphasis and to form an inclusion around verses 5-7, which contain the command to build an altar and worship. This, in effect, places worship at the center of the instructions for covenant renewal.[7]

27:1 The introduction of **Moses** in the third person signals the end of the legal section of the book and a shift to other concerns. Moses was mentioned by name in only three sections in Deuteronomy before this: 1:1-5; 4:41-46, and 5:1. In 5:1 he exhorted Israel to obey the Ten Commandments, which is similar to the situation here and links the two texts together. The **elders** were included (and the **priests** in verse 9) because the death of Moses was fast approaching and the responsibility for passing on the law was shifting to other leaders. This new responsibility for the elders (see also 31:9,28) added to their other functions as judges (19:12; 21:19-20; 22:15-18; 25:7), representatives of the village (21:2-6), and leaders (29:10[9]).

Israel was reminded that after they entered the land God had given them, they could not forget the covenant law. This command repeats that of 4:1-2; 5:1; 6:1 and other places throughout the book.[8]

---

[5]Many scholars think verses 1-13 were not originally a unit. Mayes (*Deuteronomy*, p. 340) calls it a very fragmentary chapter with little relationship between its sections. He thinks verses 5-7 are intrusive in verses 1-4 and 8, verses 9-10 go with chapters 26 and 28, and verses 11-13 are separate.

[6]P.A. Barker, "The Theology of Deuteronomy 27," *TB* 49 (1998): 277-303.

[7]The instructions here include many of the same details seen in Exod 24:3-11 at the initiation of the covenant. The law was written down, an altar was built, burnt and fellowship sacrifices were made, and stones were set up.

[8]As in the other texts "command" here is in the singular (not the plural

The law that was being repeated by Moses on the plains of Moab was not temporary, but permanent.

27:2-4 After entering the land Israel was to set up **some stones** on **Mount Ebal** on which to write the law. The stones were to be coated with **plaster** and written on with some kind of permanent ink (or maybe carved into the stone through the plaster).[9] Thus they would stand as a permanent reminder to Israel of her covenant relationship with God. Just as important was the fact that the stones were to be set up after Israel entered the land. Entering the land was proof that God had kept his promises to the patriarchs. The land was as much a permanent reminder of God's faithfulness as the stones.[10]

Erecting stelae (stone pillars) to commemorate events or publish laws was common in the ancient Near East. In Mesopotamia the custom was to incise the text into the rock. Egyptian custom included plastering rock and writing on the plaster as Moses instructed here.

All the words of this law[11] would seem to indicate at least the core of Deuteronomy, chapters 5–26. It may have included some of the historical material from chapters 1–3, the blessings and curses of chapter 28, and the exhortations of chapters 29–30. This may seem like a lot of material to write on stones, but the entire 284 laws of the Code of Hammurabi were carved on one eight-foot stele. Two pillars of similar size could probably hold the entire book of Deuteronomy.[12]

Mount Ebal was north and west of the plains of Moab where Moses was delivering the law.[13] Thus the ceremony would not take

---

of the NIV), "every commandment," indicating that the covenant law was seen as a whole.

[9]Tigay, *Deuteronomy*, p. 248.

[10]Wright, *Deuteronomy*, p. 276.

[11]The word is *tôrāh* which occurs in 1:5 (see commentary there) and would often seem to refer to most of the book (19:18,19; 28:58; 31:9-11). See the references to the Book of the Law in 30:10 and 31:26 (stones were not the only place where the law was to be written). In Exodus the Ten Commandments were engraved on stone (24:4,12; 32:15-16; 34:1,4).

[12]Merrill thinks only the Decalogue could have been written down (*Deuteronomy*, p. 342) while Driver thinks it included chapters 12–26 (*Deuteronomy*, p. 296).

[13]See on 11:29.

place immediately after Israel crossed the Jordan.[14] Mount Ebal was no doubt chosen because of its proximity to Shechem. Shechem was an important Canaanite city and had ancient covenant connections going back to Abraham. It was the first place Abraham camped when he came into the land, and where God promised him the land (Gen 12:6-7). Jacob camped there, built an altar, and purchased some land there (Gen 33:18-19). Covenant renewal at Shechem after Israel entered the land proclaimed in an emphatic way God's faithfulness to his ancient promise.[15]

In verse 13 Mount Ebal was designated as the mountain from which the curses were pronounced. Why then would the pillars with the law on them be raised on Mount Ebal rather than Mount Gerizim, the mountain of blessing (v. 12)? When compared with chapter 28, it becomes apparent that curses predominated in the covenant renewal ceremony. There was pessimism about Israel's ability to obey the law. Therefore, the stones erected on Mount Ebal perhaps functioned to expose Israel's sinfulness and uphold the curses as the more realistic possibility. Despite God's promised blessings, disobedience would more likely prevail.[16]

---

[14]The grammar of verse 4 clearly points to an indefinite future date. However, some scholars have insisted that the grammar and wording of verse 2 point to the same day that Israel crossed the Jordan, "In/on the day when . . ." (NIV, "when") (Mayes, *Deuteronomy*, p. 340; Driver, *Deuteronomy*, p. 295). But "day" plus the definite article in Deuteronomy often emphasizes the significance of the event rather than the specific time (4:32,39; 11:26; P.A. Verhoef, "יוֹם," *NIDOTTE*, 2:423; Barker, "Theology," p. 298). Joshua 8:30-35, which records the carrying out of this command, places the event after the conquest of Jericho and Ai.

[15]Shechem was also geographically in the center of the Promised Land. It guarded the major east-west pass in the central mountain range and was on the major north-south road. Later, Joseph's bones were buried there (Josh 24:32), and later still Shechem served as the first capital of the northern kingdom (1 Kgs 12:25). The book of Joshua does not record any conquest of the city before the covenant renewal ceremony in chapter 8. This has led to speculation that the Shechemites were peacefully assimilated into Israel.

[16]Barker, "Theology," p. 288. The *Samaritan Pentateuch*, the official Bible of the Samaritan sect that arose in the territory of the old northern kingdom, reads Mount Gerizim rather than Ebal in verse 4. Traditionally scholars have concluded that Samaritan scribes changed the text because they believed that Mount Gerizim was the sacred mountain where God was to be worshiped. They had their own temple there in New Testament times.

27:5-7 Erection of the stele was to be accompanied by worship, which included sacrifices and rejoicing. Building the altar was to follow the law of Exodus 20:25. Undressed stones were to be used instead of the dressed ones required for the stele.[17] Why undressed stones were used is unclear. Perhaps it set Israel apart from the Canaanites who used dressed stones. Or perhaps it had to do with the iron tools that would have required dependence on the Canaanites.[18] Two sacrifices were required, **burnt offerings** and **fellowship offerings**. These were the offerings presented at the consummation of the covenant at Sinai also (Exod 24:5). These two offerings were often combined for momentous or crisis occasions (Exod 32:6; Josh 22:27; Judg 20:26; 1 Sam 10:8; 2 Sam 6:17-18; 24:25; 1 Kgs 3:15). The burnt offering required that the sacrifice be totally consumed on the altar (Lev 1). Everything went up to God in smoke and emphasized the vertical aspect of worship. However, only the fat and entrails of the fellowship offering were burned. The rest was eaten by the worshiper and emphasized the horizontal aspect of worship (Lev 3; 7:11-18). The root of the word for fellowship offering (שׁלם, *šlm*) has a wide variety of meanings so the significance of the offering is debated.[19] The word may suggest the person presenting the sacrifice was at

---

However, there is growing opinion that the Samaritan Pentateuch is correct, and that the Hebrew text was changed as a scribal attack on the Samaritans (see the footnote by J. Hempel in BHS and Cairns, *Deuteronomy*, p. 232). On the other hand, if Jewish scribes changed the text in verse 4, then why did they not also change the text in verses 12-13, making Gerizim the mountain of cursing and Ebal the mountain of blessing?

[17]An archaeological survey a few years ago uncovered a nine foot high, nearly square structure on Mount Ebal that was identified by the excavator as an altar dating to near Joshua's time. The excavator's conclusions have been questioned. See Adam Zertal, "Has Joshua's Altar Been Found on Mt. Ebal?" *BAR* 11,1 (1985): 26-43; Aharon Kempinski, "Joshua's Altar — An Iron Age I Watchtower," and A. Zertal, "How Can Kempinski Be So Wrong?" *BAR* 12,1 (1986): 42-53; H. Shanks, "Two Israelite Cult Sites Now Questioned," *BAR* 14,1 (1988): 48-52. An Israelite altar of undressed stones from the 9th/8th century B.C. was found at ancient Arad (Amihai Mazer, *Archaeology of the Land of the Bible* [New York: Doubleday, 1990], pp. 496-498).

[18]Merrill, *Deuteronomy*, p. 343; Craigie, *Deuteronomy*, p. 329.

[19]NRSV has "sacrifice of well-being"; KJV and NASB have "peace offering"; others suggest "communion sacrifice." Richard Averbeck, "שׁלם," *NIDOTTE*, 4:135-143.

peace with God, or that he existed in a state of well-being, or that he regarded himself in close fellowship with God. Whatever the significance it was a time of **rejoicing** before God. Joyous worship was the proper context in which to renew the covenant.

The sacrifices at the heart of the covenant renewal ceremony demonstrated for Israel that even though they stood under a curse if they disobeyed (vv. 15-26; 28:15-68), their sin could be atoned for. They still could be at peace with God, for he had provided the means for atonement through sacrifice. The fellowship meal was eaten before and with God and reenacted the bond between God and Israel.[20]

27:8 Repeating the gist of verses 2-3 rounds off the instructions by emphasizing the importance of the ceremony. The inscription containing the law was to be **very clear**, out in the open for all to see. This word was used in 1:5 when Moses began to expound the law. His task was to make it plain (see on 1:5). These two occurrences of the word, along with the repetition of "this law," form a rhetorical envelope around the whole book of Deuteronomy.

The NIV translation introduces an unnecessary ambiguity into the text. **These stones** suggest that it is the altar stones that were to be written on. However, the Hebrew texts has "the stones" which points back to the large stones set up in verse 2.

27:9-10 These verses provide a transition to the arrangements for the pronouncing of the blessings and curses. They also provide a connection between chapters 26 and 28. Verse 10 is almost identical to 28:1.

At this stage in the covenant renewal ceremony the **priests** join Moses to address the people. In Joshua 8:33 they stood in front of the people with the Ark of the Covenant. The priests were sole possessors of the law as a privileged class, but they had the responsibility of teaching the law to the people (31:9-13). In verse 12 the tribe of Levi stood on the mountain with the other tribes to hear the blessings and curses.

This is the only time in Deuteronomy that the call to Israel to hear is accompanied with a command to silence (cf. Hab 2:20; Zeph 1:7; Zech 2:13). Full concentration was required for the presentation

---

[20]Barker, "Theology," p. 297; Richard Averbeck, "Offerings and Sacrifices," *NIDOTTE,* 4:1000-1001.

of the covenant law. Perhaps there was also a deliberate contrast intended with the reception of the law at Sinai. There the people responded by declaring their full compliance to the law (Exod 24:3,7). However, the intervening years had demonstrated how hollow that promise was. So here the people were cautioned not to make rash promises they could not keep.

It is striking that Israel was told **you have now become the people of the LORD your God**. How was this to be understood? Deuteronomy had already asserted their status as God's chosen people several times (4:20; 7:6-7; 9:26-29; 10:15; 14:2; 21:8). Yet the language here stresses that they now have become God's people by his special act.[21] Apparently what was intended was that within the covenant renewal ceremony the reality of Israel's relationship with God was also renewed. The historical fact of God's election had to be actualized within the people's awareness over and over. It was the very foundation of Israel's reason for being, and they could not be allowed to forget it. Israel had not just become God's people at some point in the distant past. They were continually the objects of his elective love. The ongoing existential realization of this fact had the potential of energizing Israel to loyalty and obedience, which was the main reason for renewing the covenant.

27:11-13 To prepare for the recitation of the blessings and curses the people were to arrange themselves on the two mountains, Gerizim and Ebal. Geographically there are several locations where this could have occurred. The valley that separates the two mountains is quite narrow at its east end, only 1600 feet apart. The western portion of the valley is wider, but there are two natural amphitheaters there.[22] Either place would have offered a good site.

The arrangement of the tribes seems to follow a matrilineal order. The six tribes on Mount Gerizim on the south who were to give blessings were descendants of the two wives of Jacob, Leah and Rachel. The six tribes on Mount Ebal on the north who were to give curses were descendants of Jacob's concubines, Bilah and Zilpah, with the exception of Reuben and Zebulun. Since Reuben lost his birthright because of incest with Bilhah, his tribe was counted with the lesser ones. The reason why Zebulun would have been in the

---

[21]The Hebrew uses the causative form of the verb, "caused to become."
[22]Tigay, *Deuteronomy*, p. 252.

curses group is not at all clear. Another suggestion sees the tribes arranged geographically. Those on Mount Gerizim settled in the south and central hill country. Those on Mount Ebal settled in the north and Transjordan area.[23]

H. COVENANT CURSES (27:14-26)

This section ends the covenant renewal ceremony with a list of twelve curses that were to be recited by the priests. The people would respond to the pronouncement with an affirming "Amen." Verse 12 leads one to expect that blessings would be included. Parallel blessings and curses are found in 28:3-6 and 16-19, and Joshua 8:34 relates that both were recited. But we do not find blessings here. Consequently, the curses by themselves give a somewhat negative tone to the ceremony. It is a tone reinforced by the lengthy curses in chapter 28:15-68, and the pessimistic outlook of 29:19-28; 30:1,4 and 31:16-21.[24] Unfortunately Israel's later history demonstrated that this pessimism was well founded.[25]

Scholars have proposed several solutions for the absence of the blessings. Some believe there was a blessing for each curse, but they were omitted here.[26] However, it is difficult to understand how some would have a corresponding blessing and why they would have been omitted if they did exist.[27] Others wish to rearrange the text and put 27:16-25 after 28:19.[28] Others understand the twelve curses as a counterpart to the Decalogue in Deuteronomy 5. The curses then form a frame around the stipulation section of Deuteronomy. However, since the Decalogue has Ten Commandments these scholars cannot agree if there were originally ten or twelve curses. Twelve

---

[23]Driver, *Deuteronomy*, p. 298; Cairns, *Deuteronomy*, p. 235. It is of interest that Manasseh and Ephraim are subsumed under Joseph and Levi has full tribal status.

[24]See Barker, "Theology," pp. 284-285.

[25]Ezek 22:6-12 at the end of Israel's history includes in a list of sins found in Israel many of those under curse here.

[26]Thompson, *Deuteronomy*, p. 265; Craigie, *Deuteronomy*, p. 331.

[27]Tigay, *Deuteronomy*, p. 252; Barker, "Theology," p. 281.

[28]I. Lewy, "The Puzzle of Dt XXVII 15-26: Blessings Announced, but Curses Noted," *VT* 12 (1962): 207-211.

would fit the number of the tribes.[29] Another has argued that the form of the covenant renewal in Deuteronomy is closer to the ancient land grant treaty than the vassal treaty because the land grant did not have blessings with the curses.[30]

While the curses do form, with the Decalogue, a frame around chapters 5–26, and perhaps there are twelve to correspond to the twelve tribes, it seems best to understand with Parker that the curses are intended to close the stipulation section on a pessimistic note.[31] The last curse applies to the whole law and thus brings all of Israel under a curse.

Scholars have devised different ways of grouping the curses but all agree on certain clear similarities.[32] Each begins with the imperative[33] of **curse** (אָרוּר, *'arûr*) and ends with the exclamation of **amen** by the people. The first and last curses use a relative clause to explain the action. The other ten use a participial cause. The four on sexual sins in the center (vv. 20-23) all begin with the same phrase, "cursed is the one who lies with . . . ." Verses 15 and 24 enclose the section by the reference to **in secret** and suggest a possible theme for the whole list. Verse 17 and 24 share a reference to **his neighbor**, and verses 24 and 25 deal with killing. Most seem to assume an action done in secret and known only to God or only to the perpetrator and the victim. In the latter case the victim often was not in a position to publicize the crime. The first eleven are specific while the final one is comprehensive. Perhaps the list was intended to be representative and in that sense comprehensive.[34] The curses have a variety of parallels in other parts of the Pentateuch that shall be noted below.[35]

---

[29]Compare Mayes, *Deuteronomy*, pp. 346, 348 and Merrill, *Deuteronomy*, p. 347.

[30]Andrew Hill, "The Ebal Ceremony as Hebrew Land Grant," *JETS* 31 (1988): 399-406.

[31]Phillips does see the section as an explanation for the covenant disobedience, but he dates the composition of Deuteronomy after the exile (*Deuteronomy*, p. 176).

[32]Mayes, *Deuteronomy*, p. 345, suggests there are 5 pairs plus the first and last one. Thompson understands the first and last ones to be by themselves. The rest form two groups of four and a group of two (*Deuteronomy*, p. 267).

[33]Grammatically a Qal passive form used as an imperative.

[34]Tigay, *Deuteronomy*, p. 253.

[35]See Driver, *Deuteronomy*, p. 299, for a convenient chart and Weinfeld,

The curses assumed that God was the subject and suggested that the offender was destined for divinely imposed misfortune.[36] They took the form of a solemn oath that served both as deterrent and judgment. Even if the crimes were done in secret, God would still know it and call the criminal to account. The people responded with "Amen" to affirm the truth of the curse and the necessity for divine judgment. They were also pronouncing a judgment on themselves ahead of time in case they became one of the miscreants.

27:15 The matter of idolatry had already been treated in some detail (4:16,23,25) and the danger of the Canaanite religion had been highlighted (7:1-6,25-26; 12:2-3), so it is no surprise that idolatry of any form would come under a curse. This curse reflects the first two commandments (5:8-10) which causes the curse section to begin the same way the Decalogue does, by emphasizing the vertical relationship with God. Idolatry was apostasy and public apostasy had been separately addressed already (ch. 13; see also Exod 20:23; 34:17; Lev 19:4; 26:1). However, this curse anticipated **secret** idolatry and thus required a divine judgment since it would not be open to public censure. From God's perspective it was, and is, unthinkable that anything crafted by the **hands** of a man, whether carved or cast, could represent in anyway the Lord of the universe. God revealed himself through his words, deeds, and creation, not through man-made things. The covenant and the covenant law provided a clear revelation of God's character and will. The non-Israelites had no such advantage and were left to their own imaginations for creating their gods. They ended up constructing idols.[37]

27:16 This curse is grounded in the fifth commandment (5:16). To **dishonor** or make light of the parents was the direct opposite of honoring them. The rebellious son earned the death penalty (21:18-21) as did the son who cursed his parents (Exod 21:17; Lev 20:9).

Deuteronomy and the Deuteronomic School, pp. 277-279, for parallels in the wisdom literature.

[36] In its milder form a curse could refer to merely human disapproval (Josh 9:23; Jer 20:14) but in the mouth of a prophet or God it was a powerful declaration of Divine judgment (Gen 3:14,17; 4:11; 9:25; Deut 28:16-19; Jer 11:3, etc.).

[37] Archaeologists have unearthed very few idols in the land of ancient Israel.

Dishonoring could take more subtle forms than outright rebellion and could be done in nonpublic ways. Parents were given the task of teaching the covenant law and were to be honored as God's covenant representatives. Dishonoring them not only called into question their covenant authority, but also dishonored God's authority and placed the covenant in jeopardy.

27:17 Moving a **boundary stone** was prohibited in 19:14 (see comments there). Since it was likely to be done in secret, it too required a divine censure in the form of a curse. God assigned the land to the tribes and families, and it was fundamentally his.[38] Therefore, changing a boundary was an affront to him (Lev 25:23). Boundary stones in Babylon had curses written right on them. The poor would have been especially susceptible to land theft (cf. 5:19) by the change of boundary stones since they would have lacked the means to defend themselves (see the case of Naboth, 1 Kgs 21). Apparently it was a special temptation of the nation's leaders (Hos 5:10; see Prov 22:28; 23:10).

27:18 This is the only law for the **blind** in Deuteronomy, but they would fit into the category of the poor who are often mentioned (see v. 19). However, the blind are the subject of the prohibition in Leviticus 19:14 which also included the deaf (and thus by extension all handicapped). Ill treatment of the blind would be equal to doing something in secret since the blind would be unable to identify their persecutor. Even Egyptian wisdom literature censured making fun of the blind. There is a thematic parallel between the curse in verses 18 and 19 and the curses in verses 24 and 25. All involve taking advantage of others. These two pairs of verses then form a frame around the four curses on sexual misconduct in verses 20-23.[39]

27:19 The law of 24:17 on **justice** carried no penalty, only a motivation (v. 18). The situation of **withheld** justice would have been in the same category as verses 17 and 18. Justice could have been withheld for many reasons. Village elders who acted as judges would not have been immune from family or financial influence (see below on

---

[38]A major point of the book of Joshua was the assigning of tribal lands (ch. 13-21). Protection of property boundary lines was a serious matter in the ancient Near East and was addressed in various ways in the different cultures.

[39]See Merrill, *Deuteronomy*, p. 349.

verse 25). God's concern for the poor is a consistent theme in Deuteronomy (see the discussion on 24:10-22), so it is no surprise that perpetrators would be under divine curse (see also Exod 22:21-25).

27:20 A series of four curses on sexual crimes begins with this verse. Three deal with forbidden sexual relations within the family. These were the kinds of conduct that would have been easily covered up in the family to avoid public exposure and censure.[40] Adultery was not listed perhaps because it was much more difficult to hide. In large family units that lived in close proximity to each other, temptations to these kinds of sin would have been strong. Leviticus 18 forbids a large variety of sexual relations and was the foundation for the curses here. The reason given there was that Israel was not to do as the Egyptians or the Canaanites did.

Marriage with the **father's wife** was forbidden in 22:30[23:1] (see comments there). This curse apparently refers to the stepmother, or else the mother would have been explicitly mentioned (see Lev 18:7-8). The penalty for such a shameful act was death (Lev 20:11). This conduct was also forbidden in the Hittite Laws (no. 158) and the Hammurabi code (no. 190). Such an act would have also dishonored the parents (v. 16).

27:21 Bestiality earned the death penalty in Exodus 22:19 (cf. Lev 18:23; 20:15). It would be an act difficult to prove and therefore fit the curse pattern. The biblical basis for censure of such an act was grounded in creation. There was a fundamental difference between animals and humans. Humans were created in the image of God and were placed on the earth as God's stewards over the animals. Genesis 2 reinforced the distinction. Adam reviewed all the animals but did not find a suitable mate among them. Eve was God's special creation suitable just for him. Ancient Near Eastern cultures were not as clear on bestiality. The myths portrayed sexual relations between gods and animals.[41] The Hittite laws made relations with cattle, sheep, pigs, or dogs a capital crime, but not with a horse or

---

[40]See the case of Amnon's rape of Tamar, his half-sister (2 Sam 13). Absalom, Tamar's brother, advised her to be quiet about it, and her father David did nothing when he heard about it.

[41]See *The Gilgamesh Epic* 6, 48 (*ANET,* p. 84) and a Ugaritic myth which portrays Baal having relations with a heifer (*ANET,* p. 139).

mule.[42] Perhaps a part of the reason for the curse was the association of bestiality with pagan cultic rites. If so, then its prohibition would have been grounded in the first and second commandments also (Deut 5:7-10) because it would fit the category of idolatry.[43]

27:22 This curse addresses sexual relations with a sister or a half-sister and equals Leviticus 18:9 and 20:17.[44] The Laws of Hammurabi and the Hittite laws also banned some types of incest.[45] However, the patriarch Abraham claimed Sarah was his half-sister (Gen 20:12), and Tamar seemed to think that David would let her marry her half-brother, contrary to what Amnon seemed to think (2 Sam 13:2,13). Brother-sister marriages were practiced in Egypt among the royalty to keep the crown and power in the family. In concert with verse 20 the overriding rule for sexual conduct was proper conduct within the larger family unit living together.

27:23 The parameters for forbidden sexual conduct also extended to the family of the man's wife (see Lev 18:17). Leviticus 20:14 forbade the marriage of a man to both a woman and her mother. Curses on sexual relations between a man and his stepmother (v. 20) or his mother-in-law frame the central section on sexual misconduct.

27:24 This curse does not use one of the usual words for murder, but a verb that often meant "strike down" in the sense of murder. The verb can also be used of various kinds of assault. The curse in verse 25 used the same word but adds "life" to clarify that murder is in view (Exod 21:12,15). Therefore, it is best to understand murder is in view here also. Since it was done **secretly**, the death penalty could not be imposed for there would have been no witnesses (19:15-21). The law in chapter 21:1-8 provided for the means to atone for an unsolved murder.

27:25 Taking a **bribe** would have been a secret transaction, though if discovered there would have been at least one witness. This situation could refer to a hired assassin or a false witness.

---

[42]# 187, 188, 199, 200A (*ANET,* pp. 196-197).

[43]Elizabeth Bellefontaine, "The Curses of Deuteronomy 27: Their Relationship to the Prohibitives," *No Famine in The Land: Studies in Honor of John L. McKenzie,* eds., James W. Flanagan and Anita W. Robinson (Missoula, MT: Scholars Press, 1975), p. 55.

[44]See Wenham, *Leviticus,* pp. 251-257.

[45]Laws of Hammurabi, # 154-158; Hittite Laws # 189-190.

Killing without cause purely for money went beyond reason and was pure evil. It would reflect the total breakdown in the covenant community. The shedding of innocent blood was an evil that needed to be purged out (19:13; 21:9; cf. 1 Kgs 2:31-33). Judges were forbidden to accept bribes (16:19; Exod 23:7-8), and perhaps they were the subject of this curse as well.[46] The **innocent person** was also protected by the city of refuge law (19:1-13).

27:26 This curse follows the style of verse 15 and is comprehensive. It refers to all the teaching of Deuteronomy. **This law** refers to the whole book as reflected in verse 8 (see on 1:5). This last curse reflects the fact that the previous curses were understood as representative of the whole law. The actions censured may have all been connected with secrecy, but the violation of any law would earn a curse. Penalties were provided for breaking some laws, but not others. However, this curse makes it clear that the breaking of any law was serious in God's eyes even if there was no expressed penalty.

---

[46]Weinfeld, *The Deuteronomic School*, p. 278.

DEUTERONOMY 28

I. BLESSINGS AND CURSES (28:1–29:1)

Ancient Near Eastern treaties included at or near the end a list of blessings and/or curses to provide motivation for adherence to the treaty. All the treaties from the second and first millennium BC included curses. Some also included blessings.[1] The curses predominated because negative reinforcement apparently was more effective than promises of reward for compliance.[2] These types of blessings and curses were not limited only to treaties, however. They appear in ancient law codes, building inscriptions, boundary stones and elsewhere. They seem to have been common throughout the ancient Near East for a long time.

There seems to be little question that Deuteronomy at this point follows the structure of the ancient Near Eastern treaty form.[3] The debate among scholars has centered on whether the form and content of the curses in Deuteronomy most closely fit the second millennium or the first millennium. The dividing line is basically between conservatives who see chapter 28 most closely resembling second millennium treaties[4] and the critical school that sees the curses most closely

---

[1]K.A. Kitchen, "The Patriarchal Age: Myth or History," *BAR* 21,1(1995): 48-57, 88-95.

[2]The so-called Book of the Covenant in Exodus 21–23 ends with a section that lists consequences for obeying the law and some for disobedience (23:20-33). Some of the themes are the same as in Deuteronomy 28. Also Leviticus 26 lists rewards for obedience (3-13) and negative consequences for disobedience (14-39) including many of the same themes as Deuteronomy 28 such as disease, fear, defeat by the enemy, drought, infertility, death, plague, cannibalism, and exile. But neither passage uses the words "blessing" or "curse."

[3]See Introduction, 4. Structure.

[4]Kitchen, "Patriarchal Age"; Craigie, Thompson, Merrill.

resembling the first millennium treaties.[5] As Kitchen has shown, the treaties from the two millennia have clear differences.[6] However, scholars such as Weinfeld seem to gloss over these differences, recognizing little variation among them.[7] Weinfeld is especially impressed by what he calls "direct borrowing by Deuteronomy" from the Vassal Treaty of Esarhaddon in Deuteronomy 28:26-35.[8] Weinfeld seems to go beyond the evidence in his conclusions.[9]

In any case, what is crucial to understand is the function of these blessings and curses. Throughout Deuteronomy Moses' sermonic style predominated, and he continually called for obedience to the covenant law. Obedience was the way Israel honored the LORD and demonstrated fidelity to the covenant. Moses also promised blessings for obedience (11:27; 12:15; 16:17). However, if obedience were crucial to keeping the covenant law, then disobedience certainly would earn consequences as well. Chapter 27:15-26 pronounced curses in connection with the covenant renewal ceremony at Mounts Ebal and Gerizim. But there was no expressed consequence, only a self-imposed, maledictive response by the people. In

---

[5]Weinfeld, Tigay, Cairns. Weinfeld especially appeals to the seventh century Assyrian Vassal Treaty of Esarhaddon.

[6]Kitchen, "Patriarchal Age." Numerous Hittite treaties from the 14th and 13th centuries BC have an elaborate 7-fold scheme. The Sinaitic covenant in Exodus and Deuteronomy resembles these treaties in form. The only difference between Deuteronomy and the Hittite treaties is that the blessings come before the curses in Deuteronomy. Only the later 2nd millennium treaties include blessings. The early and mid-second millennium treaties do not, nor do the first millennium treaties. The 1st millennium treaties are different in form from the 2nd millennium treaties. They mostly have 4 elements with no historical prologue, no blessings and no deposit or reading clauses. See also K.A. Kitchen, *The Bible in Its World* (Downers Grove, IL: InterVarsity, 1977), pp. 79-85.

[7]Weinfeld, *The Deuteronomic School*, pp. 59-61.

[8]Weinfeld, *The Deuteronomic School*, pp. 121-122. I will deal with the details below in the comments on those verses.

[9]See Dennis McCarthy, *Treaty and Covenant* (Rome: Biblical Institute Press, 1981), p. 175: the curse lists were common literary property that appeared in various documents in the ancient Near East. However, McCarthy is impressed by the close agreement between Deut 28:23 and 27-29 and the Vassal Treaty of Eserhaddon, and agrees with Weinfeld that some sort of direct borrowing took place.

addition, although 27:12 referred to blessings, none were given. Chapter 28 fills in these gaps with blessings and a long series of detailed curses for covenant disobedience.

Although the curses were deserved punishment for disobedience, the blessings were not earned as a reward. God's blessings on his covenant people were already there and were "the prior reality of God's grace." But they could be received only in obedience to God's will. It was a means of "appropriating God's grace and blessing, not the means of deserving it."[10]

Several interesting features mark chapter 28. The blessings and curses are of two kinds: expressed as an almost automatic consequence without direct divine causation (vv. 3-6 [blessings] and 16-19,30-34,38-44, etc. [curses]), and as directly from the LORD (vv. 7,8,9,11,12 [blessings] and 20,21,22,24,25, etc. [curses]). However, Israel was God's chosen covenant people and ultimately whatever happened to them came from God.

There is a core, poetic, blessing section (vv. 3-6) and a core curse section (vv. 16-19) that are a mirror image of each other. The curses in verses 16-19 are the reverse of the blessing in 3-6. The only anomaly is the reversal of the second and third items in the curse section (cf. vv. 17-18 with vv. 4-5). The blessing core is followed by a short section of detailed blessings that come directly from the LORD (vv. 7-14). The curse core is followed by an extensive expansion of the curse consequences (vv. 20-68) that provides great detail for certain types of curses. This long section is composed of several paragraphs, some of which have a complex interrelationship. It has three main units, each one introduced by repetition of key words from verse 1, such as "hear, obey, do" (vv. 15-44,45-57,58-68).[11] The amount of repetition in the curses, which is considerable, is part of the rhetorical style of the curse genre, designed to overwhelm the addressee with unforgettable images. The intent was to promote obedience.

---

[10]Wright, *Deuteronomy*, pp. 280-281.

[11]The curse theme of the various paragraphs and the interrelationships will be explored in the commentary below. Each paragraph will be considered separately.

1. The Blessings (28:1-14)

28:1 Chapter 28 begins with the familiar call to obey in the context of specifying the exact reward or blessing for obedience — ascendancy over the nations. This is a summary of the promise of 26:16-19. According to 4:5-8, Israel's obedience would naturally result in the admiration of the nations because the law as lived out in Israel demonstrated the nearness of God and his wisdom. This was not only a blessing but was the purpose for which God had chosen Israel, to be a witness to him among the nations. This ascendancy was a blessing, not a right, and was a result of God's grace. It was a contrast to her original, actual status for she had been the least of the nations (7:7).

The blessings focus on living in the land in safety and enjoying its produce. They emphasize that the blessings of the Abrahamic covenant (Gen 12:1-3) were coming to fruition. They were deliberately arranged in a repetitive fashion to emphasize the core themes.[12]

28:2-6 The blessings in the core section are arranged in four categories with the word "bless" repeated six times.[13] Verses 3 and 6 are composed of two pairs of opposites that express totality. **City** and **country** (v. 3) refer to the totality of space. Blessing will come wherever they undertake their activities. Verse 12 elaborates on the blessing that will come on the country (v. 16 is the opposite).

Fertility was a crucial feature of agricultural life and is addressed in verses 4 and 5. It was the most important factor for survival. An abundant or meager harvest was the difference between life and death. Abundance of food was central to a civilized society and a peaceful life in the land. Israel's ancestors had known the disruption of famine in the land of Canaan (Abraham — Gen 10:10; Isaac — Gen 26:1; Jacob — Gen 42:1; 43:1). The Israelites themselves had experienced the lack of food in the wilderness, a need God met through

---

[12]Tigay, *Deuteronomy*, p. 490, suggests a chiastic arrangement for verses 3-13. However, he leaves out verses 9-10 and his paralleling of verses 6 and 7 seems to place too great a restriction on the meaning of verse 6, applying it only to military activity.

[13]The six blessings may be related to the six tribes who were to repeat them in 27:12 (Tigay, *Deuteronomy*, p. 258).

miraculous intervention (Exod 16). The appeal of the land of Canaan was that it was flowing with milk and honey, which meant it had abundant food (1:25; 6:3; 8:7-8; 11:9; 26:9; 27:3).

The promise of fertility was the attractive appeal of the Canaanite gods Baal and Astarte, who were fertility gods. This fact underlies the often repeated exhortation to destroy the Canaanite gods and not to follow them (7:5-6,25-26; 13; 16:21-22). Hosea 2 and several passages in Kings demonstrate how often Israel failed to resist the enticements of fertility gods.

Therefore, the assertion that the LORD was the source of fertility, which came as his blessing (7:14-14; cf. Hos 2:8-9), was foundational to covenant faith and life. This fertility was comprehensive, involving the Israelites, their animals, and their crops (cf. vv. 8,11-12a). The curses of disease and drought were reversals of fertility (vv. 22-24,63). The curse section also addressed abundant crops (vv. 30-35). Further, verses 53-57 describe a particular revolting consequence of the curses that involved the **fruit of the womb**.

The last blessing (v. 6) was also comprehensive and covered all of Israel's enterprises, the whole range of activity from farming to business. Israelite farmers lived in the villages and went out daily to tend the fields, orchards, and vineyards. Business and commerce were conducted at the city gate and merchants would enter into the gate complex to conduct their affairs. The phrase **to go out** and **to come in** is applied elsewhere in the Old Testament to the ability of an individual to function successfully in all areas of life (31:2; Josh 14:11; 1 Kgs 3:7).[14]

The blessings in verses 3-6 are phrased in short, pithy poetry. Five of them are only three words in the Hebrew text. Only verse four is longer. They could have easily been incorporated into some kind of liturgical affirmation and regularly used in worship so that the Israelite was continually reminded of his dependence on God.

28:7-14 The poetic blessings of verses 3-6 are expanded in the following prose section. The LORD is the direct author of the blessings in this section, occurring as the subject seven times. There seems to be a parallel, concentric arrangement of the topics: verses 7 and 12b-13a

---

[14]All these references are translated nonliterally in the NIV. See also Ps 121:8; Isa 37:28.

deal with foreign relations, verses 8 and 11-12a deal with domestic affairs (fertility), and verses 9-10 deal with relations with the LORD.[15]

Blessing included ascendancy over other nations (1,7,12b-13a). Israel would be victorious in battle (7, cf. Lev 26:7-8) and gain economic power over other nations (12b). This would enable her to become a world power and at the head of all other nations (13a). This would be a significant triumph for a nation that began as the fewest among all the nations (7:7). This blessing corresponds to other passages in Deuteronomy that promised victory over enemies (20:1,14; 21:10; 23:14; 33:29). Security in the land to enjoy its fruits could only be possible if Israel were safe from other nations. However, disobedience could result in the reverse of the blessing (v. 25 is the precise opposite of v. 11; vv. 43-44 are the exact opposite of vv. 12b-13a).

Blessing also included Israel's special relationship with God as his holy people (v. 9) a concept at the heart of Deuteronomy's theology (cf. 4:37; 7:6; 14:2,21; 26:19; 29:13; 33:3). This blessing had a missionary consequence because it would influence the nations (v. 10). Israel's ultimate purpose was to be a witness to the nations, and living in the land under God's blessing would spark that witness. The abundance and prosperity they had was not just for their benefit. It was to inspire reverence and honor for God among their neighbors (cf. 4:6-8). The spreading knowledge of God's name was a future prospect that would extend to the whole world if Israel were faithful. It was the method by which the promise to Abraham would be realized (Gen 12:3, "all the peoples on earth will be blessed through you."). To know **the name of the LORD** was the first step in the salvation of the nations (Amos 9:11-12; cf. Acts 15:16-17; Isa 2:2-4; 19:19-22; Jer 12:14-17).[16]

The blessing section concludes with another call to obedience, reminding Israel of the conditional nature of the promises (v. 14). However, Moses did not use the conventional language that he had used before, but the more vivid **do not turn aside . . . to the right or to the left**. They were to stay firmly on the path and not deviate from it (5:32; 17:11,20; Josh 1:7). The story of Balaam and his donkey

---

[15]Thompson, *Deuteronomy*, p. 270.

[16]Wright, *Deuteronomy*, p. 281. Abimelech recognized that Abraham's and Isaac's prosperity were proof of God's blessing (Gen 21:22-23; 26:26-32).

(Num 22:21ff) provides a vivid background to the expression. The road on which Balaam rode gradually narrowed and became hemmed in by vineyard walls until there was no room to the right or the left (v. 36).[17] Diverting off the path would be exhibited by **following other gods to serve them**, an exact reversal of Deuteronomy 10:12-13 (cf. 11:28).

2. The Curses (28:15–29:1)

The curses are intended to spell out just exactly what disobedience will earn. If the promises for obedience were not strong enough motivators then perhaps spelling out the consequences for disobedience would be. The basic theme is the reversal of the blessings. God will turn both nature and foreign nations against Israel, and ultimately reverse her own history of deliverance from bondage in Egypt.

Blessings Reversed (28:15-19)

28:15 This introductory verse to the first main section of curses (vv. 15-44) is the verbal opposite of verse 1. The blessings can be reversed.

28:16-19 These curses are in poetic form and are the exact reverse of verses 3-6. The blessings were not guaranteed, and they could be turned around and operate against Israel. Obedience and disobedience would have the precise opposite effects.

Disease and Drought (28:20-24)

28:20-24 The calamities that God will bring on Israel would first of all be characterized by disease and drought. This paragraph is notable for its emphasis on God's action through the curse to destroy Israel (vv. 20,21,22,24; cf. vv. 45,48,51,61,63).[18] This divine plan is grounded in 4:26 that had already revealed what God would

---

[17]This expression reminds the Christian of Jesus' words about the narrow road and small gate that lead to eternal life (Matt 7:13-14).

[18]By using the two key words *šmd* and *'bd* 11 times in verses 20-63, the ultimate outcome of the curses is made clear.

do if Israel deviated into idolatry.[19] Total destruction was what God intended to do to Israel's enemies as part of the process of giving Israel the land he had promised (7:20-23; 8:19,20; 9:3). It seems incredible that God would end up treating his covenant people as he treated the nations. But Moses had repeatedly made clear this consequence for disobedience (6:15; 7:4; 9:8; 11:17), so it was no surprise. The suffering brought by this reversal in God's plans is illustrated by the causes of the destruction, **curses, confusion and rebuke** (v. 20).[20] Confusion was what God had planned for Israel's enemies to cause their defeat (7:23; cf. also Josh 10:10; Judg 4:15; 1 Sam 5:11; 7:10) not for Israel.

Devastating **diseases** (vv. 21-22) were the common experience of all ancient cultures (and many contemporary ones as well). Israel had experienced disease in a salvific way when God struck the Egyptians with the plague of boils (Exod 9:8-12). But now disease would strike Israel. Literally "pestilence will cling to" them (NRSV). It is significant that further references to diseases in the chapter refer to them as the diseases "of Egypt" (vv. 27,60). These would be of such a severe nature that they "would bring an end to" Israel (NIV, **until he has destroyed you**).

The list of diseases (v. 22) includes seven afflictions, probably to express completeness. The first two occur in the curse list of Leviticus 26:16 also. The exact nature of some of the terms is unclear. **Wasting disease** is perhaps tuberculosis. The feverish nature of the others matches the conditions in nature that produced **scorching heat and drought**.[21] God did in fact use physical diseases in Israel's history to execute judgment (2 Sam 24:13-15; 1 Kgs 8:37; Ezek 5:12; Amos 4:10). The **blight and mildew**[22] were crop diseases. Therefore, the judgment was to be comprehensive, striking people and plants alike. Both humans and the land would become ill.

---

[19]See commentary above on 4:26.

[20]This triad of afflictions is alliterative in Hebrew: *me'ērāh, mehûmāh,* and *mig'ereth* which Tigay renders as "curse, confusion, and cumbrance" (*Deuteronomy*, p. 261). The third word occurs only here in the Hebrew Bible and its meaning is unclear. NRSV has "frustration" while the LXX has "consumption."

[21]The Hebrew has "sword" not drought, but it does not fit the context well. Changing one vowel in the Hebrew, *ḥereb* to *ḥoreb*, gives "drought" which is preferable. The Latin Vulgate also has "drought."

[22]See the pairing of these two words in 1 Kgs 8:37; Amos 4:9; Hag 2:17.

The devastating drought was prefigured by vivid hyperbole (v. 23). A **bronze sky** would give no rain and an **iron ground** would not receive any moisture even if it did rain. Many, especially in the farming community, have probably experienced the anxiety and distress of a hot, dry period when the sky did indeed seem to turn to brass, and the ground became hard as rock. This was no doubt a common experience in the ancient Near East; an area often plagued by famine and drought.[23] Leviticus 26:19 used the same imagery but reversed the image: the sky will be iron and the ground bronze. The imagery was apparently common in the ancient Near East as the same language occurs in Assyrian treaties.[24]

The consequence of drought in the Near East was (and is) a hot wind from the desert (the sirocco), which would grow stronger and stronger, bringing dust and dirt with it and scorching everything in its path (v. 24). The devastation wrought was terrifying and ultimately fatal to an agriculturally based economy.[25]

Military Defeat (28:25-37)

This section details the consequences of military defeat as a curse. The result will be severe devastation, privation, total helplessness, and exile. Thompson has suggested a helpful chiastic structure that shows the development of thought.[26]

   A. Defeat: 25a
      B. A horror to the nations: 25b-26
         C. Boils: 27
            D. Madness: 28
               E. Oppression: 29

---

[23]See above on verses 2-6. This curse reverses the blessing of verse 12 and reflects the threat of 11:17.

[24]The Vassal Treaty of Esarhaddon in one part reads: "May they [the gods] make your ground like iron so that no one can plough it. Just as rain does not fall from a brazen heaven, so may rain and dew not come upon your fields and pastures." (lines 528-531 as quoted in Weinfeld, *The Deuteronomic School*, p. 117). The imagery is similar to Deuteronomy, but the form in which it is expressed is different.

[25]Closely related to the main themes in this part of chapter 28 is the familiar prophetic triad: sword, famine, and pestilence (Jer 21:7; 32:24; 38:2; 43:17; Ezek 5:12; 7:15; cf. Lev 26:25).

[26]Thompson, *Deuteronomy*, 273.

F. Frustration: 30-32
E′. Oppression: 33
D′. Madness: 34
C′. Boils: 35
A′. Defeat: 36
B′. A horror to the nations: 37

The displacement of B′ is perhaps to emphasize the fact that the ultimate outcome of the curses will be the opposite of what God intended for Israel. Rather than being a light and witness to the nations she will become reviled and abhorred.[27]

28:25a God's intention was that Israel should enter the Promised Land and defeat her enemies. A blessing of living in the land would be continued victory over them (v. 7; 6:19; 12:10; 20:4; 21:10) and the nations' acknowledgement of Israel's special status (v. 10; 4:6-8). But the consequence of disobedience was reversal of this divine plan. This reversal is a key component of the curse section (vv. 31,48,49,52,55,57) because it illustrated so vividly God's abandonment of his covenant people.

28:25b-26 Israel's defeat would make them a spectacle before the nations of such negative scope that the nations would recoil in **horror**, far removed from what God intended their impact to be.[28] Verse 37 expands the vocabulary of scorn and ridicule to drive home the utter devastation of the LORD's curse.[29]

There was nothing worse in death than to have one's unburied body exposed to the elements. In fact, it was a fate worse than death. This was a part of the scene that horrified the onlookers, dead bodies being scavenged by birds and animals (Jer 7:33; 16:4; 19:7; 34:20). According to the law unburied bodies desecrated the land (21:23). This is an ironic and tragic reversal in this aspect of the curses: God intended Israel to feed from the land (vv. 4-5,8,11) but because of disobedience she would become food instead.

---

[27]Tigay proposes a chiasm that begins in verse 23 and ends with verse 42, which agrees in many details with Thompson (*Deuteronomy*, p. 491). See above on chapter 8 where the chiasm also has some displacement for the purpose of emphasis.

[28]This concept of horror is used by Jeremiah in the same way (15:4; 24:9; 29:18; 34:17).

[29]This additional vocabulary is also picked up in Jeremiah (5:30; 18:16; 19:8; 25:18).

28:27 The disease aspect of the curse is repeated here by specifying that boils would be the malady, boils like those the Egyptians received (Exod 9; cf. vv. 60-61). Verse 35 elaborates on the particular body parts the boils would attack. Ultimately they would spread over the entire body (cf. Job 2:7-8). The final outcome of the whole process would be an actual, not virtual, return to Egypt (v. 68).

28:28 This aspect of the curse focuses on the results of the extreme suffering brought on by the disease and defeat. The people would be driven out of their right mind. The three words used here (**madness, blindness and confusion of mind**) are also used in Zechariah 12:4 to describe the panic that seizes horses and horsemen in the midst of a losing battle. The blindness was probably not physical but metaphorical (Isa 29:18; 42:6-7,16; 43:8; 56:10).[30] They would lose their capacity to see and understand things clearly. Verse 34 adds that the blindness will be caused by what they see: their land devastated and their children taken captive (cf. v. 67).

28:29 Failure would follow everything they did so that they would suffer oppression, both economic and other kinds. This included others benefiting from their work (v. 33). Oppression of the poor classes was forbidden throughout Deuteronomy, but Israel would not be able to escape it. **Like a blind man in the dark** is an unusual expression for a blind man is always in the dark. The following line seems to explain what the expression means: they would not have the ability to accomplish anything. Driven mad by separation from God, Israel would be at the mercy of others with no way out.

28:30-35 The cause of the horror and affliction that would lead to madness and oppression would be the multitude of privations the people would experience. These included the ravishment of their wives (a common military tactic), loss of houses, produce, and animals, and the capture and exile of their children as they stood helplessly by.

The first two privations reflect the instruction for warfare (20:5,7) when men who had a new bride or house were exempt. The other privations are the reversal of the blessings of verses 4,8 and 11. These reversals were also a part of the threats of the prophets (Amos 5:11; Micah 6:15; Jer 6:12; 8:10; Hag 1:6). The most fundamental

---

[30]Merrill, *Deuteronomy*, p. 361.

activities that supported life would fail. Subsequent death is implied (cf. vv. 38-42).[31]

28:36 The final consequence of defeat was exile, a common result of war in the ancient Near East. Exile was the way for the victor to incapacitate the vanquished and assume total control over the conquered nation. The disruption in family and national life was enormous. This was the ultimate reversal of the blessings of verses 1 and 13 (cf. v. 64) and had already been threatened in 4:27-28.[32]

Reversal of Fortune and Status (28:38-44)

28:38-42 This paragraph focuses on the economy of Israel and, by a series of contrasting statements, highlights points already made. The blessings explained so well in verses 3-14 were not guarantees but conditional. Reversal could occur. Specifically the blessings on the "fruit of the womb and the crops of the land" (v. 4a) could be nullified and the curse of verse 18 is made specific (cf. vv. 30-33). Already in 7:13 the three staple crops, grain, new wine, and oil, were

---

[31]It is in verses 26-35 that Weinfeld finds the closest parallels between Deuteronomy 28 and the Vassal Treaty of Esarhaddon (*The Deuteronomic School*, pp. 116-123), parallels that lead him to posit direct borrowing by Deuteronomy. The most remarkable parallel is that the order of the six curses in verses 27-33 is identical to the order of the treaty curses (lines 419-430). The parallel in order is more impressive than the parallel in the actual written form of the curses. Several times the parallel in wording is only one or two words in a sentence. According to Weinfeld the order of the maledictions was dictated by the Assyrian pantheon, for each curse was associated with the activity of a god, beginning with the high god, Ashur, and progressing down the ranks. However, Weinfeld does admit that the direct association of curses with gods goes back to the Old-Babylonian period (mid-second millennium BC), and is not particularly Assyrian. Thus his conclusion that Deut 28:27-29 was "transferred from a copy of a Mesopotamian treaty to the book of Deuteronomy" and "that there was direct borrowing by Deuteronomy from Assyrian treaty documents" (pp. 121-122) seems to go beyond the evidence. Deuteronomy could have just as well been drawing from an old common fund of ancient Near East curse formulas. Craigie (*Deuteronomy*, pp. 339-340) points out that adaptation is more likely than direct borrowing. Furthermore, there are significant differences between the two bodies of material, and some of the curses have close parallels to earlier sections of Deuteronomy.

[32]See comments there.

promised as a result of blessing (cf. 6:11; 8:8; Micah 6:15; Lev 26:20; Jer 12:13; Isa 5:10). However, the people under curse would initiate the growing process as usual, but never harvest the produce. **Locusts** would eat **field** crops like wheat and barley (vv. 38,42).[33] **Worms** would eat the **grapes** (v. 39), and **olive trees** would develop diseases that would cause them to **drop** their fruit (v. 40). Children who were needed to help with the harvest would be taken into **captivity** (v. 41; cf. v. 32).

28:43-44 A further economic reversal would involve the resident **alien** (vv. 43-44). Usually in Deuteronomy, aliens in Israel were listed among the oppressed (10:19; 24:17-21) and were the object of special care along with the widow and orphan. But the economic situation would become so dire that these poorest of the poor would gain economic and political ascendancy, a position God had intended for Israel (vv. 12b-13a). In the blessing section it was the nations over whom Israel would gain power, but in the reversal it was the lowly alien in Israel, not a foreign nation, who would be elevated. This was perhaps to heighten the humiliation that Israel would experience.[34]

Military Siege (28:45-57)

After a brief introduction that reprises why the curses will occur (vv. 45-48), the awful consequences of a military siege are laid out in gruesome detail (vv. 49-57). Laying siege to cities was a conventional military tactic in the ancient Near East. The suffering of the citizens in the besieged city would have been common knowledge. It was one of the worst possible experiences a community would ever endure.

28:45 Verse 45 introduces the section by repeating the themes from verse 15. Verse 15 itself was a reversal of verse 1. Verse 45 provides a summary to the whole section of curses (vv. 15-68) at midpoint in the litany of destruction.[35] The intent of God to **destroy** his

---

[33]Locusts were a particularly destructive force from time to time in the ancient Near East. The eighth plague in Egypt was locusts (Exod 10), and the prophets used imagery of a locust plague for God's devastating judgement (Joel 1:2-12; 2:1-11). Cf. *IDB*, 3:144-148, s.v. "Locusts." The reference to locusts in verses 38 and 42 form an envelope around the 4 reversal statements.

[34]Merrill, *Deuteronomy*, p. 364.

[35]The word order of verse 45 is the reverse of verse 15. Some commentators see verses 45-46 as a conclusion to the previous paragraph (Merrill, *Deuteronomy*, p. 364; Thompson, *Deuteronomy*, p. 275).

people is repeated, but now with greater force for the details have been given. But even worse things were to come.

28:46 The calamities would be so great that they would become a lasting memorial to God's action. **Signs and wonders** are a word pair often used of God's powerful intervention to save his people, especially of the events in Egypt culminating in the Exodus (Deut 4:34; 6:22; 7:19; 26:8; 29:3; 34:11). A new paradigm is introduced which will reverse the old one. From now on Israel will remember the destructive power of God, not his saving power.

28:47 Service to Israel's enemies will replace service to God (vv. 47-48), another reversal of blessing. God's blessing of prosperity, if not received with humility and joy, could be misinterpreted and lead to arrogance and self-satisfaction (6:10-12; 8:11-17). Failure to obey would lead to poverty and hard servitude would result. Service is the key word. Israel showed her loyalty and covenant faithfulness by walking after God, loving him, fearing him and serving him (10:12-13), which meant obeying him. Serving God **joyfully and gladly** was a mark of this obedience, for service to him was not burdensome. In fact it was a beautiful relationship Israel had with God. God had freed them from slavery so that they could serve him.

28:48 However, their unfaithfulness would lead to the reverse. They would return to servitude of others and experience again the fruit of hard service — **hunger, thirst, nakedness and dire poverty**. **Iron yoke** was a familiar metaphor for submission to the rule of gods and kings in the ancient Near East. Yokes were usually of wood so an iron yoke would signify a particularly heavy servitude.[36]

Jeremiah, preaching just prior to the exile, envisioned captivity as a yoke (27:7-8). But he also anticipated the time beyond the exile when the yoke would be broken and Israel would return to the land (28:14; 30:8)

28:49-52 The calamity of siege would be initiated by a distant nation **from far away, from the ends of the earth**. A distant nation brought in to wreak havoc in judgment is a familiar motif in the prophets (Isa 5:26-30; 13:5 [on Babylon]; Jer 4:16; 5:15 [quoting Detueronomy]; 6:22; Hab 1:6). Usually for Israel the distant nation

---

[36]For more of the yoke metaphor see Lev 26:13 — the LORD had broken the bars of their yoke; Isa 10:27; Jer 2:20; 27; 28; 30:8; Ezek 30:18; 34:27.

was Assyria or Babylon, although Aram (Syria) and Egypt occasionally caused difficulty as well (1 Kgs 15:18ff; 20; 2 Kgs 6:24ff; 16; 23:29-30). Supporters of the late date for Deuteronomy interpret the imagery in these verses as referring to the Babylonians. However, this kind of language consists of stock phrases describing an enemy and could apply to several countries who were enemies of Israel. The earliest to fit the imagery was Assyria, who began to cause trouble in Israel in the eighth century. Eventually Assyria conquered Samaria and took the people captive in 722 B.C. (2 Kgs 17:1-6). The Assyrians had a reputation for fierce and aggressive warfare and unparalleled cruelty. The author of Kings describes the fall of Samaria in language similar to Deuteronomy (2 Kgs 17:15-16). Therefore, there seems little reason to apply the language only to Babylon.[37]

Lengthy sieges devastated the countryside as the invaders sought food, supplies, and material for siege ramps and engines. Whereas locusts and disease were the cause of the destruction of food in the previous section (vv. 38-42), the invading army would do the destruction during a siege (v. 51). It was this destruction of food that led to the awful practice of cannibalism (vv. 53-57). A city could store only a limited supply of food, and starvation by a lengthy siege was the preferred method of conquest. There was no need to risk soldiers' lives when the city's defenders could be forced into submission by hunger. The Assyrians besieged Samaria for three years before it fell (2 Kgs 17:5).[38] Even strongly fortified cities were vulnerable to siege and therefore **trust** in their walls was misplaced. Israel was to trust in God not armies or cities.

28:53-57 The ghastly practice of cannibalism would accompany the siege. With starvation imminent, a besieged city could surrender and submit to the subsequent slaughter and cruelties, or hold out to death. If it held out, the chance of its inhabitants turning on each other was highly likely. The gruesome picture here is that of a mother eating her own child. Such a situation is recorded only once in the

---

[37]Merrill, *Deuteronomy*, p. 366; Thompson, *Deuteronomy*, p. 276. Eagle imagery is also common, cf. Hos 8:1; Jer 4:13; 48:40; 49:22.

[38]In the 20th century the siege of Leningrad by the Germans in the Second World War provides a modern example (see H.E. Salisbury, *The 900 Days: The Siege of Leningrad* [New York: Harper and Row, 1969]).

Old Testament (2 Kgs 6:24-31). It was also anticipated in the curses in the Vassal Treaty of Esarhaddon.[39]

Details that need no elaboration reflect the horror of the situation. Children who were to be cherished and raised in instruction of the LORD (Deut 6) would become food for the parents. Mothers would even hoard the child as her special food source and not share with her husband.

Concluding Warning (28:58-68)

The third major section in the curses is introduced by the familiar warning from verses 15 and 45. The curse consequences that follow are of two types already listed several times in the chapter: disease (vv. 59-64) and exile (vv. 65-68). Two references to Egypt (vv. 60,68) and the nature of the curses give this section a "reverse Exodus" theme, which climaxes in verse 68 with the assertion that God will send Israel back to Egypt. In essence, God would overturn his salvation of his covenant people. In the context of Deuteronomy, that would mean abandoning his love for Israel and violating his oath to the fathers (cf. 7:8), reversing everything he had done for her.

28:58 It is clear that **this law** (tôrāh)[40] was conceived as being written down in document form, as were the ancient Near Eastern treaties (cf. v. 61). Outside of the instruction for the king to produce his own personal copy of the law in 17:18,[41] this is the first reference to the tôrāh being written in a book.[42] The material in view was at least chapters 5-26. After chapter 28 there are six more references to this covenant document, twice as "this book" (29:20,27[19,26]) and four times as "this book of the law" (29:27[26]; 30:10; 31:24,26). There can be little doubt that a written document was meant, a document to be preserved, passed on, and periodically read before the covenant community.[43]

---

[39]*ANET*, pp. 298, 300. See also Lev 26:19; Isa 9:19-20; Jer 19:9; Ezek 5:10. Lam 2:20; 4:10 suggests it also happened during the siege of Jerusalem.

[40]Occurring 15 times in Deuteronomy, it refers to the full instruction of God and probably includes chapters 5-26; see comments on 1:5.

[41]NIV, "scroll," which is the same Hebrew word as here.

[42]Which of course would be in scroll form, see Jeremiah 36.

[43]See below on 31:9-13,24-27. This would seem to imply an early concept of an authoritative written law from God that defined the covenant community, something like a canon (cf. M. Kline, *The Structure of Biblical*

The ultimate purpose for the laws was to foster honor and reverence for God. His wisdom and love for his people in providing for them instruction for living life to the fullness he intended should elicit a thankful response. That it did not can only attest to the debilitating self-centered arrogance of Israel (and all humans).

The **name** was a reverential way of referring to God (cf. ch. 12) and was used often, especially in poetry. "One loves and fears God's name, blesses, thanks, and praises it, while sinners scorn and revile it."[44] It is usual to find "his name" or "your name." **The name** as an independent expression is rare and occurs one other time (Lev 24:11).[45]

28:59-60 Moses returns to disease as a covenant curse, but goes beyond previous descriptions (vv. 21-22,35) by stressing their severity and length. This is perhaps to be understood as the consequence of the siege described in the previous section. During a siege, congestion, poor diet, decaying corpses, foul water, and decreased resistance through starvation and contaminated food would foster epidemics of typhus, typhoid, scurvy, and dysentery.[46] The harshness of the afflictions is highlighted by the reference to **all the diseases of Egypt** (v. 60; cf. v. 27). God had protected Israel from the plagues during the Exodus and had promised to continue to do so (Deut 7:15). These diseases were to be for Israel's enemies. But in this situation of covenant reversal the old promise becomes a threat. Not only would the diseases strike Israel, they would **cling to** her.

28:61 Furthermore, the diseases would go beyond anything yet experienced. They would be comprehensive, far beyond what could be expressed. The prophets frequently saw this very thing coming to pass, though some of their descriptions may be a metaphorical way of referring to spiritual sickness.[47]

Authority [Grand Rapids: Eerdmans, 1972]). The standard critical interpretation of this verse and related references is that they are a "very late" addition to Deuteronomy (Mayes, *Deuteronomy*, p. 357).

[44]Tigay, *Deuteronomy*, p. 271. See Ps 5:11(12); 54:6(7); 61:5(6); 145:1,2; Mal 1:6; Isa 52:5; Ps 74:10,18.

[45]Cf. "the name of the LORD" in Isa 59:19. A common way of referring to God in modern Judaism is "Ha-Shem" (the name); cf. *EncJud,* s.v. "God, Names of," 7:683.

[46]See Jer 14:15-16; 21:1-10.

[47]Isa 1:6 – Israel was sick from the sole of the feet to the top of the head; Jer 6:7; 30:12-15; Hos 5:13. In Modern Hebrew the expression "a plague

28:62-63 The obvious result of such severe suffering would be a decimated people. Death by sword, famine, and plague would reduce the population to a few lucky people. This is a deliberate reference to the promise to Abraham, which was often expressed in the phrase **as numerous as the stars in the sky** (Gen 15:5; 22:17; 26:4; Exod 32:13; Deut 1:10; 7:7; 10:22). The most foundational of blessings that controlled the destiny of the covenant community would be reversed. The proof of God's care, love, and blessing would be destroyed, and Israel would no longer be able to take comfort in the promise fulfilled or experience security under the protection of God.

28:64 Exile would be certain (cf. vv. 36-37; Lev 26:33). The most devastating outcome of exile, besides the loss of family and independence, would be the loss of the security of living under God. The covenant provided Israel with both security and purpose, and distinguished her from the angst-ridden nations who never could trust their gods nor appease them enough. This sense of security reflected Israel's conviction that history had a direction and purpose. This conviction was a major breakthrough in the ancient world. It has been called the gift of the Jews to civilization.[48] But God gave them over (Rom 1:24) to the desires of their hard hearts. Their longings to serve other gods would be fulfilled (4:28; 11:28). God would cease attempting to call them back to himself and protecting them from the result of following other gods. They would learn the awful consequences of living outside of his covenant. They would enter the world of the pagans and discover its true nature.

28:65-67 The exile would be a time of no rest, **an anxious mind, eyes weary with longing, a despairing heart, constant suspense**, full of **dread and terror**. It has often been said that the ancient world was filled with anxiety, but what is pictured here goes beyond anxiety to the utter limits of human endurance. One can live in such a dreadful state of mind only so long. The enormous emotional benefits of

---

that is not written in the Torah" refers to a severe and unusual affliction (Tigay, *Deuteronomy*, p. 272).

[48]Thomas Cahill, *The Gifts of the Jews: How a Tribe of Desert Nomads Changed the Way Everyone Thinks and Feels* (New York: Doubleday Anchor Books, 1998). Cahill asserts that this new way of thinking "is the only new idea that human beings have ever had" (p. 5)! He would not, however, attribute the idea to revelation from God.

living under the care of God become starkly apparent when compared to life apart from God.

28:68 Return to Egypt would be the ultimate exile and the ultimate reversal of all that God had done. The picture is of Israel going by sea back to Egypt. What God had forbidden Israel to do (17:16), he himself would cause.[49] They would be so reduced in circumstances that they would have to sell themselves into slavery. But no one would want them.

It is a fact that before and after the fall of Jerusalem in 587 B.C. many Judeans did go to Egypt (against God's instructions, Jer 41:16–44:30). Eventually a sizable community was established there, and the Hebrew Bible was first translated into a foreign language (Greek).[50]

Conclusion (29:1)

29:1[28:69]. This verse is clearly transitional. The different versification between the English and Hebrew Bibles illustrates the different opinions on its function.[51] Does it conclude chapter 28 or begin chapter 29? The Hebrew division appears to be the better interpretation. The verse forms the logical conclusion to the core covenant document, and its language is comparable to that of Deuteronomy 1:1-5, thus concluding what began there. The repetition of "these are the words . . . which Moses" (1:1), Moab as a setting (1:5) and Horeb as the prior setting (1:2), demonstrate the relationship and make these verses an inclusio for the covenant document. There are also some subtle connections with 4:44-48. The "words of the covenant" (NIV, "terms of the covenant") clearly refer to the legal sections and exhortations that have preceded chapter 28, not the material that follows. The verse also echoes 5:2 at the

---

[49]See Exodus 14:13 — the Egyptians would never see Israel again.

[50]A colony of Jews settled on Elephantine Island in the Nile River south of Thebes sometime before 525 B.C. They had their own temple and spoke Aramaic. We know of their existence from a collection of papyri found on the island. See *IDB*, 2:83-85, s.v. "Elephantine Papyri."

[51]English translations follow the LXX translation rather than the Hebrew text. This interprets the verse as going with the following material, not the preceding.

beginning of Moses' second speech.[52] Though this covenant in Moab is said to be **in addition to the covenant** at Horeb, there is little difference between them. Deuteronomy constitutes an exhortation on the covenant at Horeb and includes much of the same material.[53]

This longest of chapters in Deuteronomy with its shocking language and pictures is summarized by Wright. 1) The suffering pictured did not spring from a morbid imagination but from the grim reality of ancient life. 2) Israel's history was inverted with the negative echoes of the blessing of Abraham and the exodus. 3) There is a polemic against idolatry implied. Idolatry ultimately brings the opposite of what false gods promise. That includes the modern false gods of consumerism, individualism, etc. 4) The conditional nature of this section should be understood. There is nothing inevitable about the sufferings described here. They were intended as warnings. But they do make a powerful statement that choices matter and have consequences.[54]

---

[52]Scholars differ on this point. Dennis McCarthy sees a new covenant formula in chapters 29–30 which is introduced by 28:69 (*Treaty and Covenant*, pp. 199-205). He is followed by Miller, *Deuteronomy*, pp. 200-202.

[53]See above on 1:5; Tigay, *Deuteronomy*, p. 274.

[54]Wright, *Deuteronomy*, pp. 281-283.

DEUTERONOMY 29

III. THE THIRD SPEECH OF MOSES (29:2–30:20)

A. THE COVENANT RATIFIED IN MOAB (29:2-29[29:1-28][1])

Chapters 29 and 30 constitute Moses' third and last formal speech and are introduced by the customary formula **Moses summoned all the Israelites and said to them** (5:2).[2] This formula suggests a new major section and adds to the weight of the argument above that 29:1 concludes chapter 28 as in the Hebrew text.

The purpose of Moses' third speech was to call all Israel to ratify the covenant that had just been presented in chapters 5–28. The speech is filled with exhortations and warnings, using familiar language and themes found throughout the book. Moses concluded the speech with a clear call to decision: Israel can choose life or death (30:15-20).

The expected and appropriate conclusion to a covenant document (as found in ancient Near Eastern treaties), the instructions for the reading and deposit of the document, does not come until 31:9ff. There we learn that the law was to be preserved by the Levites who carried the Ark of the Covenant. They were to read it every seven years (31:9-13) and deposit the book of law in the ark (31:24-26).

Therefore, chapters 29–30 might seem out of place. But Moses did not slavishly adopt the covenant form, and he had his reasons

---

[1]For simplicity's sake the English versification will be followed in the commentary. Those who want to consult the Hebrew text will have to subtract one number. See discussion above on 29:1[28:69].

[2]See also 1:1, "These are the words Moses spoke . . ." The NIV obscures the parallel between 5:1 and 29:2 by translating "all Israel" as "all Israelites." The phrases are identical in Hebrew though 29:2 is slightly longer with the addition of "to them."

for placing a summons to ratification here. Before he rounded off
the covenant presentation in the plains of Moab, he called Israel
once more to obedience, anticipated her covenant rebellion, and
looked to the future. There is a strong sense of failure in these two
chapters (30:1-10) and a looking ahead to a better time. The section
concludes with a ringing call to decision that echoes down through
the Bible and continues until today: choose life.

Since the section presents a covenant ratification demand, it is
not surprising to find in it elements of the covenant document formula. However, the form seems less complete than some have suggested.[3] The most obvious components are the historical prologue
(29:1-8), the curses (29:20-28), and the witnesses (30:19a). Theologically the section presents the main themes of Deuteronomy in com-
pact form.[4] The exhortations and warnings have all been sounded
before, but now, coming at the end of the document, they take on a
new urgency and immediacy. If Israel were to survive the next giant
step forward in her salvation history, the conquest of the land, it was
vital that she commit herself fully to God.

1. Historical Prologue (29:2-8)

29:2-3. The section begins with a historical reprise that has many
affinities with chapters 1–3 and other passages in the book that look
back to God leading Israel out of Egypt. This review serves as a motivation for action.[5] God's intent was for Israel to see his mighty
actions when he delivered her from Egypt and to trust in him to
guide her into the land. Chapter 1 described Israel's first failure to
trust even though the miracles were done before her very eyes. In
this section Moses reiterates that it was not just hearsay evidence of
God at work (vv. 2-3). As verse 5 makes clear the **signs and wonders**
included the guidance of God through the wilderness. The Israelites
who gathered in the Plains of Moab to hear Moses had experienced
the exodus as children and may have been excused for not develop-
ing trust in God. But as adults they had enjoyed God's guidance

---

[3]McCarthy, *Treaty and Covenant*, pp. 199-205; Miller, *Deuteronomy*, p. 201.
[4]Miller, *Deuteronomy*, p. 202.
[5]See especially 1:30-32; 11:2-7.

through the wilderness and therefore were personal recipients of his grace. Most recently they had witnessed God's leading them in victory over Sihon and Og (vv. 7-8; 2:24–3:11), and the allocation of their land to Reuben, Gad, and Manasseh.[6]

29:4 This statement is difficult to interpret. The idea seems to be that up to now God had not given them understanding, but now he has.[7] This raises the important question whether God's people can understand his word and ways only if he gives them the understanding. If so, then how could he hold them accountable for not understanding, as he does in Deuteronomy? Deuteronomy is full of calls to obey and choose (30:19). Are they to be taken seriously or do we have a fundamental contradiction in the book?

The solution to this problem is that God grants insight in conjunction with the seeking heart, but he withholds it from the non-seeking heart. God will reward those who sincerely desire to understand and obey his will with insight and knowledge. Physical seeing will lead to spiritual insight. But if the hearing and seeing are dulled and not matched with a heart and mind that desires to know God, then no amount of observing events or hearing God's word would suffice. That God was at work in Israel's life was a matter of faith. An event or word was open to more than one interpretation. Therefore, the interpretive word from God was necessary to clarify what in fact was really going on.[8] Isaiah 6:9-10 provides an example of preaching that, because of Israel's hard heart, engendered refusal, not understanding.[9]

---

[6]This appeal to their experience with God is a common Mosaic theme: 1:19; 4:9; 11:1-9 (see comments there).

[7]The function of the Hebrew עַד, *'ad*, "until" (NIV, "But to this day") means up to the present but not through the present.

[8]Christians have the Bible that interprets the divine words and events for them. Even then not everyone has found the evidence compelling enough to believe.

[9]See Tigay, *Deuteronomy*, p. 276; Cairns, *Deuteronomy*, p. 255. Jesus and Paul quote Isa 6:9-10 to explain resistance to both Jesus' teaching and the gospel message (Mark 4:12; Acts 28:26-27). Paul quoted Deut 29:4 in Rom 11:8 to explain why Jews in his day did not believe. This was a negative application of the verse, but it appears in a context of hope that hardened Israel will believe.

Later, Moses stated that God would give them a receptive heart (30:6). However, it would still not be against their will, but would happen only as they sought to understand and know him.[10]

29:5-6 God's provision for Israel in the wilderness was intended to be educative (8:2-4). The wilderness period was for the current generation in the Plains of Moab what the exodus had been for their parents, a direct experience of God's loving care and provision through miraculous means. The purpose was that they **might know** who God was (4:35). The provision of food and preservation of clothing was a daily occurrence. Without it Israel would have perished. This interactive experience with God was what it was to know God. The Old Testament constantly attests to the fact that God again and again proved that he was God to those able to understand (Exod 6:7; 7:5,17; 8:10,22; 9:14; 10:2; 14:4; 1 Kgs 20:13; Ezek 6:7,10, 13-14, etc.).

29:7-8 This generation had followed God into battle and experienced victory. This had happened just prior to the assembly in the plains of Moab and was fresh in their minds (Num 21:21-31; Deut 2:24–3:11). That victory became not only a signifier of Israel's trust in God but a paradigm for future conquests in the land (31:4).

2. Ratifying the Covenant (29:9-15)

29:9 This verse is sometimes taken as a conclusion to verses 2-8, but the reference to **this covenant** seems to fit more naturally with the section that follows and is matched by "this covenant" in verse 14 that provides an inclusion for the paragraph.[11]

Israel had often been called to follow the covenant in Deuteronomy as we have seen. However, this is the only passage that explicitly links obedience to prosperity, although other texts have implied

---

[10]See comments on 2:30 and the hardening of Sihon's heart. Both God and Sihon were active in the process. In an insightful book, Henry T. Blackaby and Claude V. King (*Experiencing God* [Nashville: Broadman and Holman, 1998]) repeat again and again that we come to understand the will of God only as we earnestly seek a love relationship with him.

[11]Agreeing with Merrill, *Deuteronomy*, p. 377, against the MT paragraph division. The preceding verses function as an introduction to covenant talk, but have nothing in them about covenant.

the link (for example ch. 8). To **prosper** is a word that belongs also to the wisdom tradition. It does not suggest specific material prosperity, but general success in life from paying attention to God-given wisdom, understanding, prudence, and insight (Jer 9:23; Prov 1:3; 21:11; 16:23; 10:5,19; Dan 1:17; 9:22; Ps 32:8; 64:9[10]; 106:7; Josh 1:7-8; 1 Sam 18:14,30).[12] The blessings in Deuteronomy are often interpreted in a very materialistic way, but that is a mistake. Material well-being is not excluded from Deuteronomy's blessing but it is not the main point. God's law provided the parameters for a full life under God in every aspect: spiritually, emotionally, relationally, psychologically, and materially. God naturally knows the deepest human needs of his people and how they can be met.

29:10-11 The covenant ratification was a comprehensive act that included everyone in the covenant community, not just the men and leaders. Israel, as a nation and covenant people, was responsible to God as a group, and the individual was often subsumed under the group. But when it came time to pledge covenant loyalty, each individual was expected to respond.[13] It was an individual choice as well as a national decision. The list in these two verses is comprehensive and intends to include everyone in Israelite society, even the lowliest of classes, the **aliens** who did the menial tasks of drawing **water and chopping wood.**[14]

29:12-13 Covenant ratification required verbal confirmation. The **LORD** confirmed or established the covenant and Israel accepted it. The word **oath** is used only three times in Deuteronomy, all in this chapter (see also vv. 14,19). The concept here is that Israel was put under an oath in the form of a curse that would come upon them if they disobeyed (see Gen 26:28). Literally the Hebrew text says God made a covenant and oath, (v. 12) which is a comprehensive phrase encompassing the entire relationship between God and Israel.[15] The

---

[12]See Terrence Fretheim, "שׂכל," *NIDOTTE*, 3:1243.

[13]See 12:12,18; 31:10-13; 16:11 (but 16:16, for the three major feasts, mentions only the males).

[14]In Gen 24:11-13 and Exod 2:16-19 the women were responsible for getting water. The reference in Deuteronomy may be a subtle hint of the later Gibeonite deception of Joshua. The Gibeonites were punished by assigning them the lowest of tasks (Josh 9).

[15]Merrill, *Deuteronomy*, p. 379. The NIV "sealing with an oath" does not give the true sense of the phrase.

implied curse element is made explicit in verses 20-21. Anyone who thought he could break the covenant would have the curses of chapter 28 come upon him.[16] Therefore, the people's ratification of the covenant included a solemn affirmation that they would accept the curses if they broke the covenant.

The LORD's commitment to the covenant went back to his promise to Abraham in Genesis 12. His steadfastness was beyond question. This moment, therefore, marked the culmination of divine integrity that had been demonstrated over hundreds of years. **His people** and **your God** are fundamental covenant terms. They express the nature of the intimate relationship God sought with Israel and the nature of his commitment.[17] Moses ended his third speech in 30:20 with a similar affirmation.

God's promise to the forefathers is a central feature in Deuteronomy as we have seen. It was a major basis for the LORD choosing Israel, bringing them out of Egypt, and giving them the land (7:8; 8:1; 9:5; 10:11, etc.). On this basis it was not too little for God to expect loyalty from Israel; in fact, it was the only proper response.

To **confirm** Israel as **his people** was technical language for divine affirmation and establishment of the relationship. Thus God had established the covenant with Noah (Gen 6:18) and Abraham (Gen 17:7,19; Exod 6:4). Furthermore, he would establish a future covenant with Israel (Ezek 16:62). The covenant was a bedrock commitment from God on which Israel could stake her present and her future.[18]

29:14-15 The covenant was not just for the current generation but for all future generations. The covenant community was designed to span the centuries. It was God's intention to always have a special community committed to him who would bear witness to

---

[16]See Robert P. Gordon, "אלה," *NIDOTTE,* 1:403-405.

[17]See the same terminology in Hos 1:10 and 2:23. Hosea used the language to provide an envelope for his extended discussion of the covenant relationship between God and Israel utilizing the marriage metaphor. Israel had violated the covenant by committing spiritual adultery, but God through his love and compassion would restore the nation to an intimate relationship again.

[18]The Hebrew root for "confirm" is קוּם, *qwm*, and is used only here in Deuteronomy.

him in the world. Therefore, the affirmation of the current generation placed obligations on the future generations (see 5:3 — the Decalogue was not given to the fathers but to the current generation on the plains of Moab; see 11:5-7 also). This was the case in ancient Near Eastern treaties as well and is familiar even in current national and international customs. International treaties are not renewed every generation. The nation as an entity continues even as the generations of people come and go. This sense of the unity and continuity of God's people is a central biblical concept that is often missed in modern western cultures with their stress on individualism and personal freedom.[19]

However, the concept of continuity did not preclude each generation from making its own affirmation of the covenant. The purpose of reading the covenant periodically (31:9ff) was to provide a reminder to the people and offer the opportunity for recommitment.

3. Warning against Individual Disobedience and Subsequent Penalities (29:16-28)

This section is a pessimistic conclusion to the covenant ratification procedure that warns against idolatry and anticipates God's punishment for disregarding the warning. It is a warning to any individual who might think that since the nation made a commitment to God, his personal conduct was not important to the welfare of the community. It included the person who felt he could get by with violating the covenant as long as he said the right things.

The section is grounded in the curses in chapter 28 as well as in the numerous previous warnings against idolatry (4:15-20; 7:25-26; 12:1-3; 13; 16:21-22). It is marked by repetition of key words and the familiar concentric structure. The focus is on God's **burning anger** in reaction to covenant breaking.[20]

---

[19]In the light of the biblical (both Old and New Testament) concept of the people of God as community we need to question some modern Christian ideas about individual accountability (or lack of) and "independent" churches.

[20]God's "wrath" will "burn" against the perpetrator (v. 20). As a result the land will "burn" (v. 23) because of God's "fierce, burning anger" (vv. 27-28). The repeated phrase "all the curses written in this book" (vv. 20,21,27) also binds the section together.

The thought develops in three steps: a warning to the individual about idolatry and God's anger (vv. 16-21); reaction of later generations and foreigners who see the devastated land and ask why (vv. 22-24); the answer to the question: because of idolatry (vv. 25-28).

29:16-18 These verses echo chapters 2–4. This generation of Israel had passed through the foreign territory of Sihon and Og to get to the plains of Moab. Some had been especially enticed by Baal of Peor (4:3-4; Num 25:1-9). The memory of the zeal of Phinehas was fresh. Therefore, this warning needed no more details and is briefer than earlier ones.[21] In light of the final call to national covenant ratification, it was important that no individual misinterpret his or her responsibility. National commitment meant individual commitment as well. The warning first occurred in chapter 13. Individuals could have strong influence, positively or negatively.

A **root** that **produces bitter poison** was Moses' idiomatic way of suggesting the harmful influence of rebellious individuals. The idiom means that an individual idolater could have a very damaging, long-lasting influence on the nation. A root that would remain after a tree was cut down could sprout again (Isa 11:1,10) and would be difficult to eradicate. We would say that one rotten apple spoils the whole container.[22] **Bitterness** (wormwood) often refers to the devastating results of idolatry (Jer 9:15[14]; 23:15; Amos 5:7; 6:12).

29:19 This warning anticipates that an individual might think that as long as he verbalized loyalty to the covenant, God was somehow obligated to bless him as part of the covenant community, even if he was disobedient (this may refer to the secret sins of 27:14-26). He might feel that as an individual he counted for little in the broader scheme of the national responsibility. It is notable that it is a self-

---

[21]The words for "detestable images and idols" in verse 17 are strongly pejorative and occur only here in Deuteronomy, though they are frequent in the prophets. "Detestable image" (שִׁקּוּץ, *šiqqûṣ*) refers to something especially revolting. It is parallel to "abomination" in several places. It is one of the strongest negative terms for an idol. "Idol" (גִּלֻּלִים, *gillulîm*) is also strongly pejorative because it sounds like the word for excrement (*qālāl*). Ezekiel used the word nearly 40 times in reference to foreign idols. Moses considered the idols not only to be unacceptable alternatives, but to be filthy things that should be deeply abhorred.

[22]For the metaphorical use of "root" see Prov 12:12 (positive); Isa 14:29; Hos 9:16; Mal 4:1[3:19].

blessing that the person pronounced, not a blessing from God.[23] The person may think he was safe (all is well) but he was seriously deluded. He was following his stubborn heart (Prov 14:12) not the will of God.[24]

The meaning of the phrase **disaster on the watered land as well as the dry** is unclear. It may refer to the fact that the consequences of individual sin would be nationwide and wipe out the guilty and innocent together. On the other hand, it may refer to a natural disaster that would sweep away everything. But either way the general idea is clear: private sin has public consequences.

29:20-21 The punishment would be absolute and devastating with no possibility of forgiveness. The LORD's **burning wrath** refers to his stance against all sin. It is his judgment on rebellion grounded in his **zeal** for the love and loyalty of his people. It is just and fair. There is nothing arbitrary about it.

The perpetrator was **singled out** because he had sought to hide behind the community. The consequence was blotting out any memory of him, a fate worse than death (and contrary to the law, 25:6; see also 9:14; 25:19).

29:22-24 The picture of the consequences of judgment on the land uses ideas from the destruction of Sodom and Gomorrah (Gen 19), an event so terrible it became a paradigm for God's destructive judgment (Isa 1:9; 13:19; Jer 49:18; 50:40; Amos 4:11; Zeph 2:9). The burning of the land paralleled God's burning anger on the sinners. The judgment would be a reversal of the Promised Land of milk and honey (compare also the curses in 28:16-18,24,38-40,59,61).

Such destruction could only arouse questions from later generations and even foreigners. Much of the language and many ideas in this chapter parallel similar sections in ancient Near Eastern treaties concerned with ratification and sanctions (see also Judg 9:45; Jer 48:9).

---

[23]God is almost always the subject of blessing in Deuteronomy. The particular verb form used here for blessing spotlights the self-blessing act and occurs nowhere else in the book.

[24]This self-centeredness was the first sin portrayed in Genesis 3. Adam and Eve succumbed to following their own stubborn will, grounded in pride not obedience. The temptation was "to be like God." In like matter the stubborn worshiper follows his own will in defining how he will relate to God. The desire to create one's own god or religion is no different than the desire to be like God.

29:25-28 The conclusion to the section repeats what had already been said in answer to the hypothetical question in verse 22. The devastation of the land was the consequence of divine judgment on a sinful people. Throughout Deuteronomy, idolatry was seen as a premier danger and the worst sin (see 5:6-10). It was the most obvious act of disloyalty and the most persistent of all temptations to Israel. Unfortunately, the history of Israel from the earliest time (Exod 32) to the end was marked by idolatry (see 2 Kgs 17:7-18).

As it is now (v. 28) is a phrase scholars often use to date this section of Deuteronomy to the time of the exile.[25] The verse describes exile and the phrase indicates that the exile was now, at the time of the author. It could not be from Moses they say, but from a period hundreds of years later and after the fact. On the other hand, Moses casts this section, which begins with verse 22, into the future. Future generations and foreigners will ask the question in verse 24. The answer is given in verses 25-28. The phrase, then, is in keeping with Moses' perspective on the future, and serves as a vivid warning to the current generation of Israelites who were ratifying the covenant.

4. Secret Things (29:29)

29:29 The conclusion of the section is an enigmatic statement. What are the **secret things** and the **things revealed**?

The "things revealed" seem to be defined by the following phrase and subsequent reference to **all the words of this law**. Israel did not have access to all knowledge, but God had revealed to them in his law everything they needed to live in accordance with his will.[26] The law was sufficient and necessary and complete for them. Since it was in written form, it could be passed to future generations who also could use it as a guide to the will of God. This covenant law was a gracious gift from God, and they were committing themselves to fidelity to it in the covenant renewal ceremony being described in these chapters.

In light of this interpretation the later paragraph in 30:11-14 would be a further explanation of the revealed things. The law was

---

[25]Cairns, *Deuteronomy*, p. 261; Mayes, *Deuteronomy*, p. 367.
[26]Craigie, *Deuteronomy*, p. 360.

easily accessible to Israel and not something esoteric or incomprehensible. It was given directly to them to obey.[27]

The "secret things" then would be what God had not revealed in the covenant law, the kind of knowledge that belonged only to him, such as the future. The human mind was limited and unable to encompass all the depth and breadth of God's mind (Isa 55:8-9). There was some knowledge that was God's alone. Israel did not have access to that sort of knowledge. However, that was not a human defect or an evil thing. It was the way things were. It was unnecessary that a human should know everything.

Other interpreters though, especially in the Jewish tradition, have understood the meaning of this verse in connection with verses 16-19 that address the secret sins of the individual. From this perspective, the statement would assume that the nation would not be held responsible for those secret sins (see 27:15-25).[28] Merrill offers a third option. He prefers to see the verse as connected to the immediate context, and as an answer to the question of the nations in verse 24, "Why would God treat his people so?" The answer was that it was a secret that would not be revealed to the nations. But Israel had received revelation through the law, and she knew why God had done what he had done.[29]

---

[27]Cairns, *Deuteronomy*, p. 262.

[28]Tigay, *Deuteronomy*, p. 283. This is an unsatisfactory interpretation. A further enigma is that in the Hebrew text the words "to us and to our children" have a dot over each letter. Usually the scribes used these dots to mark words that should be omitted. But it is not clear why the dots occur here.

[29]Merrill, *Deuteronomy*, p. 385. This interpretation is not significantly different from the first, preferred interpretation listed above.

DEUTERONOMY 30

B. FINAL EXHORTATION (30:1-20)

1. Return and Restoration (30:1-10)

In this section Moses responded to the dire picture presented in the last part of chapter 29 which left Israel in exile because of idolatry. Now Moses reveals some of the secret things (29:29) of God's future for his people. Beyond the judgment of exile, a promise of return and restoration would be offered. This paragraph parallels 4:29-31 in theme, and reverses many of the curses detailed in chapter 28.[1] For a reversal of the curses compare verse 5 and 28:62-63, verse 7 and 28:60, verse 8 and 28:1, verse 9 and 28:18, verse 10 and 28:58.[2] These reversals are highlighted by the repeated use of the root שׁוּב (šûb) in verses 1-10. šûb has several nuances in meaning ranging from "apostasy" to the opposite idea of "repentance," or "return and restoration."[3]

The thought of verses 1-10 develops in the familiar concentric fashion that places the focus on verse 6. Verses 1-2 and 10 parallel the ideas of obeying God and returning to him with heart and soul.

---

[1]Chapter 4:25-28 also has parallels to 29:22-29 which shows that the structure of the two passages that surround Deuteronomy 5–26 are similar. These are a part of what Christensen calls the "inner frame," (*Deuteronomy*, p. 6).

[2]See Craigie, *Deuteronomy*, p. 363. The curses themselves in 28:15-68 are a reversal of the blessings in 28:1-14.

[3]A. Rofé calls verses 1-10 a "majestic fugue on the theme of šûb" ("The Covenant in the Land of Moab (Dt 28,69–30,20): Historico-literary, Comparative, and Formcritical Considerations," *Das Deuteronomium*, ed., Norbert Lohfink [Leuven: Leuven University Press, 1985], p. 311). šûb appears in verses 1,2,3 (twice),8,9,10 (for a total of seven times). The NIV translates the word in various ways: v. 1, "you take them" to heart, v. 2, "return," v. 3, "restore" (omits second occurrence), vv. 8 and 9, "again," and v. 10, "turn."

Verses 3-5 and 8-9 emphasize prosperity in the land as a blessing from God for obedience. But verse 6 points out that this could happen only if God intervened to change Israel's heart, so that she can love him with all her heart and soul.[4]

30:1-4 A long conditional statement that sets the stage for the possible return from exile begins the section. The NIV **When** suggests a temporal sense which can also be interpreted conditionally. Israel must accomplish certain things before she can return to the land: she must take to heart the blessings and curses (v. 1) and return (which equals repent) to the LORD and obey his commands (v. 2). Then the LORD will restore her to the land (v. 3).

Verses 1-3 view the return as a certainty. However, verse 10 is clearly conditional. The two parallel passages juxtapose the certainty of God's actions toward Israel with the reality that ultimately God's response was based on Israel's response to him. God's purposes were clear but responsibility for the outcome was placed squarely on Israel.[5] It appears that the exilic experience would be such a traumatic event that the rebellious nation would finally come to its senses and realize what had happened and why. It would change her forever. Yet such change was also seen as the result of a deliberate intervention by God (v. 6).

It is unfortunate that it would take such devastation for the nation to practice the obedience that Moses had been pleading for throughout Deuteronomy.[6] Apparently, implementation of the horrible curses of chapter 28 was the only way to get Israel's attention. It was only this that would lead them to repentance, or **to return to the LORD**. And only this repentance would finally enable them to obey God with their whole being (**heart and soul**, vv. 6 and 10; 6:5; 10:12; 11:13).[7]

The reversal of God's judgment was highlighted by the contrast between **scattering** among the nations (4:27; 28:64) and a return that

---

[4]Wright, *Deuteronomy*, p. 286. Tigay sees a slightly different structure based on the use of *šûb* with verse 8 as the center (*Deuteronomy*, p. 284).

[5]Wright, *Deuteronomy*, p. 289.

[6]Note how obedience is a central theme in chapter 30: verses 2,8,10,12,13, 17,20.

[7]For the significance of the phrase see comments on 6:5. To love God with heart and soul was a fundamental requirement of the covenant. Love for God was equal to obeying God in Deuteronomy.

would **restore** their **fortunes**. This linguistic formulation made a strong impact on the prophets. It was more than just a return from captivity (the scattering), it reflected the restoration of the previous prosperity that was a consequence of God's covenant blessing on his people.[8] This was a wonderful promise and expressed God's overwhelming grace, for restoration could occur only as a gift from him (v. 6).

30:5 The return to the land and the promise of numerical growth recalls the promise to the patriarchs (Gen 12:1-3) and the numerous reminders of the promise in Deuteronomy (1:10; 6:3; 7:13; 8:1; 11:21, etc.). The focal point of the blessing would have been restoration to the land and prosperity through growth. This was at the heart of God's generous promise to Israel that he had nurtured diligently over the centuries. Such an increase would be ultimate proof that God had engineered Israel's rescue from oppression.

Jeremiah saw the return from exile as a new salvation event that would initiate a new exodus paradigm (Jer 16:14-15; 24:4-7; 31:16-17; 29:10-14). He also saw that the return would require a wholehearted seeking after God.[9]

30:6 The central point of the paragraph openly reflects the paradox of the intermingling of human and divine activity. The basis for Israel's restoration to this point was her repentance and return to God. Through obedience (v. 2) she would be restored. However, such a drastic change in the will could occur only by divine action on the heart. Actual circumcision removed the male foreskin. Likewise the hardness of the Israelite heart needed removing if the nation were going to be able to return (10:16). Ultimately this had to be an operation performed by God. The heart was the seat of the intellect and would need a dramatic reorientation. All impediments to wholehearted devotion had to be removed.[10]

---

[8]The Hebrew combination is שְׁבוּת . . . שׁוּב (šûb . . . šᵉbût), "turn/return the turning" and has a broader meaning than just return from exile. It includes complete restoration (*NIDOTTE*, 4:58). The early prophets Hosea (6:11) and Amos (9:14) picked up on this promise. Jeremiah especially took up this theme in chapters 30–33. The NIV is not consistent in its translation of the phrase, sometimes rendering it "bring back from captivity." As Jeremiah expanded his vision of the future in wider circles, he saw the restoration of foreign nations as well: 48:47; 49:6,39 (Moab, Ammon, Elam).

[9]See comments on v. 6 below.

[10]The uncircumcised heart was equated with pride and hostility toward

Verses 2 and 10 suggest repentance would lead Israel to *obey* God with all her heart and soul. In verse 6, God's circumcision of heart would enable Israel to *love* God with all her heart and soul, and accomplish the demand of 6:5. The two concepts are not contradictory. The whole of Deuteronomy can be summed up in this one affirmation: to love God was to obey him and to obey him was to love him (10:12-13).

Later, the prophets' reflected on the place of the heart in an intimate relationship with God. Jeremiah pictured the future covenant as a new covenant written on the heart (31:31-34) in contrast to the old covenant written on stone. However, Ezekiel recognized another step was needed. He anticipated the time when God would give his people a new heart altogether (36:26-27; 11:19).[11]

30:7-10 The second half of the paragraph reiterates the main idea of the first half in reverse order (vv. 1-5), but in slightly different ways. The **enemies** whom God would use as instruments of his curses in chapter 28 (vv. 25,31,48, 53,55,68) would, after the restoration, bring the curses on themselves (v. 7). The blessings and prosperity foreseen in the first part of chapter 28 would become a reality, thus proving that the curses were not the end of Israel. God had plans for her beyond the judgment he would bring.[12]

God in Lev 26:40-41. Later, Jeremiah, no doubt influenced by Deuteronomy, also equated repentance with circumcision of the heart (4:1-4). He condemned those who were circumcised only in the flesh and not in the heart (9:25-26).

[11]Paul built on these points in his argument in Romans 2 that having the law did not automatically make the Jews righteous. Physical circumcision was useless without obedience to the law. The real Jew was one whose heart was circumcised by the Spirit (vv. 25-29). Paul's Jewish opponents could not fault him at this juncture, for he was in total agreement with Deuteronomy and the prophets.

[12]Solomon concluded his prayer at the dedication of the temple with a passage based on Deuteronomy 30:1-10. It also has some grounding in 29:17-27. The main difference is that, although Solomon expressed hope that God would forgive his people and attend to them in exile, he did not project Israel's return as Moses did. See J. Gordon McConville, "1 Kings VIII 46-53 and the Deuteronomic Hope," *VT* 42 (1992): 67-79.

2. The Nearness of God's Word (30:11-14)

The concluding section to chapters 29–30 turns to Moses' final challenge to Israel — to choose for God. The covenant relationship was founded on commitment. It was imperative that Israel commit herself to God. That was the purpose of the covenant renewal in these chapters.

30:11-14 Moses first established that what he was demanding was not too difficult for Israel to accomplish. The commandment that he was giving was not new but well known to them. He was referring to the law that he had already delivered to them.[13] It was the covenant law, the body of written material contained in chapters 5–26. It was a concrete document that indeed was near them and in their heart (see the "book of the law" in 28:61; 29:21; 30:10; 31:26, and the "words of the law," 27:8).

The law was not mysterious (**in heaven**) or far away (**beyond reach**), nor was it something that required an arduous search (**cross the sea**).[14] It was readily available to them; something they had heard and could learn by heart. The expressions in verse 14 reflect an oral culture that educated its members by oral recitation and memorization (see 6:6-7,20-21). The nearness of the law in this section is equal to the nearness of God in 4:1-8. These words are a positive response to the negative implications of 29:22-28 and 30:1-10. If it looked like Israel's disobedience were certain, it was not because of the difficult, esoteric nature of the law. It could be understood and obeyed. Israel's failure was her fault, not God's.

The implications of these verses may strike many Christians as unrealistic or idealistic. But we must put aside our prejudices against the Old Testament law that are informed more by Paul's attack on legalistic Judaizers than by the Old Testament itself. Moses reflects

---

[13]The literal Hebrew is "this commandment which I am commanding you today." The NIV "what I am commanding you today" is somewhat misleading. Moses uses an expression he had used throughout Deuteronomy to refer to the law of Deuteronomy (6:25; 11:22; 15:5; 19:9).

[14]See Eccl 7:24 — wisdom was far off and undiscoverable. In Mesopotamian literature crossing the sea was seen as an especially difficult task and only the gods or heroes could do it. In the Gilgamesh Epic, Gilgamesh had to go far beyond the sea in search for life.

the Old Testament perspective that the law was accessible and for everyday life. It was not easy to obey, but it was simple to understand. There was no elitism or mystery to it. It was intended for the common person and offered directions for a full life lived out in the varied circumstances of daily existence. Obedience did not earn salvation (a legalistic understanding), but obedience was expected from a nation already established as God's covenant people.

The Psalmist understood the blessings that came from adopting the law as a guide to life and an object of meditation (Ps 1). The joys of living by the law were fully expressed (Ps 119). The Psalmists recognized that they sinned and fell short of God's will, but it was not the law's fault (Ps 51). They depended on God for cleansing from sin, but such confidence in God's grace did not suggest to them that they should abandon the law. Paul's statement that the law was holy, righteous, and good (Rom 7:12) is in total agreement with Psalm 19:7-11. The words of the mouth and the meditation of the heart that were pleasing to God (Ps 19:14) were no doubt the recitation of, meditation on, and obedience to the law.[15]

The Old Testament clearly understood that central to the efficacy of the law was its internalization in the mind and heart. It was no mere external code.[16]

3. Choose Life (30:15-20)

30:15-20 Moses' final challenge was simple. Israel had a choice[17] between two starkly different alternatives — **life or death**. There was no other alternative. It was life or death, **prosperity or destruction**.[18] The nature of the choice was clearly defined. Obedience to the law

---

[15]Perhaps Ps 19:14 was a deliberate reflection of Deut 30:14. Compare the frequent combination of mouth and heart in the Psalms: 51:15,17; 37:30-31; 40:8-9; 119:11-13,108,111-112; 141:3-4.

[16]Wright, *Deuteronomy*, p. 291.

[17]The challenge of choosing is emphasized by the fact that throughout Deuteronomy God is the subject of the verb "choose." Specifically he chose Israel and the places they were to worship him. But in this one case all of God's choosing could be overturned if Israel chose against him.

[18]Hebrew, "good or evil," which are to be understood in terms of receiving the blessings or the curses.

would lead to life, disobedience would lead to death (vv. 16-17; see 11:26-28, blessings and curses were set before them).[19] This call to life was not new. Deuteronomy is full of admonitions that obedience to the law will result in life (4:1; 5:33; 6:2,24; 8:1; 16:20; 22:7; 32:47).[20]

God's desire was to give Israel the land and bless them with long life in the land as he had promised Abraham. However, long life was not automatic. It was contingent on obedience to the law. Life was grounded in God and his word. "Man does not live by bread alone but by every word that comes from the mouth of God" (Deut 8:3; Ps 119:93).

Eventually the choice came down to God or not God. God is the author of life and a decision to obey him is a decision to live. The law was not an end in itself but a means to an end — life in intimate relationship with God.

This is a fitting climax to Deuteronomy that brings into focus the main themes and concentrates them into one formula — choose God and live. The book of Deuteronomy begins in 1:8, "see I have set before you the land; go in and take possession" of it. Chapter 30:15 closes the book with "see I have set before you this day life and good." The way was clear. Possessing the land and living in it in obedience was the path to life and blessing for Israel. The book of Deuteronomy sets forth exactly how that could be done.

---

[19]The challenge was set forth in the typical concentric pattern and the repetition of key words: vv. 15-16, Moses sets before them life and death; they should choose life so they could live in the land; vv. 17-18, if they are disobedient, they will not live long in the land; vv. 19-20: they should choose life so that they may love God and live long in the land.

[20]Verb, noun, and adjective forms of life occur 38 times.

DEUTERONOMY 31

IV. THE LAST WORDS OF MOSES: 31:1–33:29

A. FINAL INSTRUCTIONS: 31:1-30

Chapter 31 begins the final major section of Deuteronomy. This section contains miscellaneous material that does not seem to fit easily into the covenant document form that has prevailed up to this point. However, the chapters conclude the book with several important affirmations: succession in leadership (31:1-8,23);[1] the necessity for a periodic reading of the covenant document (31:9-13);[2] two long poems which have traditionally been called the Song of Moses (ch. 32) and the Blessing of Moses (ch. 33). These are a fitting conclusion to the book and affirm its character as a treaty document (see below).

Chapters 31–33 plus 34 belong to what Christensen calls the "Outer Frame" and correspond to chapters 1–3 at the beginning of the book.[3] There is a clear parallel between the wording of 1:1 and 31:1, and 3:23-29 has the same concerns addressed in 31:1-2, God's forbidding Moses to cross the Jordan River with the people. Therefore, in the overall structure of the book, the parallels between chapters 1–3 and 31–34 form an envelope around the center portion of the book, the covenant law with its sanctions in chapters 5–28. This deliberate arrangement and the sermonic orientation calls attention to both the law and Israel's failure to obey and fear God. The latter is a major theme of chapters 2–3 and 31–32.

---

[1]This was an important part of ancient Near Eastern treaties. See Kline, *Treaty*, pp. 19-20, 35-37.

[2]This too was an important part of ancient treaties.

[3]Christensen, *Deuteronomy*, p. 6.

Scholars do not agree on the structure and development of chapter 31. Verse 24, with its statement that Moses had finished writing "this law," seems to naturally follow verse 13. Therefore, verses 14-23 are called a digression.[4] However, a close analysis suggests there are two major sections to the chapter, the second much briefer than the first. The two sections repeat the same material with alternating speakers, God and Moses. This repetition is a variation on the familiar chiastic pattern that occurs often in the book. In this case the repetition occurs in a linear way. Part 1 of the chapter includes verses 1-22. First, Moses speaks (vv. 1-13) then God speaks (vv. 14-21). Part 2 is verses 23-29. First, God speaks (v. 23) then Moses speaks (vv. 24-29). Thematically, what Moses says in part 1, God says in part 2, and what God says in part 1, Moses says in part 2. Thus Moses commissioned Joshua (vv. 1-8), then God did (v. 23). God warned of Israel's disobedient future (vv. 15-21) which Moses then repeated (vv. 24-29).

Three themes are interwoven in the chapter. 1) Moses finished writing the Torah and provided for its disposition (vv. 1,9-13,24-28). Up to now God had spoken directly to Moses who reported orally to the people. But now Moses' death was imminent (cf. vv. 2,14,16,27, 29), and he would no longer be able to speak to them. Moses' written word however would continue after him and provide direction and guidance for the people. This was a significant shift in the way that God would be heard. But the written word assured Israel that the law of Deuteronomy would survive Moses and provide guidance for following generations. 2) Joshua was appointed as Moses' successor (vv. 2-8,14-15,23). Moses' impending death signaled a crucial leadership crisis. God needed to provide a new leader. The three groups of verses show a progression that gradually removes Moses from the scene and focuses on Joshua.[5] 3) The Song of Moses was introduced (vv. 16-22,30) to function, like the law, as a witness to Israel.[6]

---

[4]Tigay, *Deuteronomy*, p. 288, and others.

[5]In verses 2-8 Moses summons Joshua and commissions him. In verse 23 God commissions Joshua, and Moses is not even mentioned (Olson, *Deuteronomy*, p. 134).

[6]See Cairns, *Deuteronomy*, p. 269. He sees these three themes as the product of different editors, an unnecessary conclusion.

1. Moses Commissions Joshua (31:1-8)

31:1 The first verses provide a strong sense of transition that are echoed in the grammar. Verse one is a bridge to introduce new concerns, for final matters needed to be wrapped up.[7] Not only was the law completed, Moses' impending death meant new leadership would be needed as Israel was poised to enter the land. Israel's confidence in the future required that Moses address these matters.

31:2 There is great sadness and resignation in Moses' words. He had already shared with Israel the reason God would not let him enter the Promised Land (1:37) and recorded his plea for God's reconsideration (3:23-29). But there was no blaming or arguing here, only recognition that this was the end for him. The sense of resignation is accompanied by a sense of completeness.

Moses was a **hundred and twenty years old**. This marked the end of the third cycle of his life and rounded off his service to God. Moses was forty when he fled Egypt (Acts 7:23), eighty at the time of the Exodus (cf. Deut 2:7), and now 120.[8] Now at the end of the third cycle he was no longer able to carry out his leadership functions.[9] The end had come for Moses not because of deteriorating health

---

[7]A textual variant in the Qumran scroll and LXX make the transitional nature of the verse very clear. They read "When Moses had finished speaking all these words, he said . . . ." In this case the first half of the verse is a conclusion to the preceding section and "these words" refer backward not forward. In Hebrew the only difference between "went out" and "finish" is a reversal of the last two letters of the verb root, *ykl* for *ylk*. Scholars are divided on which is the best reading. In either case the transitional nature of the verse seems clear.

[8]There is probably some symbolism at work here. The ideal age in Egypt was 110, the age of Joseph at his death (Gen 50:26). In ancient Syria the ideal age was 120 (Walton and Matthews, *Genesis–Deuteronomy*, p. 265). In the OT 120 years was the limit to life after the flood (Gen 6:3). Moses' full life of service had been under the careful watch of God and was now complete. In the Old Testament forty was the number that signaled a full and complete period of service (Eli — 1 Sam 4:18; David — 2 Sam 5:4; Solomon — 1 Kgs 2:11; Joash — 2 Kgs 12:1) or a full generation (Judg 3:11; 5:31b; 8:28). Moses' life spanned three such periods.

[9]For explanation of the Hebrew idiom, "to go and come," see comments on 28:6. The idea here perhaps was that he was no longer able to provide military leadership (cf. 1 Sam 18:13-16 and Cairns, *Deuteronomy*, p. 271).

(see 34:7), but because his role in God's plan was at an end. A new task called for new leadership.

31:3-6 Though it was time for new human leadership, Moses' first addressed the people. He reminded them of a central theological truth: God was Israel's leader. This foundational fact could not be denied and had been demonstrated over and over in Israel's brief history. The current generation that had wandered in the wilderness had ample proof of the fact. They had seen military victories over **Sihon and Og**. These victories were a paradigm for the future. Israel had trusted God then, and they could do so now. Ultimately it mattered little who the human leader was if the people would remain faithful and trust in God (7:1-2; 9:3; 12:29).

God would **cross over** to the Promised Land ahead of Israel and defeat the nations. No matter what would happen at the human level, God would be in control and assure Israel the victory. Moses reminded Israel that God was their leader, their divine warrior who went ahead of them (Josh 5:13-15). Therefore, the nation had nothing to fear (v. 6).

> The confidence of God's people in the face of an unknown future is not *primarily* secured by the presence of a capable leader, though that ingredient follows. Overcoming anxiety and fear is found first in the realization of the Lord's powerful presence with the people. Where the sense of the presence of God in the ongoing life of the people is real, fear about "what will happen to us" can be set aside.[10]

Joshua would also **cross over ahead** of Israel. He would be Moses' replacement at the head of the people. Israel already knew this. From early times Joshua had a special place as Moses' assistant (Exod 17:8-16; 24:13; Num 11:28). He had already been designated as Moses' successor (Num 27:15-23; Deut 1:38; 3:23-39). This promise merely affirmed God's earlier word, but it was important reassurance. God and Joshua crossing the Jordan ahead of the people into the Promised Land was a clear signal of victories to come. God would keep his often-mentioned promise to the fathers. Moses' death would not be the end of divine leadership for the people.

---

[10]Miller, *Deuteronomy*, pp. 218-219.

The imperatives of verse 6 reflect the powerful theology of divine (and human, v. 7) leadership of Deuteronomy. God's people and leaders were to exhibit resolute courage in the face of every task. Israel was expected to stand firm with a strong heart. The command to be firm is balanced by two negative imperatives that mark out godly people also, **do not be afraid or terrified**. These negatives occur throughout the Bible in circumstances that require trust in God.[11] One difference in Moses' words from such demands elsewhere in the Old Testament is the three reasons Moses gives for trusting in God. All three declare one truth, the steadfast presence of God. First, God would always **go with** Israel. He would accompany Israel in all of her adventures; he would "walk with" them. This was a counterpoint to the many admonitions in the book for Israel to "walk with" God (10:12-13). They could walk with him because he walked with them (1:30,33; 8:2,15; 29:5[4]).

Secondly, God would never **leave** Israel nor, thirdly, **forsake** her. These verbs were another way of saying that Israel could count on the presence of God in her midst. He was not some distant deity who occasionally looked in on Israel to catch up on her circumstances. He was present with her (so the importance of the tabernacle) and traveled with her everywhere.

Therefore, in this crucial time of transition and uncertain future, Israel could have a robust confidence in God. He was totally and unconditionally committed to her and her welfare. Israel was assured entrance into the Promised Land and victory over the Canaanites. It was God's will to establish Israel in the land promised to the forefathers, and he would do it. Israel's part was to trust and obey him.

31:7-8 Moses repeated the same assurance and challenge to Joshua. Not only must the people trust God, their new leader must also have full confidence in divine guidance. It is important to understand that Joshua's leadership was not a matter of obtaining a position of power. He was not being invested with status or filling an office. Joshua was being equipped for a specific task, the task of leading the people into the land. Courage and fearlessness were proper equipment for leadership; they were results of complete trust in God (cf. Josh 1:6,7,9).

---

[11]See comments on 1:29; 7:21 above.

These words were Moses' important public endorsement of Joshua. Moses had already laid his hands on Joshua to give him the spirit of wisdom and a measure of his own authority (Num 27:18-23). These words were a challenge to Joshua and the people to carry out the task before them. Moses could speak from his own experience, for his initial reaction had been fear (Exod 3:11; 4:10-17). However, God had been faithful and brought the people out of Egypt through Moses' leadership. Inheriting the land was the next step for Israel, and Joshua could be certain that God would equip him for the task.

The repetition of encouraging words to Joshua demonstrated the incarnation of God's presence and leadership in Joshua. He was the visible and human embodiment of God who went before them. The people could follow Joshua with confidence.

The book of Joshua is proof of the veracity of God's promise. Joshua led Israel in occupation of the land (Josh 1–12), and he divided up the inheritance for the people (Josh 14–21). Centuries after God made the first promise to Abraham (Genesis 12), fulfillment was at hand.

Many have seen in these verses a formal commissioning pattern for the Bible. A commission began with words of encouragement followed by a description of the task. Reassurance of God's presence completed the commissioning.[12]

2. Instructions for Reading the Law (31:9-13)

31:9 Moses' impending death also had implications for other leaders in Israel: the priests and elders. They were made custodians of the law that Moses had received from God and written down. Both the religious and civil leaders shared the responsibility of preserving the law for the people.

The book of Deuteronomy continually conceives of the law as being written down (4:13; 5:22; 9:10; 10:2,4), whether referring to the Decalogue, or the whole law (28:58,61; 30:10), or the curses (29:19,20). This conception of the law in written form fits well into the ancient Near Eastern background. The earliest law codes, from

---

[12]Miller, *Deuteronomy*, pp. 220-221.

2000 B.C. and through the following centuries, exist in written form. These include the laws of Ur-Nammu, Litpit-Ishtar, Eshnunna, Hammurabi, the Hittites, and the Middle Assyrian laws. Kings and rulers thought it was important to compile laws and write them down to demonstrate that they were doing their duty in maintaining justice.[13] The ancient practice of making written copies of treaties between nations is also in the background of Deuteronomy's concern for the written law.[14] In written form the law would be continuously available to each new generation in Israel. It would also take on a new authority for the nation.[15] Though the shift was made from sermon to document, the law was still to be read to the people (v. 11). The majority of the nation would still hear the word as an oral word, subject to memorization and reflection. The fathers would still teach the children (6:7) verbally. But because the law was written down, it would not be easily subjected to revision and change. It had achieved a permanent status. Deviation or false teaching could always be checked out against the written document. We see here Scripture in the making.[16]

31:10-11 Ancient treaties between nations included a clause requiring a public reading of the documents to remind both parties of the relationship between the nations. Some treaties called for a reading three times a year.[17] Moses' instructed that the law be read

---

[13]Walton and Matthews, *Genesis–Deuteronomy*, p. 265. See *ANET*, pp. 159-198.

[14]See *ANET*, pp. 199-206.

[15]Tigay, *Deuteronomy*, Excursus 28. This was the first step toward canonization and implied several things about the law. It was divinely inspired, it was intended for all the people not just the elite, everyone should be trained in it, and everyone, not just the leaders, should know their rights and duties (p. 498).

[16]The early attestation of written laws in the ancient Near East and the emphasis on the writing down of the law in Deuteronomy negate suggestions that Deuteronomy underwent a long period of oral transmission and subsequent revision and change. The widely varying opinions about what was original and what was added show the subjective nature of such an approach.

[17]Walton and Matthews, *Genesis–Deuteronomy*, pp. 265-266. A well-known example is the Hittite treaty between Suppiluliumas and Kurtiwaza which calls for the treaty to be read "regularly" (*ANET*, p. 205).

every seven years at the **Feast of Tabernacles**.[18] The Feast of Tabernacles was one of the three major feasts when all males were to assemble before the LORD (Deut 6:13-16). A festival that followed the harvest, it was a time of great joy and thanksgiving. The law specified that the people should live in temporary shelters during the feast to commemorate the Exodus (Lev 23:33-43).

Every seventh year meant that the law was to be read in the Sabbatical year, when all Israelite debt slaves were released (Deut 15). The associations with harvest and debt release would have made the Feast of Tabernacles a fitting occasion to reflect on the law of Deuteronomy. Its concern for the poor and oppressed, and constant call to trust in God and obey him would have been especially powerful at that time. The reading guaranteed that each new generation heard the law and was called to obedience. This would have been crucial to the survival of the people of God.

It is somewhat puzzling that the Old Testament records only two times that the law was read on such an occasion. Josiah apparently read and responded to Deuteronomy's law with repentance and continued religious reform (2 Kgs 23:1-3). The second time was after the exile. Nehemiah and Ezra had led in resettlement in the land, and proclaimed a day of repentance and reading of the law. A time of confession and covenant renewal followed the reading (Neh 8:13–9:38).[19]

31:12-13 The law was for everyone, not just the elite, a fact that has been often noted in Deuteronomy. Everyone included the **men, women, children and aliens**. Only the males were required to attend the three yearly feasts, but when the law was read, all the covenant people were to be there. The women were involved as a parent responsible for raising the children. The alien was involved because several of the laws addressed their concerns. The children were involved because they were the next generation responsible for

---

[18]Also called "succoth" or "booths."

[19]A public reading of Deuteronomy can be done in about two and one-half hours. Its sermonic form and repetitious style make it an excellent book for oral presentation. W. Holladay has attempted to find evidence of the regular reading of the law in the late seventh century by studying the book of Jeremiah. He found evidence in Jeremiah 2–3; 11:1-7 and 36:9 and suggested the dates of 608, 601, and 594 BC ("A Proposal for Reflections," pp. 326-328).

covenant continuity. Consequently, everyone needed to learn the law and obey it. The periodic reading of the law ensured that especially the children heard it and learned it in public as well as private settings (cf. 6:5-9,20-25). This guaranteed the continuation of the covenant from generation to generation. Furthermore, when the people gathered to hear the law, the children would gain a powerful sense of the whole covenant community to which they belonged. A solid sense of community is based on both faithfully passing on traditions and sharing of community life. Therefore, the public reading of the law was essential to the continued preservation and welfare of the nation of Israel. Israel's later failure to keep the covenant perhaps can be traced, in part, to a failure to follow Moses' instructions in this text.

3. God's Final Warning (31:14-22)

31:14 God appeared to Moses and Joshua to share a final warning with Moses about the people, and to commission Joshua. The **tent of meeting** was a pretabernacle tent that was placed outside the camp where Moses met with God (Exod 33:7-11). Moses would go into the tent and God would appear at the entrance in the cloud. Joshua was the only other one who could approach the tent. Apparently the tent continued in use even after the tabernacle was built. Perhaps it was a special place that God used for communicating with Moses in situations when God refused to appear in Israel's midst in the tabernacle because the purity of the people was in question.[20]

---

[20]Childs, *Exodus*, pp. 590-593. The fact that the phrase "tent of meeting" is applied to the tabernacle over 130 times creates some confusion. Some have suggested that the two structures were the same (Walton and Matthews, *Genesis–Deuteronomy*, p. 266), but the text here refutes that. Others think there were two different (conflicting) ideas about where God could be met in Israel, the tabernacle or the tent of meeting (Tigay, *Deuteronomy*, p. 293). But the Bible does not confuse them. The tent of meeting seemed to be more Moses' private place to meet God as opposed to the public tabernacle (see Exod 18:7-16; Num 11:16,24,26; 12:4; Merrill, *Deuteronomy*, p. 401; *NBD*, s.v. "Tabernacle," p. 1157). At the tent of meeting God met Moses in the cloud at the entrance. At the tabernacle the cloud filled the tent so that Moses could not go in (Exod 40:34-35).

31:15 The **pillar of cloud** was the typical manifestation of the presence of God in the wilderness (Exod 13:21-22; 14:19-24; 19:19; 34:5; Num 11:25) and represented his glory (Exod 16:10). It was a continuation of the manifestation of God on Sinai (Exod 19:9,16-19; 24:15-18). It both revealed God (he spoke from the cloud) and concealed him, for no one could see God and live. Through its movement he led the people. At night the pillar of fire manifested his presence.

31:16-18 God's message to Moses was grim. It was painful for two reasons. Moses' demise was imminent[21] and his people's apostasy after his death was certain. Even though Moses had already anticipated apostasy (29:19-28; 30:1), divine affirmation erased any doubt as to the future of the nation.

Moses had often warned Israel about forsaking God and following after other gods (7:1-6; 12:1-3; 13; 28:20). But God's language was much stronger. For him apostasy was to **prostitute** oneself to the gods. This conceives of spiritual unfaithfulness with a gross term (Lev 17:7; 20:5). It is the only time the term is used in Deuteronomy, though it is common in the prophets beginning with Hosea and continuing in Jeremiah and Ezekiel.[22] Committing prostitution was a serious breach of the marriage covenant and marriage faithfulness. The covenant relationship between God and Israel was similar to a marriage and perfect faithfulness was required. Therefore, prostitution was a vivid, and fitting metaphor for apostasy. It reflected the fact that apostasy was more than an addition of gods to worship; it was an unholy act of the most sordid kind (cf. Ezekiel 16 and 23). Such an act overturned God's carefully planned relationship with Israel and was a direct affront to his grace.

To commit prostitution can be taken in a factual sense also. Canaanite religion included sexual fertility rites. If Israel adopted that religion, it meant the people engaged in actual prostitution as well.[23]

---

[21]"Rest with your fathers" was a common Old Testament idiom for dying. It was connected to the verb, *škb,*,"to lie down in sleep." But it also reflected the practice in ancient Israel of burial of bodies in a family tomb. A person who died actually did lie down with the fathers (cf. Gen 47:30; 1 Kgs 1:21; 2:10; 11:21,43; 14:20, and often of the kings).

[22]See Gary H. Hall, "זנה," *NIDOTTE*, 1:1122-1125.

[23]See Hosea 1–3 and especially 4:13-14.

That Israel could **forsake** God is difficult to imagine. It is probably true that they did not forsake him in the sense that they gave up worshiping him.[24] They would have only added to his worship the worship of other gods. But from God's perspective the demand of covenant loyalty was exclusive and the inclusion of other gods violated that demand. It was therefore the same as abandoning God and breaking the covenant.

If Israel forsook God, then he would **forsake** them (v. 17). This reversed the promise of verse 6. Nothing could annul the promise of God except the disobedience of Israel. Moses had warned her about God's burning **anger** (6:15; 7:11; 11:17; see also 29:26) for disobedience. God said it would become a fact. God would also remove his protective presence from Israel (**hide my face**) so that they would be exposed to the world, without defense (cf. Isa 54:28; 59:2; Micah 3:4; Ps 27:9).[25] Because of that, **disasters** would come upon them. The disasters were certainly those promised in the curses of chapters 28 and 29. There is a clear sense of the punishment fitting the crime in these verses. Israel would forsake God and turn her face to other gods. Therefore, God would forsake Israel and hide his face from her.

Israel could never say in the future that she had not been warned about disobedience and its consequences. The unfortunate fact is that hindsight is always better than foresight. Centuries later the author of 2 Kings affirmed that apostasy led to Israel's downfall (2 Kgs 17). The consequences also had a profound effect on the people in Nehemiah's day after the exile (Neh 8–9). But by then the permanent consequences of sin had worked themselves out in Israel's life through Jerusalem's destruction and the exile.

31:19 As a further witness and affirmation of Israel's future disobedience Moses was instructed to write down a **song** for Israel. This song is contained in chapter 32 (cf. vv. 22 and 30). The song, like the law, was to be taught to the people.

The song would function as a **witness** against them in the same way that the law did. A witness is an independent entity who functions in a court of law to give testimony about the factuality of a

---

[24]Tigay, *Deuteronomy*, p. 294.
[25]These passages stand in sharp contrast to the priestly blessing of Num 6:25-26.

charge (Deut 17:6,7; 19:15,16,18).[26] Therefore, when future generations recited the song, it would stand as a reminder of the history of their failure. They would remember that God had fully warned them about their future disobedience but that they had not paid attention. Even if future generations might be tempted to blame their affliction on God, the song would remind them that they were at fault, not God.[27]

31:20-21 These verses juxtapose God's grace and Israel's sin. God's promise to bring Israel into **the land flowing with milk and honey** was certain. He would be faithful to his promise. But Israel's sin was also certain (affirming what was said in verses 16-18).

31:22 This verse provides a rhetorical balance to verse 19. Moses, in obedience to God, wrote down the song and taught it as commanded. He is placed in opposition to Israel who was not obedient.

4. God Commissions Joshua (31:23)

31:23 God's action confirmed Moses' commissioning of Joshua in verses 7-8. Thus Moses' words of encouragement were founded on the divine word. Joshua could stand firm in the knowledge that he was God's choice to replace Moses. God would use him as the instrument to fulfill his promise. The verse begins Part 2 of the chapter in which the topics are repeated but the speakers are reversed. This was a rhetorical device to affirm the seriousness of the words.

The commissioning was repeated a third time in Joshua 1:6-9. These three texts tie the last part of Deuteronomy closely to the book of Joshua and suggest that Deuteronomy 31–34 functions as a transitional section between the two books.[28]

---

[26]Heaven and earth were also called as witnesses against Israel: 4:26; 30:19; 31:28. In ancient Near Eastern treaties the gods functioned as witnesses between the parties. In Josh 24:22 the people would stand as witnesses against themselves. Isa 30:8 and Hab 2:2-3 mention writing down prophecies as witnesses.

[27]See comments below on chapter 32 for full discussion of the form of the song as a witness to the covenant. The fact that it was in poetic form would have made it easier to memorize.

[28]Cairns, *Deuteronomy*, p. 270.

5.Moses' Final Warning (31:24-30)

31:24-26 Moses concluded what he began in verse 9 and provided for the preservation of the law document. The document was to be placed in the care of the Levites and kept with the Ark of the Covenant.[29] This arrangement assured its safety and availability when it was to be brought out for reading.[30] Its proximity to the Decalogue that was in the Ark suggests the law and the Ten Commandments were of equal authority. The law expounded the commandments and was to be obeyed in the same way.[31] This physical arrangement mimics the literary arrangement of the book of Deuteronomy. The Ten Commandments are given first in chapter 5. The explanatory statutes, judgments, and commandments follow in chapters 6–26.[32] Ancient Near Eastern treaties were stored in the major temple of each country, suggesting the deity was the custodian of the treaty. For Israel, the Ark of the Covenant was seen as symbolic of God's presence and was kept in the Holy of Holies in the tabernacle. Therefore, the law was placed in God's care.

Moses probably did not write in a **book** as modern society understands it. Books as we know them were not invented until the Christian era. The idea here is some sort of document[33] which, in ancient times, could refer to a brief or long document written on any one of numerous surfaces: stone, plaster, pottery, papyrus, parchment, or clay. Probably a scroll was intended in this case (see Jer 32:11; 36).

Merrill points out that the song and the law provided two witnesses against Israel. This was the minimum number required for conviction of a crime according to Deuteronomy 19:15.[34]

---

[29]Some have suggested that these verses follow logically verses 9-13. That is correct temporally, but rhetorically this chapter has been arranged in a topical order. Theories of later additions or intrusions need not be constructed to account for the structure of the chapter.

[30]Presumably the law would be kept in a jar for safety. It joined two other items that were kept beside the ark: a jar of manna (Exod 16:33-34) and Aaron's rod that budded (Num 17:10). Only the two copies of the Decalogue were kept in the Ark (Deut 10:1-6).

[31]Cairns, *Deuteronomy*, p. 277.

[32]Miller, *Deuteronomy*, p. 222.

[33]The Hebrew word is *sēpher*.

[34]Merrill, *Deuteronomy*, p. 404.

31:27-29 Moses' pessimism for the future of Israel matched God's in verses 16-18. Moses used vocabulary from previous sermons to repeat the dismal picture. His experience had been that Israel was **rebellious and stiff-necked** from the beginning (9:4-6,13; 10:16).

These were some of Moses' hardest and saddest words. He had given a major part of his life and energy to shepherd Israel out of Egypt toward the Promised Land. He was eager to see them receive the benefits of the longstanding promise of God. He earnestly desired to go in with them. Yet at this crucial moment of fulfillment he not only was forbidden to accompany them into the land, he saw that Israel would fail. His pleading for obedience and admonitions to faithfulness in his final sermon to his people would go unheeded. Israel would fail at the central point of covenant faithfulness: they would turn to worship man-made gods.

This preview of Israel's future apostasy was also part of Moses' song in the following chapter (33:15-18). These words are so pessimistic and accurate that many scholars see them as a later addition to the book, written after the fact.[35]

Moses' words may seem pessimistic, but they reflect the truth expressed in Genesis 2–3. Mankind, when faced with a decision between obedience to God and the temptation to become like God, will almost inevitably choose for the latter. Pride has a firm grip on human nature from which even God's people are not immune. Israel created her false gods in her image.

31:30 God had commanded Moses to write down a song in verses 19-22. Its contents were outlined in those verses. Verse 22 tells us that Moses wrote down the song, and this verse tells us that he **recited** it to the people. This verse follows logically verse 22 and serves to introduce chapter 32, the song that Moses wrote. The song served, with the law, as a future witness against Israel.

---

[35]Mayes, *Deuteronomy*, p. 379.

DEUTERONOMY 32

B. THE SONG OF MOSES: 32:1-47

God instructed Moses in 31:19 to write a song and teach it to the Israelites, which he did (v. 22). Chapter 32 is that song. The Song can be studied as an independent psalm, but its meaning is tied closely to its context and the narrative of chapter 31. It is Moses' last address to Israel.[1]

The Song presents two challenges to the interpreter. First, its form is uncertain because of the varied nature of its contents. Second, its poetic genre is a style not encountered in Deuteronomy before.

Chapter 31:19 described the purpose of the Song as a "witness" for God against the people. Since witnesses belong to the courtroom, Deuteronomy 32 would seem to function as part of a lawsuit God brought against Israel. Many scholars have affirmed that this is its genre.[2] The following lawsuit elements occur: accusation (vv. 4-6); refutation of the defendant's arguments (vv. 7-14); specific indictment (vv. 15-18); divine sentence (vv. 19-29).[3] This is a "broken" lawsuit because nonlegal elements appear in the Song. For example, verse 2 reflects wisdom literature, and verses 30-43 relieve the tension of the suit by providing a message of hope through God's offer of salvation.

---

[1]See Steven Weitzman, "Lessons from the Dying: The Role of Deuteronomy 32 in its Narrative Setting," *HTR* 87 (1994), pp. 377-393. Chapter 33 is a blessing, not a sermon or address.

[2]For a convenient survey and bibliography see Weitzmann, "Lessons," pp. 377-378.

[3]This is called the *rib* form after the Hebrew verb which is translated as "charge, lawsuit." See George E. Wright, "The Law-Suit of God: A Form-Critical Study of Deuteronomy 32," *Israel's Prophetic Heritage*, eds. Bernhard W. Anderson and Walter Harrelson, (New York: Harper and Row, 1962), pp. 26-67. See page 43 for his outline.

The Song as a covenant lawsuit provided the model for the same genre in the prophets (Isa 1; Jer 2:4-13; Micah 6:1-8). It also shares several theological themes with the prophets and perhaps was a common source for their preaching (cf. Hos 13:4-10).[4]

The wisdom literature elements in the Song have led other scholars to different conclusions. They see it as a teaching poem that drew lessons from Israel's history,[5] or as a poem with mixed genres such as didactic, hymnic and prophetic elements. Consequently, these scholars deny its covenant lawsuit setting.[6]

However, the Song is best understood as a covenant lawsuit. In the book of Deuteronomy it follows the covenant renewal of chapters 29–30 and the indictments of 31:16-18,27-29. Thematically, it agrees with the covenant emphasis of the book, even if the covenant is not explicitly referred to in the Song. But its form is mixed. It was intended as both a lawsuit and a teaching tool (the purpose of wisdom). It reminded the nation of its status before God and instructed each generation concerning their relationship with God.[7] The Song's conclusion held out hope for Israel despite her rebellious nature. This would have been an important message for the future.

Many scholars agree that the Song is old and date it prior to the 10th century B.C., although a few have suggested a date as late as the 6th and 5th centuries. Most scholars would not date the Song as early as the time of Moses, however. In support of an early date are the Song's language and major themes, certain archaic linguistic forms, and the absence of issues that concerned the later prophets.[8]

---

[4]Tigay, *Deuteronomy*, pp. 510-511. Excursus 30 in Tigay's work addresses the complex issues of Deuteronomy 32's genre and date.

[5]Driver, *Deuteronomy*, p. 345. He compares it to Ps 78, 105, 106; Ezek 16; 20; 23. See also James R. Boston, "The Wisdom Influence upon the Song of Moses," *JBL* 87 (1968): 198-202.

[6]Tigay, *Deuteronomy*, pp. 509-510; George Mendenhall, "Samuel's 'Broken Rib': Deuteronomy 32," *A Song of Power and the Power of Song*, pp. 169-180.

[7]We must not confuse form and function (Merrill, *Deuteronomy*, p. 409). Just as we freely mix forms (eg., a personal letter can contain poems, quotes, instructions, stories, etc.), biblical writers were certainly free to adapt genres for their purpose.

[8]Mendenhall proposed an 11th century date associated with the Philistine crisis in 1 Sam 7. He suggested Samuel was the author ("Deuteronomy 32," pp. 174-176). Tigay prefers an earlier time during the period of the judges because of affinities with Judg 5:8; 10:14 (*Deuteronomy*, pp. 512-513).

Furthermore, the Song enlarges on God's brief comments in 31:16-18 and Moses' words in 31:27-29. Its view of the future is similar to other Deuteronomy passages that address Israel's rebellious spirit and God's future punishment (ch. 9, 27, 28, 30). Consequently, one can be justified in tracing the Song back to Moses himself.[9]

The second challenge of the Song is its poetic style, a new kind of literature in Deuteronomy. Hebrew poetry requires that the interpreter pay attention to its structure. Normally two lines will parallel each other in expression and meaning. Sometimes three lines will be related (v. 17). The related lines will repeat a thought, or the second will build on the first, or the second will posit an opposite idea.[10] Poetry is also characterized by figurative language, such as simile, metaphor, symbolism, allusion, apostrophe (address of someone not present), personification, and hyperbole.[11] Word plays and alliterations are abundant in Hebrew poetry but cannot be reproduced in English translations. These poetic devices appeal to the imagination and emotions and make poetry easier to memorize. The Song was to be taught to the people (31:19), so its poetic style is appropriate to the occasion.

1. Summons and Introduction (32:1-2)

32:1 God, as initial speaker in the lawsuit, summons the **heavens and earth** to **listen** to what he is going to say. The covenant lawsuits in the prophets have the same feature (Isa 1:2; Jer 2:12; Micah 6:2 [mountains and foundations of the earth]; Ps 50:4). Heaven and earth were called to testify or witness against Israel in Deuteronomy 4:26; 30:19; 31:28. However, their function here seems to be different. They are only to listen to the speech as an audience who observes what is occurring. As objective onlookers they would see that God had a case against his people.[12]

---

[9]As of course the Bible suggests. See George A. Knight, *The Song of Moses: A Theological Quarry* (Grand Rapids: Eerdmans, 1995), pp. 3-7.

[10]The term for this in Old Testament studies is parallelism.

[11]See Leland Ryken, *How to Read the Bible as Literature* (Grand Rapids: Zondervan, 1984), pp. 94-102.

[12]Tigay: this is a literary device (*Deuteronomy*, p. 299). Scholars debate this point. In ancient Near Eastern treaties, the gods were called in as witnesses

32:2 This verse points to the didactic aspect of the Song. **Teaching** is a word that belongs to the instructional genre (Prov 1:5; 4:2; 7:21; 9:9; 16:21,23). Moses was to "teach" the Song to Israel in 31:19.[13] Therefore, the Song was not intended to reflect a one-time forensic action. It was an exemplar for future generations and defined the character of God, his dealings with Israel and Israel's defective response.

The image of God's word bringing precious moisture to the plants was a vivid one for ancient Israel. Rain was plentiful in only a few places in the Promised Land. In general it rained only in the fall and spring. Southern regions were very dry. Hot winds and drought were a real threat to tender, new plants. **Dew, showers, and rain** were life-giving phenomena and brought pleasant images to the mind.[14]

2. Moses Praises God's Character (32:3-4)

32:3 The speaker changes from God to Moses. Proclamation and praise are hymnic language that is found in many of the Psalms. To **proclaim the name of the LORD** was to announce his qualities, just as God had pronounced his own qualities in Exodus 34:5-7. God's character was the basis for the covenant and also the basis for the covenant lawsuit. His **greatness** (or majesty) was especially worthy of note.[15] It is this greatness of character that sets God apart from both Israel and the other gods in this Song.

---

to the treaty, presumably to hold the nations accountable. The gods, of course, had no function for ancient Israel. G.E. Wright suggests that the heavens and earth are symbols for the heavenly hosts and nations of the world, who witness to the covenant (cf. Ps 97:6; Wright, "Law-Suit," pp. 45-49). Mendenhall thinks they are the natural forces through whom are mediated the blessings and curses ("Deuteronomy 32," p. 177).

[13]A different word, לִמַּד (lmd), is used in 31:19. lmd is used often in Deuteronomy to refer to the action of helping someone learn. "Teaching" in 32:2 is a noun that refers to the content (לֶקַח, leqaḥ).

[14]For God's beneficent rain see Deut 11:14; 28:12; Job 5:10; Ps 72:6. For dew see Deut 33:13,28; Ps 133:3; Prov 19:12; Isa 26:19; Hos 14:5(6). It is interesting how verse 2 here mirrors verse 1. The first half reflects what comes from heaven, the second half what is on earth.

[15]This term occurs only 13 times in the OT, five in Deuteronomy (3:24; 5:24; 9:26; 11:2; 32:3).

32:4 This verse states the main theme of the poem. God is entirely reliable and just. He is reliable because he is a **rock**. The metaphor is grounded in the geography of the land. Canaan was full of rocky hills and craggy cliffs. The image, which is used of God often in the OT, portrays God as stable and solid, a sanctuary and refuge.[16] But he is not static. As a rock he offers safety and deliverance for his people (vv. 15,18). In this song the image was used to emphasize that he was faithful in contrast to faithless Israel. He was the true God in contrast to the other gods. They too were rocks, but powerless ones (vv. 31,37).

This image of rock projects the most important virtues of his character. Six virtues are singled out; all portray his absolute reliability and trustworthiness. Consequently, **his works are perfect**. What he has done for Israel is whole and flawless, just like his ways (Ps 18:30[31]) and his law (Ps 19:7[8]).[17] **Just, faithful, upright** are all terms proper for the law court but they also describe the nature of God. They suggest absolute fairness and justice. God was also one who **does no wrong**. Nothing he does deviates from his perfect ways. Moses preempts any attack on God's character. Israel could not defend herself by accusing God of some fault. Furthermore, these virtues were not abstractions. God had abundantly demonstrated in Israel's history that he was just and reliable.

3. Accusation (32:5-6)

Moses presented the accusation against Israel. The essence of the charge was that she was the opposite of God as just described. She was a covenant breaker, unstable, unreliable, faithless, full of flaws, little interested in righteousness and justice.

32:5 Israel had **acted corruptly toward** God. She had violated the covenant by committing apostasy (9:12; 31:29). Such shameful acts

---

[16]God is referred to as a rock 33 times in the OT. See, for example, 1 Sam 2:2; 2 Sam 22:3,32,47; Ps 18:2(3); 19:14(15); 28:1; 31:2(3); 78:35; Isa 30:29; 44:8; Hab 1:12. See also M.P. Knowles, "'The Rock, His Work is Perfect': Unusual Imagery for God in Deuteronomy 32," *VT* 39 (1989): 307-322.

[17]The word "perfect" was used of Noah, but most often in Leviticus and Numbers of the flawless lambs used for the offering.

made her God's non-child.[18] She was morally blemished just like a physically blemished lamb that was prohibited from the sacrifice.[19] More was expected of her. In Deuteronomy children were to be obedient and teachable (21:18-21; 6:20-24). They were to honor and respect their parents (5:16). They were to accept discipline from their father for their own good (8:5). But Israel was unable to conduct herself as a responsible child for she was **warped** and devious, **crooked** and perverse.[20]

32:6 Moses expressed profound astonishment that Israel could have treated God like she did. They were **foolish** and **unwise**, without sense and witless. The foolish were those who declared there was no God (Ps 14:1), the kind of children who brought grief to the father (Prov 17:21),[21] the dull and ignorant. It was difficult to understand their lack of sense.

How could they treat their **Father** and **Creator** like they did? By mixing metaphors Moses established the basis of Israel's unique relationship with God. He was her maker and lord, but also her concerned father. God's action toward her was one of love, concern and patience but also discipline and correction (Exod 4:22; Deut 1:31; 8:5; Ps 103:13; Jer 31:9,20; Hos 11:1).[22] Israel was expected to be obedient and faithful, but she consistently violated this expectation (Isa 1:2; 30:9; Jer 3:4,19; Mal 1:6).

The basis for the covenant lawsuit was established. God was blameless but his people were faithless. The next step was to submit proof.

---

[18]This is one of several curt, dismissive phrases in the Song. See "nonwise," v. 6; "no-gods," vv. 17,21; "no-people," v. 21.

[19]"Blemish" (NIV, "shame") and "perfect" (v. 4) are antonyms and are frequently used of sacrificial animals. Although the Hebrew words of this verse make sense, the word order is not clear. See the NIV footnote and NRSV for other possibilities.

[20]For a biblical commentary on the terms used in verse 5 see Ps 18:27 and Prov 8:8.

[21]Nabal, whose name derives from the root for foolish (*nbl*), was the quintessential fool in the OT (1 Sam 25).

[22]The concepts associated with the father-son relationship fit well the covenantal framework of Deuteronomy (D. McCarthy, "Notes on the Love of God in Deuteronomy and the Father-Son Relationship between Yahweh and Israel," *CBQ* 27 [1965]: 144-147).

4. History of God's Care (32:7-14)

Moses makes the case for God by briefly reviewing how God had cared for Israel in her past. God had been consistent in providing everything they needed.

32:7 Memory plays an important role in Deuteronomy. Israel was commanded to **remember** eleven times. Nearly half of these refer to remembering that she was a slave in Egypt and that God had brought her out.[23] The past was important to the present. What God had done was proof of his care and grounds for his lawsuit.

In this case what Israel was to remember went back before the Exodus to early times, even before the patriarchs. It was something their **fathers** could tell them (cf. 6:20-24).[24]

32:8-9 God's care for Israel began before he chose the patriarchs and long before the Exodus. It began apparently with the events recorded in Genesis 10-11. At that time God[25] **divided** the nations on earth, giving each its own territory.[26] In other words Israel's God was the sovereign God who controlled the whole world. Each nation was the object of his care. His plan for Israel to become his chosen nation included preparing a place for her by assigning other nations to their place as well (see Amos 9:7). This included establishing the **boundaries** for each nation. Israel had some knowledge of these facts already. God told them that he had given Moab and Ammon their land (2:9,19) and that it was not for Israel. Israel's land was Canaan that God had been preparing for them for centuries.

---

[23]5:15; 15:15; 16:12; 24:18,22; also 7:18; 8:2,18; 9:7; 24:9; 25:17.

[24]This verse is an example of Hebrew poetic parallelism. The first two lines are parallel in thought: "remember" equals "consider" and "days of old" equals "generations long past." However, the second line is not the same in meaning but calls for further reflection on the idea being expressed. The third and fourth lines function in the same way. An additional feature is that the verb "ask" does double duty; it serves as the verb for both lines.

[25]"Most High" is a general word for God used some in Genesis and often in the Psalms (Gen 14:18,19,20,22; Ps 7:17[18]; 9:2[3]; 18:13[14]; 21:7[8], etc.). It seems to be used when the more universal aspect of God's nature and claims are being emphasized. Its use here is appropriate in a poetic reference to God's universal action in an early period.

[26]Genesis 10:5,32 uses the same word for "divide" (NIV, "spread out"). Genesis 11 describes the reason why the world was divided (cf. v. 8).

God's preparation also included a symbolic symmetry to the world. There was a correlation between the nations and the **sons of Israel**. This perhaps refers to the correspondence between the number of nations in Genesis 10 (70) and the descendants of Jacob who went into Egypt (70; Gen 46:27; Deut 10:22).[27] This would have provided a satisfying sense of completeness and balance for ancient Israel.[28]

Out of all the nations God had chosen Israel as his **allotted inheritance**. God had planned it from the beginning. Her special place in his purpose was secure. Her current situation was proof as well. She was ready to take the land, which was her heritage. But prior to that was the fact that she was God's heritage.[29]

32:10 God's selection of and provision for Israel was reviewed as further proof of his faithfulness. In verses 10-14 Moses uses some of his most vivid metaphors.

God's election of Israel is placed in the wilderness period (he **found him in a barren and howling waste**). God's history with her predates the wilderness, but the Song is outlining her precarious position and God's loving care. The contrast was between her previous poverty and current plenty.[30] The desert was a place of danger because of the lack of food and water and the presence of wild animals.[31] In those desperate circumstances God intervened to protect

---

[27]Merrill, *Deuteronomy*, p. 413; Driver, *Deuteronomy*, pp. 355-356.

[28]However, both a Hebrew text from Qumran and the Septuagint have a textual variant: "sons/angels of God." This suggests the number of nations was equal to the number of heavenly hosts, and that perhaps each nation had an angel assigned to it (cf. Isa 24:21; Ps 82:6; Dan 10:20-21). In this case God assigned the nations to other heavenly beings but kept Israel for himself. Several commentators prefer this interpretation (Tigay, *Deuteronomy*, p. 303; Craigie, *Deuteronomy*, p. 379). Miller's suggestion that the text means that God also allotted the other nations their gods and religions seems to go beyond the text (*Deuteronomy*, p. 229).

[29]Verse 9 is an example of inverted parallelism. "The LORD's portion" equals "his allotted inheritance" and "his people" equals "Jacob." Again the repetition of ideas promotes deeper reflection on the truth being expressed.

[30]Perhaps Egypt is in mind here as well (Craigie, *Deuteronomy*, p. 380). The prophets also see the wilderness period as the special time when God and Israel developed their relationship: Hos 13:5-6; Jer 2:2; Ezek 16:4-8.

[31]"Barren" is used of the uninhabited world of Genesis 1:2.

(**shield**, literally, "surround") Israel. **Apple of the eye** refers to the pupil, the most sensitive and important part of the eye (cf. Ps 17:8; Prov 7:2). It was thus the most carefully cared for and protected. Any threat to the eye causes an involuntary blink or duck of the head. God's protection was gentle and personal.

32:11 God was also like an **eagle** who tenderly cared for her young. When the eaglet was old enough to fly, the parent eagle would gently force it out of the nest. It would also hover nearby as the eaglet took its first flight, and even support it with its own wings if necessary.[32]

32:12 God **alone** did all of this for Israel. There were no other **gods** to help. That is why Israel's turning to other gods was so tragic. They were not just other gods, they were **foreign** gods, strange and unknown deities who had no claim on Israel and no interest in her.[33] This verse grounds the Song in the first commandment (5:6-7). Israel could have no other gods because no other gods had any claim on her.

32:13-14 God's care for Israel included copious provisions.[34] He gave them the best and richest food. He provided for them even from the **rock** and **flinty crag**. This could be poetic hyperbole or reality. Rocky caverns provide shelter for bees and olive trees grow well in rocky soil and on rocky slopes.

The provision of food matches the description of the land in chapter 8:7-9, and the many references to it as a "land of milk and honey" (6:3; 11:9; 26:9; 27:3; 31:20). The point is that everything Israel needed, God provided for her from the beginning. He provided the best, and plenty of it, not just the bare necessities. Israel had no complaint. The land that God planned to give her before he even chose her from the nations was able to meet her needs. Everything that indicated prosperity and plenty was there: **curds,**

---

[32]Cf. Exod 19:4. The image of the eagle provided several vivid metaphors for divine activity in the OT. The best known is Isa 40:31. On the other side, eagle imagery is also used in texts about God's judgment (Ezek 17:3,7; Hos 8:1). See *Dictionary of Biblical Imagery*, s.v. "Eagle," p. 223.

[33]Cf. 31:16.

[34]The future gift of the land and Israel's experience in it is assumed in the Song as Moses casts a vision of the future. Merrill however thinks the Song could be describing the transjordan area of Gilead and Bashan, which was rich and fertile (*Deuteronomy*, p. 415).

milk, fattened lambs, choice rams, wheat, and wine.[35] God had made his case. What fault could Israel find in him? What more could he have done for them?

5. The Indictment of Israel (32:15-18)

Israel's reaction to God's generous provision was not gratitude and obedience, but rebellion and apostasy. Prosperity made her self-centered and arrogant. The warnings of 6:11-12 and 8:11-20 became reality. Israel interpreted her comfortable situation as a consequence of worshiping other gods (see Hos 2:8). She did not know that it was her covenant God who had provided for her.

Each characteristic and blessing from God was countered by an opposing action from Israel.[36] God's provision of plenty (vv. 13-14) was greeted with self-indulgence and disdain (v. 15). God's election and guidance of Israel through the wilderness (vv. 10-11) was met with worship of other gods (vv. 16-17). God, the Rock, Father, and Creator (vv. 4-9), was forgotten (v. 18).[37]

32:15 Jeshurun was apparently a pet name for Israel, though rarely used (33:5,26; Isa 44:2). Israel was supposed to be the "upright one" because she belonged to God who was upright (v. 4b).[38] But she was anything but upright. Usually the fat animal is docile and lazy, but Israel **kicked**. She became obstinate and rebellious. She renounced God and treated him disdainfully.[39]

32:16-17 Israel's idolatry made God **jealous**. It aroused his zeal for his people and concern for their loyalty.[40] His contempt for the object of Israel's worship when they turned from him could not be

---

[35]God's provision of physical food is also assurance of his spiritual provision as Isaiah preached (55:1-3).

[36]Merrill, *Deuteronomy*, p. 416.

[37]Note the chiastic arrangement of the items.

[38]"Jeshurun" comes from the root *yāšar*, "to be upright." There could be a play with the name Israel as well since Israel and *yāšar* have the same first three letters (ישר, counting the *shin* and *sin* as similar letters).

[39]The NIV "reject" is too mild. This is the same verb used for the son who dishonored the father (Micah 7:6), and for God treating Nineveh with contempt (Nahum 3:6).

[40]See comments on 5:9 and 6:15.

harsher. Israel had turned to **foreign gods** (cf. v. 12), but these were not really gods. They were nothings, "no-gods."[41] Israel had never **known** them, had never had a relationship of any kind with them. They were newly on the scene and were not known to the fathers.[42] There was nothing about them that was powerful or attractive. Israel's apostasy was incomprehensible.

32:18 A child who rebelled against its parents was subject to the death penalty (21:18-21). Israel had done that and worse. The Song combines the metaphor of Rock (v. 4) and Father (v. 6) with the imagery of a mother to emphasize the point. It is the mother who **gives birth**,[43] not the father. The poetry rounds out the picture of God as parent by bringing out his mothering side. The rebellion of the child was total, against both parents.

The indictment was complete. Despite Moses' earlier warning Israel did **forget** God. She had lost memory of him and had abandoned him. The calls to remember had not been heeded. The Song now would become a witness to later Israel. It would explain the reason for her devastation, and provide another opportunity to learn from the past.

6. The Divine Sentence (32:19-25)

Israel was found guilty of the crimes with which she was charged. Whatever defense she could have mustered would have been futile for there was no doubt about the truth of the charges. The Song turns to explaining the sentence of God the judge. It is a powerful picture of God's wrath. The rejected father treated the children like they treated him as the parallels with 31:16-22 show.

---

[41]"Demons" refer to spirits who have no divine powers rather than to demonic forces. See the no-children and no-people of verses 5 and 21.

[42]In some cultures, even in modern times, an older religion is considered to be a better religion. For example, since Buddha was born before Jesus Christ, Buddhism for people in Thailand is a superior religion (David Filbeck, *Yes, God of the Gentiles, Too* [Wheaton, IL: The Billy Graham Center, 1994], pp. 59-60). That seems to be the point of verse 17. How could Israel be interested in such no-gods that had appeared so recently?

[43]The verb refers to the writhing in pain of the mother as she labors to give birth (Isa 26:17,18; 45:10; 51:2; Jer 4:31; Micah 4:10).

32:19-20 The loving parent was justified to **reject** the children because he was provoked to **anger** (cf. v. 21). His anger was righteous, filled with regret and pain, not revenge. The child must be shown that the chosen path of rebellion was fatal to her existence. She could not turn against her parent without consequences.

God was faithful (v. 4) but Israel was **unfaithful** (v, 20; literally "no faith was in them"). Therefore, God would **hide** his **face from them**. Because Israel had turned from God (31:29), he would turn from her by removing his protective care (31:17,18). "To hide the face" meant that God would abandon the covenant with Israel.

32:21-22 God would do to Israel exactly what she had done to him (cf. v. 16). The second half of verse 21 parallels the first half. Israel had made God **jealous** and **angry**. He would make them **envious** (jealous) and **angry**. He would use the same method. Israel had turned to gods who were nothings (**no god**, v. 16) so God would use a nation who was nothing (**not a people**). This nothing nation would be God's instrument of judgment that would produce the havoc described in verses 23-25. The punishment fit the offense. In this way God displayed his justice. His punishment was neither too little nor too much. There was an ironic balance in his action.

Other word plays emphasize the foolishness of Israel. The idols of the nations were **worthless** (*hebel*). They had no use and would vanish like the mist (this is the same word used in Eccl 1:2). Furthermore, the nations were without **understanding** (*nābāl*, a similar sounding word used of Israel in v. 6).[44] God would use the foolish things of the world to judge his people.

God's **wrath** of judgment was like a **fire** that would destroy the whole world (v. 22). This was not a new idea. In 4:25 and 6:15 God was described as a jealous God and a consuming fire (7:4; 11:17; 29:20,27). Fire as a powerful, destructive force presented a terrifying image of God's wrath. The NT also adopts the image (Matt 5:22; 18:8; Rev 17:16; 18:8; 20:14,15).

The **realm of death** describes the netherworld, the abode of the dead (Hebrew, *sheol*; cf. NIV footnote; Ps 9:17; 16:10; 139:8; Isa 14:9; Amos 9:2). It has nothing to do with the NT concept of hell and a place of judgment for the wicked. It is used as a part of the language

---

[44]The same consonants are used in the verb for "rejected" in verse 15.

for the comprehensive destructive force of God's action. No place in the created world will escape it.

32:23-25 The language that described the actual judgment pictured a conquering army bringing devastation on Israel. This language was typical of the covenant curses of chapter 28.[45] Everyone would be felled by one of God's **arrows**. Seven **calamities** were listed. No one would escape: young or old, men of military age or **young women**, people in the open or seeking refuge inside. The destruction would be complete. Israel would come to an end. All this would be brought by the "no-people" of verse 21.

Paul considered at length the future of the nation of Israel in God's plan after the coming of the Messiah (Rom 9–11). Part of his discussion was based on the concept of "no people" becoming the people of God. The prophet Hosea had pictured Israel becoming a "no people" (Hosea 1:9; 2:24). Paul quoted Hosea but applied the text to the Gentiles. They were the "no people" who would become the people of God (Rom 9:24-25). It is interesting that Paul's identification of the Gentiles with the "no people" is more in tune with Deut 32:21 than Hosea.

7. The Stupid and Corrupt Enemy (32:26-33)[46]

A major shift occurs in this section and the next. Though justice had been served, God's zeal for his honor and his gracious love for Israel would transform Israel's future.

32:26-27 I said refers to God's thoughts as he reflected on his course of action. His goal was the total erasure of even the **memory** of Israel because she had broken the covenant.[47] But he knew that the enemy would look at what God had done to Israel and misinterpret the cause. Israel was a witness to God in the world and proof of his covenant love. Her disappearance would be evidence to the nations of God's demise as well, or at least of his powerlessness. This would be vexing to God (**the taunt of the enemy**) for it would seem to signal the defeat of his plan for the world.

---

[45]28:22,27-28,51-52,59-61.

[46]This is Miller's title (*Deuteronomy*, p. 231).

[47]On the importance of maintaining the remembrance of a person see comments on 7:24; 25:19.

God's actions are always open to misunderstanding, even by his own people. Self-centered, arrogant humans will always misinterpret situations. If a nation defeated Israel, it would immediately think it had done so by its own power and might. What God had done to bring honor to himself would end in dishonor for him. In addition the nations' blindness would be detrimental to them. Assyria made such a blunder and earned its destruction (Isa 10:5-19). Therefore, God determined to devise another plan to prevent this from happening.[48] It was vital for the nations' well-being that they recognize God for who he was.

32:28-29 If the nations[49] had wisdom and understanding so that they could evaluate situations correctly, then God would not have to take the action he will take. The terms used here came from the arena of wisdom. They indicate a lack of the common sense needed to survive in the world. The nations are like the simpleton and fool of Proverbs who never understand how to be successful in the world. The foundation of that success was a proper relationship with God. Without that proper relationship a person or nation is totally lacking in the tools necessary to realistically interpret the world. How much like modern culture this sounds. How often are problems misunderstood, situations misinterpreted, and solutions misguided because God is left out of the equation?

32:30-31 Evidence for the hand of God at work was the enemy's astounding victory over Israel. How could it have been managed unless the LORD had allowed it? First Samuel 4-6 provides an example of this happening. The Philistines did not understand that their victory over Israel was God's doing.[50]

---

[48]God was not caught by surprise and forced to rethink his actions. The text does not reflect on God's sovereignty, but is designed to allow the reader access to the reason behind God's actions. It is similar to Gen 6:5-6, Exod 32, and Hos 11:8-9. It is answering the question: Why did not God utterly destroy Israel as he said he would?

[49]Commentators have different interpretations of "they" of verse 28. Several see this as a return to talking about Israel while others see it as a continuing reference to the enemy of verse 27. The third person pronouns in verses 31-33 that refer to the enemy support the latter interpretation.

[50]One to a thousand was indicative of an extraordinary feat of victory. For Israel the idiom expressed God fighting on her side (Lev 26:8; Josh 23:10) or fighting against her (Isa 30:17). See also the women's song extolling David's exploits (1 Sam 18:7).

The victory was possible because of the superiority of Israel's God over all other gods. These "no gods" were "no rock" in comparison with the **Rock**. They were so-called rocks. The enemies were forced to acknowledge this truth, at least, those who might be wise enough. This was the real dividing line between Israel and the nations. Their gods were entirely different.[51]

32:32-33 The sources of the enemies' beliefs and power were corrupt. They were therefore morally degenerate in every way and deserved the punishment that Israel received. **Sodom** and **Gomorrah** were the premier examples of evil for OT writers (Gen 19; Isa 1:10; 3:9; Jer 23:14; Lam 4:6; Ezek 16:44; see also Matt 10:15; 11:23-24). The enemies of Israel would suffer the same fate as Sodom and Gomorrah. Pagan worship of idols resulted in death not life. It was as fatal as drinking **poison** (cf. Jer 25:15-29 — the nations were to drink the cup of wine of God's wrath).

8. The Vindication of God and His People (32:34-43)

The Song ends with a bold statement about the nature of God. It provides the solution to the situation created by God's judgment on Israel that was raised in verses 26-27.

32:34-36 God's plans and purposes are known only to him, except to the extent that he decides to reveal them (cf. 29:29). The revelation was **sealed** away. He would provide it in his own time.

The nations that God used to execute his judgment on Israel would think that they had done it by their own power. How could God deal with their stupidity and maintain his honor? The answer given in these verses is twofold: God would hold the nations accountable for their actions and he would rescue his people.

God will **avenge** or take vengeance on his enemies and **repay** them for their arrogance (v. 35; cf. v. 41b). This idea must be care-

---

[51]There was pluralism in the ancient world, but it was not accepted in the Bible. All religions were not the same, and Israelite faith was substantially different. Many religions today have radically different understandings of God. Some do not even acknowledge the existence of a god. It is difficult to reconcile these facts with the sentiment that all religions believe in a similar god and are headed in the same direction.

fully explained for it is open to misunderstanding. Vengeance is usually thought of as a negative concept, associated with arbitrary cruelty and illegitimate feelings: revenge and vindictiveness. The second century heretic, Marcion, used this concept to contrast the OT God with the NT God. Subsequently, he rejected the OT altogether.

In the OT, vengeance (נקם, *nqm*) is a positive concept associated with lawfulness, justice and salvation. It is grounded in the character of God, who is holy and just. God is usually the subject of the verb. If the verb is applied to human action, it is in the negative sense. Humans were not to take vengeance.

Vengeance is the just retribution of God who is the sovereign King of the universe and faithful to his covenant. He will vindicate his glorious name, watch over his justice, and act to save his people. It is usually disciplinary in nature when applied to his covenant people and aims at their restoration. Vengeance aimed at the nations means judgment on them, for they are controlled by a lust for power. They rise up against God or his people and injure God's honor.

The two-sided force of vengeance is apparent in these verses. The time for the destruction of the nations was close at hand (v. 35). At the same time God will see the hopelessness of his people and because of his compassion rescue them and restore them (v. 36). This is one of the "gems of grace" scattered throughout Deuteronomy.[52] God's law upheld the plight of the poor and oppressed, the widow, orphan, and alien (24:10-22). That same divine compassion prompted the rescue of the helpless nation at the very moment it was about to be overwhelmed by the enemy. The same theology was expressed passionately in Hosea 11 (cf. Isa 54:7-8).

This double act of vengeance restores order to the universe. The wicked are held accountable for their evil, and God's honor is vindicated by his rescue of his people. The arrogant and mighty are brought low. The weak and lowly are saved. Justice is restored. God's holiness and sovereignty are acknowledged. He is vindicated.[53]

---

[52]Wright, *Deuteronomy*, p. 303.

[53]See Miller, *Deuteronomy*, pp. 233-234; H.G.L. Peels, "נקם," *NIDOTTE*, 3:154-156; Phillip J. Nel, "שלם," *NIDOTTE*, 4:130-135. This principle, which in the OT is understood in the context of God's relationship to the nations, is given a more individual application in the NT (Rom 12:19; Heb 10:30).

32:37-38 God's action will demonstrate the total powerlessness of the pagan gods to which Israel had turned. They were "no gods" (v. 21; cf. Judg 10:14; Jer 2:28) and were proven to be completely ineffective. They did not save Israel from her enemies and could not save the enemy from God's judgment. About all they could do was deplete the resources of the people through **sacrifices and offerings**.

32:39 God's vindication also demonstrated the absoluteness of his power and authority. No god could stand up to him. Beside him there was no other (4:35,39; 5:7; 7:9). The declarative divine "I" dominates these verses. He is the Creator God over all creation (v. 6). He controls **death** and **life**. From the practical level of everyday life to national fortunes he is the only active and effective God because he is the only One (cf. 1 Sam 2:2; 2 Sam 22:32; Isa 44:6; 45:5,6,21,22; 46:9).

32:40 Therefore, what he says he will do, he will do. "As God lives . . . ." was a typical oath formula in ancient Israel (2 Sam 12:5; 1 Sam 19:6; 26:10; Jer 4:2). But when God took the oath, he could only swear by himself, **as I live** (Num 14:21; Isa 45:23; 49:18).

32:41-42 The vengeance that God announced in verse 35 is depicted as taking place. The war imagery used of Israel's destruction (vv. 23-25) is here used of the enemies'. The **arrow** and **sword** will predominate and the destruction will be complete. This was just retribution because the enemy merited it.[54]

32:43 The Song ends with a call to rejoice. The Song also ends like it began, with a proclamation about the actions of God (32:1-4). The **nations** are to join the **people** in honoring God for his justice and holiness. It seems ironic that the nations who had just suffered destruction at the hands of God should end up praising him. However, vindication of Israel meant that the nations also could be vindicated if they would turn from their sin to God. This was the ultimate missionary appeal of the OT that found its fulfillment in Jesus Christ.

That **atonement** was needed introduces a new idea to the Song. But theologically it was necessary to introduce it. If blood had been shed on the land, then atonement was required by the one who shed the blood in order to cleanse the land (Num 35:33).[55]

---

[54]The prophet Isaiah expresses the same theology in chapter 10.

[55]The footnotes in the NIV reflect the fact that there are textual difficulties with the first part of the verse. Both the Deuteronomy text from

32:44 This verse parallels 31:30 and provides the closure to the Song. It is typical of Hebrew poetic style to provide an inclusio around a poem. A variant form of Joshua's name (Hoshea) is used in the Hebrew text.

C. NARRATIVE INTERLUDE (32:48-52)

A brief narrative section provides a bridge to chapter 33 that contains the blessing that Moses pronounced on the tribes. Moses solemnly admonishes the people to obey (vv. 45-47). Then he receives word about his death (vv. 48-52).

32:45-47 Moses' command includes all of the **words** of the covenant text of Deuteronomy. **This law** normally refers to all of the instruction in the book (cf. 17:19; 27:3,8,26; 28:58; 31:12,24). The instruction was to be internalized (**take to heart**). It was to be memorized and appropriated as a guide to doing God's will. It was not enough that one generation commit themselves to obedience. The **children** were also to **obey carefully** the law. Deuteronomy consistently emphasized the important role of parents teaching the children and children adhering to the instruction (4:9-10; 5:29; 6:2,7,20-24; 11:19,21; 12:25,28). Continuation of the covenant was not automatic. Each generation had to renew its allegiance to God and his law. Personal commitment guaranteed the continuation of the covenant, not family line or cultural continuity.

The words of the law were not empty (NIV, **idle**). They were God's words and full of power and authority. Israel would find **life** in them (cf. 4:1; 8:3; 30:15-18,20) because the words came from the author of life. Conformity to them meant life lived as God intended it to be lived. It would be a full life that God would bless in every way. That meant particularly for Israel a **long** life **in the land**.

Moses began the book of Deuteronomy with exhortations to Israel to go in and take the land that God had promised them (1:8). His final words address the same theme. He repeats in a few powerful words what he had told Israel throughout the book. Obedience

---

Qumran and the LXX have alternative readings. They have "Rejoice, O heavens" for "Rejoice, O nations." This does make better sense and parallels verse 1. The overall meaning remains the same, however.

to God's instruction (*torah*) would ensure their permanent settlement in the Promised Land.

32:48-52 God's final words to Moses here and repeated in chapter 34 form a frame around chapter 33. They bring final resolution to Moses' appeal to go into the land with the people in chapter 3:23-28. Both times God told him that he could not do so.

Verses 48-51 are almost identical to Numbers 27:12-14 with a few additions. The verses here add more precise details about the geographical locations.

Moses, along with Aaron, was forbidden to enter the Promised Land for two reasons. They **broke faith** with God, and they **did not uphold** God's **holiness among the Israelites**. Numbers 27 asserts that they rebelled against God (NIV, "disobeyed my command").

The accusation refers to the event recorded in Numbers 20:1-13. The Israelites grumbled because there was no water. Moses and Aaron went to the Tent of Meeting and prayed. God told them to go to a rock with Aaron's rod and speak to the rock, and it would provide water. Moses took the rod, assembled the people, spoke to them harshly asking, "Must we bring you water from the rock?" and struck the rock twice with the rod. Water came out for the people and their livestock. Immediately God addressed Moses and Aaron. Their lack of trust to honor him as holy meant they would not enter the land.

The nature of the rebellion ("to break faith" and "to rebel" are similar ideas) was twofold. Moses seemed to be laying claim to his ability to bring out water, and he struck the rock when God had said to speak to it. Moses' failure was in his inability to rely solely on the power of God's word. He was commissioned only to speak to the rock. That was sufficient. It was arrogance to go further and add the dramatic striking of the rock two times. It drew attention to Moses and not God. This was a serious breach of trust. It did not honor God's holiness. It left the impression that God was not able to meet the needs of the people and that he was not the sufficient and only provider for them. It suggested that he needed human help. God's holiness included his unique status in Israel as the sole God. He could and would meet their every need. He was fully trustworthy and faithful. Moses called this status into doubt.

Aaron had already died six months earlier **on Mount Hor** for his rebellion (Num 20:22-29).[56] Moses' death would be similar to his in location (on top of a mountain) and cause.

Scholars debate the differences between Deuteronomy 1:37 and this text. In chapter 1 Moses blamed the people for being barred from the land, which seems to conflict with the reason given here and in Numbers.[57] However, Moses' charge in 1:37 is unclear and imprecise. If we understand that he was being defensive and not telling the whole story in chapter 1, there is no fundamental conflict with the reasons in chapter 32.[58]

Moses was to view the land from **Mount Nebo**. In 3:27 he was to view the land from Mount Pisgah. Both are a part of the **Abarim** range. This is the high mountain ridge east of Jericho and the Dead Sea that extends south down the length of the Dead Sea. Mount Pisgah was probably a ridge on Mount Nebo, or a second peak, from which one could get a better view of the land.[59] Israel had just come through the plateau area and down to the plains of Moab. Moses would have to backtrack to the mountain and up the ridge. From this point one could easily see Mount Hermon to the north, all the Jordan Valley, and the central hills down to and south of the Dead Sea. It is sad that this is all that Moses would be able to experience of the Promised Land.[60]

---

[56]It is interesting that the rebellion by the brothers in Num 20:2-13 is immediately preceded by the death of their sister Miriam (20:1). By the end of the chapter Aaron was dead also. All three siblings who had such a pivotal role in the formation of Israel died because of rebellion.

[57]See Tigay, *Deuteronomy*, p. 425.

[58]See comments above on 1:37.

[59]See comments above on 3:27. Mount Nebo was at the north end of the ridge. It is 2,740 feet high and about 10 miles east of the Jordan River where the river enters the north end of the Dead Sea.

[60]See chapter 34 for the record of his death and burial.

DEUTERONOMY 33

D. MOSES' BLESSING ON ISRAEL (33:1-29)

The last words of Moses to Israel recorded in Deuteronomy are in the form of a blessing on each tribe. Moses plays the role of the father of Israel who, before his death, pronounces divine benefactions upon his family. This was the custom in ancient Israel (Gen 27:27-29; 49:1-28).

The chapter is related thematically to both chapters 28 and 32. The blessing theme continues the short blessing section in 28:1-14 and helps counter the extended curses section of that chapter. Chapter 33 also fills out chapter 32. Chapter 32 ended with assertions concerning Israel's final vindication. Chapter 33 illustrates how that vindication will work out through the concrete blessings on the tribes. The chapter ends the book of Deuteronomy on an uplifting and positive note, in contrast to the many warnings Moses had customarily given.

Chapter 33 is poetic, full of metaphors and figures of speech, and constructed with pairs of synonymous parallel lines. It contains several word plays on the names of the tribes. There are similarities to Jacob's blessing on his sons in Genesis 49 and some similarities to Deborah's song in Judges 5. However, the order of the tribes is listed differently from Genesis 49 which lists the sons in order of birth. Deuteronomy 33 seems to list them in geographical order of their territory in Canaan. The list begins with Reuben in the Transjordan, then moves west to Judah and north through Samaria to the tribes in the Galilee area. The listing also seems to be grouped according to the mothers.[1] The tribe of Simeon is absent which seems to reflect a time after it had been absorbed into Judah (Josh 15:26-32,42; 19:1-8).

---

[1] The first three listed are Leah's sons, then Rachel's two sons, then Leah's two last sons. The last four are the sons of the concubines. The slight devi-

The text is difficult to interpret in several places. It has several rare words and some opaque allusions. Some of the problems may be due to its poetic style and early age.

Most scholars date the poem as one of the earliest in the OT. There is a general consensus that it comes from the 12th to 11th centuries B.C. The historical situation the poem reflects seems to fit well into the period of the judges and prior to the rise of the Davidic monarchy. Pre-Davidic evidence includes: no hint of the split after Solomon's death; the Thummim and Urim (see below on v. 8) fell out of use after David; the blessing on Judah, the tribe of David, is modest; Dan had already migrated to the north. These and other factors point to the eleventh or tenth century.[2]

Moses, as the prophet par excellence, could very well have given predictions about the fortunes of the tribes in the near future. On the other hand, Moses' final words to the tribes could have been updated soon after his death by someone in agreement with his words and with the whole of Deuteronomy.[3]

1. Introduction (33:1-5)

The poem begins with an introduction that is addressed to all of Israel. It is closely related to the conclusion in verses 26-29. The emphasis in both sections is on the unity of the tribes, and God's protection and provision for the nation as a whole. This puts the

---

ations from the birth order can be explained by the ordering according to geography (Tigay, *Deuteronomy*, p. 522).

[2]Cairns, *Deuteronomy*, p. 294. The tone is of prosperity and optimism. Gad's territorial expansion was complete and Simeon had been absorbed into Judah. F.M. Cross and D.N. Freedman, *Studies in Ancient Yahwistic Poetry* (Missoula, MT; Scholars Press, 1975), pp. 97-122, give the most detailed argument for an early date. See also D.N. Freedman, "'Who Is Like Thee among the Gods?' The Religion of Early Israel," *Ancient Israelite Religion: Essays in Honor of Frank Moore Cross,* ed. Patrick D. Miller, Jr., Paul D. Hanson, and S. Dean McBride (Philadelphia: Fortress, 1987), pp. 315-335. He suggests a 12th to 11th century date for both Genesis 49 and Deuteronomy 33.

[3]Thompson, *Deuteronomy*, p. 306. However, according to Joel D. Heck there is nothing in the blessing incompatible with the traditional view that it comes from Moses ("A History of Interpretation of Genesis 49 and Deuteronomy 33," *BibSac* 147 [1990]: 16-31).

individual blessings into their proper theological context. Individual blessings are possible on each tribe because each one is part of a larger covenant community.

The introduction and conclusion exhibit an interrelationship that follows a chiastic order.

A. The LORD comes to deliver his people: v. 2
    B. The LORD protects and provides for his people: vv. 3-4
        C. God is king over Jeshurun: v. 5
        C'. There is none like the God of Jeshurun: v. 26
    B'. Israel is secure in and blessed by the LORD: vv. 27-28
A'. Israel is delivered by the LORD: v. 29[4]

The arrangement also includes the mention of three important names in reverse order in the first and second half: LORD, Jacob, Jeshurun and Jeshurun, Jacob, LORD.

33:1 The poem is called a **blessing** although the verb is rare in the text (vv. 11,13,20,24; noun in v. 23). Some of the verses are phrased as wishes or petitions. Nevertheless, the poem is the final benediction of Moses on the tribes of Israel.

Moses was called a **man of God,** a phrase usually reserved for prophets in the OT. Chapter 18 had already considered Moses among the prophets, and Deuteronomy closes with an epitaph on Moses' prophetic status (34:10-12).[5] The man of God was a holy man to whom one could appeal for assistance, and from whom one expected a word from God. Therefore, the poem is to be understood as a blessing from God, not just Moses.

33:2 God is pictured as coming from the mountains of the south with his heavenly army to protect and provide for his people. The theology of God's appearance is grounded in the giving of the law at Mt. **Sinai.**[6] There he appeared in all his glory in the clouds, light-

---

[4]From Duane Christensen, "Two Stanzas of a Hymn in Deuteronomy 33," *Biblica* 65 (1984): 382-389. This close relationship has led some scholars to suggest that the verses were originally an independent hymn into which verses 6-25 were later inserted (Mayes, *Deuteronomy*, p. 396; Cairns, *Deuteronomy*, p. 294).

[5]See also Josh 14:6; Ps 90:1; Ezra 3:2; 1 Chr 23:14; 2 Chr 30:16. "Man of God" is mostly used for prophets in the historical books, especially Elijah and Elisha (29 times for the latter).

[6]This is the only appearance of Sinai in Deuteronomy. The usual designation is Horeb.

ning, and thunder (cf. v. 26). From there he led Israel through the
wilderness to Canaan. He marched out as the warrior God at the
head of the heavenly hosts and led his people in defeat of their enemies. He came as the bright sun, armed in battle gear to save Israel
(cf. Ps 80:1-3).[7] The mighty God of Sinai was also celebrated in
Judges (5:4-5), Habakkuk (3:3-6) and the Psalms (68:7-8).

33:3-4 This sovereign Warrior was the same God who had
demonstrated that he did **love the people**. Because of that love he
gave Israel the **law** so that she might **receive instruction** on how to
live in obedience to him. The entire book of Deuteronomy has been
an exposition of this theological truth. This concrete revelation of
God and his character distinguished him from the other gods and
initiated an intimate relationship with Israel. He was much more
than a divine warrior riding on the clouds.

33:5 Through his victory at Sinai and his gift of the law, God
demonstrated his **kingship** over Israel. This is not a frequent expression for God in the OT but the idea of his rule and dominion is common. It was first celebrated when God won a victory over the
Egyptian army at the Red Sea (Exod 15:18). Later Balaam, the pagan
prophet, acknowledged that God's kingship protected Israel (Num
23:21). Subsequently, Israel celebrated God's reign in her hymns (Ps
97:1; 99:1). God's rule over Israel meant the **tribes** could have confidence in him.

The introduction prepared the way for the main part of the
blessing by laying a foundation of assurance that the blessings had
power. The conclusion in verses 26-29 celebrates the wonderful
security the tribes had in their God/King.

---

[7]"Seir" and "Mount Paran" are mountains located to the south of Canaan
and are in poetic parallel to Sinai. References to them reinforce the imagery
of God coming from the south. The NIV footnote reflects the difficulty in
understanding the last line in verse 2. Several emendations of the text have
been offered. The NRSV reflects a popular solution in its translation: ". . . at
his right, a host of his own." This agrees with the LXX that has "messengers
[angels] with him." See Merrill, *Deuteronomy*, p. 435, and Patrick D. Miller,
Jr., "Two Critical Notes on Psalm 68 and Deuteronomy 33," *HTR* 57 (1964):
240-243.

2. The Blessings on the Tribes (33:6-25)

33:6 Reuben was the oldest son and the first one listed in Genesis 49:3-4. In Genesis the "blessing" was negative because of his sin with Jacob's concubine (Gen 35:22). The wish here seems to be positive. It is for longevity and increase in numbers. However, **nor** (NIV) could be read as "and" which would bring the thought in line with Genesis 49. Reuben received land in the Transjordon (Deut 3:12-17; Num 32) but was pressured by surrounding nations. Eventually the tribe suffered attrition at the hands of Syria (2 Kgs 10:32-33) and was never a significant part of the nation.[8]

Simeon, the second son, is notably absent. The book of Joshua provides evidence that the tribe was absorbed into Judah early.[9] Judah and Simeon campaigned together early in the settlement period (Judg 1:3,17). Therefore, the poem seems to reflect the fact that Simeon had little independent status.

33:7 The geographical sequence required **Judah** to be listed next. His territory was west of the Dead Sea and encompassed all the land south of Jerusalem to the Negev. Judah received one of the longest blessings in Genesis 49:8-12. It was totally positive, picturing widespread prosperity. Judah also received the famous scepter promise in Genesis 49:10. The picture in Deuteronomy is of a tribe under attack and a wish for its success. The situation in view is not clear. In Judges 1:1-20 Judah and Simeon took unconquered land by themselves. They then lived under the threat of the Canaanites. On the other hand, in Numbers 2:9 Judah was to march at the head of the army as a vanguard which would have placed the tribe in great danger. The wish could be the hope that they would not become separated from the rest of the army.

The second half of the verse contains a word play between *Yehuda* (Judah) and *yadav* (his hands). This is similar to the word play in Genesis 49:8 where *yoduka* ("praise"; cf. Gen 29:35) and *yadeka* (your hand) occur with *Yehuda*.

33:8-11 The blessing on **Levi** is second only to Joseph in length

---

[8]The Syrian aggression was under God's direction during the time of King Jehu (2 Kgs 10:32-33; 842–815 B.C.).

[9]Compare Josh 19:1-8 with 15:26-32,42. All of Simeon's listed cities end up in Judah's territory.

(vv. 13-17). Levi had no territory and is placed here after his younger brother, Judah (Gen 29:34-35). The words contrast sharply with Genesis 49:5-7. Jacob cursed Levi and Simeon together because of the violence they did to the Shechemites (Gen 34:25-31) in defense of Dinah, their sister. They both would be scattered and dispersed.

The rallying of the Levites to Moses' side in Exodus 32 is clearly reflected in verse 9. In carrying out Moses' command they made no distinction between family and nonfamily members (v. 27,29). They were the only ones zealous for the **covenant**. The Levite Phinehas emulated that same zeal at Peor in Moab (Num 25). These pious actions were part of the reason the tribe gained ascendancy in God's eyes.

As the priestly tribe, the Levites were entrusted with the **Thummim and Urim**, an early method of discovering God's will (Num 27:21). These objects were kept in the breastplate (ephod) of the high priest (Exod 28:30).[10] They are last mentioned in 1 Samuel 28:6 though the references to the ephod in 1 Samuel 30:7-8 and 2 Samuel 2:1 probably refer to the Thummim and Urim also. How they worked is unclear.[11]

The reference to **Massah** and **Meribah** (v. 8) is puzzling, for the Levites were not singled out in those episodes nor was Israel tested by God at those times. The events in Exodus 17:1-8 and Numbers 20:1-13 were occasions when Israel tested God. A possible solution to this problem is that Moses and Aaron in this episode were understood to represent the Levites. Psalm 81:7 indicates that part of Israel was tested in the wilderness. Or it could be that the Levites supported Moses on those occasions as they did in Exodus 32, but it was not recorded in the biblical text.[12]

The responsibilities of the Levites were twofold: **teach** the **law to Israel** and preside at the offerings (v. 10).[13] These mediatory roles

---

[10]The reference to "the man you favored" could be to the high priest. The NRSV translation "to your loyal one" is more accurate than the NIV. The word is *ḥasîd* which the NIV usually translates as "saint, faithful, godly, devoted, holy."

[11]The Urim perhaps gave a negative response. It may have come from the root, *'rr,* "to curse." The Thummim would have given a positive answer. It may be related to the root, *tam,* "to be perfect, complete."

[12]Cairns, *Deuteronomy,* pp. 296-297.

[13]See 31:9-13 and Lev 10:11 for the teaching function. In Deuteronomy

were crucial to the spiritual health of the nation. Passing on the instruction contained in the *torah* was foundational for the future of the covenant people (ch. 6).

The blessing includes a wish for the success of everything the Levites tried to accomplish (v. 11a). Protection against unjust attack was also crucial for the spiritual leaders of the nation (v. 11b). Unlike the other tribes, the Levites had no military component. Yet their history included times of rebellion (Korah against Aaron, Num 16), danger, and attack (Saul and the priests of Nob, 1 Sam 22:6-22).[14]

33:12 Benjamin received a tender blessing that contrasts with the picture of Benjamin as a ravenous wolf in Genesis 49:27. The latter probably reflects Benjamin's reputation for bravery and skill in war. Benjaminites were noted left-handed slingers (Judg 20:16), and the tribe produced Ehud (Judg 3:15) and Saul (1 Sam 9:1).[15]

Benjamin means "son of the right hand." Jacob personally named him, reversing Rachel's chosen name (Gen 35:18). He was Jacob's favorite after Joseph (Gen 42:4,38; 44:10) and deeply loved. **Beloved** perhaps plays on these associations. Elsewhere Israel was the beloved of the LORD (Isa 5:1; Jer 11:5) or Solomon (as noted in his personal name, Yedidyah, 2 Sam 12:25 [Jedidiah]).

Benjamin's territory was small but occupied an important position. It was a narrow strip of land north of Judah that included Jerusalem (Josh 18:28). Its land provided an important buffer zone for Judah after the division of the nation.

Benjamin's special status was reflected in God's special care. He rested on the back of God (**between his shoulders**). This is a picture of tender protection and security and is equal to holding one close in the bosom.[16] God emulated Jacob's love for Benjamin in his compassion for the tribe.[17]

---

further duties for the Levites included judicial (17:9; 21:5) and medical functions (24:8). See also Deut 10:8-9.

[14]Attacks could be verbal as well. Psalm 69 uses language similar to 11b for verbal accusations.

[15]The apostle Paul was from the tribe of Benjamin also (Rom 11:1).

[16]Merrill, *Deuteronomy*, p. 440. See Num 11:12; Ruth 4:16; 2 Sam 12:3; Isa 40:11.

[17]In the Hebrew the subject of the phrase is ambiguous. The NIV supplies "the one the LORD loves." Hebrew has "he." If God is the subject then the reference would perhaps be to God, in the form of his sanctuary, resting

33:13-17 Joseph received the longest blessing as he did in Genesis 49:22-26. The blessing is twofold: fertility and strength. This is very similar to the tone of the blessing in Genesis. Joseph did not receive any territory himself but was represented by his two sons, Ephraim and Manasseh (v. 17b; Josh 14:2-4). Together the two tribes received the largest portion of land of all the tribes. Manasseh settled in part of Gilead, Bashan (Deut 3:13), and the northern half of Samaria. Ephraim occupied the southern half of Samaria (Joshua 16–17). These areas were some of the most fertile in the Transjordan territory and in the Promised Land. However, Ephraim gained ascendancy as Jacob had predicted (Gen 48:19-20), even giving his name to the northern kingdom (Isa 7:2; 9:9; 11:13; Jer 7:15; Ps 60:7, and often in Hosea). Fruitfulness (מֶגֶד, *meged*) dominates the blessing and occurs five times (vv. 13,14[twice],15,16).[18] All of God's creation was a source of blessing for the tribes: heaven, sun, moon, mountains, and earth. The natural world was not divine, or gods, as the ancient cultures thought, but under God's control and a conduit of his grace. The bounty of the land described here is reminiscent of chapter 8.

The blessing of fruitfulness is also a word play on Ephraim's name. The root of his name is *prh*, "to be fruitful" (Gen 41:52). There may be some connection to Joseph's name also, which meant "may he increase" (Gen 30:23).

Him who dwelt in the burning bush (v. 16) is a rare reference to Exodus 3:1-6. The one who was over all nature came to Moses within nature, manifested in the burning bush. Moses met God there and received his commission to lead Israel out of Egypt.[19] At the end of his life Moses still was reflecting on his initial call.

Joseph's preeminence over his brothers (v. 16b) reflects his dream (Gen 35:5-11) and the events in Egypt. The language is taken word for word from Genesis 49:26b. Joseph's power over the

---

among the hills (shoulders) of Benjamin (Tigay, *Deuteronomy*, p. 326). It seems best to follow the NIV.

[18]The idea is difficult to track in the NIV because of the varied translations of *meged*: verse 13 — "precious dew"; verse 14 — "best, finest"; verse 15 — "choicest gifts"; verse 16 — "best gifts."

[19]Tigay suggests a word play between bush, *seneh*, and the name Manasseh (*Deuteronomy*, p. 328).

nations is expressed by a common metaphor for strength, **the horns of a wild ox** (Num 23:22; Job 39:9-12; Ps 22:21).

33:18-19 Zebulun and **Issachar** were the sixth and fifth sons of Leah (Gen 30:19-20). The positive blessing here contrasts to the negative one for Issachar in Genesis 49:14-15 where he was pictured as submitting to forced labor. The land of these two tribes in lower Galilee and the Jezreel valley was some of the richest in the northern part of the Promised Land. The reference to **sea** and **sand** in verse 19b and in Genesis 49:13 is puzzling since neither tribe had land near the sea. Perhaps at one time Zebulun had control of territory to the Mediterranean Sea, which Asher later took over. The blessing perhaps indicates that their location gave them control over important trade routes. In that case, they would have had access to seafood, shells, and other products from both the Mediterranean and Chinnereth (Sea of Galilee).

The mountain of verse 19a is unnamed. Mount Tabor was on the border of Issachar and Naphtali, which would make it the logical mountain for the reference. But there is no mention in the OT of Tabor being a place for worship, though Hosea condemned an altar there (Hos 5:1). Perhaps in pretemple times that altar was a legitimate place of worship, and the tribes enjoyed the blessing of leading others in paying respect to God.[20]

33:20-21 Gad is blessed for his strength and his leadership. In Genesis 49:19 he was celebrated for defending himself against raiders. Gad received some of the good land of Gilead (Num 32:1-5). This gave him a leadership position among the tribes. The tribe played a pivotal role in the conquest of Canaan (Josh 22:1-8) also. There is some evidence that Gad grew in size and importance over the years while Reuben, who had the land to the south, declined. When the Moabite king, Mesha, freed himself from Israelite control in the mid-ninth century B.C. he referred to the Transjordan area as Gad.[21]

When the heads of the people assembled may be a reference to the well that was dug in the Transjordan. When it was done, the people gathered to celebrate it with song and rejoicing (Num 21:16-18).

---

[20]There could be a word play between Zebulun and sacrifice, *zbh*.

[21]Moabite Stone, line 10; cf. 2 Kgs 3:4. For a convenient description and translation see D. Winton Thomas, ed., *Documents from Old Testament Times* (New York: Harper and Row, 1958), pp. 195-198.

Gad is one of the few tribes to receive a direct blessing. Blessing may be associated with a word play on Gad, for the name means "good fortune" (Gen 30:11).

33:22 The statement on **Dan** is cryptic and quite different from Genesis 49:16-18. In the latter, he is both a leader for justice (a play on his name)[22] and a snake by the road that caused terror. **Lion's cub** is similar to the figure of lion in verse 20 and refers to strength and power. It was used of Judah in Genesis 49:9.

Dan originally received land near the seacoast (Josh 19:40-48) but could not settle there because of the strength of the Amorites (Judg 1:34-35). The tribe eventually migrated to the far north and conquered the city of Laish (Judg 18), renaming it Dan. The geographical pattern for the sequence of the tribes in this poem seems to presuppose that Dan had moved north.

The northern territory of Dan was a fertile, lush area on the border of the nation. It was near the head of the Hulah Valley and its springs provided one of the major sources of the Jordan River. Laish was an ancient, well-fortified site and the Israelites made it one of their important cities. After the division of the nation it became the site of one of the altars and high places for the calves that Jeroboam set up (1 Kgs 12:25-33).[23]

The metaphor of the cub **springing out of Bashan** may refer to Dan's conquest of Laish. Bashan, the modern Golan Heights, rises above Laish/Dan to the east. The people of Dan struck swiftly, as if they had leaped from the hills onto the city.

33:23 Naphtali received one of the most positive blessings of the tribes. He received both the LORD's **favor** and **blessing**. The LORD's favor was a bestowal of protection and prosperity (Ps 106:4-5). In Genesis 49:21, Naphtali was pictured as a fertile doe. These blessings would have been realized as Naphtalites moved into their assigned territory. It included the rich Hulah valley, much of upper Galilee,

---

[22]The verb for "to bring justice" in Hebrew is *dîn*.

[23]Decades of excavations at the site of Dan have uncovered many important artifacts. These include the area of the altar and high place, much of it intact, the extensive ninth century city gate, and a complete eighteenth century B.C. mud brick gate. Today the site is still green and beautiful. The state of Israel has made it into a National Park. See Avraham Biran, *Biblical Dan* (Jerusalem: Israel Exploration Society, 1994).

and the west side of the Sea of Chinnereth (Galilee). His territory was adjacent to Zebulun and Issachar to the south and southwest.

This area was later associated with Messianic expectations. Isaiah saw a great light coming from here (Isa 9:1-2[8:23–9:1]). The NT asserts that Jesus was that great light since much of his Galilean ministry was in the tribal areas of Zebulun and Naphtali (Matt 4:12-17). The famous trio of cities where Jesus often ministered, Capernaum, Chorazin, and Bethsaida, were all in Naphtali territory. The Christian can proclaim that the land did indeed experience the great favor of God.

33:24-25 Asher was the most **blessed** of the tribes, but his **favor** was from his brother tribes. His name is perhaps related to the word for happy or fortunate (*'ašrāy*) (cf. Gen 30:12-13 and v. 29 below). Both Genesis 49:20 and the blessing here hint at the rich land Asher inherited. It was located in upper Galilee and along the coast of the Mediterranean Sea. The upper Galilee was noted for its abundant olive trees (**bathe his feet in oil**). The territory was next to Tyre and controlled the coastal highway. Therefore, security would be essential to the tribe's well-being (v. 25).

3. Conclusion (33:26-29)

The poem ends with a blessing on all of Israel (v. 29). This conclusion is closely related to the introduction in verses 1-5 (see above). The cosmic leader and king is also the protector of Israel who enables her to live in safety and security.

33:26 The source of Israel's security was the power of her unique God. **There is no one like** him (cf. v. 29; 32:39; 3:4; 4:35-39). He came to her aid riding **on the clouds**. Mythological language was borrowed here to describe the coming presence of the LORD. It was a typical way to express divine **majesty** and glory.[24] The image was appropriate for Palestine that depended on rain coming at the right time for fertility.

33:27 There was no confusion with the Canaanite gods, however, for Israel's God was the only one who was **eternal** (Gen 21:33;

---

[24]"Rider of the Clouds" is a common epithet for Babylonian and Canaanite gods, cf. *ANET*, pp. 66, 132, 138.

Hab 1:12; Ps 74:12; Isa 51:9). He was the only one who could carry Israel protectively in his **everlasting arms** as he had done since the Exodus.[25]

33:28 Consequently, Israel's life in the Promised Land would be **secure** and she would live on the bounty of the land. Joseph's blessing was similar, but the language in verse 28b is almost identical to Isaac's blessing on Jacob (Gen 27:28). The physical blessings for an abundant life were available for the whole nation in the new land.

33:29 The conclusion rings with confidence and joy. **Blessed** is not the *brk* of earlier verses but the *'ašrāy* of Psalm 1:1. "How happy are you, **O Israel**."[26] Nothing could surpass the sweet contentment and quiet security of living in God's land under his protection. He was a **shield** to Abraham (Gen 15:1) from the beginning and continued his care. Israel's security was guaranteed by her victory over her enemies.[27]

Israel faced untold dangers and threats as it prepared to move into the land. Moses had repeatedly admonished the people to trust in God and rely on him to drive out the Canaanites. He had again and again lifted up obedience to the law as the way to live in security in the land. He had often pointed out the blessings that awaited Israel. Here, at the end of his last address to the people, he reiterates the arguments. The providential care and help of the LORD was theirs. Under his protection and leadership they could cross into the land and live under his blessing there. Their future was secure. It was now time to move into that future.[28]

---

[25]Usually, references to God's arm in Deuteronomy are about his powerful ability to rescue Israel from Egypt (4:34; 5:15; 7:19; 26:8; cf. Exod 6:6; 15:16). However, here it refers to God's eternal care and protection. Moses used the phrase in his complaint to God in Num 11:12: Why should he have to carry the nation like an infant in his arms?

[26]Or, how joyful or contented. The NRSV has "Happy are you."

[27]The NIV footnote, "tread upon their bodies," is preferred over the translation in the text, "trample down their high places." Victory over enemies in the ancient Near East was commonly portrayed as the victor placing the foot on the back or neck of the victim (Gen 3:15).

[28]See Miller, *Deuteronomy*, p. 241.

DEUTERONOMY 34

V. THE DEATH OF MOSES (34:1-12)

The final major section in Deuteronomy is brief. It contains a short
narrative about Moses' death (vv. 1-8), a note on Joshua his successor
(v. 9), and a succinct epitaph extolling Moses' stature (vv. 10-12).

34:1-3 These verses are a natural sequel to 32:48-52 where Moses
was commanded to go up on Mount Nebo and view the land of
Canaan (32:49). The Blessing of Moses in chapter 33 interrupted the
narrative sequence. These narratives frame the Blessing and set it in
the context of Moses' last words, giving them greater power.

Moses climbed **Mt. Nebo** to **the top of Pisgah.**[1] Nebo was at the
northern end of the Abarim range and Pisgah was a parallel peak or
ridge on Nebo.[2] From there one could see a major portion of the
Promised Land. The **LORD showed** Moses a sweeping view of the
land in a counterclockwise panorama. **Gilead** was straight north on
the east side of the Jordan River and south of Bashan (the modern
Golan Heights). It was the territory given to Gad. **Dan** was in the
northernmost part of the land, located in the foothills of Mt.
Hermon. Mt. Hermon, 100 miles to the north, would have been
clearly visible. **Naphtali** was in upper Galilee and west of the Sea of
Chinnereth (Galilee). It would have represented the tribal territory
of all of Galilee west of the sea that would not have been visible.
Ephraim and Manasseh represented the central hill country that
became the northern kingdom. Moses would have seen Mt. Gilboa
and Mts. Ebal and Gerizim (ch. 27). **Judah** lay directly west and to
the south. Its territory went down to the **western sea** (the

---

[1]Moses began his relationship with God on a mountain (Exod 3) and
ended it on a mountain (Merrill, *Deuteronomy*, p. 451).

[2]See comments on 3:27 and 32:48-52.

Mediterranean) though the sea would not have been visible. The **Negev** was the semiarid land in southern Judah that formed the southern boundary of the Promised Land. The panoramic sweep concluded with a view directly down the Jordan River valley that would have included **Jericho**, the Dead Sea, and **Zoar**. Zoar apparently designated the area to the south of the Dead Sea. The view Moses saw was representative, for not every parcel of the land would have been visible, especially the territory beyond the central mountain range. But he saw the general sweep of the land and gained a perspective on what God planned for Israel. Moses' view would have equaled the breadth of land which was later described as "from Dan to Beersheba" (Judg 20:1; 1 Sam 3:20; 2 Sam 3:10; 17:11; 1 Kgs 4:2).

There is a certain parallel between this passage and Genesis 13:14-17. In both instances a man of God was shown the land which his descendants, or people, would inherit. The ancient promise to Abraham was close to actualization when Moses saw the land. There may be some legal action implied also. In ancient law codes the two parties viewed the property together before transferring the land.[3]

34:4 The connection with the promise to Abraham was made explicit (Gen 12:1,7; 13:15; 18:18; 28:13; Deut 1:8,21,25). This verse is almost identical to Exodus 33:1. The long journey that began in chaos with the golden calf incident was coming to a close. God was going to keep his promise because he was faithful.

The reason Moses would **not cross over into** the land was not mentioned. This had been done several times before (1:37; 3:23-29; 31:2,14,16,27-29; 32:28-52). The purpose of these last words was to commend Moses and his place in God's plan, not detract from his character.

34:5-6 Moses died and was buried with only God in attendance. He received the highest accolade — he was a **servant of the LORD**. The phrase suggests the highest status and implies an intimate relationship with God. Although the designation "servant of the LORD" is applied to many in the Old Testament, including Abraham, David, Jacob, Joshua, and the prophets, it is used most often of Moses (cf. Deut 3:24; Josh 1:1,2,7,13,15; 8:31,33; 9:24, etc.). He was the servant par excellence. This had already been confirmed when Miriam and

---

[3]Cairns, *Deuteronomy*, pp. 303-304.

Aaron had criticized Moses. God told them Moses was not just an ordinary prophet but his servant, to whom he spoke face to face (Num 12:6-8).

Consequently, Moses was designated as God's chosen one (Ps 106:23).[4] It is even possible Moses provided the model for Isaiah's extensive reflection on the servant of the Lord who became a suffering servant (Isaiah 42–55). Since Deuteronomy attributed Moses' death to the disobedience of the people (1:37; 3:26), in some sense he was the servant who suffered and took upon himself their sin (Isa 53:4-6).[5]

God **buried** Moses **in Moab, in the valley opposite Beth Peor**. This was the same place that Moses expounded the law to Israel (Deut 3:29; 4:46). Yet no one knew where the **grave** was.[6] There are several possible reasons why the location would be secret. Most importantly, it prevented veneration of the site that could have been a distraction to Israel (cf. 18:10-11). Later Jewish tradition developed several legends about circumstances surrounding Moses' death; one is alluded to in Jude 9.[7] Moses' subsequent appearance in the New Testament (Matt 17:3; Mark 9:4; Luke 9:30) proved that he lived on and still held an honored place in God's kingdom.

---

[4]Isaiah brought the two terms, servant and chosen one, together in 42:1.

[5]Patrick D. Miller, Jr., "'Moses My Servant:' The Deuteronomic Portrait of Moses," *Int* 41 (1987): 245-255.

[6]The German scholar, Martin Noth, speculated that Moses was not an important figure in early Israel's history. Only when the people came across his grave in the Transjordan did they begin to develop traditions about him as a leading person in their past. For Noth the most certain fact about Moses was that he died and was buried in the location mentioned (Martin Noth, *A History of Pentateuchal Traditions*, trans. Bernhard W. Anderson [Englewood Cliffs, NJ: Prentice-Hall, 1972], pp. 171-173). This speculation is counter to everything the Pentateuch says about Moses.

[7]The reference in Jude is apparently from an apocryphal work "The Assumption of Moses." However, the only copy of the Assumption available does not contain the account Jude alludes to. It is known from references in early Christian documents. See H.F.D. Sparks, ed., *The Aprocryphal Old Testament* (Oxford: University Press, 1987), pp. 601-616, and Bo Reicke, *The Epistles of James, Peter and Jude* (New York: Doubleday, 1964), p. 202.

34:7-8 Moses did not die from old age. He was still vigorous and strong though he was no longer able to lead (31:2).[8] He died at God's command (like Aaron, Num 33:38) because he had completed his role in God's plan. His life had spanned three generations (**120 years**; see on 31:2) and was full and complete. His death closed one era and prepared for a new one.[9] Israel was now ready to enter the land, and God had raised up new leadership in Joshua (v. 9).

The Israelites mourned for Moses as they did for Aaron, **thirty days** (Num 20:29). This was fitting for his status as a great leader.[10]

34:9 Joshua had been in line to succeed Moses since Exodus 17:8-16 where he proved his skills in the Amalekite war. He was also on Mount Sinai with Moses (Exod 24:12-13) and served with him in many capacities. In Deuteronomy, provisions had already been made for him to take over at Moses' death (1:38; 3:28; 31:3-8,14-23). His possession of the **spirit of wisdom** was crucial to his success. He had received this, as well as some of Moses' authority, at Moses' hand (Num 27:15-22). The spirit of wisdom was a critical element in equipping Joshua to lead Israel. Great leaders needed this gift. Solomon asked for it (1 Kgs 4:2), and Isaiah promised a leader in the future with such a gift (Isa 11:1-5). The gift also certified to Israel that Joshua was qualified to lead her.

However, Joshua was not Moses, and God did not speak with him face to face. Joshua's success depended on his obedience to the law that God had given Moses (Josh 1:7-9).

34:10-12 The closing words of Deuteronomy are an epitaph for Moses, extolling his virtue and uniqueness as God's servant. Moses in Deuteronomy had stressed the incomparability of God; now Moses' incomparability is stressed.[11] God's knowledge of Moses comes to the fore, not Moses' knowledge of God.

---

[8]Strong or weak eyes is one idiom the Old Testament uses to express age and vigor. Old men had weak eyes (Gen 27:1; 1 Sam 4:15; 1 Kgs 14:4). The same idiom occurs in Egyptian and Babylonian texts (*ANET*, pp. 412b, 561c).

[9]Moses' death also closed the Torah; Miller, *Deuteronomy*, pp. 244-245.

[10]Mourning times varied in the OT. Deut 21:13 mentions 30 days also, but the period was seven days for Jacob (Gen 50:10) and Saul (1 Sam 31:13). Thirty days is the norm in modern Judaism (Tigay, *Deuteronomy*, p. 194).

[11]Wright, *Deuteronomy*, p. 313.

Previously in chapter 18:15-22 Moses had been described as the model prophet who would be the first of many. Any true prophet who followed had to speak a word of God that would come to pass. Only God's word could shape the future. Therefore, faithfulness to God's word and God's future for the prophet was essential. The fact that **no prophet had risen in Israel like Moses** (v. 10) was not a contradiction of chapter 18. The words here emphasize Moses' unique intimacy with God and the fact that he was the first in the prophetic line. In this respect there was not, nor could there be, anyone like him, for he was far more than a prophet.

Only Moses had known God **face to face** (Exod 33:11; Num 12:6-8).[12] In other words, Moses had the most direct contact with God of anyone. God spoke to him in person and without mediation. The people might be "face to face" with God but there was still a distance between them, for God spoke to them from the fire or cloud (5:4,22-27; 4:12,15). Moses mediated God's word to Israel, but there was no mediator for him.

Moses was also unique as a prophet in the **signs and wonders** he displayed as God's servant. In the Exodus this proved that his words and deeds were from God. Everything that he did and said was at God's initiative.

This elevation of Moses upheld his authority as God's man. But more than that, it also upheld the authority of the book of Deuteronomy, which was Moses' last words to Israel. Any future servant, prophet, or teacher would have to be measured against Moses and his teaching. Deuteronomy, as Moses' last words, was to be the foundation for Israelite practice and belief.[13]

Many great prophets came and went. Elijah, Hosea, Amos, Isaiah, Jeremiah, and a host of others were great men of God. But none were like Moses. Ultimately, however, One like Moses did arise (John 1:45). Jesus was a new Moses as the New Testament affirms. He spent his forty days (one day for each year) in the wilderness like Moses, and he presented his own new teaching with authority (Matthew

---

[12]The Numbers text says literally "mouth to mouth."

[13]These last words to the book of Deuteronomy cannot be from Moses as everyone recognizes. Who added them and when is unknown. However, they ring true and certainly reflect divine intention.

4,5–7). However, he was greater than Moses (Heb 3:3). He was not only a prophet and servant, he was the Son of God. Moses made his last appearance in Scripture on another mountain talking with the new Moses about another "exodus" (Luke 9:28-31, Greek; NIV, "departure"). This new exodus (Jesus' death and resurrection) was one example of Jesus' superiority, for it was for the benefit of all nations, not just one.[14]

---

[14]Luke 9:31 says, "They spoke about his departure, which he was about to bring to fulfillment at Jerusalem." The Greek word translated "departure" is exodon, *exodon*. The LXX uses this word for the Exodus in Psalm 104(Eng. 105):38 and 113(Eng. 114):1.